Goal Concepts in Personality and Social Psychology

WITHDRAWN

Goal Concepts in Personality and Social Psychology

**EDITED BY
LAWRENCE A. PERVIN**
Rutgers University

Stafford Library
Columbia College
10th and Rodgers
Columbia, MO 65216

LEA LAWRENCE ERLBAUM ASSOCIATES, PUBLISHERS
1989   Hillsdale, New Jersey   Hove and London

Copyright © 1989 by Lawrence Erlbaum Associates, Inc.
All rights reserved. No part of this book may be reproduced in any form, by photostat, microfilm, retrieval system, or any other means, without the prior written permission of the publisher.

Lawrence Erlbaum Associates, Inc., Publishers
365 Broadway
Hillsdale, New Jersey 07642

Library of Congress Cataloging-in-Publication Data

Goal concepts in personality and social psychology / edited by
  Lawrence Pervin.
      p.   cm.
   Bibliography: p.
   Includes index.
   ISBN 0-8058-0069-7.   ISBN 0-8058-0383-1 (pbk.)
    1. Goal (Psychology)   2. Personality.   3. Social psychology.
   I. Pervin, Lawrence A.
BF504.G63   1988
155.2—dc19   88-24698
                                                         CIP

Printed in the United States of America
10 9 8 7 6 5 4 3 2 1

Contents

1 Goal Concepts in Personality and Social Psychology:
A Historical Perspective *1*
LAWRENCE A. PERVIN
Historical Overview of Goal Concepts *2*
Goals and Motivation *7*
Goals and Social Cognition *10*
Contributions to This Volume *12*
References *12*

2 Self-Regulation of Motivation and Action
Through Internal Standards and Goal Systems *19*
ALBERT BANDURA
Attribution Theory *20*
Expectancy-Value Theory *22*
Goal Theory *26*
Self-Regulation Through Moral Standards *64*
Acknowledgment *78*
References *78*

3 The Personal Striving Approach to Personality *87*
ROBERT A. EMMONS
Introduction *87*
Current Conceptions of Motivation *88*

Historical Background *91*
Personal Strivings as Units of Analysis *92*
Relation to Motives and Values *95*
Assessing Personal Strivings *102*
Acknowledgments *120*
References *121*

4 Ups and Downs of Life Tasks in a Life Transition *127*
NANCY CANTOR AND CHRISTOPHER A. LANGSTON

Illustrative Methods for Life Task and Strategy Analysis *132*
Themes in a Social Intelligence Analysis *145*
Acknowledgments *163*
References *163*

5 Energization and Goal Attractiveness *169*
REX A. WRIGHT AND JACK W. BREHM

Introduction *169*
Empirical Support for the Model *173*
A Theoretical Perspective and Selected Problems *200*
The Model in Summary *206*
References *207*

6 Possible Selves: Personalized Representations of Goals *211*
HAZEL MARKUS AND ANN RUVOLO

The Representation of Goals within the Self-System *212*
The Self-System and Motivation Related Approaches *214*
Why Frame Goals in Terms of the Self? *217*
Possible Selves: Empirical Studies *219*
The Role of Possible Selves in the Motivational Sequence: How Does It Work? *227*
Concluding Comments *236*
References *237*

7 Goals and the Self-Identification Process: Constructing Desired Identities *243*
BARRY R. SCHLENKER AND MICHAEL F. WEIGOLD

The Nature of Self-Identification *244*
Desirable Images *253*
Active and Passive Self-Identification *271*
Summary *281*

8 Goal Setting Theory and Job Performance 291
THOMAS W. LEE, EDWIN A LOCKE, AND GARY P. LATHAM

Introduction 291
The Historical Context 292
Goal Setting Theory 298
Current and Emerging Research Directions 312
The Goal Setting Process 318
Summary 321
References 321

9 Interpersonal Goal Conflict 327
DONALD R. PETERSON

The Data of Interpersonal Goal Conflict 331
Conceptions of Interpersonal Goal Conflict 338
Acknowledgement 359
References 359

10 The Role of Goal Categories in the Representation of Social Knowledge 363
JERZY TRZEBINSKI

Action-Oriented Representations of Social Knowledge 364
Basic Assumptions 366
Goal Categories in the Representation of Event Knowledge 368
Goal Categories in the Representation of Person Knowledge 373
Goal Categories in the Representation of Knowledge About Social Organization 389
Goal Categories in the Representation of Self-Knowledge 394
Conclusions 403
References 406

11 Inter-Personalism: Toward a Goal-Based Theory of Persons in Relationships 413
STEPHEN JOHN READ AND LYNN CAROL MILLER

General Framework 415
Person Structures 427
Situational Structures 434
Perceiving and Understanding Others 435
Inter-Personalism in Process: The Planning and Coordination of Behavior 451
Issues: Implications of this Approach 460
References 467

12 Goal Concepts: Themes, Issues, and Questions *473*
LAWRENCE A. PERVIN
The Goal Concept: Definition and Essential Features *473*
Goal Systems, the Dynamics of Goal System Functioning, and Will *476*
Goals and Social Cognition *478*
Conclusion *478*
References *478*

Author Index ***481***
Subject Index ***497***

1 Goal Concepts in Personality and Social Psychology: A Historical Introduction

LAWRENCE A. PERVIN
Rutgers University

Is behavior motivated? And, if so, can it be motivated by the anticipation of future events? What role does cognition play in such motivational processes? And, further, what role does motivation play in ongoing cognitive activity? Questions such as these provide the foundation for this book. More specifically, the chapters in this book address the question of the utility of goals concepts in studying motivation and social cognition.

These questions may seem obvious. Yet, the history of the field suggests otherwise and careful consideration leads one into issues that have preoccupied philosophers for centuries. Only a decade ago a review of 24 years of the distinguished Nebraska Symposium on Motivation suggested that the concept of motivation had ceased to be of major concern to the field and was of questionable utility as a scientific construct (Benjamin & Jones, 1978). As noted by Cofer (1981), the demise of drive theory toward the end of the 1960s was associated more generally with a decline in motivation theory. Though a chapter on cognition did not appear in the *Annual Review of Psychology* until 1966 (Van de Geer & Jaspars, 1966), cognition and information processing rapidly displaced motivation as a dominant issue of concern to psychologists. That is, not only did cognition rise as an area of interest, but it supplanted other areas of interest, such as motivation (Pervin, 1980). Thus, Cofer (1981) noted that most cognitive theorists did not consider issues traditionally addressed by motivation theorists and asked: "Where, in cognitive theory, are the strong urges and the 'hot' emotions or passions that have been central to our thinking in respect to motivation and emotion for so long?" (p. 51).

Yet, to juxtapose cognition and motivation in relation to one another may unduly simplify the matter. First, the "New Look in Perception" of the 1940s and 1950s emphasized the role of motivation in perception and thinking (Bruner, 1951). Second, at least some early information processing models of cognition did attend to the relation between motivation and cognition (Simon, 1967). More recently, theories in personality and social psychology, derived primarily from the cognitive revolution, are leading the way in exploring relations between motivation and cognition. Thus, the cognitive revolution that initially was associated with the demise of key components of motivation theory now provides the bulwark for a return to interest in purposive, goal-directed behavior.

Both thinking and motivation, cognition and goal-directed behavior, have been of interest and concern to psychologists since the beginning of the field. They form part of the triad so often defined as the areas of concern to psychologists—conation, cognition, and emotion. To understand, then, the issues addressed in the papers in this volume, it may be useful to place them in a historical context (Boden, 1972; Brody, 1983; Ryan, 1970; Silver, 1985).

HISTORICAL OVERVIEW OF GOAL CONCEPTS

Modern day action theorists, concerned with goal-directed behavior, trace their roots to Wundt and early German psychology (Frese & Sabini, 1985). At the same time, it is clear that early functionalist thought, with its roots in James, touched on many key issues of concern to goals theorists. James (1890) defined the phenomena of interest to psychologists as including feelings, desires, and cognitions and suggested that "the pursuance of future ends and the choice of means for their attainment are thus the mark and criteria of the presence of mentality in a phenomenon" (p. 8). James used words that are beginning to reappear in the psychological literature (e.g., wish, will, volition, desire) and was concerned with fundamental issues, such as the following: Does goal-directed behavior (mind, mentality) exist in lower mammals? What is the relation of consciousness to the unfolding of an organized, reflex-like pattern of movements? What is the relation between cognition of an end result and action; that is, how do we account for the translation of consciousness to the unfolding of an organized, reflex-like pattern of movements? What is the relation between cognition of an end result and action; that is, how do we account for the translation of wish into will? How do we account for disturbances of will such as where normal action becomes impossible (obstructed will) or where an abnormal action becomes irrepressible (explosive will)? His description of the situation that provides, in miniature form, the basis for an entire psychology of volition remains worthy of our consideration today:

> We know what it is to get out of bed on a freezing morning in a room without a fire, and how the very vital principle within us protests against the ordeal. Probably most persons have lain on a certain morning for an hour at a time unable to brace themselves to the resolve. We think how late we shall be, how the duties of the day will suffer; we say, "I *must* get up, this is ignominious," etc.; but still the warm couch feels too delicious, the cold outside too cruel, and resolution faints away and postpones itself again and again just as it seemed on the verge of bursting the resistance and passing over into decisive act. Now how do we *ever* get up under such circumstances? (James, 1892, p. 424)

The suggestion has been made that behaviorism displaced the concept of action with behavior (Frese & Sabini, 1985). Discussion then focuses on the debate between Tolman and Hull (Silver, 1985). Such a historical account, however, leaves out the enormously important work of McDougall (1908, 1930). Whereas Watson (1930) described images as "ghosts of sensations" and rejected both mentalism and teleology in favor of more mechanistic views, McDougall rejected a stimulus-determined view of behaviorism in favor of an emphasis on active strivings toward anticipated goals. Whereas the science of his day rejected teleological notions because they smacked of religion, McDougall was impressed with motivation as it was expressed in the foresight of goals:

> We foresee a particular event as a possibility; we desire to see this possibility realized; we take action in accordance with one desire, and we seem to guide the course of events in such a way that the foreseen and desired event results. To explain an event as caused in this way was to invoke teleological causation, a causal activity thoroughly familiar to each man through his own repeated experiences of successful action for the attainment of desired goals. (McDougall, 1930, p. 5)

McDougall was so struck with the goal-seeking quality of behavior that he announced himself to be a purposive psychologist and defended the view called hormic psychology. Purposive behavior was defined by seven characteristics: (1) spontaneity of movement, (2) persistence of movement, (3) variation of direction of persistent movements, (4) cessation of movement when a particular change in the situation has occurred (goal reached), (5) preparatory movement for a new situation, (6) improvement in the effectiveness of behavior when placed repeatedly in similar situations, and (7) participation of the whole organism in the activity. Variation in the direction of activity was held to be the most distinguishing feature of purposive behavior and what most differentiated it from stimulus governed, reflexive behavior.

Although McDougall is frequently dismissed as an instinct theorist, he can still be read with profit. Beyond his emphasis on goals and purposive strivings, he emphasized the interrelationships among cognition, affect, and conation. His concept of instinct included cognitive and affective components, as well as motor aspects. In higher animals, instinctive behaviors could increasingly be performed with awareness of a goal or end point and could be initiated by ideas of objects and by the objects themselves! The cognitive (perceptual) and motor aspects were seen as being highly modifiable so that, as a result of experience and learning, the same emotional response could become associated with many objects and result in many different behaviors. In sum, McDougall emphasized the system (cognitive, affective, behavioral) functioning of the organism in relation to goal-directed striving.

Writing in roughly the same time period as McDougall, but from a very different perspective, Alfred Adler was similarly led to an emphasis on individuals as goal-directed and motivated by their expectations of the future. Whereas often much is made of Adler's split with Freud over the emphasis on sexual instincts, of perhaps equal importance was Adler's emphasis on expectations of the future as opposed to experiences of the past. Consider, for example, the following: "Causes, powers, instincts, impulses, and the like cannot serve as explanatory principles. The final goal alone can explain man's behavior. Experiences, traumata, sexual development mechanisms cannot yield an explanation, but the perspective in which they are regarded, the individual way of seeing them, which subordinates all life to the final goal, can do so" (Adler, 1930, p. 400). Anticipating later developments in psychology, Adler replaced the concept of drives with that of values and goals. His emphasis on concepts such as the individual's hierarchy of goals, guiding self-ideal, and style of life, would appear to be similar to current concepts such as possible selves (Markus & Nurius, 1986) and action style (Frese, Stewart, & Hanover, 1987).

The Ansbachers (1956), who did so much to bring Adler's views to the attention of American psychologists, note that Adler was quite sympathetic to the personalistic psychology of William Stern, who so much influenced Gordon Allport, and that in many ways his ideas paralleled those of Gestalt psychology.

The Gestalt psychologists emphasized molar behavior, the total action of the organism, goal-directed action and the related positive and negative valences of objects, and differences between drivelike, involuntary action and intentional action (Kohler, 1929; Lewin, 1935, 1951). Tolman (1925a, 1925b), influenced both by the work of the Gestalt psychologists and the emphasis of E. B. Holt on wish and purpose, was led to the position of purposive behaviorism. In contrast with Skinner (1953), who rejected teleology as a "spector" and viewed expressions of goals or purpose as abbreviations for statements about operant conditioning, and with Hull (1943) who, while accepting purposive behavior in principle remained committed to a molecular, mechanistic view, Tolman suggested that behavior reeks of purpose and cognition: "Behavior as behavior, that is, as molar, is purposive and is cognitive. These purposes and cognitions are of its immediate warp and woof" (1932, p.6). One could observe a *readiness to persist* and a *docility* in purposive behavior, characteristics that were noted to be similar to those emphasized by McDougall. However, whereas McDougall inferred purpose, Tolman identified purpose with specific behavioral characteristics and demonstrated the variability of means-ends relationships, which were seen as essential to purposive behavior. Although lost from the attention of many current psychologists, Tolman anticipated some of the key elements of social learning theory and made a valiant effort to capture systematically the patterned, organized, purposive quality of behavior.

F. H. Allport (1937) similarly was impressed with the "teleonomic" quality of behavior, that is, its purposive or goal-directed characteristics. He contrasted a dynamic emphasis on behavior trends (goals) with static trait descriptions of behavior. His brother, G. W. Allport (1937), remained committed to a trait point of view but similarly emphasized the motivated, organized, purposive, intentional aspects of personality. G. W. Allport rejected traditional instinct and drive concepts of motivation as too limited to be expressive of the individual. At the same time, he was concerned that trait concepts seemed insufficiently dynamic. Thus, he asked whether traits were self-active and, after first suggesting that strictly speaking they were not, he went on to suggest that "in another sense traits do initiate behavior" (1937, p. 321). His conclusion was that although not all motives were traits and not all traits were motives, there was overlap between the two. However, it was the traits with a motivational component, what he called its "telic significance," that played a particularly significant role in personality. Thus, it was the striving towards goals, or what he later called propriate strivings (Allport, 1955), that was important for the organization and unity of personality.

As noted earlier, for some time the concept of motivation was closely tied to that of drive. Thus, when evidence mounted that made the drive concept untenable (Berlyne, 1960; White, 1959), interest in the concept of motivation waned. Although goals concepts remained part of the thinking of some psychologists, and an emphasis on expectations concerning the future played a role in some theories of motivation (Atkinson, 1958; Bindra, 1969; McClelland, 1961; Rotter, 1954), psychologists appeared ready to turn to different concerns and models. The beginning of the cognitive revolution can probably be traced back to the late 1950s, or just about the period of the demise of drive theory. In 1958 Newell, Shaw, and Simon presented their theory of human problem solving, emphasizing an information processing model, and in 1960 Miller, Galanter, and Pribram published their influential book *Plans and the Structure of Behavior*. Thereafter, interest in cognition increased to the extent that it has nearly dominated the field. Not only did the field of cognitive psychology emerge, but personality and social psychology went cognitive. Clinical psychologists initially went behavioral (behavior modification and behavior therapy), but eventually they too became cognitive (cognitive behavior therapy). Missing in all of this, however, were the issues typically addressed by motivation theorists, the "strong urges and the hot emotions or passions" noted by Cofer.

It is interesting to note in this regard that goals concepts have almost always been part of cognitive models, and motivational questions were never completely ignored. The *general problem solver* model involved means-ends relationships and a hierarchy of goals and subgoals. Further, Simon (1967) addressed the issue of motivational and emotional controls of cognition. And, the Miller, Galanter, and Pribram (1960) model suggested that plans are associated with goals that have motivational properties because of their value for the organism. Despite this emphasis on goals and concern with certain motivational questions, however, most cognitive models have tended to leave the organism left in thought. In particular, such models have had little to say about the kinds of goals people have, how goals and goal systems develop, and how they are integrated into other aspects of personality functioning. Although Miller, Galanter, and Pribram were critical of cognitive theorists for leaving the organism a spectator rather than a participant in the drama of life, as if people only collect maps but never go on trips, they did not provide a satisfactory answer to the problem. For the most part they too leave the person as a collector of plans or maps, with little said about how images or trips become attractive to the person and how selections are made among alternative desired outcomes.

In sum, the cognitive revolution left unanswered, and in many cases unaddressed, questions of historical significance for motivation psychologists. Yet, at the same time, it provided a possible solution for questions that had been of historical concern to purposive, teleological psychologists. In particular, advances in cybernetics (Wiener, 1948) and control theory (Powers, 1973, 1978) provided a conceptual analysis and machine demonstration of how behavior or system functioning could be regulated toward reaching some end point. The problem of how the future could determine the present was hardly a problem at all—the current image, the idea of a goal, governed purposive behavior (Boden, 1972). Organisms could now be oriented toward some end point just as a thermostat regulated temperature toward some set point and an antiaircraft gun adjusted its fire through the use of feedback. Despite arguments by some behaviorists, such as Skinner (1953), that concepts such as goals and purpose could be reduced to principles of reinforcement, psychology appeared to have found "a respectable teleology" (Silver, 1985). As we shall see in the following sections, in time the concept of goals was found to be useful in addressing the relation between motivation and social cognition.

GOALS AND MOTIVATION

In the words of George Kelly (1955), motivation theories have typically been of two kinds—the stick and the carrot, the former emphasizing the push of drives and the latter the pull of incentives. What is common to both drive and incentive theories is an emphasis on the presence of stimuli to activate and direct the organism, either an internal drive stimulus or an external environmental incentive. The concept of goals as a motivational construct has a number of advantages over internal drive and external incentive concepts. First, by emphasizing the cognitive representation or image of a goal, the organism gains freedom from the immediacy of current stimuli. Now the organism is able to be oriented toward the future, as far into the future as its cognitive capacities permit. Second, by distinguishing between *goals*, or end points the organism seeks to achieve, and *plans*, or the means through which goals are achieved, a flexible and adaptive element is added to the functioning of the organism. No longer is behavior to be viewed in terms of reflexes, stimulus-response bonds, or fixed action patterns. Rather, recognition is given to the fact that there may be multiple routes to a goal and that the organism may select the best route or plan suggested by circumstances. Third, the concept of a hierarchically organized goal system (Broadbent, 1985; Pervin, 1983; Powers, 1973) suggests that different parts of the organism are interdependent with one another and that the attainment of certain goals may be facilitative of, or incompatible with, the attainment of other goals. This adds an element of considerable complexity to the organism's functioning. Available now is the potential for the simultaneous achievement of multiple goals, as well as the potential for conflict. And, taken together with the emphasis on an anticipatory or future perspective, there is the potential for an incredible array of alternatives for sequencing the achievement of various goals. That is, with the increasing complexity of a goal system and a cognitive representational system, the organism is faced not only with the task of selecting among goals, but also that of developing strategies for achieving short-term and long-term, single and multiple goals. This indeed is a functional, molar view of behavior, which, while ignoring neither states internal to the organism nor the effects of incentive stimuli immediately present in the environment, goes far beyond either traditional reinforcement theory or expectancy-value theory.

As indicated in the introduction to this chapter, the concept of goals has been present throughout the history of psychology: James, Wundt, Ach, McDougall, Kohler, Lewin, Tolman, F. Allport, and G. W. Allport. Although interest in motivation declined following the end of the glory days of drive theory, at least some theorists continued to work in this area and to emphasize the persistent, goal-directed quality of animal and human behavior (Irwin, 1971). For example, Young (1949, 1959, 1961) raised significant questions concerning how goals arise and how goal-directed activity is regulated. He emphasized the role of affective processes in the development, organization, and regulation of motivational activity. Developments in achievement motivation theory, though based in Murray's (1938) need theory framework, similarly emphasized the importance of affective processes and goals (Atkinson, 1964; Atkinson & Raynor, 1974; McClelland, 1955).

However, at least two things are striking about relevant work over the past two decades: the number of individuals developing research programs associated with the goals concept and the variety of theoretical perspectives making use of the goals concept. In terms of the latter, an emphasis on goals and plans can be seen in such diverse perspectives as information processing theory, cognitive social learning theory, psychoanalytic theory, and action theory (Bandura, 1986; Carver & Scheier, 1982; Dweck, 1986; Frese & Sabini, 1985; Gedo, 1979; King & Sorrentino, 1983; Klinger, 1977; Kuhl & Beckman, 1985; Little, 1983; Mischel, 1973; Mook, 1987; Nuttin, 1984; Pervin, 1983; Rosenblatt & Thickstun, 1977; Schafer, 1976; Staats & Burns, 1982). For example, one recent development in psychoanalytic theory seeks to do away with Freud's "mechanistic constructs" and "Aristotle's artificial categorization of human aims into cognitive, affective, and volitional varieties" in favor of a view of personality as a hierarchy of personal aims or goals: "Personality as a whole is most fruitfully understood as a hierarchy of potentials for actions, i.e., of both organismic and subjective goals, as modified by a system of values. In my view, goals are to be understood as mental dispositions to action *ipso facto* laden with affect" (Gedo, 1979, pp. 11–12). Illustrative goals are autonomy, perfection, and intimacy. Emphasis is placed on the development of standards (moral values) and the self-system as the central organizing principle of the personal goals hierarchy. In relation to the latter, reference is made to Powers' (1973) control theory and the suggestion is made that the self represents the ninth or highest level of control and effort at integration of goal system functioning. The emphasis on the nuclear self and self-objects as associated with aims-goals (Goldberg, 1980) strikingly parallels Markus and Nurius' (1986) emphasis on possible selves and, to a certain extent, Cantor and Kihlstrom's (1987) emphasis on self-goals.

The preceding psychoanalytic emphasis on goals can be compared with that of cognitive social learning theory. In his cognitive social learning reconceptualization of personality, Mischel (1973) suggested that, in addition to the regulation of action by external consequences, individuals regulate their own behavior by self-imposed goals (standards) and self-produced consequences: "Even in the absence of external constraints and social monitors, persons set performance goals for themselves and react with self-criticism or self-satisfaction to their behavior depending on how well it matches their expectations and criteria" (pp. 273–274). More recently Bandura (1986) has suggested that most human behavior is purposive and regulated by forethought: "Self-motivation is best maintained by explicit proximal subgoals that are instrumental in achieving larger future ones" (p. 475). Bandura makes the noteworthy point that the motivating factor is not the goal itself but the evaluation of performance in relation to standards; that is, it is the ongoing cognitive comparison of performance against standards and the associated evaluative response (e.g., pride or self-criticism) that provides for the motivational effect. Finally, the effects of goal systems on motivation are mediated not only by self-evaluative mechanisms but also by self-efficacy mechanisms.

The cognitive social emphasis on the implications of goals and performance feedback information for motivation has also been addressed by other investigators. For example, Dweck (1986) reports research demonstrating the differing motivational effects of success and failure for individuals with learning as opposed to performance goals. The focus is on the effects of adaptive and maladaptive motivational patterns that, although influenced by external contingencies and internal affective states, are largely determined by organizing cognitive variables: "The study of motivation deals with the causes of goal-oriented activity . . . Adaptive motivational patterns are those that promote the establishment, maintenance, and attainment of personally challenging and personally valued achievement goals. Maladaptive patterns, then, are associated with a failure to establish reasonable, valued goals, to maintain effective striving toward those goals or, ultimately, to attain valued goals that are potentially within one's reach" (Dweck, 1986, p. 1040). There is evidence that depression is associated with the blockage of achievement of self-defining goals (Higgins, 1987; Higgins, Klein, & Strauman, 1985; Hyland, 1987; Oatley & Bolton, 1985) and that goal conflict is associated with stress and negative affect (Emmons & King, 1987; Paterson & Neufeld, 1987; Pervin, 1983; Srull & Wyer, 1986).

What is seen here is a clear linkage between motivation and cognition, a point that is developed further in the following section.

GOALS AND SOCIAL COGNITION

The concept of goals is important for consideration of social cognitive processes in two ways. First, there is the question of the extent to which goals concepts form part of the structure people use for thinking about the world; that is, to what extent do people think about others and social interaction in terms of goals categories? Second, there is the question of the effect of the person's goals on their cognitive processes, that is, is how we process information influenced by the particular purposes or goals functional at that time?

Much of social psychology during the past decade has been influenced by attribution theory, dating back to the seminal work of Heider (1958). It is noteworthy in this regard that so much of attribution theory has focused on traits as person units, rather than on motives (goals) as originally suggested by Heider. According to Heider, attributions are made to people in terms of the inferred characteristics of power (ability) and trying (intention and desire). Intention and desire were viewed by him as directed toward goals, with action being a consequent of motives and perceived means-end requirements dictated by the situation. In other words, common sense psychologists were portrayed more as motivation or dynamic psychologists than as trait theorists. In a recent study along these lines, Pervin and Furnham (1987) compared the effects of situation characteristics and person goal characteristics on perceived probabilities of behaviors for self and others. It was found that person (goal) characteristics affected expectations of behavior more than did situation characteristics and, in an apparent reversal of the "fundamental attribution error," this was even more true for self ratings than for other ratings.

The goals concept, of course, has been fundamental to artificial intelligence efforts to study human information processing (Carbonell, 1981; Carroll & Payne, 1976; Graesser & Clark, 1985; Schmidt, 1976). Goals concepts are seen as basic organizing categories (Barsalou, 1983; Murphy & Medin, 1985), used both in organizing information concerning situations (Argyle, Furnham, & Graham, 1981; Graham, Argyle, & Furnham, 1980; Stokols, 1981) and social interaction (Read, 1987; Trzebinski, 1985; Wegner & Giuliano, 1983). The perception of the motives of others, for example, is seen as a critical variable in establishing trust in close relationships (Rempel, Holmes, & Zanna, 1985) and in understanding conflicts between partners (Peterson, 1983). From a developmental standpoint, there is evidence that children at an early age understand the concepts of motive and intention and make associated inferences concerning the behavior of others (Berndt & Berndt, 1975; Bruner, 1981; Butzin & Dozier, 1986; Shantz, 1983). There also is some evidence that the belief that people act "intentionally" precedes development of the concept that things may occur "untentionally" or by accident (Sedlak, 1979). Further, there is some basis for the suggestion that trait judgments represent summary statements for perceived regularities in the goals of others (Carbonell, 1979; McArthur & Baron, 1983; Murphy & Medin, 1985). Despite such findings, there has not been systematic investigation of developmental aspects of children's understanding of their own motives and those of others.

Attributions of goals and intentionality to others represents one dimension of the relevance of the goals concept for social cognition. A second involves the ways in which the person's goals influence all aspects of social information processing (Anderson & Hastie, 1974; Showers & Cantor, 1985; Wyer & Srull, 1986). The goals of the perceiver-actor influence the perceptual focus (Jones & Thibaut, 1958), the concepts-schema used (Cohen & Ebbesen, 1979; Hoffman, Mischel, & Mazze, 1981), the preferred level of personality description (Hampson, John, & Goldberg, 1986), the assignment of intention to others (Jones & Davis, 1965; Thibaut & Riecken, 1955), and what is remembered (Moore, Kagan, & Haith, 1978).

Although not ordinarily treated within a motivational framework, the social psychological literature on impression management involves study of the effects of an actor's goals upon social behavior (Jones & Pittman, 1982; Schlenker, 1985; Tetlock & Manstead, 1985). A necessary part of such impression management, indeed of all social interaction, is an accurate assessment of the goals and plans of others as well as the behaviors-scripts most appropriate for the situation (Darley & Fazio,

1980; Schank & Abelson, 1977). In sum, social interaction and social cognition involve actors with goals, with their goals affecting their behavior, their organization of information, and their ascription of goals to others. Beyond this may be some assumptions about the goals others perceive to be part of the actor and some effort to manage such impressions. Complex social interaction involves complex cognitive-motivational processes, with the potential for error, misjudgment, and misunderstanding, as well as the potential for trust and intimacy. Given the complexity of such processes, it is not surprising that people develop strategies to simplify the world (e.g., ascribe a few basic motives to the self and a few basic motives to others). And, given the selective influence of goals on information processing and the potential for simplification in the ascription of motives to self and others, it is not surprising that human relationships are so filled with misunderstanding. In fact, one may be surprised that the degree of conflict and misunderstanding is not greater than it is. Whether this is testimony to the accuracy and self-correcting aspects of our social cognitive processes, or whether in many circumstances people are prepared to accept large margins of error, remains unknown. In any case, it is clear that goals influence social cognition and social behavior, and that feedback from the environment and one's own internal evaluative processes further influences the course of goal-directed activity.

CONTRIBUTIONS TO THIS VOLUME

Having set forth the historical context for considering goals concepts in relation to motivation and social cognition, we are in a position now to turn to the chapters in this volume. The contributors represent some of the leading figures in personality and social psychology. Thus, the fact that so many distinguished psychologists can come together to address the goals concept is testimony to its importance in current thinking in the field. At the same time, as we shall see, the chapters represent differing perspectives and serve to focus attention on major issues that remain to be addressed and pursued. It is to these chapters that we now turn, to return in the concluding chapter to consideration of the critical questions and issues that remain.

REFERENCES

Adler, A. (1930). Individual psychology. In C. Murchison (Ed.), *Psychologies of 1930*, (pp. 395–405). Worcester, MA: Clark University Press.

Allport, F. H. (1937). Teleonomic description in the study of personality. *Character and Personality, 5,* 202–214.
Allport, G. W. (1937). *Personality: A psychological interpretation.* New York: Holt, Rinehart, & Winston.
Allport, G. W. (1955). *Becoming: Basic considerations for a psychology of personality.* New Haven: Yale University Press.
Anderson, J. R., & Hastie, R. (1974). Individuation and reference in memory: Proper names and definite descriptions. *Cognitive Psychology, 6,* 495–515.
Ansbacher, H. L., & Ansbacher, R. R. (Eds.) (1956). *The individual psychology of Alfred Adler.* New York: Basic Books.
Argyle, M., Furnham, A., & Graham, J. A. (1981). *Social situations.* Cambridge: Cambridge University Press.
Atkinson, J. W. (1958). *Motives in fantasy, action, and society.* Princeton: Van Nostrand.
Atkinson, J. W. (1964). *An introduction to motivation.* Princeton: Van Nostrand.
Atkinson, J. W., & Raynor, J. (Eds.) (1974). *Motivation and achievement.* Washington, D.C.: V. H. Winston.
Bandura, A. (1986). *Social foundations of thought and action: A social cognitive theory.* Englewood Cliffs, NJ: Prentice-Hall.
Barsalou, L. W. (1983). Ad hoc categories. *Memory and Cognition, 11,* 211–227.
Benjamin, L. T. Jr., & Jones, M. R. (1978). From motivational theory to social cognitive development: Twenty-five years of the Nebraska Symposium. *Nebraska Symposium on Motivation, 26,* ix-xix.
Berlyne, D. (1960). *Conflict, arousal, and curiosity.* New York: McGraw-Hill.
Berndt, T. J., & Berndt, E. G. (1975). Children's use of motives and intentionality in person perception and moral judgment. *Child Development, 46,* 904–912.
Bindra, D. (1969). A unified interpretation of emotion and motivation. *Annals of the New York Academy of Sciences, 159,* 1071–1083.
Boden, M. A. (1972). *Purposive explanation in psychology.* Cambridge: Harvard University Press.
Broadbent, D. (1985). Multiple goals and flexible procedures in the design of work. In M. Frese & J. Sabini (Eds.), *Goal directed behavior: The concept of action in psychology.* Hillsdale, NJ: Lawrence Erlbaum Associates.
Brody, N. (1983). *Human motivation: Commentary on goal-directed action.* New York: Academic Press.
Bruner, J. S. (1951). Personality dynamics and the process of perceiving. In R. R. Blake & G. V. Ramsey (Eds.), *Perception: An approach to personality.* New York: Ronald.
Bruner, J. S. (1981). *Intention in the structure of action and interaction.* Norwood, NJ: Ablex.
Butzin, C. A., & Dozier, M. (1986). Children's use of ulterior motive information. *Child Development, 57,* 1375–1385.
Cantor, N., & Kihlstrom, J. F. (1987). *Personality and social intelligence.* Englewood Cliffs, N.J.: Prentice-Hall.
Carbonell, J. G. (1981). Politics: An experiment in subjective understanding and integrated meaning. In R. C. Schank, & C. K. Riesbeck (Eds.), *Inside computer understanding: Five programs plus miniatures.* Hillsdale, NJ: Lawrence Erlbaum Associates.
Carroll, J. S., & Payne, J. W. (Eds.) (1976). *Cognition and social behavior.* Hillsdale, NJ: Lawrence Erlbaum Associates.
Carver, C. S., & Scheier, M. F. (1982). Control theory: A useful conceptual framework in personality-social, clinical and health psychology. *Psychological Bulletin, 92,* 111–135.
Cofer, C. N. (1981). The history of the concept of motivation. *Journal of the History of the Behavioral Sciences, 17,* 48–53.
Cohen, C. E., & Ebbesen, E. B. (1979). Observational goals and schema activation: A

theoretical framework for behavior perception. *Journal of Experimental Social Psychology, 15*, 305–329.

Darley, J. M., & Fazio, R. H. (1980). Expectancy confirmation processes arising in the interaction sequence. *American Psychologist, 35*, 867–881.

Dweck, C. S. (1986). Motivational processes affecting learning. *American Psychologist, 41*, 1040–1048.

Emmons, R. A., & King, L. A. (1987). Goal striving conflict: Immediate and long-term implications for psychological and physical well-being. Unpublished manuscript.

Frese, M., & Sabini, J. (Eds.) (1985). *Goal directed behavior: The concept of action in psychology.* Hillsdale, NJ: Lawrence Erlbaum Associates.

Frese, M., Stewart, J., & Hannover, B. (1987). Goal orientation and planfulness: Action styles as personality concepts. *Journal of Personality and Social Psychology, 52*, 1182–1194.

Gedo, J. E. (1979). *Beyond interpretation: Toward a revised theory for psychoanalysis.* New York: International Universities Press.

Goldberg, A. (Ed.). (1980). *Advances in self psychology.* New York: International Universities Press.

Graesser, A. C., & Clark, L. F. (1985). *The structures and procedures of implicit knowledge.* Norwood, NJ: Ablex.

Graham, J. A., Argyle, M., & Furnham, A. (1980). The goal structure of situations. *European Journal of Social Psychology, 10*, 345–366.

Hampson, S. E., John, O. P., & Goldberg, L. R. (1986). Category breadth and hierarchical structure in personality: Studies in asymmetrics in judgments of trait implications. *Journal of Personality and Social Psychology, 51*, 37–54.

Heider, F. (1958). *The psychology of interpersonal relations.* New York: Wiley.

Higgins, E. T. (1987). Self-discrepancy: A theory relating self and affect. *Psychological Review, 94*, 319–340.

Higgins, E. T., Klein, R., & Strauman, T. (1985). Self-concept discrepancy theory: A psychological model for distinguishing among different aspects of depression and anxiety. *Social Cognition, 3*, 51–76.

Hoffman, C., Mischel, W., & Mazze, K. (1981). The role of purpose in the organization of information about behavior: Trait-based versus goal-based categories in person cognition. *Journal of Personality and Social Psychology, 40*, 211–225.

Hull, C. L. (1943). *Principles of behavior.* New York: Appleton-Century-Crofts.

Hyland, M. E. (1987). Control theory interpretation of psychological mechanisms of depression: comparison and integration of several theories. *Psychological Bulletin, 102*, 109–121.

Irwin, F. W. (1971). *Intentional behavior and motivation.* Philadelphia: J. B. Lippincott.

James, W. (1890). *Principles of psychology.* New York: Holt.

James, W. (1892). *Psychology: A briefer course.* New York: Holt.

Jones, E. E., & Davis, K. E. (1965). From acts to dispositions: The attribution process in person perception. In L. Berkowitz (Ed.), *Advances in experimental social psychology.* New York: Academic Press.

Jones, E. E., & Pittman, T. S. (1982). Toward a general theory of strategic self-presentation. In J. Suls (Ed.), *Psychological perspectives on the self.* Hillsdale, NJ: Lawrence Erlbaum Associates.

Jones, E. E., & Thibaut, J. W. (1958). Interaction goals as bases of inference in interpersonal perception. In R. Tagiuri & L. Petrullo (Eds.), *Person perception and interpersonal behavior.* Stanford: Stanford University Press.

Kelly, G. A. (1955). *The psychology of personal constructs.* New York: Norton.

King, G. A., & Sorrentino, R. M. (1983). Psychological dimensions of goal-oriented situations. *Journal of Personality and Social Psychology, 44*, 140–162.

Klinger, E. (1977). *Meaning and void: Inner experience and the incentives in people's lives.* Minneapolis: University of Minnesota Press.
Kohler, W. (1929). *Gestalt psychology.* New York: Holt.
Kuhl, J., & Beckmann, J. (Eds.) (1985). *Action control: From cognition to behavior.* Berlin: Springer-Verlag.
Lewin, K. (1935). *A dynamic theory of personality.* New York: McGraw Hill.
Lewin, K. (1951). Intention, will, and need. In D. Rapaport (Ed.), *Organization and pathology of thought.* New York: Columbia University Press.
Little, B. R. (1983). Personal projects: A rationale and method for investigation. *Environment and Behavior, 15,* 273–309.
Markus, H., & Nurius, P. (1986). Possible selves. *American Psychologist, 41,* 954–969.
McArthur, L. Z., & Baron, R. M. (1983). Toward an ecological theory of social perception. *Psychological Review, 90,* 215–238.
McClelland, D. C. (1955). Some social consequences of achievement motivation. In M. R. Jones (Ed.), *Nebraska symposium on motivation.* Lincoln: University of Nebraska Press.
McClelland, D. C. (1961). *The achieving society.* Princeton, NJ: Van Nostrand.
McDougall, W. (1908). *An introduction to social psychology.* London: Methuen.
McDougall, W. (1930). Autobiography. In C. Murchison (Ed.), *A history of psychology in autobiography.* Worcester, MA: Clark University Press.
Miller, G. A., Galanter, E., & Pribram, K. (1960). *Plans and the structure of behavior.* New York: Holt.
Mischel, W. (1973). Toward a cognitive social learning reconceptualization of personality. *Psychological Review, 80,* 252–283.
Mook, D. G. (1987). *Motivation: The organization of action.* New York: Norton.
Moore, M. J., Kagan, J., & Haith, M. M. (1978). "Memory" and motives. *Developmental Psychology, 14,* 563–564.
Murphy, G. L., & Medin, D. L. (1985). The role of theories in conceptual coherence. *Psychological Review, 92,* 289–316.
Murray, H. A. (1938). *Explorations in personality.* New York: Oxford University Press.
Newell, A., Shaw, J. C., & Simon, H. A. (1958). Elements of a theory of human problem-solving. *Psychological Review, 65,* 151–166.
Nuttin, J. (1984). *Motivation, planning, and action.* Hillsdale, NJ: Lawrence Erlbaum Associates.
Oatley, K., & Bolton, W. (1985). A social-cognitive theory of depression in reaction to life events. *Psychological Review, 92,* 372–388.
Paterson, R. J., & Neufeld, R. W. J. (1987). Clear danger: Situational determinants of the appraisal of threat. *Psychological Bulletin, 101,* 404–416.
Pervin, L. A. (1980). The cognitive revolution and what it leaves out. Unpublished manuscript.
Pervin, L. A. (1983). The stasis and flow of behavior: Toward a theory of goals. In M. Page (Ed.), *Personality: Current theory and research.* Lincoln: University of Nebraska Press.
Pervin, L. A., & Furnham, A. (1987). Goal-based and situation-based expectations of behavior. *European Journal of Personality, 1,* 37–44.
Peterson, D. (1983). Conflict. In Kelley, H. H., Berscheid, E., Christensen, A., Harvey, J. H., Huston, T. L., Levinger, G., McClintock, E., Peplau, L., & Peterson, D. (Eds.), *Close relationships.* New York: Freeman.
Powers, W. T. (1973). *Behavior: The control of perception.* Chicago: Aldine.
Powers, W. T. (1978). Quantitative analysis of purposive systems: Some spadework at the foundations of scientific psychology. *Psychological Review, 85,* 417–435.
Read, S. J. (1987). Constructing causal scenarios: A knowledge structure approach to causal reasoning. *Journal of Personality and Social Psychology, 52,* 288–302.

Rempel, J. K., Holmes, J. G., and Zanna, M. P. (1985). Trust in close relationships. *Journal of Personality and Social Psychology, 49,* 95–112.

Rosenblatt, A. D., & Thickstun, J. T. (1977). Modern psychoanalytic concepts in a general psychology. *Psychological Issues,* Monograph 42–43.

Rotter, J. B. (1954). *Social learning and clinical psychology.* Englewood Cliffs, NJ: Prentice-Hall.

Ryan, T. A. (1970). *Intentional behavior: An approach to human motivation.* New York: Ronald.

Schafer, R. (1976). *A new language for psychoanalysis.* New York: Aronson.

Schank, R., & Abelson, R. (1977). *Scripts, plans, goals, and understanding.* Hillsdale, NJ: Lawrence Erlbaum Associates.

Schlenker, B. R. (Ed.) (1985). *The self and social life.* New York: McGraw-Hill.

Schmidt, C. F. (1976). Understanding human action: Recognizing the plans and motives of others. In J. S. Carroll & J. W. Payne (Eds.), *Cognition and social behavior.* Hillsdale, NJ: Lawrence Erlbaum Associates.

Shantz, C. U. (1983). Social cognition. In P. H. Mussen (Ed.), *Handbook of child psychology.* New York: Wiley.

Showers, C., & Cantor, N. (1985). Social cognition: A look at motivated strategies. *Annual Review of Psychology, 36,* 275–305.

Silver, M. (1985). "Purposive behavior" in psychology and philosophy: A history. In M. Frese & J. Sabini (Eds.), *Goal directed behavior: The concept of action in psychology.* Hillsdale, NJ: Lawrence Erlbaum Associates.

Simon, H. A. (1967). Motivational and emotional controls of cognition. *Psychological Review, 74,* 29–39.

Skinner, B. F. (1953). *Science and human behavior.* New York: Macmillan.

Srull, T. K., & Wyer, R. S., Jr. (1986). The role of chronic and temporary goals in social information processing. In R. M. Sorrentino & E. T. Higgins (Eds.), *Handbook of motivation and cognition.* New York: Guilford.

Staats, A. W., & Burns, G. L. (1982). Emotional personality repertoire as cause of behavior: Specification of personality and interaction principles. *Journal of Personality, 43,* 873–881.

Stokols, D. (1981). Group x place transactions: Some neglected issues in psychological research on settings. In D. Magnusson (Ed.), *Toward a psychology of situations.* Hillsdale, NJ: Lawrence Erlbaum Associates.

Tetlock, P. E., & Manstead, A. S. R. (1985). Impression management versus intrapsychic explanations in social psychology: A useful dichotomy? *Psychological Review, 92,* 59–77.

Thibaut, J. W., & Riecken, H. W. (1955). Some determinants and consequences of the perception of social causality. *Journal of Personality, 24,* 113–133.

Tolman, E. C. (1925a). Purpose and cognition: The determiners of animal learning. *Psychological Review, 32,* 285–297.

Tolman, E. C. (1925b). Behaviorism and purpose. *Journal of Philosophy, 22,* 36–41.

Tolman, E. C. (1932). *Purposive behavior in animals and men.* New York: Appleton-Centry-Crofts.

Trzebinski, J. (1985). Action-oriented representations of implicit personality theories. *Journal of Personality and Social Psychology, 48,* 1266–1278.

Van de Geer, J. P., & Jaspars, J. M. F. (1966). Cognitive functions. *Annual Review of Psychology, 17,* 145–176.

Watson, J. B. (1930). *Behaviorism.* Chicago: University of Chicago Press.

Wegner, D. M., & Giuliano, T. (1983). Social awareness in story comprehension. *Social Cognition, 2,* 1–17.

White, R. W. (1959). Motivation reconsidered: The concept of competence. *Psychological Review, 66,* 297–333.

Wiener, N. (1948). *Cybernetics*. New York: Wiley.
Woodfield, A. (1976). *Teleology*. Cambridge: Cambridge University Press.
Wyer, R. S., Jr., & Srull, T. K. (1986). Human cognition in its social context. *Psychological Review, 93*, 322–359.
Young, P. T. (1949). Food-seeking, drive, affective process and learning. *Psychological Review, 56*, 98–121.
Young, P. T. (1959). The role of affective processes in learning and motivation. *Psychological Review, 66*, 104–125.
Young, P. T. (1961). *Motivation and emotion*. New York: Wiley.

2 Self-Regulation of Motivation and Action Through Internal Standards and Goal Systems

ALBERT BANDURA
Stanford University

Social cognitive theory distinguishes between two broad classes of motivation (Bandura, 1986). One class of motivators is biologically based and includes physiological conditions arising from cellular deficits and external aversive events that activate behavior through their physically painful effects. The second major source of motivators is cognitively based. In cognitively-generated motivation, people motivate themselves and guide their actions anticipatorily through the exercise of forethought. They anticipate likely outcomes of prospective actions, they set goals for themselves, and they plan courses of action designed to realize valued futures.

The capability for self-motivation and purposive action is rooted in cognitive activity. Future events cannot be causes of current motivation or action. However, by cognitive representation in the present, conceived future events are converted into current motivators and regulators of behavior. Forethought is translated into incentives and action through the aid of self-regulatory mechanisms.

Forms of Cognitive Motivators

One can distinguish three different forms of cognitive motivators around which different theories have been built. These include *causal attributions, outcome expectancies,* and *cognized goals*. The corresponding theories are attribution theory, expectancy-value theory, and goal theory, respectively. Figure 2.1 summarizes schematically these alternative conceptions of cognitive motivation. We shall see later that certain basic mechanisms of personal agency, such as perceived self-efficacy, operate in all of these variant forms of motivation.

ATTRIBUTION THEORY

According to the attribution theory of motivation (Weiner, 1985), retrospective judgments of the causes of one's performances have motivational effects. People who credit their successes to personal capabilities and their failures to insufficient effort will undertake difficult tasks and persist in the face of failure. This is because they see their outcomes as influenceable by how much effort they expend. In contrast, those who ascribe their failures to deficiencies in ability and their successes to situational factors will display low achievement strivings and give up readily when they encounter obstacles.

Some writers have argued that reasons offered retrospectively should not be regarded as causes. This is obviously true for past actions, where actions precede ascribed causes and would therefore involve backward causation. But reasons for past performances that affect beliefs of personal control can serve as causes of future actions. Thus, people who believe they failed because they did not work hard enough are likely to strive harder, whereas those who believe they failed because they lack the ability are apt to slacken their efforts and become easily discouraged.

Covington and Omelich (1979) conducted a prospective test of whether causal attributions function as causes of motivation and behavior. Students who performed poorly on an academic examination made causal attributions for their failures and rated their degree of negative affect and performance expectations for a second examination taken after a period of mastery learning. Causal attributions for failure had little effect on either affective reactions, performance expectations,

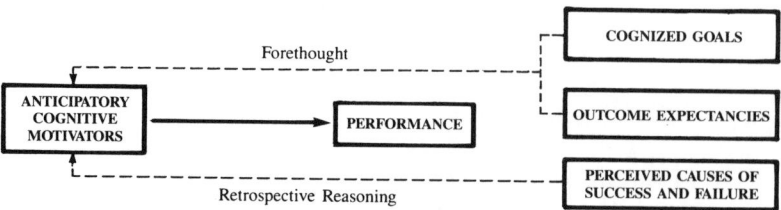

FIG. 2.1 Schematic representation of conceptions of cognitive motivation based on cognized goals, outcome expectancies and causal attributions.

or subsequent level of achievement. Only performance expectations predicted achievement level. The higher the students' judgments of their performance capabilities the better they performed later. Covington and Omelich concluded that causal attributions function as self-serving excuses rather than as causes of achievement motivation.

The role of attributional processes in achievement strivings is further clarified by research in which causal attributions for ongoing cognitive performances are varied by arbitrary attributional feedback and changes in perceived self-efficacy are measured. The results indicate that causal attributions can influence achievement strivings, but the effect is mediated almost entirely through changes in perceived self-efficacy (Relich, Debus, & Walker, 1986; Schunk & Gunn, 1986; Schunk & Rice, 1986). *Ability* attributions are accompanied by strong self-beliefs of efficacy which, in turn, predict subsequent performance attainments.

Effort attributions have variable effects on self-efficacy beliefs. These diverse findings raise the issue of the conception of ability in attribution theory. Attribution theorists usually treat ability as a fixed or stable internal property. High effort needed to achieve an outcome is taken as an indicant of low ability (Kun, 1977; Nicholls & Miller, 1984). In actuality, people vary in their conceptions of ability (M. Bandura & Dweck, 1988; Dweck & Elliot, 1983). The presumptions of attributional theory fit the subgroups of people who regard ability as a stable entity. However, many individuals construe ability as an acquirable skill that is developed through effort. The harder you try the more capable you become. For them, errors reflect inexperience in the activity rather than basic inability. High effort that begets rising accomplishments can enhance self-beliefs of efficacy (Schunk & Cox, 1986).

In judging their efficacy from performance attainments, people use much more varied sources of enactive efficacy information than the four causal factors (effort, ability, task difficulty, chance) routinely assessed in attributional research. In addition to perceptions of task difficulty and amount of effort expended, they consider whether they performed under favorable or unfavorable circumstances, the amount of external aid they received, their physical and emotional state at the time, and the pattern of their successes and failures with continued engagement in the activity. Positive or negative biases in the self-monitoring, cognitive representation, and retrieval of past successes and failures further affect self-efficacy judgment (Bandura, 1986).

The impact of effort attributions on self-efficacy beliefs may vary under different conceptions of ability and different configurations of efficacy-relevant information. Given these complicating factors, it is not entirely surprising that effort attributions do not bear a uniform relationship to self-efficacy beliefs. However, regardless of whether effort attributions correlate positively or negatively with perceived efficacy, the stronger the self-efficacy belief, the higher the subsequent performance attainments (Schunk & Cox, 1986; Schunk & Gunn, 1986; Schunk & Rice, 1986).

The overall evidence reveals that causal attributions, whether in the form of ability, effort, or task difficulty, generally have weak or no independent effect on achievement strivings. The types of factors singled out by attributional theory serve as conveyors of efficacy-relevant information that influence performance attainments mainly by altering people's beliefs in their efficacy. Occasionally, ability attribution emerges as an independent contributor to achievement, but such direct effects tend to be small and equivocal.

Subjective weighting of attributional factors and self-efficacy appraisal involves bidirectional, rather than unidirectional, causation. The relative weight given to information regarding adeptness, effort, task complexity, and situational circumstances will affect self-efficacy appraisal. Self-beliefs of efficacy, in turn, bias causal attribution. Thus, children who regard themselves as highly efficacious tend to ascribe their failures to insufficient effort, whereas those who regard themselves as inefficacious view the cause of their failures as stemming from low ability (Collins, 1982).

EXPECTANCY-VALUE THEORY

People also motivate themselves and guide their actions anticipatorily by the outcomes they expect to flow from given courses of behavior. Expectancy-value theory was designed to account for this form of incentive motivation (Atkinson, 1964; Fishbein, 1967; Rotter, 1954; Vroom, 1964). These various formulations all assume that strength of motivation is governed jointly by the expectation that particular actions will produce specified outcomes and the value placed on those outcomes. They differ mainly in what additional determinants are combined with expectancy and outcome value. Atkinson adds an achievement motive; Rotter adds a generalized expectancy that actions control outcomes; Fishbein adds perceived social pressures to perform the behavior and proneness to compliance; Vroom adds belief that the behavior is achievable through effort.

In its basic version, the expectancy-value theory predicts that the higher the expectancy that certain behavior can secure specific outcomes and the more highly those outcomes are valued, the greater is the motivation to perform the activity. The findings generally show that outcome expectations obtained by adding or multiplying these cognitive factors predict performance motivation (Feather, 1982; Mitchell, 1974; Schwab, Olian-Gottlieb, & Heneman, 1979). However, much of the variance in effort or performance remains unaccounted for. This has stimulated spirited debates about the scope of the expectancy-value theory, its major assumptions, and the methodologies used for assessing and combining the cognitive factors.

According to maximizing expectancy models, people seek to optimize their outcomes. Questions have been raised, however, concerning the assumptions about how decisions are usually made. As several authors have correctly observed, people are not as systematic in considering alternative courses of action and in weighing their likely consequences as expectancy-value models assume (Behling & Starke, 1973; Simon, 1976). Alternatives are often ill-defined. People rarely examine all the feasible alternatives or give detailed thought to all the consequences of even the options they do consider. More typically they pick, from a limited array of possibilities, the course of action that looks satisfactory rather than search studiously for the optimal one. Moreover, they are sometimes inconsistent in how they order alternatives, they have difficulty assigning relative weights to different types of outcomes, they let the attractiveness of the outcomes color their judgments of how difficult it might be to attain them, and they opt for lesser outcomes because they can get them sooner. When faced with many alternatives and complexly contingent outcomes, they use simplifying decision strategies that may lead them to select alternatives that differ from those they would have had they weighed and ordered the various factors as presupposed by the maximizing model.

The issue in question is not the rationality of the judgmental process. People often have incomplete or erroneous information about alternatives and their probable consequences, they process information through cognitive biases, and what they value may be rather odd. Decisions that are subjectively rational to the performer, given the basis on which they were made, may appear irrational to others. Subjective rationality often sponsors faulty choices. There are too many aspects to a judgmental process where one can go astray to achieve objective rationality (Brandt, 1979). The main issue in dispute concerns the correspondence between the postulated judgmental process and how people actually go about appraising and weighing the probable consequences of alternative courses of action.

The types of anticipated incentives singled out for attention is another dimension on which expectancy-value theory often departs from actuality. Some of the most valued rewards of activities are in the satisfaction derived from fulfilling personal standards. The self-satisfaction for a job well done may be valued more highly than tangible payoffs.

Because incentive theories tend to neglect the affective self-evaluative rewards of performance attainments, self-incentives rarely receive the consideration they deserve in the option-outcome calculus. Predictiveness is sacrificed if influential self-incentives are overlooked. With regard to the scope of the expectancy-value model, even the elaborated versions include only a few cognitive motivators. In actuality, forethought of outcomes influences effort and performance through additional intervening mechanisms.

People act on their beliefs about what they can do, as well as their beliefs about the likely effects of various actions. The effects of outcome expectancies on performance motivation are partly governed by self-beliefs of capabilities. There are many activities which, if done well, guarantee valued outcomes, but they are not pursued by people who doubt they can do what it takes to succeed (Beck & Lund, 1981; Betz & Hackett, 1986; Wheeler, 1983). Self-perceived inefficacy can thus nullify the motivating potential of alluring outcome expectations. Conversely, a strong sense of personal efficacy can sustain efforts in the face of uncertain or repeated negative outcomes.

In activities that call upon competencies, self-efficacy beliefs affect the extent to which people act on their outcome expectations. Some expectancy-value theories include an expectancy that effort will beget requisite performances (Vroom, 1964). It should be noted, however, that perceived self-efficacy encompasses much more than effort determinants of performance. Effort is but one of many factors that govern the level and quality of performance. People judge their capacity for challenging activities more in terms of their perceptions of the knowledge, skills, and strategies they have at their command than solely on how much they will exert themselves. Performances that call for ingenuity, resourcefulness, and adaptability depend more on adroit use of skills and specialized knowledge than on dint of effort. People who cope poorly with stress expect that marred performances in intimidating situations will be determined by their self-debilitating thought patterns rather than by how much effort they mount. Indeed, the harder they try, the more they may impair their execution of the activity. Expectancy theorists probably singled out effort as the sole cause of performance because the theory has usually been concerned with how hard people work at routine activities. Hence, the aspect of self-efficacy that is most germane to how much is accomplished is people's perceived perseverant capabilities—that is, their belief that they can exert themselves sufficiently to attain designated levels of productivity.

Some confusion has been introduced into the expectancy literature by misconstruing the specifying criteria of a performance level as its outcomes. A *performance* is conventionally defined as "an accomplishment" or "something done;" an *outcome* as "something that follows as a result or consequence of an activity." Three major classes of outcomes can be distinguished: material consequences, social reactions, and self-reactions. Thus, in a high jump field event performance levels are defined in terms of height of jumps. A 6-foot leap is the realization of a particular performance not the outcome that flows from it. The outcomes are the results a 6-foot leap produces—the social recognition, applause, trophies, monetary prizes, and self-satisfaction if it represents a superior attainment, or the social disappointment, forfeiture of material rewards, and self-criticism if it represents a deficient level of attainment. Similarly, in assessments of academic performance, letter grades of *A, B, C, D, F* are the specifying criteria of performance level not the outcomes. Remove the letter indicants of performance level, and one is left with an indefinite or indescribable performance. The social reactions, personal benefits, costs, and affective self-reactions anticipated for an *A*-level performance, or for an *F*-level performance, constitute the outcome expectations. To conceptualize a performance level as the outcome of itself is to destroy the conventional meanings of performance and outcome.

The degree to which outcome expectations contribute independently to performance motivation is partly determined by the structural relation between actions and outcomes in a particular endeavor. Because activities vary in their structural contingencies, there is no single relationship between judgments of self-efficacy and outcome expectations. Rather, the relationship between these two types of cognitions depends on how tightly contingencies are structured, either inherently or socially, in a given domain of functioning. For many activities, competency level dictates outcomes. Hence, the types of outcomes people anticipate depend largely on how well they believe they will be able to perform in given situations. Students do not expect to be showered with academic honors or prizes regardless of the adequacy of their scholarship. In most social, intellectual, and physical pursuits, those who judge themselves highly efficacious will expect favorable outcomes, whereas those who expect poor performances of themselves will conjure up negative outcomes. Thus, in activities in which outcomes are highly contingent on quality of performance, self-judged efficacy accounts for most of the variance in expected outcomes. When variations in perceived self-efficacy are partialed out, the outcomes expected for given performances do not have much of an independent effect on behavior (Barling & Abel, 1983; Barling & Beattie, 1983; Godding & Glasgow, 1985; Lee, 1984a,b; Williams & Watson, 1985).

Self-efficacy beliefs account for only part of the variance in expected outcomes when outcomes are not completely controlled by quality of performance. This occurs when extraneous factors also affect outcomes, or outcomes are socially tied to a minimum level of performance so that some variations in quality of performance have no differential effects. In work situations, for example, compensation is fixed to some normative standard but a higher level of productivity does not bring larger weekly pay checks. Perceived self-efficacy to fulfill the minimal standard will produce better expected outcomes than perceived self-inefficacy to reach that level. However, variations in perceived self-efficacy above the minimal standard would not give rise to different expected outcomes. And finally, expected outcomes are independent of perceived self-efficacy when contingencies are discriminatively structured so that no level of competence can produce desired outcomes. This is illustrated in pursuits that are rigidly segregated by sex, race, age, or some other factor. Under such circumstances, people in the disfavored group expect poor outcomes however efficacious they judge themselves to be. Thus, for example, when athletes were rigidly segregated by race, black baseball players could not gain entry to the major leagues and the attendant benefits no matter how well they pitched or batted.

GOAL THEORY

The capacity to exercise self-influence by personal challenge and evaluative reaction to one's own attainments provides a major cognitive mechanism of motivation and self-directedness. Motivation through pursuit of challenging standards has been the subject of extensive research on goal setting. Investigations of varied domains of functioning under both laboratory and naturalistic conditions provide substantial converging evidence that explicit challenging goals enhance and sustain motivation (Latham & Lee, 1986; Locke, Shaw, Saari, & Latham, 1981; Mento, Steel, & Karren, 1987). Goals operate largely through self-referent processes rather than regulate motivation and action directly. The self-reactive influences by which personal standards create powerful motivational effects are analyzed in some detail in the sections that follow.

Self-Reactive Influences as Mediators of Goal Motivation

Motivation based on standards involves a cognitive comparison process. By making self-satisfaction conditional on matching adopted goals, people give direction to their actions and create self-incentives to persist in their efforts until their performances match their goals. The anticipated

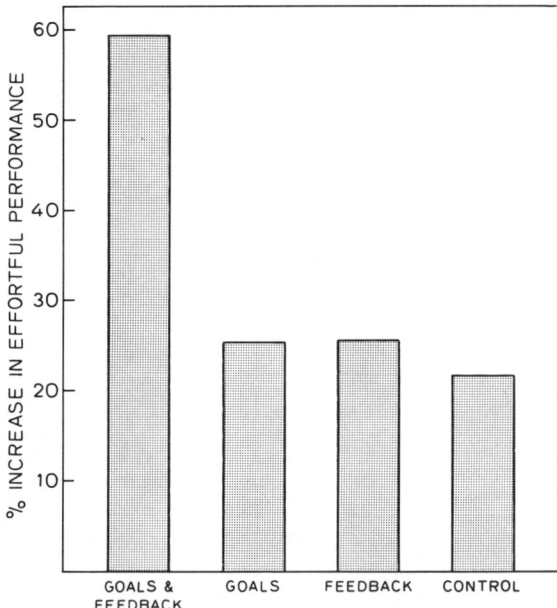

FIG. 2.2 Mean percentage change in level of motivation under conditions combining goals with performance feedback, goals alone, feedback alone, or with none of these factors (Bandura & Cervone, 1983).

self-satisfaction gained from fulfilling valued standards provides one source of incentive motivation for personal accomplishments. Perceived negative discrepancies between performance and the standard individuals seek to attain creates self-dissatisfaction that serves as another incentive motivator for enhanced effort. The motivational effects do not stem from the goals themselves, but rather from the fact that people respond evaluatively to their own behavior. Goals specify the conditional requirements for positive self-evaluation.

Activation of self-evaluation processes through internal comparison requires both comparative factors—a personal standard and knowledge of the level of one's own performance. Neither performance knowledge without standards nor standards without performance knowledge provides a basis for self-evaluative reactions. Studies in which goals and performance feedback are systematically varied yield results consistent with this formulation, whatever the nature of the pursuit (Bandura & Cervone, 1983; Becker, 1978; Strang, Lawrence, & Fowler, 1978). Simply adopting a goal, whether an easy or challenging one, without knowing how one is doing, or knowing how one is doing in the absence of a goal, has no lasting motivational impact. In marked contrast, the combined influence of goals with performance feedback heightens motiva-

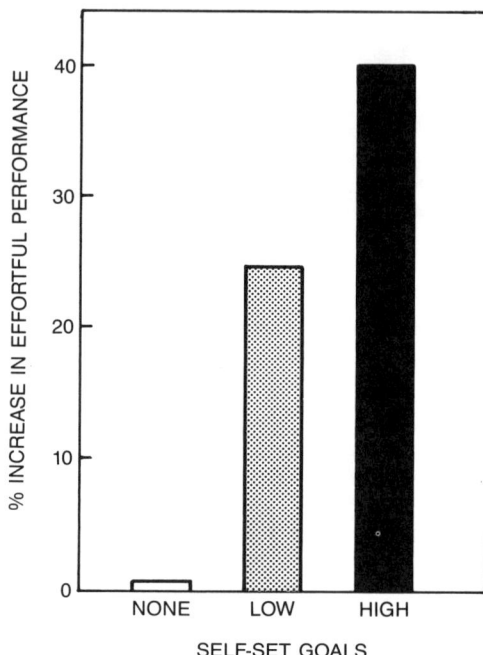

FIG. 2.3 Mean increases in motivational level under conditions of performance feedback alone depending on whether people continue to perform the activity without goals or spontaneously set low or high goals for themselves (Bandura & Cervone, 1983).

tion substantially. This is shown Figure 2.2, which summarizes the level of self-motivation when both, only one, or none of the comparative factors was present.

Although performance feedback alone is not a dependable motivator, it produces substantial variance in motivation that is explainable by the comparative structures individuals create for themselves. When they engage in an ongoing activity and are informed of their performance attainments, some set goals for themselves spontaneously (Bandura & Cervone, 1983). Variations in personal goal setting are reflected in diversity in motivation (Figure 2.3). Those who set no goals for themselves achieve no change in effort and are surpassed by those who aim to match their previous level of effort who, in turn, are outperformed by those who set themselves the more challenging goal of bettering their past endeavor. However, without knowledge of one's performance, self-set goals alone do not, in themselves, have any continuing motivational impact. These results from self-created comparative structures lend further support for the influential role of cognitive comparison processes in motivation through personal standards or goals.

Cognitive motivation based on goal intentions is mediated by three types of self-influences: affective self-evaluation, perceived self-efficacy for goal attainment, and adjustment of personal standards. As already pointed out, goals motivate by enlisting self-evaluative involvement in the activity. People seek self-satisfactions from fulfilling valued goals and are prompted to intensify their efforts by discontent with substandard performances.

Perceived self-efficacy is another cognitive factor that plays an influential role in the exercise of personal control over motivation. It is partly on the basis of self-beliefs of efficacy that people choose what challenges to undertake, how much effort to expend in the endeavor, how long to persevere in the face of difficulties, and affect their vulnerability to stress and despondency in the face of difficulties and failures (Bandura, 1982; 1986). Whether negative discrepancies between personal standards and attainments are motivating or discouraging is partly determined by people's beliefs that they can attain the goals they set for themselves. Those who harbor self-doubts about their capabilities are easily dissuaded by failure. Those who are assured of their capabilities intensify their efforts when they fail to achieve what they seek and they persist until they succeed.

That strong belief in one's efficacy heightens level of effort and perseverance in difficult pursuits is corroborated by evidence across diverse domains of functioning for both children and adults (Bandura & Cervone, 1983; Brown & Inouye, 1978; Cervone & Peake, 1986; Jacobs, Prentice-Dunn, & Rogers, 1984; Schunk, 1984; Weinberg, Gould, & Jackson, 1979). Consider a few examples of tests of whether self-efficacy beliefs operate as causal factors in motivation. Some of these tests of causality introduce a trivial factor devoid of information to affect competency but that can alter perceived self-efficacy. The impact of the altered self-efficacy beliefs on level of motivation is then measured. Studies of anchoring influences show that arbitrary reference points from which judgements are adjusted either upward or downward can bias the judgments because the adjustments are usually insufficient. Cervone and Peake (1986) used arbitrary anchor values to influence self-efficacy judgments. Judgments made from an arbitrary high starting point biased students' perceived self-efficacy as a problem solver in the positive direction, whereas an arbitrary low starting point lowered students' judgments of their efficacy (Figure 2.4). The higher the instated perceived self-efficacy, the longer they persevered on difficult and unsolvable problems before they quit.

In a related study (Peake & Cervone, 1988), efficacy judgment was biased simply by having people judge their self-efficacy in relation to ascending or descending levels of possible attainments. The initial levels in these sequences served as anchoring influences that lowered or raised self-efficacy beliefs, respectively. Elevated self-beliefs of efficacy heightened effort, whereas lowered self-beliefs lessened effort on troublesome

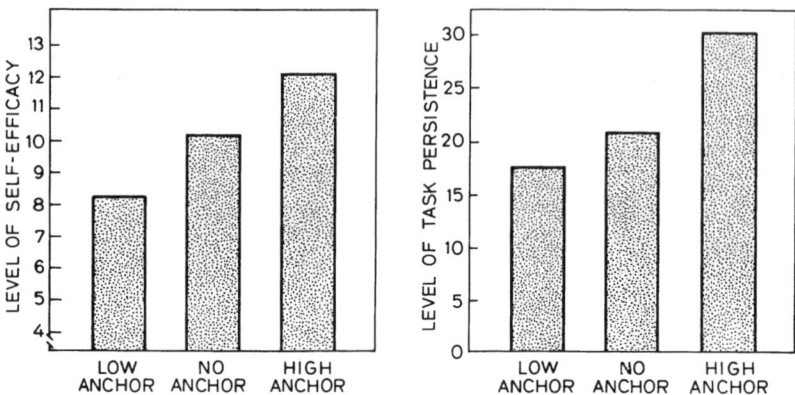

FIG. 2.4 Mean changes induced in perceived self-efficacy by anchoring influences and the corresponding effects on level of subsequent perseverant effort (Cervone & Peake, 1986).

problems. In a further study, Cervone (1985) biased self-efficacy judgment through differential cognitive focus on things about the task that might make it troublesome or tractable. Dwelling on formidable aspects weakened people's belief in their efficacy, but focusing on doable aspects raised self-judgment of capabilities. The higher the altered self-efficacy beliefs, the longer people persevered in the face of repeated failure. In these various experiments, perceived self-efficacy predicts variance in motivation within treatment conditions, as well as across treatments. Mediational analyses reveal that neither anchoring influences nor cognitive focus has any impact on motivation when variations in self-efficacy beliefs are controlled. These external influences thus exerted their effect on motivation entirely through the mediation of changes in self-efficacy beliefs.

A number of studies have been conducted in which self-efficacy beliefs are altered by bogus feedback unrelated to one's actual performance. People partly judge their capabilities through social comparison. Using this type of induction procedure, Weinberg, Gould, and Jackson (1979) showed that physical stamina in competitive situations is mediated by perceived self-efficacy. They raised the self-efficacy beliefs of one group by telling them that they had triumphed in a competition of muscular strength. They lowered the self-efficacy beliefs of another group by telling them that they were outperformed by their competitor. The higher the illusory beliefs of physical strength, the more physical endurance subjects displayed during competition on a new task measuring physical stamina (Figure 2.5). Failure in the subsequent competition spurred those with a high sense of perceived self-efficacy to even greater physical effort, whereas failure further impaired the performance of those whose perceived self-efficacy had been undermined. Self-beliefs of physical efficacy illusorily heightened in females and illusorily weakened in males obliterated large preexisting sex differences in physical strength.

Jacobs, Prentice-Dunn, and Rogers (1984) used another variant of social self-appraisal—bogus normative comparison—as a way of raising or weakening beliefs of cognitive self-efficacy. Heightened self-efficacy produced stronger perseverant effort (Figure 2.6).

The combined evidence that divergent modes of efficacy induction produce convergent effects on motivation across a variety of pursuits adds to the explanatory and predictive generality of the efficacy mediator. Perceived self-efficacy determines not only level of effort expenditure, but how productively that effort is deployed. People who have a strong sense of efficacy follow more efficient analytic strategies to discover the optimal rules of performance than do the self-doubters (Wood & Bandura, 1988; Wood, Bandura, & Bailey, 1988). When faced with complex decisions, those who distrust their efficacy become erratic in their strategic thinking. Perceived self-efficacy can thus enhance performance through its effects on deployment of strategies, as well as on motivation.

In activities in which deficient performances can have untoward consequences, perceived self-inefficacy can impair functioning by generat-

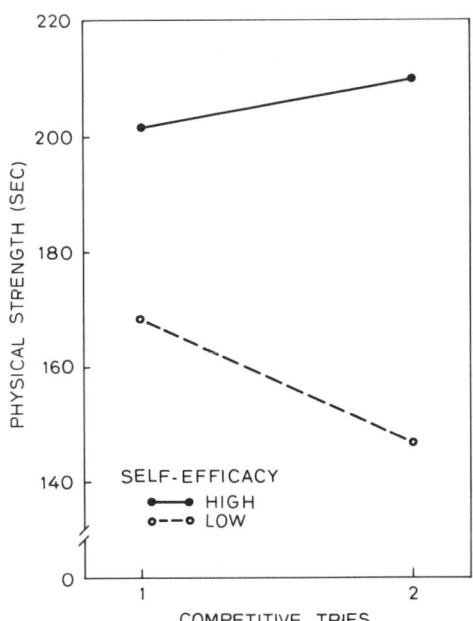

FIG. 2.5 Mean level of physical stamina mobilized in competitive situations as a function of illusorily instated high or low self-percepts of physical efficacy (Weinberg, Gould, & Jackson, 1979).

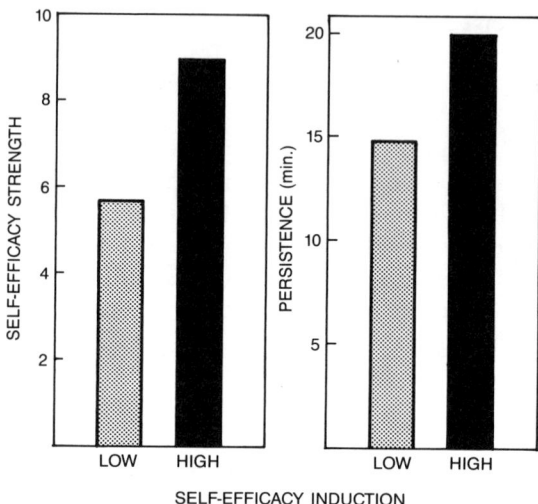

FIG. 2.6 Mean changes in perceived self-efficacy induced by arbitrary normative comparison and the corresponding effects on level of subsequent perseverant effort (Jacobs, Prentice-Dunn, & Rogers, 1984).

ing disruptive cognitions and avoidant actions. People who have a strong sense of efficacy deploy their attention and effort to the demands of the situation and are spurred by obstacles to greater effort. In contrast, those who judge themselves inefficacious in coping with environmental demands dwell on their personal deficiencies and cognize potential difficulties as more formidable than they really are. Such self-referent misgivings create stress and undermine effective use of personal competencies by diverting attention from how best to proceed to concern over personal failings and possible repercussions of mistakes (Lazarus & Launier, 1978; Meichenbaum, 1977; Sarason, 1975). The weaker the perceived coping efficacy, the higher the subjective distress, and the greater the activation of autonomic arousal, stress-related hormones, and neurotransmitters (Bandura, 1988a).

Environmental events are not always completely under personal control, and most human activities contain some potential risks. The exercise of control over anxiety arousal, therefore, requires not only development of behavioral coping efficacy but also efficacy in controlling dysfunctional apprehensive cognitions (Bandura, 1988e). It is not anxious cognitions *per se* but the perceived inefficacy to exercise control over such ruminative thinking that is most perturbing (Kent & Gibbons, 1987). People base their actions on perceived self-efficacy rather than on anxiety arousal in situations they regard as risky. Thus, perceived self-efficacy predicts avoidant behavior when anticipated anxiety is partialled out, whereas anticipated anxiety has little or no independent effect on avoidant behavior when perceived self-efficacy is controlled (Bandura, 1988b; Williams, 1987).

The goals people set for themselves at the outset of an endeavor are likely to change, depending on the pattern and level of progress they are making (Campion & Lord, 1982). They may maintain their original goal, lower their sights, or adopt an even more challenging goal. Thus, the third constituent self-influence in the ongoing regulation of motivation concerns the readjustment of personal goals in light of one's attainments. Csikszentmihalyi (1979) examined what it is about activities that fosters continuing deep engrossment in life pursuits. The common factors found to be conducive to enduring motivation include adopting personal challenges in accordance with one's perceived capabilities and having informative feedback of progress.

Studies in which discrepancy levels are varied systematically and the self-reactive influences are measured antecedently to motivational change shed light on how the self-reactive influences operate in concert in the regulation of motivation through goal systems. One experiment examined how self-evaluative and efficacy mediators contribute to motivation under a moderate negative goal discrepancy (Bandura & Cervone, 1983). As shown in Figure 2.7, affective self-evaluation and perceived self-efficacy are good predictors of the degree of change in motivation when attainments fall short of the goal being pursued. Discontent over a substandard performance combined with high perceived self-efficacy for goal attainment produces a marked heightening of effort. A low sense of self-efficacy with low discontent over a substandard performance mobilizes little effort. Either high discontent or high perceived self-efficacy alone, results in a moderate increase in motivation. The joint operation of the self-reactive influences even predicts whether motivation is enhanced, sustained, or debilitated over the course of a given attempt. The discontented self-efficacious ones intensified their effort as time went on, whereas those who judged themselves inefficacious to reach the goal and were satisfied with a substandard performance slackened their efforts and displayed a substantial decline in motivation as they continued the task.

The three self-reactive influences exert differential impact on motivation when attainments diverge from the comparative standard over a wide range of discrepancies (Bandura & Cervone, 1986). After performing a strenuous task, individuals received prearranged feedback that their effort fell either markedly, moderately, or minimally short of the adopted standard, or that it exceeded the standard. They then recorded their perceived self-efficacy for goal attainment, their self-evaluation, and self-set goals, whereupon their motivational level was measured.

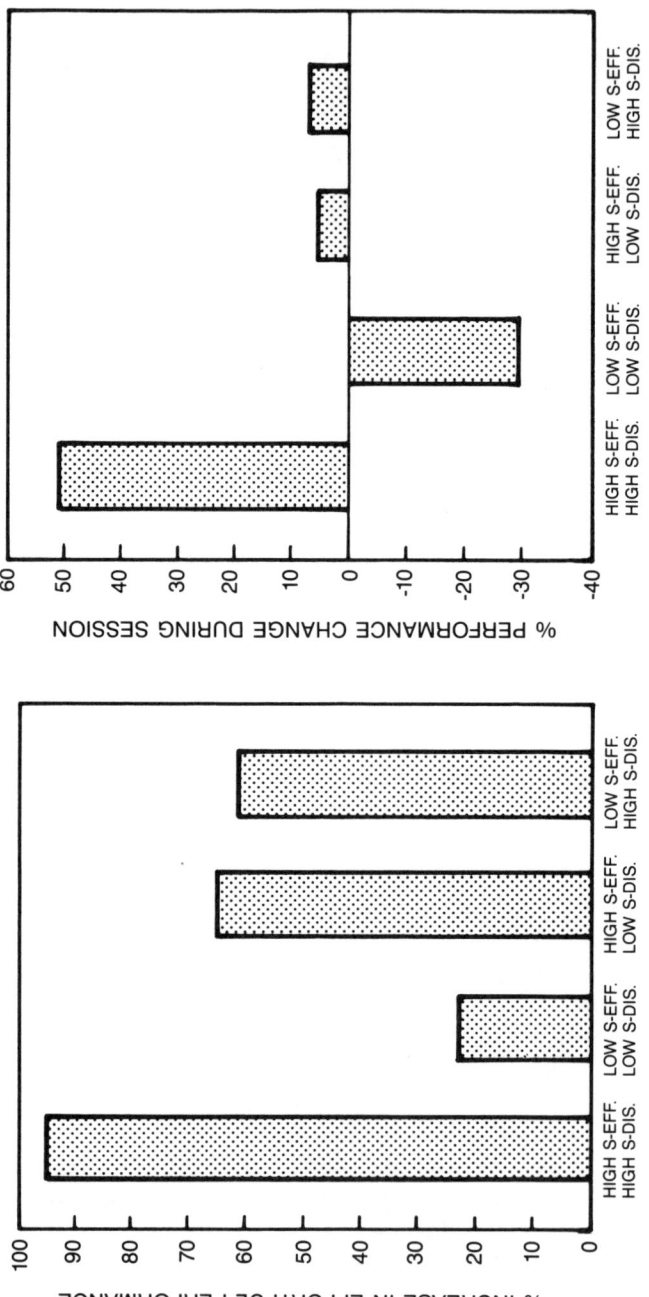

FIG. 2.7 Mean percentage changes in motivational level under conditions combining goals and performance feedback as a function of different combinations of levels of self-dissatisfaction (**S-DIS**) and perceived self-efficacy for goal attainment (**S-EFF**). The left-hand panel shows the mean change in motivation for the entire session: The right-hand panel shows the mean motivational change between the initial and the final segment of the session (Bandura & Cervone, 1983).

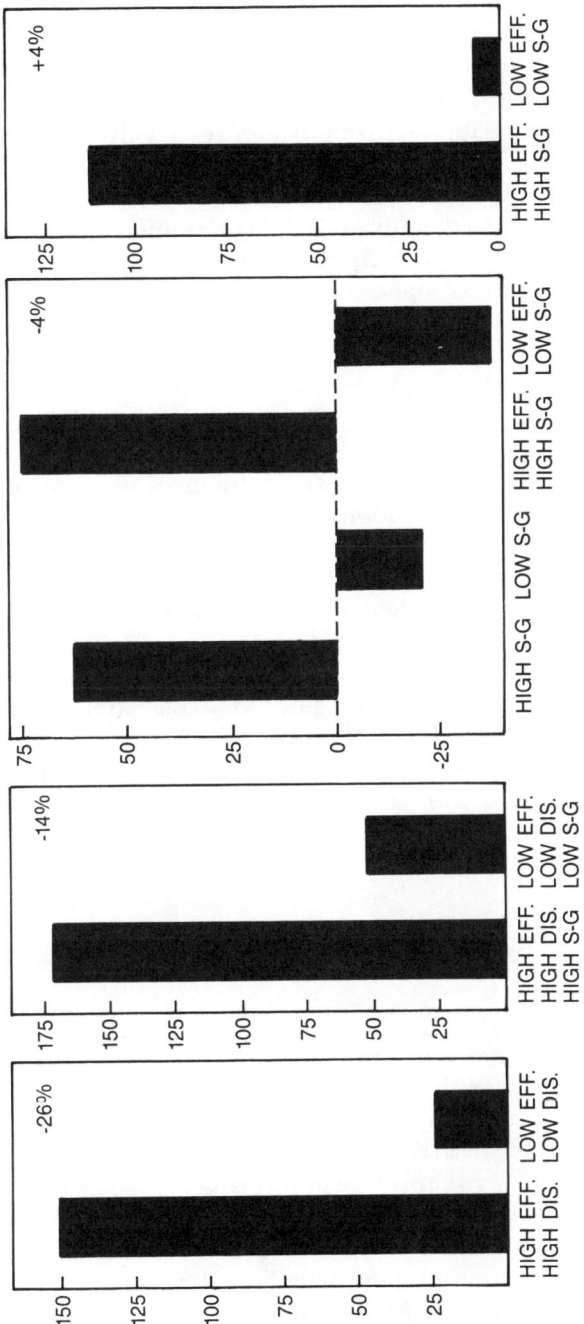

FIG. 2.8 Mean percentage changes in motivational level by people who are high or low in the self-reactive influences identified by hierarchical regression analyses as the critical motivators at each of four levels of preset discrepancy between a challenging standard and level of performance attainment. **EFF** signifies strength of perceived self-efficacy to attain a 50% increase in effort; **DIS** the level of self-dissatisfaction with the same level of attainment as in the prior attempt; and **S-G** the goals people set for themselves for the next attempt. The second set of graphs at the −4% discrepancy level summarize the results of the regression analysis performed with perceived self-efficacy averaged over the 30%–70% goal attainment range (Bandura & Cervone, 1986).

Figure 2.8 portrays graphically how the self-influences operate in concert at each discrepancy level in the regulation of motivation.

Perceived self-efficacy contributes to motivation at all discrepancy levels. The stronger the people's self-efficacy beliefs that they can meet challenging standards, the more they intensify their efforts. Discontent operates as an influential affective motivator when attainments fall substantially or moderately short of a comparative standard. The more self-dissatisfied people are with substandard attainments, the more they heighten their efforts. However, if they are quite satisfied with approximating or matching the standard again, they do not invest increased effort in the pursuit. As people approach or surpass the initial standard, the new goals they set for themselves serve as an additional motivator. The higher the self-set goals, the more effort invested in the endeavor. Taken together this set of self-reactive influences accounts for the major share of variation in motivation.

Self-reactive influences predict the impact of success, as well as of failure, on motivation. When attainments surpass challenging goals, people's beliefs in their efficacy and their self-set goals determine their level of motivation (Figure 2.8). Those who hold a strong belief in their efficacy motivate themselves by setting even higher goal challenges that create new discrepancies to be mastered. Thus, notable attainments bring temporary satisfaction, but people enlist new challenges as personal motivators for further accomplishment. Those who doubt they could muster the same level of effort again lower their goals. Their motivation declines.

Self-Regulation and the Negative Feedback Model

Many theories of self-regulation are founded on a negative feedback control system (Carver & Scheier, 1981; Kanfer, 1977). The basic structure of this type of regulatory system includes a behavior monitoring operation, a comparator, and an error correction routine. The system functions as a motivator and regulator of action through a discrepancy reduction mechanism. Perceived discrepancy between performance and the reference standard automatically triggers action to reduce the incongruity. Discrepancy reduction clearly plays a central role in any system of self-regulation. However, in the negative feedback control system, if performance matches the standard the person does nothing. A regulatory process in which matching a standard begets inertness does

2. SELF-REGULATION OF MOTIVATION

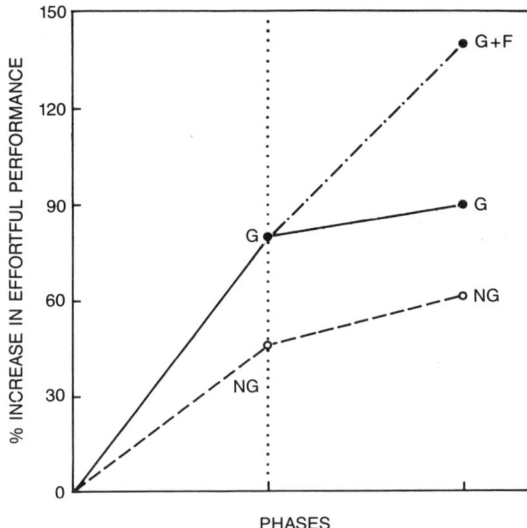

FIG. 2.9 Portrayal of how anticipatory feedforward and feedback systems operate in the initiation and continued regulation of motivation. Initially, subjects performed with goals **(G)** or no goals **(NG)**. In the next phase, the goal subjects continued to perform with goals only **(G)** or with goals and feedback **(GF)** (Bandura & Cervone, 1983).

not characterize human self-motivation. Such a feedback control system would produce circular action that leads nowhere. Nor could people be stirred to action until they receive feedback that their performance is discrepant from the standard.

Although comparative feedback is essential in the ongoing regulation of motivation, people can initially raise their level of motivation by adopting goals before they receive any feedback regarding their beginning effort (Bandura & Cervone, 1983). Negative feedback may help to keep them going, but it is not present antecedently to start them. That different self-regulatory systems operate in the initiation and continued control of motivation is shown in Figure 2.9. In the initial phase of the endeavor, individuals who had adopted a challenging goal enlisted a higher level of effort than those who performed without goals other than to do their best. As they went on with the activity, those who continued to perform it with goals only or without goals displayed no further increases in motivation, whereas the individuals who had the benefit of goals and performance feedback raised their level of motivation substantially. A theory of motivation control must explain how each new goal adoption motivates from the outset before the first performance feedback. The motivating starter is the anticipatory estimate of the level of effort needed to match the goal. Subsequent feedback provides instructive information on the corrective adjustments in motivation needed to attain the goal.

Human self-motivation relies on both *discrepancy production,* and *discrepancy reduction.* It requires *feedforward control* as well as *feedback control.* People initially motivate themselves through feedforward control by adopting valued performance standards that create a state of disequilibrium and then mobilizing their effort on the basis of anticipatory estimation. Feedback control comes into play in subsequent adjustments of effort expenditure to achieve desired results. After people attain the standard they have been pursuing, they generally set a higher standard for themselves. The adoption of further challenges creates new motivating discrepancies to be mastered. Similarly, surpassing a standard is more likely to raise aspiration than to lower subsequent performance to conform to the surpassed standard. Self-motivation thus involves a dual cyclic process of disequilibrating discrepancy production followed by equilibrating discrepancy reduction.

An evaluative executive control system with a feedforward component can, of course, be superimposed on a negative feedback operation that keeps changing aspirational standards with progressive performance attainments. To capture the complexity of human self-regulation, such an executive control system must be invested with the evaluative agentive properties previously shown to play an important role in self-directedness. These include (1) predictive anticipatory control of effort expenditure, (2) affective self-evaluative reactions to one's performances rooted in a value system, (3) self-appraisal of personal efficacy for goal attainment, and (4) self-reflective metacognitive activity concerning the adequacy of one's efficacy appraisals and the suitability of one's standard setting. Evaluation of perceived self-efficacy relative to task demands indicates whether the standards being pursued are within attainable bounds or beyond one's reach.

In human endeavors, goals adjustments do not follow a neat pattern of ever-rising standards after personal accomplishments, nor do failures necessarily lower aspirations. Rather, because of interacting factors, feedback of discrepancy has diverse effects on the self-reactive influences that mediate motivation and standard setting. This is shown in the previously cited study (Bandura & Cervone, 1986), in which people were led to believe that their attainments diverged from their original goal over a wide range of discrepancies. The variations in perceived self-efficacy and self-set goals at each discrepancy level are plotted in Figure 2.10.

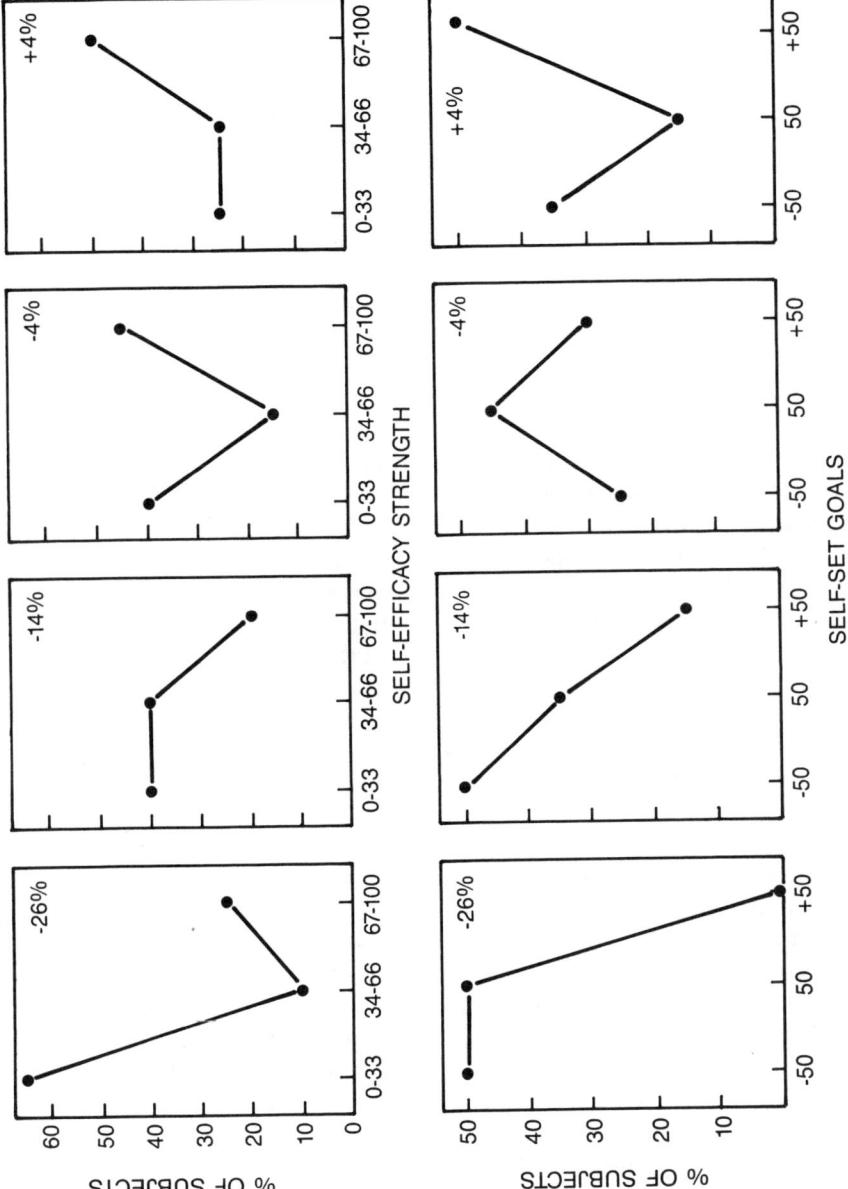

FIG. 2.10 Patterns of perceived self-efficacy to attain a 50% increase in effort and whether this difficult goal was adhered to, abandoned for a lower goal, or raised to an even more challenging goal at each of four levels of preset discrepancy (−26%, −14%, −4%, +4%) between the difficult goal and level of performance attainment (Bandura & Cervone, 1986).

Impact of Goal Discrepancy on Perceived Self-Efficacy

When people fail to fulfill a challenging standard, some become less sure of their efficacy, others lose faith in their capabilities, but many remain unshaken in their belief that they can attain the standard (see Figure 2.10). Surpassing a taxing standard through sustained strenuous effort does not necessarily strengthen self-beliefs of efficacy. Although, for most people, high accomplishment strengthens their self-beliefs, a sizable number who drive themselves to hard-won success are left with self-doubts that they can duplicate the feat.

The latter findings raise the important issue of resiliency of self-beliefs of efficacy in the face of difficulties. There is a growing body of evidence that human accomplishments and positive well-being require an optimistic and resilient sense of personal efficacy (Bandura, 1986; White, 1982). This is because ordinary social realities are usually fraught with difficulties. They are full of impediments, adversities, failures, setbacks, frustrations, and inequities. Success usually comes through renewed effort following failed attempts. To abort efforts prematurely limits personal accomplishments. Therefore, people must have a robust sense of personal efficacy to sustain the perseverant effort needed to succeed. White (1982) vividly documents that the striking common characteristic of people who eventually achieved eminence in their respective fields was an inextinguishable sense of self-efficacy that enabled them to override innumerable rejections of their early work. Their resilient self-efficacy was combined with a steadfast belief in the worth of what they were doing.

Affective and Achievement Benefits of Optimistic Self-Efficacy Belief. It is widely believed that misjudgment produces dysfunction. Certainly, gross miscalculation can get one into trouble. But optimistic self-appraisals of efficacy that are not unduly disparate from what is possible can be advantageous, whereas veridical judgments can be self-limiting. Human skill is a variable, rather than a fixed, property. What people can do depends on how well they orchestrate their subskills and stratagems and how hard they work at the task. The same capability, therefore, can give rise to performances that are subpar, ordinary, or extraordinary for a particular person. When people err in their self-appraisal they tend to overestimate their capabilities. This is a benefit rather than a cognitive failing to be eradicated. If self-efficacy beliefs always reflected only what people can do routinely, they would rarely fail but they would not mount the extra effort needed to surpass their ordinary performances.

Evidence suggests that it is often the so-called normals who are distorters in self-appraisal. Anxious and depressed people have been compared in their skills and their self-beliefs with those who are unburdened by such problems. The groups differ little in their actual skills. But they differ substantially in their beliefs about their efficacy. People who are socially anxious are often just as socially skilled as the more sociable ones. But socially active people judge themselves much more adept than they really are (Glasgow & Arkowitz, 1975).

Depressed persons usually display realistic self-appraisals of their social competencies. The nondepressed view themselves as much more adroit than they really are. As depressed people improve in treatment, they show the self-enhancing biases that characterize the nondepressed (Lewinsohn, Mischel, Chaplin, & Barton, 1980). A similar pattern of advantageous self-appraisal is revealed in laboratory tasks in which people perform actions and outcomes occur, but the actions exert no control over the outcomes. The depressed are quite realistic in judging they lack control. In contrast, nondepressed people believe they are exercising a good deal of control in such situations (Alloy & Abramson, 1979). After nondepressed people are made temporarily depressed they become realistic in judging their personal control. When depressed people are made to feel happy, they overestimate the extent to which they exercise control (Alloy, Abramson, & Viscusi, 1981). Thus, the depressed appear as realists, the nondepressed as confident distortionists.

Social reformers strongly believe that they can mobilize the collective effort needed to bring social change (Bandura, 1986, Muller, 1979). Although their beliefs and the collective sense of efficacy they instill in others are rarely fully realized, they sustain reform efforts that achieve lesser, but important, gains. Were social reformers to be entirely realistic about the prospects of transforming social systems, they would either forego the endeavor, or fall easy victim to discouragement. Realists may adapt well to existing realities, but those with a tenacious self-efficacy are likely to change those realities.

The emerging evidence indicates that the achievers, the innovators, the sociable, the nonanxious, the nondespondent, and the social reformers take an optimistic view of their personal efficacy to exercise influence over events that affect their lives. If not unrealistically exaggerated, such self-beliefs foster personal and social accomplishments.

Impact of Goal Discrepancy on Personal Goal Setting. Self-beliefs of capability affect personal goal setting. The more capable people judge themselves to be, the higher the goals they set for themselves (Bandura & Cervone, 1986; Wood, et al. 1988), and the more firmly committed they remain to their goals (Locke, Frederick, Lee, & Bobko, 1984). Hence, the variable impact of discrepancy feedback on perceived self-efficacy is also reflected in personal goal setting. As can be seen in Figure 2.9, variation in the size of the performance discrepancy produced substantially different patterns of personal goal setting. When people receive prearranged feedback that their efforts fell markedly or moderately short of the goal they were pursuing, they either adhere to it or lower their goal. A strenuous effort that falls just short of a difficult standard has diverse effects on personal goal setting. Many continue to strive for it, others lower their sights, and still others set themselves an even greater challenge.

It is widely assumed that accomplishments raise performance standards. Studies of level of aspiration show that, indeed, people generally set their goals slightly above their preceding attainment (Festinger, 1942; Ryan, 1970). However, the use of simple tasks that call for little effort limits the generality of the results from this line of research. This is because, in everyday life, significant accomplishments usually require arduous effort over an extended period. In such endeavors, many interacting determinants, including fortuitous factors, contribute to achievement. Therefore, people do not necessarily expect to outdo each past accomplishment in an ever-rising series of triumphs. Knowledge of having surpassed a demanding standard through laborious effort does not automatically lead people to raise their aspiration (see Figure 2.9). Those who have a high sense of self-efficacy set themselves more challenging goals to accomplish. But some are left with self-doubts that they can muster the same level of laborious effort again, and they set their sights on simply trying to match the standard they had previously pursued. Having driven themselves to success, others judge themselves inefficacious to repeat a demanding feat and lower their aspirations.

Goal Properties and Self-Motivation

Goal intentions do not automatically activate the self-reactive influences that govern level of motivation. Certain properties of goal structures determine how strongly the self-system will become enlisted in any given endeavor. The relevant goal properties are addressed next.

Goal Specificity. The extent to which goals create personal incentives and guides for action is partly determined by their specificity. Explicit standards regulate performance by designating the type and amount of effort required to attain them, and they generate self-satisfaction and build self-efficacy by furnishing unambiguous signs of personal accomplishments. General intentions, which are indefinite about the level of goal to be reached, provide little basis for regulating one's efforts or for evaluating how one is doing. In studies of the regulative function of goals differing in specificity, clear, attainable goals produce higher levels of performance than general intentions to do one's best, which usually have little or no effect (Locke et al., 1981; Bandura & Cervone, 1983). Specific performance goals serve to motivate the unmotivated and to foster positive attitudes toward the activities (Bryan & Locke, 1967).

Goal Challenge. The amount of effort and satisfaction that accompany variations in goals depends on the level at which they are set. Strong interest and involvement in activities is sparked by challenges. When self-satisfaction is contingent on attainment of challenging goals, more effort is expended than if easy ones are adopted as sufficient. Locke (1968) postulates an increasing linear function between goal level and performance motivation. A large body of evidence does show that the higher the goals the harder people work to attain them and the better is their performance (Mento, et al., 1987). However, the linear relationship is assumed to hold only if they accept the goals and remain strongly committed to them. Most people, of course, eventually reject performance goals they consider unrealistically demanding or well beyond their reach. However, people remain surprisingly steadfast to goals they have little chance of fulfilling, even when given normative information that others reject them as unrealistic (Erez & Zidon, 1984). When assigned goals are beyond their reach and failure to attain them carries no cost, people try to approximate high standards as closely as they can rather than abandon them altogether (Garland, 1983; Locke, Zubritzky, Cousins, & Bobko, 1984). As a result, they achieve notable progress even though the accomplishment of distal goal aspirations eludes them.

The generality of evidence of unshaken pursuit of unreachable goals must be qualified, however, by the fact that laboratory simulations may differ from actual conditions on several important dimensions: The endeavor usually involves only a brief effort, failure carries no costs, and no opportunities exist for alternative pursuits. Unattainable goals are more likely to be abandoned when the activities require extensive investment of effort and resources, failure to meet the goals brings aversive consequences, and other activities are available in which to invest one's efforts. When goals are set unrealistically high, strong effort produces repeated failure that can weaken motivation by undermining perceived self-efficacy.

Proponents of expectancy-value models interpret evidence that harder goals produce higher performances as support for their theory. In this view, motivated performance is the product of the subjective probability of success and the value of attaining it. They reason that the incentive value of goal attainment is higher for difficult than for easy goals. Hence, people will exert more effort to succeed at high goals

(Matsui, Okada, & Mizuguchi, 1981). However, in experiments in which different possible determinants of performance effort are varied, goal difficulty and perceived capability predict effort, whereas goal value and expectancy of success do not when other factors are controlled (Mento, Cartledge, & Locke, 1980). High value and expectancy of success increase the likelihood that assigned goals will be accepted as personal goals. Value and success expectancy thus affect performance indirectly, through their influence on goal acceptance, rather than by operating directly on performance. When success expectancy affects performance directly, its independent contribution is small compared to that of personal goals (Garland, 1984).

Much of the experimentation on level of goal challenges involves a single effort to achieve an individual goal. Social cognitive theory distinguishes between complementary regulative functions of distal goals and a graduated system of proximal subgoals in ongoing endeavors (Bandura, 1986). Superordinate distal goals give purpose to an activity and serve a general directive function, but subgoals are better suited to serve as the proximal determinants of specific choice of activities and how much effort is devoted to them. Self-motivation is best sustained through a series of proximal subgoals that are hierarchically organized to ensure successive advances to superordinate goals. The relationship between probability of goal attainment and effort expenditure will differ for subgoals and for end goals. Pursuit of a formidable distal goal can sustain a high level of motivation provided it is broken down into subgoals that are challenging but clearly attainable through extra effort (Bandura & Schunk, 1981). To strive for unreachable subgoals is to drive oneself to unrelenting failure. By making complex tasks easier through subdivision into more manageable units, one can perhaps retain the power of goals that tend to have lesser impact on complex than on simpler activities (Wood, Mento, & Locke, 1987).

The complementary regulation of motivation by hierarchical goals of differential achievability characterizes most of the strivings of everyday life. Long-range aspirations may remain unfulfilled, but personal and social advancements are realized in the process of successful striving. In an ongoing pursuit, of course, the perceived difficulty of a superordinate goal does not remain constant. Progress toward a superordinate goal in the distant future alters subjective estimates of eventual success. As one comes closer to realizing distal goals, their attainment appears less formidable than when originally viewed from far down the line.

Goal Proximity. As suggested in the preceding discussion, the effectiveness of goal intentions in regulating motivation and action depends greatly on how far into the future they are projected. A proximate standard serves to mobilize self-influences and direct what one does in the here and now. Distal goals alone are too far removed in time to provide effective incentives and guides for present action. In the face of many competing atrractions, focus on the distant future makes it easy to put off matters in the present on the belief that there is always ample time to mount the effort later.

Subgoals not only enlist self-reactive motivators, they also figure prominently in the development of self-efficacy (Bandura & Schunk, 1981). Without standards against which to measure their performances, people have little basis for gauging their capabilities. Subgoal attainments provide rising indicants of mastery for enhancing self-percepts of efficacy. By contrast, distal goals are too far removed in time to serve as favorable markers of progress along the way to ensure a growing sense of personal efficacy.

The standards against which attainments are compared also contribute, in several ways, to the development of intrinsic interest in the things being pursued. People develop enduring interest in activities at which they feel self-efficacious and from which they derive self-satisfaction. Challenging standards enlist sustained involvement in tasks needed to build competencies that foster interest. Moreover, when people aim for and master valued levels of performance, they experience a sense of satisfaction (Bandura & Cervone, 1983; Locke, Cartledge, & Knerr, 1970). The satisfactions derived form goal attainments build intrinsic interest. However, when distal goals are used as the comparative standard, current attainments build intrinsic interest. However, when distal goals are used as the comparative standard, current attainments may prove disappointing because of wide disparities with lofty future standards. As a result, interest fails to develop even though skills are being acquired in the process. To the extent that proximal subgoals promote and authenticate a sense of efficacious agency, they heighten interest through enhancement of perceived personal causation (Bandura & Schunk, 1981). Perceived self-efficacy is thus a better predictor of intrinsic interest than is actual ability (Collins, 1982).

These diverse effects of proximal self-motivation are revealed in a study in which children who were grossly deficient and uninterested in mathematics pursued a program of self-directed learning under conditions involving either proximal subgoals leading to a distal goal, only the distal goal, or without any reference to goals (Bandura & Schunk, 1981). Within each of the goal conditions, children could observe how many units of work they had completed in each session and their cumulative attainment. Under proximal subgoals children progressed rapidly in self-directed learning, achieved substantial mastery of mathematical operations, and developed an increased sense of efficacy (Figure

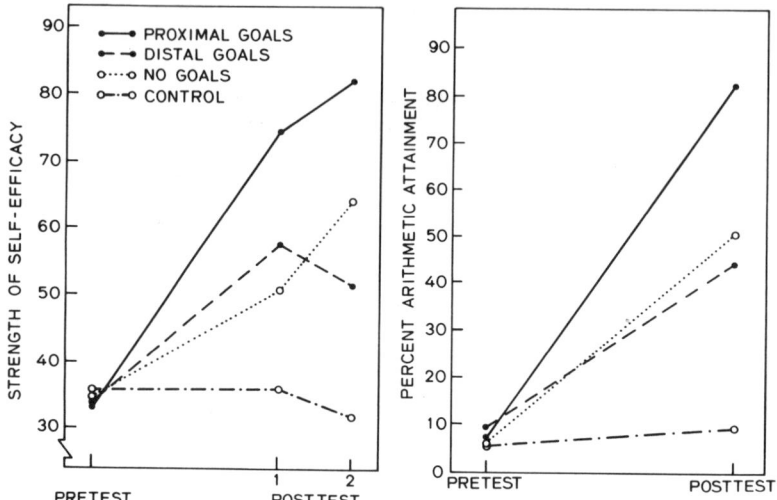

FIG. 2.11 The left panel shows the strength of children's perceived arithmetic efficacy at the beginning of the study (pretest), after they completed the self-directed learning (Post 1) and after they took the arithmetic posttest (Post 2). Children in the control group were assessed without the intervening self-directed learning. The right panel displays the children's level of arithmetic achievement before and after the self-directed learning (Bandura & Schunk, 1981).

2.11). Distal goals had no demonstrable effects. Subgoal attainments also created intrinsic interest in arithmetic initially holding little attraction for the children (Figure 2.12). The value of proximal subgoals in cultivating interest is further corroborated by Morgan (1985) in a study designed to improve the academic activities of college students over an extended period. People not only perform better under goal proximity, but they much prefer a proximal to a distal focus (Jobe, 1984).

Like any other form of influence, goals can be applied in ways that breed dislikes rather than nurture interests. As already noted, personal standards that subserve valued aspirations promote interest. But if goals assigned by others impose severe constraints and burdensome performance requirements the pursuit can become onerous. Because the effects of goals depend on their properties, propositions about the impact of goals on interest must be qualified by the nature and structure of the goals. Mossholder (1980) reports that goals enhance interest in dull tasks by infusing them with challenge but reduce interest on interesting tasks. Self-development would be poorly served if aspirations and challenges became dysfunctional for activities that normally hold some interest. Fortunately, this is not the case. An interesting activity with a rising standard for success, which continues to present challenges, enhances intrinsic interest, whereas the same activity with a low level of challenge does not (McMullin & Steffen, 1982). If subgoals for an interesting activity are easily attainable, then more distal goals, which pose more of a challenge, may hold greater interest (Manderlink & Harackiewicz, 1984). Routine successes with no corresponding growth of competence create little enjoyment. Doing more of a tedious activity under the influence of performance goals will not increase liking of it (Latham & Yukl, 1976; Umstot, Bell, & Mitchell, 1976). In the studies in which proximal goals cultivate perceived self-efficacy and intrinsic interest, each subgoal presents new challenges in mastery of new subskills (Bandura & Schunk, 1981).

The combination of perceived self-inefficacy, self-devaluation, and diminished interest creates a state of self-demoralization. Subgoal structuring of pursuits can reduce the risk of such self-demoralization through high aspiration. Significant performance gains judged against lofty distal standards do not provide much of a sense of accomplishment because of the wide disparity between current attainment and aspiration. Thus, people can be making good progress but downplaying their accomplishments and getting discouraged. Hierarchical subgoals minimize disspiriting mismatches. We shall return shortly to the self-debilitating affective consequences of unfulfilled striving.

Goal proximity should be distinguished from specificity of planning, which includes not only temporal variation in goals but a host of other factors. For example, in studies comparing daily specific plans with

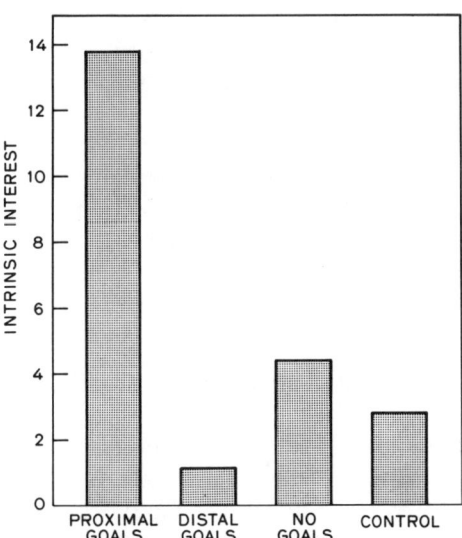

FIG. 2.12 Level of intrinsic interest in arithmetic activities shown by children in different goal conditions when given free choice of activities (Bandura & Schunk, 1981).

monthly general plans, the detailed proximal system prescribes more onerous busywork in creating daily flow charts of when and where activities will be performed and in monitoring and recording one's performances than does the distal general system (Kirschenbaum, Humphrey, & Mallet, 1981; Kirschenbaum, Tomarken, & Ordman, 1982). Self-influence requiring excess busywork is usually less faithfully applied with less beneficial results. The motivating potential of goal proximity is best revealed by varying only whether attainments are compared to close or distant standards without confounding proximal goals with more bothersome and time-consuming overseeing routines.

Efforts to clarify how goal proximity operates in self-regulatory mechanisms often encounter methodological obstacles because of spontaneous goal transformations during the course of pursuits. When encouraged to set themselves distal goals, many people quickly improvise their own more helpful proximal goals. They simply partition desired future attainments into more easily realizable subgoals (Bandura & Simon, 1977; Dubbert & Wilson, 1984). Performances become the product of self-created aspirations rather than of externally assigned goals. Similarly, even when people simply monitor their performances, without any reference to goals, many begin to create goals for themselves (Bandura & Cervone, 1983). Self-set goals predict subsequent levels of performance motivation. The motivational advantage of goal proximity becomes most evident under conditions that minimize transformation of distal goals into proximal ones (Bandura & Schunk, 1981).

Variations in personal goal setting under prescribed distal goals illustrate the dual self-processes of exercising and undergoing influence. Regardless of whether studies of self-regulatory processes focus on self-monitoring of progress or on goal setting, people are not simply reactors to situational influences. They often transform them into self-influences that differ from what others intend. Theories that attempt, through regressive causal analysis, to reduce self-regulatory processes to situational control overlook the fact that people are not merely objects of change; they act as agents who give new form to situational influences. Such bidirectionality of influence supports a reciprocal model of self-regulation (Bandura, 1986).

Hierarchical Structure of Goal Systems

Thus far, the discussion has centered on goal systems as a directive and motivational device and the self-referent mechanisms through which they exert their effects. Goal systems, of course, usually involve a hierarchical structure in which the goals that operate as the proximal regulators of motivation and action subserve broader goals reflecting matters of personal import and value. However, proximal goals are not simply subordinate servitors of valued loftier ones. Through engagement of the self-system, they invest activities with personal significance. As previously shown, proximal goals generate self-satisfaction from personal accomplishments that operates as its own reward during the pursuit of higher level goals. When the reward of personal accomplishment is linked to indicants of progress, individuals contribute a continuing source of self-motivation quite apart from the incentive of the loftier goal. Indeed, subgoal challenges often outweigh the lure of superordinate goals as ongoing motivators (Bandura & Schunk, 1981). In this motivational process, people gain their rewards in mastering an activity rather than suspend any sense of success in their endeavors until the superordinate goal is attained. The model of self-motivation as a process of recurrent proximal self-challenge and evaluative reward differs from one in which a linear series of subordinate goals is powered entirely by a superordinate one. Self-motivation through proximal self-influence does not imply any restriction in the future time perspective of aspirations. Progress toward valued futures is best achieved by combining distal aspirations with proximal self-guidance.

Generic Goal Orientations

People impose goal preferences on activities that reflect their basic orientations to achievement across a wide range of situations. This process has been the focus of research on how people's conceptions of ability affect the goals they pursue which, in turn, determine the quality of their intellectual functioning (M. Bandura & Dweck, 1988; Dweck & Elliott, 1983; Nicholls, 1984). Two major conceptions have been identified. In one perspective, intelligence is construed as an *incremental skill* that can be continually enhanced by acquiring knowledge and perfecting one's competencies. People with this conception adopt a learning goal. They seek challenging tasks providing opportunities to expand their knowledge and develop their competencies. Errors are regarded as a natural, instructive part of an acquisition process—one learns from mistakes. Such an outlook sustains task-oriented, perseverant effort in face of failures. Capabilities are judged more in terms of personal progress than by comparison against the achievements of others. Mastery through effort is rewarding, whereas easy successes are boring or disappointing.

In the contrasting perspective, intelligence is construed as a more or less *stable entity*. Because quality of performance is regarded as diagnostic of intellectual capability, errors and performance insufficiencies carry personal threat and arouse concern over social evaluation of incompetence. Consequently, people adopting the entity view tend to favor performance goals and to prefer tasks that minimize risk of errors and permit ready demonstration of proficiency at the expense of learning something new. Prolonged expenditure of effort, which is the way in which most competencies are built, also poses threats because high effort is taken as indicative of low ability. Those aiming to look smart through proficient performance are prone to measure their capabilities by comparison with the achievements of others. Effort is rewarded by a feeling of pride or relief over validation of intellectual status without having had to expend much effort.

The impact of these differential goal orientations on psychological functioning is revealed in experiments in which children have to cope with failure experiences (Elliott & Dweck, 1988). Children who view intelligence as an entity and perceive themselves as deficient in it are easily debilitated by failures, whereas those subscribing to an incremental view take failures in their stride. It should be noted that the processes and correlates discussed here concern goal orientations, not types of people. Thus, when performance-oriented children are encouraged to adopt a learning goal by portraying intelligence as an acquirable skill, they manage failure much more effectively.

Self-Regulatory Dynamics in Organizational Accomplishments

Virtually all of the research on cognitive motivators has been concerned with how self-regulatory dynamics operate in personal accomplishments. Many human endeavors are directed at group goals that are achieved in organizational structures through socially-mediated effort. In exercising control over organizational outcomes, decision makers have to rely on the concerted efforts of others, whereas at the individual level, they need regulate only their own efforts. Socially-mediated regulation of a group involves considerably more complex paths of influence than does direct self-regulation. Therefore, functional relationships established at the individual level may require qualifications at the group level.

Much of the research on human decision making examines single judgments in static environments (Hogarth, 1981; Beach, Barnes, & Christensen-Szalanski, 1986). Judgments made under such conditions may not provide a sufficient basis for developing either descriptive or normative models of decision making in dynamic naturalistic environments, which entail learning and motivational mechanisms. In such environments, decision makers must weight and integrate a wide array of information from diverse sources. Decisions must be made during a continual flow of activity so that actions taken at one point affect the options and effects of later decisions. Moreover, many of the decisional rules for exercising control over dynamic environments must be learned through exploratory experiences in the course of managing the ongoing organizational activities. It requires a reliable knowledge base and effective use of cognitive skills to ferret out relevant information, construct options, and to test or revise one's knowledge based on the results of decisional actions.

Because organizational outcomes must be achieved through the coordinated efforts of others, some of the most important managerial decisions are concerned with how best to use human talent and how to guide and motivate human effort. In executing this role, managers have to cope with numerous obstacles, failures, and setbacks, which often carry perturbing self-evaluative implications, as well as social consequences. These affective factors can undermine self-conceptions and motivation in ways that impair good use of decision making skills. Effective decision making thus involves more than applying a set of cognitive operators to existing knowledge for desired solutions. Self-regulatory influences have considerable impact on how well cognitive-processing systems operate (Bandura, 1986).

The mechanisms and outcomes of managerial decision making do not lend themselves readily to experimental analysis in actual organizational settings. The governing processes are usually influenced by a multiplicity of interacting factors that are difficult to identify let alone exercise experimental control over them. Advances in this complex field can be achieved by experimental analyses of decision making in simulated organizational environments. One such computer simulation encompasses the types of decisional activities required in complex dynamic environments (Wood & Bailey, 1985). People serve as managerial decision makers in which they have to match employee attributes to production subfunctions and to learn a complex set of decision rules on how best to guide and motivate those they oversee. The managerial rules concern the optimal use of goals, supervisory feedback, and social incentives to enhance the level of organizational performance. They have to integrate the set of rules into a cognitive model of organizational functioning that can serve as a guide for decisions regarding different group members. Knowing rules does not ensure optimal implementation of them. The managers also have to gain proficiency in tailoring the applications of the rules to individual members of the group and to apply them in concert to achieve desired group results. The self-regulatory factors are measured at periodic intervals as the managerial task is performed over a series of trials.

In the management of such dynamic environments, self-regulatory mechanisms govern organizational attainments as they do individual accomplishments (Wood & Bandura, 1988; Wood, et al., 1988). Perceived managerial self-efficacy enhances organizational performance both directly and indirectly through its influence on analytic strategies. The higher the perceived self-efficacy, the more systematic people are in applying analytic strategies to discover optimal decision rules. Analytic strategies contribute to organizational attainments beyond that of perceived self-efficacy.

The multifaceted nature of managerial activities and their mazy linkage to organizational accomplishments introduces complexities in the relation between personal goals and group attainment. Personal goals are readily translatable into performance attainments when people possess the knowledge and means to exercise control. Goals can affect performance directly by channeling attention and by mobilizing effort and sustaining it in the face of obstacles (Locke et al., 1981). In most of the research demonstrating that goals enhance accomplishments, the performers already possess the means of control and need only to intensify their efforts (Mento et al., 1987). Even on tasks that are directly controllable by effort alone, goal effects are weaker for more complex activities (Wood et al., 1987). Sheer managerial effort alone does not ensure attainment of group goals. Until the optimal managerial rules are identified, goals can produce more effortful and discerning cognitive processing of outcome information, but not necessarily immediate improvements in organizational performance. To complicate further the effects of goals on group performance, efforts to enhance the level of organizational functioning often require constituent changes in particular aspects of the social structure and the way in which social resources are allocated. If grounded in sound judgment, such fractional changes would eventually raise organizational attainments without necessarily producing sizable gains in the short run.

In the simulation studies, personal goals exert their impact on group performance by promoting effective managerial rule-learning strategies. However, they do not have a direct effect on performance. When faced with the task of managing a complex social environment, assigned goals that are difficult to fulfill undermine managers' perceived self-efficacy, which detracts from organizational attainments (Wood et al., 1988).

The way in which people construe ability has substantial impact on self-regulatory mechanisms that govern ongoing motivation and group accomplishments (Wood & Bandura, 1988). Substandard performances are likely to carry markedly different diagnostic implications depending on whether ability is construed as an acquirable skill or as a relatively stable entity. When performances are viewed as skill acquisition in which one learns from mistakes, perceived self-efficacy is unlikely to be adversely affected by substandard performances. This is because errors become normative instructive elements in the acquisition of competencies rather than as indicators of basic personal deficiencies. Construal of performances as diagnostic of underlying cognitive capability greatly increases vulnerability to the adverse effects of failure. Frequent experience of substandard performances can take a heavy toll on perceived self-efficacy.

Seasoned managers who perform the challenging managerial task under an induced entity conception of ability are beset by increasing doubts about their managerial efficacy. They become more and more erratic in their decisional activities, they lower their organizational aspirations, and they achieve progressively less with the organization they were managing (Figure 2.13).

In marked contrast, an induced conception of ability as an acquirable skill fosters a highly resilient sense of personal efficacy. Even though assigned taxing goals that elude the managers, they remain steadfast in their perceived managerial self-efficacy, they continue to set themselves challenging organizational goals, and they use analytic strategies in ways that aid discovery of optimal managerial decision rules. Such a self-efficacious orientation, which is well suited for handling adversity, pays off in uniformly high organizational attainments.

Induced differential conceptions of ability bias how similar substandard performances at the outset are cognitively processed. Construal of substandard attainments as indicants of personal deficiencies gradually creates an inefficacious self-schema in the particular domain of functioning, whereas construal of substandard attainments as instructive guides for enhancing personal competencies fosters an efficacious self-schema. Such evolving self-beliefs further bias cognitive processing of outcome information and promote actions that create confirmatory behavioral evidence for them. This produces an exacerbation cycle of motivational and performance effects.

Two aspects to the exercise of control are especially relevant to organizational change (Bandura, 1986; Gurin & Brim, 1984). The first concerns the level of personal efficacy to effect changes by productive use of capabilities and enlistment of effort. This constitutes the personal side of the transactional control process. The second aspect concerns the

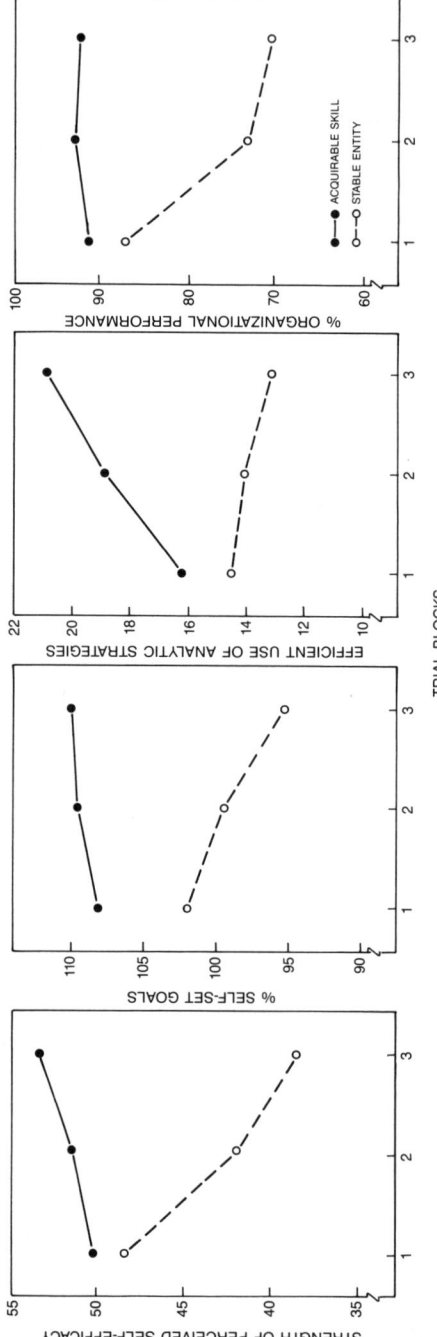

FIG. 2.13 Changes in perceived managerial self-efficacy, self-set goals relative to the preset standard, effective analytic strategies, and achieved level of organizational performance across blocks of trials under acquirable skill and entity conceptions of capability. Each trial block comprises six different production orders (Wood & Bandura, 1988).

changeability or controllability of the environment. This facet represents the level of system constraints and opportunities to exercise personal efficacy. Human behavior is, of course, governed by perceptions of personal efficacy and social environments rather than simply by their objective properties. Thus, individuals who believe themselves to be inefficacious are likely to effect little change even in environments that provide many potential opportunities. Conversely, those who have a strong sense of efficacy, through ingenuity and perseverance, figure out ways of exercising some measure of control in environments containing limited opportunities and many constraints.

In the transactions of everyday life, beliefs regarding self-efficacy and environmental controllability are not divorced from experiential realities. Rather, they are products of reciprocal causation (Bandura, 1986). Thus, when people believe the environment is controllable on matters of import to them, they are motivated to exercise fully their personal efficacy, which enhances the likelihood of success. Experiences of success, in turn, provide behavioral validation of personal efficacy and environmental controllability. If people approach situations as largely uncontrollable, they are likely to exercise their efficacy weakly and abortively, which breeds failure experiences. Over time, failures take an increasing toll on perceived self-efficacy and beliefs about how much environmental control is possible.

Organizational simulation research underscores the influential impact of perceived controllability on the self-regulatory factors governing group attainments (Bandura & Wood, 1988). People who manage a simulated organization under a cognitive set that organizations are not easily changeable quickly lose faith in their managerial capabilities, even when performance standards are within easy reach and they lower their sights for the organization (Figure 2.14). Those who operate under a cognitive set that organizations are controllable display a resilient sense of managerial efficacy, set themselves increasingly challenging goals, and use good analytic thinking for discovering effective managerial rules. The divergent changes in these self-regulatory factors are accompanied by large differences in organizational attainments.

Path analyses reveal that as managers begin to form a self-schema concerning their efficacy through further experience, the performance system is powered more extensively and intricately by self-conceptions of efficacy (Figure 2.15). Perceived self-efficacy influences performance both directly and through its strong effects on personal goal setting. Personal goals, in turn, enhance organizational attainments directly and via the mediation of analytic strategies.

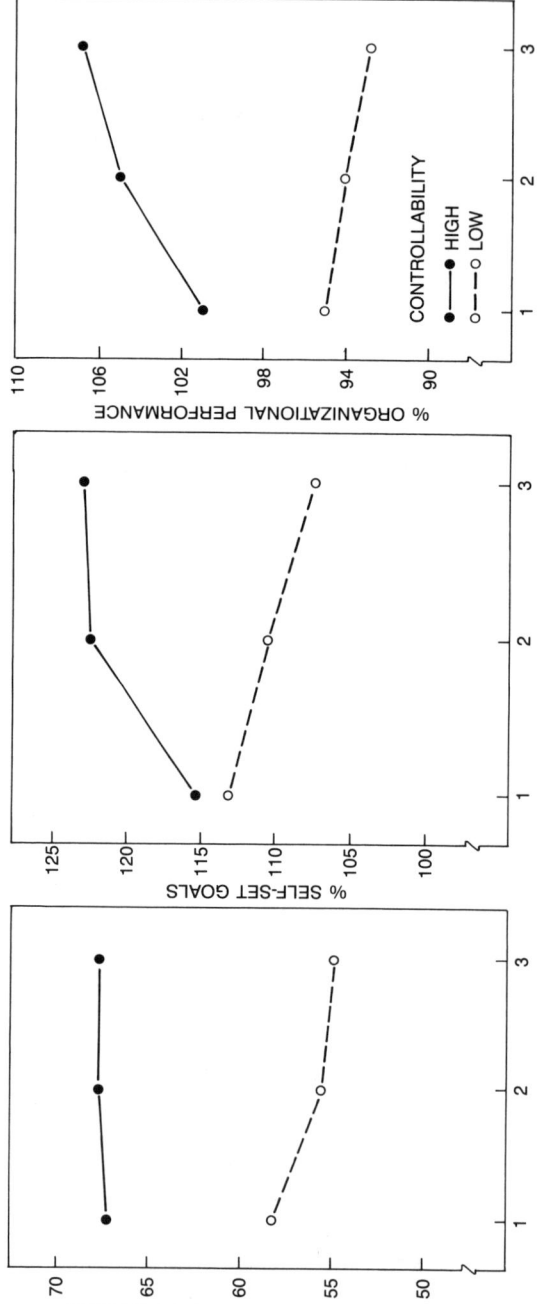

FIG. 2.14 Changes in strength of perceived managerial self-efficacy, the performance goals set for the organization, and level of organizational attainment for managers who operated under a cognitive set that organizations are controllable or difficult to control (Bandura & Wood, 1988).

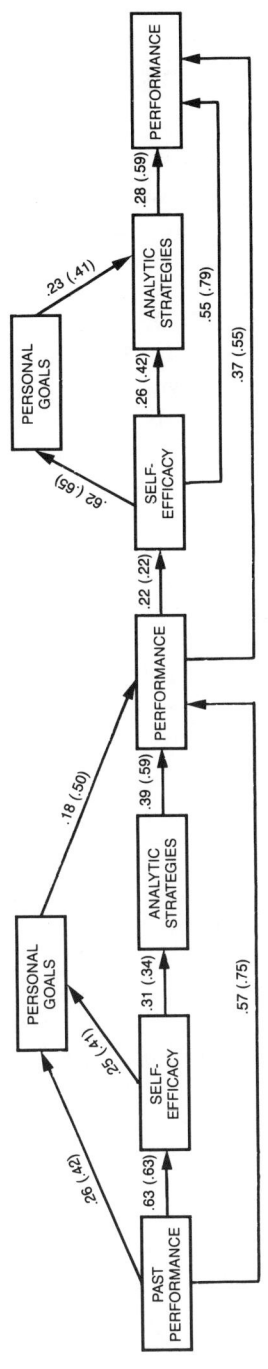

FIG. 2.15 Path analysis of causal structures. The initial numbers on the paths of influence are the significant standardized path coefficients ($ps<.05$); the numbers in parentheses are the first-order correlations. The network of relations on the left half of the figure are for the initial managerial efforts, and those on the right half are for later managerial efforts (Wood & Bandura, 1988b).

Aspirational Standards, Achievement Motives, and External Incentives

Self-motivation through self-reactive influence is a significant ingredient in a variety of motivational phenomena that comes under different names. Achievement motivation is one such instance. High achievers tend to invest their self-satisfaction in attainment of challenging goals; low achievers adopt easy goals as sufficing. The higher the aspirational standards people set for themselves, the harder they strive to fulfill them and the more likely they are to excel in their attainments.

Personality theories often portray human strivings and accomplishments as products of achievement needs or motives. The achievement motive said to direct and energize action is usually inferred from responses to items containing cues relevant to achievement. The functional properties ascribed to the achievement motive are much the same as those that characterize aspirational standards. However, there is a major conceptual difference between a motive force and self-generated incentives arising from internal standards and self-reactive influence. Motives impel behavior; self-incentives motivate and direct behavior through cognitive anticipatory mechanisms.

Research in which achievement motive and aspirational standards are measured shed some light on these alternative motivational mechanisms. Matsui, Okada, and Kakuyama (1982) found that achievement motivation has no influence on performance independently of personal goals. The relationship between achievement motivation and performance disappears when level of self-set goals is controlled. The goals people set for themselves predict their performance level and self-satisfaction better than do the traditional personality measures of need for achievement (Arvey & Dewhirst, 1976; Ostrow, 1976; Yukl & Latham, 1978).

The inclination of high need achievers to select high goals does not necessarily mean that performance standards are the products of an underlying motive as is commonly assumed. Personal standards of excellence may lead people to endorse achievement statements on personality tests rather than such endorsements verifying an achievement motive fueling aspiring standards. Evidence that standard setting is a better predictor of ongoing level of performance than are indicies of achievement motives lends causal priority to standard setting. Moreover, goal theory can explain rapid shifts in motivational level through changes in mediating self-processes, that pose explanatory difficulties for a dispositional motive determinant.

Self-influence through internal standards also contributes to the motivational effects of extrinsic feedback and incentives. Extrinsic incentives can motivate partly by activating personal goals for progressive improvement. Indeed, a series of studies conducted by Locke and his associates shows that incentives increase performance to the extent that they encourage people to set motivating goals for themselves (Locke, Bryan, & Kendall, 1968). In research reporting mixed results on whether incentives influence performance partly by their effect on self-set goals, performers were given no information about their level of performance (Pritchard & Curtis, 1973). Self-evaluative motivators are not effectively activated in the absence of knowledge of how one is doing (Bandura & Cervone, 1983). People are certainly motivated by the prospect of valued extrinsic outcomes. But by applying evaluative standards to their ongoing performances, they create motivating challenges and fulfill them to please themselves as well. Even simple feedback of progress or trivial extrinsic incentives can enhance performance motivation once self-satisfaction becomes invested in the activity. Satisfaction in personal accomplishment becomes the reward.

Affective Consequences of Goal Discrepancies

Self-regulatory processes affect mood as well as motivation. Negative discrepancies between attainments and standards selected as indicies of personal merit can give rise to self-devaluation and despondent mood. A growing body of evidence reveals that negative cognitive biases in the constituent processes of self-regulation increase vulnerability to depression (Kanfer & Hagerman, 1981; Rehm, 1982). Of special interest is evidence that faulty goal setting may be conducive to despondency and performance debilitation. Compared to nondepressed persons, the depressed tend to set higher standards for themselves relative to their attainments and to react less positively to similar successes and more self-critically to similar failures (Golin & Terrill, 1977; Loeb, Beck, Diggory, & Tuthill, 1967; Schwartz, 1974; Simon, 1979). Goal stringency is a relational characteristic reflecting the match between personal capabilities and goals, not a matter of absolute level. Depression is most likely to arise when personal standards of merit are set well above one's perceived efficacy to attain them (Kanfer & Zeiss, 1983).

Negative discrepancies in self-appraisal of capabilities by social comparison can also breed despondency. Perceived self-inefficacy to accomplish valued performances that others find readily attainable creates a depressive mood and impairs cognitive functioning (Davies & Yates, 1982). Much attention has been given to the adverse effects of unfavorably social comparison. In studies that vary the social performance standard for comparative appraisal, the higher the accomplishments of similar others, the less self-satisfied people are with their own performance attainments (Simon, 1979). The self-belittling effect of adverse social comparison is especially evident in persons who are prone to depression. When exposed to high attainments of others, the depressed judge their own accomplishments as less praiseworthy than do the nondepressed (Ciminero & Steingarten, 1978). Self-devaluative reactions to adverse social comparative appraisal is even more pronounced in depressed females (Garber, Hollon, & Silverman, 1979).

To mitigate the deleterious effects of social comparison, it is often recommended that human endeavors be structured so that people judge themselves in reference to their own capabilities and standards, rather than by comparing themselves against others. Self-comparative standards provide the benefits of personal challenge and success experiences for self-development without the cost of invidious social comparison. However, in competitive, individualistic societies, social comparison inevitably enters into self-appraisal. Domains of activities in which one person's success is another person's failure force social comparison unless one cedes such pursuits.

Continued progress in a valued activity does not necessarily ensure perpetual self-fulfillment. The strides at which activities are mastered can drastically alter self-evaluative reactions (Simon, 1979). Accomplishments that surpass earlier ones bring a continued sense of self-satisfaction. But people derive little satisfaction from smaller accomplishments, or even devalue them, after having made larger strides. Early spectacular accomplishments reflecting notable proficiency can thus be conductive to later self-dissatisfaction even in the face of continuing personal attainments. For example, it is not uncommon for great achievers to suffer depression upon receiving a prized award if they judge their current accomplishments as falling short of the earlier triumphs that brought them the social acclaim. When Linus Pauling was asked what one does after winning the Nobel Prize, he replied, "*Change fields, of course!*" After a phenomenal long jump that shattered the existing record by two feet, Beamon avoided self-disfavor by never jumping again. In short, self-discontent can be created by self-comparative standards just as it can by social-comparative standards.

Self-regulatory theories of motivation and of depression make seemingly contradictory predictions regarding the effects of negative discrepancies between attainments and standards. Standards that exceed attainments are said to enhance motivation through goal challenges, but negative discrepancies are also invoked as activators of despondent mood. Moreover, when negative discrepancies do have adverse effects, they may give rise to apathy rather than to despondency. A conceptual

2. SELF-REGULATION OF MOTIVATION

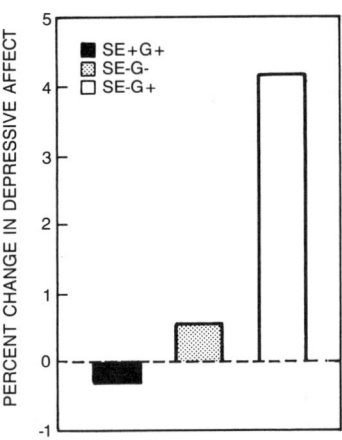

FIG. 2.16 Percentage change in depressive mood for people combining strong perceived self-efficacy with goal adherence (SE+G+); weak perceived self-efficacy with goal adherence (SE-G+); and weak perceived self-efficacy with goal abandonment (SE-G-) (Bandura & Abrams, 1986).

scheme is needed that differentiates the conditions under which negative discrepancies will motivate, depress, or induce apathy.

Social cognitive theory posits that the directional effects of negative goal discrepancies are predictable from the relationship between perceived self-efficacy for goal attainment and level of self-set goals (Bandura, 1986). Whether negative discrepancies are motivating or depressing will depend on beliefs in one's efficacy to match them. Negative disparities are likely to give rise to high motivation and low despondent mood for people who believe they have the efficacy to fulfill a difficult goal and continue to strive for it. Negative disparities are likely to diminish motivation and generate despondent mood for people who judge themselves as inefficacious to attain a difficult goal but continue to demand it of themselves. People who judge they lack the efficacy for goal attainment and abandon the difficult goals as unrealistic for themselves are likely to display the apathetic reaction. This would be reflected in lowered motivation without despondent mood.

Evidence for these differential processes comes from a study in which students received arbitrary feedback that their attainments on an intellectual task fell considerably short of a goal they had initially adopted (Bandura & Abrams, 1986). Their perceived self-efficacy for goal attainment, self-set goals, mood, and subsequent level of motivation were then measured. Different subgroups were identified in terms of whether they judged their efficacy for goal attainment to be high or low, and whether they held to the difficult goal or had abandoned it. The subgroups did not differ initially in mood or performance motivation. Figures 2.16 and 2.17 show how they changed in despondent mood and motivation after feedback that they had failed to fulfill the standard.

Continued adherence to the difficult goal with perceived self-inefficacy to fulfill it induced despondent mood (see Figure 2.16). The same level of failure did not create despondency in students who judged they had the efficacy to attain the goal and continued to pursue it, or those who viewed the goal as beyond their capabilities and thus lowered their aim.

For men, failure heightened motivation in self-efficacious goal strivers but attenuated the efforts of the self-inefficacious ones, regardless of whether they were goal strivers or goal abandoners (see Figure 2.17). Failure had a more generalized adverse impact on women. Not only did the perceived self-inefficacious ones find it hard to motivate themselves but even the self-efficacious goal strivers had difficulty mounting a high level of effort. Other data from subjects who judged their level of productivity in the absence of performance feedback shed some light on the differential gender effects of failure. Women were realists in judging their productivity, whereas men had an inflated view of how much they had produced. This self-enhancing bias in males may account for the gender differences in the motivational impact of failure. Viewed from an inflated perceived level of accomplishment, the failure feedback would be especially jarring for men. The self-efficacious ones redoubled their efforts; the self-inefficacious ones could not get more out of themselves. For women, who downplayed their accomplishments, the negative feedback would simply validate their impression that this is a difficult task at which to excel.

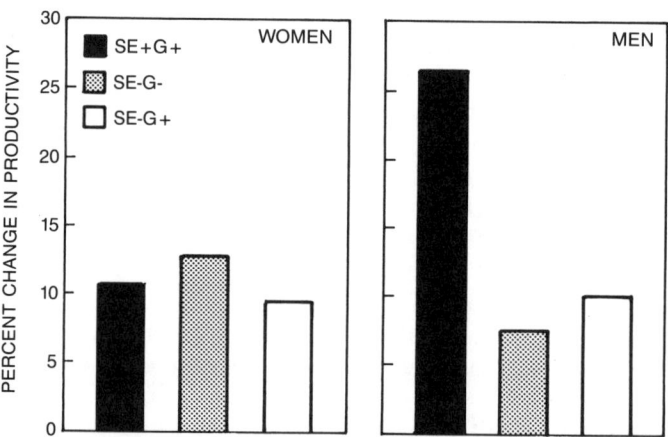

FIG. 2.17 Percentage change in level of motivation for people combining strong perceived self-efficacy with goal adherence **(SE+G+)**; weak perceived self-efficacy with goal adherence **(SE–G+)**; and weak perceived self-efficacy with goal abandonment **(SE–G–)** (Bandura & Abrams, 1986).

Thus far the discussion has been concerned with depression arising from perceived self-inefficacy to fulfill valued standards of achievement. Perceived self-inefficacy to exercise control over other things people long for can also be depressing. This may involve social relationships (Holahan & Holahan, 1987; Stanley & Maddux, 1986), child rearing (Cutrona & Troutman, 1986), or other aspects of life that mean a great deal (Devins, et al., 1982; Rosenbaum & Hadari, 1985). The greater the perceived self-inefficacy, the higher the depression.

Two biasing processes have been postulated on how mood can affect self-efficacy judgment. According to the affective priming theory proposed by Bower, past successes and failures are stored as memories along with their affect (Bower, 1983). The set of memories provides the data base on which judgmental processes operate. Mood activates, through an associative mood network, the subset of memories congruent with it. Thus, negative mood activates the failure subset, whereas a positive mood activates the success subset. The spread of activation from the emotion node makes mood-congruent memories salient. Self-appraisal of efficacy is enhanced by selective recall of past successes but diminished by recall of failures. In the cognitive priming view, specific successes or failures that induce the affect also produce cognitions that cue thoughts of other past successes and failures. This view places greater emphasis on the thought content of the inducing event than on the aroused affect as the primer of other positive or negative thoughts. Cognitive availability biases self-efficacy judgment.

Kavanagh and Bower (1985) have shown that, indeed, induced positive mood enhances perceived self-efficacy, whereas despondent mood diminishes it (Figure 2.18). The impact of induced mood on self-efficacy judgment is widely generalized across diverse domains of functioning.

Mood and perceived self-efficacy undoubtedly influence each other bidirectionally. Kavanagh (1983) tested whether inducing events exert their effects on self-efficacy judgment through affective or cognitive priming. Happy and sad moods were induced by vivification of either a personal triumph or failure, or a positive or negative fortuitous experience devoid of successful or failed efforts. The results, though qualified by gender differences, indicate that affect, rather than thought content, is the main carrier of the effect. Self-appraisal of efficacy was raised in a positive affect state and lowered in a negative affect state, irrespective of references to success or failure. People then act in accordance with their mood-altered efficacy beliefs, choosing more challenging tasks in a self-efficacious frame of mind than if they doubt their efficacy. The relationship between perceived efficacy and challenge seeking is strongest under fortuitously induced affect. Despondency can thus lower self-efficacy beliefs, which spawns poor performance, breeding even deeper de-

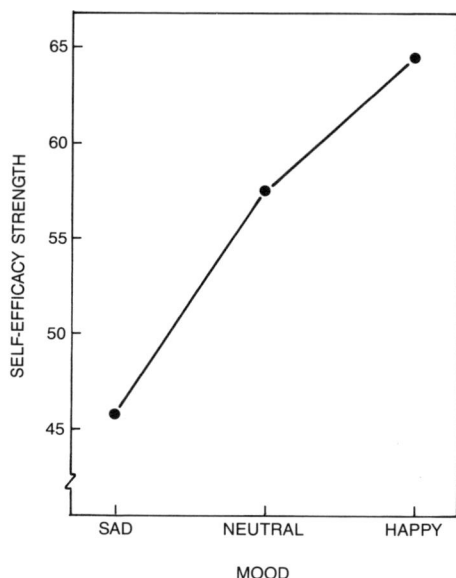

FIG. 2.18 Mean strength of self-perceived efficacy across heterosexual, social, and athletic domains of functioning when efficacy judgments were made in a positive, neutral, or negative mood state (Kavanagh & Bower, 1985).

spondency. In contrast, by raising perceived self-efficacy that facilitates accomplishments, good mood can set in motion an affirmative reciprocal process.

SELF-REGULATION THROUGH MORAL STANDARDS

The preceding discussion analyzed the mechanisms through which aspirational standards regulate motivation and personal accomplishments. In areas of functioning involving achievement strivings and cultivation of competencies, the internal standards that are selected as a mark of adequacy are progressively altered as skills and knowledge are acquired and challenges are met. In many areas of social and moral behavior, the internal standards that serve as the basis for regulating one's conduct are relatively stable. That is, people do not change from week to week in what they regard as right or wrong or as good or bad. Moreover, violation of moral standards is more likely to generate much stronger affective self-reactions to transgressive conduct than are performances that may fall short of aspirational standards.

In social cognitive theory (Bandura, 1988f), transgressive conduct is regulated by two major sources of sanctions: social sanctions and internalized self-sanctions. Both mechanisms operate anticipatorily. In fear control, people refrain from transgressing because they fear that such conduct will bring them social censure and other adverse consequences. In self-control, they behave prosocially to produce self-satisfaction and self-respect and they refrain from transgressing because such conduct will give rise to self-reproach. Because people continuously preside over their own behavior in countless situations presenting little or no threat of external sanctions, the exercise of self-sanction must play a central role in the regulation of moral conduct.

In the course of socialization, people develop moral standards from an assortment of influences that include direct tuition, the evaluative reactions to their conduct by significant persons in their lives, and the moral standards modeled by others (Bandura, 1986). People do not passively absorb standards of conduct from whatever influences happen to impinge upon them. Rather, they construct generic standards from the numerous evaluative rules that are prescribed, modeled, and taught. Once moral standards are acquired, they serve as guides and deterrents to conduct by the consequences that people produce for themselves (Bandura, 1986; Kurtines & Gewirtz, 1984). Self-regulation of conduct by self-reactive influence operates through a set of subfunctions. To exert influence over their own conduct people have to monitor what they do. However, self-monitoring alone provides little basis for self-directed reactions. Actions give rise to self-reactions through a judgmental function in which conduct is evaluated in relation to personal standards and environmental circumstances. Situations with moral implications contain many judgmental ingredients that not only vary in importance but may be given lesser or greater weight depending on the particular constellation of events in a given moral predicament. In dealing with moral dilemmas, therefore, people must extract, weigh, and integrate the morally relevant information in the situations confronting them. Factors that are weighed heavily under some combinations of circumstances may be disregarded or considered of lesser import under a different set of conditions. This process of moral reasoning is guided by multidimensional rules for judging conduct. Evaluative self-reactions provide the mechanism by which standards regulate conduct. The anticipatory self-pride and self-criticism for actions that correspond to, or violate personal standards serve as the regulatory influences. People do things that give them self-satisfaction and a sense of self-worth. They refrain from behaving in ways that violate their moral standards because it will bring self-condemnation. Self-sanctions thus keep conduct in line with internal standards.

The self-regulation of conduct is not entirely an intrapsychic affair. Rather, it involves a reciprocity of influence between thought, conduct, and a network of social influences. Under social conditions in which transgressive behavior is not easily self-excusable, conduct is likely to be

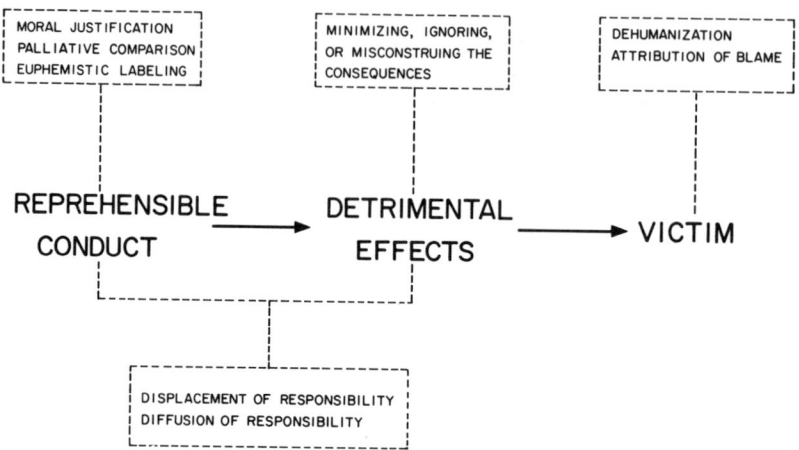

FIG. 2.19 Mechanisms through which internal control is selectively activated or disengaged from conduct at different points in the regulatory process (Bandura, 1986).

congruent with moral standards. But self-regulation of moral conduct can be weakened or nullified by exonerative moral reasoning and social circumstances. The forms that these mechanisms of moral disengagement take are analyzed in the sections that follow.

Selective Activation and Disengagement of Internal Standards

Moral standards do not function as fixed internal regulators of conduct. Self-regulatory mechanisms do not operate unless they are activated, and there are many processes by which self-sanctions can be disengaged from inhumane conduct (Bandura, 1986; 1988c). Selective activation and disengagement of internal control permits different types of conduct with the same moral standards. Figure 2.19 shows the points in the self-regulatory process at which internal moral control can be disengaged from detrimental conduct.

These mechanisms of moral disengagement have been examined most extensively in the expression of violent conduct. But selective disengagement of moral self-sanctions is by no means confined to extraordinary inducements to violence. People often experience conflicts in which behavior they themselves devalue can serve as the means for securing valued benefits. As long as self-sanctions override the force of external inducements behavior is kept in line with personal standards. However, in the face of strong external inducements, such conflicts are often resolved by selective disengagement of self-sanctions. This enables otherwise considerate people to perform self-serving activities that have detrimental social effects.

Moral Justification

One set of disengagement practices operates on the construal of the behavior itself. People do not ordinarily engage in reprehensible conduct until they have justified to themselves the morality of their actions. What is culpable can be made righteous through cognitive reconstrual. In this process, detrimental conduct is made personally and socially acceptable by portraying it in the service of moral purposes. People then act on a moral imperative.

Radical shifts in destructive behavior through moral justification is most strikingly revealed in military conduct. People who have been socialized to deplore killing as morally condemnable can be transformed rapidly into skilled combatants, who may feel little compunction and even a sense of pride in taking human life. The conversion of socialized people into dedicated combatants is achieved not by altering their personality structures, aggressive drives, or moral standards. Rather, it is accomplished by cognitively restructuring the moral value of killing, so that it can be done free from self-censuring restraints (Kelman, 1973; Sanford & Comstock, 1971). Over the years, much reprehensible and destructive conduct has been perpetrated by ordinary, considerate people in the name of religious principles, righteous ideologies, and nationalistic imperatives (Rapoport & Alexander, 1982).

Euphemistic Labeling

Language shapes people's thought patterns on which they base many of their actions. Activities can take on a very different appearance depending on what they are called. Euphemistic language thus provides a convenient device for masking reprehensible activities or even conferring a respectable status upon them. Through convoluted and sanitizing verbiage, detrimental conduct is made benign, and those who engage in it are relieved of a sense of personal agency. People behave much more inhumanely when reprehensible behavior is given a sanitized label than when it is called for what it is (Diener, Dineen, Endresen, Beaman, & Fraser, 1975).

In an insightful analysis of the language of nonresponsibility, Gambino (1973) identifies the different varieties of euphemisms. One form, palliative expressions, is widely used to make the reprehensible respectable. The agentless passive form serves as another linguistic device for creating the appearance that culpable acts are the work of nameless forces, rather than the perpetrators being the agents of their own actions (Bolinger, 1982). The specialized jargon of a legitimate enterprise can also be misused to lend an aura of respectability to an illegitimate one.

Advantageous Comparison

Whenever events occur or are presented contiguously, the first one colors how the second one is perceived and judged. By exploiting the contrast principle, moral judgments of conduct can be influenced by expedient structuring of what it is compared against. Self-deplored acts can be made righteous by contrasting them with flagrant inhumanities. The more outrageous the comparison practices, the more likely it is that one's own destructive conduct will appear trifling or even benevolent. Advantageous historical and contemporary social comparisons are also invoked in the reconstrual and justification of reprehensible conduct.

Cognitive restructuring of behavior through moral justifications and palliative characterizations is the most effective psychological mechanism for promoting conduct that ordinarily violates personal standards. This is because moral restructuring not only eliminates self-deterrents but engages self-approval in the service of deleterious conduct. What was once morally condemnable becomes a source of self-valuation. After deleterious means become invested with high moral purpose, people work hard to become proficient at them and take pride in their accomplishments.

Displacement of Responsibility

Another set of dissociative practices operates by obscuring or distorting the relationship between actions and the effects they cause. People will behave in ways they normally repudiate if a legitimate authority accepts responsibility for the consequences of the conduct (Diener et al., 1975; Milgram, 1974). Under conditions of displaced responsibility, people view their actions as springing from the dictates of authorities rather than their being personally responsible for them. Since they are not the actual agent of their actions, they are spared self-prohibiting reactions. Displacement of responsibility not only weakens restraints over one's own deleterious actions but diminishes social concern over the well-being of those mistreated by others (Tilker, 1970).

A number of social factors affect the ease with which responsibility for one's actions can be surrendered to others. High justification and social consensus about the morality of an enterprise aid in the relinquishment

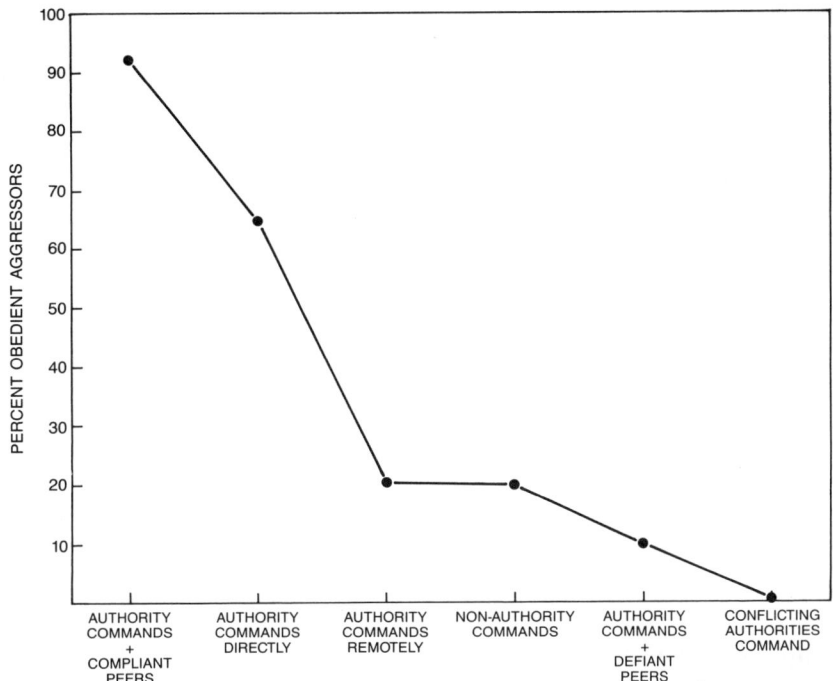

FIG. 2.20 Percentage of people fully obedient to injurious commands as a function of the legitimation and closeness of the authority issuing the commands (plotted from data by Milgram, 1974).

of personal control. The legitimacy of the authorizers is another important determinant of how readily people are willing to defer to them. As can be seen in Figure 2.20, the greater the legitimation and closeness of the authority issuing injurious commands, the higher the level of obedience. It is difficult to continue to disown personal agency in the face of evident harm following directly from one's actions. People are, therefore, less willing to obey authoritarian orders for injurious behavior when they see firsthand how they are hurting others (Milgram, 1974; Tilker, 1970).

Obedient functionaries do not cast off all responsibility for their behavior as though they were mindless extensions of others. If this were the case, they would act like automatons, only when told to. In fact, they are much more conscientious and self-directed in the performance of their duties. It requires a strong sense of responsibility to be a good functionary. In situations involving displaced responsibility, people carry out orders partly to honor the obligations they have undertaken (Mantell & Panzarella, 1976). Therefore, one must distinguish between two levels of responsibility—duty to one's superiors and accountability for the effects of one's actions. The self-system operates most efficiently in the service of authority when followers assume personal responsibility for being dutiful executors while relinquishing personal responsibility for the harm caused by their behavior. Followers who disowned responsibility without being bound by a sense of duty would be quite unreliable.

Diffusion of Responsibility

The deterrent power of self-sanctions is weakened when the link between conduct and its consequences is obscured by diffusing responsibility for deleterious behavior. This is achieved in several ways. Responsibility can be diffused by division of labor. Most enterprises require the services of many people, each performing fragmentary jobs that seem harmless in themselves. The fractional contribution is easily isolated from the eventual function, especially when participants exercise little personal judgment in carrying out a subfunction that is related by remote, complex links to the end result. After activities become routinized into programmed subfunctions, attention shifts from the import of what one is doing to engrossment in the details of one's fractional job (Kelman, 1973).

Group decision making is another common bureaucratic practice that enables otherwise considerate people to behave inhumanely because no single individual feels responsible for policies arrived at collectively. Where everyone is responsible no one is really responsible. Social organizations go to great lengths to devise sophisticated mechanisms for obscuring responsibility for decisions that will affect others adversely. Collective action is still another diffusion expedient for weakening self-restraints. Any harm done by a group can always be ascribed, in large part, to the behavior of other members. People, therefore, act more harshly when responsibility is obfuscated by a collective instrumentality than when they hold themselves personally accountable for what they do (Diener, 1977; Zimbardo, 1969). Figure 2.21 shows the level of punitiveness of individuals given punitive power over others under conditions in which the severity of their sanctions was determined personally or jointly by a group (Bandura, Underwood, & Fromson, 1975).

Disregard or Distortion of Consequences

Additional ways of weakening self-deterring reactions operate through disregard or misrepresentation of the consequences of action. When

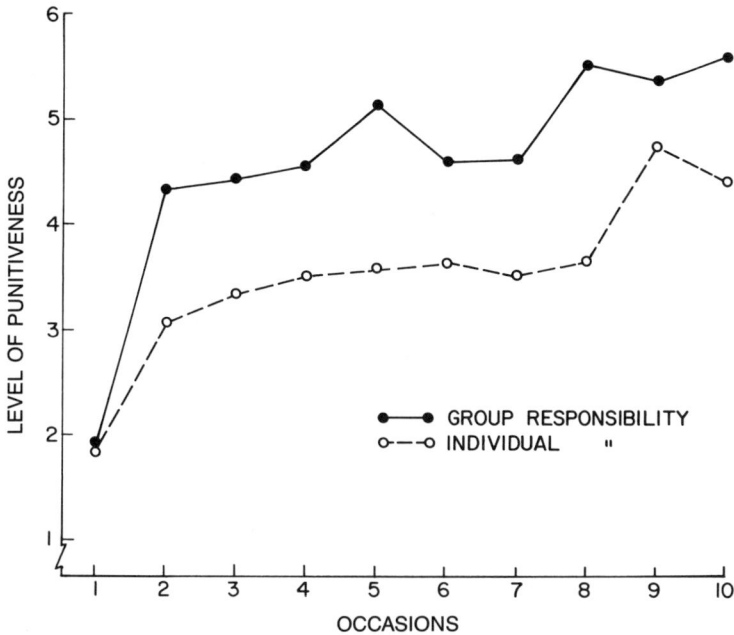

FIG. 2.21 Level of punitive sanctions imposed by individuals under conditions in which their punitiveness was determined personally or jointly by a group. Occasions represent successive times at which punitive sanctions could be applied (Bandura, Underwood, & Fromson, 1975).

people choose to pursue activities harmful to others for personal gain, or because of social inducements, they avoid facing the harm they cause or they minimize it. They readily recall prior information given them about the potential benefits of the behavior but are less able to remember its harmful effects (Brock & Buss, 1962; 1964). People are especially prone to minimize injurious effects when they act alone and, thus, cannot easily escape responsibility (Mynatt & Herman, 1975). When people can see and hear the suffering they cause, vicariously aroused distress and self-censure serve as restraining influences. For example, in studies of commanded aggression, Milgram (1974) obtained diminishing obedience as the victim's suffering becomes more evident and personalized (Figure 2.22). In addition to selective inattention and cognitive distortion of effects, the misrepresentation may involve active efforts to discredit evidence of the harm they cause. As long as the detrimental results of one's conduct are ignored, minimized, distorted, or disbelieved, there is little reason for self-censure to be activated.

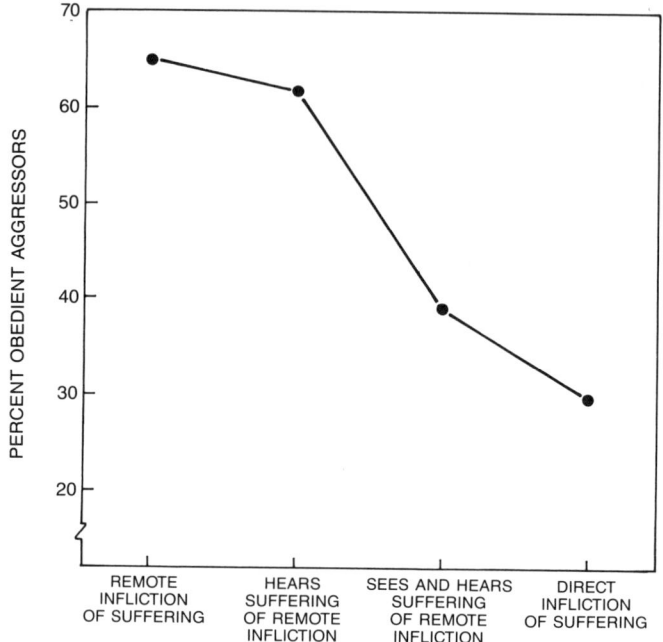

FIG. 2.22 Percentage of people fully obedient to injurious commands issued by an authority as the victim's suffering becomes more evident and personalized (plotted from data by Milgram, 1974).

Dehumanization

The final set of disengagement practices operates on the recipients of deleterious acts. The strength of self-evaluative reactions to harmful conduct partly depends on how the perpetrators view the people toward whom the behavior is directed. To perceive another as human enhances empathetic or vicarious reactions through perceived similarity (Bandura, 1988d). The joys and suffering of similar persons are more vicariously arousing than are those of strangers or individuals who have been divested of human qualities. Personalizing the adverse effects experienced by others also makes their suffering much more salient. As a result, it is difficult to mistreat humanized persons without risking self-censure.

Self-sanctions against cruel conduct can be disengaged or blunted by divesting people of human qualities. Once dehumanized, they are no longer viewed as persons with feelings, hopes, and concerns but rather as subhuman objects. Subhumans are regarded as insensitive to maltreatment and influenceable only by harsh methods. If dispossessing antagonists of humanness does not blunt self-reproof, it can be eliminated by attributing bestial qualities to them (Gibson & Haritos-Fatouros, 1986). When persons are given punitive power, they treat dehumanized individuals much more punitively than those who have been invested with human qualities (Figure 2.23). Dehumanization fosters different self-exonerative patterns of thought (Bandura, et al., 1975). People seldom condemn punitive conduct and they create justifications for it when they direct it toward individuals who have been deprived of their humanness. However, people strongly disapprove of punitive actions and rarely excuse their use toward individuals depicted in humanized terms.

When several disengagement factors are combined, they potentiate each other rather than simply produce additive effects. Thus, combining diffused responsibility with dehumanization greatly escalates the level of punitiveness, whereas personalization of responsibility, along with humanization, have a powerful self-deterring effect (Figure 2.24).

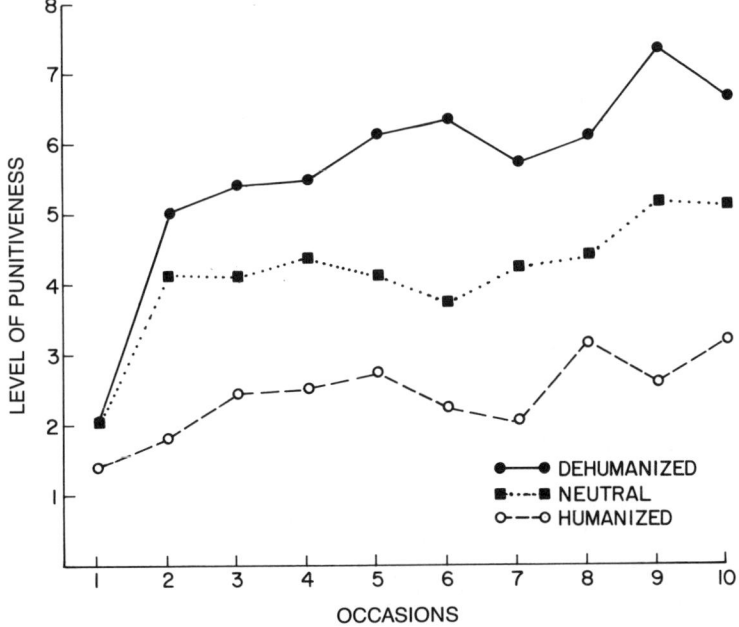

FIG. 2.23 Level of punitive sanctions imposed on repeated occasions on people characterized in humanized terms, not personalized with any characterization (neutral), or portrayed in dehumanized terms (Bandura, Underwood, & Fromson, 1975).

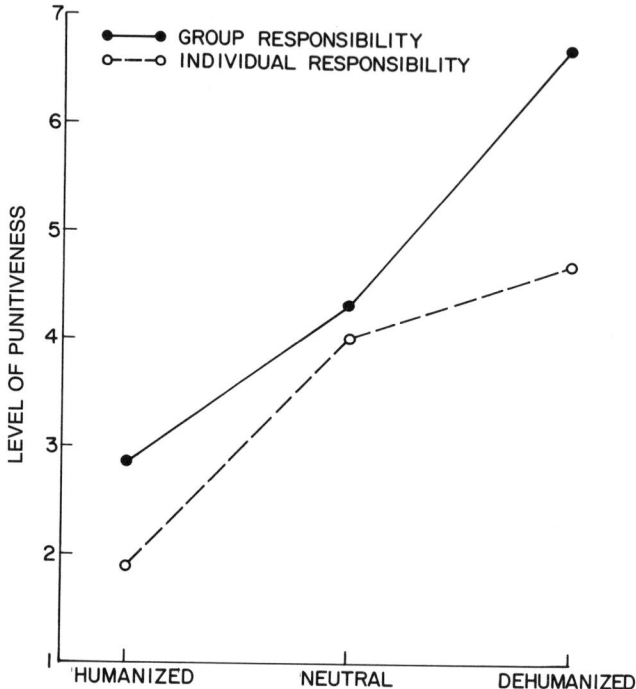

FIG. 2.24 Level of punitive sanctions imposed as a function of diffusion of responsibility and dehumanization of the recipients (Bandura, Underwood, & Fromson, 1975).

Psychological research tends to focus extensively on how easy it is to bring out the worst in people through dehumanization and other self-exonerative means. However, of considerable theoretical and social significance is the power of humanization to counteract cruel conduct. Studies examining this process reveal that it is difficult for individuals to behave cruelly toward others when they are humanized or even personalized a bit (Bandura, et al., 1975). Even under conditions in which punitive sanctions are the only means available and they are highly functional in producing desired results, those exercising that power cannot get themselves to behave punitively toward humanized individuals (Figure 2.25). In contrast, when punitive sanctions are dysfunctional because they usually fail to produce results, punitiveness is precipitously escalated toward dehumanized individuals. The failure of degraded individuals to change in response to punitive treatment is taken as further evidence of their culpability that justifies intensified punitiveness toward them.

2. SELF-REGULATION OF MOTIVATION

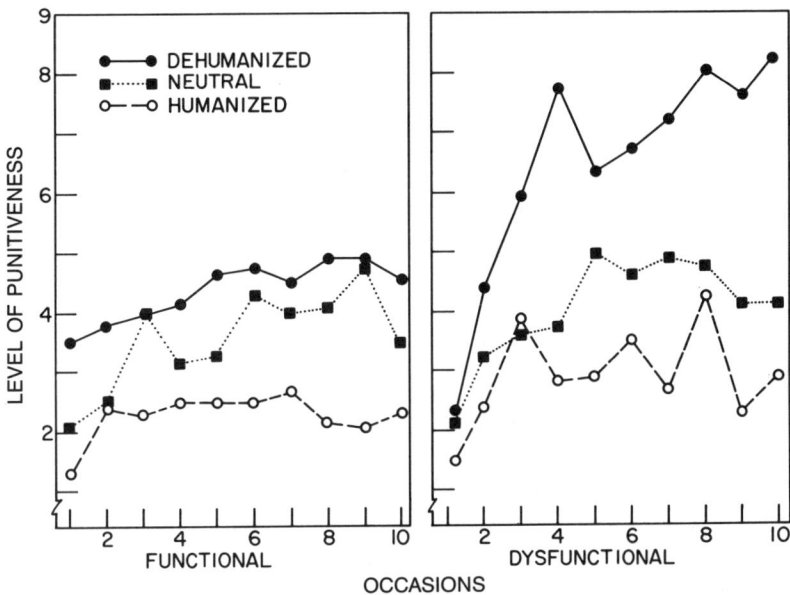

FIG. 2.25   Level of punitive sanctions imposed on repeated occasions as a result of dehumanization and the effectiveness of the punitive actions. Under the functional condition, punishment consistently produced good results; under the dysfunctional condition, punishment usually failed to achieve desired results (Bandura, Underwood, & Fromson, 1975).

Attribution of Blame

Imputing blame to one's antagonists is still another expedient that can serve self-exonerative purposes. One's own violent conduct is viewed as compelled by forcible provocation. Deleterious interactions usually involve a series of reciprocally escalative actions, in which the antagonists are rarely faultless. One can always select from the chain of events an instance of the adversary's defensive behavior and view it as the original instigation. Injurious conduct thus becomes a justifiable defensive reaction to belligerent provocations. Self-exoneration is similarly achievable by viewing one's destructive conduct as forced by circumstances rather than as a personal decision. By blaming others or circumstances, not only are one's own actions excusable but one can even feel self-righteous in the process.

Observers of maltreatment can be disinhibited in much the same way as perpetrators are by the tendency to infer culpability from misfortune. Seeing others suffer maltreatment for which they are held partially responsible leads observers to derogate them (Lerner & Miller, 1978).

The devaluation and indignation aroused by ascribed culpability, in turn, provides moral justification for even greater maltreatment.

Disengagement of Self-Sanctions and Self-Deception

The issue arises as to whether disengagement of self-sanctions involves self-deception. Because of the incompatibility of being simultaneously a deceiver and the one deceived, literal self-deception cannot exist (Bok, 1980; Champlin, 1977; Haight, 1980). It is logically impossible to deceive oneself into believing something, while simultaneously knowing it to be false. Efforts to resolve the paradox of how one can be the agent and the object of deception at the same time have met with little success (Bandura, 1986). These attempts usually involve creating split selves and rendering one of them unconscious. The split-self conceptions fail to specify how a conscious self can lie to an unconscious self without some awareness of what the other self believes. The deceiving self has to be aware of what the deceived self believes in order to know how to concoct the deceptions. Different levels of awareness are sometimes proposed as another possible solution to the paradox. It is said that "deep down" people really know what they believe. This attempt to reacquaint the split selves only reinstates the paradox of how one can be the deceiver and the one deceived at the same time. People, of course, often misconstrue events; they lead themselves astray by their biases and misbeliefs, and they act uninformedly. However, to be misdirected by one's beliefs or ignorance does not mean that one is lying to oneself.

Self-deception is often invoked when people choose to ignore possibly countervailing evidence. It could be argued that they must believe its validity in order to avoid it; otherwise they would not know what to shun. This is not necessarily so. Staunch believers often choose not to waste their time scrutinizing opposing arguments or evidence because they are already convinced of their fallacy. When confronted with evidence that disputes their beliefs, they question its credibility, dismiss its relevance, or twist it to fit their views. However, if the evidence is compellingly persuasive, they alter their original beliefs to accommodate the discrepant evidence.

People may harbor some doubts concerning their beliefs but avoid seeking certain evidence because they have an inkling the evidence might disconfirm what they wish to believe. Indeed, they may engage in all kinds of maneuvers, both in thought and in action, to avoid finding out the actual state of affairs. Suspecting something is not the same as knowing it to be true. Inklings can always be discounted as possibly being ill-founded. As long as one does not find out the truth, what one believes is not personally known to be false. Both Haight (1980) and Fingarette (1969) give considerable attention to processes whereby people avoid painful or incriminating truth by either not taking actions that would reveal it or not spelling out fully what they are doing or undergoing that would make it known. They act in ways that keep themselves intentionally uninformed. They do not go looking for evidence of their culpability or the harmful effects of their actions. Obvious questions that would reveal unwelcome information remain unasked so that they do not find out what they do not want to know. Implicit agreements and social arrangements are created that leave the foreseeable unforeseen and the knowable unknown.

In addition to contending with their own self-censure, people are concerned about how they appear in the eyes of others when they engage in conduct that is morally suspect. This adds a social evaluative factor to the process. Haight (1980) argues that, in much of what is called self-deception, persons are aware of the reality they are trying to deny, but they create the public appearance that they are deceiving themselves. Others are thus left uncertain about how to judge and treat persons who seem to be sincerely deluding themselves in efforts to avoid an unpleasant truth. The public pretense is designed to head off social reproof. When people are caught up in the same painful predicament, the result may be a lot of collective public pretense.

The mechanisms of disengagement involve cognitive and social machinations but not literal self-deception. In moral justification, for example, people may be misled by those they trust into believing that destructive means are morally right because the means will check the human suffering of tyranny. The persuasive depictions of the perils and benefits may be accurate, exaggerated, or just pious rhetoric masking less honorable purposes. The same persuasory process applies to weakening of self-censure by dehumanizing and blaming adversaries. In the rhetoric of conflict, opinion shapers ascribe to their foes irrationalities, barbarities, and culpabilities that color public beliefs (Ivie, 1980). In these different instances, those who have been persuaded are not lying to themselves. The misleaders and the misled are different persons. When the misleaders are themselves operating under erroneous beliefs, the views they voice are not intentional deceptions. They seek to persuade others into believing what they themselves believe. In social deception, public declarations by others may belie their private beliefs, which are concealed from those being deceived.

In reduction of self-censure by ignoring, minimizing, or misconstruing the deleterious effects of their actions, people lack the evidence to disbelieve what they already believe. The issue of self-dishonesty does not arise as long as one remains uninformed or misinformed about the outcomes of one's actions. When disengagement of self-censure is promoted by diffused and displaced responsibility, functionaries carry out the orders of superiors and often perform only a small subfunction, at that. Such arrangements enable people to think of themselves merely as subordinate instruments, rather than as agents, of the entire enterprise. If they regard themselves as minor cogs in the intricate social machinery, they have little reason to believe otherwise concerning their initiatory power. This is not to say that disengagement of self-censure operates flawlessly. If serious disbeliefs arise, especially at the point of moral justification, people cannot get themselves to behave inhumanely, and if they do, they pay the price of self-contempt.

ACKNOWLEDGMENT

Preparation of this chapter was facilitated by Public Health Research Grant MH-5162-25 from the National Institute of Mental Health. A major portion of this chapter originally appeared in V. Hamilton, G. H. Bower, & N. H. Frijda (Eds.), *Cognitive perspectives on emotion and motivation.* (pp. 37–61). Dordrecht: Kluwer Academic Publishers 1988.

REFERENCES

Alloy, L. B., & Abramson, L. Y. (1979). Judgment of contingency in depressed and nondepressed students: Sadder but wiser? *Journal of Experimental Psychology, 108,* 441–487.
Alloy, L. B., Abramson, L. Y., & Viscusi, D. (1981). Induced mood and the illusion of control. *Journal of Personality and Social Psychology, 41,* 1129–1140.
Arvey, R. D., & Dewhirst, H. D. (1976). Goal-setting attributes, personality variables, and job satisfaction. *Journal of Vocational Behavior, 9,* 179–190.
Atkinson, J. W. (1964). *An introduction to motivation.* Princeton, NJ: Van Nostrand.
Bandura, A. (1982). Self-efficacy mechanism in human agency. *American Psychologist, 37,* 122–147.
Bandura, A. (1986). *Social foundations of thought and action: A social cognitive theory.* Englewood Cliffs, NJ: Prentice-Hall, Inc.
Bandura, A. (1988a, in press). Self-efficacy mechanism in physiological activation and health-promoting behavior. In J. Madden, IV, S. Matthysse, & J. Barchas (Eds.), *Adaptation, learning and affect.* New York: Raven Press.
Bandura, A. (1988b). Perceived self-efficacy: Exercise of control through self-belief. In J. P. Dauwalder, M. Perrez, & V. Hobi (Eds.), *Annual series of European research in behavior therapy* (Vol. 2, pp. 27–59). Lisse (NL): Swets & Zeitlinger.
Bandura, A. (1988c). Mechanisms of moral disengagement in terrorism. In W. Reich (Ed.), *The psychology of terrorism: Behaviors, world-views, states of mind.* Cambridge: Cambridge University Press.

Bandura, A. (1988d, in press). Social cognitive theory and social referencing. In S. Feinman (Ed.), *Social referencing and social construction of reality.* New York: Plenum.

Bandura, A. (1988e, in press). Self-efficacy conception of anxiety. *Anxiety Research 1.*

Bandura, A. (1988f, in press). Social cognitive theory of moral thought and action. In W. M. Kurtines & J. L. Gewirtz (Eds.), *Moral behavior and development: Advances in theory, research and applications* (Vol. 1). Hillsdale, NJ: Lawrence Erlbaum Associates.

Bandura, A., & Abrams, K. (1986). *Self-regulatory mechanisms in motivating, apathetic, and despondent reactions to unfulfilled standards.* Unpublished manuscript, Stanford University, Stanford.

Bandura, A., & Cervone, D. (1983). Self-evaluative and self-efficacy mechanisms governing the motivational effects of goal systems. *Journal of Personality and Social Psychology, 45,* 1017–1028.

Bandura, A., & Cervone, D. (1986). Differential engagement of self-reactive influences in cognitive motivation. *Organizational Behavior and Human Decision Processes, 38,* 92–113.

Bandura, A., & Schunk, D. H. (1981). Cultivating competence, self-efficacy and intrinsic interest through proximal self-motivation. *Journal of Personality and Social Psychology, 41,* 586–598.

Bandura, A., & Simon, K. M. (1977). The role of proximal intentions in self-regulation of refractory behavior. *Cognitive Therapy and Research, 1,* 177–193.

Bandura, A., Underwood, B., & Fromson, M. E. (1975). Disinhibition of aggression through diffusion of responsibility and dehumanization of victims. *Journal of Research in Personality, 9,* 253–269.

Bandura, A., & Wood, R. E. (1988). Effect of perceived controllability and performance standards on self-regulation of complex decision-making. Manuscript submitted for publication.

Bandura, M. M., & Dweck, C. S. (1988). The relationship of conceptions of intelligence and achievement goals to achievement-related cognition, affect and behavior. Manuscript submitted for publication.

Barling, J., & Abel, M. (1983). Self-efficacy beliefs and performance. *Cognitive Therapy and Research, 7,* 265–272.

Barling, J., & Beattie, R. (1983). Self-efficacy beliefs and sales performance. *Journal of Organizational Behavior Management, 5,* 41–51.

Beach, L. R., Barnes, V. E., & Christensen-Szalanski, J. J. J. (1986). Beyond heuristics and biases: A contingency model of judgmental forecasting. *Journal of Forecasting, 5,* 143–157.

Beck, K. H., & Lund, A. K. (1981). The effects of health threat seriousness and personal efficacy upon intentions and behavior. *Journal of Applied Social Psychology, 11,* 401–415.

Becker, L. J. (1978). Joint effect of feedback and goal setting on performance: A field study of residential energy conservation. *Journal of Applied Psychology, 63,* 428–433.

Behling, O., & Starke, F. A. (1973). The postulates of expectancy theory. *Academy of Management Journal, 16,* 373–388.

Betz, N. E., & Hackett, G. (1986). Applications of self-efficacy theory to understanding career choice behavior. *Journal of Social and Clinical Psychology, 4,* 279–289.

Bok. S. (1980). The self deceived. *Social Science Information, 19,* 923–936.

Bolinger, D. (1982). *Language: The loaded weapon.* London: Longman.

Bower, G. H., (1983). Affect and cognition. *Philosophical Transactions of the Royal Society of London* (Series B), *302,* 387–402.

Brandt, R. B. (1979). *A theory of the good and the right.* Oxford: Clarendon.

Brock, T. C., & Buss, A. H. (1962). Dissonance, aggression, and evaluation of pain. *Journal of Abnormal and Social Psychology, 65,* 197–202.

Brock, T. C., & Buss, A. H. (1964). Effects of justification for aggression and communica-

tion with the victim on postaggression dissonance. *Journal of Abnormal and Social Psychology, 68,* 403–412.
Brown, I., Jr., & Inouye, D. K. (1978). Learned helplessness through modeling: The role of perceived similarity in competence. *Journal of Personality and Social Psychology, 36,* 900–908.
Bryan, J. F., & Locke, E. A. (1967). Goal-setting as a means of increasing motivation. *Journal of Applied Psychology, 51,* 274–277.
Campion, M. A., & Lord, R. G. (1982). A control systems conceptualization of the goal-setting and changing process. *Organizational Behavior and Human Performance, 30,* 265–287.
Carver, C. S., & Scheier, M. F. (1981). *Attention and self-regulation: A control-theory approach to human behavior.* New York: Springer-Verlag.
Cervone, D. (1985). *Self-efficacy judgement under uncertainty: Availability biases in perceived self-efficacy and behavior.* Unpublished doctoral dissertation, Stanford University.
Cervone, D., & Peake, P. K. (1986). Anchoring, efficacy, and action: The influence of judgmental heuristics on self-efficacy judgments and behavior. *Journal of Personality and Social Psychology, 50,* 492–501.
Champlin, T. S. (1977). Self-deception: A reflexive dilemma. *Philosophy, 52,* 281–299.
Ciminero, A. R., & Steingarten, K. A. (1978). The effects of performance standards on self-evaluation and self-reinforcement in depressed and nondepressed individuals. *Cognitive Therapy and Research, 2,* 179–182.
Collins, J. L. (1982, March). *Self-efficacy and ability in achievement behavior.* Paper presented at the annual meeting of the American Educational Research Association, New York.
Covington, M. V., & Omelich, C. L. (1979). Are causal attributions causal? A path analysis of the cognitive model of achievement motivation. *Journal of Personality and Social Psychology, 37,* 1487–1504.
Csikszentmihalyi, M. (1979). Intrinsic rewards and emergent motivation. In M. R. Lepper & D. Greene (Eds.), *The hidden costs of reward* (pp. 205–216). Morristown, NJ: Lawrence Erlbaum Associates.
Cutrona, C. E., & Troutman, B. R. (1986). Social support, infant temperament, and parenting self-efficacy: A mediational model of postpartum depression. *Child Development, 57,* 1507–1518.
Davies, F. W., & Yates, B. T. (1982). Self-efficacy expectancies versus outcome expectancies as determinants of performance deficits and depressive affect. *Cognitive Therapy and Research, 6,* 23–35.
Devins, G. M., Binik, Y. M., Gorman, P., Dattel, M., McCloskey, B., Oscar, G., & Briggs, J. (1982). Perceived self-efficacy, outcome expectations, and negative mood states in end-stage renal disease. *Journal of Abnormal Psychology, 91,* 241–244.
Diener, E. (1977). Deindividuation: Causes and consequences. *Social Behavior and Personality, 5,* 143–156.
Diener, E., Dineen, J., Endresen, K., Beaman, A. L., & Fraser, S. C. (1975). Effects of altered responsibility, cognitive set, and modeling on physical aggression and deindividuation. *Journal of Personality and Social Psychology, 31,* 328–337.
Dubbert, P. M., & Wilson, G. T. (1984). Goal-setting and spouse involvement in the treatment of obesity. *Behaviour Research and Therapy, 22,* 227–242.
Dweck, C. S., & Elliott, E. S. (1983). Achievement motivation. In P. H. Mussen (General Ed.) & E. M. Heatherington (Vol. Eds.), *Handbook of child psychology: Socialization, personality & social development* (4th Ed., Vol. 4, pp. 644–691). New York: John Wiley.
Elliott, E. S., & Dweck, C. S. (1988). Goals: An approach to motivation and achievement. *Journal of Personality and Social Psychology, 54,* 5–12.
Erez, M., & Zidon, I. (1984). Effect of goal acceptance on the relationship of goal difficulty to performance. *Journal of Applied Psychology, 69,* 69–78.

Feather, N. T. (Ed.) (1982). *Expectations and actions: Expectancy-value models in psychology.* Hillsdale, NJ: Lawrence Erlbaum Associates.

Festinger, L. (1942). A theoretical interpretation of shifts in level of aspiration. *Psychological Review, 49,* 235–250.

Fingarette, H. (1969). *Self-deception.* New York: Humanities Press.

Fishbein, M. (Ed.) (1967). *Readings in attitude theory and measurement.* New York: Wiley.

Gambino, R. (1973, November–December). Watergate lingo: A language of nonresponsibility. *Freedom at Issue* (No. 22), 7–9, 15–17.

Garber, J., Hollon, S. D., & Silverman, V. (1979, December). *Evaluation and reward of self vs. others in depression.* Paper presented at the meeting of the Association for the Advancement of Behavior Therapy, San Francisco.

Garland, H. (1983). Influence of ability, assigned goals, and normative information on personal goals and performance: A challenge to the goal attainability assumption. *Journal of Applied Psychology, 68,* 20–30.

Garland, H. (1984). Relation of effort-performance expectancy to performance in goal-setting experiments. *Journal of Applied Psychology, 69,* 79–84.

Gibson, J. T., & Haritos-Fatouros, M. (1986, November). The education of a torturer. *Psychology Today,* 50–58.

Glasgow, R. E., & Arkowitz, H. (1975). The behavioral assessment of male and female social competence in dyadic heterosexual interactions. *Behavior Therapy, 6,* 488–498.

Godding, P. R., & Glasgow, R. E. (1985). Self-efficacy and outcome expectations as predictors of controlled smoking status. *Cognitive Therapy and Research, 9,* 583–590.

Golin, S., & Terrill, F. (1977). Motivational and associative aspects of mild depression in skill and chance tasks. *Journal of Abnormal Psychology, 86,* 389–401.

Gurin, P., & Brim, O. G., Jr. (1984). Change in self in adulthood: The example of sense of control. In P. B. Baltes & O. G. Brim, Jr. (Eds.), *Life-span development and behavior* (Vol. 6, pp. 281–334). New York: Academic Press.

Haight, M. R. (1980). *A study of self deception.* Atlantic Highlands, NJ: Humanities Press.

Hogarth, R. (1981). Beyond discrete biases: Functional and dysfunctional aspects of judgmental heuristics. *Psychological Bulletin, 90,* 197–217.

Holahan, C. K., & Holahan, C. J. (1987). Self-efficacy, social support, and depression in aging: A longitudinal analysis. *Journal of Gerontology, 42,* 65–68.

Ivie, R. L. (1980). Images of savagery in American justifications for war. *Communication Monographs, 47,* 270–294.

Jacobs, B., Prentice-Dunn, S., & Rogers, R. W. (1984). Understanding persistence: An interface of control theory and self-efficacy theory. *Basic and Applied Social Psychology, 5,* 333–347.

Jobe, L. D. (1984). *Effects of proximity and specificity of goals on performance.* Unpublished doctoral dissertation, Murdoch University, Western Australia.

Kanfer, F. H. (1977). The many faces of self-control, or behavior modification changes its focus. In R. B. Stuart (Ed.), *Behavioral self-management* (pp. 1–48). New York: Brunner/Mazel.

Kanfer, F. H., & Hagerman, S. (1981). The role of self-regulation. In L. P. Rehm (Ed.), *Behavior therapy for depression: Present status and future directions* (pp. 143–180). New York: Academic Press.

Kanfer, R., & Zeiss, A. M. (1983). Depression, interpersonal standard-setting, and judgments of self-efficacy. *Journal of Abnormal Psychology, 92,* 319–329.

Kavanagh, D. J. (1983). *Mood and self-efficacy.* Unpublished doctoral dissertation, Stanford University, Stanford, CA.

Kavanagh, D. J., & Bower, G. H. (1985). Mood and self-efficacy: Impact of joy and sadness on perceived capabilities. *Cognitive Therapy and Research, 9,* 507–525.

Kelman, H. C. (1973). Violence without moral restraint: Reflections on the dehumanization of victims and victimizers. *Journal of Social Issues, 29,* 25–61.

Kent, G., & Gibbons, R. (1987). Self-efficacy and the control of anxious cognitions. *Journal of Behavior Therapy & Experimental Psychiatry, 18,* 33–40.

Kirschenbaum, D. S., Humphrey, L. L., & Malett, S. D. (1981). Specificity of planning in adult self-control: An applied investigation. *Journal of Personality and Social Psychology, 40,* 941–950.

Kirschenbaum, D. S., Tomarken, A. J., & Ordman, A. M. (1982). Specificity of planning and choice applied to adult self-control. *Journal of Personality and Social Psychology, 42,* 576–585.

Kun, A. (1977). Development of the magnitude-covariation and compensation schemata in ability and effort attributions of performance. *Child Development, 48,* 862–873.

Kurtines, W. M., & Gewirtz, J. L. (Eds.) (1984). *Morality, moral behavior, and moral development.* New York: Wiley.

Latham, G. P., & Lee, T. W. (1986). Goal setting. In E. A. Locke (Ed.), *Generalizing from laboratory to field settings* (pp. 101–117). Lexington, MA: Heath.

Latham, G. P., & Yukl, G. A. (1976). Effects of assigned and participative goal setting on performance and job satisfaction. *Journal of Applied Psychology, 61,* 166–171.

Lazarus, R. S., & Launier, R. (1978). Stress-related transactions between person and environment. In L. A. Pervin & M. Lewis (Eds.), *Perspectives in interactional psychology* (pp. 287–327). New York: Plenum.

Lee, C. (1984a). Accuracy of efficacy and outcome expectations in predicting performance in a simulated assertiveness task. *Cognitive Therapy and Research, 8,* 37–48.

Lee, C. (1984b). Efficacy expectations and outcome expectations as predictors of performance in a snake-handling task. *Cognitive Therapy and Research, 8,* 509–516.

Lerner, M. J., & Miller, D. T. (1978). Just world research and the attribution process: Looking back and ahead. *Psychological Bulletin, 85,* 1030–1051.

Lewinsohn, P. M., Mischel, W., Chaplin, W., & Barton, R. (1980). Social competence and depression: The role of illusory self-perceptions. *Journal of Abnormal Psychology, 89,* 203–212.

Locke, E. A. (1968). Toward a theory of task motivation and incentives. *Organizational Behavior and Human Performance, 3,* 157–189.

Locke, E. A., Bryan, J. F., & Kendall, L. M. (1968). Goals and intentions as mediators of the effects of monetary incentives on behavior. *Journal of Applied Psychology, 52,* 104–121.

Locke, E. A., Cartledge, N., & Knerr, C. S. (1970). Studies of the relationship between satisfaction, goal setting, and performance. *Organizational Behavior and Human Performance, 5,* 135–158.

Locke, E. A., Frederick, E., Lee, C., & Bobko, P. (1984). Effect of self-efficacy, goals, and task strategies on task performance. *Journal of Applied Psychology, 69,* 241–251.

Locke, E. A., Shaw, K. N., Saari, L. M., & Latham, G. P. (1981). Goal setting and task performance: 1969–1980. *Psychological Bulletin, 90,* 125–152.

Locke, E. A., Zubritzky, E., Cousins, E., & Bobko, P. (1984). Effect of previously assigned goals on self-set goals and performance. *Journal of Applied Psychology, 69,* 694–699.

Loeb, A., Beck, A. T., Diggory, J. C., & Tuthill, R. (1967). Expectancy, level of aspiration, performance, and self-evaluation in depression. *Proceedings of the 75th Annual Convention of the American Psychological Association, 2,* 193–194.

Manderlink, G., & Harackiewicz, J. M. (1984). Proximal versus distal goal setting and intrinsic motivation. *Journal of Personality and Social Psychology, 47,* 918–928.

Mantell, D. M., & Panzarella, R. (1976). Obedience and responsibility. *The British Journal of Social and Clinical Psychology, 15,* 239–246.

Matsui, T., Okada, A., & Kakuyama, T. (1982). Influence of achievement need on goal setting, performance and feedback effectiveness. *Journal of Applied Psychology, 67,* 645–648.

Matsui, T., Okada, A., & Mizuguchi, R. (1981). Expectancy-theory prediction of the goal theory postulate, "The harder the goals, the higher the performance." *Journal of Applied Psychology, 66,* 54–58.
McMullin, D. J., & Steffen, J. J. (1982). Intrinsic motivation and performance standards. *Social Behavior and Personality, 10,* 47–56.
Meichenbaum, D. H. (1977). *Cognitive-behavior modification: An integrative approach.* New York: Plenum Press.
Mento, A. J., Cartledge, N. D., & Locke, E. A. (1980). Maryland vs Michigan vs Minnesota: Another look at the relationship of expectancy and goal difficulty to task performance. *Organizational Behavior and Human Performance, 25,* 419–440.
Mento, A. J., Steel, R. P., & Karren, R. J. (1987). A meta-analytic study of the effects of goal setting on task performance: 1966–1984. *Organizational Behavior and Human Decision Processes, 39,* 52–83.
Milgram, S. (1974). *Obedience to authority: An experimental view.* New York: Harper & Row.
Mitchell, T. R. (1974). Expectancy models of job satisfaction, methodological, and empirical appraisal. *Psychological Bulletin, 81,* 1053–1077.
Morgan, M. (1985). Self-monitoring of attained subgoals in private study. *Journal of Educational Psychology, 77,* 623–630.
Mossholder, K. W. (1980). Effects of externally mediated goal setting on intrinsic motivation: A laboratory experiment. *Journal of Applied Psychology, 65,* 202–210.
Muller, E. N. (1979). *Aggressive political participation.* Princeton: Princeton University Press.
Mynatt, C., & Herman, S. J. (1975). Responsibility attribution in groups and individuals: A direct test of the diffusion of responsibility hypothesis. *Journal of Personality and Social Psychology, 32,* 1111–1118.
Nicholls, J. G. (1984). Achievement motivation: Conceptions of ability, subjective experience, task choice, and performance. *Psychological Review, 91,* 328–346.
Nicholls, J. G., & Miller, A. T. (1984). Development and its discontents: The differentiation of the concept of ability. In J. G. Nicholls (Ed.), *Advances in motivation and achievement* (Vol. 3). *The development of achievement motivation* (pp. 185–218). Greenwich, CT: JAI Press.
Ostrow, A. C. (1976). Goal-setting behavior and need achievement in relation to competitive motor activity. *The Research Quarterly, 47,* 174–183.
Peake, P. K., & Cervone, D. (1988). Sequence anchoring biases in self-efficacy judgments and performance. Manuscript submitted for publication.
Pritchard, R. D., & Curtis, M. I. (1973). The influence of goal setting and financial incentives on task performance. *Organizational Behavior and Human Performance, 10,* 175–183.
Rapoport, D. C., & Alexander, Y. (Eds.) (1982). *The morality of terrorism: Religious and secular justification.* Elmsford, NY: Pergamon Press.
Rehm, L. P. (1982). Self-management in depression. In P. Karoly & F. H. Kanfer (Eds.), *Self-management and behavior change: From theory to practice* (pp. 522–567). New York: Pergamon.
Relich, J. D., Debus, R. L., & Walker, R. (1986). The mediation role of attribution and self-efficacy variables for treatment effects on achievement outcomes. *Contemporary Educational Psychology, 11,* 195–216.
Rosenbaum, M., & Hadari, D. (1985). Personal efficacy, external locus of control, and perceived contingency of parental reinforcement among depressed, paranoid, and normal subjects. *Journal of Personality and Social Psychology, 49,* 539–547.
Rotter, J. B. (1954). *Social learning and clinical psychology.* Englewood Cliffs, NJ: Prentice-Hall.
Ryan, T. A. (1970). *Intentional behavior.* New York: Ronald Press.

Sanford, N., & Comstock, C. (1971). *Sanctions for evil.* San Francisco: Jossey-Bass.
Sarason, I. G. (1975). Anxiety and self-preoccupation. In I. G. Sarason & D. C. Spielberger (Eds.), *Stress and anxiety* (Vol. 2, pp. 27–44). Washington, DC: Hemisphere.
Schunk, D. H. (1984). Self-efficacy perspective on achievement behavior. *Educational Psychologist, 19,* 48–58.
Schunk, D. H., & Cox, P. D. (1986). Strategy training and attributional feedback with learning disabled students. *Journal of Educational Psychology, 78,* 201–209.
Schunk, D. H., & Gunn, T. P. (1986). Self-efficacy and skill development: Influence of task strategies and attributions. *Journal of Educational Research, 79,* 238–244.
Schunk, D. H., & Rice, J. M. (1986). Extended attributional feedback: Sequence effects during remedial reading instruction. *Journal of Early Adolescence, 6,* 55–66.
Schwab, D. P., Olian-Gottlieb, J. D., & Heneman, H. G., III (1979). Between-subjects expectancy theory research: A statistical review of studies predicting effort and performance. *Psychological Bulletin, 86,* 139–147.
Schwartz, J. L. (1974). Relationship between goal discrepancy and depression. *Journal of Consulting and Clinical Psychology, 42,* 309.
Simon, H. A. (1976). *Administrative behavior: A study of decision-making processes in administrative organization* (3rd ed.). New York: Free Press.
Simon, K. M. (1979). *Effects of self comparison, social comparison, and depression on goal setting and self-evaluative reactions.* Unpublished manuscript, Stanford University, Stanford, CA.
Stanley, M. A., & Maddux, J. E. (1986). Investigation of a combined protection motivation and self-efficacy model. *Basic and Applied Psychology, 40,* 101–114.
Strang, H. R., Lawrence, E. C., & Fowler, P. C. (1978). Effects of assigned goal level and knowledge of results on arithmetic computation: Laboratory study. *Journal of Applied Psychology, 63,* 446–450.
Tilker, H. A. (1970). Socially responsible behavior as a function of observer responsibility and victim feedback. *Journal of Personality and Social Psychology, 14,* 95–100.
Umstot, D. D., Bell, C. H., Jr., & Mitchell, T. R. (1976). Effects of job enrichment and task goals on satisfaction and productivity: Implications for job design. *Journal of Applied Psychology, 61,* 379–394.
Vroom, V. H. (1964). *Work and motivation.* New York: Wiley.
Weinberg, R. S., Gould, D., & Jackson, A. (1979). Expectations and performance: An empirical test of Bandura's self-efficacy theory. *Journal of Sport Psychology, 1,* 320–331.
Weiner, B. (1985). An attributional theory of achievement motivation and emotion. *Psychological Review, 92,* 548–573.
Wheeler, K. G. (1983). Comparisons of self-efficacy and expectancy models of occupational preferences for college males and females. *Journal of Occupational Psychology, 56,* 73–78.
White, J. (1982). *Rejection.* Reading, MA: Addison-Wesley.
Williams, S. L. (1987). On anxiety and phobia. *Journal of Anxiety Disorders, 1,* 161–180.
Williams, S. L., & Watson, N. (1985). Perceived danger and perceived self-efficacy as cognitive mediators of acrophobic behavior. *Behavior Therapy, 16,* 136–146.
Wood, R. E., & Bailey, T. (1985). Some unanswered questions about goal effects: A recommended change in research methods. *Australian Journal of Management, 10,* 61–73.
Wood, R. E., & Bandura, A. (1988, in press). Impact of conceptions of ability on self-regulatory mechanisms and complex decision-making. *Journal of Personality and Social Psychology.*
Wood, R. E., Bandura, A., & Bailey, T. (1988, in press). Mechanisms governing organizational productivity in complex decision-making environments. *Organizational Behavior and Human Decision Processes.*

Wood, R. E., Mento, A. J., & Locke, E. A. (1987). Task complexity as a moderator of goal effects: A meta-analysis. *Journal of Applied Psychology, 72,* 416–425.

Yukl, G. A., & Latham, G. P. (1978). Interrelationships among employee participation, individual differences, goal difficulty, goal acceptance, goal instrumentality, and performance. *Personnel Psychology, 31,* 305–324.

Zimbardo, P. G. (1969). The human choice: Individuation, reason, and order versus deindividuation, impulse, and chaos. In W. J. Arnold & D. Levine (Eds.), *Nebraska symposium on motivation,* 1969 (pp. 237–309). Lincoln: University of Nebraska Press.

3 The Personal Striving Approach to Personality

ROBERT A. EMMONS
University of California, Davis

INTRODUCTION

Recently it has become trendy to study motivation. Although pioneers such as Murray, Allport, Lewin, and McClelland all stressed the dynamic striving character of behavior, this was a perspective that personality psychology appeared to abandon until recently, having emphasized instead traits and behavioral (un)predictability. However, the presence of this volume, along with others recently published (Frese & Sabini, 1985; Sorrentino & Higgins, 1986) signal a revival of interest in motivational concepts in personality and social psychology. Some have even argued (Emmons, 1987; Little, 1986) that we are embarking upon a conative revolution. Whereas some of this work has taken place within a personological framework (e.g., McAdams, 1985; McClelland, 1985), others have adopted a heavily experimental social-cognitive point of view (e.g., Cantor & Kihlstrom, 1987; Sorrentino & Higgins, 1986). The purpose of this chapter is to outline the beginnings of a motivational approach to personality, focusing on idiographic goal strivings, or "personal strivings." An objective of this chapter is to demonstrate that this approach has the potential to integrate the personological and social-experimental orientations to motivation.

Recently there has been a welcome infusion of new directions and fresh perspectives into the field of personality. These new directions range from interest in biological influences on behavior (Buss, 1984;

Kenrick, Montello, & McFarlane, 1985) to studying the naturally occurring stream of behavior using innovative methods (Buss & Craik, 1983; Emmons, Diener, & Larsen, 1986; Singer, 1987) to a resurgence of interest on lives and persons (McAdams, 1988). It would appear that personality psychology has survived the doldrum period that plagued the field since Mischel's *Personality and Assessment* was published in 1968. It is perhaps not coincidental that a major influence in this resurgence has been the revitalization of motivational concepts, most notably in the form of "goals" (Frese & Sabini, 1985; Pervin, 1983). As this volume attests, several approaches have recently emphasized that knowledge of the types of goals that individuals pursue in social interactions is critical to an understanding of personality and social behavior.

CURRENT CONCEPTIONS OF MOTIVATION

Current motivational perspectives on personality fall into one of two types, shown in Table 3.1. One way to differentiate them is in terms of their adoption of a nomothetic or idiographic conception of motivation.

First is the motive disposition concept as defined by McClelland (1951, 1985) and his colleagues (Atkinson & Birch, 1970; McAdams,

Table 3.1
Current Definitions of "Motive" and Related Concepts

1. McClelland (1985) McAdams (1985) Winter & Stewart (1978) Atkinson & Birch (1970)	*motive disposition/social motive* "An enduring, recurring affectively toned cognitive cluster . . . a cluster of recurrent experiential preferences"
2. McAdams (1985)	*imago* "An idealized and personified image of the self"
3. Cantor & Kihlstrom (1987)	*life task* "Problems that people are currently working on"
4. Little (1983)	*personal project* "An interrelated sequence of actions intended to achieve some personal goal"
5. Klinger (1977, 1987)	*current concern* "The state of an organism between commitment to a goal and either attainment of the goal or disengagement from it"

1985; Winter & Stewart, 1978). These authors define a motive disposition as a class or cluster of affectively tinged goals and propose that a small number of social motives, such as achievement, intimacy, and power, are sufficient to describe and explain behavior and experience. A more recent exemplar of this approach is McAdams' (1985) concept of "imago," defined as "an idealized and personified image of the self" (p. 178). Imagoes are the central elements of a person's identity and represent instantiations of two fundamental thematic lines in people's lives: agency (power/mastery/separation) and communion (intimacy/surrender/union). Imagoes are broad, superordinate constructs, which encompass interpersonal styles, values and beliefs, and personal needs and motives (McAdams, in press).

The other major type of motivational unit being adopted by investigators is idiographic in nature. There has been an increasing trend recently toward the adoption of more circumscribed, idiographic units. Klinger (1977) developed the notion of a "current concern" out of dissatisfaction with the failure of the motive dispositions to predict spontaneous thought content. A current concern is a hypothetical motivational state in between two points in time: the identification of a goal and either the attainment of the goal or disengagement from it. This hypothetical state guides a person's ongoing thoughts, emotional reactions, and behavior during the time it is active. People simultaneously possess a number of current concerns, as there is a different concern for each goal to which a person is committed. The range of potential concerns is diverse, as each individual possesses an idiographic set than frequently changes. Examples of current concerns are going on a trip, keeping a dentist appointment, losing weight, and eating lunch tomorrow. Klinger, Barta, & Maxeiner (1981) found that certain properties of current concerns, especially value and degree of commitment, predicted naturally occurring thought streams.

A similar though independently developed concept is the personal project (Little, 1983, 1987; Palys & Little, 1983). Rooted in Murray's (1951) concept of a serial program, personal projects are "an interrelated sequence of actions intended to achieve a personal goal" (Palys & Little, p. 1223). Personal projects are things that people think about, plan for, carry out, and sometimes, but not always, complete (Little, 1983). The concept is promoted by Little as an interactional unit, taking into account both situational and personal parameters. Examples of personal projects, taken from Little (1983), are "going to the prom with Brad," "finding a part-time job," and "shopping for the holidays." Applying the concept to life satisfaction, Palys and Little (1983) found that individuals who were involved in short-term important projects that were highly enjoyable and moderately difficult were more satisfied with their lives than individuals who possessed projects that were of longer range but from which they derived little immediate enjoyment.

Finally, Cantor (Cantor, Brower, and Korn, 1985; Cantor et al., 1987; Cantor & Kihlstrom, 1987) recently developed the concept of life tasks, defined as "problems that people are currently working on" (p. 4). These life tasks, consensual in nature, organize and give meaning to a person's everyday activities and are especially salient during life transitions, such as marriage or graduation from college. Cantor et al. (1987) show how individual differences in cognitive strategies in dealing with social and academic life tasks are related to actual-ideal self-concept discrepancies in those domains.

An interesting feature of current concerns, personal projects, and life tasks is that they are all idiographic *and* nomothetic. That is, the specific list of concerns, projects, and tasks is unique to each individual. Yet these concerns, projects, and tasks can be compared along such nomothetic dimensions as value, expectancy for success, complexity, and difficulty, among others; and in this sense, comparisons among individuals can be made. In addition, these nomothetic properties tie these concepts to cognition, emotion, and action. For example, Klinger et al. (1981) reported that people tend to think about concerns that are valued, nonroutine, and for which little time is remaining before something must be done about them. With these common properties, general statements tying goals to affective, cognitive, and behavioral outcomes can be made that are likely to transcend the idiographic content of these units.

As useful as these three mixed idiographic-nomothetic approaches have been, they possess limitations when attempting to apply them to personality. By definition, personality consists of those attributes manifested by an individual with some regularity over time and across situations (Snyder & Ickes, 1985). Thus, stability and consistency are properties that personality descriptors must possess. Current concerns, personal projects, and life tasks fail in this respect as they are frequently changing. In the case of a current concern, once the goal is consummated the concern disappears. Similarly, personal projects have a clear termination stage (Little, 1983). Life tasks are salient during a particular life transition (Cantor & Kihlstrom, 1987).

Another problem is that it is often difficult to distinguish among these concepts. Perhaps most critically, current concerns, personal projects, and life tasks are not articulated in such a way that would yield meaningful descriptions about the psychological propensities of individuals. Examples of current concerns and personal projects, such as "picking up a pair of pants at the cleaners" (Klinger et al., 1981) or "having lunch tomorrow" (Little, 1983) seem a retreat from G. Allport's (1937) definition of personality as "the dynamic organization within the individual of those psychophysical systems that determine one's unique adjustment to the environment" (p. 48).

Thus, the field of personality does not appear to possess in its armamentarium a concept that accomplishes exactly what is required here. A gap exists between the broad, nomothetic motives on the one hand and these specific, everyday concerns and goals on the other. A concept is needed that captures the recurring, typical, goal-seeking behavior that defines a person's individuality. The remainder of this chapter presents the case for a concept designed to fill this gap, the personal striving.

HISTORICAL BACKGROUND

In 1937, Floyd Allport published an article in *Character and Personality* entitled "Teleonomic description in the study of personality." In this article, he proposed that personality traits are fundamentally inadequate for describing the personality of an individual. An individual's personality might be better described, according to Allport, in terms of what the person seems to be "trying to do" or the purpose or purposes that a person seems to be trying to carry out. Allport coined the term "teleonomic trend" to describe these behavioral tendencies, which he claimed were more dynamic and discriminating than trait terms. Allport also suggested that these teleonomic trends could be used to understand apparently inconsistent behavior, thus representing an early, though unheeded solution to the behavioral consistency controversy (Pervin, 1983). Allport's concept of teleonomic trend became the topic for many of his students' doctoral dissertations, some of which were published (Frederiksen & Allport, 1941; Gregory, 1945; Morse & Allport, 1952; Musgrave & Allport, 1941; Solomon & Allport, 1939; Tannenbaum & Allport, 1956). Unfortunately, the influence of the concept did not spread far from Syracuse University and had limited influence upon the field of personality as a whole. A possible reason for this may have been the cumbersome method of assessing these trends, which required observers ratings from a large number of peers. Allport did not believe that what an individual said about his or her motives should be taken at face value. There is reason to believe, however, that the concept was abandoned prematurely. With the current emphasis on goal-directed behavior and idiographic approaches to motivation (Frese & Sabini, 1985; Pervin, 1985), the time seems ripe for its renewal. To this end, we have been developing the concept of a "personal striving," a modern day descendant of the teleonomic trend.

PERSONAL STRIVINGS AS UNITS OF ANALYSIS

Gordon Allport (1953) stated that "When we set out to study a person's motives we are seeking to find out what that person is trying to do in this life, including what he is trying to avoid, and what he is trying to be" (p. 112). This struck me as being not an unreasonable place to begin. Personal strivings are idiographically coherent patterns of goal strivings and represent what an individual is typically trying to do. In other words, personal strivings refer to the typical types of goals that a person hopes to accomplish in different situations. Each individual can be characterized by a unique set of these "trying to do" tendencies. For example, a person may be "trying to appear attractive to the opposite sex," "trying to be a good listener to his or her friends," and "trying to be better than others." Additional examples of personal strivings are given in Table 3.2.

Personal strivings can be thought of as superordinate abstracting qualities that render a cluster of goals functionally equivalent for an individual—in other words, that places them into broad equivalence classes. In this sense, a striving is similar to the definition of a motive disposition given earlier. However, the critical difference lies in the idiographic nature of the personal striving. A personal striving is a unifying construct—it unites what may be phenotypically different goals or actions around a common quality or theme. Thus, a striving can be

Table 3.2
Examples of Personal Strivings

Make attractive women notice me
Do as many nice things for people as I can
Get to know new people
Maintain an above average beauty
Force men to be intimate in relationships
Have as much fun as possible
Avoid being dependent on my boyfriend
Make it appear that I am intelligent
Avoid arguments when possible
Make life easier for my parents
Become financially independent from others
Show that I am superior to others
Make a good impression
Avoid maliciously gossiping about others
Set aside time for "emotional rest" each day

3. THE PERSONAL STRIVING APPROACH 93

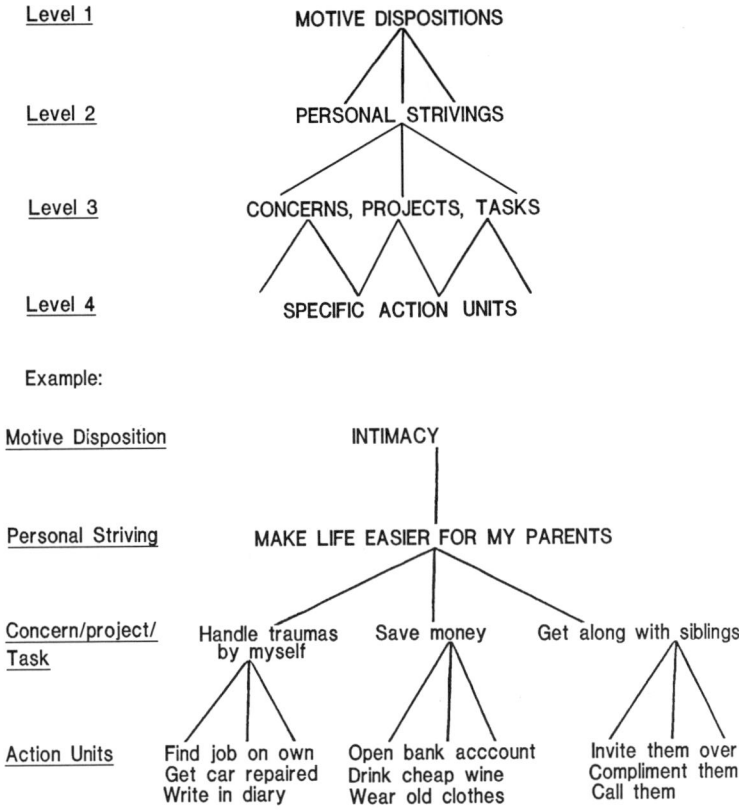

FIG. 3-1. Hierarchical Model of Motivation.

achieved in a variety of ways and satisfied via any one of a number of concrete goals. For instance, a person with the striving to "be physically attractive" may have separate goals about exercising, dressing a certain way, having a new wave hair style, etc. A person who has the striving "trying to gain prestige" may have separate goal concerns of publishing in prestigious journals, owning a Mercedes, and vacationing in Europe. It is useful to conceptualize personal strivings as occupying a position in a hierarchical control of action, as shown in Figure 3.1.

In this hierarchy, personal strivings are situated between global, diffuse motives and concrete, specific actions. Personal strivings, being at the second level in this four-level hierarchy, are presumed to generate lower level concerns, goals, tasks, or projects, which in turn lead to specific behavioral actions. The subordinate actions are in the service of the middle level goal units, which are in turn in the service of the more abstract strivings. The example given is undoubtedly an oversimplification, as many strivings flow from a given motive. This conceptualization is compatible with other hierarchical models (Carver & Scheier, 1981; Martindale, 1980; McAdams, 1985; Powers, 1973; Schank & Abelson, 1977; Vallacher & Wegner, 1985). In addition to the vertical structure, there is also a horizontal structure, which refers to the relationships that personal strivings have upon each other, for example either instrumental or conflictful (discussed in more detail later in this chapter).

Unlike teleonomic trends, personal strivings are not restricted to the behavioral domain. They may be cognitive, affective, or behavioral in nature. For example, a person may be trying to "achieve a spiritual oneness with God" or "trying to see the best in difficult situations," for which it would be difficult to specify behavioral referents. Personal strivings are also intended to depict what a person is currently typically trying to do, and, as such, represents current self-conceptions. However, their goal-directed nature permits them to encompass future, possible self-conceptions as well (Markus & Nurius, 1986). Personal strivings also are not normally terminated by successful or unsuccessful experiences. For example, a person who is trying to "see the best in difficult situations" is not likely to be content with a single accomplishment of this striving and from then on adopt a pessimistic orientation to situations. One could refer to personal strivings, then, as "enduring" as opposed to "current" concerns.

The personal striving approach to personality is compatible with the recently advanced control theory of self-regulation (Carver & Scheier, 1981, 1982; Hyland, 1987). These authors view behavior as a discrepancy reduction process operating in terms of a negative feedback loop, where individuals act to minimize the discrepancy between their present condition and a desired standard or goal. Carver and Scheier borrow from Powers' (1973) notion of hierarchical levels of control, where various levels of behavioral standards differing in abstraction are posited as guiding behavior. These behavioral standards, or goals, are arranged in a hierarchy from the broadest, most abstract organizing principles to the narrowest, most specific actions. From the present perspective, a personal striving can be viewed as a superordinate standard of comparison for a person's subordinate goal strivings. The personal striving is equivalent to the principle level in Powers' hierarchy. A principle is a quality and abstraction, which can be realized through many different courses of action. The principle, in turn, specifies reference values to the next level of control, the program level, which is equivalent to more circumscribed concerns or projects in the personal striving scheme. The program, in turn, specifies a specific course of behavioral action, which is in the service of the higher order program, which is in turn in the service of the superordinate principle. For example, someone may have the striving of "trying to become independent from my parents" and use it as a general guiding principle. The striving will specify reference values, or goals, at a lower level of abstraction. The person may have the plan of going away to college, for instance, as one way of seeking independence. This plan, in turn, will specify more concrete behavioral prescriptions, such as renting an apartment or opening a checking account. Thus, the personal striving perspective is compatible with Carver and Scheier's and Powers' hierarchical control theories.

The hierarchical model of personality presented here is also similar with several other formulations. Murray (1938) postulated actones (specific actions), needs, and complexes arranged in a hierarchical system. Similarly, Martindale (1980) proposed a hierarchy of control consisting of action units, plans, dispositions, and subselves. McAdams (1985) has recently proposed that imagoes (personified self-images) specify motives, which in turn specify action units. (personified self-images) specify motives, which in turn specify action units. Vallacher & Wegner (1985, 1987) hypothesize that a given action can be identified at different levels, ranging from the broadest purpose to the most specific behavior.

RELATION TO MOTIVES AND VALUES

Several motivational terms have been used more or less interchangeably in the past, so some clarification is needed before moving on to the assessment of personal strivings. How do personal strivings differ from other motivational concepts, such as goals, need, motives, and values? As indicated earlier, a motive refers to a tendency to strive for a general class of incentives that are highly fused with affect (McAdams, 1985; McClelland, 1985; Winter & Stewart, 1978). This definition in itself is quite similar to the personal striving construct. The crucial difference lies in the idiographic nature of the personal striving. One could also refer to strivings as "idiomotives" or "personal dispositions" in G. Allport's (1937) terminology. Personal strivings represent individualized instantiations of nomothetic motives. For example, a person with a high need for achievement may have separate strivings of trying to do a good job, trying to get things accomplished, or trying to get attention from others and believes that achieving something is the best way to attain those objectives. Clearly, motives can be expressed in many different ways, and these "ways" can take the form of personal strivings.

Although not included in the hierarchical model, another related construct is a *value* (Rokeach, 1973). A value is a cognitive representation (belief) about the desirable. It is a mixture of a person's needs, social norms, and societal and institutional demands. A value indicates what one *ought to do,* whereas a striving indicates what one *wants to do.* Needless to say, conflict can often arise between values and strivings. Values are also nomothetic: According to Rokeach (1973), "all men possess the same values (a small number) in different degrees" (p. 3). Finally, values have a more passive and indirect role in goal-directed behavior because they are higher than strivings in the hierarchy of controlling influences on behavior. For example, a person who values "friendship" may have separate strivings of "trying to help others," "trying to meet new people," or "trying to avoid disagreements."

ASSESSING PERSONAL STRIVINGS

The Personal Striving Assessment Packet (PSAP) (Emmons, 1986) consists of four separate measurement instruments. Each will be described in some detail.

Generation of Striving Lists

The first instrument asks respondents to list all of his or her personal strivings. The instructions are quite detailed to ensure correct understanding of what is being required. Individuals are given the definition of a personal striving as "the things that you typically or characteristically are trying to do in your everyday behavior." They are then provided with several examples, such as "trying to persuade others that one is right," "trying to seek new and exciting experiences," and "trying to avoid being noticed by others." It is stressed that these strivings are phrased in terms of what the person is "trying" to do, regardless of whether the person is actually successful. They are also instructed that the strivings may be either positive or negative and that the striving must refer to a repeating, recurring goal, not to a one-time concern. Respondents are also cautioned to keep their attention focused on themselves and not to compare the things that they typically do with what others try to do. In addition, they are told to try to recall instances of actual behavior that was intended as opposed to what might have been the result. Respondents then complete two pages of open-ended statements, the stem of which is "I typically try to_____." None of the subjects in several studies conducted to date has failed to produce a list of his or her strivings in this manner. The number of strivings listed by individual subjects has ranged from 10 to over 40, with an average of around 16.

An objection might be raised that we are requiring respondents to make judgments for which they are ill-equipped. Subjects are required to make inferences about their personality characteristics, inferences that under certain conditions have been shown to be fallible (Nisbett & Wilson, 1977). As should be apparent from the instructions used in eliciting the strivings, every attempt is made to stay as close as possible to concrete behavioral experiences, thus minimizing inferential leaps that may be difficult to make. We also believe that we are assessing the content of personal strivings, rather than process. We are not asking subjects to speculate on the origin (process) of their strivings. Under these conditions, we believe that the likelihood of self-report errors are minimized.

Nevertheless, alternative means for eliciting strivings are desirable. We are currently experimenting with a sentence completion task to elicit personal strivings. Subjects complete the thought begun in stems such as "The most important thing to me is_____" and "I find myself thinking a great deal about_____". By probing in this manner, we are hoping to introduce a bit more structure into the elicitation task and perhaps uncover striving-related material that respondents might not otherwise freely produce. Sentence completion tasks have been shown to be effective in assessing motives in the past (Aronoff, 1967; see Rabin & Zlotogorski, 1985 for a review). We have also recently collected peer ratings of strivings, and are examining the degree of correspondence between peer-nominated and self-reported strivings. It will be interesting, for example, to see if all of a person's associates attribute to that person a striving such as "trying to prove their superiority to others," while the person themselves indicates that they were merely "trying to do a good job." There has been some work on the recognition of goals in others (Schmidt, 1976, this volume), and the personal striving approach may offer insight into this age-old problem.

Before proceeding to the second assessment task, subjects are told to select from their original striving lists 15 strivings that they feel best describe themselves. The purpose of this is so that each subject has the same number of strivings, for ease of data manipulation. Because the average number of strivings listed in the open-ended format has been around 16, not much information is being lost by shortening the list to 15.

Striving Specification Task

Following the generation of the striving lists, subjects explore in more depth the nature of each striving, in order to increase the salience of the cluster of goals that each striving is referring to. Respondents are asked to consider the actual ways that they go about trying to succeed in each of their strivings. This is referred to as the Striving Specification Task. Respondents are asked to consider the particular goals that they have and the plans for trying to reach these goals for each striving. For example, if the striving is "trying to spend more time relaxing," they are asked to consider the actual ways (drinking, going to movies, exercising) in which they try to accomplish the striving. These ways can consist of very specific goals, plans, or behaviors. They are instructed to write down as many as possible for each striving. On the average, about four to five ways are listed for each striving. By breaking down each striving into its subordinate components, respondents are in a better position to complete the remaining two assessment steps in the PSAP. We have yet to fully exploit these strategies listed, but some of the uses of this measure are described elsewhere in the chapter.

Striving Assessment Scales

The crux of the PSAP are the Striving Assessment Scales (SAS). These consist of 18 dimensions, identified in previous research (Klinger et al., 1981; Little, 1983, Wadsworth & Ford, 1983) as important dimensions along which goals can be described. Respondents are asked to rate each of their 15 strivings on the following dimensions: *valence* (positive or negative); value, which is assessed by two questions (a) happiness felt upon successful consummation and (b) unhappiness felt upon failure (after Klinger et al., 1981); *ambivalence,* which is assessed by asking how much unhappiness is felt upon successful consummation (again after Klinger et al.); *commitment, importance; past attainment; probability of success; confidence in probability of success; probability of success given no action; environmental opportunity; effort; difficulty; causal attribution* (does success depend more on internal or external factors); *social desirability; clarity of means; instrumentality;* and *satisfaction with progress.* In selecting these dimensions, every attempt was made to be comprehensive, which perhaps lead to a little redundancy among the dimensions. Factor analyses of these 18 dimensions (Emmons, 1986) resulted in three interpretable factors: (a) *degree of striving,* on which value, importance, and commitment loaded highest; (b) *success,* on which past attainment, satisfaction with progress, and probability of success loaded highest; and (c) *ease,* on which probability if no action, environmental opportunity, and difficulty (negative) loaded most highly. As has been argued cogently in support of other mixed idiographic-nomothetic measures of motivation (Klinger, 1987; Little, 1983), these nomothetic dimensions permit comparisons across individuals even though the motivational content is idiosyncratic. The 18 SAS dimensions also appear to possess a reasonable degree of stability over time. Emmons (1986) computed both 3- and 6-month stability coefficients for the 18 dimensions. The stabilities of the individual scales ranged from .58 to .91 for the 1-month interval (with a mean of .73), and from .47 to .70 for the 3-month period (with a mean of .60). Social desirability and importance were the most stable (perhaps being less affected by immediate experiences), whereas effort and impact were the least stable (perhaps being most susceptible to immediate experiences. I argue elsewhere (Emmons, 1986) that we should not expect these to be high because of the dynamic nature of the phenomena being assessed: People undoubtedly evaluate their strivings differently at different points in time, and, of course, the strivings themselves can change over time. We have found that in a sample of 40 undergraduates after 18 months, 45% were still present (with minor wording changes). Although the strivings are reasonably stable, they are certainly not immutable given certain life changes and transitions. Certainly our vision of what we are trying to do can and does change at various points in our lives, and personal strivings reflect continuing development throughout the life span.

Striving Instrumentality Matrix

The final step in the PSAP is the Striving Instrumentality Matrix (SIM). A 15 by 15 matrix is constructed for each person in which both the rows and columns list the personal strivings for that person. Subjects are asked to compare their first striving with their second and to ask themselves: "Does being successful in this striving have a helpful or harmful (or no effect at all) on the other striving?" The rating is made on a 5 point scale, where -2 = very harmful effect, -1 = somewhat harmful effect, 0 = no effect at all, $+1$ = somewhat helpful effect, and $+2$ = very helpful effect. The comparison process is continued until the entire matrix is filled out. An example of two strivings that were seen as having a harmful effect on each other by one subject were "to appear more intelligent than I am" and "to always present myself in an honest way." An example of two strivings that were seen as having a helpful or instrumental effect on each other identified by the same subject were "to help others when they are in trouble" and "to get to know others better." For the matrix as a whole, the average amount of conflict or instrumentality in the person's striving system is determined and is used as a variable in between-subject analyses. We have employed the concept of conflict as measured in this way in studies that are described later in the chapter.

Coding of Strivings

Personal strivings, are, by definition, idiographic. For certain research purposes, however, a more abstract level of analysis is desirable. Strivings can be categorized into thematically relevant content categories. We have been attempting to develop a system for coding personal strivings into the major motive systems—achievement, power, affiliation, and intimacy—using the criteria developed by other investigators coding verbal or written material (McClelland, 1961; McAdams, 1980; Winter & Stewart, 1978). In addition to these social motives, we have added some additional categories, such as personal growth/health and self-presentation. The categories and examples of strivings representative of each category are shown in Table 3.3.

The majority of the categories show a sufficient degree of rater reliability, and we plan to continue to refine the definitional criteria and perhaps develop additional content categories in the future. The ability to code personal strivings into these or other categories will enable researchers to traverse the territory between idiographic and nomothetic levels of analysis.

Unconscious Motivation

Before we consider empirical work that has employed the personal striving concept, two fundamental questions on the assessment of personal strivings remain to be addressed. First, are people aware of all that they are trying to do? Second, are they willing to tell us? It might be wondered whether people are aware of their strivings and can con-

Table 3.3
Striving Content Categories

Category	Example
Positive	"Think of the needs of others"
Negative	"Not let too many people get close to me"
Intrapersonal	"Avoid worrying about financial setbacks"
Interpersonal	"Persuade others that I am right"
Achievement	"Work toward higher athletic capabilities"
Affiliation	"Be friendly with others so they will like me"
Intimacy	"Help my friends and let them know I care"
Power	"Force men to be intimate in relationships"
Personal Growth/Health	"Develop a positive self-worth"
Self-Presentation	"Be concerned about my physical appearance always"
Autonomy	"Make decisions on my own"

sciously report them, since the possibility of unconscious goals has recently arisen (Pervin, 1983). The position taken here is that people *are able* to report when solicited what they are trying to accomplish. However, there is also no requirement that individuals be consciously aware of their strivings all of the time. Surely there is no reason for us to be chronically aware of the strivings that unite our separate goals concerns. Strivings are postulated to function in much the same manner as schemas, scripts, or other superordinate organizing structures and guiding principles (Singer, 1987).

It is recognized, however, that although people are likely to be aware of their personal strivings when asked about them, they may lack insight into the consequences of them (Gregory, 1945). Or people may be unaware of the faulty, maladaptive foundation of some of their strivings. For example, a person may be aware that they are trying to prove that they are superior to others but not realize that others dislike them because of this striving. Most current perspectives agree that people do have access to their goals. Klinger et al. (1981) believe that the case for unconscious goals has been overstated and conclude that "life would be far more chaotic than it is if substantial portions of people's goal strivings were for goals about which the striver was unconscious" (p. 171). Pervin (1983) speculates that persons might not be able to verbally articulate the details of a plan formed to obtain a goal, even though the person is aware of the goal and is capable of acting on it. Wadsworth and Ford (1983) in their research found that people were able to discuss their personal goals, describe various means-end relationships, and describe their goals in relation to everyday behavioral activities. There is also much to admire in Weiner's (1986) declaration that "the royal road to the unconscious is less valuable than the dirt road to consciousness" (p. 285).

Thus, other perspectives and previous work provide reasons to believe that individuals will be able to tell us what their personal strivings are. What may elude them is how these strivings came about in the first place, for example, *why* they are trying to get attention from others, or *why* they are trying to hurt another's feelings, but we do not ask them to speculate on the origins of these strivings. They simply describe what they are trying to do through their everyday behavior in current life situations. Of course, the possibility that people may not be willing to admit their strivings cannot be totally eliminated. Our interest up to now has simply been in what individuals consciously admit to trying to do. No claim is being made that the true motives of individuals is being unearthed, and we are not claiming that personal strivings represent the complete picture of the motivational aspects of personality.

EMPIRICAL WORK ON PERSONAL STRIVINGS

The heuristic value of the personal striving concept has now been demonstrated in a number of studies, including predicting levels of subjective well-being (Emmons, 1986), the influence of conflict and ambivalence on psychological and physical well-being (Emmons & King, 1988); the impact of conflict over expressing emotion on well-being (Emmons & King, 1987); and the relationship between self-complexity and affective reactivity (Emmons & King, in press). Each of these will be considered in turn.

Subjective Well-Being

In the initial study that employed the personal striving framework, (Emmons, 1986) 40 subjects generated lists of their personal strivings and rated them on the Striving Specification Task, Striving Assessment Scales, and Striving Instrumentality Matrix. The purpose of the study was to examine the relationship between aspects of the personal strivings (the as assessed by the SAS and SIM) and three components of subjective well-being: positive affect, negative affect, and life satisfaction. Positive and negative affect has been found to be relatively independent of each other in people's lives (Diener & Emmons, 1984), and the third component, satisfaction, is only moderately related to affect (Campbell, Converse, & Rodgers, 1976). There is widespread belief in our culture that possessing and progressing toward meaningful life goals is a prerequisite for well-being and happiness. Although several subjective well-being theories (Diener, 1984) are telic in nature, there have been few empirical attempts to chart the relations between these two domains. The personal striving perspective offers a framework within which to test such speculations. Subjects in the study recorded their moods and thoughts by use of an experience-sampling method (ESM) four times a day for 21 consecutive days. The ESM consists of signaling individuals at random moments throughout the course of their waking hours and having them record aspects of their immediate experience. We have used the ESM and variations of it in a number of studies (Diener & Emmons, 1984, Diener, Larsen, Levine, & Emmons, 1985; Emmons & Diener, 1985, Emmons & Diener, 1986), and it is ideally suited to the study of private experience (see Hormuth, 1986 and Larson & Csikszentmihalyi, 1983 for details on the method).

In accordance with expectancy-value formulations (Klinger, 1977), commitment was strongly associated with value and expectancy for success. Some other predictable relationships that were found between the

Table 3.4
Multiple Regression Analyses, Subjective Well-Being Variables

Well-Being Dimension	R	R	R increase	F	P<
Positive Affect					
Value	.39	.15	.15	6.49	.02
Effort	.45	.20	.05	4.34	.05
Past attainment	.51	.25	.05	3.84	.05
Negative Affect					
Probability of success	.34	.12	.12	5.13	.05
Conflict	.44	.20	.08	4.28	.05
Ambivalence	.71	.50	.30	21.04	.01
Life Satisfaction					
Instrumentality	.34	.12	.12	5.12	.01
Importance	.59	.35	.23	11.41	.05
Probability of success if no action	.65	.42	.07	3.92	.05

SAS was that difficulty was negatively associated with both striving clarity and environmental opportunity, and effort was negatively associated with probability of success given no action. These correlations provided evidence for the validity of the SAS.

Regarding subjective well-being, multiple regression analyses, shown in Table 3.4, revealed that positive affect was found to be best predicted by value, importance, and past fulfillment of strivings. Negative affect was best predicted by probability of success (negative), conflict, and ambivalence. Life satisfaction was best predicted by instrumentality, importance, and probability of success given no action.

In general, each component of well-being was related to a different set of predictors, providing further evidence that these components are relatively independent of each other (Diener, 1984, Diener & Emmons, 1984, Watson & Tellegen, 1985). In addition, these personal striving characteristics tended to account for greater amounts of variance in subjective well-being than personality traits had in previous studies (Costa & McCrae, 1980; Emmons & Diener, 1985). This supports the contention that subjective well-being might be better understood in terms of individuals' perceptions of their idiosyncratic goal strivings rather than in terms of nomothetic traits.

Conflict Among Strivings and Well-Being

Some of the more intriguing results in the aforementioned study involved the two measures of personal striving conflict: ambivalence and conflict as rated in the instrumentality matrix. Individuals who experienced much negative affect and who were low in life satisfaction reported greater ambivalence over their strivings as well as greater conflict between their strivings. This was to be expected given the recognition that conflict between and within one's goals is likely to be psychologically injurious (Epstein, 1982a; Pervin, 1983). Theorists and researchers beginning with Freud and including self-theorists such as Lecky (1945) and Epstein (1982a) have stressed the necessity of avoiding inner conflict by maintaining consistency and harmony among aspects of the self. These formulations led us to more closely examine the effect of conflict and ambivalence on both psychological and physical well-being. Conflict refers to situations in which one striving is seen by the person as interfering with other strivings in the individual's striving system. Ambivalence refers to the person's feeling that he or she has a desire to achieve and yet not achieve the same striving, and it is assessed by asking subjects to estimate the amount of unhappiness experienced upon successful consummation of the striving. Conflict and ambivalence are distinct, thought related, in that conflict between two strivings is likely to engender ambivalence toward one or both of the offending strivings. There is reason to believe that chronic motivational conflict involving strivings should be associated with lower physical well-being. For example, McClelland and his associates have documented the role of the inhibited power motive syndrome in producing physical illness (McClelland & Jemmott, 1980; McClelland, 1982; see Jemmott, 1987, for a review). Individuals that experienced chronic motivational conflict, such as conflict over expressing power, had higher blood pressure than others who did not possess this motive combination. Furthermore, long-term inhibited power motive syndrome has been associated with a weakening of the immune system and subsequent susceptibility to stress-related illnesses (McClelland, Floor, Davidson, and Saron, 1980).

Two separate samples (a total of 88 individuals) participated in this study (Emmons & King, 1988). In addition to the Striving Assessment Packet, they also completed a number of well-being measures, including daily reports of positive and negative affect, neuroticism, and physical and psychological symptomatology. The relationship between these variables and conflict for sample 2 are shown in Table 3.5.

Conflict and ambivalence were found to be associated with high levels of neuroticism, depression, negative affect, and psychosomatic complaints. The relationship between conflict and physical symptoms held after partialing both neuroticism and depression out of the relationship. Conflict between strivings was also related to the number of visits made to the student health center, as well as the total number of different illnesses based on physician ratings at the center.

Table 3.5
Correlations of Striving Conflict and Ambivalence With Psychological and Physical Well-Being

Psychological Well-Being	Conflict	Ambivalence
Psychological		
Positive Affect	−.11	−.34[b]
Negative Affect	.21	.18
DPQ Well-Being Scale	−.07	−.11
Anxiety	.17	.27[a]
Depression	.19	.34[b]
Physical		
Somatization	.24[a]	.19
Daily Symptoms	.14	.13
Health Center Visits	.27[a]	.12
Number of Illnesses	.31[b]	.21

Note. N = 48; [a]$p < .05$, [b]$p < .01$.

Forty of the subjects (Sample 1) were mailed follow-up questionnaires a year later to investigate whether conflict is a prospective predictor of physical illness. We correlated the ambivalence and conflict measures at time 1 with reported symptomatology at time 2 (1 year later, partialing out initial symptom levels). The correlations were stable over time, and actually rose slightly, though nonsignificantly (from $r = .28$ to $r = .31$). These partial correlations indicate that conflict does appear to lead to physical illness over time.

How does one account for these findings? We believe that Pennebaker's inhibition model of psychosomatic illness is a promising candidate (Pennebaker, 1985; Pennebaker & Bealls, 1986). Pennebaker and his colleagues have found that individuals who inhibit their desire to confide in others about traumatic life events are more likely to develop later physical illnesses, such as flus, ulcers, and respiratory infections. A desire to confide, coupled with a fear of confiding (i.e., conflict) about potentially embarassing events, such as rape or incest, results in increased rumination, chronic autonomic arousal, and eventual physiological distress and illness. According to Pennebaker, the inhibition of the desire leads the person to obsess over the traumatic incident. Lack of expressing emotion to others is associated with increased autonomic nervous system arousal, which, when chronic, can lead to the development of a number of psychosomatic disorders. It has now been well documented that there exists a negative relationship between expressiveness and autonomic arousal, particularly skin conductance

(Buck, 1984; Lanzetta & Kleck, 1970; Pennebaker, 1985), and that long-term chronic arousal is associated with a variety of maladies. For example, the personality style of repressive-defensiveness has been linked to the development, diagnosis, and progression of a variety of serious illnesses, including cancer and hypertension (Friedman & Booth-Kewley, 1987; Jensen, 1987).

We believe that the inhibition model can be used to account for the relationships between conflict and lower well-being. Although not stated in such terms, Pennebaker indirectly points to a conflict situation, conflict between wanting to confide in others coupled with a fear of confiding, which results in increased rumination about the trauma, chronic autonomic arousal, and eventual physiological distress. The inhibition model would predict that individuals should avoid acting on strivings over which they were ambivalent and strivings that were in conflict with other strivings. The model would also predict that individuals would tend to obsess or ruminate over these conflicting strivings.

To test these hypotheses, we (Emmons & King, 1988, Study 3) had subjects write down what they were thinking about and what activity they were engaged in at random times on four occasions a day over a 3-week period, using an experience-sampling method. After the 3-week period, we had subjects review their thoughts and activites and indicate whether each was related to any of their 15 strivings, and, if so, which ones. This gave us an estimate of the amount of time spent thinking about and acting on each striving. We then correlated these two indices with the conflict and ambivalence ratings. Consistent with the inhibition model, individuals spent more time thinking about conflicting and ambivalent strivings (r's = .17 and .14, both P's < .01), yet they spent less time acting on them (r's = −.27 for ambivalence and −.17 for conflict, both P's < .01). Although these correlations are not large, they are impressive given the multitude of influences on naturally occurring thought and action. Conflict appears to lead both to the inhibition of behavior and to increased rumination, which, over time, have been shown to lead to aversive psychological and physical illness. This study was also notable because it showed that people are aware of and are able to report on intrapsychic conflict, that conflict can be measured in a meaningful idiographic way, and that conflict of this type has measurable consequences for both psychological and physical well-being.

Conflict Over Expressing Emotion and Well-Being

We then became curious about the nature of the strivings that were causing people conflict. What sorts of strivings are people ambivalent and conflicted over? Interestingly, in the two samples that we have studied most extensively, many of the strivings rated high in ambivalence seem to be centered on the expression of emotion. Some of the strivings of this genre include "keep jealousy under control," "express myself honestly," and "deal with anger constructively." Given the premium that is placed on curtailing expression in our culture, and given that expression is viewed as the "normal" culmination of emotional experience (Baumeister & Tice, 1987) it is perhaps not surprising that issues surrounding the expression of emotion cause people a good deal of conflict. Of course, the individuals in Pennebaker's research suffer from conflict involving the desire to confide or express their feelings to others and the fear that such free expression might bring negative consequences, such as ostracization or censure. As we perused lists of strivings, we continued to encounter strivings dealing with the expression, management, or regulation of emotion.

Given the centrality of these concerns in our subjects' lives, we decided to develop a questionnaire designed specifically to tap ambivalence over expressing emotion, which we have come to call the Ambivalence Over Expressing Emotion Questionnaire (AEQ) (Emmons & King, 1987). The AEQ consists of 28 items based largely on strivings generated by subjects in our two samples. Items tap both positive and negative emotions. Example items include "I try to honestly criticize others for their own good, but I worry that they will be angry with me if I do so," and "Often I'd like to show others how I feel, but something seems to be holding me back," and "I try to show people that I love them, although I am afraid that it may make me appear weak or vulnerable." The scale is unidimensional, has a high internal consistency (alpha = .88), has shown a 2-month test-retest reliability of .83 (Emmons & King, 1987), is positively associated with a measure of trait ambivalence (Raulin, 1984), and correlates slightly negatively with social desirability. An attempt was made to word items in the personal striving framework, asking what the person tries to do as opposed to what they actually do, because these may not correspond. Indeed, we found that the AEQ correlated only −.24 with a measure of actual expressiveness, the Affective Communication Test (ACT; Friedman, Prince, Riggio, & DiMattea, 1980). Conflict or ambivalence over expressing emotion can take on different forms, from wanting to express but not being able to, to expressing but not necessarily wanting to, to expressing and later regretting it. Items were written so as to represent all of these possibilities.

We were interested in examining the extent to which both ambivalence over expressing emotion and actual emotional expressiveness (self-rated) were associated with psychological and physical well-being. The 48 individuals who were the subjects in one of the samples in Emmons &

King (1988) were also administered the AEQ, a measure similar to the ACT, which was expanded by items that we generated, a measure of family expressiveness (Halberstadt, 1986) and a battery of psychological and physical well-being measures. Results showed that high expressiveness ambivalence was related to anxiety; depression; obsessive-compulsiveness; neuroticism; and daily reported negative moods, headaches, and chest pains and was negatively related to patterns of expression within the family. Contrary to expectations, however, we did not find actual expressiveness negatively associated with these measures of psychological and physical distress. Apparently, expression alone is no guarantee against the problems that have been associated with emotional inhibition.

We believe that these findings can help clarify the sometimes contradictory relationship that is found between emotional expressiveness and well-being. The correlations between the EAQ and distress measures and lack of a correlation between the ACT and these measures suggest that it is ambivalence over expressing emotion, rather than a lack of expression per se, that is detrimental to well-being. This would indicate that individuals who are expressive but who are in conflict over expression may actually be worse off than less expressive individuals who feel no conflict over expression emotion. Encouraging expression in these "natural inhibitors" may be an added source of stress, as Tavris (1984) and Hochschild (1983) have shown. The focus should not be on expression as an end to itself. Rather, the individual goals and attitudes that underly expressive or inhibitory behavior may be more directly relevant to resulting psychological and physical distress than to the observed behavior itself. These notions are once again compatible with Pennebaker's inhibition model, in that conflict over expression results in an inhibition of expressiveness, an increase in chronic autonomic arousal, and a raised susceptibility to psychosomatic illnesses over time.

If the preceding speculations are true, then individuals who are ambivalent over expressing emotion should show higher baseline levels of arousal such as skin conductance and should also show fewer spontaneous expressive behaviors. We are currently engaged in further attempts to validate the scale along these lines with a variety of self- and peer-report, behavioral, and physiological indicators. Other future plans in this line of research include developing a taxonomy of conflict, using the writings of Bakan (1966) and Erikson (1959) among others as theoretical guidelines; examining how people resolve or otherwise deal with conflict among their strivings, and tracking sex and age differences in the content and preferred styles of conflict resolution.

Self-Complexity and Affective Reactivity

A final study to be mentioned here examined the relationship between personal striving self-complexity and affective reactivity (Emmons & King, in press). In an intriguing series of studies, Linville (1982, 1985) has demonstrated that the complexity of self-representation in terms of traits or social roles is inversely related to the extremity and variability of affective experience. While Linville's work has been limited to the trait and social role domains, the personal striving construct represents an ideal vehicle for extending this model into other domains.

Complexity is a structural attribute of personal striving systems. It refers to the degree of interdependence (low complexity) and independence (high complexity) among the elements (strivings) in the system, as well as the integration of these elements. In keeping with Linville's use of the term complexity, we examine only the differentiation and not the integration component. Some striving systems are characterized by a great deal of complexity. This would occur, say, when a person possesses strivings pertaining to achievement, affiliation, self-presentation, intimacy, etc., strivings that are for the most part independent of each other. Independent strivings are those in which the attainment of one has no impact upon the attainment of others. Neither an instrumental nor a conflictful relationship exists between independent strivings. Simplicity in the striving system is characterized by a greater interdependence among the strivings, which could occur, for example, when most of the strivings pertain to affiliation/intimacy, or most pertain to achievement/power. Interdependent strivings are strivings that affect, in an instrumental or conflicting way, other strivings within a person's striving system. Greater similarity among one's strivings is also indicative of simplicity, whereas greater differentiation is a sign of complexity in the system. Complexity also refers to the number of different plans, or means-end connections, that are associated with each striving. Complex strivings in this case are strivings that can be successfully achieved in a variety of different ways. Note that this meaning of complexity refers to individual strivings, whereas the previous use of complexity referred to the striving system as a complete unit.

We hypothesized that complexity within the striving system would be positively associated with affective reactivity. Affective reactivity encompasses both intensity and variablity of day-to-day mood. It is obvious that individuals vary widely in their emotional reactions to daily life events. We have identified this characteristic as an important parameter of emotional experience (Diener et al., 1985; Larsen, Diener, & Emmons, 1986; Larsen & Diener, 1987). According to the arousal-regulation theory of affect intensity (Larsen & Diener, 1987), individuals are motivated to maintain an optimum level of physical arousal, and affective intensity is one mechanism by which such regulation occurs. We predicted that emotionally intense individuals would structure their lives in such a way so as to obtain maximum affective experience, whereas the opposite would be true for low intensity subjects. One way to achieve such a structure would be to construct a complex goal-striving system. Notice that these predictions are opposite to the results that Linville has reported. At the same time, we predict that high intensity subjects would possess fewer plans for accomplishing each striving. By "putting their eggs into one basket" (Linville, 1985) intense individuals are creating the conditions that allow them to feel extreme elation or extreme despair upon successful or unsuccessful experiences.

Eighty-eight subjects in two samples completed the Striving Assessment Packet and rated their moods, either twice of four times a day, for 21 consecutive days. Personal striving complexity was assessed in three ways. One was a straightforward dissimilarity rating, where they rated the degree of dissimilarity (on a 9-point scale) between all possible pairs of strivings. Complexity was indicated by a high average dissimilarity score. The second index of complexity was derived from the Striving Instrumentality Matrix (SIM). Recall that in this measure, the degree of conflict, instrumentality, or independence tht exists between all possible pairs is rated. Complexity scores were computed by counting the number of "0" instrumentality ratings in the matrix. Such a count indicates the number of independent striving pairs in each subject's striving system and is consistent with Linville's (1985) conceptualization of complexity as the degree of independence/interdependence among the aspects of self-representation. The third measure of complexity was derived from the Striving Specification Task described earlier. We counted the number of "ways" that each subject indicated were the means by which they planned to accomplish each striving. A large number of ways indicated high complexity, whereas a small number indicated low complexity.

Daily emotional intensity was computed in the standard way (see Diener et al., 1985) by taking the mean positive affect on occasions when positive affect exceeded negative and the mean negative affect on occasions when negative exceeded positive and summing these two. We also administered the Affect Intensity Measure (AIM) (Larsen et al., 1986), an individual difference measure of emotional intensity. Affect variability was the standard deviation from the mean positive and negative affect ratings. The correlations among the three complexity measures and the affective reactivity measures are shown in Table 3.6.

As predicted, affective reactivity, both the variability and intensity of

Table 3.6
Correlations Between Affective Reactivity
and Striving Complexity Measures

	Variability		Intensity		AIM	
	1	2	1	2	1	2
Dissimilarity Ratings	.28[a]	.25[a]	.29[a]	.30[a]	.02	.14
Independent Pairs	.30[a]	.21	.29[a]	.30[a]	.32[a]	.25[a]
Plan Complexity	−.06	.05	−.33[a]	−.36[b]	.07	−.13

Note. 1 = Sample 1, N = 40; 2 = Sample 2, N = 48.
[a]$P < .05$; [b]$P < .01$. AIM = Affect Intensity Measure.

mood, were positively associated with the two measures of striving system complexity. However, the plan complexity measure was negatively associated with the intensity of daily mood. Thus, reactive individuals are characterized by a greater complexity across their striving system, but less complexity within their strivings. They have more strivings that are unrelated and dissimilar to each other than their less reactive counterparts, yet they have a limited number of means available in their repertoire for achieving each striving. These findings are consistent with more with Larsen & Diener's arousal-regulation theory than with Linville's self-complexity/affect extremity theory. Intense individuals do appear to seek out emotionally charged, stimulating situations as a means of regulating arousal levels. Complex life structures fall into the realm of emotion-provoking activities. Such a position is compatible with the view that persons actively seek out, create, and manipulate their environments in accordance with their psychological propensities (Buss, 1987; Emmons & Diener, 1986). This is also in keeping with Tomkins' (1979) view that a major motivational tendency is to experience and express affect.

In the remainder of the chapter, the relevance of the personal striving approach for a number of different themes is discussed. These include the relationship between personal strivings and personality traits, similarities between action identification theory (Vallacher & Wegner, 1987) and the personal striving approach, personal strivings and the self-concept, clinical implications of the personal striving concept, and the development of personal strivings.

Personal Strivings and Personality Traits

Without a doubt, the major unit of analysis adopted by the majority of investigators of personality has been the trait. Although the concept of a trait has had a rocky history, Buss and Craik (1983) have recently restored respectability to the summary-frequency use of trait in their act-frequency analysis. According to this perspective, a trait such as extraversion or dominance is simply a category made up of members (which in this case are acts) differing in their prototypicality. To say that a person is dominant means that they have performed a number of prototypically "dominant" acts. It would be instructive at this point to consider the differences between traits and personal strivings. Personal strivings provide different information about a person than does a trait ascription as it exists at a different level of analysis. As a simple example, three individuals might be said to be equally conscientious, yet they may be trying to do different things through their conscientious behavior. One person may be trying to be well liked, another simply trying to keep things neat and orderly, and the third trying to fulfill his or her obligations. The three might achieve similar scores on a trait measure of conscientiousness, may have performed a similar number of prototypically conscientious acts, and may be rated as equally conscientious by observers; yet each individual is aspiring to different objectives through his or her behavior.

Traits are qualities that a person presumably possesses a certain amount of and thus derive their meaning from a normative scale of reference (Lamiell, 1987). The existence of a trait, in other words, is dependent on individual differences with regard to that trait. Personal strivings, on the other hand, are idiographic in nature, and the description of an individual in terms of these strivings is not dependent on the presence of the same striving in other people. Also, trait description takes into account the effects of the behavior. For example, to describe someone as "dominant" or "friendly" implies that they are successful in dominating others or in making friends. However, ascribing a personal striving to someone is independent of the effects of that striving. A person may be trying to be dominant or trying to be friendly but may not be succeeding because any one of several factors, ranging from a lack of opportunity, to a lack of social skills, to conflict with other strivings. Personal strivings then, as personalized motives, are independent of skill level, as are motive dispositions (McClelland, 1985). Buss and Craik (1983) state that "Efforts to clarify the conceptual and empirical interrelations among various middle-level personality approaches to the categorization of acts and to explanatory systems . . . is likely to occupy personality theorists in a profitable fashion . . . during the 1980's" (p. 124). Alston (1970, 1975) in two penetrating analyses which seem to have been largely ignored, also argues for the separation of and a detailed analysis between motivational and trait concepts. I believe that the personal striving concept can serve as a vehicle for clarifying some of these interrelations. What is the relationship of these personal strivings to personality traits? It is clear that simple relations will not normally exist between them. As Pervin (1983) has noted, a given goal can lead to many different behaviors, and a given behavior can be in the service of different goals. Abstracting from behaviors to traits, a given striving may underlie different traits, and several strivings may be reflected in a single trait. The preceding conscientiousness example represents the latter case. As an example of the former, a striving such as "trying to get ahead" could produce such behaviors as doing what others say, dressing neatly, and smiling frequently, which in turn could lead to trait attributions of submissiveness, neatness, and friendliness. One way the degree of relatedness between traits and strivings could be assessed is through relevance ratings, where the relevance of a number of traits for a given striving is ascertained (e.g., How relevant is submissiveness for trying to get ahead?).

One can classify acts into traits categories, as in the act-frequency approach (Buss & Craik, 1983); however, acts can also be classified in terms of what the person is trying to do, as in the personal striving approach. Buss and Craik (1983) give as an example of the act of "complaining about a tough steak" as a maifestation of the trait of dominance. Alternatively, they suggest, the act may be viewed as a manifestation of the striving "trying to impress his boss," which the person does by taking charge in the restaurant. Given the theoretical supremacy of a motivation-based account of personality (Alston, 1970, 1975), such a categorization scheme would seem preferable to the categorization of acts without regard to the intentions behind them. These two theoretical systems offer different ways for classifying everyday experience. I concur with Buss and Craik (1983) that interrelations between these concepts are not likely to be definitively understood in the near future.

The personal striving approach might also offer insight into the continuing behavioral consistency controversy. It has been suggested that behavior need not be consistent at the surface or phenotypic level for there to be consistency or coherence at a deeper, genotypic level (Alker, 1972; Block, 1968; McClelland, 1981; Pervin, 1985). Although such a position has always seemed intuitively appealing, the problem has been a lack of agreement as to how best conceptualize the genotype. The relationship between surface structure and deeper structure has long been a theoretical thorn in personality's side (Sanford, 1956). Personal strivings offer one possibility, as it has been pointed out that personal strivings are unifying constructs that tie together phenotypically dissimilar actions around a common theme. As a simple example of how a personal striving can account for behavioral inconsistency, consider a man who is aggressive, dominant, and competitive at work. At home, however, he is passive, submissive, and cooperative. Merely counting behaviors is likely to paint a picture of a severely disheveled personality. Actually, his actions become increasingly lawful (McClelland, 1981) if we consider *what he is trying to do*. Perhaps he has the striving "trying to be liked by others." At work, he seeks the approval of his superiors and so acts competitively and aggressively. At home, he recognizes that those same actions are not going to produce the desired outcome, so his behavior is an abrupt about-face with his wife and children. What appears to be inconsistency at the surface level is lawful and understandable with recourse to the genotype (McClelland, 1981). Thus, for people to be consistent with themselves, their behavior must often be inconsistent (Hogan, 1983, makes a similar point), as the same striving will often lead to very different actions in different situations. Of course, this approach to personality entails a deeper level of understanding of individual dynamics than does a trait-based account. The personal striving concept can help render such inconsistent actions intelligible, while at the same time recognizing the discriminativeness of behavior (Mischel, 1984).

Personal Strivings and Action Identification Theory

In their action-identification (AI) theory, Vallacher and Wegner (1985, 1987) propose a hierarchy consisting of levels of act identities ranging from the most abstract purposes for which an action is carried out (high level identities) to the most concrete action units (low-level identities). For example, the act of "seeing if someone is at home" can also be identified by lower level identities, such as "pushing a doorbell" and "moving a finger" (1987, p. 4) at successively lower levels. Three principles characterize action identification theory: (a) People maintain action in accord with their prepotent identity for the action, (b) people embrace high level identities when these become available, and (c) failure to maintain action under one identity will force movement to a lower identity level. From the personal striving perspective, there is considerable similarity between what a person is trying to do (personal striving) and knowing what one is doing (action identification). Personal strivings may be viewed as act identities at a high level of abstraction. It might be said that one's personal strivings represent all of the high level identities that characterize a person at a particular time. The second principle states that prepotent identities, or identities at higher levels in the action hierarchy, are preferable to lower level identities. High level identities, such as "getting exercise" (Vallacher and Wegner, 1987, p. 9) possess a range of interchangeable means available for maintaining the action, just as personal strivings can be achieved in a variety of different ways. In addition, these various means may be phenotypically dissimilar, providing a context for which to interpret seemingly inconsistent behavior (Vallacher & Wegner, 1987).

One difference between action identification theory and the personal striving approach is that the hierarchies in the former are behavioral by definition. In the personal striving approach, they need not be limited to behavior. For example, a person who is trying to "achieve a spiritual oneness with God" may not necessarily engage in observable actions to try to achieve this striving. Also, action identification theory is not concerned with what motives people have, whereas the personal striving approach takes this, and the relationship between these motives, as its fundamental datum. In AI theory, motives are referred to as "act identities at a relatively high level that serve to integrate more basic identities" (Vallacher & Wegner, 1985, p. 118) apparently failing to recognize that motives are cognition-affect-action complexes that cannot be reduced to action alone.

The aspect of action identification theory most relevant here occurs in the links between action and self. Act identities at high levels provide information on what the person is like, and Vallacher and Wegner refer to this as "the ascriptive component" of act identities (1985, p. 187). Ascriptive components, or ascriptive themes, represent the highest level of action identification and tap an individual's goals, values, and other self-defining attributes. For example, an ascriptive theme for the low level act of playing the piano might be "expressing myself," "demonstrating talent," or "releasing tension," any one of a number of which might appear on a list of personal strivings. Furthermore, these ascriptive themes provide for a sense of continuity and stability in everyday behavior, as do personal strivings.

Action identification theory maintains that action control flows in two directions. Action is maintained from the top-down (action maintenance); however, action also emerges from the bottom-up (action emergence). In the latter case, acts take on new identities that may be different from the original identity that the actor had in mind when initiating the action. The personal striving approach keeps open the possibility that new strivings can emerge in a similar way. A person may come to find that what he or she is trying to do or even typically try to do is different from what was originally intended. A person who spends a lot of time interacting with others may come to believe that he or she is "trying to get to know others better" without consciously intending to do so from the beginning. In fact, it may not be surprising that such a process occurs, as the personal striving instructions ask respondents to focus on their past behavior.

Personal Strivings and the Self-Concept

The self-concept has been recently portrayed as dynamic (Markus & Wurf, 1987). Self-concept, according to this view, consists of the incentives, standards, plans, rules, and scripts for behavior, which are encompassed under declarative and procedural knowledge (Cantor & Kihlstrom, 1987). Motivation is thus accorded a central role in the dynamic self-concept, albeit in a format different from traditional personological formulations. It is evident from this literature that self-conceptions need not be limited to static, traitlike qualities. Certainly personal strivings also represent features of the dynamic self-concept. Self-conceptions of what one is trying to do and the means by which the strivings are realized are self-defining qualities that emerge in the description of the self in the personal striving assessment procedure. The working self-concept (Markus & Wurf, 1987) refers to those strivings that are salient at any point in time. These personal strivings are likely to influence the perception of others, choice of situations (Emmons & Diener, 1986), and other attentional and perceptual processes.

In their work on the motivational facets of the self, Greenwald (1982) and Breckler and Greenwald (1986) identify ego tasks as important elements of the self-concept. Ego tasks are goals and strategies that are concerned with establishing and maintaining a favorable self-evaluation and are accomplished by obtaining self- or other-approval. These ego tasks could be viewed from within the personal striving perspective. For example, strivings can be categorized in terms of whether they are enacted either to please the self or to please others. Ego tasks, like personal strivings, are not terminated by success and continue to serve as salient guides for action.

Some forms of personal striving conflict discussed earlier can be viewed within Higgins' (1987) self-concept discrepancy theory. According to this theory, discrepancy among different domains of the self (actual, ideal, and ought) leads to characteristic negative emotional states, such as sadness, anxiety, and depression. Conflict among personal strivings represents "contradictions among one's self-perceived attributes" in Higgins' terminology. It is conceivable that what a person is trying to do could result from the wishes of others, thereby representing "oughts." For example, the striving of "trying to make life easier for my parents" could be the result of perceived familial obligations and could come into conflict with a self-generated striving like "trying to have as much fun as possible." This would be an instance of an actual/own:ought/other discrepancy that is predicted to produce anxiety-related emotions according to self-discrepancy theory.

Clinical Implications

The description of personality in terms of personal strivings opens up a host of other possibilities for clinical application. In keeping with the control theory perspective, problems may arise at two stages. First is what Carver and Scheier (1982) refer to as the *absence* of regulation, or the inability to specify reference values. This occurs when individuals have a superordinate concern in mind but are unclear as to what actions will lead them in the direction of it. An individual may be trying to become independent from his or her parents but have little idea of the concrete steps that need to be taken to achieve this independence. In action identification theory, this occurs when the prepotent act identity is at too high a level for it to be an effective guide to action. Thus, clinical intervention could focus on breaking down the superordinate concern into manageable subgoals, and each of these focused on separately. Indeed, this is the rationale underlying many cognitive-therapeutic strategies (Kanfer, 1979). Similarly, Vallacher and Wegner (1987) advise identifying the action at a lower level when identities are at too high a level for the action to be successfully executed.

A second problem may arise when individuals are *misregulating* (Carver & Scheier, 1982). This occurs when people are regulating their behavior in a maladaptive way (i.e., when the goal or reference value is erroneous to the superordinate concern). For example, one person in a past study had the striving "trying to get attractive women to notice me." This individual may rely on a certain opening line when confronting a potential admirer in a social situation as one of his strategies for accomplishing this striving. It does not require much imagination to see that contrary to helping him achieve this striving, the behavior may actually be moving him farther from the superordinate concern. Clinical intervention could focus on providing the individual with insight into his or her maladaptive strategies and suggest new and more efficient courses of action.

From a different perspective, many of the faulty and irrational beliefs identified in rational-emotive therapy (Ellis & Harper, 1975) may have their basis in personal strivings. That is, personal strivings may consist of things that people feel they *must* or *should* or *have* to do or feel. This is best illustrated by a subject in one study ("Poofy") who possessed strivings such as "behave in such a way that I am accepted by everyone," "perform at perfection in my job," "be accepting of everyone," and "appear 'together' all of the time." Perhaps not surprisingly, "Poofy" was troubled by extreme anxiety and was actually taking antianxiety medication under a physician's advice. Clinical intervention could pinpoint the irrational nature of strivings such as these and show the person the faulty reasoning behind them.

Methodologically, the Striving Instrumentality Matrix (SIM) is a useful way of assessing the degree on self-perceived conflict between one's strivings. We have also found that objective raters are reasonably accurate at judging the degree of conflict between a target individual's strivings. Because conflict is often viewed as a culprit in personal and interpersonal difficulties, the SIM would appear to possess a great deal of applicability. Individuals that have completed the SIM have remarked to us that it was extremely useful to have thought about their strivings in this way and that it helped them identify problem areas in their life.

On the Origin of Personal Strivings

Where do personal strivings come from? Why do individuals decide to try to achieve certain outcomes but not others? The persepective to be developed here represents a synthesis of a variety of theoretical viewpoints, including those of Adler (1956), Aronoff and Wilson (1985), Epstein (1982b), Hogan (1983, 1987), Maddi (1980), Maslow (1970), McAdams (1985), and Tomkins (1979). Although the following scenarios are clearly speculative, they are not incompatible with these influential theoretical formulations.

In beginning this line, I borrow from Maddi's (1980) distinction between the core and periphery of personality. The core of personality is reflected in the genotypical constitution of the individual and refers to features common to all individuals. The periphery, on the other hand, refers to learned attributes that develop as a result of experience. The peripheral characteristics have a more direct yet circumscribed effect on behavior than do the core characteristics. The core and periphery, according to Maddi, are linked through developmental processes.

With this as a metatheoretical blueprint, I begin with the assumption that at the core, humans possess three basic needs: (a) safety/predictability/control, (b) social approval/intimacy/belongingness, and (c) self-esteem/competence/mastery. Aronoff and Wilson (1985) demonstrate that a number of personality theories converge on these three fundamental motivational tendencies. For example, Maslow's (1970) middle three in his need hierarchy (safety, belongingness, and esteem) are equivalent to these three. More recently, Hogan (1983, 1987) in his socioanalytic theory, assumes the importance of three social motives: structure and predictability, attention and social acceptance, and status and popularity.

I next assume that people possess, at a preconscious level (Epstein, 1982b) implicit beliefs regarding what must be done in order to satisfy these basic needs (i.e., to obtain what is desired in life and to avoid what is feared). The core needs become transformed, through experience, into implicit beliefs regarding goal attainment and subsequent need satisfaction. These implicit beliefs, then, lead to goal-directed behavior organized around an individual's personal strivings. For example, a person might believe "In order to be competent, I must become independent from my parents," which could lead to the striving of "trying to become financially independent from my parents." Similarly, an implicit belief that "In order to be liked by others I must help them" may lead to the striving "Trying to help others who are upset." One who believes in the importance of a financially secure future may develop the striving of "trying to achieve high grades in order to get into medical school."

This position is somewhat similar to the one adopted by Aronoff and Wilson (1985), who assert that the deprivation of the three core needs (security, belongingness, esteem) results in adaptational behaviors that take the form of peripheral motives and are maintained because they are successful in alleviating anxiety associated with this deprivation. I would claim, however, that such a process is more likely to lead only to negative, avoidance strivings, as opposed to positive, approach strivings. For example, deprivation of belongingness is more likely to engender strivings dealing with avoiding loneliness as opposed to becoming intimate with others, with the latter being more likely to result from favorable past experiences. Personal strivings are not necessarily compensating for or correcting earlier developmental deficiencies. Nevertheless, the positions converge on the notion that these core tendencies are transformed through learning into peripheral motives, or personal strivings.

What are the processes by which the core needs become transformed into the peripheral strivings? A variety of mechanisms are undoubtedly responsible. From the standpoint of goal theory (Pervin, 1983), classical, operant, and observational learning all play a role. Some strivings may also be compensatory in origin (Adler, 1956). For example, feeling interior to others may lead to trying to prove one's superiority; failing to get along with others may lead one to try to be indifferent to the reactions of others (Gregory, 1945). What sort of experiences are likely to lead to the development of strivings? Out of a multitude of life experiences that each of us have, those especially salient or noteworthy are the most likely candidates. These could be viewed as either nuclear episodes (McAdams, 1985) or nuclear scenes (Tomkins, 1979). Nuclear episodes and scenes refer to psychologically significant events accompanied by high levels of affect that play a major role in the development of the individual. McAdams (1985) differentiates between episodes that lead to continuity and affirmation of the self versus those that represent a transformation or turning point in the person's life. Personal strivings could result from either process, the former lending stability and continuity to what the person is trying to do and the latter representing a change in what the person is trying to do. A heated parental argument, for instance, could lead an adolescent to try to become independent from his or her parents, a theme that could be played out again and again (Tomkins, 1979). McAdams (1985) found associations between the social motives of intimacy and power and recollection of thematically related events in autobiographical memory. By the same token, we would expect that the content of the person's current personal strivings would be related to the recall of thematically related events from his or her past.

Conclusions

There has been a clear shift in personality psychology in recent years toward naturally occurring units of analysis (Buss & Craik, 1983; Little, 1986). These refer to actions that occur without coercion from an experimenter. The act-frequency approach (Buss & Craik, 1983), personal projects (Little, 1983), current concerns (Klinger, 1977, 1987), life tasks (Cantor & Kihlstrom, 1987), and now personal strivings are all examples of this "new look" in personality. The personal striving construct is envisioned as providing a link between traditional personological formulations of the motive concept (Aronoff & Wilson, 1985; Hogan, 1982; McAdams, 1985; McClelland, 1985; Pervin, 1983), and recent social-cognitive perspectives (Cantor & Kihlstrom, 1987; Mancuso & Mascolo, 1987; Sorrentino & Higgins, 1986; Srull & Wyer, 1986; Vallacher & Wegner, 1985), thereby satisfying protagonists from each camp. Certainly our understanding of social behavior must be predicated on knowing what individuals are trying to do in social situations. At the same time, there exists considerable coherence in what a person is trying to do over time. In the future, special attention should be directed toward identifying the optimal level of analysis for various explanatory and predictive purposes.

Attention should also be directed toward developing criteria for distinguishing among the various idiographic motivational units. Surely if we asked a subject to provide us with a separate list of his or her personal strivings, personal projects, current concerns, and life tasks there would be some overlap. To what degree would a person's current concerns overlap with his or her life tasks? Would life tasks or personal strivings emerge from a clustering analysis of the current concerns? Some, perhaps even most, concerns and projects would not achieve status as life tasks or personal strivings, even though they might serve as compelling temporary guides for thought and action.

What are the advantages of focusing on personal strivings as units of personological analysis rather than subordinate concerns and projects or superordinate motives? The position taken here is that personal strivings are at the level of analysis that conveys an optimal amount of information about an individual. More discriminating than global motives yet more stable than specific plans, personal strivings occupy a desirable yet unexplored position in the hierarchy of personality functioning. A number of studies have suggested the usefulness of the concept for understanding differences in mood and physical and psychological well-being. The heuristic value of the concept for other domains awaits future theoretical and research endeavors.

ACKNOWLEDGMENTS

This chapter has benefited from earlier discussions with Joel Aronoff, Eric Klinger, and Dan P. McAdams. Stephen Briggs, Ed Diener, Laura King, Thomas Reischl, and Thomas K. Srull provided helpful feedback on an earlier draft of the chapter. I am grateful to Norman Frederiksen, Ray S. Musgrave, Richard Solomon, Arnold Tannenbaum, Theodore Vallance, and John Valentine for sharing with me their published and unpublished papers with Floyd Allport.

REFERENCES

Adler, A. (1956). *The individual psychology of Alfred Adler.* New York: Basic Books.
Alker, H. A. (1972). Is personality situationally specific or intrapsychically consistent? *Journal of Personality, 40,* 1–16.
Allport, F. (1937). Teleonomic description in the study of personality. *Character and Personality, 5,* 202–214.
Allport, G. W. (1937). *Personality: A psychological interpretation.* New York: Holt, Rinehart, & Winston.
Allport, G. W. (1953). The trend in motivational theory. *American Journal of Orthopsychiatry, 23,* 107–119.
Alston, W. P. (1970). Toward a logical geography of personality: Traits and deeper lying personality characteristics. In H. D. Kiefer & M. K. Munitz (Eds.), *Mind, science, and history* (pp. 70–105). Albany, NY: SUNY Press.

Alston, W. P. (1975). Traits, consistency, and conceptual alternatives for personality theory. *Journal for the Theory of Social Behavior, 5,* 17–48.
Aronoff, J. (1967). *Psychological needs and culture systems.* Princeton, NJ: Van-Nostrand.
Aronoff, J., & Wilson, J. P. (1985). *Personality in the social process.* Hillsdale, NJ: Lawrence Erlbaum Associates.
Atkinson, J. W., & Birch, D. (1970). *The dynamics of action.* New York: Wiley.
Bakan, D. (1966). *The duality of human existence.* Boston: Beacon Press.
Baumeister, R. F., & Tice, D. M. (1987). Emotion and self-presentation. In R. Hogan and W. H. Jones (Eds.), *Perspectives in personality* (Vol. 2, pp. 181–200). Greenwich, CT: JAI Press.
Block, J. (1968). Some reasons for the apparent inconsistency of personality. *Psychological Bulletin, 70,* 210–212.
Breckler, S. J., & Greenwald, A. G. (1986). Motivational facets of the self. In R. M. Sorrentino & E. T. Higgins (Eds.), *Handbook of motivation and cognition* (pp. 145–164). New York: Guilford Press.
Buck, R. W. (1984). *The communication of emotion.* New York: Guilford Press.
Buss, D. M. (1984). Evolutionary biology and personality psychology: Toward a conception of human nature and individual differences. *American Psychologist, 39,* 1135–1147.
Buss, D. M. (1987). Selection, evocation, and manipulation. *Journal of Personality and Social Psychology, 53,* 1214–1221.
Buss, D. M., & Craik, K. H. (1983). The act-frequency approach to personality. *Psychological Review, 90,* 105–126.
Campbell, A., Converse, P. E., & Rodgers, W. L. (1976). *The quality of American life.* New York: McGraw-Hill.
Cantor, N., Brower, A., & Korn, H. (1985). Cognitive bases of personality in a life transition. In E. E. Roskam (Ed.), *Measurement and personality assessment* (pp. 323–331). New York: Elsevier Science Publishers.
Cantor, N., Norem, J., Niedenthal, P., Langston, C., & Brower, A. (1987). Life tasks, self-concept ideals, and cognitive strategies in a life transition. *Journal of Personality and Social Psychology, 53,* 1178–1191.
Cantor, N., & Kihlstrom, J. F. (1987). *Personality and social intelligence.* Englewood Cliffs, NJ: Prentice-Hall.
Carver, C. S., & Scheier, M. F. (1981). *Attention and self-regulation: A control theory approach to human behavior.* New York: Springer-Verlag.
Carver, C. S., & Scheier, M. F. (1982). Control theory: A useful conceptual framework for personality-social, clinical, and health psychology. *Psychological Bulletin, 92,* 111–135.
Costa, P. T., & McCrae, R. R. (1980). Influence of extraversion and neuroticism on subjective well-being: Happy and unhappy people. *Journal of Personality and Social Psychology, 38,* 668–678.
Diener, E. (1984). Subjective well-being. *Psychological Bulletin, 95,* 542–575.
Diener, E., & Emmons, R. A. (1984). The independence of positive and negative affect. *Journal of Personality and Social Psychology, 47,* 1105–1117.
Diener, E., Larsen, R., Levine, S., & Emmons, R. A. (1985). Intensity and frequency: Dimensions underlying positive and negative affect. *Journal of Personality and Social Psychology, 48,* 1253–1265.
Ellis, A., & Harper, R. A. (1987). *A new guide to rational living.* North Hollywood, CA: Wilshire Book Company.
Emmons, R. A. (1986). Personal strivings: An approach to personality and subjective well-being. *Journal of Personality and Social Psychology, 51,* 1058–1068.
Emmons, R. A., & Diener, E. (1985). Personality correlates of subjective well-being. *Personality and Social Psychology Bulletin, 11,* 89–97.

Emmons, R. A., & Diener, E. (1986). Situation selection as a moderator of response consistency and stability. *Journal of Personality and Social Psychology, 51,* 1013–1019.
Emmons, R. A., Diener, E., & Larsen, R. J. (1986). Choice and avoidance of everyday situations and affect congruence: Two models of reciprocal interactionism. *Journal of Personality and Social Psychology, 51,* 815–826.
Emmons, R. A. (1987, August). *Current status of the motive concept.* Paper presented as part of a symposium entitled "Fifty Years of Personality Psychology" (K. Craik & R. Hogan, Chairs) at the 95th Annual Convention of the American Psychological Association, New York.
Emmons, R. A., & King, L. A. (1988). Conflict among personal strivings: Immediate and long-term implications for psychological and phsysical well-being. *Journal of Personality and Social Psychology, 54,* 1040–1048.
Emmons, R. A., & King, L. A. (1987, August). *Ambivalence over expressing emotion: Psychological and physical implications.* Presented at the 95th Annual Convention of the American Psychological Association, New York.
Emmons, R. A., & King, L. A. (in press). *Personal striving complexity and affective reactivity. Journal of Personality and Social Psychology.*
Epstein, S. (1982a). Conflict and stress. In L. Goldberger & S. Breznitz (Eds.), *Handbook of stress* (pp. 49–68). New York: The Free Press.
Epstein, S. (1982b). The unconscious, the preconscious, and the self concept. In J. Suls & A Greenwald (Eds.), *Psychological perspectives on the self* (Vol. 2, pp. 219–247). Hillsdale, NJ: Lawrence Erlbaum Associates.
Erikson, E. H. (1959). *Identity and the life cycle.* New York: International University Press.
Frederiksen, N., & Allport, F. H. (1941). Personality as a pattern of teleonomic trends. *Journal of Social Psychology, 13,* 141–182.
Frese, M., & Sabini, J. (1985). *Goal directed behavior: The concept of action in psychology.* Hillsdale, NJ: Lawrence Erlbaum Associates.
Friedman, H., & Booth-Kewley, S. (1987). The "disease-prone personality:" A meta-analytic view of the construct. *American Psychologist, 42,* 539–555.
Friedman, H., Prince, L., Riggio, R., & DiMatteo M. R. (1980). Understanding and assessing nonverbal communication of emotion: The Affective Communication Test. *Journal of Personality and Social Psychology, 39,* 333–351.
Greenwald, A. G. (1982). Ego task analysis: An integration of research on ego-involvement and self-awareness. In A. H. Hastorf & A. M. Isen (Eds.), *Cognitive social psychology.* New York: Elsevier Publishers.
Gregory, W. S. (1945). The application of teleonomic description to the diagnosis and treatment of emotional instability and personal and social maladjustments. *Character and Personality, 13,* 179–211.
Halberstadt, A. G. (1986). Family socialization of emotional expression and nonverbal communication styles and skills. *Journal of Personality and Social Psychology, 51,* 827–836.
Higgins, E. T. (1987). Self-discrepancy: A theory relating self and affect. *Psychological Review, 94,* 319–340.
Hochschild, A. (1983). *The managed heart: Commercialization of human feeling.* Berkeley, CA: University of California Press.
Hogan, R. (1982). On adding apples and oranges in personality psychology. *Contemporary Psychology, 27,* 851–852.
Hogan, R. (1983). A socioanalytic theory of personality. In M. M. Page (Ed.), *Nebraska symposium on motivation* (pp. 55–90). Lincoln, NB: University of Nebraska Press.
Hogan, R. (1987). Personality psychology: Back to basis. In A. Rabin, J. Aronoff, & R. Zucker (Eds.), *The emergence of personality* (pp. 79–104). New York: Springer.
Hormuth, S. (1986). The random sampling of experiences *in situ. Journal of Personality and Social Psychology, 54,* 262–293.

Hyland, M. E. (1987). Control theory interpretation of psychological mechanisms of depression: Comparison and integration of several theories. *Psychological Bulletin, 102,* 109–121.

Jemmott, J. B. (1987). Social motives and susceptibility to disease: Stalking individual differences in health risks. *Journal of Personality, 55,* 267–298.

Jensen, M. R. (1987). Psychobiological factors in predicting the course of breast cancer. *Journal of Personality, 55,* 317–342.

Kanfer, F. H. (1979). Self-management: Strategies and tactics. In A. P. Goldstein & F. H. Kanfer (Eds.), *Maximizing treatment gains.* New York: Academic Press.

Kenrick, D. T., Montello, D. R., & MacFarlane, S. (1985). Personality: Social learning, social cognition, or sociobiology? In R. Hogan & W. H. Jones (Eds.), *Perspectives in personality* (Vol. 1, pp. 201–234). Greenwich, CT: JAI Press.

Klinger, E. (1977). *Meaning and void: Inner experience and the incentives in people's lives.* Minneapolis, MN: University of Minnesota Press.

Klinger, E. (1987). The interview questionnaire technique: Reliability and validity of a mixed idiographic-nomothetic measure of motivation. In J. N. Butcher and C. D. Spielberger (Eds.), *Advances in personality assessment* (Vol. 6, pp. 31–48). Hillsdale, NJ: Lawrence Erlbaum Associates.

Klinger, E., Barta, S. G., & Maxeiner, M. E. (1981). Current concerns: Assessing therapeutically relevant motivation. In P. C. Kendall & S. Hollon (Eds.), *Assessment strategies for cognitive-behavioral interventions* (pp. 161–195). New York: Academic Press.

Lamiell, J. T. (1987). *The psychology of personality: An epistemological inquiry.* New York: Columbia University Press.

Lanzetta, J. T., & Kleck, R. E. (1970). Encoding and decoding of non-verbal affect in humans. *Journal of Personality and Social Psychology, 16,* 12–19.

Larsen, R. J., & Diener, E. (1987). Affect intensity as an individual difference characteristic: A review. *Journal of Research in Personality, 21,* 1–39.

Larsen, R. J., Diener, E., & Emmons, R. A. (1986). Affect intensity and reactions to daily life events. *Journal of Personality and Social Psychology, 51,* 803–814.

Larson, R., & Csikszentmihalyi, M. (1983). The experience-sampling method. *New Directions for Methodology of Social and Behavioral Sciences, 15,* 41–56.

Lecky, P. (1945). *Self-consistency: A theory of personality.* New York: Island Press.

Linville, P. W. (1982). Affective consequences of complexity regarding the self and others. In M. S. Clark & S. T. Fiske (Eds.), *Affect and cognition* (pp. 79–109). Hillsdale, NJ: Lawrence Erlbaum Associates.

Linville, P. W. (1985). Self-complexity and affective extremity: Don't put all of your eggs in one basket. *Social Cognition, 3,* 94–120.

Little, B. R. (1983). Personal projects: A rationale and method for investigation. *Environment and Behavior, 15,* 273–309.

Little, B. R. (1986). Personality and the environment. In D. Stokols & I. Altman (Eds.), *Handbook of environmental psychology.* New York: Wiley.

Little, B. R. (1987). Personal projects and fuzzy selves: Aspects of self-identity in adolescence. In T. Honess & K. Yardley (Eds.). *Self and identity: Perspectives across the life span.* (pp. 230–245). New York: Routledge Kegan Paul

Maddi, S. R. (1980). *Personality theories: A comparative analysis.* Homewood, IL: Dorsey Press.

Mancuso, J. C., & Mascolo, M. F. (1987). Re-cognizing achievement motivation. *Motivation and Emotion, 11,* 323–330.

Markus, H., & Nurius, P. (1986). Possible selves. *American Psychologist, 41,* 954–969.

Markus, H., & Wurf, E. (1987). The dynamic self-concept: A social psychological perspective. *Annual Review of Psychology, 38,* 299–327.

Martindale, C. (1980). Subselves: The internal representation of situational and personal dispositions. In P. Shaver (Ed.), *Review of personality and social psychology* (Vol. 1, pp. 193–218). Beverly Hills, CA: Sage Publications.

Maslow, A. H. (1970). *Motivation and personality* (2nd ed.). New York: Harper & Row.

McAdams, D. P. (1980). A thematic coding system for the intimacy motive. *Journal of Research in Personality, 14,* 413–432.

McAdams, D. P. (1985). *Power, intimacy, and the life story: Personological inquiries into identity.* Homewood, IL: Dorsey Press.

McAdams, D. P. (1988). Biography, narratives, and lives: An introduction. *Journal of Personality, 56,* 1–18.

McAdams, D. P. (in press). Personal needs and personal relationships. In S. Duck (Ed.), *Handbook of research on personal relationships.* New York: Wiley.

McClelland, D. C. (1951). *Personality.* New York: Dryden.

McClelland, D. C. (1961). *The achieving society.* Princeton, NJ: Van Nostrand.

McClelland, D. C. (1981). Is personality consistent? In A. Rabin, J. Aronoff, and R. Zucker (Eds.), *Further explorations in personality* (pp. 87–113). New York: Wiley.

McClelland, D. C. The need for power, sympathetic activation and illness. *Motivation and Emotion,* 1982, *6*(1), 31–41.

McClelland, D. C. (1985). *Human motivation.* Glenview, IL: Scott, Foresman, & Company.

McClelland, D. C., & Jemmott, J. B. (1980). Power motivation, stress, and physical illness. *Journal of Human Stress, 6,* 6–14.

McClelland, D. C., Floor, E., Davidson, R. J., & Saron, C. (1980). Stressed power motivation, sympathetic activation, immune function and physical illness. *Journal of Human Stress, 6,* 11–19.

Mischel, W. (1984). Convergences and challenges in the search for consistency. *American Psychologist, 39,* 351–364.

Morse, N. C., & Allport, F. H. (1952). The causes of anti-Semitism: An investigation of seven hypotheses. *Journal of Psychology, 34,* 197–233.

Murray, H. A. (1938). *Explorations in personality.* New York: Oxford University Press.

Musgrave, R. S., & Allport, F. H. (1941). Teleonomic description in the study of behavior. *Character and Personality, 9,* 326–343.

Nisbett, R. E., & Wilson, T. D. (1977). Telling more than we can know: Verbal reports on mental processes. *Psychological Review, 84,* 231–259.

Palys, T. S., & Little, B. R. (1983). Perceived life satisfaction and the organization of personal project systems. *Journal of Personality and Social Psychology, 44,* 1221–1230.

Pennebaker, J. W. (1985). Traumatic experience and psychosomatic disease: Exploring the roles of behavioral inhibition, obsession, and confiding. *Canadian Psychology, 26,* 82–95.

Pennebaker, J. W., & Bealls, S. K. (1986). Confronting a traumatic event: Toward an understanding of inhibition and disease. *Journal of Personality and Social Psychology, 95,* 274–281.

Pervin, L. A. (1983). The stasis and flow of behavior: Toward a theory of goals. In M. M. Page (Ed.), *Nebraska Symposium on Motivation* (pp. 1–53). Lincoln, NB: University of Nebraska Press.

Pervin, L. A. (1985). Personality: Current controversies, issues, and directions. *Annual Review of Psychology, 36,* 83–114.

Powers, W. T. (1973). *Behavior: The control of perception.* Chicago: Aldine.

Rabin, A. I., & Zlotogorski, Z. (1985). The sentence completion method—recent research. *Journal of Personality Assessment, 49,* 641–647.

Raulin, M. L. (1984). Development of a scale to measure intense ambivalence. *Journal of Consulting and Clinical Psychology, 52,* 63–72.

Rokeach, M. (1973). *The nature of human values.* New York: The Free Press.

Sanford, N. (1956). Surface and depth in the individual personality. *Psychological Review, 63,* 349–359.

Schank, R., & Abelson, R. P. (1977). *Scripts, plans, goals and understanding.* Hillsdale, NJ: Lawrence Erlbaum Associates.

Schmidt, C. F. (1976). Understanding human action: Recognizing the plans and motives of others. In J. S. Carroll and J. W. Payne (Eds.), *Cognition and social behavior.* Hillsdale, NJ: Lawrence Erlbaum Associates.

Singer, J. L. (1987). Private experience and public action: The study of ongoing conscious thought. In A. I. Rabin, J. Aronoff, & R. A. Zucker (Eds.), *The emergence of personality* (pp. 105–148). New York: Springer.

Snyder, M., & Ickes, W. (1985). Personality and social behavior. In G. Lindzey & E. Aronson (Eds.), *Handbook of social psychology* (pp. 883–947). New York: Random House.

Solomon, R. S., & Allport, F. H. (1939). Lengths of conversations: A conformity situation analyzed by the telic continuum and J-curve hypothesis. *Journal of Abnormal and Social Psychology, 34,* 419–464.

Sorrentino, R. M., & Higgins, E. T. (1986). *Handbook of motivation and cognition: Foundations of social behavior.* New York: Guilford.

Srull, T. K., & Wyer, R. S. (1986). The role of chronic and temporary goals in social information processing. In R. M. Sorrentino & E. T. Higgins (Eds.), *Handbook of motivation and cognition* (pp. 503–549). New York: Guilford Press.

Tannenbaum, A. S., & Allport, F. H. (1956). Personality structure and group structure: An interpretative study of their relationship through an event-structure hypothesis. *Journal of Abnormal and Social Psychology, 53,* 272–280.

Tavris, C. (1984). On the wisdom of counting to ten: Personal and social dangers of anger expression. In P. Shaver (Ed.), *Review of personality and social psychology* (pp. 170–191). Beverly Hills, CA: Sage.

Tomkins, S. S. (1979). Script theory: Differential magnification of affects. In R. A. Dienstbier (Ed.), *Nebraska symposium on motivation* (Vol. 26, pp. 201–236). Lincoln: University of Nebraska Press.

Vallacher, R. R., & Wegner, D. M. (1985). *A theory of action identification.* Hillsdale, NJ: Lawrence Erlbaum Associates.

Vallacher, R. R., & Wegner, D. M. (1987). What do people think they're doing? Action identification and human behavior. *Psychological Review, 94,* 3–15.

Wadsworth, M. W., & Ford, D. H. (1983). The assessment of personal goal hierarchies. *Journal of Counseling Psychology, 30,* 514–526.

Watson, D., & Tellegen, A. (1985). Toward a consensual structure of mood. *Psychological Bulletin, 98,* 219–235.

Weiner, B. (1986). Attribution, emotion, and action. In R. M. Sorrentino & E. T. Higgins (Eds.), *Handbook of motivation and cognition* (pp. 281–312). New York: Guilford Press.

Winter, D., & Stewart, A. J. (1978). The power motive. In H. London & J. E. Exner, Jr. (Eds.), *Dimensions of personality* (pp. 391–448). New York: Wiley.

4 Ups and Downs of Life Tasks in a Life Transition

NANCY CANTOR
CHRISTOPHER A. LANGSTON
University of Michigan

There are many cogent reasons to think that the goals concept is a critical one in personality and social psychology: Goals are the individual's cognitive representation of personal motivation (Markus, 1983; Bandura, 1986; Emmons, 1986); goals are critical components in social cognition (Trzebinski, this volume); goals serve as standards in action control (Kuhl & Beckmann, 1985). As such, it can be argued that an understanding of goals—their form, function, and interindividual variation—is essential to explicating the cognitive basis of both interpersonal interaction and self-regulation (Pervin, 1983, 1985; Sorrentino & Higgins, 1986). Recent conceptualizations of social intelligence provide one fruitful orientation toward the study of goals and problem solving (Cantor & Kihlstrom, 1987; 1988). In particular, intelligence can be viewed as a multifaceted repertoire of social knowledge, developed within, and fine tuned to meet the demands of, personal, social, and cultural life contexts (e.g., Sternberg, 1984). Individuals bring their social intelligence to bear in the hopes of solving their currently pressing life tasks (i.e., to reach their desired self-goals).

Cantor & Kihlstrom (1988) have suggested that the study of personality and problem solving can proceed in a manner paralleling current treatments of intelligence:

Intelligence is displayed in real-world problem-solving behavior, on tasks related to the goals encouraged by the individual's social life context. Understanding social intelligence, then, requires some characterization of the expertise that people bring to bear in solving life problems, the contexts that render certain problems more important than others, and the pragmatic considerations that define the goals to be achieved in an intelligent solution (p. 20)

As noted by Sternberg (1984) and others (e.g., Baltes, 1986; Denney, 1984), this emphasis on expertise, context, and pragmatics of everyday problem-solving behavior, suggests important assumptions about the domain specificity of people's expertise and about the powerful impact of life contexts and of personal goals on performance. These assumptions, in turn, seem to fit well with intuitions and data about social intelligence.

The social intelligence framework highlights both a set of units of analysis—life tasks and strategies—and several key themes to develop in the investigation of individuals' goal-directed activity. Individuals have many goals and tasks at any one time in life, and they bring to bear multiple strategies to work on these diverse tasks. Certain goals and strategies take on particular meaning for individuals as a function of demands set up by the life contexts in which they operate (Veroff, 1983). Similarly, individuals change their tasks and their strategies over time, and, as their life contexts change, our analyses need to be sensitive to these contextual demands and to these changes. Finally, for any given task and strategy there are usually several standards—some quite personal and idiosyncratic and some quite consensually defined—against which to evaluate the success of people's goal-directed efforts. Even the most apparently self-defeating activity can serve some functions for the individual that contribute to well-being, and it is important to understand personal and autobiographical forces that contribute to individuals' task goals and strategies.

The present analysis of goals and problem-solving accords special emphasis, therefore, to the *interpretive contexts* for individuals' choices of tasks and strategies, to the *sensitivity* of these goals and problem-solving orientations to features of domains and of life experience, and to the complex *pragmatics* that underlie individuals' strategic choices. In the following discussion, we will first develop further the *units of analysis* derived from our social intelligence framework, illustrating these units with empirical work on college students' efforts to negotiate the transition from home and high school to college life. Then, we will return to a more detailed consideration of these three themes, as they are manifest in the lives of these students, in the hopes of demonstrating the heuristic value of a social intelligence perspective in the analysis of goals and problem solving.

Goals, Life Tasks, and Strategies

Our treatment of the goals concept places it within a problem-solving framework in which *goals* are made concrete as *life tasks* on which individuals work in particular life periods and within specified life contexts (Cantor, Norem, Niedenthal, Langston, & Brower, 1987; Little, 1983). The test anxious individual with a driving need to achieve scholastically feels particularly energized to solve this life task during his or her college years, and more specifically, within mainly testing situations at college. Once out of college, the self-goal as a calm, cool, success story comes to the fore as a slightly different concrete version of the achievement life task; in that life period, a pressing life task is one of feeling comfortable in authority positions, and the relevant contexts are occupational, rather than educational (Veroff, 1983). Goals, then, are instantiated for individuals in the life tasks that are currently time-consuming, self-relevant, and self-defined as important, and in the set of contexts in which those particular self-ideals can be realized or lost.

When goals are considered within a problem-solving framework, a critical aspect of the goal is that it represents an end state that is somehow different from a current state, thus establishing a focus for the person's activity—the *task* of trying to reach that goal (Anderson, 1981; Gagne, 1984). In some cases, the life-task goal, if reached, would constitute a clearly different state than is currently true for that person, as when a depressed individual works to become happier, less immobilized, and more active. In those instances, there is a clear, usually articulatable, self-concept discrepancy (Higgins, Klein, & Strauman, 1985) that represents the magnitude of the change in state to be reached in that life task. At other times, especially when a person enters a new life period or life situation, the life task may not be as dramatically different from those of the past, and the life-task goal, similarly, may represent a state that has been reached before but in other life contexts. The first-year college student, for example, is often consumed with the life task of "making friends" to achieve a goal of "interpersonal intimacy" (or more simply, to find "social distractions from achievement pressures"). For some students, this "social self" is indeed quite discrepant from their previous "high school self," whereas for others, the task of "making friends" is pressing, but not self-discrepant, more like an old task in a new context (Langston & Cantor, 1987; Cantor, Markus, Niedenthal, & Nurius, 1986). Whether dramatic or not, these *self-concept discrepancies* are important markers of the process of life-task problem solving—markers of each individual's current and hoped-for state with regard to that particular self-relevant domain of life activity.

Life Tasks. Traditionally, theorists interested in life tasks have defined them fairly explicitly by linking them to basic, evolutionarily adaptive motives or functions (e.g., Plutchik, 1980), to lifelong strivings established early on in a person's development (e.g., Adler, 1931), or to stages of psychosocial growth (e.g., Erikson, 1950). As in the more recent treatments of "personal strivings" (Emmons, 1986), "current concerns" (Klinger, 1977), or "personal projects" (Little, 1983), we prefer a more eclectic, less well-defined construction of the task concept. In our view (Cantor & Kihlstrom, 1987) life tasks vary considerably from individual to individual and for any given person from one life period to the next. They vary as to *scope* (e.g., from big tasks of "becoming a good person" to relatively more contained ones of "getting good grades"), *persistence* (e.g., recurrent themes of "finding intimacy" versus more or less circumscribed tasks of "getting married"), and *source* (e.g., externally-encouraged tasks of "finding a job" versus relatively self-initiated tasks of "learning the violin").

Keeping this diversity in mind, we limit the definition of life tasks simply to encompass those tasks that individuals find highly salient and attention consuming and that are seen as organizing daily life activity around self-goals. In our empirical investigations of life tasks, we try to allow individuals first to define the tasks and relevant life task activities in their own words, at their own preferred level of abstraction, encouraging them subsequently to work "up and down" the ladder of abstraction so as to provide a set of abstract, often consensually-shared tasks, in addition to the list of sometimes unique projects that instantiate those molar tasks in their current lives (see, Little, 1983).

As a rule, we (Cantor et al., 1987) typically start with individuals' self-articulated life tasks, though we do not assume that all such tasks—or all aspects of a given task—are easily or even frequently the subject of conscious reflection (see Klinger, 1977). In fact, we choose to study life-task problem solving in the context of major life transitions, when people experience significant changes in their interpersonal, physical, and work worlds, in large part because these times of change tend to encourage individuals to think about their self-goals and about the life tasks and specific activities through which these goals can now be pursued (e.g., Levinson, 1978). Periods of life transition are also interesting contexts for the study of changes in individuals' life tasks (Stewart & Healy, 1985); they provide a nice real-life analog to a laboratory task that balances familiarity and novelty of demands (Sternberg, 1984; Baltes, Dittman-Kohli, & Dixon, 1984).

Strategies. Another very critical aspect of the life-task problem-solving framework is that it focuses attention on the process, the *problem-solving strategies,* by which individuals work to solve their current life tasks. Goals as self-ideals (end states) can be represented or described in a static form; goals as life tasks must be conceptualized as dynamic regulators of action (Pervin, 1983; Markus, 1983; Bandura, 1986). When the "shy person" tries on an assertive face, this strategy of social interaction provides new meaning, self-relevance, and organization to a whole set of thoughts, feelings, and actions related to the task of overcoming social anxiety (Goldfried, Padawer, & Robins, 1984). Most important, there are usually multiple strategies to effect any given life task goal (e.g., an assertive strategy or a submissive strategy might both be attempts to achieve status), and, therefore, a full understanding of how people frame their life tasks requires careful attention to their strategies of problem solving in relevant domains.

We define strategies as patterns of appraisal, planning, retrospection, and effort whose elements span a temporal period before, during, and after, relevant events and have functional coherence because they relate to a life task goal (see Cantor et al., 1987). In this way, the "self-handicapper" (Jones & Berglas, 1978) achieves his or her attributional self-protective goal via a constellation of strategic efforts before, during, and after, tests of competence: embracing excuses and distractions before the test, unobtrusively working quite hard on the test, protecting the self before the outcome is known with inflated appraisals of task difficulty, and, finally, securing full self-protection with pronouncements of post-hoc attributions that vary as a function of success or failure (C. R. Snyder, 1985). As this example indicates, the elements of a strategy are diverse in content, involving thoughts, feelings, and effort, sometimes directed towards the self, and other times more focused on influencing others or on controlling the task activity itself. Strategies specify a particular reading of a generic life-task goal, one that often reflects the person's interpretation of readiness for the task: Self-handicappers, for example, seem willing to sacrifice actual performance by embracing obstacles before a test, perhaps because they are actually unsure of their ability to control performance outcomes, and opt thus for a self-protective version of an achievement task goal (Berglas, 1985). As a result, it is not always an easy matter to evaluate, as an outsider, the effectiveness of a life-task strategy (i.e., sometimes the objective indicators of success and failure do not coincide with the goals most uppermost in a person's mind).

We specifically do not intend to embrace some implications associated with the colloquial meaning of the term strategy in our delineation of these problem-solving strategies. For instance, achievement strategies like self-handicapping or defensive pessimism are not necessarily or even typically consciously executed (Kihlstrom, 1987), though with only the slightest of encouragement individuals can often tell you in retrospect how they characteristically tackle certain problems (Norem & Cantor, 1986b). Similarly, since these strategies usually reflect pressing personal intentions or goals (Kuhl, 1985) and are often associated with the person's own reading of his or her competence and past experience in relevant domains (Bandura, 1986), it makes most sense to view them as primarily *self*-regulatory in nature, rather than as directed mainly at interpersonal manipulation. Finally, in informal usage, we tend to think of people as having quite consistent, generalized styles of problem solving (e.g., "he is a true repressor" or "she always sees the bright side of things"). Yet, to the extent that strategies are intimately linked, at least in principle, to particular life-task goals and domains of life-task activity, individuals should be able to vary their strategic orientations in line with their different readings of their self-in-situations (Kihlstrom & Cantor, 1984; Pervin, 1976). The status in reality of such an assumption of flexibility in social intelligence remains very much an open question, one to which we will return in the following discussion of life-task problem solving.

ILLUSTRATIVE METHODS FOR LIFE TASK AND STRATEGY ANALYSIS

In order to give substance to this discussion of the life task and strategy approach to personality, we will present several of the empirical research efforts that it has inspired. The research will attempt to describe the path from life task appraisals to problem-solving strategies and finally to outcome measures of performance and health. First, an overview of the Honors Project (Cantor, et. al, 1987) will be provided, focusing on the utility of this life task strategy approach for understanding the transition of undergraduates from high school to college. Second, two "packages" of appraisals and strategies, defensive pessimism and social constraint, will be described. These two analyses show how the understanding of individuals' goals and strategies can improve our understanding of individual differences. This presentation of the methods and types of data involved will give the reader a feel for the concrete applications of the theory and subsequently provide fodder for additional discussion of issues in this perspective.

The Honors Project (Cantor et al., 1987) has tracked a core group of 147 undergraduates from their first year at college through their senior year, focusing on their perceptions of their life tasks and their strategic activities, as well as on standard outcome measures. In several of the data collection waves, only subsets of the sample have been called upon to participate, and additional subjects have been acquired at some points of data collection for comparison purposes. Table 4.1 summarizes the data collected thus far in each of the four main phases in the project. Outcome assessments were collected in each of the years of the study, covering areas of academic and social performance, perceived life stress (after Cohen et al., 1983) and health and well-being (junior year only). The following discussion presents a selective review of some of our key methods for assessing life tasks and strategies.

Assessing Students' Current Life Tasks

In the first survey of the project, subjects were asked to list their current life tasks (i.e., those things they felt they were working on in their lives) and to rank order them with regard to importance. On average, 8.3 tasks were reported per subject, suggesting that current life tasks were readily accessible and plentiful in our sample. Tasks ranged greatly in specificity, from very abstract (e.g., "maturing beyond my high school mentality") to quite concrete and immediate (e.g., "finding a girlfriend"). Most of the tasks listed seemed to reflect aspects of the students' new environment but also represented larger life themes such as affiliation and achievement.

The students were also asked to self-code their tasks according to a pretested scheme of more generic, consensual college life-task categories in achievement and interpersonal domains (Brower, 1985). They successfully categorized 81% of their freely-generated tasks into at least one of the six consensual categories: achievement tasks—(a) getting good grades, (b) setting goals—planning for the future, (c) managing time; and interpersonal tasks—(d) being on one's own away from family, (e) developing an identity, and (f) making friends. A significant number of tasks were apportioned into each of the categories, further supporting the relevance of the consensual categories. They were also able to use these generic task categories as an organizational structure for generating their concrete life situations at college and their specific plans for handling these tasks. A substantial number of situations were produced for each consensual category (M=5.6 per category), showing the everyday applicability of the categories. The degree of detail in the students' plans for handling task-relevant situations (labeled as plan reflectivity)

Table 4.1
Overview of Three-Year Longitudinal Honors Project

Time	Data Collection Phase	Sample Measures and Sources of Coding Schemes
Wave One Fall '84	*Questionnaire One* 2 hour Mail Survey N = 181 of Honors College first year class	Family background data; self-concept discrepancy (Higgins et al., 1985); life-task listing & appraisals (Little, 1983); Coping plans: Reflectivity (Spivak et al., 1976) and negativity; Optimism-Defensive Pessimism Strategy Prescreening (Norem & Cantor, 1986 ab).
Wave Two Winter '85	*Questionnaire Two* 20 Minute Mail Survey N = 147 Core Sample[a] N = 110 Comparison Sample[b]	Achievement performance: GPA; Adjective checklist on satisfaction (Lubin, 1965); Social performance: satisfaction rating and adjective checklist; 14 Item Perceived Stress Scale (Cohen et al., 1983); life-task listing (Little, 1983)
Spring '85	*Social Event Study* Two sessions, one hour each n = 21 from core sample	Plans and expectations for on-campus Marti-Gras event; Behavior and affect checklist reports of event; "Social" self-concept discrepancy (Higgins et al. 1985)
Spring '85	*Experience Sampling Study* Electronic Pagers with 5 "beeps" per day, 10 days n = 24 from core sample	Activity reports (see Hormuth, 1986)—approx 37 per ss; Social interactions for each report (after Wheeler, Reis, & Nezlek, 1983); 10 Mood-emotion scales for each report (after Little, 1983). [10 days of nightly diary reports on some material.]

(continued)

Table 4.1
(continued)

Time	Data Collection Phase	Sample Measures and Sources of Coding Schemes
Wave Three Spring '86	*Questionnaire Three* 1 hour, group sessions n = 97 from core sample	Life-task Conflict Grid (Little, 1983); Coping plans (Spivak et al., 1976); 14 Item Perceived Stress Scale (Cohen et al., 1983); Academic and social performance & satisfaction
Spring '86	*Interview Studies* Two one-on-one videotaped sessions each approx. 1 hour n = 67 from core sample	*Session 1:* Moos & Moos (1981) Family Environment scale; Interview on academic & social life tasks and strategies with videotaped interviews coded by two trained raters with 92 item Q-Sort "strategy" Deck; Block, 1971 for method). *Session 2:* Problem-solving talk-aloud interview in which student is "challenged" with obstacles; coding of videotaped interviews for *flexibility* and *optimism-pessimism*.
Wave Four Spring '87	*Telephone Interview* Six minute phone interview conducted by I.S.R. field office n = 127 of core sample	4-Item Perceived Stress Scale (Cohen et al., 1983); Symptom checklist (after Verbugge, 1980); Report on medication use & health visits; Academic & social life performance, satisfaction, and confidence

[a]N = 147 completed both Q1 & Q2;
[b]N = 110 comparison group completed only Q2

was related to subsequent measures of academic performance (even though these highly reflective students did not come to college with any better records than their less reflective peers, see Cantor et al., 1987 for details). In other words, subjects seemed to find it relatively easy to move "up and down a life-task ladder" from their personal current tasks to more abstract achievement and interpersonal task categories, and then back to the concrete level of life task situations and plans; and their ability to do this kind of self-reflection had predictable associations with subsequent performance.

To understand more about how these students were appraising and anticipating their life tasks, we also asked them to rate each of these six consensual tasks on 11 meaning dimensions (importance, enjoyment, difficulty, control, initiative, stress, progress, challenge, absorption, time spent, and others' view) (after Little, 1983). The students provided these ratings at two time periods, in the beginning of their first term at college (wave one) and after a year and a half of college life experience (wave three), allowing us to assess changes in patterns of life task appraisal. As we will discuss later, the three achievement tasks were consistently appraised as more difficult, more challenging, more stressful, less controllable, less enjoyable, and showing less progress as compared to the three interpersonal tasks, though other changes in the content and pattern of appraisals did emerge in this time period.

Both sets of appraisal ratings were analyzed using factor analytic techniques to uncover any latent appraisal structure. In the first wave data, separate analyses of the ratings for each of the six consensual tasks converged on a similar, three-factor, orthogonal solution. Therefore, the loading matrices of each task were rotated to approximate the average of the loading matrices using a least squares Procrustean technique. A similar result of a converging three-factor solution occurred in the third wave data, although the particular factor loadings are different from those in the first wave data. The three factors and their salient loadings for the first and third waves of data are displayed next to one another in Table 4.2.

In the first wave data, the first factor, labeled as anxiety-absorption, seems to represent the negative aspects of the tasks: the degree to which they were viewed as stressful, difficult, and time consuming. The next two factors seem to represent the positively-valued concepts of personal responsibility (control, initiative, and progress) and reward (enjoyment, progress, and absorption). In contrast, departures from this structure are clearly apparent in the factor solution of the third wave appraisal data. The first factor of the original solution (anxiety-absorption) has decomposed into two separate factors, one loading primarily on the negatively-toned dimensions (e.g., stress and difficulty) and the other

Table 4.2
Loading of Eleven Life-Task Appraisal Dimensions on Three Orthogonal Factors in First and Third Wave Data

Appraisal Dimensions	WAVE 1			WAVE 3		
	Anxiety-Absorption	Personal Responsibility	Rewardingness	Importance Absorption	Stressfulness	Reward-Control
Importance	.42			.62		
Enjoyment			.45			.55
Difficulty	.52				.60	
Control		.66				.70
Initiative		.74				.59
Stress	.57				.70	
Progress		.30	.40			.70
Challenge	.67			.38	.60	
Absorption	.66		.36	.66		
Time spent	.62			.67		
Others' view	.29			.33		

representing importance and absorption. At the same time, the second and third factors of the original solution (personal control and rewardingness) have fused in the third wave ratings into a single component representing both ideas. A possible interpretation is that under the stresses of the first year in college, life tasks that are important and absorbing are also stressful, perhaps because of the inexperience with, and uncertainties of, the new environment. Students may, after the first rush of a life transition, feel more confident and able to take a more differentiated view of their tasks.

In the third wave survey, a new procedure was also employed to measure the students' perceptions of the relationships among their various life-task activities: They were asked to judge the extent to which working on one of the six consensual tasks facilitated or conflicted with each of the other tasks (after Little, 1983). The procedure had subjects judge the degree to which working on each task conflicted or facilitated each other on a five-point scale, ranging from a great deal of conflict to a great deal of facilitation, with a midpoint of indifference (no effect). Judgments were made directionally, so that, for example, the impact of "getting good grades" upon "making friends" was measured separately from the impact of "making friends" upon "getting good grades." Our intent was to look for life tasks that might have significant, asymmetrical impacts on other tasks in the system, indicating their conceptual centrality (Table 4.3).

Table 4.3
Facilitation-Conflict Grid Representing Averaged Ratings
of Inter-Task Impact

		Task Impacted Upon					
		Getting Good Grades	Setting Goals	Making Friends	Being on Ones Own	Identity	Managing Time
Task Causing Impact	Getting Good Grades	—	1.25	−.48*	.23	.46	.67
	Setting Goals	1.3	—	.55	.96	1.35	.74
	Making Friends	−.38*	.53	—	.92	1.11	.06*
	Being on One's Own	.33	1.01	1.07	—	1.33	.75
	Identity	.60	1.44	1.19	1.38	—	.29
	Managing Time	.49	.71	−.24*	.57	.36	—

Note. Ratings were made on a scale of +2 to −2, positive numbers indicating more facilitation. Starred (*) numbers representing the facilitation-conflict among "Getting Good Grades," "Managing Time," and "Making Friends." The grand mean of the ratings was .69, indicating significant facilitation.

In general, students seemed to feel that working on one task facilitated progress on others; the mean facilitation score was significantly above the midpoint of the rating scale. However, students tended to see particular conflict between the achievement-oriented tasks of "getting good grades" and "managing time" and the interpersonal task of "making friends." These data suggest a psychological opposition in the students' minds between academic and social life task pursuits.

Assessing Life Task Experience

During the spring of the first year, a very fruitful study of actual life-task activity was conducted using a subset (n = 24) of the core sample. The study, using random time, experience sampling, and daily diary procedures, assessed in an immediate and on-line fashion subjects' appraisals of their activities, the social and emotional character of the "events" and the time spent in various types of situations (Norem, 1987). Using this methodology an even greater proportion of reported activities (88%) were classifiable (again by the subjects) within the six consensual tasks. Moreover, the construal differences between the academic and social domains were validated; academic activities evoked more stress and challenge, whereas social activities were characterized by greater (on-the-spot) enjoyment.

Assessing Life Task Strategies

The students' achievement strategies were first assessed using a brief self-report measure of defensive pessimism and optimism included in the first questionnaire survey (Norem & Cantor, 1986a). Later, in the spring of the students' sophomore year at college, a more substantial and diverse assessment of interpersonal and achievement strategies was obtained in an interview study with a subset (n = 67) of the sample. These students participated in two, hour-long, semistructured interviews regarding their lives as students at the University of Michigan and their approaches to solving common problems. The interviews were videotaped and then coded by observers using a Q-sort procedure (after Block, 1971) with an item deck of 92 items. The Q-sort deck represented elements from a variety of well-researched self-management strategies, with component items reflecting activity in academic and in social domains (see Norem, 1987, for details on the deck content). The items covered attitudes about self, attitudes about goals, attributions about events, and behaviors that comprise a variety of different action control strategies (Kuhl, 1985), with each item phrased in terms specific to these students' experiences in academic or in social situations. These Q-sort rating data have been used subsequently to explicate in detail the components of a defensively pessimistic achievement strategy and of a social constraint strategy (see following discussion).

Assessing Students' Selves: Past, Present, and Ideal

In the service of relating patterns of life-task appraisal and strategy orientation to aspects of the students' self-perceptions and personal experiences, several different self-assessment measures were included in the project. As part of the first questionnaire survey, for example, students generated lists of ten characteristics of their actual and ideal selves, following standard procedures for assessing self-concept discrepancy (Higgins et al., 1985). Discrepancies were coded by subtracting the number of synonyms across the two lists from the number of antonyms. For a finer grained approach, the synonyms and antonyms were also coded into the particular life task categories that they represented (e.g., the self-ideal of "being more sociable" into the "making friends" task category). Thus, life-task specific self-concept discrepancies were created.

Additionally, family and background data were obtained through self-report and through information provided by the admissions office (e.g., parental education, SAT scores). The Moos (1974) Family Environment Scale was also administered to a subset of the students (those who participated in the life task interviews, n = 67). This is a self-report instrument that retrospectively assesses characteristics of an individual's family life experience. These data proved invaluable in our attempts to understand the basis for students' specific strategic reactions to these college life tasks, attempts to which we will now turn.

Illustrative Life Task–Strategy "Packages"

Defensive Pessimism. One of the first fruits of the social intelligence approach has been an analysis of the strategy of defensive pessimism (Norem & Cantor, 1986a, 1986b; Cantor, et al, 1987). Defensive pessimists typically engage in cognitive activity in anticipation of achievement tasks involving "playing out worst case scenarios," setting low expectations, and taking concrete steps to prepare for task demands. In contrast, those who use an optimistic strategy typically have high expectations and feel less anxiety in anticipation of a performance task. In the research conducted so far, both strategies have been shown to lead to positive performance on achievement tasks.

In the context of the Honors Project research program we have attempted to integrate this strategy analysis with the life-task approach. Distinguishing optimists (n = 43) and defensive pessimists (n = 34) initially on the basis of a questionnaire measure of defensive pessimism, a number of important differences were found. Although defensive pessimists did not differ from optimists in their high school grade point averages (GPA), they set lower expectations for first semester GPA and showed generally more negative appraisals of academic tasks (e.g., more difficult, stressful, challenging, and time consuming; and less controllable and likely to show progress). Importantly, this harsh appraisal was not generally characteristic of defensive pessimists; there were no significant differences in appraisal of social tasks. Defensive pessimists performed better when they reflected in detail in their plans for academic problems, regardless of the negative thoughts revealed in those plans. However, pessimists' planned-for fears did not materialize: they performed as well on average in their first semester as the optimists (GPAs M = 3.34 and M = 3.38, respectively).

Figure 4.1 summarizes the ways in which the components of the two strategies function differently within the two self-management systems. For those who adopted an optimistic strategy, high expectations (in the form of expected GPA) was a strong positive associate of good acedemic performance. Discrepancy between perceptions of self and ideal, degree of reflectivity in academic situation plans, and the negativity of those plans were all negatively associated with positive outcomes. Also, the perceived reward of academics (factor 3 from the first wave factor analysis) was unrelated to performance. In essence, the ability of an optimist to focus on positive performance expectancies and not to think about other, more negative aspects of the problem was essential for his or her success.

Within the group of defensive pessimists, however, the patterns of relationships were very different. For defensive pessimists, performance expectations had no consistent association to performance. Discrepancy between perceptions of self and ideal and degree of reflectivity in academic situation plans were strong *positive* associates of good academic performance. Surprisingly, even negativity of those situation plans was not negatively related to performance, although the positive relation was weak. Also, the perceived reward of academic effort played an important and positive role in achieving performance success. For pessimists, the ability to focus and reflect on the discrepancy between one's and one's self goals seems central to success. We suspect that this anxiety-provoking focus allows the defensive pessimist to take control of the situation by constructively channeling energy in preparing to succeed. Also important is the fact that the goal must be perceived as rewarding, in order we suspect to justify the use of such an exhausting strategy (Cantor & Norem, 1987).

Despite defensive pessimism's tendency to perpetuate anxiety and tension, it seems to be an adaptive strategy that brings success to those who use it. Moreover, defensive pessimism must be evaluated in the context of the persons who have adopted the strategy. Their retrospective reports on the Moos (1974) Family Environment Scale reveal that defensive pessimists felt that their family life was lacking in structured guidance, making gaining control of difficult situations likely to be a particular concern. With this autobiographical frame of reference in mind, defensive pessimism seems perhaps more reasonable as a way to "harness anxiety" in the service of confronting important achievement task goals.

Social Constraint. An even more recent development is the analysis of a strategy of social constraint and other-directedness in interpersonal task settings (Langston & Cantor, 1987, 1988). The strategy seems similarly

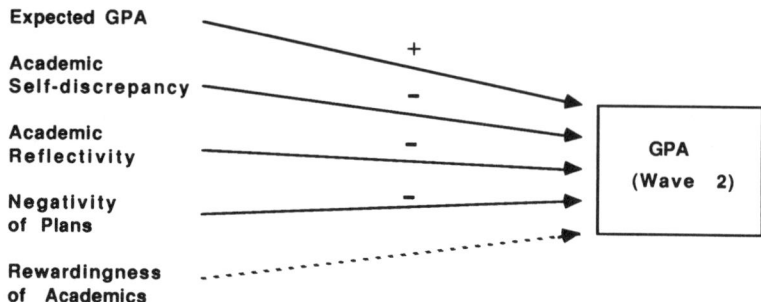

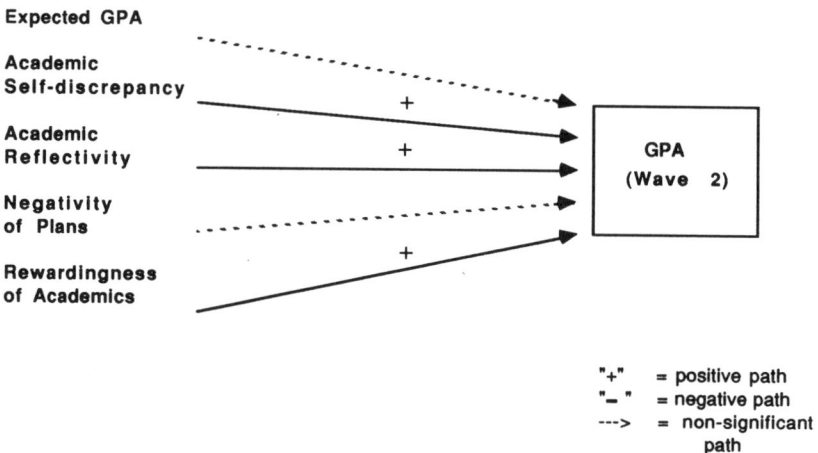

FIG. 4.1. Influence of strategy components on performance (GPA) for optimists and defensive pessimists.

motivated as defensive pessimism; however, it is focused on performance in the social/interpersonal goal domain. This strategy also differs from defensive pessimism in that it seems to be more clearly self-defeating in terms of at least some of the goals that it is "intended" to serve.

A significant subset of our sample (n = 27) distinguished themselves with a divergent pattern of appraisal of social versus academic tasks, in comparison with the modal student (n = 84). At odds with the consensus view of social tasks as far more enjoyable and far less difficult and stressful than academic or achievement-oriented tasks, these students were relatively negative in their appraisals of the social domain. As well as seeing the social domain in a harsher light than the norm, those characterized by the social contraint strategy also saw themselves as relatively less competent in the social arena.

Nevertheless, these students did characterize their social tasks as important and worthwhile. Their ratings of hoped-for satisfaction in the social domain did not differ from the majority of the Honors College sample. These students did not withdraw their concern or commitment from the social domain. It is important to note that these negative appraisals did not generalize to all domains of life; overall negativity and depressive cognitions did not differ between those using the strategy and those who did not.

These students' "deviant" appraisals (of social tasks), however, were linked to a pattern of behavior characterized by a lack of self-directed and self-enhancing action and by a tendency to follow other's lead in the social domain; we labeled this action pattern as a social constraint strategy on the basis of the observers' Q-sort ratings of the interviews. In those Q-sort codings of the interviews, there were significant differences between the social constraint group and the modal group of students regarding all of the previously mentioned components. The *task appraisal* items "low social expectations," "finds social tasks in general to be stressful," and "finds social tasks to be [un]manageable," for example, were more characteristic of the social constraint group than of the modal student. The *self-appraisal* items "sees discrepancy between actual and ideal social self," "focuses attention on self after social failure," and "makes self-deprecating comments" were also more characteristic. These differences confirm the appraisal differences assessed via the various self-report measures used in the first and second wave of data collection. In addition, items reflecting *effective action*, for example, "takes effective action," "picks friends and social commitments that facilitate accomplishing own goals," and "manipulates environment to help accomplish own goals" were less characteristic of the social constraint group. Finally, items indicating *other-directedness*, for example, "is comfortable with and desirous of having structure imposed by others," "thinks about having social support," and "uses perceived similarity of self to typical others in situations as [a] guide in decision making" were more characteristic. These four aspects cohere as the strategy of social constraint.

For those characterized by social constraint there may have been a self-esteem protective function of the strategy. They seemed to prefer not to expose themselves by standing out in leading social activities, but rather to participate as followers and observers. This motivation for the strategy of constraint was further illuminated by the fact that those who used it reported their family environments to have relatively little open and easy communication and expression of emotions. In the social intelligence framework, it might be argued that the strategy, therefore, was in part an adaptation to a deficit that the students perceived as a result of their lack of experience with intimate others who were skilled in interpersonal interaction.

The use of this strategy was also associated with significantly lowered social satisfaction ratings. Figure 4.2 schematically shows the process by which harsh construals of social life tasks influenced the adoption of the social constraint strategy and the strategy affected social satisfaction (Langston & Cantor, 1988). Appraisals themselves did not seem to have a major impact on performance except insofar as they determined the selection and function of behavior as part of a coherent problem-solving strategy. The indirect effect of appraisal on outcome is important in the life-task approach in that it highlights the flexibility of peoples' attempts to solve their life tasks. The social constraint strategy was not the only observed response to negative appraisals in this sample: As the data suggest, some students with negative appraisals of social life tasks managed to find a route to social satisfaction (i.e., there was no direct, inevitable negative impact on social satisfaction of the initial negative task appraisals).

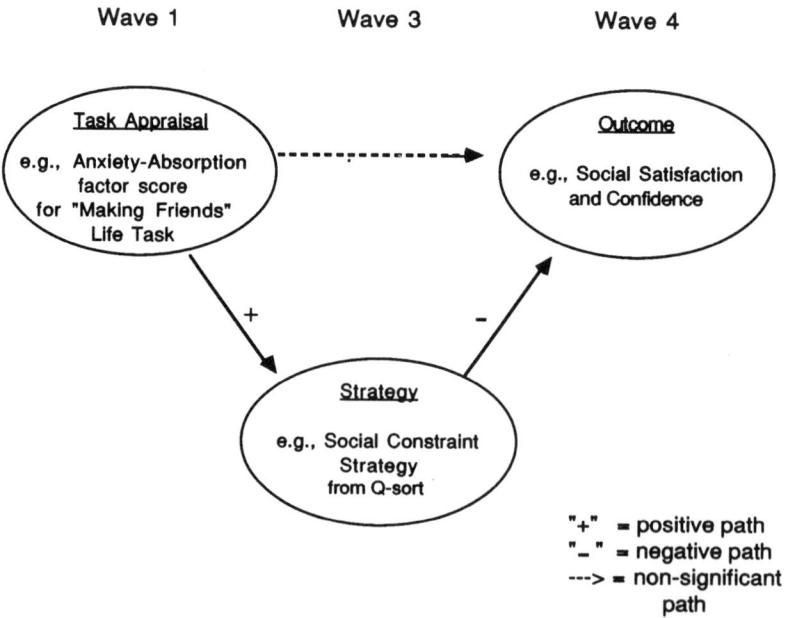

FIG. 4.2. Path model of influence of appraisals of social life tasks via their impact on the use of the social constraint strategy.

In one regard, the social constraint strategy seemed to be adaptive in that it presumably protected those who adopted it from damage to self-esteem (in their own minds at least) and provided a mechanism for participation in interpersonal activities. These students were not immobilized or perpetually "stuck" in state-oriented (Kuhl, 1985) musings about generalized self-inadequacies, and they did find a way to take part in social life activities. However, their orientation toward these activities certainly did not fully satisfy all of their relevant social goals and desires.

THEMES IN A SOCIAL INTELLIGENCE ANALYSIS

The foregoing discussion was intended to provide a look at the methods of choice, and the favored units of analysis, in a social intelligence approach to life-task problem solving. In order to show individuals actively at work on life tasks, we followed this group of students in a major life transition, using self-report, experience-sampling, and observer Q-sort techniques to uncover patterns in the ways in which they construed and appraised their important life-task goals at college and in their strategic reactions to those tasks. The transition experience provided a context of shared social demands for these students within which individual patterns of problem solving emerged. As the analysis of the defensive pessimism and social constraint strategies suggested, not surprisingly, individuals differ considerably in the ways in which they pursue these shared life-task goals, differences that seem to reflect unique perspectives on the self and on the task at hand. These characteristic strategies, in turn, have predictable consequences for performance and for well-being, sometimes, as in the case of these two strategies, allowing individuals to meet some goals (e.g., of performance, of self-protection) but also exposing them to other (new) tasks (e.g., containing stress and fatigue, being interpersonally assertive). These illustrative examples, therefore, highlight the complexity of the patterns and consequences of individuals' problem-solving orientations, even within a fairly structured period of life transition. We turn now to consideration of these complexities from the perspective of a social intelligence analysis, drawing further on the experiences of these students as they negotiate college life.

Interpretive Contexts for Life Tasks and Strategies

The social intelligence model accords special status to the role of *context* as an interpretive framework in individuals' selection and appraisal of life tasks and in the choice of strategies that individuals pursue to reach those life-task goals. Because this is a largely cognitive model of personality, rather than focus on physical, objective features of individuals' life contexts that might well influence their goals and strategic choices, we chose, instead, to pay particular notice to contextual determinants that can be characterized as psychological or subjective in nature. In fact, for our purposes, contexts are best thought of as *interpretive frameworks* in the heads of individuals—the background set of messages, ideas, feelings, memories that come to mind for the individual as they approach particular periods in their lives and particular domains of life-task activity. These interpretive frameworks, of course, derive often fairly directly from experiences with the values, demands, and tasks encouraged by familial, subcultural, and social-institutional life settings (Veroff, 1983). However, by concentrating on contexts as interpretive frameworks in the head of the actor, we can also keep track of instances when the individual's construction of reality diverges significantly from the modal or "normative" version in his or her current life setting. In this way, we can thus attend to the typical ways in which individuals' choices of tasks to pursue, their appraisal or construal of those tasks, and the strategies they embrace, are constrained by their social life settings and simultaneously keep open to the powerful impact of personal histories—the cognitive baggage that sometimes only quite indirectly reflects actual social pressures, perceptions, or norms.

Contextual determinants of life-task goals and strategies come in many forms. For example, there are the interpretive frameworks set up by the demands that society typically places on individuals to be a certain kind of person in each life epoch (Higgins & Parsons, 1983; Erikson, 1950) and, correspondingly, the individual's own autobiographical context for transforming those normative demands into personal desires (Reich & Zautra, 1983). In this vein, every student knows that they are supposed to "come to grips with being on my own," though for some this college life task does not seem to constitute a major challenge; in fact, they integrate the task rather automatically (and perhaps unreflectively) into their other daily chores, whereas for others it is an imposing and important obstacle to satisfaction with college life (Zirkel & Cantor, 1988). In our analyses of goals in the transition to college life, as previously described, three aspects of the general interpretive framework within which students appear to select and pursue their life tasks emerged as especially powerful: a social or normative context, a context of self-perceptions and self-ideals, and, relatedly, an autobiographical context of goal-relevant experiences. We will now consider those data again with an eye toward illustrating these contextual frameworks.

Normative Frameworks. One very critical interpretive context for individuals' choices of life tasks to pursue, and their subsequent appraisal of those tasks, is a set of age-graded social-cultural expectations that delineates the "appropriate" or "normative" pursuits for each phase of life (see Higgins & Parsons, 1983; Ryff, 1987). These age-graded prescriptive messages are often articulated directly to individuals as they move into a new life transition. College students, for example, are told in orientations that the next phase of their lives will involve tasks of independence, identity development, goal consolidation, and so forth (Marcia, 1980; Cutrona, 1982). More subtle messages come from the institutional structure within which the individual will operate in each age-graded phase of life; time and effort are differentially allocated to different life-task activities in each institutional context. The young child, for example, stays wedded to family life pursuits in part because the week is structured to include a great deal of time for such activities; the college student confronts a different set of messages about "going home" in which vacation time is restricted and clearly demarcated as separate from "regular" school life (Csikszentmihalyi & Larson, 1984). Institutions also structure the amount of time spent alone, in groups, as a subordinate, as a leader, with peers or with "teachers" and "learners." These aspects of the typical organization of activity within institutional settings provide important information to participants about the culturally valued life task pursuits (Caspi, 1987; Veroff, 1983).

The college students in our sample frequently mentioned the presence of large blocks of "time on my own" or "time to structure myself" as a new feature of college life, and they seemed to see in this new "freedom" a *task* of identity development and independence (Cantor et al., 1987). In fact, in the experience-sampling study, we (Moore & Cantor, 1988) found that students spent significantly more time in college life activities that were relevant to aspects of their self-concept that they had initially mentioned as areas for personal development (i.e., attributes they would ideally like to have but had not yet mastered) than in pursuits for which they were already well suited. For example, if a student had described himself or herself on our first questionnaire measure as actually being quite a procrastinator and as wanting to be better organized and more prompt with school work, then he or she quite likely to be spending time in "time management" activities in the experience-sampling study, more time, in fact, than on other self-relevant activities (e.g., "hanging out with friends") about which he or she had expressed more of a "self-fit" (e.g., "I'm low-key and socially at-ease"). One way to interpret these experience-sampling data is that the students were in a sense accepting the institutional challenge to structure their own time so as to facilitate their particular domains identity and goal development. An interesting corollary of spending time on these "self-discrepant" life-task goals is that such identity development activity is quite emotionally taxing. The students felt much better and more satisfied when pursuing their more "comfortable" life tasks (i.e., in activities that fit well with their current self-concepts). Goal-directed activity is perhaps more fulfilling in retrospect than it is fun at the time that the effort is being exerted!

The structure of life within institutions, and the age-graded messages given as individuals enter new life periods, have fairly direct influences on the nature of the life tasks that participants pursue, and their commitment to those life-tasks goals. Our data also suggest that there is a somewhat more subtle effect of the social-normative context on individuals' *appraisals* of the life tasks (i.e., their vision of how stressful, difficult, enjoyable, rewarding, and so forth, the tasks will be to pursue in this life setting). For example, the students in our sample were quite uniform in their appraisals of achievement life tasks as far more threatening and imposing and less rewarding than interpersonal life tasks, though they viewed their social life goals as highly self-relevant and important. These differential expectations about academic versus social life tasks were reflected in their appraisals of the tasks, the detail in their plans for coping with these tasks (achievement > interpersonal), and in the content of the gaps between their actual and ideal self-concepts when they first entered college (Cantor et al., 1987). Although there may well be some reality to this modal perception that achievement tasks are more demanding and stressful and less immediately rewarding than interpersonal life tasks, it is important to note that this particular sample of Honors College students had much to be pleased about their past achievement successes and that much that is strikingly new about college life is best viewed as social in nature (e.g., the forum for academic pursuits changes far less drastically from high school to college than does the forum for interpersonal interaction and the demands of out-of-classroom life). In fact, judging from their own reports of satisfaction with their social lives at the end of their first college term (e.g., average ratings equivalent to a 2.7, or B-, when rescaled on a 4-point grading scale), these students' social life tasks were not all that easy to accomplish, especially since they reported having hoped to achieve considerably higher levels of social life satisfaction (e.g., average rescaled ratings of hoped for social satisfaction of 3.3, or B+).

Whether correctly or not, these students seemed to carry this interpretive framework (of achievement-interpersonal task comparisons) with them throughout the three years of college experience in which we followed them. For example, in the spring of their freshman year at

4. UPS AND DOWNS OF LIFE TASKS   **149**

college, students in the experience-sampling study were reporting far more negative and less positive emotional experiences on average in achievement than in social situations, and in the spring of their sophomore year, students across the whole sample rated their achievement tasks of "getting good grades" and "managing time" as the tasks causing most conflict within their task systems (i.e., the tasks most likely to interfere with progress on their other important tasks).

These expectations and feelings about achievement versus interpersonal *life-task activity* persisted against a background of relative satisfaction on these students parts with their actual academic *performances*. For example, on adjective checklist assessments these students reported being relatively satisfied with their first-terms GPAs. The average discrepancy between their obtained and hoped for GPA was actually smaller than the comparable discrepancy for social satisfaction; the average first term GPA was B+, and the average hoped for GPA was between B+ and A–. In their junior year at college they reported being just as satisfied with their academic performance as with their social lives. The consistency and strength of their negative expectations for, and appraisals of, achievement life-task activity, standing as it does in sharp contrast to their own satisfaction with their performance in the domain and to the presence for them of some fairly taxing social life tasks, suggests to us the influence of a shared interpretive context for their feelings about college life tasks. The zeitgeist of undergraduates generally suggests that coursework is *the* difficult aspect of college, whereas to outsiders there are other life tasks of equal stature and difficulty.

Personal frameworks. The normative contexts (of age-graded demands, institutional structuring of life activity, and shared perceptions of task difficulty) for students' choices of and approaches toward task goals, seemed quite clear in our data on the transition to college life. More striking, however, are the individual interpretive frameworks that seemed also to be operating as particular students reflected on those shared demands and appraisals in constructing their personal life tasks, current concerns, or projects (Klinger, 1977; Little, 1983; Cantor & Kihlstrom, 1987, 1988). These personalized patterns occurred not only in the students' investment in and appraisal of commonly shared life tasks, but even in the content of the issues that they saw as being at stake in these shared or normative life tasks (i.e., in the very framing of the tasks themselves). When the students in our sample listed the situations and activities at college that they viewed as relevant to the life task of "being on my own," for example, a rather clear division was apparent: One group of students (n = 42) viewed the independence task as intimately linked to separating from their prior family life (e.g., a construal that emphasized personal growth *out* of the past and sometimes *into* the future), whereas a majority (n = 84) group expressed more present-centered, less developmentally-oriented, construals that focused on the chores to be performed at college (Zirkel & Cantor, 1988). As we will detail, these differing task construals were associated with different patterns of task activity and of adjustment at college. Our data contain several such instances of a personalized pattern of life-task construal that seems to reflect an individual's unique interpretive framework on this shared life transition.

Grappling with independence and lost identities. One of the central life tasks articulated by our college student sample was that of "independence—being on my own," for which students listed situations ranging across a variety of interpretations of the independence task, such as new responsibilities and tasks at college (e.g., paying bills, making sure not to crash the car), new freedoms at college (e.g., being able to go out all night), future selves (e.g., getting married and settling down), relationship to family and homesickness (e.g., missing mom's cooking; not neglecting family), replacing past identities (e.g., developing an identity outside of being so-and-so's kid) (see Zirkel & Cantor, 1988 for a more complete categorization scheme). This was clearly a life task that lent itself to very different sorts of construals across our student sample.

In pursuing these alternative constructions of the independence life task, Zirkel & Cantor (1988) distinguished a group of 42 students who found the independence task to be especially intimidating absorbing, and stressful (as measured by appraisal ratings), as compared to the modal pattern of construal. These students were highly invested in their independence life task, as measured both by the number of situations and activities that they generated as relevant to this task (at the beginning of their college experience), and by the amount of time they actually spent in independence-related activity, as measured by behavior reports from a subsample of the group who participated later in the experience-sampling study. Moreover, this "deviant" group seemed to have an interpretive framework for the independence task that differed in content and emphasis from the modal or normative pattern of construal in our sample: They were more likely to describe their task of "being on my own" in terms of the loss or absence of family life and support and in terms of the need to develop new skills and attributes to replace this "child" identity. In contrast, the modal pattern of construal, appraisal, and investment suggested a more routine or mundane interpretation of this task with less emphasis on the past, less intimidation about the present, and less time spent carving out domains of new self-identity. In a sense, the "deviant" group actually looked more like the prototype of a "college student searching for an independent voice," though they also suffered much more stress and dissatisfaction with college life in the process, by comparison with the more "down-to-earth" approach of the typical student. The independence life task was one that lent itself to multiple interpretations, with correspondingly different patterns of activity that followed from those unique construals.

Autobiographical frameworks. The individual's current perceptions of self, embedded within a rich store of autobiographical knowledge (Kihlstrom & Cantor, 1984), provide a critical evaluative context for personal interpretations of these shared life-task goals (Bandura, 1977, 1982). As Cantor & Kihlstrom (1987) suggest, individuals frame specific versions of commonly held life tasks and select strategies based on their readings of personal experience, capacities, and efficacy in relevant domains (Paulhus & Martin, 1987). Again, a critical assumption here is that the operative context for life tasks and strategies is the individual's thoughts, feelings, and judgments about his or her past, present, and possible selves more than the consensually agreed upon account of his or her competence or past performance (Norem & Cantor, 1988). We view this personal-autobiographical interpretive context as a powerful and relatively direct determinant of life task appraisal and strategic orientation and believe that often this framework constitutes a rather different vision of the person's potential than might be obtained from relevant members of his or her social world.

Getting good grades and making friends. To illustrate the influence of these quite unique personal frameworks for life-task appraisal and strategic orientation, we turn to two domains, the achievement and interpersonal domains, in which there was strong consensuality among our student sample about the meaning and nature of the relevant goals and activities. Unlike the independence task, the life tasks of "getting good grades" and "making friends" are relatively concrete, and most students view them as involving generally the same set of activities (e.g., studying while friends are partying; finding people to hang out with; being myself among strangers; and so on). This background of shared construal of the tasks, as well as strong commitment to the tasks, allows us to see in particularly striking form the role played by self-perceptions in shaping students' unique reactions to achievement and interpersonal tasks.

When we investigated student's appraisals of these two important life tasks of "getting good grades" and "making friends," as noted earlier, there emerged in each domain a distinct minority pattern of appraisal that had clear repercussions for students' strategic orientations to their life tasks. In the achievement arena, the defensive pessimists (Cantor et al., 1987) reported being especially intimidated by their achievement life tasks, relative to the average Honors Program student's appraisal, even though they acknowledged their past academic successes and continued to be quite satisfied in college with their specific achievements. In the interpersonal task domain, students in our sample who embraced a strategy for social interaction of inhibited action and other-directedness (Langston & Cantor, 1988) were also especially likely to have appraised the social life tasks as threatening, stressful, and unrewarding—a distinctly unusual pattern of perception for our student sample with respect to this life task arena.

In both of these groups, the students who evidenced these rather unusual patterns of appraisal seemed to be operating with particular visions of their relevant past experiences and of their current self-images in the domain, perceptions that we feel functioned as critical interpretive frameworks for their strategic orientations. The defensive pessimists, though quite "normal" for this sample in their appraisals of their "social selves," saw especially large gaps between their current and ideal "student" selves. In contrast, the students with "deviant" appraisals of the "making friends" task emphasized bothersome discrepancies between their actual and ideal selves in the social domain and did not seem to be especially "down on themselves" in the academic arena. For the former group (of defensive pessimists), the discrepancy between their personal interpretive framework in the achievement domain, and objective assessments of their abilities, and performances in this domain were very apparent (Norem & Cantor, 1988). For the latter group with "deviant" appraisals in the interpersonal domain, there is less evidence that their relatively negative self-appraisals contradicted objective assessments of their social skills or past performances, though these self-perceptions served to perpetuate their less than ideal social experiences through the medium of their self-effacing social constraint strategy (see, Baumeister & Scher, 1987 for a discussion of self-defeating shyness strategies).

These interpretive self-perception frameworks were also reflected in, and probably bolstered by, unique retrospections about their family lives: The defensive pessimists reported experiencing unusually little structured guidance within their families, whereas the social constraint students reported that their families were especially likely to be affectively restrained and expressively inhibited in family interactions (as measured by self-reports on the Moos [1974] Family Environment Scale). These perceptions of family life no doubt contributed to the pessimists' anxieties about successfully carrying through on achievement tasks (Norem & Cantor, 1988) and to the social constraint students' fears of social embarrassment, as well as to their inclination to let others take the lead in social interactions. Autobiographical retrospections about family life probably constitute one of the main interpretive contexts for students' assessments of self-efficacy in various life-task domains, and, in turn, for the ways in which they frame the specific task to be solved in each domain (i.e., the self-goal to pursue in the achievement and interpersonal arenas) (Cantor & Kihlstrom, 1987).

It is, of course, difficult to know from these retrospective reports whether their family environments did indeed fail to provide the necessary models for confident and assertive achievement or interpersonal strategies, respectively. However, their reports do indicate that both sets of families were perceived by their children as placing a value on achievement and on interpersonal tasks, yet there appeared to be some discomfort on the students' parts about their personal preparation for handling such tasks. For defensive pessimists, these self-perceptions would likely *not* be shared by their families, in light of these students' consistently superior academic records. For the social constraint students, the veridicality of these perceptions remains a more open question, perhaps one that might be addressed by finding out whether other family members also experienced an absence of freewheeling social interactions, and whether they too felt constrained in their interpersonal relations by this history. In any case, whether a veridical reflection of past experience or not, these autobiographical perceptions seemed to set the tone for the kinds of readings that these students gave to their current life-task goals.

Context Sensitivity and Development and Change

An important corollary of these normative and personal contexts for life-task activity in different domains is that individuals' life-task appraisals and their strategic orientations towards those task goals are quite likely to be specifically tailored to fit each interpretive framework. Thus, it would be misguided to expect to find broad-based consistencies in individuals' styles of task appraisal and action. Each task is seen at a normative level to require a specific response with particular amounts of difficulty (Paulhus & Martin, 1987), and each reading of the individual's task goal reflects his or her quite intricate assessment of highly specific sets of personal past experiences (Kihlstrom & Cantor, 1984). This pattern of context sensitivity in appraisal and in action is apparent throughout our data set on the transition to college life. The defensive pessimists in this study were reflecting anxieties in the achievement domain; the social constraint students were inhibited in interpersonal assertiveness and not in their achievement pursuits. Although their respective strategies each had clear repercussions for performance and well-being in other life task domains, the initial impetus for their reactions was clearly linked to a particular life task with its own elaborated meaning and history for the individual. As we consider the pragmatics of life-task problem solving, and the potential malleability of individuals' strategic orientations, it becomes increasingly important to keep in mind these domain-specific origins of goals and of strategies.

Of particular importance with regard to the context sensitivity of life task appraisals and strategies are the implications for development and change. Although it is widely acknowledged that life tasks undergo fairly "revolutionary" change in periods of life transition, more subtle evolutionary changes may also take place within life epochs, as different aspects of the normative and personal contexts become salient. For example, in our Honors Project data, there was a significant decline in the harshness with which the academic task of "getting good" grades was appraised, between the first and third waves of data collection. Although the academic task remained more harshly appraised than its "matching" social task of "making friends," some of the negativity surrounding it had mellowed. Part of this change is undoubtedly due to the changes in performance feedback that typically occur once first year students survive introductory courses and find particular academic niches. However, students' grade point averages actually changed very little between the first and third semesters ($M=3.27$ and $M=3.43$, respectively). Part of the change in students' appraisal, therefore, may be due to changes in the normative climate of opinion regarding the importance of grades and what they can reveal. The anxious and eager first-year student segues, with a fair share of peer group encouragement, into the "experienced" and jaded sophomore.

Another important and revealing change, traceable perhaps to shifts in the normative context, was the increased importance of the task of "setting goals and planning for the future." Between the first and third waves this task category moved from the fifth to the second most commonly used, supplanting both the categories "getting good grades" and "managing time." After the intense pressure of the first year is over, students must begin to plan courses of study, majors, important summer jobs, and (in these career conscious days) even careers. The normative, age-graded messages about student life encourage this disengagement, such that the prototypical second semester senior typically begins to withdraw effort from academic pursuits in preparation for the life transition to employment; "getting good grades" now lacks almost all of its motivating force.

Aspects of the person's sense of control over the normative, institutional context also seem to affect the structure of appraisals, as well as the appraisals of particular tasks. As was reported previously, the factorial structure underlying appraisal ratings changed between the first and third waves of data collection. The anxiety-absorption factor decomposed itself into separate aspects of (negatively-toned) stress and difficulty and (more positively-valued) importance and absorption. The increasing order provided by mastery of the environment during the students' first year seems likely to have allowed and promoted this differentiation in the perception of life tasks. Similarly, as people crossing a life transition become more familiar with the new circumstances their great concern with personal control of their lives may cease to be such a central issue. Thus, we saw the fusion of the personal control and rewardingness factors of the first wave appraisal ratings in the third wave data.

An important component built into experience in an institutional setting, is the history of positive and negative feedback—either externally- or self-generated feedback—that accrues over time. In this regard, feedback that an individual interprets in "failure" terms is likely to have special impact in the development and change of life tasks. One possible reaction to failure feedback in a life task is, of course, to withdraw effort from that task. For example, the negative experiences in premedical courses of many students entering college with the goal of becoming doctors often leads to the abrupt abandonment of that life task (Grant et al., 1986). However, the observable consequences of such an abandonment of a previously important life task may be lessened by post hoc reevaluation of the appraisal of the life task to protect self-esteem. Similarly, self-esteem might be effectively enhanced by increased investment in some other aspect of an individual's life (Linville, 1985). These two processes were suggested in a small group of students in our sample (n = 16) who seemingly withdrew from and devalued their interpersonal tasks (which they had appraised as very intimidating and difficult) and committed themselves to a great degree to academic achievement concerns (Langston & Cantor, 1987).

It seems likely, in a similar but perhaps more constructive vein, that some portion of the defensive pessimist and socially constrained subjects in our sample will eventually alter their characteristic strategies because of the self-produced stress and discomfort that they engender. The stress produced by predicting the worst, and the dissatisfaction of inhibiting social action, will likely lead to either reevaluations of the tasks for which the strategies are used or (more adaptive) reevaluations of the usefulness of the strategies themselves (Cantor & Norem, 1987; Baumeister & Scher, 1987). One likely evolution of these strategies would be for the students to learn some control over their use, by restricting them to just those academic or social situations that arouse particular anxieties about self-failure or self-embarrassment.

Fortunately for all of us, not all feedback from others, or from our own self-reflections, is negative. Positive feedback also will cause change and development in life tasks. Some tasks may be well enough defined and specific enough that completion or satisfaction of the task may be easily obtained and observed. For some students in their transition to college, the task of "being on one's own" may be instantiated by something as simple as learning to do one's laundry. The task continues to demand to be addressed but, framed in that way, it is relatively easily mastered. The experience of mastering a task may also cause it to be discarded or devalued because it has become too easy, not challenging enough, or boring. Some tasks may be especially circumscribed and temporally bounded and thus become easily passed and discarded. Life tasks, such as to get through the semester, to get into a fraternity, or to have one date, are relatively closed-ended, so that once they have occurred, by definition they are over. It seems likely that such tasks are really only reflections of more complex underlying tasks that will soon sprout anew; however, the passing of such milestones may still bring satisfaction and enhance perceptions of control and efficacy (Levinson, 1978). In this sense, it is difficult to evaluate the relative importance of different life tasks; occasionally, it is nice to experience the easy accomplishment of a personal goal, even though others may not view the resulting change as noteworthy.

The other side of the coin of life task abandonment, when individuals come to recognize the infeasibility of a life-task goal, is, of course, far less rewarding. For example, among honors college students there is often (even typically) little personal experience with failure, especially in academic tasks. Therefore, the process of abandoning a task that is inappropriate may be particularly difficult for our students. A common complaint is that in high school "they were able to do everything" but that they can no longer succeed in all of their endeavors. Their inability to recognize defeat and to gracefully disengage from nonproductive commitments can be a major source of distress in the early phases of the transition to college life. Indeed, a criterion for adjustment in the social intelligence framework (Cantor & Kihlstrom, 1987) is the person's proclivity to notice and to respond to feedback that indicates the need or opportunity for such change. Responsiveness to feedback is not likely to be a generalized personal attribute, and most people are probably better able to engage in corrective self-change in domains that are somewhat peripheral to their key life task goals (Swann, 1987; Tesser & Campbell, 1983; Markus, 1977, 1983). Yet individuals do sometimes put aside the blinders of self-enhancement and self-verification motives and work to effect change in their negative self-images (Wurf, 1988) or in their especially frustrating life-task involvements, demonstrating as they do, an encouraging sign of social intelligence.

Complex Pragmatics of Life-Task Problem Solving

The contextual framing of life tasks and strategies suggests not only that individuals' problem solving efforts will likely be domain specific or temporally bounded, but also that the pragmatics underlying these efforts will be very complicated, to the extent that life tasks are open to alternative cognitive constructions, then there are multiple goals embedded in these tasks and so several different standards of evaluation must be adopted. Ill-defined tasks rarely have single, best solutions; and life tasks are typically ill-defined (Cantor & Kihlstrom, 1987, 1988). We have seen in our data from the honors project (Cantor et al., 1987), that the problems that individuals see when they give a personal reading of an age-graded task like "making friends" or "being on my own" or "getting good grades" are frequently not apparent from, or synonymous with, those encouraged by the shared normative assessments of the tasks. The personalizing of age-graded tasks makes the process of evaluating individuals' strategic solutions all the more difficult.

The case of defensive pessimists (Cantor & Norem, 1987) provides a good example of the complex pragmatics of life-task problem solving. The defensive pessimists' anxiety and negative thinking is quite out-of-line with the reality of their past performance in achievement tasks and quite perplexing to others in their social environment. This clash between the consensual reading and defensive pessimists' personal readings of the "realities" of their achievement task makes for quite different standards of evaluation of the costs-benefits of the defensive pessimists' strategic orientation in these life task situations. Why, asks the optimist, would any one with the superior record of achievement of these individuals waste their time preparing ahead of time for potential obstacles to success in a task, when the obviously best strategy is to assume the best until proven otherwise, and relax to conserve energy for the task itself? To the typical "outsider," even to a well-intentioned advocate of the pessimist, the wear and tear and emotional ups and downs of the defensive pessimist's preparatory strategy seems totally unwarranted, overly costly, and even slightly irrational and annoying (e.g., "they deserve that exhaustion and stress; they brought it on themselves, unnecessarily".

Yet, for defensive pessimists, with their particular, perhaps peculiar autobiographical frame of reference for their achievement tasks, the strategy seems essential to accomplishing their task goals. Pessimists feel the need to control their anxieties, to motivate persistence at the tasks, to "take control" before the fact; for them, these subgoals take precedence and must be met before the successful achievement end state will be reached. In a sense, their personal goals in the situation provide a rationale that makes the stress and strain of their characteristic strategy seem, at least for a while, to be justified, or at the least, an inevitable corollary to success (Cantor & Norem, 1987).

It is tremendously difficult to do a fair or balanced job of cost-benefit accounting when life-task problem solving involves personal and normative readings of tasks, with layers of goals to be met by any solution. This is true even in cases for which there is a less obvious discrepancy, than with defensive pessimists, between personal and consensual readings of individuals' readiness for a life task. For example, consider the typical reaction to a shy person's characteristic reticence in a social interaction task: The extraverted observer is annoyed, and the shy actor feels disappointed once again (Zimbardo, 1977). Such is the experience of dissatisfaction on the part of students in our sample who embraced a social constraint strategy (Langston & Cantor, 1987). However, even with this more clearly dysfunctional strategy, there was a set of personal goals of self-protection against social embarrassment being served, and, so, the cost-benefit ratio was not totally onesided. Clearly one would hope in the case of the social constraint strategy, and perhaps even for defensive pessimism, that it is a short-lived means towards a more confident and assertive end; but the necessary life span of the strategy may be somewhat protracted in light of the history behind the person's current interpretive framework. Moreover, it seems to take a significant amount of time and negative feedback before individuals start to feel the costs accruing from their life task strategies and to identify the source of negativity as personally generated and perhaps avoidable (Cantor & Norem, 1987).

Evaluating Social Intelligence:
No Simple Quotient

One is tempted, because of the complex pragmatics underlying life-task problem solving, to stand somewhat back from the specifics of a person's different tasks and strategies and instead to evaluate his or her "social intelligence" with rather global measures of well-being, health, and perceived stress. Such assessments, though appealing in their simplicity, are, in our opinion, problematic, especially when used as indirect indices of "social I.Q." (Cantor & Kihlstrom, 1987, 1988). There are several problems with letting well-being measures stand in as arbiters of life-task problem solving (or, social intelligence), and we would like to end the present discussion with a brief consideration of some of the pitfalls to which our own and others' work are prone.

The first and most obvious problem with these global measures of well-being is that they blur the boundaries of an individual's performance across different domains of life-task activity. Although it is often true that stress, dissatisfaction, and discomfort engendered in one life-task domain will overwhelm the individual's general state of well-being, it is too easy to forget the domain-specific source of the difficulty, leading to the potentially mistaken inference of generalized social I.Q. deficits. Generalized deficits seem to be the exception not the rule in social intelligence. More typically, self-efficacy varies considerably for an individual across different life task domains (Bandura, 1986; Paulhus & Martin, 1987), and individuals construct different task goals and use differentially effective strategies to meet those goals in the various domains of their goal-directed pursuits. It is thus somewhat misguided to assume, a priori, that global well-being derives from, in any meaningful or direct way, underlying social I.Q. This inferential leap becomes especially problematic with regard to issues of predictive utility and therapeutic interventions. With those objectives in mind, it is much better to work first with each salient life situation for the individual, assessing behavioral outcomes relative to the person's competence in each situation independently (Wright & Mischel, 1987), and framing interventions to undermine dysfunctional strategies that are often problematic precisely because they are overgeneralized and too rigidly applied across different task situations (Dodge & Cole, 1987).

Another, and perhaps more subtle, pitfall to evaluating life-task problem solving via measures of well-being and perceived stress and satisfaction is that such an approach constitutes a static assessment of a fundamentally dynamic or change-oriented process. By definition, life-task problem solving is a forward-looking endeavor, aimed at achieving changes in the self in important, self-definitional life contexts. Such a process is quite likely to engender stress, to be difficult to accomplish, to involve highs and lows, and to be experienced with some fair share of conflict and ambivalence at disrupting an equilibrium, even when the old state was itself dissatisfying. Even in the best of circumstances, individuals often find themselves in conflict over which important project or task or striving to pursue, and that conflict takes its toll on health and well-being (e.g., Emmons, this volume). The experience of self-concept discrepancy—feelings, however vaguely articulated, that one isn't living up to one's ideals—are psychologically disturbing and disruptive of well-being (Strauman & Higgins, 1987; Salovey & Rodin, 1985). Consequently, it is very hard to know how to characterize individuals' states of adjustment in the context of efforts at self-change.

As we noted earlier, students in our sample experienced considerable negative affect and discomfort as they worked on life tasks that constituted challenges for their self-concepts (Moore & Cantor, 1988). Those students who were highly invested in working through their independence task, in growing beyond their childhood selves, were also experiencing substantial discomfort and stress in their daily lives, as well as reporting dissatisfaction with their current lives (Zirkel & Cantor, 1988). For these students, and we suspect for most people, the process of life-task problem solving was a difficult one, and measures of global well-being reflected their struggles. An assessment of these students focusing exclusively on their current problems in living runs the risk of ignoring the potentially *constructive* nature of their efforts to navigate the transition from home and high school to independence at college and in their later lives.

We are not trying to argue strongly for the virtues of a life filled with conflict, self-doubt, and distress, a position that certainly has advocates in the psychoanalytic tradition. We have little doubt that for some of the students in our sample the distress they were experiencing in college may well signal problems that go beyond their current efforts at life-task problem solving. And, both popular wisdom and recent experimental data support the benefits for long-term health and well-being of an optimistic, relatively conflict-free, self-confident outlook on life (Taylor & Brown, 1987; Scheier & Carver, 1985). However, it is also possible that in our swing away from the conflict-ridden clinical portrait of self-growth, the field has forgotten some of the struggle and stress that may well accompany goal-directed pursuits quite naturally, especially in domains that tap into age-graded, socially-prescribed life tasks. Furthermore, unfortunately even with longitudinal methods, it is often difficult to tell whether such disturbances in well-being are temporary, or whether the person is indeed caught in a self-perpetuating and self-defeating cycle (Baumeister & Scher, 1987). Even so, it seems important to remain open to the possibility that some struggle is constructively directed at "taking control" of one's life in the service of reaching an important life-task goal.

In this regard, although we do not endorse simple, unitary, or averaged assessments of individuals' social intelligence, there do seem to be some criteria of effective, assertive problem solving that can be applied in a way that remains faithful to the complex, domain-specific nature of goals and strategies. For example, as Klinger (1975) pointed out in his powerful analysis of cycles of commitment to and disengagement from goals to which individuals are prone, investment of time, thought, and energy in goal-directed activity—even when accompanied by emotional upheaval—is a reasonable measure of constructive problem solving. One is tempted to worry about an individual's well-being when declarations of personal inadequacies and unreached self-ideals are accompanied by signs of effort withdrawal, fatigue, and immobilization (Carver & Scheier, 1985; Kuhl, 1985). In contrast, the defensive pessimist's negativity and self-doubts, occurring in the context of a highly mobilized and active problem solver, cause far less alarm, even when the stress level soars (Cantor et al., 1987). Similarly, the students in our sample who were "schematic for independence," although not experiencing satisfaction in their college life activities, appeared to be constructively engaged because of their investment in time and thought in relevant tasks (Zirkel & Cantor, 1988). Accordingly, the kinds of data that one can obtain through experience-sampling methods (Hormuth, 1986) seem invaluable aids to the assessment of social intelligence (Larsen, 1987).

In addition to assessment organized around engagement-disengagement in life task activity, an important criterion for effective problem solving is the extent of flexibility (vs. rigidity) in an individual's goals, tasks, and strategies, as evidenced both across situations and over time (Cantor & Kihlstrom, 1987, 1988; Paulhus & Martin, 1987). For example, Norem (1987) has argued that defensive pessimism becomes a very costly strategy when it is overgeneralized, such that every achievement situation evokes the same magnitude of anticipatory stress; and even some social situations that heretofore had not been construed as tapping into achievement goals come to elicit this preparatory, self-protective strategy. To the extent that defensive pessimists cannot modulate their strategic reactions, such that they react with alarm rather indiscriminantly, then the accrued costs in psychological stress are indeed likely to outweigh the gains in self-protection. Berglas & Jones (1978) made a similar point about underachievement and self-handicapping: When individuals start making self-handicapping a habitual strategic response to situations that challenge their competence image, then they come too often to sacrifice performance, ultimately establishing a self-defeating cycle (see, also, Taylor, Collins, & Skokan, 1987, on coping flexibility).

For life-task problem solving to be "intelligent" it should be highly discriminative, reflecting the individual's sensitive reading of the demands in each important life situation (Wright & Mischel, 1987). Failures to discriminate are readily apparent in psychopathology and in less extreme clinical disorders (e.g., Peterson & Seligman, 1984). Another important form of overgeneralization occurs as individuals fail to take advantage of changes in environmental demands across the lifespan (Caspi, 1987; Ryff, 1987), foisting old goals, tasks, and strategies on new life environments. The students in our study, for example, who embraced the social constraint strategy, may not have taken sufficient risks in their new college social environment, failing thus to generate a new personal history of reinforcing interpersonal interactions. In fact, one senses from the consistency with which they construed negatively their interpersonal world and shrank from assertive action in that area that they were entrapped in a self-defeating pattern that precluded future creative solutions to their pressing social life tasks (Cheek, Melchior, & Carpentieri, 1986).

To fully assess this aspect of social intelligence it is imperative that individuals' tasks and strategies be monitored both within and across the different contexts marked by major life transitions (Veroff, 1983). These shifts in life contexts are especially critical as tests of creative problem solving in social relations. It is often necessary for people to enter a new life period or setting in order to "shed" the constraints of personal reputations (e.g., Snyder & Swann, 1978), especially when those reputations inhibit attempts at self-change (Nasby & Kihlstrom, 1986). In this regard, cognitive-behavioral assessments and therapeutic interventions are aimed frequently at helping a client to take advantage of the new "freedom" and life-task opportunities accompanying changes in life circumstances. To make real progress, it is critical to see the unrealistic aspects of current goals and the negative repercussions of habitual strategies (Nasby & Kihlstrom, 1986) and to generate a new, more rewarding set of task goals and strategies in challenging life-task domains (see, Ingram & Hollon, 1986; Winfrey & Goldfried, 1986).

Summary and Conclusion

In this chapter we have shown how personality psychology's concern with individual differences and enduring regularities in behavior and social psychology's concern with social-situational and normative influences on behavior can be addressed in the life-task framework. This perspective looks for flexible intelligence in people's approaches to their enduring goals. People "work on" their self-relevant and self-defining life tasks in light of their perceptions of normative, personal, and autobiographical contexts. In the process of struggling with these life tasks, individuals use strategies that organize their behavior in *functionally* coherent ways. These life-task-strategy packages often expose individuals to a complex set of experienced outcomes, some positive, some negative, with some losses and some gains. Consequently, it seems to us that no simple comparisons on dimensions of social I.Q. will succeed in assessing the utility of any particular package, at any particular time in a person's life; this is instead a more monumental life task.

ACKNOWLEDGMENTS

We would like to thank Nancy Exelby for technical assistance and the following colleagues for comments on this work: Aaron Brower, David Buss, John Kihlstrom, Harold Korn, Hazel Markus, Ethel Moore, Paula Niedenthal, Julie Norem, Christopher Peterson, Abigail Stewart, David Winter, and Sabrina Zirkel.

The research reported in this article was supported by National Science Foundation grant (BNS 84-11778) to Nancy Cantor and Harold Korn and the University of Michigan Regent's Fellowship to Christopher A. Langston.

REFERENCES

Adler, A. (1931). *What life should mean to you.* Boston: Little, Brown & Co.
Anderson, J. R. (1981). *Cognitive psychology and its implications.* San Francisco: Freeman.
Baltes, P. B. (1986). *The aging of intelligence: On the dynamics between growth and decline.* Unpublished manuscript, Max Planck Institute, Berlin.
Baltes, P. B., Dittman-Kohli, F., & Dixon, R. A. (1984). New perspectives on the development of intelligence in adulthood: Toward a dual-process conception and a model of selective optimization with compensation. In P. B. Baltes & O. G. Brim, Jr. (Eds.), *Life-span development and behavior* (Vol. 6, pp. 33–76).
Bandura, A. (1977). Self-efficacy: Toward a unifying theory of behavioral change. *Psychological Review, 84,* 191–215.
Bandura, A. (1982). Self-efficacy mechanism in human agency. *American psychologist, 37,* 122–147.
Bandura, A. (1986). *Social Foundations of Thought and Action: A Social Cognitive Theory.* Englewood Cliffs, NJ: Prentice Hall.
Baumeister, R., & Scher, S. (in press). Self-defeating behavior patterns among normal individuals. *Psychological Bulletin.*
Berglas, S. (1985). Self-handicapping and self-handicappers: A cognitive/attributional model of interpersonal self-protective behavior. In B. Maher (Ed.), *Perspectives in personality* (Vol. 1). (pp. 235–270). Greenwich, CT: JAI Press.
Berglas, S., & Jones, E. E. (1978). Drug choice as an internationalization strategy in response to noncontingent success. *Journal of Personality and Social Psychology, 36,* 405–417.
Block, J. (1971). *Lives through time.* Berkeley, CA: Bancroft Books.
Brower, A. M. (1985). *Personality constancy and change in the transition to college life.* Unpublished dissertation, University of Michigan.
Cantor, N., & Kihlstrom, J. F. (1987). *Personality and social intelligence.* Englewood Cliffs, NJ: Prentice-Hall.

Cantor, N., & Kihlstrom, J. F. (in press). Social intelligence and cognitive assessments of personality. In R. S. Wyer & T. K. Srull (Eds.), *Advances in Social Cognition*, Vol 2. Hillsdale, NJ: Lawrence Erlbaum Associates.

Cantor, N., Markus, H., Niedenthal, P., & Nurius, P. (1986). On motivation and the self-concept. In R. M. Sorrentino & E. T. Higgins (Eds.), *Motivation and cognition: Foundations of social behavior*. New York: Guilford Press.

Cantor, N., Norem, J. K. (1987 in press). Defensive pessimism and stress and coping. *Social Cognition*.

Cantor, N., Norem, J. K., Niedenthal, P. M., Langston, C. A., & Brower, A. M., (1987). Life tasks, self-concept ideals, and cognitive strategies in a life transition. *Journal of Personality and Social Psychology, 53*(6).

Carver, C. S., & Scheier, M. F. (1985). A control-systems approach to the self-regulation of action. In J. Kuhl & J. Beckmann (Eds.), *Action control*. New York: Springer-Verlag.

Caspi, A. (1987). Personality in the life course. *Journal of Personality and Social Psychology, 53*(6), 1203–1213.

Cheek, J. M., Melchoir, L. A., & Carpentieri, A. M. (1986). Shyness and self-concept. In L. M. Hartman & K. R. Blankstein (Eds.), *Perception of self in emotional disorder and psychotherapy* (pp. 113–131). New York: Plenum.

Cohen, S., Kamarick, T., & Mermelstein, R. (1983). A global measure of perceived stress. *Journal of Health and Social Behavior, 24*, 385–396.

Csikszentmihalyi, M., & Larson, R. (1984). *Being adolescent*. New York: Basic Books.

Cutrona, C. E. (1982). Transition to college: Loneliness and the process of social adjustment. In L. A. Peplua & D. Perlman (Eds.), *Loneliness: A sourcebook of current research, theory, and therapy*. New York: Wiley.

Denney, N. (1984). A model of cognitive development across the life span. *Developmental Review, 4*, 171–191.

Dodge, K. A., & Cole, J. D. (1987). Social-information-processing factors in reactive and proactive aggression in children's peer groups. *Journal Personality and Social Psychology, 53*(6), 1146–1158.

Emmons, R. A. (1986). Personal strivings: An approach to personality and subjective well-being. *Journal of Personality and Social Psychology, 51*(5), 1058–1068.

Erikson, E. H. (1950). *Childhood and Society*. New York: Norton.

Gagne, R. M. (1984). Learning outcomes and their effects: Useful categories of human performance. *American Psychologist, 39*, 377–386.

Goldfried, M. R., Padawer, W., & Robins, C. (1984). Social anxiety and the semantic structure of heterosocial interactions. *Journal of Abnormal Psychology, 93*, 87–97.

Grant, L., Arnold, L., Blaustein, E. H., Brown, D. R., Eder, S., & Meiselas, L. (1986). Combined premedical-medical programs: Program structure and student outcomes at four universities. *Journal of Medical Education, 20*, 95–108.

Higgins, E. T., & Parsons, J. (1983). Social cognitions and the social life of the child: Stages as subcultures. In E. T. Higgins, D. N. Ruble, & W. W. Hartup (Eds.), *Social cognition and social development*. New York: Cambridge University Press.

Higgins, E. T., Klein, R., & Strauman, T. (1985). Self-concept discrepancy theory: A psychological model for distinguishing among different aspects of depression and anxiety. *Social Cognition, 3*, 51–76.

Hormuth, S. (1986). The random sampling of experiences in situ. *Journal of Personality, 54*, 262–293.

Ingram, R. E., & Hollon, S. D. (1986). Cognitive therapy of depression from an information processing perspective. In R. E. Ingram (Ed.), *Information processing approaches to clinical psychology* (pp. 259–281). New York: Academic Press.

Jones, E. E. & Berglas, S. (1978). Control of attributions about the self through self-

handicapping strategies: The appeal of alcohol and the role of underachievement. *Personality and Social Psychology Bulletin, 4,* 200–206.
Kihlstrom, J. F. (1987). The cognitive unconscious. *Science, 237,* 1445–1452.
Kihlstrom, J. R., & Cantor, N. (1984). Mental representations of the self. *Advances in Experimental Social Psychology,* (Vol. 17). New York: Academic Press.
Klinger, E. (1975). Consequences of commitment to and disengagement from incentives. *Psychological Review, 82,* 1–25.
Klinger, E. (1977). *Meaning and void: Inner experience and the incentives in people's lives.* Minneapolis: University of Minnesota Press.
Kuhl, J. (1985). From cognition to behavior: Perspectives for future research on action control. In J. Kuhl & J. Beckmann (Eds.), *Action control from cognition to behavior.* New York: Springer-Verlag.
Kuhl, J., & Beckmann, J. (Eds.). (1985). *Action Control From Cognition to Behavior.* New York: Springer-Verlag.
Langston, C. A., & Cantor, N. (1987). *Life tasks and motivation.* Paper presented at 95th Annual Convention of the American Psychological Association at New York City.
Langston, C. A., & Cantor, N. (1988). *Strategies of social constraint in social life tasks.* Unpublished manuscript, University of Michigan.
Larsen, R. J. (1987). The stability of mood variability: A spectral analytic approach to daily mood assessments. *Journal of Personality and Social Psychology, 52*(6), 1195–1204.
Levinson, D. J. (1978). *The seasons of a man's life.* New York: Balantine.
Linville, P. W. (1985). Self-complexity and affective extremity: Don't put all of your eggs in one cognitive basket. *Social Cognition, 3*(1), 94–121.
Little, B. (1983). Personal projects—A rationale and methods for investigation. *Environmental Behavirol, 15,* 273–309.
Marcia, J. E. (1980). Identity in adolescence. In Adelson, J. (Ed.), *Handbook of adolescent psychology.* New York: Wiley.
Markus, H. (1977). Self-schemata and processing information about the self. *Journal of Personality and Social Psychology, 35,* 63–78.
Markus, H. (1983). Self-knowledge: An expanded view. *Journal of Personality, 51,* 543–565.
Moore, E., & Cantor, N. (1988). *Self-concept discrepancy and motivation for life tasks.* Paper presented at the meetings of Midwestern Psychological Association. Chicago, IL.
Moos, R. H. (1974). Family environment scale (Form R). Palo Alto, CA: Consulting Psychologists Press.
Nasby, W., & Kihlstrom, J. F. (1986). Cognitive assessment of personality and psychopathology. In R. E. Ingram (Ed.), *Information-processing approaches to psychopathology and clinical psychology.* (pp. 217–239). New York: Academic Press.
Norem, J. K. (1987). *Strategic realities: Optimism and defensive pessimism.* Unpublished doctoral dissertation, University of Michigan, Ann Arbor, MI.
Norem, J. K., & Cantor, N. (1986a). Anticipatory and post hoc cushioning strategies: Optimism and defensive pessimism in "risky" situations. *Cognitive Therapy and Research, 10*(3), 347–362.
Norem, J. K., & Cantor, N. (1986b). Defensive pessimism: "Harnessing" anxiety as motivation. *Journal of Personality and Social Psychology, 51*(6), 1208–1217.
Norem, J. K., & Cantor, N. (in press). Cognitive strategies, coping and perceptions of competence. In R. J. Sternberg and J. Kolligan, Jr. (Eds.), *Perception of competence and incompetence across the lifespan.* New Haven: Yale University Press.
Paulhus, D. L., & Martin, C. L. (1987). The structure of personality capabilities. *Journal of Personality and Social Psychology, 52*(2), 354–365.
Pervin, L. A. (1976). A free-response description approach to the analysis of person-situation interaction. *Journal of Personality and Social Psychology, 34* (3), 465–474.

Pervin, L. A. (1983). The stasis and flow of behavior: Toward a theory of goals. In M. M. Page (Ed.), *Nebraska Symposium on Motivation.* (pp. 1–53). Lincoln: University of Nebraska Press.

Pervin, L. (1985). Personality: current controversies, issues, and directions. In M. Rosenzweig & L. W. Porter (Eds.), *Annual Review of Psychology* (Vol. 36) (pp. 83–114). Palo Alto, CA: Annual Reviews.

Peterson, C., & Seligman, M. (1984). Causal explanations as a risk factor for depression: Theory and evidence. *Psychological Review, 91*(3), 347–374.

Plutchik, R. (1980). A general psychoevolutionary theory of emotion. In R. Plutchik & H. Kellerman (Eds.), *Emotion: Theory research and experience* (pp. 3–33). New York: Academic Press.

Reich, J. W., & Zautra, A. J. (1983). Demands and desires in daily life: Some influences on well-being. *American Journal of Community Psychology, 1,* 41–58.

Ryff, C. D. (1987). The place of personality and social structure research in social psychology. *Journal of Personality and Social Psychology, 53*(6), 1192–1202.

Salovey, P., & Rodin, J. (1985). Cognitions about the self: Connecting feeling states and social behavior. In P. Shaver (Ed.), *Review of personality and social psychology* (Vol. 6), (pp. 143–166). Beverly Hills: Sage.

Scheier, M. F., & Carver, C. S. (1985). Optimism, coping and health: Assessment and implications of generalized outcome expectancies. *Health Psychology, 4,* 219–247.

Snyder, C. R. (1985). The excuse: An amazing grace? In B. Schlenker (Ed.), *The self and social life* (pp. 235–261). New York: McGraw-Hill.

Snyder, M., & Swann, W. B., Jr. (1978). Behavioral confirmation in social interaction: From social perception to social reality. *Journal of Personality, 50,* 149–157.

Sorrentino, R. M., & Higgins, E. T. (Eds.). (1986) *Handbook of motivation & cognition: Foundations of Social behavior.* New York: Guilford Press.

Sternberg, R. J. (1984). Toward a triarchic theory of human intelligence. *The Behavioral and Brain Sciences, 7,* 269–315.

Stewart, A. & Healy, J. Jr. (1985). Personality and adaptation to change. In R. Hogan & W. Jones, (Eds.), *Perspectives on personality: Theory, Measurement, and interpersonal dynamics* (pp. 117–144). Greenwich, CT: JAI Press.

Strauman, T. J., & Higgins, E. T. (1987). Automatic activation of self-discrepancies and emotional syndromes: When cognitive structures influence affect. *Journal of Personality and Social Psychology, 53*(6), 1004–1014.

Swann, Jr., W. B. (1987). Identity negotiation: Where two roads meet. *Journal of Personality and Social Psychology, 53*(6), 1038–1051.

Taylor, S. E., & Brown, J. (1987). Illusion and well being: *Some social psychological contributions to a theory of mental health.* Unpublished manuscript, University of California, Los Angeles, CA.

Taylor, S. E., Collins, R. L., & Skokan, L. A. (1987). *The role of illusions in coping with serious illness.* Paper presented at the meetings of the American Psychological Association, New York.

Tesser, A., & Campbell, J. (1983). Self-definition and self-evaluation maintenance. In J. Suls & A. G. Greenwald (Eds.), *Psychological perspectives on the self* (Vol. 2) (pp. 1–31). Hillsdale, NJ: Lawrence Erlbaum Associates.

Veroff, J. (1983). Contextual determinants of personality. *Personality and Social Psychology Bulletin, 9,* 331–344.

Winfrey, L. L., & Goldfried, M. R. (1986). Information processing and the human change process. In R. E. Ingram (Ed.), *Information processing approaches to clinical psychology* (pp. 241–258). New York: Academic Press.

Wright, J., & Mischel, W. (1987). A conditional approach to dispositional constructs: The local predictability of social behavior. *Journal of Personality and Social Psychology, 53*(6), 1159–1177.

Wurf, E. (1988). *The functioning of negativity in the self-concept.* Unpublished doctoral dissertation, University of Michigan.

Zimbardo, P. G. (1977). *Shyness: What it is; what to do about it.* Reading, MA: Addison-Wesley.

Zirkel, S., & Cantor, N. (1988). *Independence and identity in the transition to college life.* Unpublished manuscript, University of Michigan.

5 Energization and Goal Attractiveness

REX A. WRIGHT
University of Alabama at Birmingham

JACK W. BREHM
University of Kansas

INTRODUCTION

Much of our research in recent years has centered around a theory concerned with the determinants and consequences of the mobilization of energy (Brehm, Wright, Solomon, Silka, & Greenberg, 1983; Ford & Brehm, 1987; Wright, 1987). At the core of the theory is the proposition that there is an increase in the magnitude of goal valence to the extent that an individual is energy mobilized to carry out instrumental behavior. Thus, if someone is trying to attain an attractive outcome, he or she should find that outcome increasingly desirable the more motivationally aroused he or she is. By the same token, the subjective desire to avoid a potential aversive outcome should be greater under conditions of high energization than under conditions of low energization.

What also is proposed is that energy mobilization is determined by what the individual believes can, will, and must be done to satisfy a motive. If a motive is easily satisfied, then effort and energization should be relatively low, because very little energy is required. Similarly, if a motive is impossible to satisfy, or is too difficult to satisfy to be worth the effort it requires, there should be no intention to try and, therefore, energization should be low. In short, it is only outcomes that are perceived as difficult, possible, and worthwhile that are expected to produce significant degrees of effort and motivational arousal.

The energization model is consistent with many theories of motivation in suggesting that variables such as need, incentive value, and the expectancy of motive satisfaction once instrumental behavior has been carried out (i.e., the instrumentality of behavior, Vroom, 1964) play a role in determining the amount of energy that will be expended to attain a desired state of affairs. However, it differs from most in regard to the role these variables are expected to play. Specifically, it posits that, rather than causing motivation directly, these variables combine to determine *potential* motivation, which is defined as the maximum amount of energy that an individual would be *willing* to expend to secure an outcome were it necessary or useful to do so.

The proposed distinction between actual motivation and potential motivation can be clarified by example. Consider a person who, although he normally eats three meals a day, has because of a heavy work schedule gone without breakfast, lunch, and dinner. It is 10 o'clock in the evening, and our deprived individual knows that to obtain food, he must walk 10 blocks to get to a certain restaurant before it closes. It is plausible to assume that this individual will think of himself as very hungry and that he will be quite willing to rush to the restaurant to obtain a meal. In terms of the present formulation, both potential motivation and actual motivation (i.e., energization) should be relatively high. Because energy is high, so should be the subjective desire for food.

Now imagine a similar individual who also has gone without food all day but is in a somewhat different situation. He is in a small, isolated town in which not even a vending machine is available. This individual realizes that, unless he drives 50 miles (which he is not willing to do even in his deprived state), it will be impossible to obtain food until a local restaurant opens in the morning. In this case, potential motivation would be quite high, but because there is nothing to be done until morning, energization should be low. As a consequence, the desirability of food should be relatively small.

For a third hypothetical case, picture an individual who, like the first two people, has not eaten all day but who, in contrast to them, has only to sit down at a table and manipulate his knife and fork in order to have a fine meal. Will he be motivationally aroused? Yes, but only slightly, for this individual has very little to do to obtain food. Although potential motivation is as high as in the preceding examples, only a small amount of energy is required and consequently only a small amount should be mobilized and expended. Furthermore, as in the preceding example, the desirability of food should be relatively small.

Figure 5.1 illustrates how potential motivation and the difficulty of instrumental behavior interact to determine the degree of energization and consequent effect on goal valence. The top and middle sections of the figure show how potential motivation determines the degree of difficulty at which an individual gives up on satisfying the motive. The

5. ENERGIZATION AND GOAL ATTRACTIVENESS

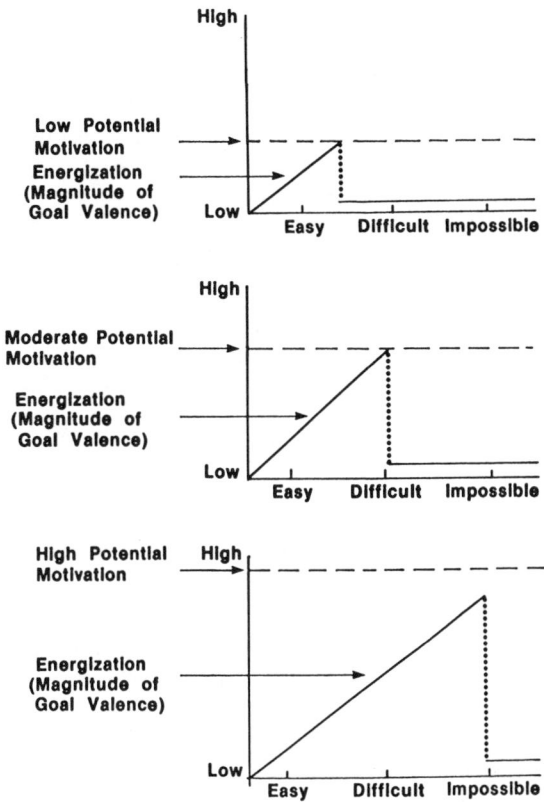

FIG. 5.1 Motivational arousal under three levels of potential motivation.

bottom section makes the additional point that where potential motivation is relatively high, giving up can be determined by the sheer impossibility of carrying out the required instrumental behavior, in which case the maximum level of energization that would be provided by potential motivation is never realized.

In summary, it is hypothesized, first, that the magnitude of goal valence increases directly with energization. Energization, in turn, is thought to vary as a function of instrumental task difficulty. Specifically, energization should increase with the perceived difficulty of motive satisfaction up to the point at which either potential motivation is reached (i.e., motive satisfaction is seen as "too difficult") or motive satisfaction is perceived as impossible. Beyond this point, effort and motivational arousal should be low. What makes an instrumental task "too difficult" is that the potential gains of performing it are outweighed by the costs of performing it. Presumably, the greater the need, the more valuable the incentive, and the greater the likelihood of motive satisfaction once an instrumental task has been carried out, the greater will be potential motivation.

Although the present theoretical argument holds that motivation is a function of what can, will, and must be done to attain an outcome, it should not be taken to imply that variables related to potential motivation will necessarily be dissociated from energization. To the contrary, a positive relationship between potential motivation and energy levels would be expected in circumstances in which (a) there is freedom with regard to the difficulty of instrumental activity that may be engaged in, and (b) potential gain increases with the difficulty of activity selected. In such circumstances, the activity chosen should be the most difficult perceived as possible and warranted in view of the possible benefits available there and at all other activity levels. Once a task or activity level has been chosen, energy should be mobilized in proportion to the perceived demands of that task or activity level.

To illustrate, imagine a production line worker who is told she must construct twenty items on her shift in order to receive a day's salary. If she constructs 20 items, she will receive the full salary; if she does not, she will receive no salary at all. Previously described reasoning from the energization model, of course, predicts that so long as this task (constructing the items) is perceived as possible and worthwhile, the worker will expend only as much energy as is required to do it. This should be true regardless of how much effort she would be willing to exert.

As a contrast, consider the woman's behavior at a different factory, where the rules are slightly different. Here, salary is directly proportional to the number of items produced: the more items constructed, the larger the salary for that day. Assuming the young woman can freely choose the manner in which she works, the present view predicts that she will work as fast and hard as she feels is justified, given her need for money, the increment in salary that an increase in effort is likely to achieve, and so forth.

A special instance of this kind of situation is where individuals do not know how much effort will be necessary to satisfy a motive. Here the potential gain or benefit that is related to effort is the likelihood of success on the instrumental task. Although it cannot be determined just how likely it is that a given amount of effort will result in success, it is reasonable to assume that higher levels of effort are more likely to result in success than are lower levels of effort. For example, individuals who concentrate very hard should be able to succeed at more levels of difficulty than those who are only mildly intent. Because the willingness to expend the energy required to attain higher probabilities of success should be proportional to the strength of the motive, it may be posited that energization in this circumstance will be a direct function of potential motivation. Put another way, individuals should tend increasingly to "hedge their bets" by preparing for higher levels of effort the greater the need, incentive value, and probability of motive satisfaction once instrumental activity is completed.

Only slightly different are circumstances in which task demands are ambiguous; that is, there is a perception of task difficulty, but confidence in that perception is not complete. In these cases, individuals are expected to estimate the probability of success associated with different amounts of effort that could be exerted and then exert the greatest amount of effort that is perceived to be warranted given considerations related to motive strength and the probability that that amount of effort will result in success on the task. Consequently, energization should be a function of potential motivation when a stronger motive justifies the effort required to attain a given probability of success and a weaker motive does not.

EMPIRICAL SUPPORT FOR THE MODEL

In this section we will review the evidence presently available for the preceding propositions. Our primary focus will be on experiments we and some of our colleagues have conducted, which were designed explicitly to evaluate implications of the energization model. In addition, however, we will discuss data from some pertinent studies that originally were not cast in the present theoretical language.

Task Difficulty and Goal Valence

Initial Studies. Because the idea of energization in proportion to perceived task demand appeared to apply most clearly to a motor task, one of the first experiments that examined the influence of task difficulty upon perceptions of goal attractiveness (Vought, 1977, Experiment 1) used a dynamometer (a device that measures grip strength). The purpose of the study was simply to see if the subjective desirability of a goal would be higher when subjects were confronted with a difficult grip than when subjects were confronted with an easy grip. Upon arriving for the session, subjects were asked to squeeze the dynamometer as hard as they could. It was then explained that the investigators were interested in the effects of "psyching up" on athletic performance. To study this, they were randomly assigning subjects a standard to meet, and then allowing some to "psych up" before making their grip. All subjects were told that they would be in the group that would have up to two minutes to "psych themselves up," and that if they succeeded in making their grip, they would receive a $1 prize. As soon as subjects indicated they understood the instructions, the standard was presented. It was either 75% or 150% of the subject's initial grip and was written on a card so that the experimenter would remain blind to condition. When subjects announced that they were ready, the experimenter interrupted and handed them a questionnaire containing a difficulty manipulation check and a question asking, "How attractive to you is the prize?"

As expected, difficulty ratings in the difficult condition were significantly higher than those in the easy condition, but well within the range of possibility. As also was expected, the subjective attractiveness of the $1 dollar prize was reliably greater in the difficult condition than in the easy condition. Thus, the results supported the prediction that where goal attainment is perceived as possible and worthwhile, goal attractiveness is a direct function of the perceived difficulty of attaining the goal.

Although these findings are consistent with the energization formulation, a clear interpretation of them is difficult for at least two reasons. First, it was found that subjects in the difficult condition took longer to prepare themselves for the squeeze (62 seconds) than did subjects in the easy condition (27 seconds). Thus, it is possible, though perhaps not plausible, that this could have accounted for the difference in the reported attractiveness of the goal. Second, it seems probable that the perceived likelihood of obtaining the prize differed between the two experimental conditions. Since at least one investigator Carlsmith (1962) has reported that the perceived value of a potential chance outcome varied with the probability of its occurrence, it may be that the attractiveness of the prize was determined by subjects' perceptions of the probability that they would receive it.

To reduce these ambiguities, a second experiment, using the basic procedure of the first, was carried out (Vought, 1977, Experiment 2). It contained three difficulty conditions, easy (50% the initial grip), difficult (120% the initial grip), and impossible (200% the initial grip), and two conditions in which attainment of the prize was determined solely by chance. In the latter cases, the probabilities of goal attainment were high (80%) and moderate (50%). To equate the amount of time that subjects took to prepare themselves in the difficulty conditions, all subjects there were required to "psych up" for 30 seconds.

Results of this study fully supported the relationships depicted in Figure 5.1 (see Table 5.1). Task difficulty ratings increased steadily from the easy to the impossible condition. However, goal attractiveness ratings were nonmonotonically related to the difficulty of the required grip, with higher ratings in the difficult condition than in either the easy or

Table 5.1
Goal Attractiveness as a Function of Task Difficulty and Chance

Difficulty		Chance	
Easy	4.00	High	5.46
Difficult	6.36	Moderate	6.00
Impossible	4.64		

Note: From Vought (1977, Experiment 2). Higher values represent higher goal attractiveness. High chance = 8 out of 10. Moderate chance = 5 out of 10.

impossible conditions. In addition, the chance determined conditions produced no difference in the rated attractiveness of the prize.

This demonstration involved a motor task, where the effect of difficulty on energization would seem most clear. However, the hypothesized relationship would be of considerably greater theoretical and empirical interest if it also applied to a cognitive task such as problem solving. Therefore, a variety of experiments involving cognitive tasks were conducted.

In one (Solomon & Silka, reported in Brehm et al., 1983), students at a junior college were recruited to take part in a testing program of math abilities. Subjects were told that they would receive a booklet of 10 math problems all of which were at the same level of difficulty. They also were told that there the booklets varied in difficulty levels, ranging from that appropriate for a high school freshman to that appropriate for someone with a Ph.D. in mathematics. Subjects were informed that the difficulty level they would receive would be determined randomly, and that if they worked 8 of the 10 problems correctly, they would receive $1. After these instructions were clear, a test booklet was assigned and subjects were told to familiarize themselves with the problems before starting work. This, of course, served to acquaint them with the difficulty of obtaining the goal. Some subjects received problems that were very easy (simple arithmetic), others received problems that were slightly difficult (simple algebra), and some received problems that were quite difficult (calculus and differential equations). After inspecting the booklet and indicating that they were ready to begin, subjects were asked to complete a questionnaire containing manipulation checks and a question asking how desirable they personally found the goal offered for solving 8 out of 10 problems.

Ratings of task difficulty, effort requirements, and likelihood of success all strongly confirmed the effectiveness of the difficulty manipulation. In addition, goal attractiveness ratings supported predictions derived from the energization theory. Specifically, the dollar was viewed as more attractive in the difficult condition than in the easy and extremely difficult conditions, which did not differ in this respect.

Another study of this type was conducted by Toi (1980). She led college students to believe they were taking part in a screening project for in-depth personality testing and evaluation. More precisely, subjects were told that the investigators were interested in the personalities of individuals with mathematical ability, and that only those who succeeded on an initial math exam would qualify to participate in the study proper, which was to take place some time later. As in the Solomon and Silka experiment, the problems that were assigned were designed to appear easy, difficult, and impossible. Subjects were given a brief period to inspect the test, and asked to indicate when they were ready to begin. Once they did, the experimenter administered a brief "departmental survey questionnaire" which, in addition to filler items, contained manipulation checks and a question asking, "If the present study is a project that continues, how interested are you in participating in it?"

Estimates of task difficulty again indicated that the experimental manipulation was successful. Furthermore, for men, interest ratings were in the expected nonmonotonic pattern, although the easy difficult comparison was reliable only at the 10% level of confidence. For women, on the other hand, interest ratings were relatively low in all of the difficulty conditions. Although an explanation for the latter result is not certain, one possibility is that women in the moderately difficult condition gave up. Whereas men in that condition indicated that it was fairly likely that they would be able to solve the problems, women in that condition reported that they probably could not.

Still another study of this genera (Wright, Toi, & Brehm, 1984) was designed to extend the energization model into the area of interpersonal attraction. Male subjects were told that they could qualify for a "learning session" in which they would be accompanied by a moderately attractive female student (a picture was provided) by performing well enough on a preliminary memorization task (memorizing nonsense trigrams). In some cases the preliminary task was intended to be easy (two trigrams), in others it was intended to be moderately difficult (five trigrams), and in still others it was intended to be very difficult (eight trigrams), though possible. Predictions were that the female assistant would be viewed as most desirable in the moderately difficult condition because the goal of being with her would be seen as worth the effort of the two and five trigram tasks, but not the effort required by the eight trigram task.

Results accorded with these expectations. Task difficulty ratings increased from the easy to the very difficult condition, and, even at their highest, were well within the range of possibility. Of greater theoretical interest, ratings of the target's sexiness, cuteness, and overall attractiveness were higher for subjects assigned the five-trigram task than for subjects assigned the two- and eight-trigram tasks.

A final experiment (Solomon & Greenberg, reported in Brehm et al., 1983) attempted to evaluate a dissonance interpretation of previous goal attractiveness effects. In this regard, it should be noted that in the aforementioned studies, choice and commitment were intentionally minimized to prevent the arousal of dissonance (see Wicklund & Brehm, 1976). Furthermore, subjects in the difficult conditions of most were unsure about whether they would succeed and therefore attain the goal, which should have prevented dissonance reduction through enhancing the value of the goal (Jecker, 1964). Still, it could be argued that choice was implicit and that subjective probability estimates were different from those reported on questionnaires. Therefore, an experiment was needed to address specifically this alternative interpretation.

The strategy was to have subjects evaluate an incentive immediately before they began working on easy or difficult math problems, or a few minutes after completing work (but before performance feedback was provided). It was reasoned that, if dissonance were operating, then differences in goal attractiveness as a function of task difficulty should be found after work as well as before. If the effects were due to energization, on the other hand, goal attractiveness ratings should be higher in the difficult condition only when measures were taken in immediate anticipation of task performance. After the task was completed, energy should return to baseline levels, and attractiveness values should be equivalent. Results supported the energization interpretation. The goal ($1) was rated more desirable in the difficult/immediate anticipation condition than in all other conditions, in which ratings did not differ.

In summary, the initial studies that examined goal attractiveness as a function of instrumental task difficulty presented a pattern of results that was highly congruent with theoretical expectations. To be specific, they provided evidence that, at least in the context of an appetitive paradigm, appraisals of a potential outcome are most exaggerated when imminent instrumental activity can be characterized as difficult, but possible and worthwhile. Vought's second experiment and the experiment by Solomon and Greenberg have special significance for rendering untenable dissonance and probability-of-success alternative explanations of the goal valence effects.

First Experiments Employing Avoidance Paradigms. Having garnered the initial support for the energization model, a next logical step was to examine its implications in an avoidance context. Just as moderate increases in perceived instrumental task difficulty are expected to enhance the subjective desirability of potential positive outcomes, so are they also expected to enhance the subjective aversiveness of potential negative outcomes. Unpleasant outcomes that are perceived as either "too difficult" or impossible to avoid (or escape or minimize), of course, should produce low energization and be appraised as relatively innocuous.

In the first attempt (Wright's first experiment, reported in Brehm et al., 1983), subjects were told that they would be assigned to one of two "learning groups" on the basis of their performance on a preliminary memory test. If they succeeded on this test, they would be assigned to a harmless recitation learning group. If they failed, on the other hand, they would be assigned to a punishment learning group, where participants received shock every time they responded incorrectly. The task was to memorize two, four, or six nonsense trigrams within a 2-minute period, or 20 trigrams in 15 seconds. Once the instructions were clear, subjects completed two questionnaires, one for the investigators, and one ostensibly a departmental form. The first questionnaire included mood items and manipulation checks. The departmental form included filler items intended to strengthen the cover story, and a question asking, "(People respond differently.) If you receive a shock in this experiment, how unpleasant do you personally expect it to be?"

Before presenting the results, we should point out that this study really had two purposes. Besides demonstrating energization effects in an avoidance setting, there was an aim to provide further evidence that differences in perceived task difficulty are sufficient to produce changes in the magnitude of goal valence. To do so, it was necessary to manipulate task difficulty without varying perceived probability of success. Although not easily accomplished, this should be possible since, conceptually, as perceived difficulty rises from zero there will be no change in perceive likelihood of success until individuals begin to doubt that they have the ability and/or energy to overcome the difficulty of a task. It was believed originally that this was most likely to be demonstrated in the four-trigram condition, where subjects were expected to have higher task difficulty ratings, but not lower likelihood ratings, than were subjects in the two-trigram condition.

As anticipated, there was an increase in perceived task difficulty from the two-trigram condition to the four-trigram ($P<.08$) and six-trigram ($P<.01$) conditions, and from these conditions to the 20-trigram condition ($P<.005$). Likelihood of success, on the other hand, did not vary across conditions except in the 20-trigram condition, where ratings were significantly lower than in the other conditions ($P<.01$). Likelihood means in the two-trigram, four-trigram, six-trigram, and 20-trigram conditions were 6.5, 6.0, 5.3, and 3.0, respectively (11-point scales with end points of 0 and 10). As also was predicted, shock unpleasantness ratings tended to be higher in the four- and six-trigram conditions than

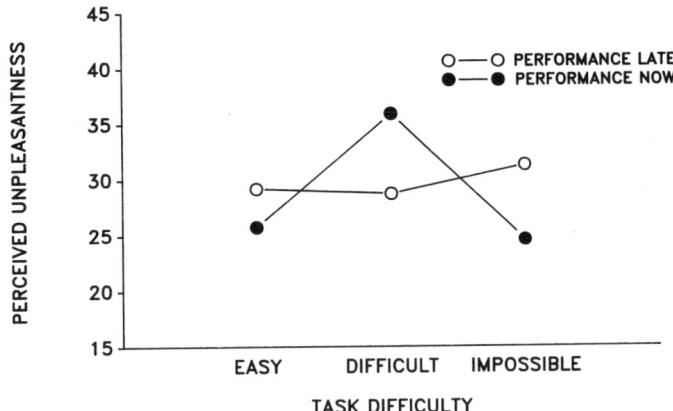

FIG. 5.2 Unpleasantness ratings as a function of task difficulty under conditions where subjects were to perform the task immediately or approximately 30 minutes later. (From Brehm et al., 1983)

in the two- and 20-trigram conditions, although only the two-/four-trigram and two-/six-trigram comparisons proved to be statistically reliable.

This study was followed by a similar experiment in which the four-trigram condition was dropped, and a timing manipulation was added (Wright's second experiment, reported in Brehm et al., 1983). As before, subjects expected to be able to avoid an aversive shock session by performing the two-trigram, six-trigram, or 20-trigram task. For half of the subjects, however, instructions stated that the period of memorization would take place approximately 30 minutes later, after an interval in which they would simply inspect art prints. For the rest, the memorization period was to take place immediately, and be followed by the art print task.

On the assumption that differences in energization should occur only when instrumental task performance is imminent, it was predicted that enhanced negative appraisals in the six-trigram condition relative to the two-trigram and 20-trigram conditions would be found only when the task was to be performed right away. This prediction was strongly supported by the results. As seen in Figure 5.2, the potential shock was rated significantly more aversive by subjects expecting to perform the six-trigram task immediately than by subjects expecting to perform the two-trigram task immediately or the 20-trigram task immediately. Unpleasantness ratings for subjects expecting to perform the tasks later, on the other hand, were moderate and did not differ as a function of task difficulty.

In a third experiment (Wright & Brehm, 1984), male subjects first listened to an unpleasant noise over headphones and then were led to believe they could avoid a second presentation of it by making a dynamometer grip that was easy (i.e., "just move the indicator needle"), moderately difficult (i.e., "squeeze your (previous) maximum squeeze level plus 5 on the dial"), or impossible (i.e., "squeeze twice your initial maximum effort"). As expected, unpleasantness ratings taken immediately before task performance were higher in the difficult grip condition than in the easy grip condition ($P<.08$). However, when the grip was impossible, ratings were no different than when the grip was difficult.

Although the unpleasantness results in the impossible condition of this study were not anticipated and may be viewed as contrary to the energization hypothesis, an explanation in terms of methodology is possible. As accounted in the research report, many subjects in this condition stated after the session was over that they were prepared to forcibly remove the headphones if the noise was loud enough. If anticipatory energization took place for this reason, then the unpleasantness ratings would make sense theoretically (i.e., goal valence should be high where energization is high). This interpretation is supported by a recent unpublished study that showed expected appraisal effects in an impossible condition where this extra-experimental means of escape was not available (Wright, Brehm, Solomon, Silka, & Crutcher, 1988).

To summarize, the first avoidance studies generally concurred with the appetitive studies in indicating a higher magnitude of goal valence under difficult but possible and worthwhile task conditions than under easy and impossible task conditions. This was demonstrated using both cognitive and motor tasks, and an aversive event subjects had (the noise studies) and had not (the shock studies) actually experienced.

Task Difficulty and Energization

In all of the experiments described thus far, it was assumed that there was anticipatory energization during the interval just before task performance. Although this assumption seems reasonable, it obviously needs to be verified because of its central place in our theorizing.

Studies of Physiologic Reactivity. We began a search for such verification with a literature review. In particular, we were interested in studies involving cardiovascular measures because the function of the cardiovascular system seems most logically related to the general process of energization with which the theory is concerned (see Cacioppo & Petty,

1982; Hassett, 1978; Surwit, Williams, & Shapiro, 1982). Fortunately, some relevant data already were available. For example, in an experiment by Elliott (1969, Experiment 2), subjects' heart rates (HR) were monitored while they performed an easy, moderately difficult, or extremely difficult tone discrimination task for money. As might be expected, there was a steady increase in HR across trials when the tones were moderately difficult to discriminate, but a decrease across trials when the tones were easy or extremely difficult to discriminate.

Complementary effects were observed by Obrist et al. (1978), who studied cardiovascular responses of subjects who believed they could avoid electric shock by responding quickly enough on a reaction time task. As the study progressed, it became clear that the required standard was easy to attain, moderately difficult to attain, or extremely difficult (actually impossible) to attain. Again, as would be predicted, elevations in HR, systolic blood pressure (SBP) and dP/dt (a measure of myocardial force) across trials were higher in the moderately difficult condition than in the easy and extremely difficult conditions, in which cardiovascular responses did not differ.

These and other experiments (reviewed by Wright, 1987) provide evidence that our initial presumptions were correct. Nevertheless, because they all sampled physiological responses during, instead of immediately before, task performance, they leave some question as to whether the goal valence effects can be attributed to group differences in *anticipatory* arousal. Consequently, a series of investigations were carried out to address this issue directly.

The earliest investigation was conducted by Tom Pysczcynski (reported in Brehm, Vought, & Pysczcynski, 1980). Subjects were met individually and told that the study concerned the physiology of behavior. Presumably, the experimental task was to try to make a number of different dynamometer grips while certain physiological responses were being monitored. There was a practice period, during which preliminary grips were taken, and then a brief rest period so that baseline measures could be obtained. After the baseline period, subjects were to turn over a card indicating the grip they were to try to reach on the first trial, which was to begin in approximately 30 seconds. As in the goal valence studies, the grip assigned was easy (a very low number on the dial), difficult ("squeeze as hard as you can"), or impossible ("squeeze to the top of the scale").

The experimental hypotheses were only partially supported by the results. On the one hand, HR elevations above baseline during the 30-second preperformance interval were greater in the difficult grip condition than in the easy grip condition, and there tended to be greater digital vasoconstriction during the preparatory period when the grip was difficult than when the grip was easy ($P<.10$). On the other, anticipatory cardiovascular effects in the impossible grip condition were no different than those in the difficult condition.

One explanation for the results in the impossible condition is that the instructions were confusing and may have been interpreted to mean essentially the same thing as those in the difficult condition. In short, even though they could not make the assigned level, subjects in the impossible condition could at least make their best grip. Since the purported reason for conducting the research was to study physiology, it may have been assumed that the researchers would glean something from the data even if the assigned grip level was not attained.

A subsequent experiment (Wright, 1984) dealt with this problem by limiting behavioral options available to certain subjects. As in some other studies, subjects were threatened with the possibility of participating in an aversive learning session that would involve electric shock. Two thirds were told they could avoid the session by performing a motor exercise; for half of these the exercise turned out to be easy (to flip a toggle switch), whereas for the rest it turned out to be difficult (to make a strenuous dynamometer grip). The remaining subjects were told that they had been randomly assigned to a group that would not have the opportunity to avoid the session at all. Congruent with expectations, immediately before the task was to be performed, subjects in the difficult avoidance condition manifested a larger increase in HR and greater digital vasoconstriction than subjects in the easy avoidance and impossible avoidance conditions. In addition, anticipatory appraisals of how aversive it would be to receive shock tended to follow cardiovascular response levels (i.e., they were most negative when the grip was difficult).

Similar findings were obtained recently in a study in which subjects believed either that they could avoid a loud noise by performing an easy (one-trigram) or difficult (seven-trigram) memory task, or that they would not be able to avoid the noise (Wright, Brehm, & Bushman, in press). Once again, measures of HR and SBP indicated greater anticipatory cardiovascular arousal when avoidance was expected to be difficult relative to when it was expected to be easy or impossible. Elevations in diastolic blood pressure (DBP) tended to be greater in the difficult avoidance condition than in the impossible avoidance condition, but not the easy avoidance condition.

Contrada, Wright, and Glass (1984) examined the effects of the difficulty of a cognitive task on cardiovascular reactivity and the subjective desirability of a positive goal. Physiologic and subjective measures were taken just before subjects attempted to solve at least 8 out of 10 mental arithmetic problems within five minutes, with the opportunity to receive $3 if they succeeded. For half, the problems were the same as those used in the easy condition of the Solomon and Silka study, described previously. For the rest, the problems were those used in the difficult condition of that study. As expected, subjects waiting to perform the more difficult problems evinced greater SBP change above baseline than subjects waiting to perform the easier problems. Unexpectedly, however, there was no difference between these groups in ratings of how attractive the money was.

Two possible explanations were offered for the discrepancy between the cardiovascular and goal attractiveness data. First, although difficulty ratings indicated that subjects in the difficult condition viewed their problems as harder than did subjects in the easy condition, in absolute terms ratings in the difficult condition were not very high. Thus, it is conceivable that the difficulty manipulation was too weak with this (university instead of junior college) population to have subjective motivational effects. This would, of course, require the extra-theoretical assumption that SBP responses are more sensitive to manipulations of task difficulty than are perceptions of goal valence. Second, it could be that subjects were distracted from attending to the goal by the various physiologic recording instruments that were used (e.g., inflating blood pressure cuff). This makes sense theoretically if one assumes that energization can impact on goal appraisals only to the extent that attention is directed toward those outcomes. It also would be congruent with the positive goal valence results obtained by Wright (1984) because the negative incentive in that study (shock) would be expected to command greater attention than the $3 prize offered in this experiment.

As a follow-up, Wright, Contrada, and Patane (1986) conducted an experiment that employed a stronger difficulty manipulation and implemented procedures designed to maintain goal salience throughout the procedure. Subjects were told that a certain number of nonsense trigrams would be projected onto a screen, and that they would receive a pen (on display) if they memorized those trigrams within minutes. Some subjects learned later that two trigrams would be projected, others learned that six trigrams would be projected, and others learned that 20 trigrams would be projected. To strengthen the difficulty manipulation, experimental materials described the two-trigram task as very easy, the six-trigram task as very difficult but possible for most people, and the 20-trigram task as impossible for most people. After instructions were clear, lights in the room were lowered. However, to enhance the salience of the goal, a small lamp remained trained on the pens that were displayed. After a 30-second anticipation period, during which cardiovascular measures were obtained, there was an interruption and administration of the usual questionnaire.

Table 5.2
Perceived Task Difficulty, Anticipatory Systolic Blood Pressure
Responsiveness, and Perceived Goal Attractiveness

Experimental Groups	Task Difficulty	Systolic Change	Goal Attractiveness
Easy	0.87	+ 6.50	3.91
Moderately Difficult	5.91	+ 10.40	4.86
Extremely Difficult	8.00	+ 4.50	3.00

Note: Adapted from Wright, Contrada, and Patane (1986).

Table 5.2 presents the main results of this study. As is apparent, the revised procedure produced a powerful manipulation of perceived task difficulty and the predicted nonmonotonic pattern of anticipatory SBP responsiveness. In addition, the predicted correspondence between SBP change and goal attractiveness ratings was observed (both quadratic effects reliable at $P<.05$).

Although our research has been almost exclusive in its focus on cardiovascular measures, it should be clear that these are not the only response parameters that might be used to index energization. Indeed, some other responses may be more clearly indicative of energy mobilization. In this regard, it is interesting to note that Frankenhaeuser and her associates (Frankenhaeuser & Johansson, 1976; Frankenhaeuser & Lundberg, 1977) have reported data that show a correspondence between task demand and levels of urinary adrenaline. Also interesting, but less obviously related, are studies by Kahneman (1973) and his colleagues, which appear to indicate a direct relationship between pupillary dilation and the intention to try on a cognitive task.

Behavioral Studies. A very different approach to this issue is seen in recent studies that have examined behavior under conditions where motivational arousal was expected to be high or low. Hill, Fultz, and Biner (1985), for example, led subjects to believe an upcoming anagram task would be easy, difficult, or impossible, and then, just before the task was to begin, assessed performance on an incidental learning task that involved familiar and unfamiliar stimuli (names). Based on the well-known Yerkes-Dodson principle (Yerkes & Dodson, 1908), it was predicted that confronting a difficult task (relatively high motivation), as compared to an easy or impossible task (low motivation), would enhance the recall of familiar names (a simple task) and inhibited the recall of unfamiliar names (a complex task). Consistent with this prediction, the most familiar names and the fewest unfamiliar names were recalled in the difficult condition.

Similar reasoning was the basis of a study by Ford, Wright, and Haythornthwaite (1985). By combining (a) the hypothesis that there is a monotonic relationship between energization and the magnitude of goal valence, with (b) the Yerkes-Dodson law, which states there is a curvilinear relationship between motivation and performance, these investigators derived the hypothesis that (c) a curvilinear relation might be found between goal valence and performance. In accordance with this, they found that individuals who rated a performance incentive moderately attractive performed better on a moderately difficult anagram task than did subjects who rated the incentive unattractive and extremely attractive.

A final experiment (Esqueda, 1985) took a somewhat different tack. Rather than measuring performance quality, it assessed the speed and strength of several noninstrumental behaviors. Specifically, subjects were confronted with an easy, difficult, or impossible memorization task, and then required at different points to (a) write down their student identification number, (b) indicate orally that they were "ready," and (c) press a button to indicate they were ready. Records were made of how long it took to write down the identification number, how loud the verbal response was, and how long the indicator button was pressed. Unexpectedly, the results for voice loudness were complicated by experimenter effects. However, as predicted, subjects wrote quicker and held the button down longer in the difficult condition than in the easy and impossible conditions.

Summary. Together, the studies presented in this subsection comprise a reasonably compelling body of evidence that energization varies with task difficulty in the expected manner, both immediately before and during task performance. It is especially noteworthy that positive effects have been obtained consistently using different tasks, goals, and measures of energization, given that the early goal valence experiments were so diverse.

Interaction of Task Difficulty and Potential Motivation

An obvious implication of the energization model is that instrumental task difficulty should interact with potential motivation to determine energization and the magnitude of goal valence. That is, whether or not a given activity is perceived as "too difficult" should depend on the level of potential motivation. If potential motivation is high enough, it is expected that a difficult task will be viewed as worthwhile, and consequently that energization and the magnitude of goal valence will be relatively high. On the other hand, if potential motivation is sufficiently low, it is expected that the same task will be seen as too difficult and that energization and the magnitude of goal valence will be low.

This point is illustrated nicely in a recent experiment by Biner (1987), which manipulated potential motivation by varying the value of an incentive offered for good performance. Subjects were presented with three, eight, or 45 nonsense trigrams and told that they could earn either a modest incentive ($1) or a relatively valuable incentive (a record album) by succeeding on it. It was anticipated that the record would be perceived as worth an attempt at all of the tasks, whereas the dollar would be perceived as worth an attempt at the three- and eight-trigram tasks only. Accordingly, predictions were that goal attractiveness ratings taken immediately before the task performance period would increase steadily with task difficulty when the goal was the record, but be nonmonotonically related to task difficulty (i.e., highest in the eight-trigram condition) when the goal was the dollar. Findings were largely congruent with these expectations. For subjects offered the record, attractiveness ratings increased from the two-trigram condition to the eight-trigram condition, and then remained high in the 45-trigram condition. For subjects offered the dollar, on the other hand, attractiveness ratings increased from the three-trigram condition to the six-trigram condition, but then decreased in the 45-trigram condition.[1]

Other studies have manipulated potential motivation by varying the likelihood of motive satisfaction after instrumental activity was completed. In one study (Wright, Kelley, & Bramwell, in press), subjects expected to perform an easy (two-trigram) or moderately difficult (five-trigram) memory task with the opportunity to earn either a very high (14/15) or very low (1/15) chance of leaving the experiment early, and thereby avoiding an aversive reading task. Specifically, subjects were told that, if they succeeded, the experimenter would allow them to choose from a deck of cards numbered from 1 to 15. In the low likelihood conditions, subjects could leave early if they chose the 15; in the high likelihood conditions, subjects could leave early if they chose anything *but* the 15. As predicted, it was found that ratings of how unpleasant the aversive reading task would be increased with task difficulty only when success insured a high probability of avoidance. When the probability of

---

[1]It was necessary to use an exceptionally large number of trigrams in the very difficult condition of this experiment because pretesting showed that subjects were reluctant to give up even when the incentive was trivial.

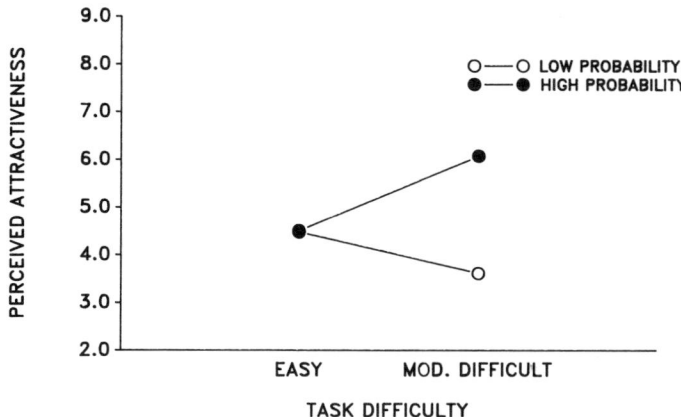

FIG. 5.3 Adapted from Wright & Gregorich (1988). Goal attractiveness ratings as a function of task difficulty under high and low likelihood conditions.

avoidance (given success) was low, unpleasantness ratings were relatively low in both memory task conditions.

A later experiment (Wright & Gregorich, 1988) used the same procedure but a different incentive. Subjects were given the opportunity to earn a very high (14/15) or very low (1/15) chance of obtaining a moderately attractive goal (a spiral notebook) by memorizing two or five nonsense trigrams in 2 minutes. Again, as predicted, positive evaluations of the goal increased with the difficulty of obtaining it in the high likelihood conditions but were relatively low regardless of task difficulty in the low likelihood conditions (Figure 5.3).

A final investigation of this type (Wright & Gregorich, in press) was conducted to examine further the assumption that effects above were due to group differences in energy mobilization. In terms of procedure, it was virtually identical to the study by Wright and Gregorich (1988). However, in addition to taking subjective measures, the researchers obtained samples of HR, SBP, and DBP during the interval immediately preceding the performance period.

Elevations on all of the cardiovascular measures tended to be greatest in the difficult/high likelihood condition; therefore, an energization interpretation of the previous goal valence effects was supported. Effects were most clearcut in the case of SBP. As seen in Figure 5.4, when the probability of goal attainment (given success) was high, anticipatory SBP reactivity was greater in the difficult condition than in the easy condition. On the other hand, when the probability of goal attainment (given success) was low, anticipatory SBP reactivity was relatively

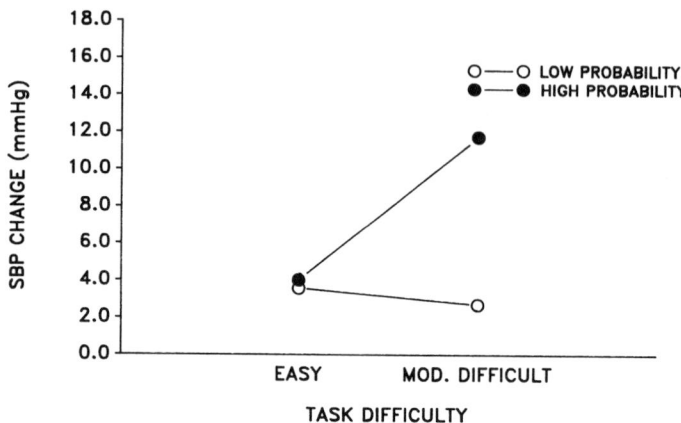

FIG. 5.4 Systolic blood pressure change as a function of task difficulty under high and low likelihood conditions. (Adapted from Wright & Gregorich, in press)

low in both task conditions. Despite the positive cardiovascular results, this study produced no group differences in goal attractiveness, perhaps because of distraction.

In addition to these experiments, which were intended to test this implication of the theory, there are a number of other investigations that provide relevant data. For example, Manuck, Harvey, Lechleiter, and Neal (1978) had subjects solve a series of easy or difficult concept formation problems, telling half that success would prevent a "noise shock" from occurring after certain trials and the rest that the noise shock would occur periodically regardless of how well they performed. It was found that, during task performance, SBP was greatest when the concept task was difficult and aversive stimulation was contigent on performance quality. When the task was easy and when stimulation was not related to performance, systolic elevations were uniformly low. These findings, of course, may be interpreted as indicating that the effort required by the difficult task was perceived as worthwhile only when it reduced the likelihood of noise (i.e., when potential motivation was relatively high).

Similar contingency effects have been reported by Contrada et al. (1982), Houston (1972), and Johnson (1963). In the study by Contrada et al., elevations in SBP and DBP were greater among subjects who could avoid noise and shock by performing well on a difficult reaction time task than among subjects whose performance on the task was unrelated to presentation of the aversive stimulus. Houston and Johnson observed higher HRs in subjects who could avoid shock by performing a difficult digit-recall task and tone discrimination task, respectively, than in subjects who performed the tasks but could not avoid the shock.

To our knowlege, only one study of this type produced different results. In it (Solomon, Holmes & McCaul, 1980), subjects performing a difficult digit-recall task manifested greater digital vasoconstriction than subjects performing an easy digit-recall task, regardless of whether performance was supposed to be related to the presentation of an electric shock. A possible explanation for this is that motives unrelated to the contingency manipulation (e.g., impression management) affected subjects' decisions of how hard to try. If so, the more difficult task may have appeared worthwhile even when it did not influence the likelihood of shock. Of course, it is not at all clear why such motives would have been operating in this study and not in the others; therefore, the reasoning must be considered speculative.

By way of summary, a variety of studies provide support for the prediction that energization and the magnitude of goal valence will depend not only on the difficulty of an instrumental task, but also on the level of potential motivation. Those we and our colleagues have conducted have been concerned chiefly with goal appraisals and produced positive findings in both appetitive and avoidant contexts. The single investigation that included measures of physiologic responsivity yielded anticipatory cardiovascular results that accorded with the goal valence data. Other studies, although they were not designed with this theoretical model in mind, obtained a pattern of cardiovascular responsivity that is highly consistent with the present formulation. Only one experiment (Solomon et al., 1980). produced unexpected effects, and it may be interpretable in terms of the model.

Potential Motivation and Energization

It is commonly believed that motivational arousal increases directly with need and the value of available incentives (e.g., Cofer & Appley, 1964; Weiner, 1972). For example, an individual who has not eaten recently might be expected to be more motivationally aroused in the presence of food than an individual who had lunch an hour earlier. By the same token, individuals should be more energy mobilized in the presence of a delectable dish than in the presence of food that is barely edible. The energization theory, on the other hand, views need and incentive value as determinants of potential motivation and predicts that they will be associated with energy levels only when instrumental activity is needed, and there is a relationship between possible gain and amount of effort expended.

At first glance, there would appear to be abundant evidence for the former point of view. For instance, a number of experiments show greater physiologic responsivity in subjects performing under high threat conditions than in subjects performing under low threat conditions (e.g., Houston, 1972; Solomon et al., 1980). Similarly, recent studies by Elliott (1969) and Fowles and his colleagues (Fowles, Fisher, & Tranel, 1982; Tranel, Fisher, & Fowles, 1982) indicate a direct correspondence between HR and monetary incentives offered for good performance. Regarding the effect of need, classic investigations by Belanger and Feldman (1962) and Hahn, Stern, and McDonald (1962) show a positive relationship between HR in animals bar pressing for water and number of hours of liquid deprivation.

Although experiments such as these often are cited as documenting conventional wisdom, they can be interpreted plausibly in terms of the energization theory. That is, in the studies involving humans, the experimental tasks usually were unfamiliar and demanding (digit recall, color-word conflict, difficult reaction time, motor coordination). Further, subjects rarely were given the opportunity to practice. As a result, task demands may have been unclear, in which case, as explained earlier, a correspondence between motivational arousal and potential motivation might well be expected. In the animal studies, the situation depicted also would appear to be one in which there is freedom to exert more or less effort and a correspondence between the effort exerted and potential gain. That is, the animals could bar press at any speed, and the faster they pressed (i.e., the harder they worked) the faster they would obtain water. Because the tendency to exert effort under these conditions should increase directly with deprivation, so should energy levels during task performance.

These interpretations, of course, are post hoc, and therefore only speculative. However, additional data lend credence to them. With respect to the first interpretation, we would point to an experiment by Elliott (1965) in which subjects performed a reaction time task for one of three amounts of money over a series of 10 experimental sessions. During the early sessions (sessions 1 through 4), when task requirements probably were vague, findings were similar to those cited above: HR increases were directly proportional to the monetary incentive. During the later sessions (sessions 7 through 10), on the other hand, when task demands should have been clearer, HR was unrelated to incentive value.

With regard to the second interpretation (i.e., of the animal studies), it is noteworthy that both Belanger and Feldman (1962) and Hahn et al. (1962) measured the frequency of bar pressing and found that response frequency increased with deprivation up to a point (around 48 hours) and then decreased. The first portion of these data obviously accords

5. ENERGIZATION AND GOAL ATTRACTIVENESS   **191**

with our explanation of the HR effects. Although decreased responding at very high levels of deprivation would seem contradictory at first, a careful analysis suggests that it may not be. In discussing these results, Hahn et al. (1962) point out that when animals are deprived of water for a long time, they may have to exert more effort to execute a relatively few bar presses than less deprived animals do to execute many bar presses. Thus, HRs in the highest deprivation conditions may indicate great, but relatively ineffective, effort. In support of this are additional data indicating significant weight loss in animals who were deprived of water for 72 or more hours.

The only studies we know of that provide direct tests of our reasoning concerning the conditions under which energy levels will and will not be associated with variables that determine potential motivation are presented below. They all address the question of how people respond motivationally when there is a call for action, but instrumental task demands are not known. As will be recalled, the present formulation predicts that energization in this circumstance will be a direct function of potential motivation. Put simply, people should be prepared to expend the maximum energy they are willing to, given the significance of success. The first of these studies was carried out by Bruce Roberson (1985, Experiment 1).

Male college students served as subjects. They were informed that the investigation was concerned with three issues: women's ability to choose partners with whom they can work effectively, the importance of being able to choose a partner, and first impressions. In the experimental session, the subject, a female student, and another male student were to describe themselves over an intercom, and then the female would choose which man she wanted to work with on a creativity task. Presumably, the man who was not selected would work later on a card-sorting task in a study of perception. Thus, making a better impression was a task instrumental to being with the woman and to avoiding the card-sorting task. Presentations by the woman and other man actually had been prerecorded on tape.

There were four experimental conditions. In one (easy), the competing man gave a very poor performance, so that subjects should have perceived it as relatively easy to make a better impression and thereby be chosen by the woman and avoid the card-sorting task. In another (difficult), the competing man gave a credible presentation, expressing interests and abilities that might be considered typical of college men. As a consequence, making a better impression should have seemed harder, but possible. In a third condition (impossible), subjects were told that the woman had been randomly assigned to work with the other man, and, therefore, there was nothing they could do to be chosen. Finally, in a

Table 5.3
Ratings of the Female Target and the Card-Sorting Task

Experimental Conditions	Female is Nice	Like to Work With Female	Like to Work on Card-Sorting Task
Easy	6.43	2.00	−1.07
Difficult	7.64	2.29	−1.36
Impossible	6.50	1.36	0.00
No Information	7.92	2.93	−2.00

Note: From Roberson (1985, Experiment 1). Higher values indicate greater niceness and liking.

fourth condition (no information), subjects were not allowed to hear the presentation of the other man, so they could not determine how much effort would be required to make a better presentation. When the instructions were clear, and the presentation period was about to begin (except in the impossible condition), the usual anticipation period questionnaire was administered.

The means presented in Table 5.3 show that the theoretical predictions received strong support. As would be expected, subjects in the difficult condition rated the woman as nicer and wanted more to work with her than did subjects in the easy and impossible conditions. More important for the present concern, ratings for both measures were highest in the no information condition. Subjects' ratings of how much they would like to work on the card-sorting tasks also are presented, and, as can be seen, they show the expected avoidance effect. When avoidance was difficult, liking ratings were *lower* (i.e., subjective aversiveness was higher) than when avoidance was easy and impossible. Further, when the difficulty of avoidance was unknown, liking ratings were lowest of all conditions.

In a follow-up study, Roberson (1985, Experiment 2) crossed an abbreviated task information factor (easy, no information) with a manipulation of potential motivation. For half of the subjects (high potential motivation), the recording presented a female target who was friendly and enthusiastic about college; for the rest (low potential motivation), the recording presented a woman speaking monotonously and negatively about college.

Before presenting the results, let us review carefully what the theoretical predictions would be. First, when the instrumental task was to be easy, energization should have been relatively low regardless of potential motivation. Consequently, the subjective desire to be with the female target and avoid the card-sorting task would be expected to be relatively low in both the easy/high potential motivation condition and the easy/low potential motivation condition. Of course, since appraisals of how nice the target is should be based, at least in part, on the objective information, a difference on that measure between the high and low potential motivation conditions would not be suprising. Second, because energization should attain the peak of potential motivation when task demands are not known, motivational arousal in the no information conditions should have been higher than that in the easy conditions, and proportional to the level of potential motivation. Thus, measures of subjective desire should have been greater when demands were unknown than when they were known (easy), and greatest in the high potential motivation/no information condition.

The support for these predictions was, in fact, limited at best. Ratings did indicate that subjects thought the woman was nicer and more desirable to work with in the no information conditions than in the easy conditions. Further, the desire to work on the card-sorting task tended to be lower when task demands were unknown relative to when they were known. However, there was no indication of a greater difference on these measures as a function of potential motivation in the no information conditions as compared to the easy conditions. Instead, subjects in both task information conditions tended to rate the woman more positively and the card-sorting task more negatively when potential motivation was high than when potential motivation was low.

The most puzzling aspect of these data from the point of view of the present theory is that they seem to contradict the notion that motivational arousal will not correspond to incentive value when instrumental task demands are known (and there is no potential gain via the expenditure of extra energy). On the other hand, an alternative interpretation is possible. To wit, it may be that demands in the easy conditions were not as apparent as was intended and originally believed. After all, a self-presentation task of this sort would be novel for most people. Even though they knew that the other subject had done poorly and, therefore, that their task should be easier, these subjects may have had doubts about how to go about doing a better job. Indeed, this could account for the mean difficulty rating in this condition (3.30) being only slightly below the midpoint of the scale (0 = not at all difficult; 10 = extremely difficult). If subjects were not sure about how much effort they had to exert, then greater energization when potential motivation was relatively high might be anticipated.

Fortunately, there is a means of assessing this argument, indirectly at least. A recent experiment by Wright, Heaton, and Bushman (1988) employed a similar design but used a slightly different procedure. In particular, there was an effort to insure that task demands were quite clear in the easy conditions. Subjects were led to believe they could earn a fairly trivial incentive (a pen) or a relatively valuable incentive (a record album) by memorizing trigrams. Some learned subsequently that their task would be extremely easy—one trigram. The rest were told that they could receive one, three, five, seven, or 15 trigrams, but that they would not find out what task they were assigned until the performance period began. Subjective and cardiovascular (SBP, DBP, HR) measures were taken just before performance.

Predictions were similar to those for Roberson's second experiment. When assignment of the one-trigram task was all but certain, task demands should have been clear and minimal; and, therefore, anticipatory energy mobilization should have been low irrespective of the value of the incentive offered for good performance. When there was an equal likelihood of receiving each of the memorization tasks, on the other hand, anticipatory energization should have been moderate and proportional to the value of the incentive (i.e., relatively greater for subjects working for the record). Because HR and SBP are believed to be more sensitive than DBP to group differences in effort (Obrist et al., 1978; Obrist, Light, McCubbin, Hutcheson, & Hoffer, 1979), it was expected that they would be more likely to reflect the impact of the experimental manipulations.[2]

Results showed no effects for anticipatory DBP or HR. However, as seen in Figure 5.5, results for anticipatory SBP were highly congruent with expectations. An analysis of covariance on the SBP change scores (baseline SBP as the covariate) yielded a significant effect for task difficulty (task information in the Roberson studies). Although there was no interaction, it can be seen that predictions regarding the impact of incentive value on energy levels in the easy and unknown conditions were generally confirmed. That is, (a) SBP change in the two incentive conditions was virtually identical when the memory task was expected to be easy, and (b) the increase in SBP reactivity from the easy to the unknown condition tended to be greater when the goal was the record than when the goal was the pen. This was borne out by pair-wise comparisons, which show that whereas reactivity in the record/unknown condition was greater than that in the record/easy condition ($P<.05$),

---

[2]Work by Obrist and his colleagues indicates that the effects of effort upon the cardiovascular system are the result of increases and decreased in sympathetic activity. Diastolic blood pressure change is not thought to be a good index of such activity because DBP is determined largely by overall peripheral resistance, which is not necessarily affected by sympathetic stimulation.

5. ENERGIZATION AND GOAL ATTRACTIVENESS   **195**

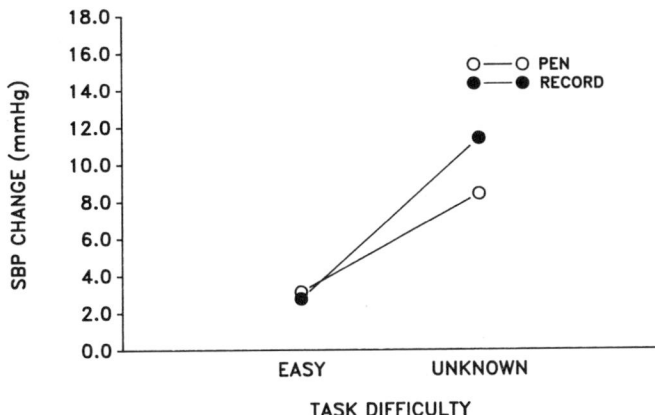

FIG. 5.5 Systolic blood pressure change in subjects offered a pen or record album under conditions where task demands were low or unknown. (From Wright, Heaton, & Bushman, 1988)

reactivity in the pen/unknown condition was not greater than that in the pen/easy condition $(P>.20)$.

Because distributions in some conditions were skewed and variances tended to be unequal, the goal attractiveness data were examined nonparametrically, in terms of the number of scores in each condition falling above and below the median for the group as a whole.[3] Figure 5.6 displays the proportion of ratings in each condition that were above the overall median. An analysis of variance performed on the arc sine-transformed proportions (e.g., Langer & Abelson, 1972; Winer, 1971) yielded both incentive and task difficulty main effects $(P<.02)$. Although again there was no interaction, it can be seen in the figure that these individual effects also accorded with predictions. The contrast of proportions in the easy and unknown conditions was reliable $(P<.05)$ when the goal was the record, but not when the goal was the pen. Moreover, whereas the proportion in the record condition was higher than that in the pen condition when the difficulty of the upcoming memory task was not known $(P<.01)$, proportions in the two incentive conditions were not reliably different when the task was expected to be easy $(P>.20)$.

The foregoing review, then, makes apparent several points. First, as many theories would predict, there is considerable evidence that increases in need and incentive value can potentiate cardiovascular re-

---

[3]Six attractiveness scores were on the median and, therefore, not included in the analysis.

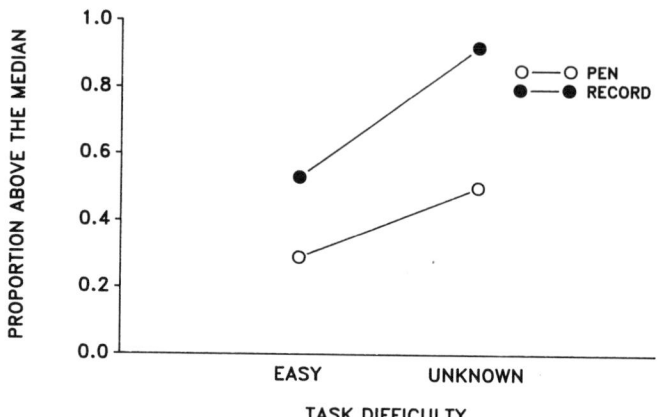

FIG. 5.6 Proportion of goal attractiveness ratings in each condition above the median overall. (From Wright, Heaton, & Bushman, 1988)

sponses. Second, these studies, without too much difficulty, can be reinterpreted in terms of the energization model. Although the validity of these interpretations has yet to be firmly established, there are data that bolster them. For instance, the study by Elliott (1965) indicates, as the energization theory would predict, that incentive effects in subjects performing tasks for more or less money are most likely to be found during the early stages of an experiment, when task demands probably are unclear. Finally, there is some direct evidence that cardiovascular reactivity and the magnitude of goal valence are proportional to potential motivation when instrumental task demands are not known and proportional to difficulty when task demands are known.

Energization and Goal Valence

We will conclude our survey of evidence by considering briefly some research performed to evaluate directly the impact of energization on goal valence. Its importance for the theory should be self-evident. Although the studies presented so far give reason to believe that energization and the magnitude of goal valence vary in the predicted fashion with the major parameters of the model, they do not establish unequivocally the expected causal relationship between these two variables. For this to be accomplished, energy levels must be manipulated independent of task difficulty.

Two experiments by Wright (1982, experiment 1 & 2) were patterned after a study of emotion by Cantor, Bryant, and Zillmann (1974). In both, subjects read passages that were arousing (erotic or violent) or nonarousing (educational), and then, shortly thereafter, were placed in the position where they could avoid an aversive learning (i.e., shock) session by performing an easy memory task (two trigrams in 2 minutes). Predictions were that there would be residual arousal in the conditions where subjects read the exciting passages (Zillmann, 1983), which would have the effect of enhancing negative appraisals of the potential shock session. As expected, anticipatory shock unpleasantness ratings were reliably higher in the erotic and violent conditions than in the educational conditions.

A pair of subsequent investigations had the same aim, but manipulated residual arousal levels differently. In one (Weeks & Wright, 1987), male subjects walked briskly up and down a flight of 14 steps three times and then went down a short hallway to a cubicle to wait for further instructions.[4] One, 5, or 9 minutes later, they received written instructions tellings them that they could leave the experiment early, and thereby avoid an aversive reading task, by unscrambling some relatively easy anagrams. Just before beginning work, they completed a questionnaire asking, among other things, how attractive the incentive of leaving was to them and how unpleasant it would be to have to stay and perform the reading task.

Following the work of Cantor, Zillmann, and Bryant (1975), it was predicted that residual arousal effects, such as those obtained by Wright (1982), would be found only when subjects waited 5 minutes before receiving the experimental instructions. In the 1-minute condition, subjects were expected to attribute excess arousal to the exercise they just performed, whereas in the 9-minute condition they should have been back to baseline. In support of these expectations were the attractiveness and unpleasantness ratings, which were significantly higher for subjects who waited 5 minutes than for subjects who waited 1 and 9 minutes.[5]

The other experiment (Weeks, Burch, & Hernandez, reported by Wright, 1987) crosscut the timing factor above with a manipulation of exercise difficulty. Half of the subjects performed the stair-stepping exercise three times, and the rest performed it only once.[6] The latter task was included because it was expected to produce little residual arousal. Accordingly, predictions were the attractiveness and un-

---

[4]Pretest data showed that systolic blood pressure was substantially above baseline at 1 and 5 minutes, and back to baseline by 9 minutes. Subjective ratings indicated that participants were aware of extent of their arousal (above baseline) at 1 minute, but not at 5 minutes.

[5]It is possible that subjects who waited only 1 minute simply were tired and distracted from the goal.

[6]In pretesting, measures of systolic blood pressure returned to baseline by 5 minutes after this task.

pleasantness ratings would be higher in the 5-minute condition than in the 1- and 9-minute conditions when subjects had performed the high-effort, but not the low-effort, exercise.

Perhaps because the procedure involved three experimenters, rather than one, the results were not as clearcut as those reported by Weeks and Wright (1987). Specifically, there were no group differences in ratings of how attractive in incentive of leaving was, and distribution/variance problems limited the interpretation of the usual analysis of variance performed on the unpleasantness data. On the other hand, an analysis of the unpleasantness ratings in terms of the number of values in each condition falling above and below the group median provided some evidence for the experimental hypotheses. In the high-effort conditions, the proportion above the median in the 1-, 5-, and 9-minute conditions were .44, .80, and .25, respectively. In contrast, corresponding proportions in the low-effort conditions were .56, .44, and .44. An analysis of variance on the arc sine-transformed proportions revealed a significant interaction ($p<.03$). Further, a planned contrast of the high-effort/ 5-minute condition against all other conditions was reliable at the 2% confidence level, with no significant residual.

To a greater or lesser degree, the preceding experiments all indicate that the magnitude of goal valence is enhanced under conditions conducive to arousal transfer relative to conditions not conducive to arousal transfer. Because so few studies have been conducted, this research cannot be considered conclusive and might even be viewed as preliminary. Nevertheless, as a body, the work clearly adds strength to the argument that energization is causal in its relationship with goal valence.

Summing Up: The Evidence in Overview

For purposes of organization, the evidence for the energization model was placed into five general categories. In the first were studies relevant to predictions regarding the impact of instrumental task difficulty on goal valence magnitude. Although they involved a variety of procedures, these investigations present a picture in terms of the theory that is fairly coherent. In a word, with minor exceptions, they show more positive appraisals of potential attractive outcomes and more negative appraisals of potential aversive outcomes when instrumental tasks were difficult, but possible and worthwhile, than when instrumental tasks were easy, too difficult, or impossible.

The second category included studies relevant to predictions about the relationship between task difficulty and energization. Those coming from outside our laboratories were concerned principally with physiologic responsivity during task performance. On the whole, they indicate that cardiovascular responsiveness, as well as reactivity on some other physiologic response measures, is greater under moderately difficult task conditions than under easy and impossible task conditions. Research we and our colleagues have carried out has been concerned mainly with anticipatory cardiovascular responses and behavior under conditions where energization is expected to be relatively high or low. Studies of the former type concur with the performance studies in indicating the predicted nonmonotonic relationship between task difficulty and cardiovascular reactivity. The behavioral studies suggest that the anticipation of difficult tasks, as compared to easy and impossible tasks, (a) facilitates performance on well-learned tasks while inhibiting performance on complex tasks, and (b) increases the speed and intensity of (simple) noninstrumental behaviors.

Experiments in the third category relate to the prediction that task difficulty and potential motivation interact to determine energy levels and the magnitude of goal valence. Those from our laboratories have included explicit manipulations of potential motivation, either varying incentive value or the likelihood of motive satisfaction, given success on the instrumental task. With but one exception, they have shown that the magnitude of goal valence increases with task difficulty only so long as the potential outcome is perceived as worth the effort required by the instrumental task. In one study, cardiovascular reactivity was assessed immediately before the task performance period, and results for those measures were congruent with the aforementioned goal valence findings. Experiments that were not cast originally in terms of the present formulation included *de facto* manipulations of potential motivation, and also show patterns of cardiovascular reactivity during task performance that are consistent with the goal valence data.

In the fourth category was research regarding the relationship between energization and potential motivation. The studies reviewed in the beginning indicate clearly that variables such as need and incentive can serve to potentiate cardiovascular reactivity during (and presumably immediately before) instrumental task performance. At first blush, these data appear contrary to the energization model. However, as was pointed out, experiments of this type may have involved special circumstances in which effort would be expected to increase with motive strength. Thus, at minimum, the findings cannot be viewed as contradictory. An energization explanation of these studies is supported by some preexisting evidence (e.g., the experiment by Elliott, 1965), as well as recent studies that generally confirm theoretical predictions about motivational responses when task demands are not known.

In the final category were recent efforts to examine the impact of energization upon the magnitude of goal valence without manipulating task difficulty. To a greater or lesser degree, these studies indicate that goal valence magnitude is enhanced under conditions that are conducive to arousal transfer effects relative to conditions that are not conducive to arousal transfer effects.

A THEORETICAL PERSPECTIVE AND SELECTED PROBLEMS

Motivation Versus Potential Motivation

The distinction between potential motivation and actual motivational arousal (energization) is necessary to the preceding review of motivational phenomena. It allows us to understand how subjective goal values and desires can fluctuate while actual goals and needs remain constant. It also allows us to understand how physiological indices of motivational arousal can vary while goals and needs remain constant, an understanding that would seem particularly valuable for the analysis of responses to stressors. The mediating variable on which we have placed central emphasis, in order to understand how actual motivational arousal can differ from potential motivation, is the perceived difficulty of carrying out instrumental behavior. We have assumed that the motivational system is conservational in nature and that mobilized energy cannot be restored to the pool of potential motivation without great loss of efficiency. Either mobilized energy is impossible to restore to the pool, can be only partially restored, or at a minimum, requires the expenditure of considerable energy to carry out the restoration process. There is the further possibility that the physiological preparation for the expenditure of energy (e.g., mobilization of free fatty acids in the blood) may have harmful long-term effects (e.g., the clogging of arteries) when the mobilized energy is not expended.

But there is a more fundamental issue involved in the distinction between potential and actual motivation. Theories of motivation that fail to take into account the need for effort and its requisite, energy, assume that an internal state of the organism (e.g., need or drive) and/or some external state (e.g., a pleasant outcome or the threat of a negative outcome) produce motivation in proportion to the magnitude of the internal and/or external state. But this assumption presents the absurd picture that an organism will be highly motivationally aroused, and perhaps act *intensely*, when little effort is required, and even when there is no behavior that will affect the internal or external state. Clearly, then, a distinction must be drawn between potential motivation and actual

5. ENERGIZATION AND GOAL ATTRACTIVENESS 201

motivation, the latter being determined in part by the amount of effort required to satisfy the motive or gain the incentive.

The notion of potential energy is quite handy for understanding certain aspects of the physical world. The electricity supplied to one's home or place of work is, at the electrical outlet, potential energy until something is connected to that outlet and turned on. When a device, whether it be a light bulb, a hair dryer, etc., is turned on, the potential energy is released to do some kind of work: emit light, heat air, blow air, and so forth. Similarly, although one does not normally think of one's water supply as a source of energy, the water that comes from the faucets has a great deal of force, enough, for example, to spray water from a lawn sprinkler over an area measuring 30 square feet. That potential energy is released only when one turns on the faucet.

These are two common systems of energy in the physical world in which energy is available but is not used until it is released to perform a specific function. What perhaps is most remarkable about these examples of the conversion of potential energy into some form of work is the ease with which storage and control of energy takes place. Consider, for example, a new flashlight battery. It is capable of lighting a bulb or running a small motor for a certain number of hours. As long as it is not connected to anything, it continues to have that capability *with no expenditure of energy*. The maintenance of potential energy does not necessarily require much expenditure of energy.

Second, the control over the release of potential energy into work of some form may be accomplished with only a small fraction of the amount of potential energy or energy released. One can easily turn the water faucet on or off, even though one cannot stop the flow of water by sticking one's finger in the spigot. An electrical outlet may contain the potential energy to run an air conditioner, a vacuum cleaner, or a clothes dryer, and yet this energy can be controlled by the flick of a switch.

Within some broad limits, then, potential energy can be stored without great expenditure of energy, and the release of this potential energy to perform work of some kind can be controlled with little expenditure of energy. What we propose, then, is that the human organism is an energy system that easily stores energy and *releases* that energy to perform work as situational requirements—the difficulty of instrumental behavior—demand. In this sense, then, the human would be a relatively efficient energy system.

In contrast, the control of a force such as potential motivation by a counterforce would be quite inefficient. Sexual deprivation provides one example. Physiological mechanisms build an urge toward sexual activity and release (orgasm). Most people would grant that such an urge can become very strong and, thus, if the only way to block the urge is to create a counter-force, the strength of the counterforce must be even greater than that of the sexual urge. What's worse, these forces are actually pressing each other, which means that if the counterforce is sufficiently strong to stop expression of the sexual urge, the amount of energy being expended in this conflict is at least twice the amount represented by the sexual urge. To return to one of our examples from the physical world, it would be like trying to turn a faucet on and off by using a cork to stop up the pipe. To stop the flow of water produced by a pressure of 50 lb/sq inch, the cork would have to be pressed into the faucet at an even greater pressure. A counterforce is an extremely inefficient way to control a force.

Control of motives by counterforces is implicit if not explicit in psychological theories of conflict and inhibition. For example, neo-Hullian theories (e.g., Miller, 1959) suggested that an approach motive [tendency] (e.g., sexual drive) could be blocked by an avoidance motive [tendency] such as learned fear if the avoidance motive [tendency] was made the stronger of the two. Similarly, the Freudian concept of repression appears to be a counterforce, though in this case the libidinal force might be redirected rather than simply blocked. Nevertheless, repression is thought to use up considerable energy, as should be true of a counterforce (Fenichel, 1945, p. 150).

To return to the main thesis, we have argued that the concept of potential motivation employs the main determinants of motivation featured in traditional motivational theories: need or drive, goals, threats of negative outcomes, and the probability that these conditions will be beneficially changed if instrumental behavior is successfully carried out. We then argued that a determinant of how much energy would be mobilized would be a direct function of the perceived difficulty of the instrumental behavior necessary, as long as the importance of the motive outweighed the required effort, and as long as the instrumental behavior was perceived as possible (within the individual's capability). We are now arguing explicitly what was implicit in the concept of potential motivation, namely, that a need and/or incentive in conjunction with the physiological system provides potential energy and that potential energy is converted to actual energy according to the perceived difficulty of required instrumental behavior. Finally, we are arguing that the mechanism that converts potential to actual energy has the characteristics of a valve or switch, that is, a mechanism that uses very little energy relative to the amount that can be controlled. However, a valve is the more apt metaphor because ideally the controlling mechanism should be able to release or convert variable amounts of potential energy. In turn, the controlling mechanism must be informed by the cognitive assessment of energy needs (i.e., judgments about the requirements for instrumental behavior).

Thus, under conditions of food deprivation, and even when food is present in the situation, the conversion of potential into mobilized energy will occur according to the assessment of energy needs. There will be little or no cost to the individual (expenditure of energy) if it is clear that the food is simply unattainable (e.g., in a vending machine when the person has no money) because not turning on the valve to release energy is easy. And it should be approximately equally easy to release a small amount of energy if the required behavior is easy (e.g., putting a coin in a slot and unwrapping a candy bar) or a large amount of energy if the required behavior is difficult (e.g., breaking into the vending machine).

The gist of our argument is that the motivational system is designed to be energy efficient (which helps to ensure survival of the organism). This means that even when a powerful motive is acting on the individual (e.g., extreme deprivation of a biological need, a very important incentive such as avoidance of mutilation or death), little or no energy will be released if there is little or no effort called for.

Subjective Motivational Effects: Functional Significance and Alternative Causal Schemes

We have suggested that the subjective appraisal of need and/or goal value is a direct function of the level of energization, and presented evidence to that effect. However, this view may be unsatisfying to some degree because it does not address the question of functional significance (i.e., it does not explain *why* appraisal should vary with energy level).

Although we have no clear answer to this question, we will suggest some possibilities worth considering. One is that the subjective effects reviewed here are the result of a process similar to that in Schachter's theory of emotion (e.g., Schachter & Singer, 1962) or the arousal transfer model (Zillmann, 1983). That is, physiological arousal (energization) may be experienced and attributed to one's need and/or to the attractiveness of the goal (or threat of a negative outcome). If so, the subjective appraisal could have no necessary functional value and may be viewed as an epiphenomenon, at least insofar as the subjective appraisal is affected by energy level.

Another possibility is that a more direct mechanism is involved which has functional utility. This view distinguishes between the physiological and psychological functions of the energy system. The argument is that the functional value of efficiency in the physiological energy system is important to survival of the organism, whereas the functional value of the appraisal of needs and goals may be purely psychological and normally secondary to survival needs.

If we assume that the mobilization or release of energy is proportional to the difficulty of instrumental behavior (where that difficulty can be assessed), the psychological consequences might be that the individual would frequently find certain discrepancies between his objective state of need or goal value (potential motivation) and his state of motivational arousal. Whenever motive satisfaction was easy or impossible, the two states would be discrepant. Thus, it seems possible that the psychological functional reason for energization level's determining subjective states of motivation is simply to make the felt need and/or desirability of the sought outcome congruent with the experience of being motivated. If, because task requirements are very easy, little energy is mobilized, it is congruent to feel little desire and see little attractiveness in the potential outcome. Similarly, if nothing can be done to satisfy the need or attain the potential outcome, the consequent lack of motivational arousal would be congruent with feeling little or no need and seeing little or no value in the potential outcome. And where the difficulty of need satisfaction or outcome attainment was great, a congruent experience would be a strong felt need and/or important potential outcome.

Both of the preceding possibilities assume that energization affects appraisal as we have proposed. It is obvious, though, that alternative causal schemes have been entirely ruled out. In particular, there is the possibility that the causal link between energization and the subjective assessment of motivational variables is reversed. As an example, it might plausibly be argued that people *magnify* the subjective appraisal of need or goal value *in order* to energize themselves. The implicit proposition in this argument is that the "objective" need or goal value is inadequate to produce the required level of energy and that the individual, therefore, voluntarily magnifies the appraisals in order to "pump himself or herself up." This indeed would be a plausible view if the research evidence on felt need or perceived magnitude of goal valence as a function of task difficulty involved only relatively insignificant goals. As seen in our review of the literature, however, a number of studies involve objectively significant outcomes: interpersonal attraction, threat of shock, LP records, for example. In addition, the explanation implies that the effect of task difficulty on goal attractiveness should increase as the objective value of the goal decreases. What little evidence there is (Biner, 1987; Brehm, 1988; Wright & Gregorich, in press, 1988; Wright, Kelley, & Bramwell, in press) supports exactly the opposite conclusion, namely that goal attractiveness ratings vary increasingly with difficulty as the objective value of the goal increases from low to moderate. Finally, this view cannot easily account for the finding that goal valence magnitude is enhanced under conditions conducive to arousal transfer relative to conditions that are not conducive to arousal transfer (e.g., Wright, 1982). Together, these points indicate that it is unlikely that the evidence we have reviewed should be interpreted as voluntary magnification of appraisals in order to effect energization.

A related possibility is that the energy system is efficiently constructed much as we have speculated, but that energy *needs* somehow determine directly subjective assessments, which, in turn, determine energization. That is, as a result of the interplay between potential motivation and task difficulty, the perceived desire and/or value of the outcome may be affected and serve to determine the release of energy from the reserve of potential energy. An appeal of this formulation is that it gives subjective appraisal of motivational dimensions more than psychological functional significance. Instead, subjective appraisal has the more important function of determining level of energization. On the other hand, this process is relatively complicated and cannot easily account for the goal valence effects in the arousal transfer studies.

Potential Motivation and Subjective Effects

It is presumably the major determinants of potential motivation, internal state, and/or potential positive or negative outcome, whose appraisal is correlated with the difficulty of instrumental behavior. Would it not follow, then, that when the appraised magnitude of the need and/or outcome is lowered as a function of low task requirements, potential motivation, too, would be lowered? The answer, of course, is no: If the organism is to survive and thrive, accurate responsiveness to its internal state and/or potential outcomes must take precedence over its energy efficiency. Thus, when an individual reports that he/she has only moderate desire to avoid an unavoidable potentially painful electric shock, the true negative character of that impending event must still register somewhere in the motivational system. Otherwise, the individual would not avoid the negative outcome if the opportunity arose. Because a potential outcome or its lack could be life threatening (dangerous electric shock, food for a starving individual), lack of responsiveness to opportunity would tend to result in nonsurvival of the species.

The foregoing argument would lead us to believe that subjective appraisal is most accurate when energization is at a maximum. From this perspective, the psychological problem is that of reducing the appraised magnitudes of need and potential outcome when energization is less than maximal. Therefore, we might suppose that there is *suppression* of appraised levels to the extent that the level of energization falls below the maximum called for by potential motivation. Note that this suppression of subjective assessment could involve psychological costs and the consequent expenditure of energy. Just because the system is designed to be energy efficient psychologically does not necessarily mean that it also will be energy efficient physiologically. An additional possible problem is that the system may be more or less successful in suppressing appraisal of need and/or outcome value whenever energization is relatively low.

In summary, the order of events presumably would be (a) the accurate perception of need and/or potential outcome value, (b) the perceived energy requirements for motive satisfaction (from task difficulty), (c) the recognition of any discrepancy between potential motivation and energy requirements, and (d) the suppression of motivational appraisal to bring it into line with required energy level. However, if the subjective appraisal of motivational dimensions falls below the objective values of potential motivation, the latter must remain intact in order to insure survival of the organism. Thus, all of the preceding explanations of why subjective appraisals may differ from objective appraisals assume that the individual somehow knows what the objective picture is, even while "seeing" a different subjective picture. Perhaps one could invoke the "hot-cool" dimension of cognition and assert that subjective assessment is hot, whereas objective is cool. Alternatively, and perhaps more cogently, one might assume that the appraisal of potential motivation is nonconscious, whereas that of energy level (feeling of motivation) is conscious. At the moment there seems to be no way to choose from among the myriad of alternative views.

THE MODEL IN SUMMARY

Whether subjective assessments of motivational variables are determinant of or determined by energy level, the following propositions summarize the model:

1. Potental motivation is a direct function of the discrepancy between one's present state of well-being and that expected to occur given a specified potential outcome. The potential outcome, of course, could produce a more positive or more negative state of well-being.

1.1 Other things equal, potential motivation increases as deprivation or need increases and as the objective magnitude of a potential positive or negative outcome increases.

1.2 The objective and subjective magnitudes of need and goal value coincide only when the individual is maximally energized to satisfy the motive.

2. The level of energy at any given time is a direct function of the expected or experienced difficulty of satisfying potential motivation, given that one is already engaged in instrumental behavior or that one anticipates immediate commencement of instrumental behavior.

2.1 The greater the perceived difficulty of the instrumental behavior, the greater the level of energization.

    2.11 Mobilization of energy will cease if required effort outweights potential motivation.

    2.12 Mobilization of energy will cease if required behavior is beyond the capabilities (e.g., strength, intelligence) of the person.

3. The subjective appraisal of own need or the value of the potential outcome is a direct function of the interplay between potential motivation and difficulty of required instrumental behavior.

3.1 With task difficulty held constant, the subjective appraisal of need and goal value will be a direct function of objective determinants such as deprivation and real world value of the goal.

3.2 With objective factors of potential motivation held constant, the subjective appraisal will be a direct function of task difficulty up to the point at which subjective appraisal equals objective appraisal or the task becomes impossible. Beyond this point, subjective appraisal will be low.

4. Potential motivation is *not* a function of energization.

REFERENCES

Belanger, D., & Feldman, S. M. (1962). Effects of water deprivation upon heart rate and instrumental activity in the rat. *Journal of Comparative and Physiological Psychology, 55,* 220–225.

Biner (1987). Effects of difficulty and goal value on goal valence. *Journal of Research in Personality, 21,* 395–404.

Brehm, J. W. (1988). *Desirability of avoiding a negative outcome as a function of the magnitude of the outcome and the difficulty of avoiding it.* Unpublished manuscript, University of Kansas.

Brehm, J. W., Vought, C., & Pysczcynski, T. (1980). *Energization and consequent goal attractiveness as a function of the perceived difficulty of a motor task.* Unpublished manuscript, University of Kansas.

Brehm, J. W., Wright, R. A., Solomon, S., Silka, L., & Greenberg, J. (1983). Perceived difficulty, energization, and the magnitude of goal valence. *Journal of Experimental Social Psychology, 19,* 21–48.

Cacioppo, J. T., & Petty, R. E. (Eds.). (1982). *Perspectives on cardiovascular psychophysiology.* New York: Guilford.

Cantor, J. R., Bryant, J., & Zillmann, D. (1974). Enhancement of humor appreciation by transferred excitation. *Journal of Personality and Social Psychology, 30,* 812–821.

Cantor, J. R., Zillmann, D., & Bryant, J. (1975). Enhancement of experienced sexual arousal in response to erotic stimuli through the misattribution of unrelated residual excitation. *Journal of Personality and Social Psychology, 32,* 69–75.

Carlsmith, J. S. (1962). *Strength of expectancy: Its determinants and effects.* Unpublished doctoral dissertation, Harvard University, Cambridge, Mass.

Cofer, C. N., & Appley, M. H. (1964). *Motivation: Theory and Research.* New York: Wiley.

Contrada, R. J., Glass, D. C., Krakoff, L. R., Krantz, D. S., Kehoe, K., Isecke, W., Collins, C., & Elting, E. (1982). Effects of control over aversive stimulation and Type A behavior on cardiovascular and plasma catecholamine responses. *Psychophysiology, 19,* 408–419.

Contrada, R. J., Wright, R. A., & Glass, D. C. (1984). Task difficulty, Type A behavior pattern, and cardiovascular response. *Psychophysiology, 21,* 638–646.

Elliott, R. (1965). Reaction time and heart rates as functions of magnitude of incentive and probability of success. *Journal of Personality and Social Psychology, 2,* 604–609.

Elliott, R. (1969). Tonic heart rate: Experiments on the effect of collative variables lead to a hypothesis about its motivational significance. *Journal of Personality and Social Psychology, 12,* 211–228.

Esqueda, L. S. (1985). *Behavior intensity as a function of task difficulty.* Unpublished doctoral dissertation, University of Kansas, Lawrence, KS.

Fenichel, O. (1945). *The psychoanalytic theory of neurosis.* New York: Norton.

Fowles, D. C., Fisher, A. E., & Tranel, D. T. (1982). The heart beats to reward: The effect of monetary incentives on heart rate. *Psychophysiology, 19,* 506–513.

Ford, C. E., & Brehm, J. W. (1987). Effort expenditure following failure. In C. R. Snyder & C. E. Ford (Eds.), *Coping with negative life events: Clinical and social psychological perspectives* (pp. 81–104). New York: Plenum.

Ford, C. E., Wright, R. A., & Haythornthwaite, J. (1985). Task performance and magnitude of goal valence. *Journal of Research in Personality, 19,* 253–260.

Frankenhaeuser, M., & Johanson, G. (1976). Task demands as reflected in catecholamine excretion and heart rate. *Journal of Human Stress, 14,* 173–184.

Frankenhaeuser, M., & Lundberg, U. (1977). The influence of cognitive set on performance and arousal under different noise loads. *Motivation and Emotion, 1,* 139–149.

Hahn, W. W., Stern, J. A., & McDonald, D. G. (1962). Effects of water deprivation and bar pressing activity on heart rate of the male albino rat. *Journal of Comparative and Physiological Psychology, 55,* 786–790.

Hassett, J. (1978). *A primer of psychophysiology.* San Francisco: W. H. Freeman.

Hill, T., Fultz, J., & Biner, P. M. (1985). Incidental learning as a function of anticipated task difficulty. *Motivation and Emotion, 9,* 71–85.

Houston, B. K. (1972). Control over stress, locus of control, and responses to stress. *Journal of Personality and Social Psychology, 21,* 249–255.

Jecker, J. D. (1964). The cognitive effects of conflict and dissonance. In L. Festinger (Ed.), *Conflict, decision, and dissonance* (pp. 21–30). Stanford, CA: Stanford University Press.

Johnson, H. J. (1963). Decision making, conflict, and physiological arousal. *Journal of Abnormal and Social Psychology, 2,* 114–124.

Kahneman, D. (1973). *Attention and effort.* Englewood Cliffs, NJ: Prentice-Hall.
Langer, E. J., & Abelson, R. P. (1972). The semantics of asking a favor: How to succeed without really dying. *Journal of Personality and Social Psychology, 24,* 26–32.
Manuck, S. B., Harvey, S. H., Lechleiter, S. L., & Neal, K. S. (1978). Effects of coping on blood pressure responses to threat of aversive stimulation. *Psychophysiology, 15,* 544–549.
Miller, N. E. (1959). Liberalization of basic S-R concepts: Extensions to conflict behavior, motivation, and social learning. In S. Koch (Ed.), *Psychology: A study of a science* (Vol. 2). New York: McGraw-Hill.
Obrist, P. A., Gaebelein, C. J., Teller, E. S., Langer, A. W., Grignolo, A., Light, K. C., & McCubbin, J. A. (1978). The relationship among heart rate, carotid dP/dt, and blood pressure in humans as a function of type of stress. *Psychophysiology, 15,* 102–115.
Obrist, P. A., Light, K. C., McCubbin, J. A., Hutcheson, J. S., & Hoffer, J. L. (1979). Pulse transit time: Relationship to blood pressure and myocardial performance. *Psychophysiology, 16,* 292–301.
Roberson, B. F. (1985). *The effect of task characteristics and motivational arousal on the perceived valence of multiple outcomes.* Unpublished doctoral dissertation, University of Kansas, Lawrence, KS.
Schachter, S., & Singer, J. (1962). Cognitive, social, and physiological determinants of emotional state. *Psychological Review, 69,* 379–399.
Solomon, S., Holmes, D. S., & McCaul, K. (1980). Behavioral control over aversive events: Does control that requires effort reduce anxiety and physiological arousal? *Journal of Personality and Social Psychology, 39,* 729–736.
Surwit, R. S., Williams, R. B., & Shapiro, D. (1982). *Behavioral approaches to cardiovascular disease.* New York: Academic Press.
Toi, M. (1980). *The effect of perceived difficulty of cognitive task on goal attractiveness.* Unpublished master's thesis, University of Kansas, Lawrence, KS.
Tranel, D. T., Fisher, A. E., & Fowles, D. C. (1982). Magnitude of incentive effects upon the heart. *Psychophysiology, 19,* 514–519.
Vought, C. (1977). *The effect of physical difficulty on goal attractiveness.* Unpublished master's thesis, University of Kansas, Lawrence, KS.
Vroom, V. H. (1964). *Work and motivation.* New York: Wiley.
Weeks, J. L., & Wright, R. A. (1987, May). *Effects of residual excitation upon appraisals of a potential aversive event.* Paper presented at the meeting of the Midwestern Psychological Association, Chicago, IL.
Weiner, B. (1972). *Theories of motivation.* Chicago: Markham.
Wicklund, R. A., & Brehm, J. W. (1976). *Perspectives on cognitive dissonance.* Hillsdale, NJ: Lawrence Erlbaum Associates.
Winer, B. J. (1971). *Statistical principles in experimental design* (2nd ed.). New York: McGraw-Hill.
Wright, R. A. (1982). Perceived motivational arousal as a mediator of the magnitude of goal valence. *Motivation and Emotion, 6,* 161–180.
Wright, R. A. (1984). Motivation, anxiety, and the difficulty of avoidant control. *Journal of Personality and Social Psychology, 46,* 1376–1388.
Wright, R. A. (1987). Coping difficulty, energy mobilization, and appraisals of a stressor: Introduction of a theory, and a comparison of perspectives. In C. R. Snyder, & C. E. Ford (Eds.), *Coping with negative life events: Clinical and social psychological perspectives* (pp. 51–79). New York: Plenum Press.
Wright, R. A., & Brehm, J. W. (1984). The impact of task difficulty upon perceptions of arousal and goal attractiveness in an avoidance paradigm. *Motivation and Emotion, 8,* 171–181.

Wright, R. A., Brehm, J. W., & Bushman, B. J. (in press). Cardiovascular responses to threat: Effects of the difficulty and availability of a cognitive avoidant task. *Basic and Applied Social Psychology*.

Wright, R. A., Contrada, R. J., & Patane, M. J. (1986). Task difficulty, cardiovascular response, and the magnitude of goal valence. *Journal of Personality and Social Psychology, 52*, 837–843.

Wright, R. A., & Gregorich, S. (in press). Difficulty and instrumentality of imminent behavior as determinants of cardiovascular response and self-reported energy. *Psychophysiology*.

Wright, R. A., & Gregorich, S. (1988). *Goal attractiveness as a function of the difficulty and effectiveness of instrumental behavior*. Unpublished manuscript, Univ. of Alabama at Birmingham.

Wright, R. A., Heaton, A., & Bushman, B. (1988). *Motivational responses when instrumental task demands are not clear*. Unpublished manuscript, University of Alabama at Birmingham.

Wright, R. A., Kelley, C. L., & Bramwell, A. (in press). Difficulty and effectiveness of avoidant behavior as determinants of evaluations of a potential aversive outcome. *Personality and Social Psychology Bulletin*.

Wright, R. A., Brehm, J. W., Solomon, S., Silka, L., Crutcher, B. (1988). *Additional evidence of a nonmonotonic relation between instrumental task difficulty and the magnitude of goal valence in an avoidance context*. Unpublished manuscript, University of Alabama at Birmingham.

Wright, R. A., Toi, M., & Brehm, J. W. (1984). Difficulty and interpersonal attraction. *Motivation and Emotion, 4*, 327–341.

Yerkes, R. M., & Dodson, J. D. (1908). The relation of strength of stimulus to rapidity of habit formation. *Journal of Comparative Neurological Psychology, 18*, 459–482.

Zillmann, D. (1983). Transfer of excitation in emotional behavior, In J. T. Cacioppo & R. E. Petty (Eds.), *Social psychophysiology: A sourcebook* (pp. 215–235). New York: Guilford.

6 Possible Selves: Personalized Representations of Goals

HAZEL MARKUS
ANN RUVOLO
University of Michigan

> Under some circumstances I need friendship or need to catch a train just as truly as under other circumstances I may need water or calcium. Where do these needs come from? . . . It has always been clear to everyone but the psychologist that these are needs of the *self*. When "I need friendship", it is the "I" that has the need. If we analyze away the "I" we lose the meaning of the motivation, just as when we analyze away the perceptual object we lose the meaning of perception. (MacLeod, 1949, p. 112)

The premise of our chapter is that needs and goals are fundamental elements of the self-system and that the precise nature of their functioning is best understood with reference to the self-system. We will argue that the crucial element of a goal is the representation of the individual *herself* or *himself* approaching and realizing the goal. Without this representation of the self, a goal will not be an effective regulator of behavior. Goals are rarely cognized in total abstraction. Most goals, whether relatively mundane like getting dressed in the morning, or more complex such as gaining tenure in a profession, occasion the construction of a "possible self" in which one is different from the now self and in which one realizes the goal. It is the "I" that holds or possesses the goal or the threat: for example, I hope to finish college; I plan to buy a car; I am afraid of failing this test. A goal will have an impact on behavior to the extent that the individual can personalize it by building a bridge of self-representations between one's current state and one's desired or hoped-for state. The critical determinant of whether a given goal will guide and sustain instrumental action is thus the ability to create and maintain the possible selves that allow one to appropriate a desired end state and to make it one's own.

In the course of this chapter we will discuss the concept of possible selves and their role with the self-system, examine the advantage of framing goals in terms of the self, review a variety of related approaches that have implicated the self, discuss several empirical studies that have formulated goals as "possible selves," and finally consider in detail how possible selves may function to enhance or impair performance.

THE REPRESENTATION OF GOALS WITHIN THE SELF-SYSTEM

Possible selves can be viewed as the future oriented components of the self-system. They represent individuals' ideas of what they might become, what they would like to become, and especially what they are afraid of becoming. "The possible selves that are hoped for might include the successful self, the creative self, the rich self, the thin self, or the loved and admired self, whereas the dreaded possible selves could be the alone self, the depressed self, the incompetent self, the alcoholic self, the unemployed self, or the bag lady self" (Markus & Nurius, 1986, p. 954). These global possible selves enable the construction or retrieval of related but more focused task-relevant possible selves (e.g., "a good student"-possible self will enable the construction of a "me successfully completing this anagram task" possible self, and an "incompetent"-possible self will facilitate the construction of a "failing this test"-possible self).

Possible selves give specific, self-relevant form, meaning, and direction to one's hopes and threats. Possible selves are specific representations of one's self in future states and circumstances that serve to organize and energize one's actions. These thoughts, images, or senses of one's self in the end state and in the intermediate states—me wearing a red shirt or me doing rounds at the hospital, or me being made fun of by co-workers, or me as a bored and underpaid clerk—are viewed as the individualized carriers of motivation. They are the manifestations of one's goals, aspirations, motives, fears, and threats.

Our concern with possible selves grows out of earlier work that formulated the self-concept as system of self-schemas. Self-schemas are affective-cognitive structures that are constructed creatively and selectively on the basis of one's experience in a given domain. They organize and direct the processing of self-relevant information and these cognitive consequences have been documented at length (e.g., Markus &

Sentis, 1982; Markus & Zajonc, 1985). People with a self-schema in a particular domain (schematics)—whether it is for their attributes of independence, creativity, or shyness; for their abilities or talents; for their expertise about sports, food, or the stock market; or for their roles as leader, teacher, parent or spouse—are defined as those who consider these domains to be of critical personal importance.

Self-schemas are not just memories of past actions or passive generalizations about ongoing actions, however. They are also claims of responsibility for one's future actions in this domain. Possible selves are thus viewed as the elements of the self-schema that give structure and meaning to the future in the individual's domains of investment and concern. One of the most important ways in which self-schemas allow the individual to "go beyond the information given" is in the anticipation of what might be, and what is possible for me in a given domain. The ability to anticipate specific futures is thus a powerful consequence of becoming *schematic* in a given domain.

Current thinking on the role of anticipation (see Neisser, 1985) suggests that imagining an action involves running at least part of the sequence of actions that would normally accompany or govern the imagined action. And imagining one's own actions through the construction of elaborated possible selves achieving the desired goal may thus directly facilitate the translation of goals into intentions and instrumental actions. Possible selves then can be seen as the elements of self-schemas that are essential for putting the self into action. They are action-oriented representations, which as Trzebinski has emphasized (see this volume), allow for more obvious connections between individuals' internal structures and their overt actions. Individuals can construct all types of possible selves; they are limited only by their imagination, and all possible selves can have some impact on behavior. Yet unless one's possible selves derive from the domains of one's current involvement and expertise, they are unlikely to be particularly effective in regulating performance.

We assume that possible selves function as they become part of the working self-concept (Markus & Kunda, 1986; Markus & Nurius, 1986). The working self-concept is drawn from the self-system, which contains a vast repertoire of self-representations (e.g., self-schemas, possible selves), plans, strategies, and rules for behavior. Some of these self-representations are core and some are more peripheral. The functional self-concept of a particular movement—the working self-concept— is a nonrandom sample from the universe of one's self-conceptions. The working self-concept can then be viewed as a continually active, shifting array of accessible self-representations. Self-representations (semantic, imaginal, enactive) become active when they are triggered by self-

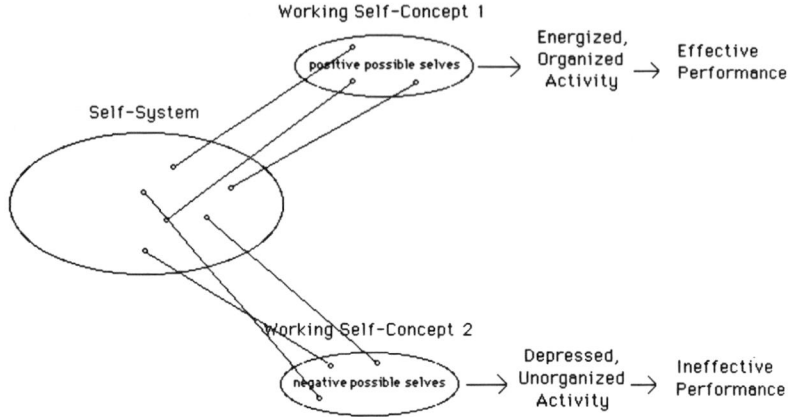

FIG. 6.1 Role of the self-system in goal-directed behavior

relevant events or when they are more deliberately invoked by the individual in response to an event or a situation. This working self-concept is instrumental in the regulation of behavior and how efficiently it can regulate behavior depends on its structure.

As indicated in Figure 6.1, as the individual approaches a goal, positive possible selves (representing the individual in the desired state) may dominate the working self-concept. To the extent that these positive possible selves can be maintained and competing or incongruent possible selves can be momentarily suppressed, the individual's actions will be focused, energized, and organized by this possible self. In contrast, when feared possible selves dominate the working self-concept, performance will be disorganized and impaired unless or until a positive possible can be recruited that will counter the negative self.

THE SELF-SYSTEM AND MOTIVATION: RELATED APPROACHES

The view that the self-system and motivated or goal-directed behavior are interwoven is seldom made explicit, yet the belief that the two must be linked can be inferred from the writing of a variety of personality and motivation theorists. Concepts like "will" or "volition" have as their essence the confluence of self and motivation, the deliberate choice of one's own actions. Wundt (1894) theorized that a cause of voluntary actions was an individual's "willing self," which was determined by motives and feelings. Similarly, James (1890) proposed a central self, which was the source of attention, effort, and will. He saw this central self as a junction between thought and action and hypothesized that the self is closely connected with the "process through which ideas become outward acts" (p. 248). McDougall (1928) theorized about the related concept of "volition," which was thought to be an aspect of the self. He claimed that "volition essentially involves a positive increase of the energy with which an idea maintains itself in consciousness and plays its part in determining bodily and mental processes" (p. 252). McDougall reasoned that if the person's whole self is brought to the support of a motive, the motive can become a volition and this volition will serve to regulate behavior.

Somewhat later, Rank (1936) built an entire theory of personality around the concept of will, which he viewed as "a positive guiding organization and integration of the self" (p. 158). In a related vein, Adler (Ansbacher & Ansbacher, 1956) described the "will-to-power" or more commonly "will power" which involved the idea of a dynamic organization of the self-system for the purpose of accomplishing some objective.

Lewin's (1948) writing on the relation between time perspective and morale also reflected the idea that a positive view of the self in a future state is critical for purposeful or goal-directed actions. He wrote

> studies in unemployment show how a long drawn-out idleness affects all parts of a person's life. Thrown out of a job, the individual tries to keep hoping. When he finally gives up, he frequently restricts his action much more than he has to. Even though he has plenty of time, he begins to neglect his home duties. He may cease to leave his neighborhood; even his thinking and his wishes become narrow. (p. 103)

The important link that Lewin established here was between constricted self-relevant possibility and impaired performance.

What Lewin called "morale" and viewed as some combination of initiative and determination, the confident sense that "I can do it" can also be thought of as will or agency, and goes by an array of other labels as well. It has been called effectance motivation (Harter, 1978; White, 1959), personal causation (deCharms, 1968), intrinsic motivation (Deci, 1975; Deci & Ryan, 1980), and control (Burger, 1985; Lefcourt, 1976; Rodin & Langer, 1977; Rotter, Chance, & Phares, 1972).

Bandura (1986) in his influential theory of self-efficacy has analyzed agency in terms of mechanisms of the self. We now know, for example, that the stronger one's perceived self-efficacy, the more effort one will exert and the more one will persist. The significant question that remains is how does this work. What are the self-relevant cognitions that create and embody these feelings of efficacy and how do they function to influence action?

Despite Bandura's rationale for the role of the self in the regulation of behavior, for the most part, the study of motivation still proceeds without the specific implication of the self-system. The classic motivation theories did not include the self as an important conceptual element (see Atkinson, 1964; Feather, 1963; McClelland, Atkinson, Clark & Lowell, 1953) and this is still true in most current theories. As an example, the most recent textbook of motivation, a volume entitled *Motivation: The Organization of Action* by Mook (1986) does not contain a single reference to the self or self-concept. In the most recent advanced treatment of motivation, a book edited by Sorrentino and Higgins (1986) entitled *Motivation and Cognition*, there are several selections that refer to the self, but these focus primarily on self-evaluation as a dominant motive, rather than on the relationship between the self-system and motivation or goals more generally.

Nuttin (1984) has argued persuasively for the need to "personalize motivation." He claims that most psychologists have been preoccupied with the impersonal, instinctual, or the unconscious nature of motivation. Like Allport (1961), Nuttin suggests that one's actions are governed not by instincts or infantile impulses but through personal, idiosyncratic motivational structures. Two individuals may each have a need for affiliation or a need for achievement, but the form that these needs will assume, and the intentions and actions that will be associated with them, depends on what the individual believes to be possible. An essential project, then, according to Nuttin, is to determine how a general need is transformed into the concrete personal goals and intentions to act of which we are more or less aware.

Personality psychologists and self-concept researchers have been relatively more concerned with personalizing goals or motivation (see Pervin, 1983). Schlenker (1985), for example, has individualized motivation by postulating "desired selves" that are determined by situational constraints and by the anticipated audience for the behavior and that process information in the setting. For Gollwitzer and Wicklund (1985), the self-concept is linked to motivation through the concept of self-definitions. They claim that an individual's most important actions are in the service of completing or operationalizing their significant self-definitions. And Cantor and Kihlstrom (1987) developed the idea of "life tasks," which are the problems that individuals work on at particular times of their lives. With this concept they have attempted to tie self-knowledge directly to self-regulation. They find that the most important life tasks, those elaborated with the most detailed self-knowledge, plans and scripts, are the most influential in explaining significant outcomes. Related concepts include personal projects (Little, 1983), personal goals (Staub, 1980), current concerns (Klinger, 1975), psychological careers (Raynor & McFarlin, 1986), personal strivings (Emmons, 1986), and life themes (Schank & Abelson, 1977).

WHY FRAME GOALS IN TERMS OF THE SELF?

With our emphasis on possible selves, we are placing the self-system squarely at the heart of motivation and action, and this has a number of conceptual advantages. When one wants or intends or has a goal to achieve something, it is the self (the "I" and the "me") that has want or the intent or the goal, and it is these self-relevant representations that are the specific instigators of motivated or goal-directed behavior. The literature is replete with terms for cognitive motivators (as opposed to biological motivators). Traditionally motivation theorists have referred to expectancies, either generalized or specific, to cognized goals, to causal attributions, to self-efficacy beliefs, and to value (e.g., Atkinson, 1964; Bandura, 1986; Nicholls, 1984) in describing the cognitive units that carry motivation.

We suggest that possible selves are the cognitive/affective elements that incite and direct one's self-relevant actions. Motivated behavior does depend on one's attributions and on one's expectancies and beliefs about the outcome, but the referent of these expectancies and beliefs and the element that is psychologically experienced and that is a durable aspect of consciousness is a possible self. Thus, by focusing on possible selves, we believe that we are phenomenologically very close to the actual thoughts and feelings that individuals experience as they are in the process of motivated behavior and instrumental action. These representations of self-relevant possibility include thoughts, images, or senses of one's self in the end state and at various substages of the end state.

Traditional formulations view motivation primarily as the joint function of the expectancy of an outcome and the value associated with that outcome (Atkinson, 1964; Fishbein, 1967; Vroom, 1964). Yet this model does not always apply; people are often quite unsystematic in selecting among outcomes to pursue. In many cases, individuals give relatively little independent weight to their chance of success and base their decisions and actions on value-related information—primarily, how much they would desire a given outcome. The strength of the cosmetic and fashion industry, for example, seems to depend on the fact that people cannot or will not realistically estimate their probability of achieving the sought after goal, but instead base their actions on how much they want a desired outcome. What seems critical in explaining actions in these cases is whether or not individuals can construct a desired possible self. If a compelling possible self can be constructed, the outcome is valued and simultaneously the expectancy of attaining it is increased.

A possible self contains both the representation of a given anticipated action or performance and the outcomes that are associated with it. Although Bandura (1986) has repeatedly argued for the importance of separating the performance and the outcome, with respect to the creation of a possible self, the two are often psychologically fused. Thus, Bandura (1987) argued that a 6 foot jump is the realization of a performance, but that the outcomes—the recognition, the applause, the prizes, trophies and the self-esteem—are distinct from this performance. Conceptually the performance and the outcome expectancies can be separated, but the possible self integrates representations of the individual producing the performance and simultaneously realizing the associated outcomes. Thus, the "champion" possible self glories in the roar of the crowd, feels the weight of the medal on her chest, declines an offer to go professional, and signs autographs. All of these representations of the self in the desired future state together create the possible self, and the more specifically elaborated it is in terms of diverse types of self-representations, the greater its hypothesized influence in energizing and organizing performance.

When individuals separate performance and outcome expectancies, it is an indication that they are unable to imagine the self unambiguously realizing the desired state. This may occur when individuals question or doubt their desires, abilities, or feelings of efficacy or when they are concerned that factors other than individual ones may control the anticipated outcome. In the latter case, for example, one may construct a possible self in which one writes a very important book but at the same time entertain a possible self of not getting the book published.

An emphasis on possible selves also allows for integration of a variety of findings related to goal effectiveness. Thus, specific, clear goals have been shown to be more effective than vague or general intentions to perform well (e.g., Locke, Shaw, Saari, & Latham, 1981). Goals of moderate difficulty have been found to be the most motivating; goals that are too easy or too difficult are less effective (Atkinson, 1964; Feather, 1982). Goals that individuals accept and that they are committed to function best and will be pursued even if they are thought somewhat difficult to maintain (Locke, 1968). And performance is best when individuals are highly self-focused, and the goals are perceived as very important (Hollenbeck & Williams, 1987). These findings on goal effectiveness are most easily understood with reference to a mediating self-system. Specific goals are relatively more effective because they allow for the elaboration of distinct possible selves. Goals that individuals feel to be important, involving, or to which they are committed are effective because these goals are self-relevant and self-defining and as a result the desired end state, even a difficult one, will be easier to form into a unit with the self (cf. Heider, 1946).

Finally, a focus on possible selves rather than more abstract or impersonal goals allows some insight into why individuals have some goals and not other goals, or why some individuals have goals that other individuals do not. The nature of one's possible selves depends on the nature of one's core self-structures or salient identities. The person who has defined herself in terms of her competence as a photographer and as a mother will have possible selves that elaborate self-relevant futures in these domains. And the individual who defines himself in terms of his running ability and his creativity will have possible selves in these self-defining domains. Goal-directed or motivated behavior and the nature of the self-system are thus reciprocally related (see also Schlenker, 1985; this volume).

POSSIBLE SELVES: EMPIRICAL STUDIES

We have proposed that realizing a desired goal depends on being able to keep the possible self that represents the self achieving this goal as a dominant or central element in the working self-concept. In general, the more elaborated the possible self in terms of semantic, imaginal, or enactive representations, the more motivationally effective it can be expected to be. When an elaborated positive possible self is active ("me successfully completing this problem"), it will both organize and energize the individual's activities in pursuit of it. Other competing possible selves will be less accessible and an aspect of the phenomenological experience will be a feeling of willfulness, capability, or efficaciousness (Bandura, 1986; Harter, 1981; White, 1959). The sense of one's self in a feared or undesired state (e.g., "me as incompetent" or "me as failing") also can be motivationally significant. It can provide vivid images or conceptions of an end state that must be rejected or avoided. When an image or sense of one's self in such a feared or undesired state dominates the working self-concept it can produce inaction or a stopping in one's tracks (cf. Atkinson, 1957).

In some cases, an individual may experience conflict between two positive possible selves (e.g., to finish reading a book, to go to bed); in this case whichever possible self is most fully elaborated in the individual's current state will succeed in dominating the working self-concept. In other cases, there may not be a single positive possible self that is sufficiently compelling to dominate the working self-concept. In the latter instance, the resulting experience may be of a lack of energy or a lack of focus or direction.

Possible Selves and Task Performance

To begin an exploration of how possible selves may influence ongoing performance, Ruvolo & Markus (1986), using a guided imagery task, attempted to activate either positive or negative possible selves in the working self-concept. Subjects were told to "imagine themselves in the future" and then were given one of four different descriptions of this future: (a) *success work*—"Everything has gone as well as it possibly could have. You have worked hard and succeeded in achieving your goals;" (b) *success luck*—"Everything has gone as well as it possibly could have. You have been very fortunate and have gotten some lucky breaks along the way;" (c) *failure work*—"Everything has gone as badly as it possibly could have. You have worked very hard but have failed to achieve your goals;" and (d) *failure luck*—"Everything has gone as badly as it possibly could have. You have been very unlucky and have had some bad breaks along the way."

In each condition, subjects answered a series of essay about what they were imagining. After the imagery manipulation, all groups were treated identically. Subjects performed a task that was designed to assess their currently accessible possible selves. A series of terms were presented on a computer screen and the subject's task was simply to respond "possible for me" or "not possible for me" to each word. The stimulus words were (a) positive words reflecting high achievement or successful affiliation with others (e.g., "prestigious", "very popular", and "high-powered;" (b) negative words reflecting lack of successful achievement or affiliation (e.g., "underachiever", "unmotivated", as "withdrawn;" and (c) control words (e.g., "tired", "calm"). During this task, we recorded responses and response times. Following this self-descriptive task, the subjects worked on a performance task that measured persistence. The task was a writing task that required subjects to copy numbers with their nondominant hand. They were instructed to stop when they wished.

As shown in Figure 6.2, the subjects in the success-work condition worked much longer on the persistence task than did the failure subjects, persisting for almost 7 minutes. The failure work subjects stopped, on the average, before 5 minutes had passed. An overall anova on these

6. POSSIBLE SELVES

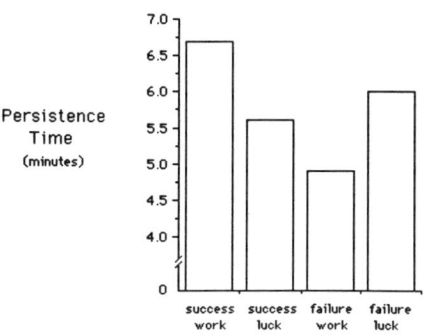

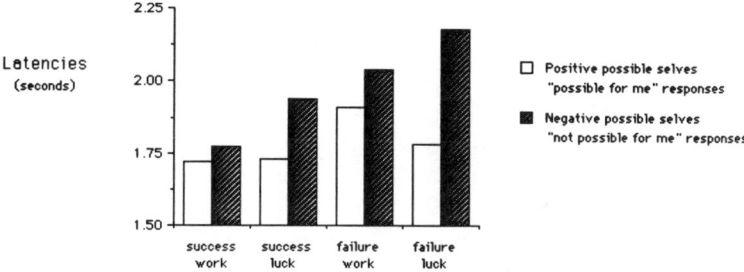

FIG. 6.2 Group means for latencies of self-descriptive responses and for task persistence times

group performance means was significant, and the contrast between the failure work and the success work conditions was highly significant. In contrast, the success-luck and failure-luck conditions did not differ significantly from each other.

We assumed that the working self-concept mediated performance on this task. To explore the nature of this working self-concept, we examined the pattern of response times. The time to respond "possible for me" or "not possible for me" was assumed to be an indicator of the current accessibility in thought and memory of these terms or of terms related to them. Thus, short affirmative response times to the question "is it possible for me" meant that a representation of the self that matched or was similar to the one indicated on the screen was highly accessible. As shown in Figure 6.2, respondents in the success work conditions were significantly faster than the failure work group to say "yes, it is possible for me" to be prestigious, win high honors, famous, etc. These subjects were also faster to say "no, it is not possible for me" to be a failure, unmotivated lazy, etc. Such a pattern of responding suggests that representations of the self as successful may have been active in the working self-concept just before performing the task and perhaps during the task as well.

Representations of the self as failing or as unsuccessful must have been temporarily inaccessible because the success respondents were very quick to deny these characterizations. Those in the failure work condition took decidedly longer to respond "no, it is not possible for me" to selves such as lazy or unsuccessful, an indication that perhaps representations of the self such as these were indeed active in the working self-concept. Further, the longer response times for the failure-work subjects to claim "yes, it is possible for me" to be successful, prestigious, and famous indicates that positive possible selves such as these may have been relatively less accessible at the time of the task performance. The luck conditions, the success-luck and the failure-luck, showed a pattern of responses indicating that some negative possible selves did intrude into the working self-concept. In both groups they took longer than those in the success-work conditions to claim that negative possibilities could not characterize them.

Together these results suggest that before performing the writing task those in the success-work condition had working self-concepts that were dominated by positive possibility. We speculate that as they began to perform the required task they were (a) relatively energized or aroused as a result of recruiting, constructing, and deploying positive representations of themselves; and (b) focused on images and conceptions of themselves as successful in the future. As a result, these subjects were able to quickly generate representations of themselves as successful on the required task, and could prepare for the task relatively efficiently. In contrast, those who had been focused on future failure were probably consumed by conceptions or images of negative possible selves. As a consequence they may have been (a) relatively depressed and thus not energized, and (b) relatively disorganized. When required to perform the task, it may have been more difficult for the failure subjects to inhibit these negative possible selves and to prepare themselves for the required task performance.

These findings are consistent with those from the test anxiety literature that suggest that impaired performance is associated with negative thoughts about one's performance (Krohne & Laux, 1982; Sarason, 1984). Such negative conceptions of the self not only detract from the performance at hand, but they prevent the recruitment and deployment of positive possible selves—"me successfully completing this task"—from becoming active and energizing and organizing performance. A question remains as to whether possible selves (or some aspects of them) are active during actual performance or whether positive possible selves are useful primarily for energizing and organizing performance and then are relatively inaccessible once action begins. Csikszentmihalyi (1975), for example, argues that the best performance occurs when individuals are "in the flow" and when they are not self-aware. Certainly for many types of performance, the activation of cognitive representations of possible selves may be decidedly detrimental.

In this study of the effect of possible selves on performance, we were primarily concerned with the nature of the working self-concept at the point of specific performance. We assumed that the working self-concept is a biased selection from one's complete repertoire of possible selves. In other research we have taken a broader view of the function of possible selves. First, we have been concerned with exploring which possible selves individuals have in their repertoire. Second, we are interested in how these possible selves may be used in a strategic way (Cantor & Kihlstrom, 1987) to produce motivational control when choosing among competing actions or deciding whether or not to engage in a given activity.

Thus Oyserman and Markus (1988) have proposed that a given possible self will have maximal motivational effectiveness when it is offset or balanced by a countervailing possible self in *the same domain*. A feared possible self will be most effective as a motivational resource when it is balanced with a self-relevant positive expected or hoped for possible selves that provides the outlines of what one might do to avoid the feared state. Likewise, positive expected selves will be stronger motivational resources, and maximally effective, when they are linked with representations of what could happen if the desired state is not realized.

In this perspective possible selves are viewed as motivational resources that provide individuals with some control over their own behavior (cf. Carver & Scheier, 1982; Kuhl & Beckmann, 1985). Although people cannot always control what becomes active in the working self-concept, we assume that individuals are often able to deliberately recruit and deploy these possible selves to motivate themselves. For example, at a given moment, a positive possible self of "finishing my assignment" may not be particularly compelling, perhaps because of competing possible selves ("me watching TV", "me playing tennis"). If the countervailing feared self of "me being late with my assignment" or "me never doing the assignment" can be recruited, the desire to avoid this negative self should shore up one's flagging motivation and keep one in pursuit of the desired possible self.

Similarly, a vivid representation of one's self in a relevant positive and desired manner ("me getting through school") can be used to counter the representation of the self in an undesired state ("me doing poorly in school" or "me dropping out") and to prevent the inaction that occurs when a dreaded possible self dominates the working self-concept. Without a positive possible self that provides an outline of a desired state that can be realized if the feared possible self is avoided, one's actions will be disorganized or subject to control by a variety of external or situational factors that will remove attention from the feared possible self. A picture of one's self as 30 pounds overweight on the refrigerator may effectively activate an undesired self in the working self-concept. This feared self is unlikely to have a systematic effect on one's current actions, however, unless it is paired with an elaborated sequence of representations of one's self dieting and exercising until a thinner self is achieved that can be recruited into the working self-concept to supplant the feared self. The more one's feared and hoped for possible selves have been individually crafted to offset each other, the more motivational control one can gain in a given domain.

Individuals with a balance between their feared and their expected selves in a given domain will have more control over their behavior in this domain because they will have more varied motivational resources available to them than will individuals without such balance. Such a dynamic balance between one's expected and one's feared selves in a given domain creates a more intense and a more directed motivational state than either an expected possible self or feared possible self alone. Individuals who have developed a self-schema in a given domain are the most likely to display this balance between expected and feared selves. A self-schema provides a sense of what one is and what one is not and also a sense of what one might become, both positive and negative. Thus, the individual with the extrovert self-schema knows that is possible to be the charming life of the party but that it is also possible to be overbearing and pushy.

Possible Selves and Delinquency

In an empirical test of the importance of balance among one's possible selves, Oyserman and Markus (1988) conducted a semistructured interview study of 238 youth between the ages of 13 and 16 who varied in the degree of their delinquency, from those with no official involvement with delinquency to those confined to the state training school for delinquent youth. They hypothesized that becoming involved and staying involved in delinquency reflects a lack of balance among one's possible selves and thus a lack of specific motivational control over one's actions. They anticipated that the delinquent youth would display the least balance between their expected and their feared possible selves.

Specifically there were four separate groups (a) youth attending seven inner-city Detroit schools formed the officially nondelinquent group (b) youth attending area schools of observation, alternative schools, and public school in connection with a delinquency intervention program (c) youth living in group homes and (d) youth living in the institution of last resort for juvenile delinquent males in the state.

Oyserman and Markus asked these youth to describe three "expected" selves and three "feared selves" for the next year. Coders then scored the number of balanced pairs of expected and feared selves. A pair of responses (an expected and a feared self) was considered "in balance" if the expected self and the feared self represented a positive and a negative aspect of the same content area. For example, an expected self of "pass ninth grade" might be paired with a feared self of "flunk out of school," an expected self of "have lots of friends" might be paired with a feared self of "lonely," an expected self of "get a job" might be paired with a feared self "can't keep a job." Each respondent received a score of 0 (no balance) to 3 (balance in each of three possible pairs of expected and feared selves).

As anticipated, significant differences in the balance of the possible selves of the four groups of youth were observed (see Figure 6.3). Over 81% of the public school respondents had at least one clear match between their feared possible selves and their expected possible selves. The number of matches was decidedly fewer among the other three more officially delinquent groups. Only 55% of the community placement youth had one or more matches among their response to these questions. For the group home and the training school youth, the figures were 39% and 37%, respectively. For 63% of the youth from the training home, no matches could be found among their responses to these questions of feared and expected possible selves, but this was true for only 19% of the nondelinquent youth. Thus, the most delinquent subsamples were those with the most asymmetrical configurations of possible selves. This measure of balance among expected and feared selves thus allowed us to order perfectly the four groups of youth according to their level of official delinquency. As shown in Figure 6.3, however, this was not the case for the self-esteem measure. A U-shaped relationship with severity of delinquency was obtained, with public school and training school youth both scoring higher than community placed and group home youth.

Using the balance measure, Oyserman and Markus (1988) also reliably predicted self-reported delinquency among the officially *non*delinquent group. Youth who lacked balance in their possible selves subsequently reported higher levels of delinquent behavior than youth

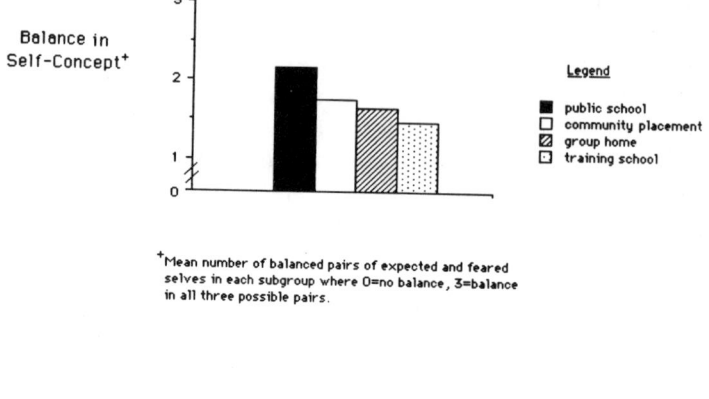

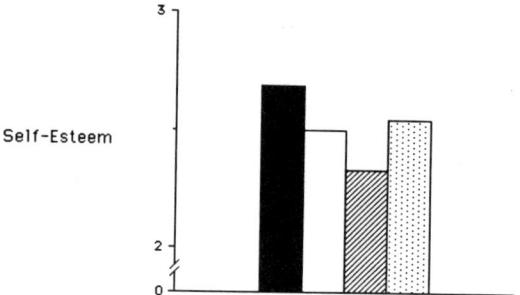

FIG. 6.3 Group means for balance in self-concept and for self-esteem

whose possible selves contained some balance. In thinking about the role of possible selves in creating and maintaining delinquency, we hypothesized that positive and negative possible selves and the links between them are important in both the initiation and maintenance of delinquent behavior. A major task of adolescence is to create the self one is going to become. Adolescents who are not successful in constructing and maintaining such positive selves, whether at home with the family, or at school with teachers and peers, may have primarily negative or feared selves in their repertoire and may thus seek out alternative domains in which to define the self. Delinquency and the chance to define one's self as independent, tough, daring, or adventurous becomes an alternative domain because there are very few other viable ones. A need for positive possible selves may first lead some youth to delinquency.

Other youth may be drawn to delinquency because they have yet to create compelling feared or "to-be-avoided" selves in their self-defining domains. Such youth may expect to finish school, or to find a good job, or to have friends but may not have elaborated self-relevant futures in which they drop out, are unemployed, or suffer the disapproval of family and friends. Expected positive selves alone may not provide these adolescents with sufficient motivation control to allow them to turn away from delinquent activity that appears exciting.

Although delinquent activity may offer a set of temporarily positive self-definitions, once initiated it is likely to elicit a set of very negative, feared possibilities (fear of prison, fear of being injured or killed) that must be added to the set of negative selves that have already been shaped. These adolescents will find it increasingly difficult to create and maintain socially sanctioned positive possibilities. As a result, their set of believable and satisfying expected selves will be increasingly narrowed and they will be left mostly with negative expectations for the future. Thus, Oyserman and Markus (1988) hypothesized that delinquency is maintained by a combination of feared and undesired selves that are not balanced by positive possibilities, and by expectations of negative possible selves.

THE ROLE OF POSSIBLE SELVES IN THE MOTIVATIONAL SEQUENCE: HOW DOES IT WORK?

In the previous sections we have theorized that possible selves are the personalized carriers of an individual's motivation. We have hypothesized that individuals will feel motivated or unmotivated depending on whether the working self-concept is configured of positive or negative possible selves, and that in some cases individuals can actively construct, recruit, or deploy these possible selves, alone or in combination, to regulate their own behavior. So far, however, we have stopped short of speculations about how these representations of the self in the future are responsible for specific action, that is, how they can enhance or impair performance.

Generally, we have hypothesized that possible selves work by personalizing the goal, that is, by making the goal one's own or, in Lewin's language putting a piece of the self in the goal space. Cognitively, affectively, somatically, the task representation and the self-representation become one, which may then serve to decrease the psychological distance between one's current state and the desired state. From research on goal gradients (Miller, 1944), we know that animals approaching the goal box speed up because of the increased presence of goal-related cues. Similarly, those individuals with a clear image, conception, or sense of themselves in a future state (e.g., successful on a given task) will have accessible more cues relevant to this future state, and this will enhance goal related performance. The construction of possible selves allows one to experience a contingency between one's now self and one's imaged or felt future self. The better one is at constructing these possible selves, the more vivid and specific they become, the more one's current state can be made similar to the desired state.

When the working self-concept is dominated by positive possibility, it is these senses, images, and conceptions that will regulate the individual's actions. This means that individuals will be extremely self-focused (cf. Carver & Scheier, 1982; Klinger, 1975), yet focused on future rather than on current selves. Further, they will be focused on actions instrumental for achieving the desired goal, rather than on their current state (e.g., how am I doing?) (cf. Kuhl & Beckmann, 1985). This can have a variety of interrelated cognitive, affective, and somatic effects, each of which will be briefly discussed.

Cognitive Consequences

We can speculate first that possible selves focus and organize one's activities. The most obvious implication of this is that information processing will be biased in the direction of stimuli that are consistent with the activated possible self. Klinger and his colleagues (1975; Klinger, Barta, and Maxeiner, 1980) found, for example, that commitment to a goal is accompanied by increased responsiveness to cues related to the goal and to an increased amount of thought about the goal. Inconsistent stimuli suggesting alternative or opposite outcomes will be slighted. This selective information processing will enable individuals to construct the bridge of self-representations between one's current state and the anticipated future state. In many cases, possible selves are elements of larger scripts or schemas that will be primed along with the possible selves; and these scripts or schemas contain the plans, strategies, and procedural knowledge that enable the performance. Locke et al. (1981), for example, stresses that strategy development is one of the important ways in which goal-setting affects performance.

Task components involving cognitive skills can be mastered more quickly when a relevant schema is available to organize information and guide information processing. Research with athletes suggests that imagining oneself performing a behavior helps people to learn the cognitive skills involved in sports performances (Feltz & Landers, 1983; Hall & Erffmeyer, 1983; Ryan & Simons, 1981). Schemas may enable people to picture task requirements clearly, organize them, and fulfill them efficiently.

The more compelling the possible self, the more vividly it can be elaborated in the present, and the more it will command attention and structure one's current activity. The person who is preparing to write a class paper, for example, will be absorbed by those activities that will produce the desired possible self. This will facilitate the production of specific plans (e.g., "me going to the third floor of the library, not reading the newspaper, checking out books, xeroxing articles, staying home Saturday night", etc). In addition, well-elaborated possible selves are engaging and lead to a type of attentional control that inhibits the processing of interesting but distracting irrelevant alternatives and that facilitates the processing of information that supports the intended performance (cf. Kuhl & Beckmann, 1985).

Other cognitive effects of possible selves include their influence on the individual's perception of the probability of success in achieving a given outcome. With respect to making decisions about the future, for example, Kahneman and Tversky (1982) suggest that people run mental simulations by constructing scenarios of alternative outcomes. The ease with which a particular event can be simulated is used to evaluate the likelihood of realizing the state. Similarly, Anderson and his colleagues (Anderson, 1983; Anderson, Lepper, & Ross, 1980) have suggested that the scripts that come most easily to mind are those that will be relied on most heavily in a decision about the future. They find that imagining one's self in a behavioral script markedly influences one's expectation about carrying out the behavior. Further, such images may influence not only one's expectations but also *actual* behavior. Thus, Gregory, Cialdini, and Carpenter (1982) found that many more people who imagined themselves with cable television subscribed to it than did those who simply listened to a persuasive message about its virtues. And Sherman and Anderson (in press) found that psychotherapy patients who imagined themselves returning for at least four sessions were less likely to drop out than did those who did not engage in this imagery. Thinking about a given end state in direct relationship to the self may make it seem more likely, and it may also make it appear more or less attractive.

After there has been an increase in an individual's subjective probability of realizing a possible self or in the value associated with it, there may be an increase in the amount of effort devoted to realizing it. Several studies have shown that people with high perceived probability of success expend more effort and persist longer at tasks than do people with low expectations. Holding low expectations may mean that a compelling and desirable possible self cannot be maintained in the working self-concept. These people may withdraw effort to protect themselves (Berglas & Jones, 1978; Smith, Snyder, & Handelsman, 1982).

Carver, Blaney, and Scheier (1979) showed that self-aware subjects with high expectations persisted longer than those with low expectations. In a correlational study, Battle (1965) showed that junior high school students with high expectations about math persisted longer on a novel math task than did students with low expectations. Feather (1963) demonstrated that those with high expectations persisted longer than those with low expectations, but only among subjects for whom the motivation to achieve success was higher than the motive to avoid failure.

Zajonc and Brickman (1969) found that just stating an expectancy was sufficient to improve performance, and they hypothesized that commitment mediated this effect. Forming an expectancy involves creating a desirable possible self that attracts and concentrates one's attentions and efforts.

Affective Consequences

By imagining a possible self, one may anticipate and actually experience part of the affect, positive or negative, associated with the end state. And the more elaborated the possible self, the more this will be true. The affect created by the activation of various possible selves can have a variety of influences on performance. Positive feelings lead children to perform more efficiently and to recall more words in a memory test than children without these feelings (Barden, Garber, Duncan, & Masters, 1981; Masters, Barden & Ford, 1979). Positive affect also increases the efficiency of decision making. Isen and Means (1983) showed that compared to control subjects, subjects who were put in a positive mood used a better decision strategy, ignored unimportant information more, and made decisions more quickly. Both groups of subjects arrived at the same decision, but the positive-affect subjects were more efficient. Further, Isen (1984) suggests that positive affect leads to enhanced creativity; she argues that people in positive moods can create larger cognitive, more diverse categories.

If, however, individuals experience negative affect with the activation of possible selves, the performance effects may be very different. Negative possible selves may be associated with anxiety which Sarason (1984) describes as "self-preoccupation about inability to respond adequately" (p. 930). Self-preoccupation is associated with internal distractors that hurt performance by reducing the amount of attention a person can give to the task. The more preoccupied the person is, the less well he or she performs (see also Wine, 1971). Covington (1986) describes anxiety as the anticipation of failure. During testing situations, anxiety is accompanied by arousal, distractability, and reduced performance. In addition to performance inhibitors, Covington describes the negative effects of anxiety that can occur before performance even starts. For example, without a positive possible self to offset the feared or negative self, and to focus and organize performance, anxious individuals may study less efficiently or use self-defeating strategies.

When a positive possible self is available to counter a negative one, the negative possible self and the associated anxiety can have beneficial effects on performance. Thus, Mahoney and Avener (1977) in a study of elite gymnasts found that the more successful gymnasts used their anxiety as a stimulus to better performance, whereas the less successful ones were overwhelmed by their anxiety. Cantor and her colleagues (Norem & Cantor, 1986) have identified individuals they call defensive pessimists who can harness their anxiety by anticipating the worst outcome and then working with great effort to ensure that it is not realized.

Somatic Consequences

Related to the affective consequences of positive selves previously described are a variety of other effects that might be generally described as somatic effects. One can speculate, for example, that by envisioning and thereby partially enacting possible selves one may be able to recruit or construct some of the visual, auditory, kinesthetic, or visceral representations of the self in the future.

The most straightforward connection between thoughts and feelings and various physical effects is through arousal. In one study, Wright, Contrada and Patane (1986) described easy, moderately difficult, or very difficult tasks to subjects who thought they would be performing them later. Those who were preparing to work on the moderately difficult task had a high increase in systolic blood pressure, but those anticipating an easy task or a very hard one experienced only slight increases. The individuals expecting a moderately difficult task were probably the most invested in the task and thus able to create a realistic sequence of possible selves, and this had an arousing or energizing effect.

The arousal engendered by activating a possible self can have diverse effects, depending on whether or not the possible self is well-elaborated and tied to a domain of one's expertise. If it is, the arousal created by anticipating the possible self is likely to enhance the emission of the correct dominant response (Spence, 1956) and performance will be enhanced. If the arousal is created by a poorly elaborated fantasy-based possible self, its activation can be expected to have a detrimental effect on performance. Similarly, an arousing possible self is likely to narrow the range of cues used (Easterbrook, 1959) in a given situation. This will have positive effects on performance if the procedures are routinized or schematicized and new input from the environment is not required; otherwise negative effects will result.

Notions about the possible physical effects of one's thoughts and feelings have, of course, a long historical precedent. Thus, for centuries some systems of medicine have centered on the assumption that the mind and body affect each other and cannot be treated separately. In ancient Greece, physicians considered patients' dreams and imagined images to be important resources in diagnosing and curing illness (Achtenberg, 1985). Navajo practitioners and traditional Chinese doctors both rely on patients' beliefs to aid healing (Sandner, 1979; Porkert 1979). The empirical support for mind/body interdependencies is scattered, however, coming primarily from health psychology or sports psychology. Some of the most compelling evidence is anecdotal but there are by now a sufficient number of small studies and demonstrations to suggest a number of intriguing hypotheses worthy of exploration.

Medical researchers are beginning to study the interrelationships between thoughts and feelings and physical health. With such diverse health problems as heart disease, alcoholism, and improper immune system functioning, studies suggest that mental activity, especially self-referent mental activity, can be linked with physical outcomes. For example, Pommer, Diederichs, Hummel, Kratzer & Offerman (1985) interviewed patients who were about to undergo kidney transplants. They found that those whose operations would later be successful had higher optimism, less fear, and more willingness to try again if the first operation were to be unsuccessful. Before the operation, patients whose transplants would be unsuccessful were more submissive, rigid, and depressive. They were also likely to have been influenced by other people when making their decisions about transplants, whereas successful candidates were those who made their own decisions about the transplant. Pommer et al. (1985) concluded that "integration of the graft starts before 'somatic incorporation' " (p. 101). The successful recipients probably formed strong possible selves of themselves as healthy transplant recipients. The unsuccessful candidates, plagued by worry and pushed to their actions by other people, probably did not have this benefit of a guiding positive possible self.

The mechanisms of such a connection between thoughts, feelings, and physical outcomes are still largely opaque; but there are numerous plausible speculations that one can make. It is possible that a keenly experienced possible self may function to focus or coordinate the autonomic, neural, or sensorimotor systems, or some aspects of these systems. In contrast, the presence of negative possible selves may disrupt the synchronous functioning of these systems.

Other mind/body effects have been demonstrated by alcohol researchers. Mental rehearsal can increase the body's alcohol tolerance. Subjects who mentally rehearsed a task were not as debilitated by the effects of alcohol when they later performed the same task (Annear & Vogel-Sprott, 1985; Vogel-Sprott, Rawana & Webster, 1984).

In another correlational study of the relationship between mind and illness, Stern, Pascale, and Ackerman (1977) observed that people who denied the seriousness of their illness had better rehabilitation after myocardial infarction than did patients who became depressed about their illness. Recently, Friedman and Booth-Kewley (1987) performed a meta-analysis of research on personality and physical illness and concluded that some factors such as depression and anxiety are linked with problems such as heart disease. These studies suggest a link between negative possible selves and poor health.

Some health practitioners believe so strongly in the relationship between mental and physical occurrences that they encourage physically ill people to alter their thought processes, hoping to alter the course of the disease. Simonton, Matthews-Simonton and Creighton (1978) advocate the active use of imagery during treatment for cancer. They suggest that patients create vivid, specific images of their bodies attacking diseased cells and being healed. These strong possible selves are thought to channel the body's energies into the healing process. Other medical researchers emphasize how important the patient's hope and faith are during the treatment of illness (Brewin, 1986; Cunningham, 1986; Stoll, 1986).

Also relevant to the somatic effects of possible selves is a seldom cited literature on the beneficial effects of mental practice. This work shows quite clearly that mental practice (the symbolic rehearsal of physical activity in the *absence* of any gross muscular movements) is very often associated with improved task performance (for reviews see Corbin,

1972; Feltz & Landers, 1983; Mackay, 1981; Richardson, 1967a, 1967b, Ryan & Simons, 1981, 1982; Zecker, 1982). Richardson (1967a) in a review of 25 studies found that mental practice or symbolic rehearsal improved performance in ring tossing, juggling, tennis, card sorting, digit substitution, muscular endurance, and mirror drawing. Consistent with these studies are statements from athletes about how they prepare for successful performance. Greg Louganis, the Olympic champion high diver, has described how he envisions every feature of his upcoming dive, mentally rotating his body through time and space. Dick Fosbury, the high jumper, reported that vividly picturing himself performing the event is vital for success (Mahoney & Avener, 1977; Ryan & Simons, 1982). Some coaches routinely train their athletes to use imagery to enhance performance. They claim that such mental practice can serve several purposes; it can help athletes when they are learning their skills, and it can help them perform optimally when they compete (Korn & Johnson, 1983; Orlick, 1986).

From the perspective of possible selves, it is interesting to note that the beneficial effects of mental imagery are strongest when the person uses what is called "internal imagery," viewing the activity as he or she would while performing it (Mahoney & Avener, 1977; Nigro, 1983; Orlick, 1986). Performance effects are less strong when the person takes an external perspective and see himself or herself as an outside observer would. Imagining from the internal perspective would seem to allow one to create possible selves not just of the end state but of the required substates or intermediate states as well, thus allowing some practice of all aspects of the performance.

In the type of mental rehearsal carried out in the preceding studies there is a rehearsal not just of the required movements but of the coordination of perceptual schemas with action schema. Finke (1980) has charted the equivalencies between imagery and actual perception and has shown that visual imagery shares portions of the visual perceptual cycle such than an individual who imagines reading a book shows a pattern of perceptual activity very similar to that of someone actually reading a book and a very different pattern from someone imagining a ship on a horizon. Such work implies a coherence among perception, imagery, and action that is only now beginning to unfold (see Volpert, 1982). Such a coherence, of course, would be especially beneficial when the anticipated performance is physical in nature. Yet even if it is mental performance that is anticipated, the anticipation may still serve to organize and energize future actions.

Ach (1910) as quoted in Kuhl & Beckmann, 1985), an early motivation psychologist, in fact, postulated a "subjective moment of volition," which gave rise to sensations in various parts of the body of the type that may actually occur during performance. This general idea has been pursued by a variety of researchers interested in the training or improvement of sports or other physical activity. There are many reports by athletes of a connection between their images of themselves and physical activity. Tennis players, for example, when thinking of a coming match note that they often anticipate various strokes by very slight muscle tensions and micromovements (Horowitz, 1978). And indeed some research indicates that when imagining performing some action, the corresponding muscles may be slightly activated (Korn & Johnson, 1983). In some small amount, motor pathways may become enervated in the same way that they are when the muscles are actively engaged in the behavior. The physical action of the muscles is mimicked during imagery, and some learning occurs.

MacKay (1981) suggested that mental and physical events have the same underlying components. He postulated a hierarchy of the neurons that regulate mental activity and muscle movements. Because of practice, activation of the pathways between nodes becomes more familiar, and transmission along the pathways becomes faster, leading to enhanced performance. This facilitation can take place even if the practice is mental because when mental nodes are activated, the corresponding muscle movement nodes are "primed" or partially activated, even though no muscle movement takes place.

Other evidence that the "priming" of muscles takes place during mental activity or imagery was reported by Bird (1984). She asked athletes to imagine themselves performing their sports. She recorded their electromyographic (EMG) activity in muscles relevant for the activity. The EMG results corresponded to the imagined activity. For one subject, EMG data could be collected while the athlete performed her sport. For her, the EMG levels collected while she practiced free throws matched the EMG levels emitted when she imagined taking the shots. Such findings suggest it is the personalization of the goal, specifically the embodiment of the desired end state—feeling one's self in the anticipated state—that enhances performance.

The exact inferences to be drawn from these findings are not unambiguous, however. Thus, Feltz and Landers (1983) assert that low level muscle activation is not responsible for the performance effects, because imagery may well energize all muscles, not just the ones involved in the action. They suggest that global physical arousal creates the beneficial effects. Similarly, Weinberg, Gould, and Jackson (1980) find that imagery increased performance on a strength task but not on a coordination or balance task, and thus they attribute the enhanced performance to general arousal.

CONCLUDING COMMENTS

Our goal in this chapter was to outline the advantages of conceptualizing goals as possible selves. We have argued that a critical feature of a goal is the personalized representation (cognitive, affective, somatic) of the individual approaching and realizing the goal. The first advantage of framing goals in terms of the self is that possible selves—senses, images, or conceptions of the self approaching and achieving a given end-state—seem to capture some elements of what is consciously experienced by individuals who are engaged in motivated or goal-directed behavior. A second advantage is that with possible selves goal effectiveness can be more fully understood. Why is it that important goals are effective, that goals to which an individual is committed are effective, and that specific goals are effective? These are all factors that encourage the individuals to put themselves into the goal and to construct the sequence of self-representations that will allow them to appropriate the goal. A third advantage is that we can begin to hypothesize quite specifically about how goals have their powerful effects on behavior. Once we can specify the various ways in which goals are personalized and given structure and form, we can examine how these representations are combined and integrated to regulate action and performance.

A final potential advantage to this approach is that it allows us to theorize about how the self-system is implicated in the production and control of action. Most theorists of the self now concur about the active, dynamic nature of the self-system. It is not just a static repository of self-representations. Instead, it is assumed to forcefully mediate and regulate ongoing action. The task that remains is to examine how this occurs. We have proposed possible selves as one of the mechanisms by which thought and feeling can be linked to action. At the cognitive level, possible selves provide focus and organization to one's intended activity. They guide the recruitment of appropriate self-knowledge, the development of plans, and the search for appropriate behavioral strategies. Possible selves are action-oriented structures (see Trzebinski, this volume) and in the course of constructing, recruiting, and deploying them parts of the required sequences of actions will be primed, partially activated, or "run." When this type of mental and somatic practice or anticipation occurs, performance is enhanced. To the extent that we can develop methods for measuring the degree of elaboration of a possible self, we should be able to predict performance more precisely than measures of level of aspiration or achievement motivation, which assess only one aspect of the individual's orientation to the goal.

REFERENCES

Achtenberg, J. (1985). *Imagery in healing: Shamanism and modern medicine*. Boston: New Science Library.
Allport, G. W. (1961). *Pattern and growth in personality*. New York: Holt.
Anderson, C. A. (1983). Imagination and expectation: The effect of imagining behavioral scripts on personal intentions. *Journal of Personality and Social Psychology, 45,* 293–305.
Anderson, C. A., Lepper, M. R., & Ross, L. (1980). Perseverance of social theories: The role of explanation in the persistence of discredited information. *Journal of Personality and Social Psychology, 39,* 1037–1049.
Annear, W. C., & Vogel-Sprott, M. (1985). Mental rehearsal and classical conditioning contribute to ethanol tolerance in humans. *Psychopharmacology, 87,* 90–93.
Ansbacher, H. L., & Ansbacher, R. R. (1956). *The individual psychology of Alfred Adler*. New York: Basic Books.
Atkinson, J. W. (1957). Motivational determinants of risk-taking behavior. *Psychological Review, 64,* 359–372.
Atkinson, J. W. (1964). *An introduction to motivation*. Princeton, NJ: Van Nostrand.
Bandura, A. (1986). *Social foundations of thought and action: A social cognitive theory*. Englewood Cliffs, NJ: Prentice-Hall.
Bandura, A. (1988). Self-regulation of motivation and action through goal systems. In V. Hamilton, G. H. Bower & N. H. Frijda (Eds.), *Cognition, motivation, and affect: A cognitive science view*. Dordrecht: Martinus Nijholl, in press.
Barden, R. C., Garber, J., Duncan, S. W., & Masters, J. C. (1981). Cumulative effects of induced affective states in children: Accentuation, inoculation, and remediation. *Journal of Personality and Social Psychology, 40,* 750–760.
Battle, E. S. (1965). Motivational determinants of academic task persistence. *Journal of Personality and Social Psychology, 2,* 209–218.
Berglas, S., & Jones, E. E. (1978). Drug choice as a self-handicapping strategy in response to noncontingent success. *Journal of Personality and Social Psychology, 36,* 405–417.
Bird, E. I. (1984). EMG quantification of mental rehearsal. *Perceptual and Motor Skills, 59,* 899–906.
Brewin, T. B. (1986). Quality of survival: Can we measure it? Can we influence it? In B. A. Stoll (Ed.), *Coping with cancer stress*. (p. 83–94). Boston: Martinus Nijholl Publishers.
Burger, J. M. (1985). Desire for control and achievement-related behaviors. *Journal of Personality and Social Psychology, 48,* 1520–1533.
Cantor, N., & Kihlstrom, J. (1987). *Personality and social intelligence*. Englewood Cliffs, NJ: Prentice-Hall.
Carver, C. S., Blaney, P. H., & Scheier, M. F. (1979). Reassertion and giving up: The interactive role of self-directed attention and outcome expectancy. *Journal of Personality and Social Psychology, 37,* 1859–1870.
Carver, C. S., & Scheier, M. F. (1982). Control theory: A useful conceptual framework for personality, social, clinical, and health psychology. *Psychological Bulletin, 92,* 111–135.
Corbin, C. B. (1972). Mental practice. In W. P. Morgan (Ed.), *Ergogenic aids and muscular performance*. (pp. 93–118). New York: Academic Press.
Covington, M. V. (1986). Anatomy of failure induced anxiety: The role of cognitive mediators. In R. Schwarzer (Ed.), *Self-related cognitions in anxiety and motivation* (pp. 247–264). Hillsdale, NJ: Lawrence Erlbaum Associates.
Csikszentmihalyi, M. (1975). *Beyond boredom and anxiety*. San Francisco: Jossey-Bass.
Cunningham, A. J. (1986). Psychological self-help by cancer patients. In B. A. Stoll (Ed.), *Coping with cancer stress*. (pp. 131–142). Boston: Martinus Nijholl Publishers.

deCharms, R. (1968). *Personal causation.* New York: Academic Press.
Deci, E. L. (1975). *Intrinsic motivation.* New York: Plenum Press.
Deci, E. L., & Ryan, R. M. (1980). The empirical exploration of intrinsic motivational processes. In L. Berkowitz (Ed.), *Advances in experimental social psychology* (Vol. 13), (pp. 39–80). New York: Academic Press.
Easterbrook, J. A. (1959). The effects of emotion on cue utilization and the organization of behavior. *Psychological Review, 66,* 183–201.
Emmons, R. (1986). Personal strivings: An approach to personality and subjective well-being. *Journal of Personality and Social Psychology, 51,* 1058–1068.
Feather, N. T. (1963). Mowrer's revised two-factor theory and the motive-expectancy-value model. *Psychological Review, 70,* 500–515.
Feather, N. T. (Ed.). (1982). *Expectations and actions: Expectancy-value models in psychology.* Hillsdale, NJ: Lawrence Erlbaum Associates.
Feltz, D. L., & Landers, D. M. (1983). The effects of mental practice on motor skill learning and performance: A meta analysis. *Journal of Sport Psychology, 5,* 25–57.
Finke, R. A. (1980). Levels of equivalence in imagery and perception. *Psychological Review, 87,* 113–132.
Fishbein, M. (Ed.). (1967). *Readings in attitude theory and measurement.* New York: Wiley.
Friedman, H. S., & Booth-Kewley, S. (1987). The "disease-prone personality": A meta-analytic view of the construct. *American Psychologist, 42*(6), 539–555.
Gollwitzer, P. M., & Wicklund, R. A. (1985). The pursuit of self-defining goals. In J. Kuhl, & J. Beckmann (Eds.), *Action control: From cognition to behavior.* New York: Springer-Verlag.
Gregory, W. L., Cialdini, R. B., & Carpenter, K. M. (1982). Self-relevant scenarios as mediators of likelihood estimates and compliance: Does imagining make it so? *Journal of Personality and Social Psychology, 43*(1), 89–99.
Hall, E. G., & Erffmeyer, E. S. (1983). The effect of visuo-motor behavior rehearsal with videotaped modeling on free throw accuracy of intercollegiate female basketball players. *Journal of Sport Psychology, 5,* 343–346.
Harter, S. (1978). Effectance motivation reconsidered: Toward a developmental model. *Human Development, 21,* 34–64.
Harter, S. (1981). A model of mastery motivation in children: Individual differences and developmental change. In W. A. Collins (Ed.), *The Minnesota Symposia on Child Psychology, 14,* 215–255.
Heider, F. (1946). Attitudes and cognitive organization. *Journal of Psychology, 21,* 107–112.
Hollenbeck, J. R., & Williams, C. R. (1987). Goal importance, self-focus, and the goal-setting process. *Journal of Applied Psychology, 72*(2), 204–211.
Horowitz, M. J. (1978). *Image formation and cognition.* Second Edition. New York, NY: Appleton-Century Crofts.
Isen, A. M. (1984). Toward understanding the role of affect in cognition. In R. S. Wyer & T. K. Srull (Eds.), *Handbook of social cognition* (Vol. 3). Hillsdale, NJ: Lawrence Erlbaum Associates.
Isen, A. M., & Means, B. (1983). The influence of positive affect on decision-making strategy. *Social Cognition, 2,* 18–31.
James, W. (1890). *Principles of psychology.* New York: Holt.
Kahneman, D., & Tversky, A. (1982). The simulation heuristic. In D. Kahneman & A. Tversky (Eds.), *Judgment under uncertainty: Heuristics and biases* (pp. 201–208). Cambridge, England: Cambridge University Press.
Klinger, E. (1975). Consequences of commitment to and disengagement from incentives. *Psychological Review, 82,* 1–25.

Klinger, E., Barta, S. G., & Maxeiner, M. E. (1980). Motivational correlates of thought content, frequency and commitment. *Journal of Personality and Social Psychology, 39,* 1222–1237.
Korn, E. R., & Johnson, K. (1983). *Visualization: The uses of imagery in the health professions.* Homewood, IL: Dow Jones-Irwin.
Krohne, H. W., & Laux, L. (Eds.). (1982). *Achievement, stress, and anxiety.* Washington: Hemisphere Publishing Corporation.
Kuhl, J., & Beckmann, J. (Eds.). (1985). *Action control from cognition to behavior.* Berlin: Springer-Verlag.
Lefcourt, H. M. (1976). *Locus of control: Current trends in theory and research.* Hillsdale, NJ: Lawrence Erlbaum Associates.
Lewin, K. (Ed.). (1948). *Resolving social conflicts.* New York: Haven.
Little, B. R. (1983). Personal projects: A rationale and method for investigation. *Environment and Behavior, 15,* 273–309.
Locke, E. A. (1968). Toward a theory of task motivation and incentives. *Organizational Behavior and Human Performance, 3,* 157–189.
Locke, E. A., Shaw, K. N., Saari, L. M., & Latham, G. P. (1981). Goal setting and task performance: 1969–1980. *Psychological Bulletin, 90*(1), 125–152.
Mackay, D. G. (1981). The problem of rehearsal or mental practice. *Journal of Motor Behavior, 13*(4), 274–285.
MacLeod, R. B. (1949). Perceptual constancy and the problem of motivation. *Canadian Journal of Psychology, 3,* 62–63.
Mahoney, M. J., & Avener, M. (1977). Psychology of the elite athlete: An exploratory study. *Cognitive Therapy and Research, 1,* 135–141.
Markus, H., & Kunda, Z. (1986). Stability and malleability of the self-concept. *Journal of Personality and Social Psychology, 51,* 858–866.
Markus, H., & Nurius, P. (1986). Possible selves. *American Psychologist, 41,* 954–969.
Markus, H., & Sentis, K. (1982). The self in social information processing. In J. Suls (Ed.), *Social psychological perspectives on the self.* Hillsdale, NJ: Lawrence Erlbaum Associates.
Markus, H., & Zajonc, R. B. (1985). The cognitive perspective in social psychology. In G. Lindzey & E. Aronson (Eds.), *The handbook of social psychology* (Vol. l), (pp. 137–230).
Masters, J. C., Barden, R. C., & Ford, M. E. (1979). Affective states, expressive behavior, and learning in children. *Journal of Personality and Social Psychology, 37,* 380–390.
McClelland, D. C., Atkinson, J. W., Clark, R. A., & Lowell, E. L. (1953). *The achievement motive.* New York: Appleton-Century-Crofts.
McDougall, W. (1928). *An introduction to social psychology.* London: Methven.
Miller, N. E. (1944). Experimental studies of conflict. In J. McV. Hunt (Ed.), *Personality and the behavior disorders* (Vol. 1). New York: Ronald.
Mook, D. G. (1986). *Motivation: The organization of action.* New York: W. W. Norton & Company.
Neisser, U. (1985). The role of invariant structures in the control of movement. In M. Frese & J. Sabini (Eds.), *Goal directed behavior: The concept of action in psychology.* (pp. 97–109). Hillsdale, NJ: Lawrence Erlbaum Associates.
Nicholls, J. G. (1984). Achievement motivation: Conceptions of ability, subjective experience, task choice, and performance. *Psychological Review, 91,* 328–346.
Nigro, G. N. (1983). Improvement of skill through observation and mental practice. Unpublished doctoral dissertation. Cornell University.
Norem, J. K., & Cantor, N. (1986). Defensive pessimism: "Harnessing" anxiety as motivation. *Journal of Personality and Social Psychology, 51*(6), 1208–1217.

Nuttin, J. (1984). *Motivation, planning, and action* (R. P. Lorion & J. E. Dumas, Trans.). Hillsdale, NJ: Lawrence Erlbaum Associates.

Orlick, T. (1986). *Psyching for sport: Mental training for athletes.* Champaign, IL: Leisure Press.

Oyserman, D., & Markus, H. (1988). Possible selves and delinquency. Paper presented at the International Congress of Psychology, Sydney, Australia.

Pervin, L. A. (1983). The stasis and flow of behavior: Toward a theory of goals. In M. M. Page (Ed.), *Nebraska symposium on motivation.* (pp. 1–53). Lincoln: University of Nebraska Press.

Pommer, W., Diederichs, P., Hummel, M., Kratzer, P. & Offerman, G. (1985). Patients' expectations from renal grafting and transplantation outcome. *Psychotherapy & Psychosomatics, 44,* 95–102.

Porkert, M. (1979). Chinese medicine: A tradition healing science. In *Ways of health: Holistic approaches to ancient and contemporary medicine.* New York: Harcourt Brace Jovanovich.

Rank, O. (1936). *Will therapy* (J. Taft, Trans.). New York: Knopf.

Raynor, J. O., & McFarlin, D. B. (1986). Motivation and the self-system. In R. M. Sorrentino & E. T. Higgins (Eds.), *Handbook of motivation and cognition* (pp. 315–349). New York: Guilford.

Richardson, A. (1967a). Mental practice: A review and discussion, Part I. *Research Quarterly, 38,* 95–107.

Richardson, A. (1967b). Mental practice: A review and discussion, Part II. *Research Quarterly, 38,* 263–273.

Rodin, J., & Langer, E. S. (1977). Long-term effects of a control relevant intervention with the institutionalized aged. *Journal of Personality and Social Psychology, 35,* 897–907.

Rotter, J. B., Chance, J. F., & Phares, E. J. (1972). *Applications of social learning theory of personality.* New York: Holt, Rinehart & Winston.

Ruvolo, A., & Markus, H. (1988b). Possible selves and motivation. Paper presented at the American Psychological Association Meetings, Washington, D.C.

Ryan, E. D., & Simons, J. (1981). Cognitive demand, imagery, and frequency of mental rehearsal as factors influencing acquisition of motor skills. *Journal of Sport Psychology, 3,* 35–45.

Ryan, E. D., & Simons, J. (1982). Efficacy of mental imagery in enhancing mental rehearsal of motor skills. *Journal of Sport Psychology, 4,* 41–51.

Sandner, D. F. (1979). Navaho Indian medicine and medicine men. In D. S. Sobel (Ed.), *Ways of health: Holistic approaches to ancient and contemporary medicine* (pp. 117–146).

Sarason, I. G. (1984). Stress, anxiety, and cognitive interference: Reactions to tests. *Journal of Personality and Social Psychology, 46,* 929–938.

Schank, R. C., & Abelson, R. P. (1977). *Scripts, plans, goals, and understanding.* Hillsdale, NJ: Lawrence Erlbaum Associates.

Schlenker, B. R. (1985). Identity and self-identification. In B. R. Schlenker (Ed.), *The self in social life* (pp. 65–99). New York: McGraw-Hill.

Sherman, R. T., & Anderson, C. A. (In press). Decreasing premature termination from psychotherapy. *Journal of Social and Clinical Psychology.*

Simonton, O. C., Matthews-Simonton, S., & Creighton, J. (1978). *Getting well again.* New York: St. Martin's Press.

Smith, T. W., Snyder, C. R., & Handelsman, M. M. (1982). On the self-serving function of an academic wooden leg: Test-anxiety as a self-handicapping strategy. *Journal of Personality and Social Psychology, 42,* 314–321.

Sorrentino, R. M., & Higgins, E. T. (1986). *Handbook of motivation and cognition: Foundations of social behavior.* New York: Guilford.

Spence, K. W. (1956). *Behavior theory and conditioning.* New Haven: Yale University Press.

Staub, E. (1980). *Social and prosocial behavior.* In E. Staub (Ed.), *Personality: Basic aspects and current research,* (pp. 237–294). Englewood Cliffs, NJ: Prentice-Hall.
Stern, M. J., Pascale, L., Ackerman, A. (1977). Life adjustment postmyocardial infarction. *Archives of Internal Medicine, 137,* 1680–1685.
Stoll, B. A. (Ed.). (1986). Faith only belongs in churches? In *Coping with cancer stress.* (pp. 9–20). Boston: Martinus Nijhoff Publishers.
Vogel-Sprott, M., Rawana, E., & Webster, R. (1984). Mental rehearsal of a task under ethanol facilities tolerance. *Pharmacology Biochemistry & Behavior, 21,* 329–331.
Volpert, W. (1982). The model of the hierarchical-sequential organization of action. In W. Hacker, W. Volpert, & M. Von Cranach (Eds.), *Cognitive and motivational aspects of action.* Berlin: Deutscher Verlagder Wissenschoflen, Amsterdam/New York: Elesevier/Worth, Holland.
Vroom, V. H. (1964). *Work and motivation.* New York: Wiley.
Weinberg, R. S., Gould, D., & Jackson, A. (1980). Cognition and motor performance: Effect of psyching-up strategies on three motor tasks. *Cognitive Therapy and Research, 4*(2), 239–245.
White, R. W. (1959). Motivation reconsidered: The concept of competence. *Psychological Review, 66,* 297–333.
Wine, J. (1971). Test anxiety and direction of attention. *Psychological Bulletin, 76,* 92–104.
Wright, R. A., Contrada, R. J., & Patane, M. J. (1986). Task difficulty, cardiovascular response, and the magnitude of goal valence. *Journal of Personality and Social Psychology. 51*(4), 837–843.
Wundt, W. M. (1894). *Lectures on human and animal psychology.* (Trans. from the 2nd German Edition by J. E. Creighton & E. B. Titchener). New York: MacMillan.
Zajonc, R. B., & Brickman, P. (1969). Expectancy and feedback as independent factors in task performance. *Journal of Personality and Social Psychology, 11,* 148–156.
Zecker, S. G. (1982). Mental practice and knowledge of results in the learning of a perceptual motor skill. *Journal of Sport Psychology, 4,* 52–63.

7 Goals and the Self-Identification Process: Constructing Desired Identities

BARRY R. SCHLENKER
MICHAEL F. WEIGOLD
University of Florida

The recent resurgence of interest in the self has brought with it a proliferation of minitheories, each focusing on a distinctive aspect of how people describe, define, or express themselves. Most approaches can be distinguished based on where they fall on two intersecting dimensions, the four quadrants of which can be characterized by the terms "self-reflection," "self-disclosure," "self-deception," and "self-presentation." The first dimension describes the actor's purported *motive for the activity*. Is the actor seeking accuracy or personal advantage? In common parlance, the terms "self-reflection" and "self-disclosure" are regarded as attempts by the actor to acquire, crystallize, or convey accurate information about the self. The motive appears to be the pursuit or expression of knowledge. In contrast, the terms "self-deception" and "self-presentation" are viewed as attempts to package or fabricate information that is in the actor's best interests. The motive is to benefit the self. As Tetlock and Levi (1982) indicated, theoretical positions can be grouped into those that emphasize the acquisition and use of logically accurate information about the self and those that emphasize motivated biases that serve to protect and enhance views of the self. The second dimension reflects the *private or public nature of the activity*. Self-reflection and self-deception are private and are performed for the self. Self-disclosure and self-presentation are public and are performed, at least in part, for others. As Tetlock and Manstead (1985) noted, theoretical positions can be readily grouped into those that emphasize intrapsychic versus interpersonal processes.

Any theory that attempts to capture more than a fragment of the phenomena associated with the self must deal with experiences that fall along both dimensions. An integrative approach cannot focus only on accuracy or only on self-interest any more than it can assign significance to only the private or public facets of self. Human beings are unique in the combination of (a) mental capabilities that permit the quest for knowledge yet allow for bias and cunning, and (b) social predilections that embed us deeply in a matrix of real or imagined other people who influence our ideas and actions, just as we influence theirs. With the objective of integration, this chapter will discuss aspects of a theory of self-identification (Schlenker, 1980, 1982, 1984, 1985, 1986a, 1987). We consider the nature and implications of self-identification as a goal-directed activity in its own right and as a component of other goal-directed social behaviors.

THE NATURE OF SELF-IDENTIFICATION

Defining and expressing one's identity is an ubiquitous feature of social activity. Social life requires that people communicate a sense of who they are and what they are likely to do, and specifying the properties of one's identity serves important intrapersonal and interpersonal functions. First, specifying one's identity (or, more properly, specifying those facets of one's identity that are considered relevant to the occasion) is an inherent component of the self-regulation of conduct. It has implications for the valuation and selection of goals; the choice of effective strategies for goal achievement; expectations of goal achievement; and the monitoring, evaluating, and correcting of goal-directed activities (Bandura, 1982; Foote, 1951; Markus & Nurius, 1986; Rosenberg, 1979; Schlenker, 1980, 1985).

Second, specifying one's identity permits a sense of understanding, prediction, and control of the environment (Berscheid, Graziano, Monson, & Dermer, 1976; Gergen, 1968; Goffman, 1959; Schlenker, 1980, 1985). Once people have categorized and evaluated one another, they can proceed with the confidence that they will generally behave consistently with the identities they construct, and others will do likewise (Gergen, 1968; Goffman, 1959; Schlenker, 1980, 1985; Tedeschi, Schlenker, & Bonoma, 1971). When identities are fixed in terms that are understandable and potentially agreeable to the parties, all other dealings can follow; the participants can relate to one another and regulate their conduct accordingly. Without these specifications, accomplished consciously or nonconsciously, confusion and tentativeness result; at the extreme social anxiety is produced (Schlenker & Leary, 1982a, 1985).

Third, identities mediate the outcomes people receive from social life. People receive (and expect to receive) outcomes that are commensurate with the types of identities they create (Alexander & Wiley, 1981; Goffman, 1959; Schlenker, 1980, 1984; Tedeschi, 1981; Tedeschi & Norman, 1985). More attractive identities, as determined by the particular social marketplace, receive more valued rewards; unattractive identities are associated with more costly, less rewarding encounters. Identities thereby determine in part the consequences of social interaction for the participants.

Self-identification is the process, means, or result of showing oneself to be a particular type of person, thereby specifying one's identity (Schlenker, 1984, 1985). Fixing and expressing identity involves systematically defining and categorizing oneself, bringing relevant evidence and experiences to bear.[1] It is accomplished privately through contemplation of oneself, and publicly through self-disclosure, self-presentation, and other activities (e.g., dress, task selection and performance) that symbolically communicate one's identity to others. Self-identification is as relevant in long-standing relationships as it is during first encounters (Schlenker, 1984) and is as vital in private settings in which people serve as audiences for their own conduct as it is in public settings in which people categorize, evaluate, and judge one another (Schlenker, 1980, 1986a). The complementary process is identification of the other, wherein a person attempts to specify, in thoughts and through actions, what the other is like.

Self-identification constructs and expresses an identity. The concept of *identity* recognizes the mutal dependency of the private and public facets of the self. Identity can be regarded as a theory of self (or a schema) that is formed and maintained through actual or imagined interpersonal agreement about what the self is like.[2] Analogous to a scientific theory, its contents must withstand the process of consensual agreement by informed, significant observers. As such, there is a constant triangulation of information between the views of the self as audi-

---

[1]Self-identification can occur through the use of descriptions, evidence, inference, analogy, or treatment and can be done linguistically or iconically. This use of identification is much broader than the classic psychoanalytic use of the term, which refers to people emulating (identifying with) someone else and incorporating the other's personality characteristics. Emulation is only one way in which we identify ourselves and involves fixing one's identity through analogy ("I am like him").

[2]When "identity" refers to a person's generalized, cumulative theory of self, it appears to be identical to how the term "self-concept" is usually used. Epstein (1973) defined the self-concept in precisely this way, as a self-theory, and analyses of the self from a social cognition perspective (Greenwald & Pratkanis, 1984; Markus, 1977; Markus & Sentis, 1982) frequently describe the self as a schema, or organized framework of information

ence for evaluating one's own conduct and other people as audiences for evaluating one's conduct (Erikson, 1959; Harre', 1983; Schlenker, 1985, 1986a). "People's ideas about themselves are expressed and tested in social life through their actions. In turn, the outcomes of these 'tests' provide the basis for crystallizing, refining, or modifying identity based in part on how believable or defensible these identity images appear to be [to various audiences]" (Schlenker, 1986a, p. 24).

Self-Identification in Context

By its nature, self-identification is a goal-directed activity in which the self is specified for some purpose to some audience. Schlenker (1985) lists three propositions that describe the basis for self-identification on a given occasion.

1. Self-identification occurs in a particular context that reflects the interaction of the person (e.g., the actor's self-concept and values), the situation (e.g., opportunities for and constraints on the satisfaction of values; social rules and rituals that provide information about normatively structured patterns of action), and one or more salient audiences for the activity (other people, imagined referents, or self).
2. An initial assessment and evaluation of self, situation, and audience evokes for the actor or prompts the actor to formulate (a) a goal or set of goals that might satisfy needs and values, (b) a script or plan for goal accomplishment, and (c) a set of desired identity images that describe the type of person the actor believes he or she can and should be on the occasion.
3. These desired identity images mediate self-identification on the occasion, acting like subscripts or subplans embedded within the overall script or plan. These images organize and regulate self-identification and may or may not correspond with images comprising the self-concept.

---

about oneself. The connotations of identity, however, highlight private and public triangulation, but the connotations of self-concept suggest a more private phenomenon.

A distinction can be drawn between identity as a cumulative theory of self and identity as it is situated or conceived in relation to particular other people in particular situations (Hewitt, 1976). The former can be called identity or the self-concept. The latter refers to a particular set of self-identifications that occur in context; these can be represented in memory as generalized self-images (or self-schemata). Discussions of social selves (James, 1890), situated identities (Alexander & Wiley, 1981), and the working self-concept (Markus & Nurius, 1986) focus on these more specific, contextually defined aspects of self.

This conceptualization assumes that people are purposive and planning; they are always thinking, always acting, and always trying to achieve particular objectives in life (see Carson, 1969; Harre' 1980; McCall & Simmons, 1978; Miller, Galanter, & Pribram, 1960; Schank & Abelson, 1977). The goal (or set of goals) that exists on an occasion can be important or mundane (e.g., getting a job or watching television with friends), specific or vague (e.g., graduating college or becoming learned), immediate or long-term (e.g., getting a date for this evening or raising a family), but it inevitably provides an objective for one's activities.

People employ scripts and plans in their pursuit of goals. Scripts and plans are cognitive representations that describe the operations (steps and procedures) required to get from a present state to a goal state (Abelson, 1976; Schank & Abelson, 1977). According to Schank and Abelson (1977), scripts are relatively specific, previously acquired and used, and available in memory as reasonably complete representations of the procedures required to achieve goals. Plans are constructed when existing scripts are unavailable or unacceptable and involve integrating general information about how people achieve goals with specific information pertinent to the situation or audience. Scripts and plans can be conscious or unconscious (Langer, 1978; Miller et al., 1960), and once activated direct the individual's thoughts and actions on the occasion, analogous to how a program directs the operations of a computer. That is, they provide templates for interpreting external events, activate sets of expectations for how interactions will evolve, and permit individuals to both regulate and respond to ongoing interactions.

Person, Situation, and Audience

Self-identifications do not occur in a vacuum. They should be regarded as *activities* (thoughts or behaviors) that occur in particular social contexts and are multiply determined. These activities reflect the transaction of the person (e.g., self-concept, values, mood), the situation (e.g., reward-cost contingencies, social rules), and an audience. This view constrasts with traditional positions that tend to focus on either personal or situational determinants. One such view holds that self-identifications are expressions of the self-concept and deals reluctantly with cases where behavior diverges from the self-concept by citing situational pressures. Another view holds that self-identifications are controlled by situational contingencies and demotes the self-concept to the status of epiphenomenon; the self-concept supposedly derives from behavior but does not influence behavior or does so only minimally. (A variation on this theme proposes that self-identifications are merely public ploys designed to achieve personal gain from others.) A third view, an individual difference variation that incorporates both of the preceding, suggests that self-identifications are genuine expressions of self for some people but manipulative ploys controlled by situational contingencies for other people (Buss & Briggs, 1984). It is curious to note that positions that emphasize personal determinants also tend to assume that people's motives are more virtuous (e.g., being motivated by authenticity, consistency, accuracy), whereas positions that emphasize situational determinants also tend to assume that people's motives are more base (e.g., being motivated by selfishness, manipulativeness, Machiavellianism); we will return to this point later.

We propose that *all* self-identifications comprise varying contributions from the person, situation, and audience. Given a particular setting, people assess its possibilities and work out objectives, strategies and tactics, and a pertinent portrait of self that permits them to take advantage of opportunities and dangers. This sequencing of events is arbitrary because goals often exist first, arising from needs and values that exist in a particular context, and stimulate people to accomplish them by selectively seeking out and constructing new environments that provide even better opportunities for goal achievement (e.g., selecting a college, a major, friends, and so forth, that will benefit one's long-term career objectives) (see Schlenker, 1985, for further discussion).

Self-identifications are not simply "pure expressions" of the self, mindless reactions to situational pressures, or Machiavellian deceits to fool the unwary. Self-identifications are contextually bound and influenced by the actor's self-concept, the situation, and the salient audience. For example, variations in an audience, even an imagined one, produce variations in self-identifications because they influence the types of acts that are regarded as appropriate and the standards that are used to evaluate the acts (Baldwin & Holmes, 1987; see also Greenwald & Breckler, 1985; Schlenker, 1986a). Even when subjects are anonymous, causing them to think of one rather than another audience will change their reactions (Baldwin & Holmes, 1987). Imagine the difference in thoughts when people reflect on their intellectual qualities before a discussion with an Ivy League interviewer versus Uncle Joe, the tow truck driver (Morse & Gergen, 1970). Variations in situational factors such as reward/cost contingencies and social rules will similarly modify people's self-identifications (Schlenker, 1985). Self-identifications are an edited, packaged version of the self meant for a particular audience and having a particular objective. Yet the actor extracts from them generalizations that, wittingly or unwittingly, comprise the self-concept. Once these generalizations are derived, they in turn influence subsequent self-identifications.

In this view, the self-concept represents an actor's cumulative, generalized theory of self. The question is not, "How accurate are public self-identifications as expressions of the self-concept?" The question is, "When will aspects of the self-concept be salient and weighed heavily relative to the other determinants of self-identifications?" With these issues in mind, we turn to a brief look at aspects of the person, situation, and audience as determinants of self-identifications (see Schlenker, 1980, 1986a, for more complete discussions).

The Person. Self-identifications are influenced by the actor's (a) personality, particularly as represented by the self-concept; (b) goals; and (c) affective state (mood). Particular self-images (or self-schemata) can be activated by elements of the situation, the audience, or the actor's goals. When activated, information contained in these self-images will be available for packaging and presentation to audiences. Some self-images have been formed and stabilized over years of personality development through continued use and validation by others, and these form the core of the self-concept (Hogan, 1982). These images are likely to be more *important* (i.e., related to valued outcomes) and *central* (i.e., more inclusive), and are therefore more likely to be represented in people's self-identifications across a variety of situations (Schlenker, 1986a). Keep in mind, however, that we are not arguing that these self-images simply emerge in self-identifications, faithfully reproduced for examination by audiences. Instead, the information contained in the self-images must be edited and packaged for consumption in the particular context.

To claim that people's self-identifications are influenced by situations and audiences does not imply that people are liars or that self-presentations are transient, unstable emissions that are unrelated to the self-concept. Studies have shown remarkable stability of facets of the self-concept over time (e.g., McCrae & Costa, 1982). This stability probably arises because of the importance and centrality of the relevant core images and the high consensual validation that is provided for these images by audiences (Hogan, 1982; Schlenker, 1985; Swann, 1983, 1985). Further, people's self-images are more likely to be highly correlated with their behaviors when people regard themselves as consistent on the relevant dimension (Bem & Allen, 1974) or when people are privately self-attentive and hence focusing on their existing self-beliefs (Carver & Scheier, 1985). In this vein, Trudeau and Schlenker (1986) found that people who perceived themselves as consistent on a trait would not shift their self-beliefs after role-played self-presentations that were greatly discrepant from their initial self-beliefs. However, people who perceived themselves as inconsistent on the trait shifted their self-beliefs to bring them in line with highly discrepant self-presentations. These findings indicate that core facets of the self-concept are relatively resistant to abrupt changes, but self-beliefs on less potent dimensions can be modified with relative ease.

There has been virtually no research on the impact of an actor's goals on the activation of specific self-images. Research does indicate, however, that a perceiver's goals influence the schemata that are activated when subjects form judgments of others (e.g., Cantor & Mischel, 1979; Jeffrey & Mischel, 1979) and that cuing a particular role context (e.g., professional life versus family life) activates schemata that are associated with the goals of the pertinent roles (e.g., schemata relevant to the business world versus parenting) (Trzebinski, McGlynn, Gray, & Tubbs, 1985). It would therefore be surprising if goals did not activate identity images that are relevant to goal completion.

People's moods also influence self-identifications. Affective states increase the accessibility in memory of commensurately toned information (Isen, 1984; Snyder & White, 1982). People who experience positive affect are more likely to focus on positive information about the self, whereas those who experience negative affect focus on negative information (Mischel, Ebbesen & Zeiss, 1973; Snyder & White, 1982).

The Situation. Situations (and audiences) influence self-identifications in at least two ways. First, they influence the opportunities and constraints available for satisfying needs and values and present actors with behavior-outcome contingencies (Schlenker, 1986a). If goal achievement is contingent on creating a particular type of identity in the situation, as it so often is, people's self-identifications are more likely to incorporate aspects of these situationally appropriate identities. Phrased differently, the more important the relevant goals and the clearer the contingency between goal achievement and creating a particular identity, the more likely it is that public self-identifications will be influenced by situational pressures rather than the constituents of one's self-concept. The literature on self-presentation demonstrates that people will vary their behavior to create the type of impression that will achieve valued outcomes (Baumeister, 1982; Jones & Pittman, 1982; Jones & Wortman, 1973; Schlenker, 1980; Tedeschi, 1981; Tedeschi & Norman, 1985).

Second, situations (and audiences) influence self-identifications through their capacity to cue particular goals, scripts, and identity images. They thus activate relevant information in memory (Schlenker, 1986a). The cued information can be more personal in nature, such as elements of the self-concept, or it can be more social in nature, such as socially appropriate goals, scripts, and roles that the person is expected to enact (largely irrespective of personal feelings or one's self-concept). Studies indicate that situations themselves can cue associated information about identity, social roles, and social expectations; and people are likely to behave in ways that are consistent with this information (Alexander & Rudd, 1981; Alexander & Wiley, 1981).

The Audience. Self-identification always involves one or more real or imagined audiences, and at least three general classes of audiences can be distinguished. The first is the *self*. Early symbolic interactionists (Cooley, 1902; Mead, 1934) emphasized people's reflexive abilities to think about and evaluate themselves; current analyses of self-regulation extend these ideas by focusing on the components of the self-evaluation process (Bandura, 1982). People's own internalized values, standards, and knowledge provide a basis for self-regulation and self-evaluation (Greenwald & Breckler, 1985; Hogan, 1982; Schlenker, 1980, 1982, 1985, 1986a; Snyder, Higgins, & Stucky, 1983). Research on private self-attention (Carver & Scheier, 1981, 1985) and, more broadly, inner orientation (Hogan & Cheek, 1983) can be seen to address the self-as-audience for social behavior. The concept of self-as-audience thus does not describe a homunculus; instead, it affirms the reflective and reflexive capabilities of people (Schlenker, 1980).

The second is *other people* with whom one interacts. Research on public self-attention (Carver & Scheier, 1981, 1985), self-presentation and self-disclosure (Baumeister, 1982; Jones & Pittman, 1982; Jones & Wortman, 1973; Schlenker, 1980; Tedeschi, 1981), and, more broadly, outer orientation (Hogan & Cheek, 1983) can be seen to focus on the impact of immediate others, often others who are strangers, on people's behavior.

The third is *reference others* who have achieved a special prominence in our lives (Schlenker, 1984, 1986a). Their opinions, values, and standards are of sufficient import that they are evoked as exemplars and evaluators across a wide variety of situations. They need not be present to be salient but may be cued by one's goals or pertinent aspects of the situation, as when a teenager contemplates her mother's admonitions about sex while on a date. Also in this category are others whom one has never met, including characters from fiction, who serve as evaluators and exemplars. As examples, the child may become concerned with how Santa Claus will evaluate her behavior as Christmas approaches, and before a battle the soldier may evoke an image of John Wayne to serve as an exemplar for conduct (see Schlenker, 1986a, for further discussion). Reference others occupy an intermediate position between public and private concerns because they reflect the impact of an external (sometimes impersonal) audience who has been internalized and comes to influence behavior even when the actor is alone.

Audiences become salient when (a) they are more immediate because of their presence or the expectation that they will soon be present, especially when they are regarded by the actor as powerful or attractive, and (b) they are cued by some aspect of the situation or one's goals (e.g., a religious icon evokes thoughts of how one's behavior might be evaluated by Jesus). Included in the last category are cases where attention is directed to a particular audience via various focusing tactics, as in the cases of the self-as-audience being evoked by the presence of a small mirror, one's classmates being evoked by a videocamera that will record one's conduct for later viewing, or reference others being evoked by mention of their names (Baldwin & Holmes, 1987; Carver & Scheier, 1985; Greenwald & Breckler, 1985; Schlenker, 1986a).

As with situations, audiences influence self-identifications through their capacity (a) to present reward/cost opportunities that influence our goals and plans (e.g., achieving love, friendship, money, power), and (b) to cue particular self-images and social roles that are relevant (e.g., a college student returns home during the holidays to find old roles reactivated). After this information is activated, actors draw upon it in their subsequent self-identifications. Audiences also provide an evaluative framework for assessing one's performance (Baldwin & Holmes, 1987; Greenwald & Breckler, 1985; Schlenker, 1980, 1985, 1986a). The audience is expected to observe, judge, and react to the activity, using particular beliefs, rules, and standards for judgment. As such, audiences also influence people's expectations of outcomes from self-identification (Schlenker, 1980, 1984, 1986a; Schlenker & Leary, 1982a, 1985). Finally, audiences provide social comparison information, whereby people evaluate their standing on an attribute by comparing themselves with reference others (Morse & Gergen, 1970).

Packaging. An often overlooked aspect of audiences is that they serve as receptors for information about the self.

> To communicate effectively requires tailoring or fitting information to the audience's knowledge and value systems, using terms, symbols, and evidence that will be comprehensible to them. Further, to communicate persuasively requires that the information be presented in ways that are expected to be most likely to be accepted and least likely to be challenged by the audience given their knowledge and values. This process requires role-taking skill in being able to place oneself in the position of the audience and anticipate how they are likely to perceive various ways of packaging desired self-identifications. (Schlenker, 1986a, p. 31)

Packaging involves arranging, interpreting, and weighting information about oneself in a fashion that is designed to create a desired impact on others, even though one might not usually arrange, interpret, or weight the information in the same way (Schlenker, 1985). It is thus basically "true" and fitted to the appropriate circumstances. There is nothing nefarious or Machiavellian about packaging information about the self. Just as a textbook writer must edit information to present it in a readable, concise fashion, so must people in everyday life edit information about themselves to provide the "best" description possible. Some people are more skilled than others at this task (Cheek, 1982; Cheek & Hogan, 1983; Snyder, 1979), but everyone must do it. There is simply too much information about oneself to do anything but provide an edited, packaged version that is relevant to the goals at hand, even when one contemplates onself while alone. The actor's goals, of course, may involve communicating truthful *or* distorted information about the self (just as a textbook writer may try to present a balanced view or become an advocate for a particular position).

Identity Images

According to self-identification theory, the confluence of person, situation, and audience produces a set of desired identity images that will guide behavior on the occasion. These images represent a fitted version of the self for the occasion. When particular identity images have been activated, they provide (a) an *organizational structure* for information, that is, people can use the images to organize and sequence relevant information; (b) an *interpretational filter*, that is, the image influences how relevant information is selected, interpreted, stored, and recalled from memory; (c) a *script for conduct* based on behavioral-prototype or response-specifying information and standards; (d) an *evaluative framework* for judging conduct, that is, they contain standards against which one's conduct can be compared; and (e) *information about the relationship between images and outcomes*, that is, the image contains information about the consequences of "being" the type of person typified by the image (see Schlenker, 1985, for discussion of each point). As such, identity images mediate our perceptions, feelings, and behavior in social settings.

DESIRABLE IMAGES

Beliefs do not exist without consequences, and these consequences partially determine why people come to endorse one belief rather than another.[3] Pragmatic philosophers such as Pierce (1878) and James

---

[3]Pascal's "wager" illustrates the potential impact of expected consequences. He argued that if people believe in God and God exists, they gain boundless reward; if they believe and God does not exist, they have lost nothing. If people do not believe in God and God exists, they have lost everything; if they do not believe and God does not exist, they have gained nothing. Ergo, the payoff matrix favors belief largely independently of any set of facts or evidence that can be marshaled.

(1907) emphasized consequences when they explicitly linked the truth of an idea to its usefulness. They argued that a "true" belief is one that permits its holder to function effectively in the world. Extrapolating, a "true" belief is one that permits a sense of being able to understand, predict, and control events better than alternative beliefs and provides satisfaction. When an idea is acted on, does it produce mistakes, errors, and the inability to achieve goals? If so, its utility, and hence truth, is low and it should be abandoned for more potentially profitable (or less costly) conceptions. Conversely, ideas that minimize errors and generate goal achievement will be perpetuated until even more useful ones come along.

The two critical elements of beliefs that emerge from this analysis are (a) *believability*, or the extent to which the belief is perceived to be an accurate, defensible construal of the available evidence; and (b) *personal beneficiality*, or the extent to which it serves the holder's values and goals (Schlenker, 1980, 1982, 1985). These two elements are components of *all* beliefs, including one's about ourselves, other people, and the environment; and together they define the "truth" as the actor sees it. When applied to self-identifications, the analysis suggests that *within the range of potentially believable identity images, that is, the set of self-beliefs that can be justified and defended based on the salient evidence, people endorse those that best serve their goals and values.* Self-beliefs that fulfill this criterion are called *desired identity images* or *desired self-identifications* (Schlenker, 1980, 1982, 1985). A formula for assessing the desirability of a self-identification has been presented elsewhere (Schlenker, 1980, 1981). In essence, the formula takes into account the expected outcomes if a belief is correct minus the expected outcomes if the belief is incorrect, with each term weighted by the perceived probability that the belief is correct versus incorrect, respectively. Among other things, the formula suggests that particular self-identifications are more desirable when (a) they are regarded as leading to the accomplishment of more valuable goals, and (b) they are expected to be accepted by audiences without serious doubt or challenge. Conversely, self-identifications are less desirable when (a) the costs of being challenged or rejected are high, and (b) the likelihood of serious challenge is high.

Desired images are neither idealistically glorifying nor faithful to what observers may regard as the fine nuances of evidence. Rather, desired images represent an integration of one's wishes (the beneficiality component) and reality (the believability component). They comprise what people believe they *should be* and *can be* on the occasion, being reality-edited yet glorified images of self. Desirable images are not ideal images; the former speak to what people believe they can be, at least under the "right" circumstances, whereas the latter speak to unreachable heights. Instead, desirable images are in the tradition of James' (1890) use of the term *pretensions,* or what we "back ourselves to be" (see also McCall & Simmons, 1978; Rosenberg, 1979; Turner, 1968). The self-concept appears to consist of these desirable self-identifications (Schlenker, 1980, 1985).

The desirability of a particular image is not a constant. Different contexts (e.g., situations, audiences) result in different weightings and values for the components (Schlenker, 1980). For example, a glorifying self-identification that may seem believable when a person is talking to a supportive spouse may seem less believable when he or she is with expert, discerning, critical others; the self-identification would be more desirable and likely to be proffered in the first than second case. Desirability probably fluctuates only within a specific range for a given person, however. Also, some images, by virtue of their importance and centrality, are likely to be more stable across situations and audiences.

To explore better the nature of desirability and its implications for self-identification, we will consider the concepts of believability and beneficiality in more detail. We will then examine research that supports the view that self-identifications are mediated by image desirability.

Beneficiality

The idea that people are motivated to regard themselves favorably has a long history. The Roman philosopher Seneca mused that, "Other men's sins are before our eyes; our own are behind our back." James (1890) contended that "self-seeking" was a "fundamental instinctual impulse" that generated vanity, pride, and superiority strivings; and Allport (1937) called defense of the ego "nature's eldest law." Numerous self-theorists have endorsed the existence of a need for self-esteem (Greenberg, Pyszczynski, & Solomon, 1986; Greenwald, 1980; Jones, 1973; Rosenberg, 1979).[4] Further, Taylor and Brown (1988) argue that overly positive self-evaluations, exaggerated perceptions of mastery, and un-

---

[4]A variation on the theme that people act to protect and enhance their self-evaluations is that people construct idealized images of self that they attempt to actualize. The concept of an ideal image of self began in the psychoanalytic literature (Freud, 1925; Horney, 1945) and was often used to explain neuroticism (e.g., excessive anxiety results from failing to achieve the unrealistically lofty standards required by the ideal self). Rogers (1959) extended the theme, proposing that people attempt to move toward their ideal self and that self-regard is based on the size of the discrepancy between the real and ideal self. Baumeister (1982) proposed that a major motive for self-presentation is the desire to convey an idealized image of self to others. Markus and Nurius (1986) suggested that "possible selves"—which are "the ideal selves that we would very much like to become" (p. 954) or types of selves that we want to avoid becoming—can act as incentives for future behavior and guide our actions.

realistic optimism are not only characteristic of normal thought, they are illusions that promote mental health.

Numerous lines of research have been cited to support the existence of a motivational bias to boost self-esteem or to construct a glorified image of self. Examples include the following:

1. The tendency to recall successes better than failures (Greenwald, 1980; Greenwald & Pratkanis, 1984)
2. The tendency to attribute responsibility to self for successes but not for failures on individual and group tasks (Greenberg et al., 1986; Miller & Schlenker, 1985; Schlenker, 1980; Schlenker & Miller, 1977; Snyder, Stephan, & Rosenfield, 1978; Weary-Bradley, 1978; Weary & Arkin, 1981)
3. The proclivity to regard one's own motives for a given behavior as primarily good and the motives of others as less good (Schlenker, Hallam, & McCown, 1983)
4. The tendency to change one's attitudes in a way that justifies negative conduct or provides greater personal acclaim for positive conduct (Schlenker, 1982; Schlenker & Goldman, 1982; Schlenker & Schlenker, 1975)
5. The tendency to deny responsibility for harming others (Harvey, Harris, & Barnes, 1975)
6. The tendency to respond positively to favorable evaluations of self and negatively to unfavorable evaluations (Jones, 1973; Mettee & Aronson, 1974)
7. The tendency to associate oneself with winners and dissociate onself from losers (Cialdini, Levy, Herman, Kozlowski, & Petty, 1976; Richardson & Cialdini, 1981).

Greenwald and Breckler (1985) argue that such effects are not just public impression management ploys but represent genuine beliefs in a "too good" self. They note that these effects can be obtained privately as well as publicly (Arkin, Appelman, & Burger, 1980; Schlenker et al., 1983) and occur even under strong constraints for honesty (Riess, Rosenfeld, Melburg, & Tedeschi, 1981). Further, favorable self-referent judgments are made rapidly (Markus, 1977; Paulhus & Levitt, 1987; Rogers, Kuiper, & Kirker, 1977), suggesting that subjects do not need to spend time contemplating how they would like to appear but are responding instantaneously with self-flattering verdicts. Finally, subjects do not merely say self-flattering things, but they act in ways indicating that they genuinely believe their statements, as when they persevere on tasks in the face of obstacles (Bandura, 1977; Feather, 1982).

Despite a pervasive tendency to massage one's own ego, it is an oversimplification to argue that people indiscriminately act to boost self-esteem or public esteem. First, people's goals influence the identities they attempt to construct. Schlenker (1980) proposed that it is often in people's best interests to present themselves as other than likable or competent. He argued that people will often present themselves as irrational and punitive (e.g., during a conflict situation in which one tries to make an opponent back down), extremely moral (e.g., a priest who dramatizes his role for parishioners in the attempt to serve as an exemplar), incompetent (e.g., a self-perceived failure who wants to receive the support and care of others; in the extreme, the self-presentations of the mental patient), or in ways that will make them disliked (e.g., a person who is trying to discourage a persistent suitor). Thus, although people spend much of their time constructing identities that will gain them approval and esteem, their short- and long-term goals frequently call for variations. Jones and Pittman (1982) subsequently described different self-presentational objectives, including intimidation (attempts to be feared), exemplification (attempts to be seen as moral and worthy), and supplication (attempts to be seen as helpless), in addition to the more traditional self-inflating strategies of ingratiation (attempts to be liked) and self-promotion (attempts to be seen as competent). According to self-identification theory, the beneficiality of an image reflects the extent to which it serves the holder's goals and values, not simply to the extent that it makes the holder appear to be "good" or boosts self-esteem.

Second, the beneficiality of a self-judgment does not have free reign. People's judgments are constrained by reality—the reality created by the fact that, when acted upon, people's beliefs have consequences for their material and social outcomes (Schlenker, 1980). We are not suggesting that a "self-esteem" motive is sometimes compromised by an "accuracy" or "consistency" motive. Instead, we are arguing that self-beliefs always represent the integration of information related to beneficiality and believability.

Believability

Believability refers to the extent to which a persuasive or at least defensible case can be constructed to support a claim. The believability of an assertion depends heavily on the relationship between the claim and the relevant data (e.g., Is the claim supported by the facts?), but it is also influenced by social considerations, including the interpersonal, persuasive skills of the advocate and the characteristics of the audience, such as their rebuttal skills and inclinations. The concept of believability can be best illustrated by drawing an analogy with the criteria scientists use to evaluate theories. Just as some scientific theories are more believable than others because they better fulfill certain criteria, so some claims to identity images are more believable. In science, theories are regarded as "better" when they (a) are consistent with existing data (empirical consistency); (b) are logically structured with no internal contradictions (logical consistency); (c) are more straightforward, easily communicable explanations for events (i.e., simplicity and communicability of a theory); (d) are more consistent with the prevalent values, beliefs, rules, and assumptions of the scientific community (background consistency); (e) are accepted by a greater number of scientists (consensus within the scientific community); and (f) are accepted by scientists who are more influential in the field by virtue of their accomplishments, reputations, and persuasive skills.

In like fashion, some self-identifications are more believable than others because they better fulfill criteria that people use to evaluate one another's claims. We suggest that self-identifications are more believable to the extent that they fulfill the following criteria, which parallel the above six "scientific criteria."

1. Empirical Consistency. Self-identifications are more believable when they are consistent with available information that is relevant to the self-identification. Claims should be consistent with information known about the actor based on past behavior, reputation, membership in social groups, and even expected future behavior. Further, claims should be consistent with information known about any objects, events, tasks, situations, and audiences that are involved (e.g., harming another person is easier to justify as self-defense if the other is known as a bully rather than a milksop; derogating a test on which one failed is easier if the instrument is regarded as having suspect rather than high validity). Considerable evidence indicates that people will adjust their self-presentations to the demands of the salient evidence (Baumeister, 1982; Baumeister & Jones, 1978; Schlenker, 1975; 1980; Tedeschi, 1981; Ungar, 1980).

2. Internal Consistency. Self-identifications are more believable when they are logically structured with no internal contradictions. William James (1890) noted the havoc wreaked by having to live up to demands created by contradictory self-identifications:

> "I am often confronted by the necessity of standing by one of my empirical selves and relinquishing the rest. Not that I would not, if I could, be both

handsome and fat and well dressed, and a great athlete, and make a million a year, be a wit, a *bon-vivant*, and a lady-killer, as well as a philosopher; a philanthropist, statesman, warrior . . . and saint. But the thing is simply impossible. The millionaire's work would run counter to the saint's; the *bon vivant* and the philanthropist would trip each other up . . ." (pp. 199–200)

We tend to select images that fit together as part of a package, thereby maintaining consistency and preserving our sanity by limiting the number of images that we must master. The literature on interrole conflicts (Sarbin & Allen, 1968), which occur when the instructions from different roles are incompatible, indicates the stress that can be created by internal contradictions.

3. Simplicity and Communicability. Self-identifications are more believable when they are more straightforward, easily communicable descriptions. The popularity of scientific theories is affected by how easily the theory can be communicated and comprehended (Becker & McClintock, 1972). The persuasion literature shows that when messages become too complex, comprehension and receptivity decline (Eagly & Chaiken, 1984). Similarly, people seem to assume that the truth comes in tidy packages; if the claim is too convoluted, its appeal suffers. For this reason, people sometimes construct convenient lies for fear that the truth will take too long to explain or be misunderstood.

4. Fitting Prevailing Assumptions and Values. Self-identifications are more believable when they are consistent with the prevalent values, beliefs, assumptions, and rules of the community. Self-identifications must be fitted to the views, values, and inclinations of audiences (Carson, 1969; Foote, 1951; Mills, 1940; Schlenker, 1980, 1982; Scheff, 1968; Scott & Lyman, 1968). Self-identifications that contradict this background information will confront questions and challenges. As examples, claims of being a ghost are untenable in most of Western society; claims of being a witch or being inhabited by the spirit of a deceased person are generally disbelieved, but one can find groups whose world view permits acceptance. Similarly, our culture endorses claims of mental illness to explain extreme deviance, but claims of demonic possession, which were acceptable in the past, now are reinterpreted as symptoms of mental illness, not veridical representations.

5. Consensual Validation. Self-identifications are more believable when they receive consensual validation (actual or imagined) from others, especially those who are significant to the actor by virtue of their family relationship, friendship, attractiveness, power, or expertise. Obtaining consensual validation enhances confidence in the validity of the identification, whereas failing to receive validation raises questions. Public validation of one's qualities, especially when questions could be raised about one's standing on those traits, has been regarded as an important consequence of self-presentation (Schlenker, 1980, 1987; Swann, 1983; Wicklund & Gollwitzer, 1982). People's self-evaluations are shaped by the feedback they receive from others (Gergen, 1982; Rosenberg, 1979; Shrauger & Schoeneman, 1979). When self-identifications are challenged by new information, people change their self-beliefs to bring them in line with the contradictory information *unless* they receive social support from friends who will verify their initial claims, in which case no changes in self-beliefs occur (Swann & Predmore, 1985). The failure to receive validation of one's self-identifications is threatening and stressful (Schlenker, 1987; Swann, 1983). It has been found that people who exhibit the greatest amounts of stress in their interpersonal relationships also have the greatest discrepancies between their self-appraisals and the perceived or actual appraisals of them by others (Lundgren, 1978).

6. Confidence and Persuasive Skills. Self-identifications are more believable when they are asserted with greater confidence, particularly by actors who have better acting skills and are attuned to the inclinations of the audience. People who appear to be confident—by using "powerful" styles of speech, making eye contact, and avoiding signs of anxiety in their voice and gestures—are more persuasive than those who do not (Erickson, Lind, Johnson, & O'Barr, 1978; Hemsley & Doob, 1978; Schlenker, 1980). Confident witnesses are believed more in simulated court cases than are nonconfident ones, even though confidence is unrelated to the actual accuracy of the testimony (Wells & Murray, 1984). Minority group members are more likely to persuade a majority when the minority is consistent and persistent in its views (Nemeth, 1986). High self-monitors, who are good actors and attuned to the preferences of others, are effective communicators who are successful at interpersonal tasks (Snyder, 1979). Even when the task is to communicate an "accurate" portrait of self and not just a self-flattering one, people with better acting skills are more effective in accomplishing their interpersonal goal (Cheek, 1982; Cheek & Hogan, 1983).

Self-presentations that are expressed with confidence are not only likely to persuade others about the veracity of one's claims, but are likely to persuade oneself as well. First, because confident assertions are more persuasive, the actor is more likely to receive feedback indicating that the self-presentation was regarded as veridical. The consensual validation then buttresses the actor's own perceptions of the truthfulness of his or her behavior. Second, because people associate confidence with "truth," a self-perception process may take place in which we judge our own confident behaviors to be more true and sincere than our behaviors that seem less confident. Just as people who smile and act happy soon begin to feel happy (Izard, 1971; Laird, 1974; Tompkins, 1962), by acting confidently, we probably directly influence perceptions of our truthfulness.

Explaining Discrepancies. When self-identifications fall short on one or more of these criteria, the actor must construct a reasonable and convincing explanation for the anomaly, otherwise audiences (oneself included) may begin to doubt the authenticity of the claim. For example, when evidence seems inconsistent with a particular self-identification, as when an actor's claims are contradicted when he fails a test or receives a negative evaluation from another person, the actor can (a) claim that the data is invalid (e.g., the instrument is unreliable or invalid, or the evaluator is biased or stupid); (b) denigrate the importance of the attribute (e.g., "It's not important to do well on that;" or "I can always hire someone to do that for me"); or (c) modify self-beliefs slightly without revising the core conception (e.g., "I am extremely wise, but do not do well in that limited, trivial area"). In science, of course, anomalous data usually receive similar initial treatment, either (a) being rejected as invalid because of measurement problems, faulty operationalizations, or other errors; (b) being denigrated as trivial, especially in light of the large quantity of supporting data; or (c) being used to generate auxiliary hypotheses that represent only minor adjustments to the theory (Hempel, 1966; Lakatos, 1970). It takes a critical mass of anomalous data to produce accommodation in long-standing beliefs, especially ones that seem to have withstood the rigors of prior challenges. In science, no theory ever receives perfect scores on all criteria. Similarly, people's self-identifications frequently seem to fall short of perfectly fulfilling all criteria. People construct self-serving explanations to deal with the apparent deviations (see Schlenker, 1980, 1982, 1987).

Desirability in Context

The desirability of a self-identification will vary across situations and audiences. The beneficiality of a particular self-identification can change over time because (a) people confront different reward-cost opportunities, bring different values, skills, and resources to bear, and have different goals (e.g., a college student wants to be seen as intelligent when interacting with a professor, but beguiling when with a girlfriend/boyfriend); and (b) people perceive that one rather than another script or plan will best achieve their goal (e.g., in order to impress a job interviewer, one person stresses her competence and accomplishments, whereas a second stresses her likability and compatibility). The believability of a particular self-identification can change because (a) different types of information about self, roles, and standards are primed by situational cues, making available in memory the corresponding aspects of self (e.g., parents and friends prompt people to think of different facets of themselves and to apply different standards when evaluating their performance), and (b) people adjust their self-identifications to make them more acceptable to the salient audience given the available "evidence" (e.g., boasts to one's spouse of being the most talented salesman in the company give way to more modest claims when interacting with co-workers who have made more sales).

An impressive amount of data indicates that people's self-identifications shift in quite predictable ways based on changes in desirability. Jones' (Jones, 1964; Jones & Wortman, 1973) pioneering research on ingratiation showed that people will become more self-enhancing when motivated to create a good impression on attractive or powerful others. People not only become more or less self-enhancing (a quantitative change), they also tailor their self-identifications to the specific attributes preferred by significant audiences (a qualitative change). For example, Zanna and Pack (1975) had female college students interact with a male who was either attractive (handsome and unattached) or unattractive (short and engaged), and who described his ideal woman as someone who fit the traditional female role or the liberated female role. They found that the women presented themselves in line with the man's preferences so long as he was attractive; unattractive men had no influence on the women's self-presentations. In general, variations in the expected consequences of particular self-identifications produce changes in self-identifying behaviors (Baumeister, 1982; Jellison, 1981; Schlenker, 1980, 1984; Tedeschi, 1981; Tedeschi & Norman, 1985; Tetlock, 1985a; Weary-Bradley, 1978; Weary & Arkin, 1981).

Of course, people cannot merely claim to be whatever their whims dictate or claim the image that would make the ideal impression on others. People are expected to be what they claim to be (Gergen, 1968; Goffman, 1959; Schlenker, 1980; Tedeschi et al., 1971). Consistency between words and deeds allows people to "participate in organized social life with good confidence that others will do what they say they will do .... Every man is under compulsion to keep his promises, and to make his acts correspond with his verbal expressions. He constantly watches others to see that they do likewise" (Dollard, 1949, p. 624). Inconsistency breeds unpredictability, and people who are unpredictable are disliked and punished (Gergen & Jones, 1963). As Gergen (1968) observed, "it is simply less taxing and perhaps less anxiety-provoking if the social environment is not in constant and capricious flux" (p. 300).

Schlenker and Leary (1982b) found that consistency between claims and performance is favorably evaluated by observers, but deviations are condemned. The greater the deviation between an actor's claims (e.g., performance on a test or in a tennis match) and the actor's actual performance, the less positively the actor was evaluated by subjects. Further, subjects especially disapproved of inaccuracy when the actor's claims occurred after the performance and, therefore, could be seen as lies, rather than before the performance, where the deviation might be discounted as a bad prediction caused by an "off day" or some other unanticipated problem. In contrast, when subjects were not given information about how the actor performed, they appeared to assume that his or her claims were accurate. Actors were evaluated more favorably when their claims were higher rather than lower. In the absence of a reason to be suspicious, people seem to assume that others' claims are truthful (DePaulo, Stone, & Lassiter, 1985; Goffman, 1959).

People's self-presentations are influenced by the information that is publicly available about them. Schlenker (1975) had subjects succeed or fail on test in private and led them to believe that they would work on a very similar set of problems as part of a group. It was explicitly noted that performance on the group problems would probably be comparable to performance on the prior problems because of the similarity of the tasks. Half of the subjects were led to expect that their personal performance as part of the group would be anonymous, where their inputs could not be clearly distinguished, and the other subjects were led to expect that their personal performance would be identifiable by the other group members. Before working on the group task, subjects were given the opportunity to present themselves to the other group members. It was found that when future performance was a matter of public record, subjects presented themselves consistently with their performance expectations. Those who expected success described themselves as more competent than those who expected failure. In contrast, when subjects' future performance would supposedly be anonymous, subjects presented themselves as quite competent irrespective of their private expectations of performance.

Similar effects have been obtained in a variety of areas. Baumeister and Jones (1978) showed that subjects would present themselves consistently with publicly known information about their past performance, but were uniformly self-enhancing when past performance was not a matter of public record. Frey (1978) found that people's attributions about their performance correspond with publicly known information but become more self-flattering when public constraints are absent. Further, subjects' reactions to interpersonal evaluations from others seem to follow a consistency pattern (e.g., preferring an accurate rather than flattering evaluator) when subjects expect their performance to be known to others, but they follow an esteem-enhancing pattern (i.e., preferring a flattering evaluator over an accurate one) when their performance will not be known publicly (Jones, 1973; Jones & Pines, 1968). In each of these studies, subjects' self-presentations tracked the conditions that Schlenker and Leary (1982b) showed will maximize the favorability of observers' evaluations: consistency when audiences are aware of performance information and self-enhancement when audiences are unaware.

Self-identifications are less self-enhancing and more consistent with available information when the criteria for evaluating the claims are clear, quantitative, and unambiguous as opposed to vague, qualitative, or open to interpretation. Thus, claims about intellectual tasks (Lefcourt, Hogg, Struther, & Holmes, 1975; Lorge & Solomon, 1960) and future academic performance (Biggs & Tinsley, 1970; Binder, Jones, & Strowig, 1970; Holland & Nichols, 1964; Keefer, 1969) are generally quite accurate, as well or better calibrated than objective measures (Shrauger, 1982). Claims concerning social competence, however, are often unrelated to observer ratings of performance (Arkowitz, Lichtenstein, McGovern, & Hines, 1975; Glasgow & Arkowitz, 1975). As Thomas Hobbes (1651/1952) observed, "For such is the nature of men that howsoever they may acknowledge many others to be more witty, or more eloquent, or more learned, yet they will hardly believe there be many so wise as themselves."

Just as the standards for evaluating claims can vary in specificity, the performance itself can be considered more or less diagnostic and valid. People can dismiss poor performances on tasks whose validity is doubtful, but they are constrained by consistent performances on valid tasks (Schlenker, Miller, & Leary, 1983; Ungar, 1980).

People's certainty in how they perform acts as a constraint on self-identifications. When people are certain they will perform at a particular level, self-identifications are held more closely in check; when people are uncertain about how they will perform, their hopes can more greatly influence their self-identifications. In support of this idea, Ungar (1980) had subjects succeed or fail on a test they believed would be a valid or invalid predictor of future performance. Subjects then selected problems to work on during a group session in which their performance would be public record. When subjects believed their prior performance would predict their public performance, they selected problems that were consistent with their expectations: Subjects who expected failure selected easier, less diagnostic problems than subjects who expected success. In contrast, when subjects believed their prior performance would not be a valid predictor of future performance, they selected more difficult problems irrespective of their prior performance. Thus, under conditions of greater certainty, subjects' expectations dictated their task selection; under conditions of uncertainty, task selection seemed to be guided by the desire to do well on more impressive tasks.

The anticipation of future tests of skills can be intimidating when people are concerned that they might fail. In general, people are more modest in their self-descriptions and attributions when they anticipate continued tests of their ability compared to when they believe they will not be tested again (Eagly & Acksen, 1971; Wortman, Costanzo, & Witt, 1973).

Desirability Is Not Positivity

According to self-identification theory, a desirable self-identification is not necessarily a "positive" self-identification (Schlenker, 1980, 1982, 1985). For one thing, people's values and long-term goals may lead them to select lifestyles and identities that are out of the mainstream. For another, short-term goals can cause people to focus on useful, but not necessarily positive, attributes, such as an image of intimidation presented to a rival.

Going beyond valuation differences, self-identifications that one believes will flagrantly overestimate (positively) one's attributes constitute a threat to self (Schlenker, 1984, 1987; Schlenker & Leary, 1982a, 1985). Because performance is always judged in relation to standards, a problem can arise if people believe their capabilities are poor or the applicable standards are too high. In such cases, people experience anxiety and, when the standards are at fault, usually try to lower them or to show that they are inapplicable.

Being overpraised provides an example. Discomfort is produced by being overpraised in public (Buss, 1980) and subjects who receive inordinate rather than mild praise engage in greater self-criticism (Davis & Brock, 1972). Kanouse and Pullan (described in Kanouse, Gumpert, & Canavan-Gumpert, 1981) praised subjects for their successful performance on a task. They found that subjects who were praised in a way that implied continued superior performance on future tasks, as compared to those who were praised in a way that did not hold future implications for performance, (a) reported greater anxiety, (b) attributed their prior success more to luck, and (c) actually performed worse on subsequent tasks.

A comparable refutation of overly high standards appears to be involved in the often poor task performance of people with low self-esteem. Maracek and Mettee (1972) found that subjects who were low in self-esteem engaged in a concerted effort to lower expectations about their performance, provided they believed they would undergo further evaluation. It is not desirable to be regarded in a way that dooms one to failure.

Similarly, Baumeister and his associates (Baumeister, 1984; Baumeister, Hamilton, & Tice, 1985; Baumeister & Steinhilder, 1984) found that people will "choke under pressure" created by high public expectations, performing more poorly when public expectations are unrealistically high rather than more manageable. Although private expectations of success are directly related to performance quality (Bandura, 1977; Feather, 1982; Locke, 1968; Locke, Shaw, Saari, & Latham, 1981), public expectations of success produce decrements in performance when they create unrealistically high standards (Baumeister et al., 1985). High public expectations increase performance only when they are accompanied by correspondingly high private expectations (Baumeister et al., 1985). Baumgardner and Brownlee (1987) found that people who are more likely to doubt their ability to perform up to social standards will fail at the outset of a task in order to lower standards.

Desirability: Response Bias or Private Belief?

It could be argued that variations in the desirability of a self-identification will influence people's public self-presentations but will not affect their private self-identifications. In other words, such findings may represent shifts in behavior, not self-beliefs, as a function of expected consequences. The data, however, support the opposite position: People's private self-reflections are affected by the desirability of alternative self-identifications.

First, manipulations of factors that affect desirability produce changes in people's private self-ratings. For example, research indicates that the manipulated importance of a trait affects people's self-descriptions and attributions even in private (McKillop & Schlenker, 1987; Miller, 1976). To illustrate, McKillop and Schlenker (1987) had some subjects confront negative information in the form of a role-played negative self-presentation about their standing on either an important or unimportant trait (i.e., a trait described as highly related to performance in business settings versus unrelated to performance). When the trait was supposedly important, subjects subsequently *raised* their private self-ratings, suggesting that they engaged in private counterarguing and polarized their standing to reaffirm the desired attribute. When the trait was unimportant, counterarguing was minimal and no changes in self-beliefs occurred. People are concerned with constructing desired identity images for the self as audience just as they are when other people are audiences.

As another example, variations in the public or private nature of a performance later influence subjects' private attributions. Frey (1978) found that subjects privately evaluated a test as more valid after a success than after a failure, and this tendency was stronger when the prior performance was public rather than private. Subjects were apparently more pleased with success and threatened by failure when these events occurred publicly, and their private attributions responded in kind.

Second, people's public self-presentations influence their own private self-beliefs and evaluations (Dlugolecki & Schlenker, 1985; Fazio, Effrein, & Fallender, 1981; Gergen, 1965; Jones, Rhodewalt, Berglas, & Skelton, 1981; Rhodewalt & Agustsdottir, 1986; Spivak, Rogers, & Schlenker, 1986). Behaviors that may have started out as exaggerations or packaged positions can come to be believed. To illustrate, Fazio et al. (1981) asked subjects a set of questions that were designed to elicit, and did elicit, either extraverted or introverted responses. Subjects in the extraverted condition subsequently rated themselves as more extraverted and actually behaved in a more extraverted fashion when they interacted with another person later (i.e., they were more likely to initiate a conversation, they talked more, and they were seen by judges as more extraverted). Thus, not only did their public self-identifications, elicited by "loaded questions," influence their private self-ratings, they also influenced their subsequent behaviors in an unrelated situation. Dlugolecki and Schlenker (1985) had subjects present themselves in a very positive fashion and similarly found effects of the self-presentations on subjects' private attitudes, memories of past relevant events, and behaviors in an unrelated situation. Clearly, people's public behaviors come to shape their own self-conceptions and future actions (see Schlenker, 1986a, for a review of research on the effects of self-presentations on self-conceptions). What may have started out as behavior designed to elicit a particular reaction from others can become internalized as part of the self-concept. These newly formed self-images can then guide people's actions in other situations until different events occur that change the self-beliefs or make different self-beliefs salient (Jones et al., 1981).

Desirability is not just a public concept (Schlenker, 1980, 1986a). Theoretically, people should be concerned with the desirability of their self-identifications in private, and the existing research indicates that they are. The same components that are taken into account when presenting an identity to others—believability and beneficiality—are integrated when we reflect on ourselves.

Desirability: What is the Motive?

According to self-identification theory, the context generates a set of desired identity images, and these images mediate people's self-identifications on the occasion. These propositions suggest a synthesizing perspective on three debates about the "ultimate motive" for self-relevant behavior.

1. Do people strive for accuracy in their self-perceptions, seeking out valid, diagnostic information about themselves, or are they motivated to seek and perceive information in a biased, self-serving fashion? (Alicke, 1987; Greenberg et al., 1986; Tetlock & Levi, 1982; Trope, 1983)
2. Are people motivated to promote self-consistency, perceiving and behaving in ways that validate their existing self-beliefs, or are they motivated to maximize their self-esteem? (Jones, 1973; Mettee & Aronson, 1974; Schrauger, 1975; Swann, 1985)
3. Do people attempt to present the real self or the ideal self to others? (Compare Swann, 1985, who contends that people attempt to verify their existing self-beliefs, with Baumeister, 1982, who proposes that people attempt to project their ideal self to others)

The opposite positions in each of these debates are usually regarded as theoretical alternatives. On the one side are motives to be accurate, consistent, and genuine, whereas on the other side are motives to be self-enhancing and self-protecting. Proponents of each side typically argue that the motive they favor is the dominant one. They attempt to explain results that conflict with their favored position and that seem to support the strength of the opposite motive by (a) introducing auxiliary hypotheses that permit conflicting results to be interpreted in line with the favored motive (e.g., self-esteem proponents suggest that people sometimes self-deprecate, thereby accruing short-term losses in esteem, in order to build credibility for long-term enhancements in esteem), or (b) suggesting that the opposite motive exists but operates only within a limited range of conditions as compared to the favored motive (e.g., consistency proponents argue that people are usually consistent but will prefer self-enhancing information when they are uncertain of their standing on an attribute).

Through an alternate set of assumptions, self-identification theory takes a different approach to these issues. Each of the opposites emphasizes phenomena that represent greater weight being placed on one of the two types of components—believability or beneficiality—that comprise all beliefs. Positions stressing accuracy or consistency give greater weight to the believability component, in that they emphasize relatively logical inferences made from evidence, often at the expense of what appears to be immediate self-interest. Positions stressing self-enhancement give greater weight to beneficiality, in that they emphasize self-glorification, often seemingly done at the expense of what observers might regard as accuracy. In contrast, we regard believability and beneficiality as coexisting components of all beliefs. It is not a matter of "truth or consequences," but rather "truth and consequences" as fused elements.

The problem is not to determine which motive exists or when each will dominate. Rather, the two components reside as factors in an equation, with their integration equaling the desirability of the self-identification (see Schlenker, 1980, 1981). In some situations, greater weight will be place on believability, as when the relevant information seems to be unambiguous, diagnostic, and leaves little room for interpretive license. In other situations, beneficiality is given greater leeway because the consequences are great and/or the evidence is ambiguous or capable of multiple interpretations. More precisely, *the likelihood that a particular self-identification will occur is increased by factors that (a) increase the expected positive outcomes if the identification is correct* (i.e., increase the expected positive consequences of actually "being" a particular type of person), *(b) reduce the expected negative outcomes if the identification is incorrect* (i.e., reduce the expected consequences of being wrong about oneself), *or (c) increase the likelihood that the salient audience will accept (or not challenge) the self-identification.* For shorthand, we use the term "beneficiality" to refer to the first two elements above and "believability" to refer to the last (Schlenker, 1980, 1981).

The difference in perspective is not merely a semantic one in which believability is substituted for consistency and beneficiality replaces self-esteem enhancement. The "needs" approach focuses on the individual and the unyielding drives assumed to characterize behavior. The self-identification approach places the individual in a social context in which his or her identity has both personal and interpersonal implications. The "needs" approach assumes the existence of primary motives and must search for conditions that suppress or overwhelm the operation of the need. The self-identification approach proposes that people are flexible and make strategic decisions in their attempts to construct desired identity images. It specifies how the factors that we term believability and beneficiality must be integrated to define desirability and what factors will influence the integration of these components.

Desirability: Cognition and Affect

Assessments of believability involve (a) integrating and evaluating information about self and performances, (b) taking the perspective of others who will hear and evaluate one's claims, (c) using psycho-logic to assess the "fittingness" and consistency of information, (d) comparing relevant information with standards that exist for making claims, and (e) choosing between alternative claims. These types of activities are usually regarded as cognitive, although they clearly have implications for the affect an actor experiences. In comparison, assessments relevant to beneficiality involve a strong affective component because they refer to likes and dislikes. Zajonc (1980) proposed that the more primitive affective system is devoted to making assessments that pertain to the well-being of the individual, and assessments of beneficiality are in precisely this category. Believability, therefore, should be closely associated with measures of cognition, and beneficiality should be closely associated with measures of affect.

As such, it is interesting to note that one attempt at resolving the debate between proponents of consistency theories and proponents of esteem theories has been to suggest that each motive operates with the domain of a different physiological system. Shrauger (1975) proposed that the cognitive system is governed by the need for cognitive consistency, and the affective system is governed by the need for self-esteem enhancement. Shrauger's review of the literature suggested that measures that tap cognitions support consistency, and measures that tap affect support esteem enhancement. More recently, Swann, Griffin, Predmore, and Gaines (1987) found support for this view, showing that subjects exhibited a preference for consistency on cognitive measures and esteem enhancement on affective measures. Appropriately, the measures of cognitions employed by Swann et al. (1987) could be regarded as assessments of believability because they asked about the accuracy and validity of the impression subjects' created on an evaluator and the competence of the evaluator who provided interpersonal feedback. From our perspective, measures that are most likely to tap the components of believability fall in the domain of items typically included under the heading "cognition;" and measures that assess the components of beneficiality tend to fall in the category of well being, threat, and affect. Our interpretation thus differs somewhat from the positions of Shrauger and Swann et al., who propose that different "needs" govern the operation of different physiological systems.

"ACTIVE" AND "PASSIVE" SELF-IDENTIFICATION

Self-identifying activities vary in the extent to which they involve greater versus lesser cognitive effort (devoted to them as opposed to other activities). Most everyday situations are relatively routinized and people's self-identifying activities proceed without much thought about or assessment of the self and contextual features (Schlenker, 1980, 1984, 1986a). Examples include dealing with familiar people in familiar settings, performing routine or frequently encountered tasks, and expressing elements of frequently performed roles. Under these conditions, self-identifications occur rather automatically, without much prior thought and planning, and are based on scripts that have been used repeatedly and successfully in similar contexts. They comprise modulated, habitual patterns of self-identifying behavior that may, in the past, have been diligently studied and practiced but now form part of the actor's battery of normal maintenance activities. These routinized behaviors permit actors to focus their cognitive efforts on other tasks.

In this nonself-reflective mode, self-identifications draw largely from private self-images and frequently enacted roles that have become internalized as part of the self-concept. They rarely represent a perceived break from values or self-beliefs. Although self-identifying behaviors are still responsive to external contingencies, people are probably unaware of the extent to which their actions are adapted to the particular setting. Self-presentational shifts in behaviors, such as variations in the positivity of one's self-descriptions, usually represent highly learned responses that are triggered automatically by particular situational cues (Cialdini, Levy, Herman, & Evenbeck, 1973; Jones & Wortman, 1973; Schlenker, 1980). Unless problems are perceived during the performance, self-identification proceeds according to the script. James (1890, p. 79) referred to such self-identifying habits as "the enormous flywheel of society," which entrap people in self-perpetuating patterns of behavior, some of which may be less than optimally satisfying. Langer (1978) used the term "mindless" behavior to describe a similar process of unconsciously engaging and using well practiced cognitive scripts.

On other occasions, people expend considerable cognitive effort in assessing and planning their performances, such as before an important date, speech, business meeting, or interview. On these occasions, people gather relevant information, plan and rehearse, and remain especially alert during the performance itself, vigilantly monitoring and assessing themselves, the task, and the context, to stay on the right track and to evaluate how they are doing. On still other occasions, an otherwise routine performance may engage cognitive effort when problems develop along the way. These problems focus attention on the self-identification process, as when an actor begins to notice that the audience is not responding in the desired fashion, or when the actor commits a faux pas during an otherwise uneventful occasion.

According to self-identification theory, there are at least two factors that produce an increase in cognitive effort devoted to self-identification (Schlenker, 1980, 1985). First is the *importance* of the values, goals, and pertinent identity images that exist on the occasion. As these increase in importance, so does the extent to which the occasion marshals the actor's mental resources. Second is the magnitude of any anticipated or encountered *impediments* to goals, scripts or plans, and the construction of desired identities. Impediments to self-identifying activities indicate that something may go wrong (or has gone wrong) and people's desired identity images may not be satisfactorily constructed or maintained. Impediments can spring from uncertainties, doubts, conflicts, or threats that are relevant to a performance. A situation may be novel or unfamiliar, causing actors puzzlement about how to behave; an audience may be intimidating, causing actors to wonder how they will come across; actors may doubt their ability to achieve their goals, causing them to expect failure; actors may be uncertain about their standing on particular attributes that are relevant to a performance, causing them to reflect on their actual characteristics; the pursuit of profits may produce conflicts with one's values and self-images, as in the dilemma of whether one should lie for personal gain. As these examples illustrate, impediments can arise from personal, audience, and situational factors. When they occur, people engage in increased assessment of information relevant to the impediment. Cognitive resources become focused on ways to eliminate or circumvent the problem. Thus, it is proposed that *the extent or thoroughness of assessments of self, situation, and audiences increases as a function of the importance of the goals that might be achieved on the occasion, and the perceived existence and magnitude of any impediments that might thwart goal achievement* (Schlenker, 1985).

The increased processing of information produced by importance and impediments implicates a more active and motivated type of cognitive activity than is implied in the more routine mode (Schlenker, 1980, 1984, 1985, 1986a, 1987). *It produces a more intensified processing of information pertinent to the salient goal(s) and the impediments. Further, it pro-*

duces intensified attempts, privately and publicly, to construct and maintain desired identity images. The increased thought and motivation to construct desired identity images focuses attention on the self and produces contemplation of self-images that are relevant to the goal. For ease of exposition, we will use the term *passive mode* to refer to the state of low cognitive effort being devoted to self-identifying activities and *active mode* to refer to the state of high cognitive effort. It is recognized, however, that these terms describe end points on a continuum of cognitive effort.[5]

Consequences of the Active Mode

In contrast to the passive mode, the active mode involves a more thoughtful assessment of one's self-identifications and the contexts in which they occur. It constitutes a more intensive processing of information that goes beyond surface features and involves argumentation (documenting and counterarguing) designed to reaffirm desired identity images (Schlenker, 1987). This assessment engages both the cognitive and motivational facets of the actor's identity.

The objective of the assessment is to construct and protect desired identity images. Phrased differently, it is to arrive at the "truth" about oneself, with truth defined in terms of the combination of beneficiality ("What type of person do I want to be in this situation?") and believability

---

[5]The distinction between passive and active modes of processing has precedence in the literature on persuasion and attitude change following counterattitudinal behavior. Petty and Cacioppo (1986) proposed that persuasion can occur via a more central route that involves thoughtful consideration of arguments and evidence, including counterarguing, or a more peripheral route in which salient situational features, such as the characteristics of the communicator, influence reactions in a nonthoughtful fashion. They proposed that ego importance of the topic of the message is the major determinant of whether processing occurs via the central (for involving messages) or peripheral (for uninvolving messages) route. Ego involvement falls in the current category of the importance of the relevant values, goals, and identity images. Similarly, Fazio, Zanna, and Cooper (1977) proposed that attitude change following counterattitudinal behavior takes place via either a passive process of self-inference, as people merely infer that their attitudes correspond with their behavior, or via a more active process of dissonance reduction, in which people become motivated to rationalize their behavior. They suggested that when actions and prior attitudes do not differ greatly (i.e., actions fall in the actor's latitude of acceptance), the passive process occurs, but when actions and attitude are greatly discrepant (i.e., actions fall within the latitude of rejection), motivated processing occurs. Discrepancy falls in the current category of impediments because highly discrepant behaviors are likely (a) to raise uncertainties about what the actor is "really like," (b) to jeopardize the desired identity images the behavior probably contradicts, and (c) to raise concerns about the actor's consistency and reliability (Schlenker, 1982).

("Based on salient evidence, what type of person am I really?"). Evidence and aspirations become fused in the integration, and actors' conclusions identify the "best" type of person they can be given the salient evidence, context, and consequences (Schlenker, 1980, 1986a). It is in the active mode that people will most closely approximate the type of mental calculations suggested by the expected value formulation of desirability. That is, in the active mode people are likely to contemplate facets of believability and beneficiality, thinking about the consequences and implications of their self-identifications.

The consequences of increased assessment can be considered in three broad categories. These include (a) intensified cognitive processing, (b) accounting, and (c) strategic activities designed to create and maintain desired identity images (see Schlenker, 1987, for more complete discussion).

Intensified Information Processing

Increased assessment channels people's cognitive efforts into avenues that usually increase the likelihood of goal achievement and overcome potential impediments. Research suggests that it produces the following:

1. More Vigilant Information Processing. The active mode involves greater attention to and consciousness of pertinent information about the self, situation, and audience (cf. Berscheid et al., 1976; Carver, 1979; Schlenker, 1984, 1985, 1986a). People are more likely to notice, attend to, and give greater weight to information that is relevant to the self-identification goal, thus processing relevant information in a more in-depth fashion. Research supports the proposition that the intensity of information processing is increased when people encounter impediments. For example, people (a) display better recall of self-threatening than nonthreatening information, suggesting they have processed it better in attempts to counterargue and refute it (Wyer & Frey, 1983), and (b) make self-descriptive judgments faster when aspects of identity are challenged by others (Swann & Hill, 1982). Accountability (being answerable) to others, a factor that should engage the active mode, has been shown to generate more intensive information processing, greater recall of relevant information, data-driven processing of information, and greater awareness of the strategies that are being employed during decision making (Schlenker, 1986b; Schlenker & Weigold, in press; Tetlock, 1985b).

2. A More Thorough Search for Information. The active mode produces a search for information (in memory or the environment) that might clarify any ambiguous, missing, or conflicting information. Research indicates that when people confront impediments, they will search for relevant information that will help in solving the problem, preferring information that supports desired identity images and refutes potential threats (Frey, 1981; Pyszczynski, Greenberg, & LaPrelle, 1985).

3. Greater Examination and Comparison of Alternatives, including alternative goals, scripts or plans, and desired identity images. It is likely that in the active mode, people contemplate possibilities and try to achieve a more optimal solution to problems. In contrast to the passive mode, where "satisficing" solutions involving simple cognitive heuristics are used, the active mode probably generates more thorough comparisons and integrations, including more complex solutions. For example, people who are accountable to others, as compared to those who are not, make more cognitively complex judgments and use more complex decision strategies (Tetlock, 1985b). In other words, in the active mode, people may abandon simple heuristics and employ more elaborate and thorough decision rules.

4. Greater Rehearsal of the Contemplated Performance. If time permits, people become more likely to practice their contemplated performance, as in the case of an important speech that is rehearsed mentally, before a mirror, and then before a supportive audience of family or friends before the actual performance.

5. Increased Salience of the Pertinent Standards for the Performance and Greater Monitoring and Control of One's Activities in the Effort to Fulfill the Standards. Self-monitoring and control are improved as a consequence of focusing attention on the relevant standards (Bandura, 1982; Carver, 1979). Indeed, people are more likely to act in ways that dramatize and assert desired identity images when these images are questioned by others rather than when no impediment occurs (Swann & Hill, 1982; Swann & Read, 1981). In the active mode, the audience's expectations and likely reactions to one's performance become more salient, so the audience has a greater potential to influence the actor's conduct (Schlenker, 1986b).

6. Increased Responsiveness to Personal Information that pertains to how well or poorly the standards are being met. In the active mode, people seem to be more sensitive to feedback from others about how they are doing, prompting them to interpret the feedback in terms of its implications for their own identities (Fenigstein, 1979; Schlenker & Leary, 1982a, 1985). In short, the active mode appears to enhance egocentrism.

Accounting

Explanations are required when people confront obstacles to their pursuit of goals. An explanation provides an interpretation of an event when its meaning is unclear or might be misinterpreted or misconstrued by audiences (Schlenker, 1982). According to self-identification theory (Schlenker, 1982, 1987), *identity-relevant explanations occur when events appear to (a) violate standards in ways that threaten desired identity images* (e.g., Was the actor responsible for "bad" conduct? Was the conduct condemnable?), *or (b) meet commendable standards, but ambiguity exists about the relevance of the event for desired identity images* (e.g., Was the actor responsible for "meritorious" conduct? Was the conduct really commendable?). Both of these conditions generate active assessment because they involve impediments to the construction and preservation of desired images; they associate the actor with negative images and dissociate the actor from positive images, respectively.

It is proposed that *people attempt to explain events in ways that validate desired identity images and repudiate undesired images* (Schlenker, 1980, 1982, 1987). To the extent that this can be accomplished, impediments are overcome, the affective consequences are more positive (or less negative); and people can continue to work toward their goals with reasonable expectations of success. The literature on egotistical biases in attributions and perceptions (Greenwald, 1980; Snyder, 1985; Snyder et al., 1978; Tetlock & Levi, 1982; Weary-Bradley, 1978; Weary & Arkin, 1981), in which people attempt to associate themselves with positive events and dissociate themselves from negative events, can be regarded as evidence of the tendency to gravitate toward desired identity images through one's explanations of events (for reviews, see Schlenker, 1980, 1982, 1987).

Further, *people resist the inference that a desirable image is unrepresentative of self or an undesirable one is representative of self*. For example, Spivak et al. (1986) induced subjects to present themselves positively or negatively to an interviewer on an important trait dimension. The experimenter's instructions emphasized that the self-presentation could be regarded as representative of self (i.e., you can exaggerate your qualities but remain generally truthful) or as unrepresentative of self (i.e., create the impression even if you have to lie, but do not be outrageous in your statements). A negative self-presentation creates a greater impediment to people's desired self-view when it can be regarded as representative rather than unrepresentative of self, whereas a positive self-presentation creates an impediment when it can be seen as unrepresentative rather than representative. When an impediment exists, greater self-assessment and counterarguing should occur, as people attempt to repudiate it. In support of this reasoning, subjects later *increased* their self-ratings on the dimension, compared to control subjects, when situational cues suggested that the negative self-presentation had been representative of self or the positive self-presentation had been unrepresentative of self. Instead of a passive self-inference process, in which subjects shift their self-appraisals to bring them in line with their behavior (Bem, 1972), these effects suggest an active, motivated processing of information designed to reaffirm desired identity images when these come under question.

Strategic Activities

Goals mobilize people's mental and behavioral resources in the service of goal achievement. When the goal is important or possible impediments are perceived, people's efforts become devoted to overcoming obstacles and developing effective plans. Schlenker (1987) reviewed evidence indicating that people who confront impediments engage in strategic activities designed to preserve and reaffirm desired identity images. These include (a) direct counterattacks against the obstacle (e.g., attempting to change the opinion of a co-worker who is constantly critical or, if this is unsuccessful, getting oneself or the co-worker transferred to a different location); (b) attempts to strengthen identity from current and future threats, including compensatory behaviors that bolster identity (e.g., the 98 pound weakling who either pumps iron to become Mr. America or studies hard to become a Nobel laureate); and (c) the pursuit of support from other people that reaffirms desired identity images (e.g., seeking validation from friends and family after being criticized by an employer).

Outcome Expectations: Optimal or Stressed Performances

According to self-identification theory, assessment generates an outcome expectation, which is the perceived likelihood that the desired images can be constructed and maintained in the context (Schlenker, 1985, 1987; Schlenker & Leary, 1982a). These self-identification outcome expectations reflect the extent to which potential problems are likely to be rectified given the nature of the audience, the situation, and the actor's attributes and personal resources (e.g., perceived social skills, supportive friends). As discussed elsewhere (Schlenker & Leary, 1982a), these expectations will be lower when (a) audiences are perceived to be more demanding, less supportive, and more evaluative; (b) the situation is more demanding, difficult, evaluative, or ambiguous (e.g., tasks on which past failures have occurred; novel situations; "test" rather than "game" situations); and (c) the actor's perceived skills and resources relevant to the task are lower (e.g., low self-regard, poor social or communication skills, high social anxiety), and he or she is especially concerned about the evaluative implications of the performance (e.g., high need for social approval, high fear of failure, high public self-consciousness).

If the outcome expectation indicates that the self-identification goal is likely to be achieved, actors experience positive affect and continue to work toward the goal. Indeed, people with higher as compared to lower outcome expectations will procrastinate less before starting difficult tasks, will work harder on them, and will persevere longer in the face of obstacles (Bandura, 1977, 1982; Feather, 1982). Higher expectations are associated with self-reaffirming ruminations, explanations, and activities (Schlenker, 1987). It is not surprising, then, that higher as compared to lower outcome expectations typically produce better performance (Bandura, 1982; Feather, 1982).

The self-identification analysis suggests that impediments can actually improve people's performance, if the actors emerge from the assessment process with reasonably high outcome expectations. The routine behaviors associated with the passive mode allow people to devote their cognitive energies to other concerns, but at the price of not fully assessing the identity-related possibilities in the situation. The active mode, triggered by important performances and/or perceived impediments, results in more intensive assessment and increases the likelihood that people's activities are better fitted to the opportunities and constraints that exist (Schlenker, 1980, 1987; Schlenker & Leary, 1982a). The contrast is between taking an interaction for granted, as in the case of the overconfident student who has not adequately prepared for a class presentation and becomes self-conscious, flustered, and confused when unexpected questions arise; and fully assessing the situation, as in the case of the well-prepared student who has anticipated a variety of questions, planned responses, and monitors and controls the performance in ways designed to meet high standards. Analogously, coaches of highly ranked athletic teams usually emphasize the strengths of upcoming, unranked opponents who might otherwise be taken for granted by his overconfident players. It is this sense in which people can improve their performance by focusing their attention on their self-presentations. The combination of the active mode and high outcome expectations results in the perception of tasks as challenges that provide the opportunity for mastery and success (Schlenker, 1987).

In contrast to these facilitating effects, low outcome expectations are associated with negative affect and suboptimal performance (Schlenker, 1985, 1987; Schlenker & Leary, 1982a, 1985). The increased intensity of information processing, which normally helps direct cognitive activity toward a solution to potential problems, becomes debilitating in the context of low expectations. If the cognitive search for solutions to impediments continually generates perceptions of failure, people become trapped in assessment and begin to focus on their deficiencies and liabilities (Carver, 1979; Hill, Weary, & Williams, 1987; Pyszczynski & Greenberg, 1987; Schlenker, 1987; Schlenker & Leary, 1982a, 1985). In addition, people attempt to withdraw, mentally or in actuality, from the difficult situation and avoid similar situations in the future. Information processing declines in effectiveness, self-monitoring and control worsens as signs of stress and anxiety leak through one's weakened guard, and people engage in protective self-presentations designed to reduce the chance of even greater losses for identity (Schlenker, 1987; Schlenker & Leary, 1985). The self-protective style is characterized by making safe, secure decisions; taking less personal responsibility for prospective good outcomes; attributing successes to external factors such as luck and failures to lack of ability; avoiding or withdrawing from the stressful situation; and expending less effort and exhibiting less endurance. Further, when in the self-protective mode, actors communicate less information about themselves and, when they must present themselves to others, they focus on neutral information. The self-protective style characterizes people who are low in self-esteem and high in anxiety and depressive tendencies (Arkin, 1981; Hill et al., 1987; Schlenker & Leary, 1985), although anyone can have the experience when they confront impediments and have low outcome expectations.

It is in this sense that self-consciously focusing on one's self-presentations can debilitate one's social performance. When the intensified cognitive activity that characterizes the active mode occurs under conditions of low outcome expectations, people begin to experience high stress and anxiety, self-doubts, and fear. Their self-presentational performance suffers.

Expressiveness Versus Self-Presentation

A popular view is that people engage in self-presentation only some of the time, such as when there are salient reward-cost contingencies related to how well they come across to others (e.g., at a job interview) or when they are in highly structured, formal settings that have clear scripts (e.g., at a wedding) (Buss & Briggs, 1984; Jones & Pittman, 1982). At other times, people are "expressive," disclosing truthful information about themselves with relatively little self-consciousness, censorship, or editing. To the extent that this view is simply an application of the idea that there are some occasions when behavior is influenced more by situational factors (e.g., audience expectations, rewards) than by personal factors (e.g., self-concept, mood), and there are other times when the reverse is true, it is rather uncontroversial. However, the argument seems to go beyond the relative influence of personal and situational forces. Instead, it contains the undercurrent that self-presentation is inherently illicit, deceitful, superficial, and immoral; and that "good" people do not do self-presentation, they are self-expressive.

We take a different view (see Hogan & Sloan, 1985, for a compatible position). Self-identification is an integral component of all social behavior. It (a) must involve editing and packaging, (b) should be affected by the particular audience and situation in order to be effective, and (c) can be guided by the objective of conveying a sincere portrait of self to others just as it can be guided by the objective of conning others about oneself. Indeed, we argue that the normal (most statistically frequent) state of social interaction is characterized by people's attempts to communicate what they regard as the "truth" about themselves, with "truth" defined in terms of desirable identity images. Self-presentation is a subcategory of self-identification that involves the attempt to control information about oneself to audiences. There is no reason to equate self-presentation with deceit. Unless, of course, one *defines* self-presentation by limiting it to cases of illicit or ulterior motives, such as by defining it as an illicit attempt to increase one's power or liking by influencing other's impressions of self. Instead of adopting a limited definition, we employ a broader use that better captures the full range of self-identifying activities that occur before audiences. Expressiveness versus deception refers to an attribution made about the motives of the actor, not the inherent properties of the act.

Nonetheless, there are differences in the extent to which people (a) invest cognitive effort in their self-identifications, (b) are phenomenologically aware of their self-identifying activities, and (c) are likely to attribute their behavior to the desire to create a particular impression on other people (irrespective of the actual existence of such a motive). People will invest more cognitive effort in self-identification when the relevant goal increases in importance and/or they perceive an impediment to constructing desired identity images. These are also the conditions under which people are more likely to be phenomenologically aware of their identities. If the self-identification is directed toward other people as the primary audience, and if the actors can profit from the type of impression they create, observers and perhaps the actors themselves will be more likely to call the behavior "self-presentation"

7. CONSTRUCTING DESIRED IDENTITIES

(with negative connotations). There are thus times when people are focused more on the self-identification process. To argue that self-presentation occurs only part-time, however, is akin to arguing that people only pursue goals some of time because they either (a) do not always invest great cognitive effort on the activities they employ to pursue those goals, (b) are not always phenomenologically aware of how they are pursuing their goals, or (c) do not always attribute their behavior to intrinsic motives.

SUMMARY

Self-identification is a goal-directed activity in which the self is specified for some purpose to some audience. According to self-identification theory, people strive to construct and maintain desired identity images. These images represent what people believe they should and could be on the occasion, being reality-edited yet romanticized views of self. Self-identifications are more desirable to the extent that they are associated with accomplishing more valued goals and are perceived as more believable; they are less desirable when the costs of being wrong about oneself are higher and believability is lower. The believability of a self-identification can be evaluated according to six criteria that parallel the criteria scientists use to evaluate a theory. Believability acts as a constraint on self-identifications by restricting the claims one can make to other people and to oneself.

It is argued that self-identifications always represent an integration of information related to "wishes" and "reality." More precisely, a particular self-identification becomes more likely when factors (a) increase the expected positive outcomes if the identification is correct, (b) decrease the expected negative outcomes if the identification is incorrect, or (c) increase the likelihood that the salient audience will accept the claim. The self-identification position provides a synthesizing perspective on debates between advocates of a grand "consistency motive" versus a "self-esteem enhancement motive."

A distinction is made between passive and active modes of self-identification, based on the amount of cognitive effort devoted to the self-identification process. The passive mode reflects habitual, modulated patterns of self-identifying behavior. The active mode reflects greater cognitive effort devoted to pursuing self-identifying goals, as people engage in assessment of the self, the situation, and the audience for the activity. It is proposed that the active mode occurs when (a) self-identifying goals are important, and/or (b) impediments to self-identification are perceived. The objective of the assessment process is to construct and protect desired identity images, and it is in the active mode that people are most aware of their self-presentations. The analysis of self-identification modes has implications for conceptualizations of self-presentation as expressive versus manipulative.

REFERENCES

Abelson, R. P. (1976). Script processing in attitude formation and decision making. In J. S. Carroll & J. W. Payne (Eds.), *Cognition and social behavior* (pp. 33–45). Hillsdale, NJ: Lawrence Erlbaum Associates.

Alexander, C. N., Jr., & Rudd, J. (1981). Situated identities and response variables. In J. T. Tedeschi (Ed.), *Impression management theory and social psychological research* (pp. 83–103). New York: Academic Press.

Alexander, C. N., Jr., & Wiley, M. G. (1981). Situated activity and identity formation. In M. Rosenberg & R. H. Turner (Eds.), *Social psychology: Sociological perspectives* (pp. 269–289). New York: Basic Books.

Alicke, M. D. (1987). Public explanation and private ratiocination: Communication between the public and private selves. In R. Hogan & W. H. Jones (Eds.), *Perspectives in personality: Theory, measurement, and interpersonal dynamics* (Vol. 2 pp., 143–180). Greenwich, CT: JAI Press.

Allport, G. H. (1937). *Personality: A psychological interpretation.* New York: Holt.

Arkin, R. M. (1981). Self-presentation styles. In J. T. Tedeschi (Ed.), *Impression management theory and social psychological research* (pp. 311–333). New York: Academic Press.

Arkin, R. M., Appelman, A. J., & Burger, J. M. (1980). Social anxiety, self-presentation, and the self-serving bias in causal attribution. *Journal of Personality and Social Psychology, 38,* 23–35.

Arkowitz, H., Lichtenstein, E., McGovern, K., & Hines, P. (1975). The behavioral assessment of social competence in males. *Behavior Therapy, 6,* 3–13.

Baldwin, M. W., & Holmes, J. G. (1987). Salient private audiences and awareness of the self. *Journal of Personality and Social Psychology, 52,* 1087–1098.

Bandura, A. (1977). Self-efficacy: Toward a unifying theory of behavioral change. *Psychological Review, 84,* 191–215.

Bandura, A. (1982). The self and mechanisms of agency. In J. Suls (Ed.), *Psychological perspectives on the self* (Vol. 1, pp. 3–39). Hillsdale, NJ: Lawrence Erlbaum Associates.

Baumeister, R. F. (1982). A self-presentational view of social phenomena. *Psychological Bulletin, 91,* 3–26.

Baumeister, R. F. (1984). Choking under pressure: Self-consciousness and paradoxical effects of incentives on skillful performance. *Journal of Personality and Social Psychology, 46,* 610–620.

Baumeister, R. F., Hamilton, & Tice, D. M. (1985). Public versus private expectancy of success: Confidence booster or performance pressure. *Journal of Personality and Social Psychology, 48,* 1447–1457.

Baumeister, R. F., & Jones, E. E. (1978). When self-presentation is constrained by the target's knowledge: Consistency and compension. *Journal of Personality and Social Psychology, 36,* 608–618.

Baumeister, R. F., & Steinhilder, (1984). Paradoxical effects of supportive audiences on performance under pressure: Home field disadvantage in sports championships. *Journal of Personality and Social Psychology, 47,* 85–93.

Baumgardner, A. H., & Brownlee, E. A. (1987). Strategic failure in social interaction: Evidence for expectancy disconfirmation processes. *Journal of Personality and Social Psychology, 52,* 525–535.

Becker, G., & McClintock, C. G. (1972). Scientific theory and social psychology. In C. G. McClintock (Ed.), *Experimental social psychology* (pp. 5–20). New York: Holt, Rinehart & Winston.

Bem, D. J. (1972). Self-perception theory. In L. Berkowitz (Ed.), *Advances in experimental social psychology* (Vol. 6, pp. 1–62). New York: Academic Press.

Bem, D. J., & Allen, A. (1974). On predicting some of the people some of the time: The search for cross-situational consistencies in behavior. *Psychological Review, 81,* 506–520.

Berscheid, E., Graziano, W., Monson, T., & Dermer, M. (1976). Outcome dependency: Attention, attribution, and attraction. *Journal of Personality and Social Psychology, 34,* 978–989.

Biggs, D. A., & Tinsley, K. J. (1970). Student-made academic predictions. *Journal of Educational Research, 63,* 195–197.

Binder, D. M., Jones, J. G., & Strowig, R. W. (1970). Non-intellective self-report variables as predictors of scholastic achievement. *Journal of Educational Research, 63,* 364–366.

Buss, A. H. (1980). *Self-consciousness and social anxiety.* San Francisco: W. H. Freeman.

Buss, A. H., & Briggs, S. R. (1984). Drama and the self in social interaction. *Journal of Personality and Social Psychology, 47,* 1310–1324.

Cantor, N., & Mischel, W. (1979). Prototypes in person perception. In L. Berkowitz (Ed.), *Advances in experimental social psychology* (Vol. 12, pp. 3–52). New York: Academic Press.

Carson, R. C. (1969). *Interaction concepts of personality.* Chicago: Aldine.

Carver, C. S. (1979). A cybernetic model of self-attention processes. *Journal of Personality and Social Psychology, 37,* 1251–1281.

Carver, C. S., & Scheier, M. F. (1981). *Attention and self-regulation: A control-theory approach to human behavior.* New York: Springer-Verlag.

Carver, C. S., & Scheier, M. F. (1985). Aspects of self and the control of behavior. In B. R. Schlenker (Ed.), *The self and social life* (pp. 146–174). New York: McGraw-Hill.

Cheek, J. M. (1982). Aggregation, moderator variables, and the validity of personality tests: A peer-rating study. *Journal of Personality and Social Psychology, 43,* 1254–1269.

Cheek, J. M., & Hogan, R. (1983). Self-concepts, self-presentations, and moral judgments. In J. Suls & A. G. Greenwald (Eds.), *Psychological perspectives on the self* (Vol. 2, pp. 249–273). Hillsdale, NJ: Lawrence Erlbaum Associates.

Cialdini, R. B., Levy, A., Herman, C. R., & Evenbeck, C. (1973). Attitude politics: The strategy of moderation. *Journal of Personality and Social Psychology, 25,* 100–108.

Cialdini, R. B., Levy, A., Herman, C. P., Kozlowski, L. T., & Petty, R. E. (1976). Elastic shifts of opinion: Determinants of direction and durability. *Journal of Personality and Social Psychology, 34,* 663–672.

Cooley, C. H. (1902). *Human nature and the social order.* New York: Scribner's.

Davis, D., & Brock, T. C. (1972). Paradoxical instigation of self-criticism by inordinate praise. *Proceedings of the 80th Annual Convention of the American Psychological Association,* 191–192.

DePaulo, B. M., Stone, J. I., & Lassiter, G. D. (1985). In B. R. Schlenker (Ed.), *The self and social life* (pp. 323–370). New York: McGraw-Hill.

Dlugolecki, D., & Schlenker, B. R. (1985, August). *Self-presentations and self-appraisals: Cognitive activity, internalization, and behavior.* Paper presented at the 93rd Annual Meeting of the American Psychological Association, Los Angeles, CA.

Dollard, J. (1949). Under what conditions do opinions predict behavior? *Public Opinion Quarterly, 12,* 623–632.

Eagly, A., & Acksen, B. (1971). The effect of expecting to be evaluated on change toward favorable and unfavorable information about oneself. *Sociometry, 34*, 411–422.

Eagly, A. H., & Chaiken, S. (1984). Psychological theories of persuasion. In L. Berkowitz (Ed.), *Advances in experimental social psychology* (Vol. 17, pp. 257–369). New York: Academic Press.

Epstein, S. (1973). The self-concept revisited: Or a theory of a theory. *American Psychologist, 28*, 404–416.

Erickson, B., Lind, E. A., Johnson, B. C., & O'Barr, W. M. (1978). Speech style and impression formation in a court setting: The effects of powerful and powerless speech. *Journal of Experimental Social Psychology, 14*, 266–279.

Erikson, E. H. (1959). Identity and the life cycle. In G. S. Klein (Ed.), *Psychological issues*. New York: International Universities Press.

Fazio, R. H., Effrein, E. A., & Falender, V. J. (1981). Self-perceptions following social interaction. *Journal of Personality and Social Psychology, 41*, 232–242.

Fazio, R. H., Zanna, M. P., & Cooper, J. (1977). Dissonance and self-perception: An integrative view of each theory's proper domain of application. *Journal of Experimental Social Psychology, 13*, 464–479.

Feather, N. T. (1982). Actions in relation to expected consequences: An overview of a research program. In N. T. Feather (Ed.), *Expectations and actions: Expectancy-value models in psychology* (pp. 53–95). Hillsdale, NJ: Lawrence Erlbaum Associates.

Fenigstein, A. (1979). Self-consciousness, self-attention, and social interaction. *Journal of Personality and Social Psychology, 37*, 75–86.

Foote, N. N. (1951). Identification as the basis of a theory of motivation. *American Sociological Review, 16*, 14–21.

Freud, S. (1925). *Collected papers*. London: Hogarth Press.

Frey, D. (1978). Reactions to success and failure in public and private conditions. *Journal of Experimental Social Psychology, 17*, 172–179.

Frey, D. (1981). Reversible and irreversible decisions: Preference for consonant information as a function of attractiveness of decision alternatives. *Personality and Social Psychology Bulletin, 7*, 621–626.

Gergen, K. J. (1965). Interaction goals and personalistic feedback as factors affecting the presentation of self. *Journal of Personality and Social Psychology, 1*, 413–424.

Gergen, K. J. (1968). Personal consistency and the presentation of self. In C. Gordon & K. J. Gergen (Eds.), *The self in social interaction* (pp. 299–308). New York: Wiley.

Gergen, K. J. (1982). From self to science: What is there to know? In J. Suls (Eds.), *Psychological perspectives on the self* (Vol. 1, pp. 129–149). Hillsdale, NJ: Lawrence Erlbaum Associates.

Gergen, K. J., & Jones, E. E. (1963). Mental illness, predictability, and affective consequences as stimulus factors in person perception. *Journal of Abnormal and Social Psychology, 67*, 348–358.

Glasgow, R., & Arkowitz, H. (1975). The behavioral assessment of social competence in dyadic heterosexual interaction. *Behavior Therapy, 6*, 488–498.

Goffman, E. (1959). *The presentation of self in everyday life*. Garden City, NY: Doubleday.

Greenberg, J., Pyszczynski, T. A., & Solomon, S. (1986). The causes and consequences of a need for self-esteem: A terror management theory. In R. Baumeister (Ed.), *Public self and private self* (pp. 189–212). New York: Springer-Verlag.

Greenwald, A. G. (1980). The totalitarian ego: Fabrication and revision of personal history. *American Psychologist, 35*, 603–618.

Greenwald, A. G., & Breckler, S. J. (1985). To whom is the self presented? In B. R. Schlenker (Ed.), *The self and social life* (pp. 126–145). New York: McGraw-Hill.

Greenwald, A. G., & Pratkanis, A. R. (1984). The self. In R. S. Wyer & T. K. Srull (Eds.),

Handbook of social cognition (Vol. 3, pp. 129–178). Hillsdale, NJ: Lawrence Erlbaum Associates.

Harre', R. (1980). *Social being: A theory for social psychology.* Totowa, NJ: Littlefield, Adams & Co.

Harre', R. (1983). Identity projects. In G. M. Breakwell (Ed.), *Threatened identities* (pp. 31–51). New York: Wiley.

Harvey, J. H., Harris, B., & Barnes, R. D. (1975). Actor-observer differences in the perceptions of responsibility and freedom. *Journal of Personality and Social Psychology, 32,* 22–28.

Hempel, C. G. (1966). *Philosophy of natural science.* Englewood Cliffs, NJ: Prentice-Hall.

Hemsley, G. D., & Doob, A. N. (1978). The effect of looking behavior on perceptions of a communicator's credibility. *Journal of Applied Social Psychology, 8,* 136–144.

Hewitt, J. P. (1976). *Self and society: A symbolic interactionist social psychology.* Boston: Allyn & Bacon.

Hill, M. G., Weary, G., & Williams, J. (1987). Depression: A self-presentation formulation. In R. F. Baumeister (Ed.), *Public self and private self* (pp. 213–239). New York: Springer-Verlag.

Hobbes, T. (1952). *Leviathan.* In R. M. Hutchins (Ed.), Great books of the western world. Chicago: Encyclopaedia Britannica (Originally published, 1651).

Hogan, R. (1982). A socioanalytic theory of personality. In M. Page & R. Dienstbier (Eds.), *Nebraska symposium on motivation* (pp. 55–89). Lincoln: University of Nebraska Press.

Hogan, R., & Cheek, J. M. (1983). Identity, authenticity, and maturity. In T. R. Sarbin & K. E. Scheibe (Eds.), *Studies in social identity* (pp. 339–357). New York: Praeger.

Hogan, R., & Sloan, T. (1985). *Self-presentation and personality: A reply to Buss and Briggs.* Unpublished manuscript, University of Tulsa.

Holland, J. L., & Nichols, R. C. (1964). Prediction of academic and extracurricular achievement in college. *Journal of Educational Psychology, 55,* 55–65.

Horney, K. (1945). *Our inner conflicts.* New York: Norton.

Isen, A. M. (1984). Toward understanding the role of affect in cognition. In R. S. Wyer & T. K. Srull (Eds.), *Handbook of social cognition* (Vol. 3, pp. 179–236). Hillsdale, NJ: Lawrence Erlbaum Associates.

Izard, C. E. (1971). *The face of emotion.* New York: Appleton.

James, W. (1890). *The principles of psychology.* New York: Holt.

James, W. (1907). *Pragmatism.* New York: Longmans-Green.

Jeffery, K. M., & Mischel, W. (1979). Effects of purpose on organization and recall of information in person perception. *Journal of Personality, 47,* 397–419.

Jellison, J. M. (1981). Reconsidering the attitude concept: A behavioristic self-presentation formulation. In J. T. Tedeschi (Ed.), *Impression management theory and social psychological research* (pp. 107–126). New York: Academic Press.

Jones, E. E. (1964). *Ingratiation.* New York: Appleton-Century-Crofts.

Jones, E. E., & Pittman, T. (1982). Toward a theory of strategic self-presentation. In J. Suls (Ed.), *Psychological perspectives on the self* (pp. 231–262). Hillsdale, NJ: Lawrence Erlbaum Associates.

Jones, E. E., Rhodewalt, F., Berglas, S., & Skelton, J. A. (1981). Effects of strategic self-presentation on subsequent self-esteem. *Journal of Personality and Social Psychology, 41,* 407–421.

Jones, E. E., & Wortman, C. (1973). *Ingratiation: An attributional approach.* Morristown, NJ: General Learning Press.

Jones, S. C. (1973). Self- and interpersonal evaluations: Esteem theories versus consistency theories. *Psychological Bulletin, 79,* 185–199.

Jones, S. C., & Pines, H. A. (1968). Self-revealing events and interpersonal evaluations. *Journal of Personality and Social Psychology, 8,* 277–281.

Kanouse, D. E., Gumpert, P., & Canavan-Gumpert D. (1981). The semantics of praise. In J. H. Harvey, W. J. Ickes, and R. F. Kidd (Eds.), *New directions in attribution research* (Vol. 3, pp. 97–115). Hillsdale, NJ: Lawrence Erlbaum Associates.

Keefer, K. E. (1969). Self-prediction of academic achievement by college students. *Journal of Educational Research, 63,* 53–66.

Laird, J. D. (1974). Self-attribution of emotion: The effects of expressive behavior on the quality of emotional experience. *Journal of Personality and Social Psychology, 29,* 475–486.

Lakatos, I. (1970). Falsification and the methodology of scientific research programmes. In I. Lakatos & A. Musgrave (Eds.), *Criticism and the growth of knowledge* (pp. 91–196). Cambridge: Cambridge University Press.

Langer, E. J. (1978). Rethinking the role of thought in social interaction. In J. H. Harvey, W. J. Ickes, and R. F. Kidd (Eds.), *New directions in attribution research* (Vol. 2, pp. 35–58). Hillsdale, NJ: Lawrence Erlbaum Associates.

Lefcourt, H. M., Hogg, E., Struther, S., & Holmes, C. (1975). Causal attributions as a function of locus of control, initial confidence, and performance outcomes. *Journal of Personality and Social Psychology, 32,* 391–397.

Locke, E. A. (1968). Towards a theory of task motivation and incentive. *Organizational Behavior and Human Performance, 3,* 157–189.

Locke, E. A., Shaw, K. N., Saari, L. M., & Latham, G. P. (1981). Goal setting and task performance: 1968–1980. *Psychological Bulletin, 90,* 125–152.

Lorge, I., & Solomon, H. (1960). Group and individual performance in problem solving related to previous exposure to problem, level of aspiration, and group size. *Behavioral Science, 5,* 28–38.

Lundgren, D. C. (1978). Public esteem, self-esteem, and interpersonal stress. *Social Psychology, 41,* 68–73.

Maracek, J. & Mettee, D. R. (1972). Avoidance of continued success as a function of self-esteem, level of esteem certainty, and responsibility for success. *Journal of Personality and Social Psychology, 22,* 98–107.

Markus, H. (1977). Self-schemata and processing information about the self. *Journal of Personality and Social Psychology, 35,* 63–78.

Markus, H., & Nurius, P. (1986). Possible selves. *American Psychologist, 41,* 954–969.

Markus, H., & Sentis, K. (1982). The self in social information processing. In J. Suls (Ed.), *Psychological perspectives on the self* (Vol. 1, pp. 41–70). Hillsdale, NJ: Lawrence Erlbaum Associates.

McCall, G. J., & Simmons, J. F. (1978). *Identities and interactions* (2nd ed.). New York: Free Press.

McCrae, R. R., & Costa, Jr. (1982). Self-concept and stability of personality: Cross-sectional comparisons of self-reports and ratings. *Journal of Personality and Social Psychology, 43,* 1282–1292.

McKillop, K. J., Jr., & Schlenker, B. R. (1987, March). *Active versus passive processing and the internalization of self-presentations.* Paper presented at the 33rd Annual Meetings of the Southeastern Psychological Association, Atlanta.

Mead, G. H. (1934). *Mind, self, and society,* Chicago: Chicago University Press.

Mettee, D. R., & Aronson, E. (1974). Affective reactions to appraisal from others. In T. L. Huston (Ed.), *Foundations of interpersonal attraction* (pp. 235–283). New York: Academic Press.

Miller, D. T. (1976). Ego involvement and attributions for success and failure. *Journal of Personality and Social Psychology, 34,* 901–906.

Miller, G. A., Galanter, E., & Pribram, K. H. (1960). *Plans and the structure of behavior.* New York: Holt, Rinehart, & Winston.
Miller, R. S., & Schlenker, B. R. (1985). Egotism in group members: Public and private attributions of responsibility for group performance. *Social Psychology Quarterly, 48,* 85–89.
Mills, C. W. (1940). Situated actions and vocabularies of motives. *American Sociological Review, 5,* 904–913.
Mischel, W., Ebbesen, E. B., & Zeiss, A. R. (1973). Selective attention to the self: Situational and dispositional determinants. *Journal of Personality and Social Psychology, 27,* 129–142.
Morse, S., & Gergen, K. J. (1970). Social comparison, self-consistency, and the concept of self. *Journal of Personality and Social Psychology, 16,* 148–156.
Nemeth, C. J. (1986). Differential contributions of majority and minority influence. *Psychological Review, 93,* 23–32.
Paulhus, D. L., & Levitt, K. (1987). Desirable responding triggered by affect: Automatic egotism? *Journal of Personality and Social Psychology, 52,* 245–259.
Petty, R. E., & Cacioppo, J. T. (1986). The elaboration likelihood model of persuasion. In L. Berkowitz (Ed.), *Advances in experimental social psychology* (Vol. 19, pp. 123–205). New York: Academic Press.
Pierce, C. S. (1878). How to make our ideas clear. *Popular Science Monthly, 12,* 286–302.
Pyszczynski, T. A., & Greenberg, J. (1987). Depression, self-focused attention, and self-regulatory perseveration. In C. R. Snyder & C. E. Ford (Eds.), *Coping with negative life events: Clinical and social psychological perspectives* (pp. 105–129). New York: Plenum Press.
Pyszczynski, T. A., Greenberg, J., & LaPrelle, J. (1985). Social comparison after success and failure: Biased search for information consistent with a self-serving conclusion. *Journal of Experimental Social Psychology, 21,* 195–211.
Rhodewalt, F., & Agustsdottir, S. (1986). The effects of self-presentation on the phenomenal self. *Journal of Personality and Social Psychology, 50,* 47–55.
Richardson, K. D., & Cialdini, R. B. (1981). Basking and blasting: Tactics of indirect self-presentation. In J. T. Tedeschi (Ed.), *Impression management theory and social psychological research* (pp. 41–53). New York: Academic Press.
Riess, M., Rosenfeld, P., Melburg, V., & Tedeschi, J. T. (1981). Self-serving attributions: Biased private perceptions and distorted public descriptions. *Journal of Personality and Social Psychology, 41,* 224–231.
Rogers, C. R. (1959). A theory of therapy, personality, and interpersonal relationships as developed in the client-centered framework. In S. Koch (Ed). *Psychology: A study of a science* (Vol. 3, pp. 184–256). New York: McGraw-Hill.
Rogers, T. B., Kuiper, N. A., & Kirker, W. S. (1977). Self-reference and the encoding of personal information. *Journal of Personality and Social Psychology, 35,* 677–688.
Rosenberg, M. (1979). *Conceiving the self.* New York: Basic Books.
Sarbin, T. R., & Allen, V. L. (1968). Role theory. In G. Lindzey & E. Aronson (Eds.), *The handbook of social psychology* (2nd ed., Vol. 1, pp. 488–567). Reading, MA: Addison-Wesley.
Schank, R., & Abelson, R. (1977). *Scripts, plans, goals, and understanding.* Hillsdale, NJ: Lawrence Erlbaum Associates.
Scheff, T. J. (1968). Negotiating reality: Notes on power in the assessment of responsibility. *Social Problems, 16,* 3–17.
Schlenker, B. R. (1975). Self-presentation: Managing the impression of consistency when reality interferes with self-enhancement. *Journal of Personality and Social Psychology, 32,* 1030–1037.

Schlenker, B. R. (1980). *Impression Management: The self concept, social identity, and interpersonal relations.* Monterey, CA: Brooks-Cole. (Distributed by Krieger Publishers, Melbourne, FL).

Schlenker, B. R. (1981, August). *Self-presentation: A conceptualization and model.* Paper presented at the 89th Annual Meetings of the American Psychological Association, Los Angeles.

Schlenker, B. R. (1982). Translating actions into attitudes: An identity-analytic approach to the explanation of social conduct. In L. Berkowitz (Ed.), *Advances in experimental social psychology* (Vol. 15, pp. 193–247). New York: Academic Press.

Schlenker, B. R. (1984). Identities, identifications, and relationships. In V. Derlega (Ed.), *Communication, intimacy, and close relationships* (pp. 71–104). New York: Academic Press.

Schlenker, B. R. (1985). Identity and self-identification. In B. R. Schlenker (Ed.), *The self and social life* (pp. 65–99). New York: McGraw-Hill.

Schlenker, B. R. (1986a). Self-identification: Toward an integration of the private and public self. In R. F. Baumeister (Ed.), *Public self and private self* (pp. 21–62). New York: Springer-Verlag.

Schlenker, B. R. (1986b). *Personal accountability: Challenges and impediments in the quest for excellence.* Technical Report for the Navy Personnel Research and Development Center, San Diego.

Schlenker, B. R. (1987). Threats to identity: Self identification and social stress. In C. R. Snyder and C. Ford (Eds.), *Coping with negative life events: Clinical and social psychological perspectives* (pp. 273–321). New York: Academic Press.

Schlenker, B. R., & Goldman, H. J. (1982). Attitude change as a self-presentation tactic following attitude consistent behavior: Effects of choice and role. *Social Psychology Quarterly, 45,* 92–99.

Schlenker, B. R., Hallam, J. R., & McCown, N. E. (1983). Motives and social evaluations: Actor-observer differences in the delineation of motives for a beneficial act. *Journal of Experimental Social Psychology, 19,* 254–273.

Schlenker, B. R., & Leary, M. R. (1982a). Social anxiety and self-presentation: A conceptualization and model. *Psychological Bulletin, 92,* 641–669.

Schlenker, B. R., & Leary, M. R. (1982b). Audiences reactions to self-enhancing, self-denigrating, and accurate self-presentations. *Journal of Experimental Social Psychology, 18,* 89–104.

Schlenker, B. R., & Leary, M. R. (1985). Social anxiety and communication about the self. *Journal of Language and Social Psychology, 4,* 171–193.

Schlenker, B. R., & Miller, R. S. (1977). Egocentrism in groups: Self-serving biases or logical information processing? *Journal of Personality and Social Psychology, 35,* 755–764.

Schlenker, B. R., Miller, R. S., & Leary, M. R. (1983). Self-presentation as a function of the validity and quality of past performance. *Representative Research in Social Psychology, 13,* 2–14.

Schlenker, B. R., & Schlenker, P. A. (1975). Reactions following counterattitudinal behavior which produces positive consequences. *Journal of Personality and Social Psychology, 31,* 962–971.

Schlenker, B. R., & Weigold, M. F. (in press). Self-identification and accountability. In R. A. Giacalone and P. Rosenfeld (Eds.), *Impression management in the organization.* Hillsdale, NJ: Lawrence Erlbaum Associates.

Scott, M. B., & Lyman, S. M. (1968). Accounts. *American Sociological Review, 33,* 46–62.

Shrauger, J. S. (1975). Responses to evaluation as a function of initial self-perceptions. *Psychological Bulletin, 82,* 581–596.

Shrauger, J. S. (1982). Selection and processing of self-evaluative information: Experimental evidence and clinical implications. In G. Weary & H. L. Mirels (Eds.),

Integrations of clinical and social psychology (pp. 128–153). New York: Oxford University Press.
Shrauger, J. S., & Schoeneman, T. J. (1979). Symbolic interactionist view of self-concept: Through the looking glass darkly. *Psychological Bulletin, 86,* 549–572.
Snyder, C. R. (1985). The excuse: An amazing grace? In B. R. Schlenker (Ed.), *The self and social life* (pp. 235–260). New York: McGraw-Hill.
Snyder, C. R., Higgins, R. L., & Stucky, R. J. (1983). *Excuses: Masquerades in search of grace.* New York: Wiley-Interscience.
Snyder, M. (1979). Self-monitoring processes. In L. Berkowitz (Ed.), *Advances in experimental social psychology* (Vol. 12, pp. 85–128). New York: Academic Press.
Snyder, M., & White, P. (1982). Moods and memories: Elation, depression, and the remembering of the events of one's life. *Journal of Personality, 50,* 149–167.
Snyder, M. L., Stephan, W. G., & Rosenfield, D. (1978). Attributional egotism. In J. H. Harvey, W. Ickes, & R. F. Kidd (Eds.), *New directions in attribution research* (Vol. 2, pp. 91–117). Hillsdale, NJ: Lawrence Erlbaum Associates.
Spivak, K. R., Rogers, S. L., & Schlenker, B. R. (1986, March). *Motivational changes in self-appraisals following self-presentations.* Paper presented at the Annual Meetings of the Southeastern Psychological Association, Orlando, FL.
Swann, W. B., Jr. (1983). Self-verification: Bringing social reality into harmony with the self. In J. Suls & A. G. Greenwald (Eds.), *Psychological perspectives on the self* (Vol. 2, pp. 33–66). Hillsdale, NJ: Lawrence Erlbaum Associates.
Swann, W. B., Jr. (1985). The self as architect of social reality. In B. R. Schlenker (Ed.), *The self and social life* (pp. 100–125). New York: McGraw-Hill.
Swann, W. B., Griffin, J. J., Predmore, S. C., & Gaines, B. (1987). The cognitive-affective crossfire: When self-consistency confronts self-enhancement. *Journal of Personality and Social Psychology, 52,* 881–889.
Swann, W. B., Jr., & Hill, C. A. (1982). When our identities are mistaken: Reaffirming self-conceptions through social interaction. *Journal of Personality and Social Psychology, 43,* 59–66.
Swann, W. B., Jr., & Predmore, S. C. (1985). Intimates as agents of social support: Sources of consolation or despair? *Journal of Personality and Social Psychology, 49,* 1609–1617.
Swann, W. B., Jr., & Read, S. J. (1981). Self-verification processes: How we sustain our self-conceptions. *Journal of Experimental Social Psychology, 17,* 351–372.
Taylor, S. E., & Brown, J. D. (1988). Illusion and well-being: A social psychological perspective on mental health. *Psychological Bulletin, 103,* 193–210.
Tedeschi, J. T. (Ed.) (1981). *Impression management theory and social psychological research.* New York: Academic Press.
Tedeschi, J. T., & Norman, N. (1985). Social power, self-presentation, and the self. In B. R. Schlenker (Ed.), *The self and social life* (pp. 293–322). New York: McGraw-Hill.
Tedeschi, J. T., Schlenker, B. R., & Bonoma, T. V. (1971). Cognitive dissonance: Private ratiocination or public spectacle? *American Psychologist, 26,* 685–695.
Tetlock, P. E. (1985a). Toward an intuitive politician model of the attribution process. In B. R. Schlenker (Ed.), *The self and social life* (pp. 203–234). New York: McGraw-Hill.
Tetlock, P. E. (1985b). Accountability: The neglected social context of judgment and choice. In B. M. Staw & L. Cummings (Eds.), *Research in organizational behavior* (Vol. 9, pp. 279–332). Greenwich, CT: JAI Press.
Tetlock, P. E., & Levi, A. (1982). Attribution bias: On the inconclusiveness of the cognition-motivation debate. *Journal of Experimental Social Psychology, 18,* 68–88.
Tetlock, P. E., & Manstead, A. R. S. (1985). Impression management versus intrapsychic explanations in social psychology: A useful dichotomy? *Psychological Review, 92,* 59–77.
Tompkins, S. S. (1962). *Affect, imagery, consciousness* (Vol. 1). New York: Springer-Verlag.

Trope, Y. (1983). Self-assessment in achievement behavior. In J. Suls & A. G. Greenwald (Eds.), *Psychological perspectives on the self* (Vol. 2, pp. 93–121). Hillsdale, NJ: Lawrence Erlbaum Associates.

Trudeau, J. V., & Schlenker, B. R. (1986, August). The internalization of self-presentations: Effects of prior self-images and misattribution. *Paper presented at the meetings of the American Psychological Association,* Washington, D.C.

Trzebinski, J., McGlynn, R. P., Gray, G., & Tubbs, D. (1985). The role of categories of an actor's goals in organizing inferences about a person. *Journal of Personality and Social Psychology, 48,* 1387–1397.

Turner, R. H. (1968). The self-conception in social interaction. In C. Gordon & K. J. Gergen (Eds.), *The self in social interaction* (pp. 93–106). New York: Wiley.

Ungar, S. (1980). The effects of certainty of self-perceptions on self-presentation behaviors: A test of the strength of self-enhancement motives. *Social Psychology Quarterly, 43,* 165–172.

Weary, G., & Arkin, R. M. (1981). Attributional self-presentation. In J. H. Harvey, W. J. Ickes, and R. F. Kidd (Eds.), *New directions in attribution research* (Vol. 3, pp. 223–246). Hillsdale, NJ: Lawrence Erlbaum Associates.

Weary-Bradley, G. (1978). Self-serving biases in the attribution process: A reexamination of the fact or fiction question. *Journal of Personality and Social Psychology, 36,* 56–71.

Wells, G. L., & Murray, D. M. (1984). Eyewitness confidence. In G. L. Wells & E. F. Loftus (Eds.), *Eyewitness testimony: Psychological perspectives.* New York: Cambridge University Press.

Wicklund, R. A., & Gollwitzer, P. M. (1982). *Symbolic self-completion.* Hillsdale, NJ: Lawrence Erlbaum Associates.

Wortman, C. B., Costanzo, P. B., & Witt, T. R. (1973). Effect of anticipated performance on the attribution of causality to self and others. *Journal of Personality and Social Psychology, 27,* 372–381.

Wyer, R. S., & Frey, D. (1983). The effects of feedback about self and others on the recall and judgments of feedback relevant information. *Journal of Experimental Social Psychology, 19,* 540–559.

Zajonc, R. B. (1980). Feeling and thinking: Preferences need no inferences. *American Psychologist, 35,* 151–175.

Zanna, M. P., & Pack, S. J. (1975). On the self-fulfilling nature of apparent sex differences in behavior. *Journal of Experimental Social Psychology, 11,* 583–591.

8 Goal Setting Theory and Job Performance

THOMAS W. LEE
Graduate School of Business Administration,
University of Washington

EDWIN A. LOCKE
College of Business and Management,
University of Maryland

GARY P. LATHAM
Graduate School of Business Administration,
University of Washington

INTRODUCTION

In writing this chapter, we assumed that our audience consists primarily of personality and social psychologists who are interested in motivation and social cognition. In a sense, we consider ourselves "outsiders" in that our backgrounds are in organizational behavior, human resource management, and industrial and organizational psychology. Moreover, our primary organizational affiliations are management departments within business schools, though we maintain secondary affiliations with the psychology departments at our universities. As outsiders then, what contribution might we offer in this book? At a general level, we hope to convey how researchers in our field approach and study motivation and social cognition. At a more specific level, this chapter presents and discusses the research on a major and influential theory of work motivation, namely, goal setting.

This chapter is divided into four major sections. The first section describes how theorists and researchers in our field have traditionally studied work motivation. The second section defines goal setting theory and delineates its components. The third section describes current and emerging research directions in goal setting theory. The fourth section presents a conceptual model of the goal setting process for the purposes of summary, integration, and stimulation of new research.

THE HISTORICAL CONTEXT

The motivation to work is often conceptualized as an aspect of the individual that *initiates, directs, and sustains* human action toward job performance (Steers & Porter, 1987). Although important, work motivation is only one of many determinants of job performance. Ability, job knowledge, and situational constraints are also important causal factors.

It is beyond the scope of the present chapter to provide a detailed history of the theories of work motivation and job performance from our field. For the interested scholar, there are numerous books (e.g., Miner, 1980; Pinder, 1984; Steers & Porter, 1987), book chapters (e.g., Campbell & Pritchard, 1976; Landy & Becker, 1987; Locke & Henne, 1986) and journal articles (e.g., Mitchell, 1982; Salancik & Pfeffer, 1977, 1978) devoted to the topic of work motivation. In this section, only a brief overview of some influential theories is presented.

As an organizing schema for the present section, portions of Locke and Henne's (1986) general model of motivation were adopted, where the major theories of work motivation were classified in terms of their specificity and causal distance from human action. The most nonspecific and causally distant from human action are the need-based theories, which are followed by the value-based theories. The most specific and causally close to human action are the theories of goals and social cognition.

Need-Based Theories

Maslow (1954) and Alderfer (1969). In an early, well-known, and influential theory of work motivation, Maslow (1954) postulated that people have five basic needs: physiological, safety, affiliation, esteem, and self-actualization. It was theorized that an unsatisfied need causes an internal state of tension, which, in turn, leads to behaviors intended to reduce that tension. When a need is satisfied and the tension is reduced, the motivational potency of that need is reduced and another need takes primacy. Furthermore, Maslow asserted that the five needs are activated in a sequential and hierarchical fashion. Only after an employee satisfies (and makes inactive) a lower order need can the next highest need in the hierarchy become an active force.

In the organizational sciences, there has been a substantial amount of research on Maslow's theory; further, there has been substantial agreement on the interpretation of the empirical evidence (e.g., Campbell & Pritchard, 1976; Locke & Henne, 1986; Miner, 1980; Pfeffer, 1982; Pinder, 1984; Wahba & Bridwell, 1987). The consensus is that (a) there is little evidence for the five distinct needs that are postulated to exist for all employees; (b) the hypothesized process for the activation and deactivation of needs has not been well supported; and (c) there is very little support for the sequential and hierarchical ordering of the five needs.

In response to the cumulative and nonsupporting evidence, Alderfer (1969) proposed several major modifications to Maslow's theory, which have become known as ERG theory. Alderfer combined Maslow's five needs into three need categories arranged semi-hierarchically: existence, relatedness, and growth (i.e., ERG). Like Maslow's theory, need dissatisfaction was theorized to create an internal state of tension that energizes one's behavior toward the elimination of that tension. Correspondingly, the reduction of tension was said to cause the deactivation of that need and leads to the activation of a higher order need. In contrast to Maslow's theory, Alderfer suggested that the continual need dissatisfaction of a higher order need can, under certain conditions, lead to the reactivation of a lower level need. Moreover, Alderfer suggested that under certain conditions multiple needs may operate. The research evidence on ERG theory, however, is also quite clear; like Maslow's theory, ERG theory suffers from numerous conceptual ambiguities and generally nonsupportive empirical testing (e.g., Campbell & Pritchard, 1976; Pfeffer, 1982).

The research interest in Maslow's theory has largely diminished in the last decade, and there appears to be little likelihood for any substantial renewal of interest. Furthermore, the research interest in ERG theory has never been great, nor does it appear likely to grow in the foreseeable future. The contemporary influence of Maslow's theory should not be overlooked, however. Its heyday occurred in the 1950s and 1960s, which is when many people who are now senior managers and executives in industry were formally educated. A residual of that formal education is that Maslow's intuitively appealing hierarchy is sometimes accepted as *the* definitive explanation of employee work motivation.

Need-based theories have not received strong empirical support because they are conceptually inadequate (Locke & Henne, 1986). Although need theories may explain, in a general fashion, why a person must act (e.g., to obtain a desired outcome like money or feelings of accomplishment), they do not explain why specific actions are chosen in specific situations to obtain specific outcomes. Moreover, need-based theories do not easily account for individual differences. Although levels of need deprivation can vary, need-based theories assume that all people have the *same* hierarchical order of needs and respond to deprivation in the *same* manner. Both of these assumptions are dubious. Even with a constant level of deprivation, many possible actions can result in the satisfaction of a need. Furthermore, people may not always be fully aware of their needs. To be valid, need-based theories should explain how subconscious mental states can lead to specific actions in specific situations. To date, need-based theories have not been able to do this.

Value-Based Theories

Value-based theories focus on what the individual wants or desires, rather than on what he or she necessarily needs to survive or to be healthy.

Equity Theory. Equity theory (Adams, 1965) focuses on a single value, namely, perceived equity (i.e., fairness or justice). Among organizational scientists, equity theory is often considered one of the more precise social exchange theories and is asserted to be a powerful means to understand social relationships. The major postulates of equity theory are that " . . . (1) perceived inequity creates tension in the individual; (2) the amount of tension is proportional to the magnitude of the inequity; (3) the tension created in the individual will motivate him or her to reduce it; and (4) the strength of the motivation to reduce inequity is proportional to the perceived inequity . . ." (Mowday, 1987, p. 93).

The empirical research has been primarily laboratory based and has centered on the effects of inequity created by overpayment and underpayment (with either hourly or piece-rate payment) on the quantity and quality of work output. (See Mowday, 1987, or Pinder, 1984, for more complete summaries on equity theory.) In general, the evidence is supportive. With underpayment on a piece-rate system, subjects tend to produce higher quantity but lower quality work output than equitably paid subjects; with underpayment on an hourly wage system, subjects tend to produce less or lower quality output than equitably paid subjects. With overpayment on a piece-rate system, subjects tend to produce less quantity but higher quality work output than equitably paid subjects; with overpayment on an hourly wage system, subjects tend to produce more or higher quality output than equitably paid subjects.

Equity researchers have indicated that there may be serious problems with experimental internal invalidity, particularly with the overpayment conditions (Mowday, 1987; Pinder, 1984). These problems center around the definitions of equity, methods of inequity resolution, choice of comparison, and potential individual differences as moderators. Nonetheless, most equity researchers agree that the existing evidence justifies additional work aimed at resolving these problems. In recent years, the research interest in equity theory has diminished somewhat, but it seems likely that equity theory will continue to generate a modest stream of empirical research.

Expectancy Theory. Unlike equity theory, expectancy theory (Vroom, 1964) has focused on values in general, rather than a single, particular value. It is also one of the most heavily researched theory of work motivation of the past 25 years. The theory has undergone several major conceptual refinements (Campbell & Pritchard, 1976; Graen, 1969; Porter & Lawler, 1968), and the empirical evidence has become so large that at least 11 major literature reviews exist (e.g., Campbell, Dunnette, Lawler & Weick, 1970; Mitchell, 1974). Despite some differences, there is substantial similarity across the versions of expectancy theory.

The three major components of the theory are expectancy, instrumentality, and valence; and these are theorized to combine multiplicatively to determine an individual's *decision* to exert work effort. The first component, expectancy, is the expectation that one's level of work effort will lead to a certain degree of job performance. The second component, instrumentality, is the belief that certain levels of job performance will lead to particular outcomes (e.g., pay, praise, promotion). The third component, valence, refers to the value an individual places on the particular outcomes. In other words, expectancy theory holds that the decision (or choice) to exert work effort results from the multiplicative combination of (a) the expectation that if one tries, one can do the job (i.e., an expectancy); (b) the belief that if one performs well, organizational rewards will follow (i.e., an instrumentality); and (c) the rewards that are important to the individual (i.e., the valence). If any of the components are low, the choice to exert work effort should be reduced.

The empirical research on expectancy theory has been conducted in both laboratory and field settings. Unfortunately, little can be said definitely on the validity of expectancy theory. Campbell and Pritchard (1976) identified numerous conceptual, measurement, and methodological problems that make the interpretation of the research evidence problematic. For example, expectancy theory concerns the multiplicative combination of expectancy, instrumentality, and valence *within* each person (Porter & Lawler, 1968; Vroom, 1964). The theory, then, clearly suggests within subject designs. Yet, researchers have more often adopted *between* subject designs, with data collected cross-sectionally. Kennedy, Fossum and White (1983) recently compared the predictive validity of three versions of expectancy theory when tested by within, versus between, subject designs. Across the three versions, studies with within subject designs consistently demonstrated greater predictive power than studies with between subject designs. Another design problem is that most studies have included only a limited number of outcomes. Little information is available on how expectancy and instrumentality operate in the presence of many desired outcomes.

Expectancy theory also requires two dubious assumptions. First, employees are assumed to seek the maximum amount of their desired rewards. Second, employees are assumed to conduct an enormous number of mental calculations in their decision to exert work effort. The seminal work of March and Simon (1958) and Simon (1947) on satisficing and the research of Tversky (1967, 1969, 1972) and Kahneman and Tversky (1984) on cognitive limitations cast some doubt on the validity of these assumptions.

In reviewing the literature, Pinder (1984) concluded that the studies since 1976 have been greatly improved conceptually and methodologically. The validity of expectancy theory, however, remains an open issue. In the last several years, the research on expectancy theory has substantially diminished.

On balance, value-based theories have considerably more empirical support than need-based theories. One reason for the increased validity may stem from the explicit inclusion and consideration of individual differences. Whereas the need theories assume that all people have the same needs, value-based theories assume that people differ in their values and the degree of importance attached to each value. For example, some undergraduate students may place a high value on employment immediately upon graduation. They may pursue a business major because they believe it to be an efficient means to employment. In contrast, others may see college as an opportunity to acquire broad and general knowledge. They may pursue a liberal arts education, even though it may have less of an immediate employment payoff. Moreover, two business majors may value employment differently. One business major may specialize in accounting, which traditionally offers very high immediate employment opportunity; whereas the other business major may concentrate on personnel (because he or she values working with people), which traditionally offers less immediate employment opportunity.

Theories that deal with multiple values (e.g., expectancy theory) have more empirical support and conceptual flexibility than single-value theories (e.g., equity theory), which also have more empirical support than need-based theories. Nonetheless, value-based theories are still overly general. Many possible actions remain that are consistent with a given value. For example, two new assistant professors may possess very strong professional career ambitions. One assistant professor may direct that ambition toward an academic career path of research, publication, and teaching. The other assistant professor may direct that ambition toward an organizational career path of university administration. A theory of work motivation should allow for a specific prediction and explanation of a specific action.

Organizational Behavior Modification

Organizational behavior modification, which is based on Skinner's (1953) work, involves four principles (Hamner & Hamner, 1976). First, observable behaviors are of primary interest. Second, response frequency is the key form of behavioral measurement. Third, clear specification and measurement of the desired behaviors must be made. Fourth, clear contingencies must be established between the job behavior and rewards or reinforcement. In the organizational literature, numerous empirical studies demonstrate the effectiveness of applying these procedures (e.g., Komaki, Barwick & Scott, 1978; Latham, Mitchell, & Dossett, 1978; Saari & Latham, 1982). Because organizational behavior modification appears to produce the intended outcomes and to be relatively straightforward to apply, we suspect that there will be continual interest in this approach as an *applied organizational technology* (e.g., Komaki, 1986).

As a theory that drives scientific research and facilitates understanding, however, the influence of organizational behavior modification is rapidly declining. The recent surge of cognitively based theory and research in psychology has demonstrated that cognitive constructs are necessary in any theory of human action (Bandura, 1986). For example, Kaufman, Baron and Kopp (1966) correctly informed one group as to how frequently their performance would be rewarded, but incorrectly informed two other groups that their behavior would be reinforced either every minute (a fixed interval schedule) or after they had performed on the average of 150 responses (a variable ratio schedule). The results demonstrated that, although everyone was on the same reward schedule, a person's beliefs about the schedule of reinforcement influenced behavior more than the actual experienced consequences. In reviews of this literature, Locke (1969, 1972, 1977, 1980) concluded that organizational behavior modification is conceptually indefensible and that in practice, it primarily involves the relabeling, in behaviorist terms, of cognitive constructs and already well-established motivational techniques.

Goal Setting Theory

Although the scientific interest in need- and value-based theories and in reinforcement technologies has declined, research on goal setting has proliferated (Miner, 1980; Pinder, 1984). Unlike the preceding motivational theories and technologies, the empirical evidence on goal setting theory has been consistent, supportive, and cumulative across methods, settings, and disciplines.

Goal setting might be viewed as the result of four decades of normal science (Kuhn, 1970). In our discipline's formative years, the initial theories (e.g., Maslow) were proposed and tested. As the evidence suggested low validity, potential improvements were hypothesized (e.g., Alderfer), and alternatives were proposed (e.g., organizational behavior modification and expectancy theory). When empirical testing revealed a new set of problems, the process repeated itself. Eventually, a theory arrived that was empirically corroborated and became well accepted within the organizational sciences (i.e., goal setting). For the foreseeable future, goal setting is the dominant theory of work motivation in the organizational sciences.

GOAL SETTING THEORY

A very strong implicit value in most business schools can be captured in the following question. "What can academicians offer to managers that *really works?*" As academically trained social scientists, we often prefer to avoid responding because our answer would frequently involve interpreting poorly specified, unvalidated theories. As university professors employed by professional schools, however, our various audiences and constituencies require us to answer the question. In departments of management within business schools, the most common and strongest answer may be captured by the title of Locke and Latham's (1984) book: *Goal Setting: A Motivational Technique That Works.*

In the organizational sciences, there is strong agreement among researchers and practitioners on the definition of "really works." It means the reliable and valid prediction and/or facilitation of the individual's job performance. In 1977, Pinder warned that it is frequently inappropriate to apply the theories of work motivation to many organizational settings because, in part, most theories have not been strongly supported by empirical research. In other words, we did not know if they *really* worked. By 1984, Pinder concluded that goal setting had been subjected to substantial laboratory and field testing and had demonstrated more scientific validity than any other theory of work motivation.

The Origins and Concepts of Goal Setting Theory

Goal setting theory originates from two traditions. One tradition is the engineering model of scientific management (Taylor, 1911) and its descendants like management by objectives (e.g., Locke, 1982; Odiorne, 1978). The other tradition is the academic model of the Wurzberg School and Kurt Lewin (a Gestalt psychologist) and their concepts of intention, task, mental set, and level of aspiration (see Ryan, 1970, for a summary). In 1968, Locke merged these two traditions into the theory of goal setting. The initial laboratory research was conducted primarily by Locke and his associates, and the initial field research was conducted primarily by Latham and his colleagues. These initial studies were intended to demonstrate that goal setting in fact "really worked" and to begin to understand why and how goal setting worked.

A goal is conceptualized as the object or aim of an action. A goal is that which one wants to accomplish; it concerns a valued, future end state. It may be selling nine new life insurance policies in a fiscal quarter, cutting a cord of wood in one day or completing ten laboratory tasks in an hour. Implicit within this thinking is that the goal is an *immediate regulator* of behavior. In the organizational sciences, related concepts include the intention to quit found in the research on employee turnover (Mobley, 1977) and attendance motivation found in the research on employee absenteeism (Steers & Rhodes, 1978, 1984).

Goal Attributes. Goals are defined as having two primary attributes, *content* and *intensity*. Goal content specifies what is to be accomplished and has at least four dimensions: difficulty, specificity, complexity, and conflict. Goal *difficulty* refers to the degree of proficiency or level of job performance required for goal attainment. For example, a goal of six articles published in scientific research journals within 2 years would be much more difficult to attain than one such article in the same time period. Goal *specificity* refers to the degree of quantitative precision required by the goal. For example, a goal of 3 published research articles per academic year for an assistant professor would be much more specific than a general goal such as "do your best." Goal *complexity* refers to the number of different intended outcomes and their interrelationships. For instance, an assistant professor at a large research university might be told that his goal of tenure includes some combination of research, publication, service, and teaching; whereas an assistant professor at a smaller teaching college might be told that his goal of tenure includes only teaching and service. Goal *conflict* refers to the degree to which achieving one valued goal inhibits achieving another desired goal. For instance, an assistant professor may discover that the goal of 6 publications in scientific research journals within 2 years involves time demands that interfere with the time requirements for a goal of achieving teaching excellence.

The second attribute of goals, intensity, concerns the process of how the goal is set and accomplished. Goal intensity involves such characteristics as the participants' commitment, perception of the goal's importance and the cognitive processes involved in goal attainment. For example, an assistant professor may be very committed to the goal of six publications within 2 years in scientific research journals. He or she may spend considerable time and energy conceptualizing and conducting research projects and may possess the intellectual ability and training necessary to attain the goal. But, the causal effect of goals on performance may greatly diminish if that assistant professor's goal commitment decreases after learning that most of the next pay increase results from achieving teaching excellence rather than conducting research and publication.

The Relationship Between Goals and Job Performance

Goal Difficulty. A basic postulate of goal setting theory is that hard goals, if accepted, lead to greater job performance than medium or easy goals. More specifically, there should be a positive monotonic relationship between goal difficulty and job performance, if the goal has been accepted. In a review of the literature, Locke, Shaw, Saari and Latham (1981) reported that 48 studies partly or wholly supported the hypothesis that hard goals lead to better job or task performance than medium or easy goals; nine studies did not support the hypothesis. In a meta analysis, Tubbs (1986) identified 56 empirical studies that directly measured goal difficulty and job or task performance and reported a corrected mean effect size of $d=.82$ between difficulty and performance. In another meta analysis, which excluded within-subject research designs, Mento, Steel, and Karren (1987) identified 70 relevant studies and reported a corrected mean effect size of $d=.55$ between goal difficulty and job or task performance. The empirical evidence clearly supports a facilitating effect of goal difficulty on job or task performance.

Goal Difficulty/Specificity. A second basic postulate of goal setting theory is that hard *and* specific goals, if accepted, lead to higher job performance than general, "do your best" or no goals. Locke et al. (1981)

reported that 51 studies partially or wholly supported the hypothesis that specific, hard goals lead to better job or task performance than do-your-best or no goals; only two studies did not support the hypothesis. Tubbs (1986) identified 48 empirical studies that directly measured both goal difficulty/specificity and job or task performance, and reported a corrected mean effect size of d=.50 between difficulty/specificity and performance. Mento et al. (1987) identified 49 relevant studies and reported a corrected mean effect size of d=.44 between goal difficulty/specificity and job or task performance. The empirical evidence also clearly supports the facilitating effect of goal difficulty/specificity on job or task performance.

Goal Specificity. Since the introduction of goal setting theory (Locke, 1968), there has been some confusion about the effect of goal specificity, per se, on job performance because the theory does *not* make a prediction about this relationship. Rather, the theory concerns the effect of goal difficulty, or the *joint* effect of goal difficulty and specificity on job performance. Nonetheless, there is a mistaken belief among some organizational scientists that goal specificity per se facilitates job performance. This is clearly incorrect because goals can be specific and *easy*, which would lead to low levels of job performance. In two studies, Locke, Chah, Harrison and Lustgarten (in press) experimentally separated the effects of goal specificity and goal difficulty. They found that goal difficulty primarily affected the mean level of performance, whereas goal specificity as such affected only the variability of performance. The more specific the goal, the lower the variablity of performance, assuming performance was controllable.

Generalizability of Results

There is strong agreement among organizational scientists that the empirical evidence supports the facilitating effect of goal difficulty and goal difficulty/specificity on job or task performance. Moreover, there is also sufficient research to address the issue of the generalizability.

Laboratory Versus Field Settings. In a review of the literature, Latham and Lee (1986) found that 37 laboratory experiments and 27 field studies supported the hypothesis that hard, specific goals lead to greater job or task performance than "do your best" or no goals. Only one laboratory and one field study did not support the hypothesis.

In his meta analysis, Tubbs (1986) identified 45 laboratory (d=.90) and 11 field (d=.52) studies that directly measured the effect of goal difficulty on job or task performance. Moreover, he identified 34 laboratory (d=.58) and 14 field (d=.43) studies that directly measured the effect of goal difficulty/specificity on job or task performance. Like Locke et al (1981) and Latham and Lee (1986), Tubbs found evidence for the facilitating effects of both goal difficulty and goal difficulty/specificity on job or task performance in both laboratory and field settings. Unlike, Locke et al. (1981) and Latham and Lee (1986), however, Tubbs found that there were stronger effects in laboratory than field settings.

In their meta analysis, Mento et al. (1987), who eliminated within-subject studies as noted earlier, also reported larger effect sizes of laboratory over field studies for both the relationships between goal difficulty and job or task performance (d=.65 versus d=.49), and between goal difficulty/specificity and job or task performance (d=.57 versus d=.35). These differences, however, were *not* statistically significant. In a supplemental analysis, Mento et al. (1987) found no evidence for a moderating effect of setting (i.e., laboratory versus field) on the relationship between goal difficulty and job or task performance, but they did find evidence for the moderating effect of setting on the relationship between difficulty/specificity and performance.

Taken together, traditional reviews of the literature and meta analyses reveal considerable evidence that goal setting facilitates performance in both laboratory and field settings. From the meta analyses, however, there may be some reason to believe that somewhat stronger effects emerge from laboratory than field settings.

Experimental Versus Correlational Designs. In the review by Locke et al. (1981) and the meta analyses of Tubbs (1986) and Mento et al. (1987), there was no evidence of a moderator effect of research design on either the relationships between goal difficulty and job or task performance, or between goal difficulty/specificity and job or task performance. The effects of goal setting can be demonstrated both with experimental and nonexperimental (correlational) designs.

Criteria of Performance. Latham and Lee (1986) examined whether hard, specific goals facilitate job performance more than nonspecific goals when performance is defined as quantity and/or quality of work, or when performance is operationalized by soft (e.g., performance ratings) and/or hard (e.g., dollar amount or countable outcomes) measures? Three laboratory experiments supported the hypothesis that hard, specific goals facilitated the *quality* of task performance more than nonspecific goals; no laboratory experiment was found that disconfirmed the hypothesis. Twenty-eight laboratory experiments supported the hypothesis that hard, specific goals facilitated the *quantity* of task performance more than nonspecific goals; only one laboratory experiment did not support the hypothesis. Furthermore, one field study supported the hypothesis that hard, specific goals facilitated the *quality* of job performance more than nonspecific goals, and seven field studies supported the hypothesis that hard, specific goals facilitated the *quantity* of job performance more than nonspecific goals. No field study was found that disconfirmed these hypotheses. For those studies that investigated *both* the quality and quantity dimensions of performance, Latham and Lee identified 14 laboratory experiments and 8 field studies that supported the hypothesis that hard, specific goals facilitated task or job performance more than nonspecific goals. No laboratory or field study disconfirmed the hypothesis.

Latham and Lee (1986) also identified 43 laboratory experiments that supported the hypothesis that hard, specific goals facilitated task performance on *hard* criteria (e.g., number of widgets produced) more than nonspecific goals; only one laboratory experiment did not support the hypothesis. There were no laboratory experiments that included only *soft* criteria (e.g., performance ratings). But four laboratory experiments that measured *both* soft and hard criteria of task performace supported the hypothesis that difficult, specific goals facilitated performance more than nonspecific goals; no laboratory experiment disconfirmed the hypothesis. Furthermore, 14 field studies supported the hypothesis that difficult, specific goals facilitated job performance on *hard* criteria more than nonspecific goals; and four field experiments supported the hypothesis that difficult, specific goals facilitated job performance on *soft* criteria more than nonspecific goals. For those field studies that measured *both* soft and hard criteria, three studies supported the hypothesis that difficult, specific goals facilitated job performance more than nonspecific goals; no study disconfirmed the hypothesis.

The cumulative evidence clearly demonstrates the applicability of goal setting theory across a broad range of job performance measures. It appears that researchers need not be overly concerned with their particular measure of job performance; virtually any reliable and valid measure may be appropriate for research purposes.

Individual Versus Group. Though the available research is more limited, Latham and Lee (1986) compared the results of goal setting studies where the unit of analysis was either the individual or the group. With the individual as the unit of analysis, 45 laboratory experiments and 17 field studies supported the hypothesis that hard, specific goals facilitate performance more than nonspecific goals; only one laboratory experiment did not support the hypothesis. With the group as the unit of analysis, one laboratory experiment and four field studies supported the hypothesis that hard, specific goals facilitate performance more than nonspecific goals; no study disconfirmed the hypothesis.

Moderators in the Relationship Between Goals and Performance

Goal setting theory predicts a facilitating effect of goals on job performance, but this effect can be strongly influenced by several moderating factors.

Knowledge of Results (or Feedback). In the initial theory, Locke (1968) proposed that the causal effect of feedback on job performance was moderated by goals. Through a series of carefully controlled laboratory experiments, Locke and his associates found that knowledge of results *without* goals did not improve performance, but *given* knowledge of results, goals were sufficient to improve performance (e.g., Locke, 1967; Locke & Bryan, 1968, 1969a, 1969b; Locke, Cartledge & Koeppel, 1968). Locke concluded that goals appear to moderate the effects of feedback (or knowledge of results) on task and job performance. Moreover, Latham, Mitchell and Dossett (1978) obtained strong corroborating evidence in a subsequent field experiment. Specifically, they found that the job performance of engineers and scientists who received feedback, praise, public recognition or money did not differ from the performance of those in the control group. Only those engineers and scientists who received goals in addition to feedback, praise, recognition, or money outperformed those in the control group.

Other studies have found that goals *without* knowledge of results did not improve performance, but *given* goals, knowledge of results were sufficient to improve performance (e.g., Becker, 1978; Komaki et al., 1978). These studies suggested that knowledge of results also appears to moderate the effect of goals on performance.

In their recent meta analyses, Tubbs (1986) and Mento et al. (1987) reported possibly conflicting evidence on the influence of feedback. Tubbs found that feedback was a strong moderator in the relationship between goal difficulty and performance ($d=.35$ for no feedback; $d=.89$ for informal feedback; $d=.76$ for formal feedback), but it was a weak moderator in the relationship between goal difficulty/specificity and performance ($d=.49$ for no feedback; $d=.46$ for informal feedback; $d=.57$ for formal feedback). Tubbs observed that many of the studies in his meta analysis were not intended to test for the moderating influence of feedback. The experimental manipulations appeared to have inadvertently *highlighted* the moderating effect of feedback on the relationship between goal difficulty and job or task performance and *masked* the effect of feedback on the relationship between goal difficulty/specificity and job or task performance. The results of his meta analysis must be viewed with caution.

Mento et al. (1987) found that although the effect sizes suggested a moderator effect, the differences were not statistically significant for either the relationships between goal difficulty and job or task performance (d=.61 with feedback; d=.57 without feedback) or between goal difficulty/specificity and job or task performance (d=.50 with feedback; d=.41 without feedback). Mento et al. concluded that there was no evidence for the moderating effect of feedback but cautioned, however, that their findings could be due to the weak statistical power of their moderator analysis.

The meta analyses of Tubbs (1986) and Mento et al. (1987) included many studies that were not designed to investigate directly the role of feedback. More important, several crucial studies on feedback had to be omitted from the meta analysis because the necessary data were not available in the published articles. Consequently, their findings and conclusions were ambiguous.

The research of Erez and others, however, was designed to investigate directly the effect of feedback. Their findings are quite clear and have greatly clarified matters. For example, Erez (1977) was the first to demonstrate that neither goals nor knowledge of results *alone* are sufficient for the improvement of task performance. Rather, *both* goals and knowledge of results must be present. Subsequent research has strongly supported this conclusion (see Locke et al., 1981, for a full summary). A third basic postulate of goal setting theory has now been accepted by organizational scientists. The facilitating effect of hard, specific goals on job or task performance is contingent on a cognitive component: Feedback which yields information about goal progress.

Goal Commitment. A fourth basic postulate of goal setting theory is that an individual must be committed to the goal before it can facilitate job performance (Locke, 1968; Locke & Latham, 1984). In the initial theory, goal acceptance referred to one's initial agreement with a goal, and goal commitment referred to the sustained agreement over time with that goal (Locke, 1968). Over the years, organizational scientists have often used the terms interchangeably. More recently, however, the term goal commitment has acquired a broader meaning among organizational scientists and refers to one's attachment or determination to attain any goal, which would include those self set, participatively set, or assigned.

Goal acceptance is viewed as a subset of commitment and refers to the commitment to a particular assigned goal (Locke, Latham, & Erez, 1988).

In the 1970s, empirical attempts to demonstrate a relationship between goal commitment and job or task performance were generally unsuccessful (Locke et al., 1981). In the 1980s, Locke and Latham (1984), and Erez and her associates observed that the research on goal commitment commonly involved measures of commitment that had very little variance. They reasoned that the absence of reliable relationships between goal commitment and job or task performance was due to this small amount of variance. If greater variability were obtained in goal commitment, then there should be a positive relationship between goal commitment and job or task performance, assuming the goal is challenging.

Erez and her associates have empirically demonstrated that *given* sufficient variance, goal commitment and job performance are, in fact, positively related (e.g., Earley, 1985; Earley & Kanfer, 1985; Erez, 1986; Erez, Early & Hulin, 1985; Erez & Arad, 1986). For example, Erez and Zidon (1984) conducted a two-phased, within-subject-design experiment that induced high variance on goal commitment. In phase one, subjects in the experimental group experienced increasingly difficult goals across trials. In phase two, the subjects in the experimental group were encouraged to question and reject difficult goals, which produced far greater variance in goal commitment than is typically reported in goal setting studies. Erez and Zidon found a positive relationship between goal difficulty and task performance (at the higher goal difficulty levels) when there was high goal commitment but a negative relationship between difficulty and performance when there was low goal commitment. The slope reversal from positive to negative relationships was due to the change from goal acceptance to goal rejection as the goals become more difficult.

In a review of the research, Locke, Latham, and Erez (1988) identified four key determinants of goal commitment. First, the *legitimate authority* to set goals should be granted to the goal setter (e.g., the immediate supervisor). The application of such authority is enhanced if the supervisor is physically present, demonstrates supportiveness, works in a climate characterized as trusting, and judiciously exerts pressure on the subordinate (i.e., excessive pressure can be dysfunctional). Second, *peer and group pressures* should be directed toward goal attainment (e.g., Matsui, Kakuyama & Onglatco, 1987). There are numerous demonstrations of the dysfunctional outcomes for the individual's goal commitment and performance when the group and company set different goals (e.g., Taylor, 1911). Moreover, the modeling of the desired behavior by peers can be a positive influence on the observer's goal commitment (Earley & Kanfer, 1985). Third, the *employee's expectation* that effort leads to performance (i.e., the "expectancy" from expectancy theory; Vroom, 1964) and *self efficacy* (i.e., from social learning theory; Bandura, 1982) should be high. Strong evidence is emerging that self-efficacy positively correlates with goal commitment (Bandura, 1987). Fourth, *incentives and rewards* also encourage goal commitment. Based on expectancy and social learning theories, a goal's general valence and instrumentality, monetary potential, and intrinsic (or self-administered) value should positively relate to goal commitment.

Another possible determinant of commitment, which has not received much attention by goal setting researchers, is *publicness*. Hollenbeck, Williams and Klein (in press) found that commitment to difficult goals was higher when commitment was public rather than private. This harks back to Lewin's (1943) classic experiments on changing food preferences. Lewin, however, never manipulated publicness separately from other variables, such as group decision making. Research on the effects of public versus private commitment to goals should be of great potential interest to social psychologists.

Task Complexity. Locke et al. (1981) theorized that goals should have less effect on complex tasks and more effect on simple tasks because the completion of complex tasks likely requires greater use of cognitive and other abilities than simple tasks. For example, Wood (1985) suggested that complex tasks may lead to suboptimal action plans for task accomplishment, whereas simple tasks may lead to efficient actions plans. Recently, Wood, Mento and Locke (1987) conducted a meta analysis of 125 studies to assess the moderating effect of task complexity on the relationship between goals and performance. As hypothesized, it was found that goal setting effects were significantly greater for easy ($d=.76$) than for complex tasks ($d=.42$).

Self Efficacy. Bandura (1986) defined self-efficacy as an individual's evaluation of his or her capabilities to determine, organize, and execute courses of action necessary to deal with prospective situations. As such, self-efficacy is intricately involved in the goal setting process. For example, Locke, Frederick, Lee, and Bobko (1984) demonstrated that self-efficacy positively and directly affected goal choice, goal commitment, and task performance. Moreover, Bandura and Cervone (1986) found that given negative feedback about job performance in relation to goals, those people with high self-efficacy achieve greater subsequent performance levels than those people with lower self-efficacy.

Ability. Campbell et al. (1970) observed long ago that any relationship between work motivation and job performance must be to some extent moderated by the individual's ability. Correspondingly, ability is theorized to moderate the effect of goals on job performance.

Participation in Goal Setting. Few topics in the psychological sciences have been more politicized than that of participation (Locke & Schweiger, 1979). Young social scientists have been educated to believe that the superiority of decisions made participatively over decisions imposed by authority figures is virtually an axiom, not to be questioned or doubted. Lewin (1943) was perhaps the first to conduct experiments related to participation (along with Lippit, White, and others), but the classic Coch and French (1948) study was the first to be conducted in the work place. Although these authors failed to make a conclusive case for participation (e.g., see Bartlem & Locke, 1981), this study is widely cited in support of the superiority of participative decision making (PDM).

The research results, however, have not been nearly as supportive of PDM as its proponents would have us believe. Field studies conducted at General Electric (French, Kay, & Meyer, 1966; Kay, Meyer, & French, 1965; Meyer, Kay, & French, 1965) of the performance appraisal process concluded that the act of setting a goal for future performance improvement had a considerably stronger effect on subsequent improvement in performance than whether the goal was set participatively. Participation sometimes led to better and sometimes to worse performance than assigned goals.

Starting in the 1970s, Latham and his colleagues began a series of 11 (seven field and four laboratory) experiments on the effects of participation on goal commitment and performance (summarized in Locke, Latham, & Erez, 1988). In one study (of uneducated woods workers) participative goal setting had better effects than assigned goals but this also could have been due to differences in goal difficulty. In one other study, participation resulted in better performance than assigned goals, but this was because of cognitive (informational) rather than motivational (commitment) reasons. In the remaining nine studies, participation goals were no more effective than assigned goals. These null findings were corroborated in a series of field studies by John Ivancevich and his colleagues at the University of Houston (see Locke, Latham, & Erez, 1988) and by Dossett, Cella, Greenberg, & Adrian (1983).

A thorough review of the PDM literature by Locke and Schweiger (1979) concluded that PDM was no more effective in promoting high performance than nonparticipative decision making. Narrative reviews of just the PDM/goal setting literature by Latham and Lee (1986) and

Schweiger and Leana (1986) reached the same conclusion as Locke and Schweiger. The goal setting meta analyses by Mento, et al. (1987) and Tubbs (1986) also concluded that the effect of participation on goal commitment or performance was minimal.

The only inconsistency in the results of the PDM/goal setting studies has been the recent series of experiments by Erez and her colleagues (Erez, 1986; Erez & Arad, 1986; Erez et al., 1985; Erez & Kanfer, 1983). In these studies it was found quite consistently that participation in goal setting led to higher commitment and higher subsequent performance than assigned goal setting.

The marked difference in the results obtained by Latham et. al. and Erez et. al. prompted them to undertake an unique collaborative effort. With Locke as third-party mediator, they jointly designed four crucial experiments (Platt, 1964) designed to isolate and test the significance of the differences in tasks, instructions, and procedures used by each in their studies. In these four studies, some eight to ten variables that could have explained the differences in results were explored and tested. The report of these studies (Latham, Erez & Locke, in press) concludes that the major factor accounting for the different results was that Erez used very curt and brief "tell" instructions when assigning goals, whereas Latham used "tell and sell" instructions in a friendly and supportive atmosphere. Other factors that played a role in the results were that Erez gave self-efficacy inducing instructions to her PDM subjects, encouraged all subjects to reject goals they did not like, had some subjects set personal goals before being assigned goals, and used goals of greater difficulty than did Latham. When tell and sell instructions are used in a supportive atmosphere, when the artifacts of self-efficacy instructions for the PDM group and of telling people to reject goals they have just been asked to accept are eliminated, and when personal goals are not set first, assigned goals work as well as participative goals. There is evidence that PDM might be slightly superior when the goal level is high, but this does not seem to be a major factor in the results.

Perhaps the final chapter (at least for now) in the PDM odyssey is a recent meta analysis of the entire PDM literature by Wagner and Gooding (1987). In one analysis, to prevent bias caused by method variance, they eliminated percept-percept relationships (e.g., between perceived participation and perceived performance motivation) and found that the mean correlation between participation and performance was approximately .10. This extremely modest finding is quite consistent with the findings at General Electric (GE), with those of Latham and of various narrative reviews and with meta analyses of goal setting studies. Clearly, participation is not a very robust variable in terms of its effects on goal commitment or performance. The bulk of the evidence seems to support the original findings at GE that the source of the goal is not as important as the fact that a goal is set.

Mediators of the Relationship Between Goals and Performance

To understand fully why goal setting affects performance, it is necessary to understand the mediators by which goals operate. Thus far, four specific mechanisms have been identified.

Direction. An accepted goal channels human attention and action toward activities relevant to that goal, rather than to nonrelevant activities. For example, Terborg (1976) found that subjects with specific goals spent a greater percentage of time looking at goal-relevant text material than subjects with vague or no goals. To demonstrate this, Locke and Bryan (1969a) provided feedback on five performance dimensions for a car driving task but set goals for only one of these five dimensions. Performance improved only on the dimension specified by the goal.

Effort. In addition to simple channeling, goals mobilize energy in proportion to the difficulty or level of the goal. The relationship between goal level and effort appears to be linear until the limits of one's ability are reached. For example, Sales (1970) found that higher work loads produced higher subjective reports of effort, faster heart rates, and higher output than lower work loads. Latham and Locke (1975) found that people work faster or harder under shorter than longer time limits.

Persistence. Persistence involves direction and effort extended over some period of time. Accepted goals are postulated to sustain the direction and effort of employee work behavior over that period of time. For example, LaPorte and Nath (1976) provided subjects with unlimited time on a prose reading task. Those subjects with the more difficult goal spent considerably more time reading than those with easy goals.

Task Strategy Development. Direction, effort, and persistence are relatively direct and immediate goal mechanisms. Moreover, these mechanisms are activated almost automatically because past experience has taught the individual that they improve one's performance on all aspects of tasks. Goals, however, may have indirect effects by stimulating action planning. Specifically, faced with a goal to be attained, the individual may search for and develop plans or methods by which to attain the accepted goal. These plans may require enacting a routinized, task-specific, behavioral pattern (e.g., a manufacturing plant's standard operating procedures), learning a new skill (e.g., how to maintain a new piece of machinery), or devising a creative problem solution (e.g., developing and enacting a new product marketing strategy). Latham and Baldes (1975) observed, for example, that truck drivers who were assigned difficult goals made small modifications to their trucks in order to increase the likelihood of goal attainment. Terborg (1976) found that subjects who were assigned difficult goals were more likely to develop and implement task strategies than easy goal subjects. We believe that the development of new skills and plans is most necessary when the task is new or complex. It is not yet known, however, under what conditions goals will lead to the development of effective versus ineffective (or detrimental) action plans.

Why Goal Setting Works

In our judgment, the empirical evidence is compelling: Goal setting works. Goal setting works best when the specified moderators are present, and goal setting works through the mediators identified above. Latham and Lee (1986) suggest that a goal is a specific symbol that allows an employee to engage in foresightful, conscious, and self-energized (i.e., motivated) action. A quantitative and specific goal simplifies an employee's identification and monitoring of the behaviors necessary for goal attainment. With the nonspecific goal, such behavioral identification and tracking can become more difficult. With a hard, specific goal, an employee can more easily attend to the appropriate *and* inappropriate (or nonoptimal goal-directed) behaviors necessary for goal attainment. Deviation from appropriate (or optimal goal-directed) behavior can trigger an adjustment toward more efficient behaviors. As discussed, a goal is a motivator only if there is commitment to the goal; the origin of the goal appears to be largely unimportant. In short, if there is commitment to the goal, job performance improves because the goal provides a regulatory mechanism that allows the employee to observe, monitor, subjectively evaluate and adjust job behaviors toward effective goal attainment.

In a complementary explanation, Bandura (in press) suggested that people routinely conduct cognitive evaluations of their performance, where the accepted goal serves as the standard by which a comparison can be made. The goal, then, provides a conditional basis for a positive or negative self-evaluation. A perceived negative discrepancy between one's performance and the accepted goal results in self dissatisfaction and such self-dissatisfaction serves as an incentive for subsequent improvement. Assuming sufficiently high self-efficacy, deviations from that standard can trigger what Latham and Lee (1986) described as adjustments toward more efficient behaviors and can be the basis for the direction and persistence of one's efforts.

A related question concerns why goal setting theory generalizes so readily? One answer may be the closeness of goals to action. Goals are a more immediate and task specific determinant of action that general variables such as values, motives, and needs. We believe (in concert with Ryan, 1970, and with modern attitude theorists such as Ajzen & Fishbein, 1977) that specific actions in specific situations are regulated to a considerable extent by the conscious goals and intentions individuals have in those situations. We hypothesize that values, motives, and needs (whether conscious or subconscious) affect specific actions through their effects on individuals' specific goals and intentions (although we cannot a priori rule out some effects of motives that are strictly subconscious).

A second answer may be simplicity (Dunnette, 1976; Latham & Lee, 1986; Pinder, 1984). That is, goal setting theory leads directly to simple experimental operations and statistical methods needed to test it. The interpretation of results from these simple operations and tests is correspondingly simple and unambiguous. Furthermore, the simplicity of the theory, research designs and statistical methods also leads very directly to a transfer of learning, via theoretical principles, among researchers. The communication among researchers, therefore, can focus on substantive theoretical concerns rather than methodological and statistical issues. Certainly, concern over method and statistics is crucial to psychology, organizational science, or any social science. But, the very simplicity of goal setting theory has necessitated that relatively little time and energy be devoted to conflicts over method. The vast bulk of researcher time and energy can be focused on content rather than method issues.

A third answer may be that goal setting taps a fundamental attribute of human behavior, namely, goal-directedness. Productive work requires purposeful actions toward some objectives. Goals make the objective explicit and direct actions toward goal attainment. Because goal directedness is central to work motivation and productivity, the goal setting effect, therefore, is a very robust phenomenon.

CURRENT AND EMERGING RESEARCH DIRECTIONS

Current Research Issues

Monetary Incentives. The early theory speculated that money affected job performance via the level of set goals (Locke, 1968). For example,

Locke, Bryan and Kendall (1968) reported that goals affected performance even when monetary incentives were partialled out but not vice versa. Latham and his associates have suggested that money may lead to "spontaneous" goal setting. For example, Saari and Latham (1980) found support for spontaneous goal setting among mountain beaver trappers on incentive pay. More recently, Locke et al. (1981) have speculated that money may affect job performance via an increase in goal commitment. At present, however, the systematic effect of money on the goal setting process is not well understood. It does appear that money has an effect on job performance, that a portion of the effect is independent of goals (Pritchard & Curtis, 1973), but that some portion of the causal effect of money on job performance does occur through goals.

Individual Differences. A substantial amount of research has looked for a moderating effect of various individual differences on the relationship between goals and job performance. The commonly studied variables include education, race, job tenure, age, sex, need for achievement, need for independence, higher order need strength, self-esteem, and internal versus external locus of control. Unfortunately, very little has been learned from this effort because few of the findings have been replicated across studies.

In the organizational sciences in general, personality and other individual differences have often been studied inadequately (Weiss & Adler, 1984). The research on goal setting in particular has been no exception. Many studies were not specifically designed to examine the effects of personality and individual differences. Most of the studied personality and individual difference variables were not selected on a theoretical basis; they tended to be very exploratory and convenience driven. The convergent and discriminant validity for many of the personality measures were often given minor consideration.

Fortunately, there is now a reasonably strong awareness of these problems among organizational scientists. Future research will likely avoid many of these problems. For example, it has been suggested that the demand characteristics of many organizational situations may minimize the effects of personality on job performance. Whereas assigned goals, for instance, would tend to negate the effects of personality, self-set goals may be a potentially powerful mediator of the relationship between personality and performance. Consistent with this idea, Taylor, Locke, Lee, and Gist (1984) investigated the effects of Type A personality on the quantity and quality of research publications among university faculty. Using path analysis, they found that self-set goals and self-efficacy were major mediators in the effect of Type A behavior on research productivity.

Goal Commitment. In addition to Locke, Latham and Erez (1988), Hollenbeck and Klein (1987) have also theorized about the individual and situational antecedents of goal commitment and the process by which these antecedents relate to goal commitment. Goal commitment was theorized to be the direct result of an interaction between the attractiveness of goal attainment (i.e., the valence) and the expectancy of goal attainment (i.e, the combination of expectancy and instrumentality). The attractiveness of goal attainment was theorized to result from many possible person-situation interactions. The situational factors included a goal's publicness, volition and explicitness (Salancik, 1977), the organization's reward structure (Ilgen, Fisher & Taylor, 1979), and level of competitiveness (Forward & Zander, 1971). The person variables included the individual's need for achievement, endurance for long and difficult work (Jackson, 1974), Type A behavior pattern, organizational commitment, and job involvement. The expectancy of goal attainment was also theorized to result from many possible person-situation interactions. The situational variables included knowledge about others' performance, goals or commitment (Festinger, 1942, Rakestaw & Weiss, 1981), task complexity (Steers & Porter, 1974), performance constraints (Peters & O'Connor, 1980) and supervisor's supportiveness (Latham & Saari, 1979b). The person variables included one's perceived ability, history of success, self-esteem, and locus of control.

Task Strategies. It was noted earlier that task strategies were an indirect mechanisms by which goals affect subsequent performance. Detailed studies of the formation, development, utilization, and effectiveness of task strategies are only beginning to be designed and carried out. We believe that this is an important area for future research. Here we will simply give a few examples of the types of studies of goals and task strategies that are now ongoing.

Earley (1986) examined whether the source of information (i.e., supervisor versus union steward) and type of information provided (i.e., task strategy versus company rationale for the work) affected goal commitment, and job performance for workers in the United States and England. As expected, goal setting facilitated job performance. Moreover, employees who received information on task strategy had higher self-efficacy and higher performance than those who received information on work rationale. Interestingly, information from the union steward facilitated performance more than information from the supervisor in England only. There was no difference in the United States.

In two laboratory experiments, Early and Perry (in press) investigated *how* goals and task strategy might operate to facilitate task performance. In both experiments, goals and information priming (i.e., providing information on how to do the task) were manipulated, and the effect on task strategy and performance was observed. Specific, challenging goals intensified the effects of task strategy on performance as compared to general goals. Task priming affected strategy and performance but only when combined with specific goals. Priming facilitated performance when the strategy was suitable to the task. When the strategy was unsuitable, performance suffered. It appears that the process of how goals affect performance may be more complicated that originally thought. The potential arises than under certain conditions (e.g., extreme time pressures), goal setting may motivate employees toward task strategies and behaviors that are dysfunctional.

Cultural Values. In the earlier discussion of the disagreements between the findings of Latham and Erez regarding PDM and goal setting, it was noted that the disagreements between the two initial sets of studies were due to procedural differences between them. An additional factor that could have been partly responsible for these differences, but that could not be tested directly in the resolution studies by Latham et al. (in press), was that of cultural differences. Some (though not all) of Erez's initial studies were carried out in Israel, a more collectivistic culture than the United States and Canada, where Latham's studies and the resolution studies were conducted. Recently Erez and Earley (1987) reexamined some of their data to determine whether there were differential effects of PDM on goal commitment and performance among U.S. and Israeli subjects. They included both Israeli urban and Israeli kibbutz subjects (who are more collectivistic than other Israelis) in their Israeli samples. There were also three degrees of participation: none (assigned goals), representative, and full (group decision). Generally it was found that the U.S. subjects responded equally well (with respect to performance) in all three conditions, whereas both Israeli samples performed significantly better under some or full PDM than with none. American subjects performed significantly better than Israelis under assigned goals. More studies of this type in other cultures (e.g., Australia, Japan, South America, West Germany) would be most interesting. (Note, however, that Erez's studies were all conducted using the same procedures described above under the participation heading.) The results indicate the possible importance of cultural values in determining the individual's response to goal setting interventions.

Emerging Research Directions

Goal Setting and Bargaining Research. When generalizing research across situations, caution is usually in order. When generalizing to topics not commonly studied in one's academic discipline, caution and further empirical study become even more important. A new (and innovative) research direction is the application of goal setting theory to facilitate the negotiation of interdependent outcomes. In a laboratory simulation of bargaining behavior, Huber and Neale (1987) studied individual and dyadic outcomes when each negotiator's performance was affected by the opponent's performance. With the individual as the level of analysis, negotiators who had specific, hard goals showed more profitability than those with nonspecific or easier goals. With the dyad as the level of analysis and when both negotiators had specific, hard goals, joint profitability was maximized; when both negotiators had nonspecific goals, joint profitability was minimal. In only partial agreement with goal setting theory, when both negotiators had difficult goals, joint profit was not maximized; when both negotiators had moderately difficult goals, or when one had a difficult and the other had a moderate goal, joint profit was maximized. To the extent that this laboratory simulation has external validity, a potentially important qualification of goal setting theory may have been discovered. For example, researchers in labor negotiation, mediation, and arbitration should be encouraged but cautious in applying goal setting theory to their studies.

Goal Setting and Leadership. The application of goal setting to theories of managerial and leadership behavior is a very natural pairing. Indeed, Locke and Somers (1987) reported a novel direction for goal setting research: the naturally occurring experiment. In the Judge Advocate's Office of the Tactical Air Command of the U.S. Air Force, official guidelines (i.e., goals) existed for the time allowed to process a court martial, but these guidelines were routinely ignored for many years as being too unrealistic. When a new colonel took command of the Judge Advocate's Office, a major "goal emphasis" program (i.e., intervention) was instituted that made very salient the goal's achievement. The program included monthly letters to various offices, telephone calls to individual offices asking about specific delays, and direct discussions of goals at conferences and site visits. After implementation of the intervention, the number of days required to process a court martial dramatically dropped in comparison to the preintervention period and declined in comparison to Judge Advocate Offices in other parts of the Air Force. Certainly, this study cannot be considered a rigorously controlled field experiment. Yet, its value may be as a demonstration that goal setting theory is effective on complex tasks. This study along with the work of others, such as Bennis and Nanus (1985) and Kotter (1982), provide evidence that goal setting can be effectively applied as a practical managerial and leadership tool.

Goal Setting and Complex Financial Tasks. Virtually all goal setting research involves psychological constructs (e.g., effort, choice, persistence), human resource management issues (e.g., effectiveness of job performance), and employee behavior. Another innovative direction is the possible meshing of goal setting and agency theories, which has become very influential in financial research (Jensen & Meckling, 1976). Specifically, Edmister and Locke (1987) looked at whether loan officers could regulate their economic performance in accordance with different weights that they placed on different goal outcomes under conditions in which they were pursuing multiple goals. It was found that, in general, they performed at a level commensurate with the weight placed on each goal. Two other interesting aspects of this study were that (a) the goals were for groups rather than individuals; and (b) the task was very complex, requiring high skill levels, computers, and 4 hours of work to complete each work session. More studies of group goal setting and goal setting with multiple goals are clearly warranted.

At a more immediate level, this study has strong practical implications for the decision policies, training, and immediate supervision of money managers, loan officers, and financial planners. At a more abstract level, this research direction may encourage the interchange of ideas, constructs, or research methods between two very different academic disciplines, namely, the psychologically oriented field of organizational behavior and the economically oriented field of finance.

Goal Setting and Self Management. Economic downturns have prompted numerous industrial layoffs. An immediate outcome of these layoffs have been calls from business executives for self-management techniques designed for the nonexempt employee. Frayne and Latham (1987) designed and implemented an organizational intervention program based on Kanfer's (1974, 1975, 1980) work in clinical psychology and goal setting theory to increase employee job attendance. Their intervention program consisted of (a) each employee identifying causes of absenteeism; (b) brainstorming solutions to overcome these causes of absenteeism; (c) setting short- and long-term attendance goals; (d) self-monitoring attendance; (e) establishing a behavioral contract for the self-administration of rewards and punishments; and (f) implementing a periodic follow-up plan. After 12 weeks, attendance for the treatment group significantly improved as compared to a control group. The psychological variable that explained this increase in employee attendance was self-efficacy. A follow-up study (Latham & Frayne, in press) showed that the results held over the subsequent 9 months. Moreover, application of the intervention program to the control group resulted in a significant increase in their self-efficacy and job attendance.

THE GOAL SETTING PROCESS

A considerable amount of theory and empirical research has been presented. Figure 8.1, which represents our conceptual summary of the empirical research, as well as some theoretical speculations as discussed in the present chapter, integrates the various classes of variables and offers a rudimentary statement on the conceptual nature of relationships between specific variables. Box 1 includes the major dimensions of the goal content. These include goal specificity and difficulty, complexity and conflict (Locke et al., 1981). Box 2 includes the main antecedents of goal commitment. These include the goal setter's legitimate authority, peer and group pressures, publicness, expectancy, self-efficacy, valence, and instrumentality.

Goal content is theorized to be a causal determinant of work behavior (Box 3; Locke, 1968; Locke et al., 1981), if there is commitment to the goal. Goal commitment is a necessary intervening construct in the relationship between goals and job performance (Locke & Latham, 1984; Locke et al., 1981; Locke et al., in press). In our conceptual model, work behavior is characterized by the attributes of individual effort, persistence, direction, and task strategy (Locke & Henne, 1986; Locke et al., 1981). The recent research of Earley and his associates (e.g., Earley, 1985, 1986; Earley & Kanfer, 1985) have confirmed that task strategy is an important part of the goal setting process. We speculate that after the employee becomes committed to the goal, the employee may begin rather directly with task strategizing. That is, the employee begins almost immediately to think about how to attain the goal.

Individual work behavior is, to some extent, affected by the employee's level of job knowledge (Box 4). Recently, Hunter (1986) has summarized literally hundreds of studies, across tens of thousands of individuals, that have investigated the relationships among general cognitive abilities, job knowledge, and job performance. Applying both meta and path analytic techniques, Hunter found evidence for (a) a very strong causal effect of general cognitive ability on job knowledge, (b) a strong causal effect of job knowledge on performance, and (c) an addi-

GOAL SETTING THEORY AND JOB PERFORMANCE

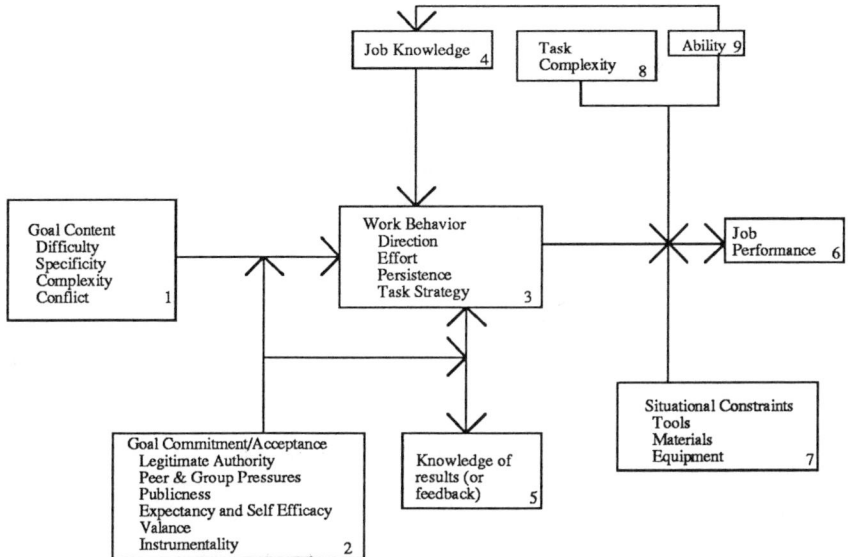

FIG 8.1 The Goal Setting Process

tional moderate and incremental causal effect of general cognitive ability directly on job performance.

Based on the empirical research summarized by Hunter (1986), we speculate that an employee's ability (Box 9) affects one's level of job knowledge, which in turn affects one's work behavior. Furthermore, we speculate that in *most* work situations, the employee has some idea of what he or she is supposed to do (i.e., job knowledge) before any actual work behavior takes place. Certainly, the time span between the mental activity and action can be very short (e.g., "sink or swim" or "on the job training" as forms of organizational socialization), but we believe that most work behavior occurs after some mental activity.

Knowledge of results (or feedback; Box 5) has been established as a necessary condition for goals to have a subsequent effect on job performance (Erez, 1977). As shown in Figure 8.1, work behavior and knowledge of results are theorized to be interdependent. Moreover, the interdependence (or simultaneity) between work behavior and knowledge of results may be so strong that in most organizational settings they are causally inseparable. In our conceptual model, knowledge of results is theorized as affecting and affected by work behavior. At the same time, knowledge of results is shown as working through goals because without goals, such knowledge does not affect performance (Locke et al., 1968).

The relationship between work behavior and job performance (Box

6) is, to some extent, moderated by such situational constraints as the availability of materials, tools, and, equipment (Peters, O'Connor & Eulberg, 1985; Box 7). More specifically, goal setting theory assumes that the employee has at least a "minimum" level of these moderators. For example, the job performance of a sales representative is frequently (appropriately or inappropriately) defined as total sales in dollars. One of the many determinants of such sales performance is simple effort (i.e., how hard the sales representative works). Yet, even a heroic work effort is unlikely to compensate for the absence of reliable customer service or shipping departments, weak economy, or poor product quality. In most organizations, the individual's work behavior is only one of many determinants of job performance. With such interdependencies, goals can only affect subsequent job performance *if* one assumes a certain level these moderators.

Recently, evidence has been reported that suggests that task complexity also moderates the goals and performance relationship (Box 8; Wood et al., 1987). More specifically, with simple tasks, goals have a strong effect on job performance; with complex tasks, goals have a weaker effect on performance. Furthermore, it is well recognized by organizational scientists that the relationship between work behavior and job performance requires a sufficient amount of individual ability (Box 9; Campbell et al., 1970).

Hunter (1986) has presented considerable evidence that general cognitive ability affects performance both indirectly through job knowledge and directly. Based on Hunter, we further speculate that task complexity and individual ability and knowledge *combine* to moderate the relationship between goals and job performance. We offer the following speculative predictions:

1. Under the conditions of high task complexity and high ability and knowledge, goals (via the work behaviors of effort, direction, persistence and task strategy) have a strong effect on job performance.
2. Under conditions of high task complexity and low ability and knowledge, goals have a weak effect on performance.
3. Under conditions of low task complexity and low ability and knowledge, goals have a moderate effect on performance.
4. Under conditions of low task complexity and high ability and knowledge, goals have a very strong effect on job performance.

It is important to recognize that our predictions carry the following assumptions: (a) a hard, specific goal has been set; (b) there is commitment to the goal; (c) feedback exists; and (d) the situation does not totally negate the effect of work motivation.

SUMMARY

This chapter has presented the dominant theory of work motivation from the organizational sciences, namely, goal setting. We have described its historical origin, evaluated the existing research, and suggested a conceptual model that integrates and summarizes much of this theory and research. We argue that goal setting is not only the dominant theory of work motivation but that it is also a dynamic and an evolving paradigm. Goal setting theory is the intellectual basis for a great deal of empirical research on work motivation and job performance. Though we know a great deal about the effects of goals, much more remains to be learned.

REFERENCES

Adams, J. S. (1965). Inequity in social exchange. In L. Berkowitz (Ed.), *Advances in Experimental Social Psychology* (Vol. 2, pp. 267–299). New York: Academic Press.

Ajzen, I., & Fishbein, M. (1977). Attitude-behavior relations: A theoretical analysis and review of empirical research. *Psychological Bulletin, 84,* 888–918.

Alderfer, C. P. (1969). An empirical test of a new theory of human needs. *Organizational Behavior and Human Performance, 4,* 142–175.

Bandura, A. (1982). Self-efficacy mechanism in human agency. *American Psychologist, 37,* 122–147.

Bandura, A. (1986). *Social foundations of thought and action: A social cognitive theory.* Englewood Cliffs, NJ: Prentice-Hall.

Bandura, A. (in press). Self-regulation of motivation and action through goal systems. In V. Hamilton, G. Bower & N. Fryda (Eds.), *Cognitive perspectives on emotion and motivation.* Dordrecht: Martinus Nijholl.

Bandura, A., & Cervone, D. (1986). Differential engagement of self reactive influences in cognitive motivation. *Organizational Behavior and Human Decision Processes, 38,* 92–113.

Bartlem, C. S., & Locke, E. A. (1981) The Coch and French study: A critique and reinterpretation. *Human Relations, 34,* 555–566.

Becker, L. J. (1978). Joint effect of feedback and goal setting on performance: A field study of residential energy conservation. *Journal of Applied Psychology, 63,* 428–433.

Bennis, W., & Nanus, B. (1985). *Leaders.* New York: Harper & Row.

Campbell, J. P., Dunnette, M. D., Lawler, E. E., & Weick, K. E. (1970). *Managerial behavior, performance, and effectiveness.* New York: McGraw Hill.

Campbell, J. P., & Pritchard, R. D. (1976). Motivation theory in industrial and organizational psychology. In M. Dunnette (Ed.), *Handbook of industrial and organizational psychology* (pp. 63–130). Chicago: Rand-McNally.

Coch, L. and French, J. R. P. (1948) Overcoming resistance to change. *Human Relations, 1,* 512–532.

Dossett, D. L., Cella, A., Greenberg, C. L., & Adrian, N. (1983). *Goal setting, participation and leader supportiveness effects on performance.* Paper presented at the annual meetings of the American Psychology Association, Anaheim, CA.

Dunnette, M. D. (1976). *Handbook of industrial and organizational psychology.* Chicago: Rand-McNally.

Earley, P. C. (1985). Influence of information, choice and task complexity upon goal acceptance, performance, and personal goals. *Journal of Applied Psychology, 70*, 481–491.

Earley, P. C. (1986). Supervisors and shop stewards as sources of contextual information in goal setting: A comparison of the United States with England. *Journal of Applied Psychology, 71*, 111–117.

Earley, P. C., & Kanfer, R. (1985). The influence of component participation and role models on goal acceptance, goal satisfaction and performance. *Organizational Behavior and Human Decision Processes, 36*, 378–390.

Earley, P. C., & Perry, B. C. (in press). Work plan availability and performance: An assessment of task strategy priming on subsequent task completion. *Organizational Behavior and Human Decision Processes.*

Edmister, R. O., & Locke, E. A. (1987). The effects of differential goal weights on the performance of a complex financial task. *Personnel Psychology, 40*, 505–517.

Erez, M. (1977). Feedback: A necessary condition for the goal setting-performance relationship. *Journal of Applied Psychology, 62*, 624–627.

Erez, M. (1986). The congruence of goal setting strategies with socio-cultural values and its effects on performance. *Journal of Management, 12*, 83–90.

Erez, M., & Arad, R. (1986). Participative goal setting: Social, motivational and cognitive factors. *Journal of Applied Psychology, 71*, 591–597.

Erez, M., & Earley, P. C. (1987). Comparative analysis of goal setting across cultures. *Journal of Applied Psychology, 72*, 658–665.

Erez, M., Earley, P. C., & Hulin, C. L. (1985). The impact of participation on goal acceptance and performance: A two step model. *Academy of Management Journal, 28*, 50–66.

Erez, M., & Kanfer, F. H. (1983). The role of goal acceptance in goal setting and task performance. *Academy of Management Review, 8*, 454–463.

Erez, M., & Zidon, I. (1984). Effect of goal acceptance in goal setting and task performance. *Journal of Applied Psychology, 69*, 69–78.

Festinger, L. (1942). Wish, expectation, and group standards as factors influencing level of aspiration. *Journal of Abnormal and Social Psychology, 37*, 184–200.

Forward, J., & Zander, A. (1971). Choice of unattainable group goals and effects on performance. *Organizational Behavior and Human Performance, 6*, 184–199.

Frayne, C., & Latham, G. P. (1987). Application of social learning theory to employee self-management of attendance. *Journal of Applied Psychology, 72*, 387–392.

French, J. R. P., Kay, E., & Meyer, H. H. (1966). Participation and the appraisal system. *Human Relations, 19*, 3–20.

Graen, G. (1969). Instrumentality theory of work motivation: Some experimental results and suggested modification. *Journal of Applied Psychology, 53*, 1–25.

Hamner, W. C., & Hamner, E. P. (1976). Behavior modification on the bottom line. *Organizational Dynamics, 4*, 8–21.

Hollenbeck, J. R., & Klein, H. J. (1987). Goal commitment and the goal setting process: Problems, prospects and proposals for future research. *Journal of Applied Psychology, 72*, 212–220.

Hollenbeck, J. R., Williams, C. R., & Klein, H. J. (in press). An empirical examination of the antecedents of commitment to difficult goals. *Journal of Applied Psychology.*

Huber, V. L., & Neale, M. A. (1987). Effects of self and competitor goals on performance in an interdependent bargaining task. *Journal of Applied Psychology, 72*, 197–203.

Hunter, J. E. (1986). Cognitive ability, cognitive aptitudes, job knowledge, and job performance. *Journal of Vocational Behavior, 29*, 340–362.

Ilgen, D. R., Fisher, C. D., & Taylor, M. S. (1979). Consequences of individual feedback on behavior in organizations. *Journal of Applied Psychology, 64*, 349–371.

Jackson, D. N. (1974). *Personality research form manual.* Port Huron, MI: Research Psychologists Press.
Jensen, M. C., & Meckling, W. H. (1976). Theory of the firm: Managerial behavior, agency costs and ownership structure. *Journal of Financial Economics, 3,* 305–360.
Kahneman, D., & Tversky, A. (1984). Choices, values, and frames. *American Psychologist, 39,* 341–350.
Kanfer, F. H. (1974). Self regulation: Research, issues, and speculations. In C. Neuringer & J. L. Michaels (Eds.), *Behavior modification in clinical psychology* (pp. 178–220). New York: Appleton-Century-Crofts.
Kanfer, F. H. (1975). Self-management methods. In F. H. Kanfer (Ed.), *Helping people change* (pp. 309–355). New York: Wiley.
Kanfer, F. H. (1980). Self-management methods. In F. H. Kanfer & A. P. Goldstein (Eds.), *Helping people change* (2nd ed., pp. 334–389). New York: Pergamon Press.
Kaufman, A., Baron, A., & Kopp, R. (1966). Some effects of instructions on human operant behavior. *Psychonomic Monograph Supplements, 1,* 243–245.
Kay, E., Meyer, H. H., & French, J. R. P. (1965). Effects of threat in a performance appraisal interview. *Journal of Applied Psychology, 49,* 311–317.
Kennedy, C. W., Fossum, J. A., & White, B. J. (1983). An empirical comparison of within-subjects and between-subjects expectancy theory models. *Organizational Behavior and Human Performance, 32,* 124–143.
Komaki, J. L. (1986). Toward effective supervision: An operant analysis and comparison of managers at work. *Journal of Applied Psychology, 71,* 270–279.
Komaki, J. L., Barwick, K. D., & Scott, L. R. (1978). A behavioral approach to occupational safety: Pinpointing and reinforcing safety performance in a food manufacturing plant. *Journal of Applied Psychology, 63,* 434–445.
Kotter, J. P. (1982). *The general managers.* New York: Free Press.
Kuhn, T. S. (1970). *The structure of scientific revolutions* (2nd ed.). Chicago: The University of Chicago Press.
Landy, F. J., & Becker, W. S. (1987). Motivation theory reconsidered. In L. Cummings & B. Staw (Eds.), *Research in organizational behavior* (Vol. 9, pp. 1–38). Greenwich, CT: JAI Press.
LaPorte, R. E., & Nath, R. (1976). Role of performance goals in prose learning. *Journal of Educational Psychology, 68,* 260–264.
Latham, G. P., & Baldes, J. J. (1975). The "practical significance" of Locke's theory of goal setting. *Journal of Applied Psychology, 60,* 122–124.
Latham, G. P., Erez, M., & Locke, E. A. (in press). Resolving scientific disputes by the joint design of crucial experiments by the antagonists: Application to the Latham-Erez dispute regarding participation in goal setting. *Journal of Applied Psychology.*
Latham, G. P., & Frayne, C. (in press). Self management techniques for increasing job attendance: A follow-up and replication. *Journal of Applied Psychology.*
Latham, G. P., & Lee, T. W. (1986). Goal setting. In E. Locke (Ed.), *Generalizing from laboratory to field settings* (pp. 101–117). Lexington, MA: Lexington Books.
Latham, G. P., & Locke E. A. (1975). Increasing productivity with decreasing time limits: A field replication of Parkinson's law. *Journal of Applied Psychology, 60,* 524–526.
Latham, G. P., Mitchell, T. R., & Dossett, D. L. (1978). Importance of participative goal setting and anticipated rewards on goal difficulty and job performance. *Journal of Applied Psychology, 63,* 163–171.
Latham, G. P., & Saari, L. M. (1979a). The effects of holding goal difficulty constant on assigned and participatively set goals. *Academy of Management Journal, 22,* 163–168.
Latham, G. P., & Saari, L. M. (1979b). Importance of supportive relationships in goal setting. *Journal of Applied Psychology, 64,* 151–156.

Lewin, K. (1943). Forces behind food habits and methods of change. *Bulletin of the National Resource Council, 108,* 35–685.
Locke, E. A. (1967). Motivational effects of knowledge on results: Knowledge or goal setting? *Journal of Applied Psychology, 51,* 324–329.
Locke, E. A. (1968). Toward a theory of task motivation and incentives. *Organizational Behavior and Human Performance, 3,* 157–189.
Locke, E. A. (1969). Purpose without consciousness: A contradiction. *Psychological Reports, 25,* 991–1009.
Locke, E. A. (1972). Critical analysis of the concept of causality in behavioristic psychology. *Psychological Reports, 31,* 175–197.
Locke, E. A. (1977). The myths of behavior mod in organizations. *Academy of Management Review, 2,* 543–553.
Locke, E. A. (1980). Latham versus Komaki: A tale of two paradigms. *Journal of Applied Psychology, 65,* 16–23.
Locke, E. A. (1982). The ideas of Frederick W. Taylor: An evaluation. *Academy of Management Review, 7,* 14–24.
Locke, E. A., & Bryan, J. F. (1968). Goal setting as a determinant of the effect of knowledge of score on performance. *American Journal of Psychology, 81,* 398–406.
Locke, E. A., & Bryan, J. F. (1969a). The directing function of goals in task performance. *Organizational Behavior and Human Performance, 4,* 35–42.
Locke, E. A., & Bryan, J. F. (1969b). Knowledge of score and goal level as determinants of work rate. *Journal of Applied Psychology, 53,* 59–65.
Locke, E. A., Bryan, J. F., & Kendall, L. M. (1968). Goals and intentions as mediators of the effects of monetary incentives on behavior. *Journal of Applied Psychology, 52,* 104–121.
Locke, E. A., Cartledge, N., & Koeppel, J. (1968). Motivational effects of knowledge of results: A goal setting phenomenon? *Psychological Bulletin, 70,* 474–485.
Locke, E. A., Chah, D., Harrison, S., & Lustgarten, N. (in press). Separating the effects of goal specificity from goal difficulty. *Organizational Behavior and Human Decision Processes.*
Locke, E. A., Frederick, E., Lee, C., & Bobko, P. (1984). Effect of self-efficacy, goals, and task strategies on task performance. *Journal of Applied Psychology, 69,* 241–251.
Locke, E. A., & Henne, D. (1986). Work motivation theories. In C. Cooper & I. Robertson (Eds.), *International review of industrial and organizational psychology 1986* (pp. 1–35). New York: Wiley.
Locke, E. A., & Latham, G. P. (1984). *Goal setting: A motivational technique that works.* Englewood Cliffs, NJ: Prentice-Hall.
Locke, E. A., Latham, G. P., & Erez, M. (1988). The determinants of goal commitment. *Academy of Management Review, 13,* 23–39.
Locke, E. A., & Schweiger, D. M. (1979). Participation in decision-making: One more look. In B. Staw (Ed.), *Research in organizational behavior* (Vol. 1, pp. 265–340). Greenwich, CT: JAI Press.
Locke, E. A., Shaw, K. N., Saari, L. M., & Latham, G. P. (1981). Goal setting and task performance. *Psychological Bulletin, 90,* 125–152.
Locke, E. A., & Somers, R. L. (1987). The effects of goal emphasis on performance on a complex task. *Journal of Management Studies, 24,* 405–411.
March, J. G., & Simon, H. A. (1958). *Organizations.* New York: Wiley.
Maslow, A. H. (1954). *Motivation and personality.* New York: Harper & Row.
Matsui, T., Kakuyama, T., & Onglatco, M. L. U. (1987). Effects of goals and feedback on performance in groups. *Journal of Applied Psychology, 72,* 407–415.
Mento, A. J., Steel, R. P., & Karren, R. J. (1987). A meta-analytic study of the effects of goal setting on task performance. *Organizational Behavior and Human Decision Processes, 39,* 52–83.

Meyer, H. H., Kay, E., & French, J. R. P. (1965). Split roles in performance appraisal. *Harvard Business Review, 43,* 52–83.
Miner, J. B. (1980). *Theories of organizational behavior.* Hinsdale, IL: Dryden.
Mitchell, T. R. (1974). Expectancy theory models of job satisfaction, occupational preference, and effort: A theoretical, methodological, and empirical appraisal. *Psychological Bulletin, 81,* 1053–1077.
Mitchell, T. R. (1982). Motivation: New directions for theory, research, and practice. *Academy of Management Review, 7,* 80–88.
Mobley, W. H. (1977). Intermediate linkages in the relationship between job satisfaction and employee turnover. *Journal of Applied Psychology, 62,* 237–240.
Mowday, R. T. (1987) Equity theory predictions of behavior in organizations. In R. Steers & L. Porter (Eds.), *Motivation and work behavior* (4th ed. pp. 89–110). New York: McGraw Hill.
Ordiorne, G. S. (1978, October). MBO: A backward glance. *Business Horizons,* 14–24.
Peters, L. H., O'Connor, E. J., & Eulberg, J. R. (1985). Situational constraints: Sources, consequences and future considerations. In K. Rowland & G. Ferris (Eds.), *Research in personnel and human resources management* (pp. 79–114). Greenwich, CT: JAI Press.
Peters, L. H. & O'Connor, E. J. (1980). Situational constraints and work outcomes: The influence of an overlooked construct. *Academy of Management Review, 5,* 391–397.
Pfeffer, J. (1982). *Organizations and organization theory.* Boston: Pitman.
Pinder, C. C. (1977). Concerning the application of human motivation theories in organizational settings. *Academy of Management Review, 2,* 384–397.
Pinder, C. C. (1984). *Work motivation.* Glenview, IL: Scott Foresman.
Platt, J. R. (1964). Strong inference. *Science, 146,* 347–353.
Porter, L. W., & Lawler, E. E. (1968). *Managerial attitudes and performance.* Homewood, IL: Dorsey.
Pritchard, R. D., & Curtis, M. I. (1973). The influence of goal setting and financial incentives on task performance. *Organizational Behavior and Human Performance, 10,* 175–183.
Rakestaw, T. L., & Weiss, H. M. (1981). The interaction of social influence and task experiences on goals, performance, and performance satisfaction. *Organizational Behavior and Human Performance, 27,* 326–344.
Ryan, T. A. (1970). *Intentional behavior: An approach to human motivation.* New York: Ronald Press.
Saari, L. M., & Latham, G. P. (1980). *Hypotheses on reinforcement properties of incentives contingent upon performance.* Unpublished manuscript, Department of Psychology, University of Washington.
Saari, L. M., & Latham, G. P. (1982). Employee reactions to continuous and variable ratio reinforcement schedules involving a monetary incentive. *Journal of Applied Psychology, 67,* 506–508.
Salancik, G. R. (1977). Commitment and the control of organizational behavior and belief. In B. Staw, & G. Salancik (Eds.), *New directions in organizational behavior* (pp. 1–54). Chicago: St. Clair Press.
Salancik, G. R., & Pfeffer, J. (1977). An examination of need satisfaction models of job attitudes. *Administrative Science Quarterly, 22,* 427–456.
Salancik, G. R., & Pfeffer, J. (1978). A social information processing approach to job attitudes and task design. *Administrative Science Quarterly, 23,* 224–253.
Sales, S. M. (1970). Some effects of role overload and role underload. *Organizational Behavior and Human Performance, 5,* 592–608.
Schweiger, D. M., & Leana, C. R. (1986). Participation in decision making. In E. Locke

(Ed.), *Generalizing from laboratory to field settings* (pp. 147–166). Lexington, MA., Lexington Books.

Simon, H. A. (1947). *Administrative behavior.* New York: Free Press.

Skinner, B. F. (1953). *Science and human behavior.* New York: Macmillan.

Steers, R. M., & Porter, L. W. (1974). The role of task-goal attributes in employee performance. *Psychological Bulletin, 81,* 434–452.

Steers, R. M., & Porter, L. W. (1987). *Motivation and work behavior* (fourth edition). New York: McGraw Hill.

Steers, R. M. & Rhodes, S. R. (1978). Major influences on employee attendance: A process model. *Journal of Applied Psychology, 63,* 391–407.

Steers, R. M., & Rhodes, S. R. (1984). Knowledge and speculation about absenteeism. In P. Goodman & R. Atkin (Eds.), *Absenteeism* (pp. 229–275). San Francisco: Jossey Bass.

Taylor, F. W. (1911). *The principles of scientific management.* New York: Norton.

Taylor, M. S., Locke, E. A., Lee, C., & Gist, M. E. (1984). Type A behavior and faculty research productivity: What are the mechanisms? *Organizational Behavior and Human Performance, 34,* 402–418.

Terborg, J. R. (1976). The motivational components of goal setting. *Journal of Applied Psychology, 61,* 613–621.

Tubbs, M. E. (1986). Goal setting: A meta-analytic examination of the empirical evidence. *Journal of Applied Psychology, 71,* 474–483.

Tversky, A. (1967). Additivity, utility and subjective probability. *Journal of Mathematical Psychology, 4,* 175–202.

Tversky, A. (1969). Intransitivity of preference. *Psychological Review, 76,* 31–48.

Tversky, A. (1972). Eliminating by aspects: A theory of choice. *Psychological Review, 79,* 281–299.

Wahba, M. A., & Bridwell, L. G. (1987). Maslow reconsidered: A review of research on the need hierarchy theory. In R. Steers, & L. Porter (Eds.), *Motivation and work behavior* (pp. 51–58). New York: McGraw Hill.

Wagner, J. A., & Gooding, R. Z. (1987). Shared influence and organizational behavior: A meta analysis of situational variables expected to moderate participation-outcome relationships. *Academy of Management Journal, 30,* 524–541.

Weiss, H. A., & Adler, S. (1984). Personality and organizational behavior. In B. Staw & L. Cummings (Eds.), *Research in organizational behavior* (Vol. 6, pp. 1–50). Greenwich, CT: JAI Press.

Wood, R. E. (1985). *Task complexity and goal effects.* Paper presented at the annual meeting of the National Academy of Management, San Diego, California.

Wood, R. E., Mento, A. J., & Locke, E. A. (1987). Task complexity as a moderator of goal effects: A meta analysis. *Journal of Applied Psychology, 72,* 416–425.

Vroom, V. (1964). *Work and motivation.* New York: Wiley.

9 Interpersonal Goal Conflict

DONALD R. PETERSON
Rutgers University

In the later years of his long career, Henry Murray came to the view that the study of individual personality could never, by itself, lead to a thorough understanding of human lives. Beyond the person, interpersonal relationships had to be explored. Beyond action, interaction had to be examined.[1] Murray's earlier personology, expressed so memorably in *Explorations in Personality* (1938), was self-consciously transactional in its philosophy. Unlike the trait psychologies of the day that ignored situational determinants of behavior, Murray's theory incorporated the environment organically, especially through the concept of press. The appreciation of psychological life as a flowing process rather than of personality as a constellation of fixed entities was clear in all of Murray's writing, both early and late. But the later conceptions, rarely cited and apparently seldom read, are fundamentally different from the early ones in their focus on social interaction rather than individual action as a subject of scientific inquiry.

> In this paper I shall attempt to elucidate the widely preached but narrowly practiced assumption that the social scientist's 'real entity' . . . is a temporal unit of interacting processes, the simplest being a short interpersonal proceeding, say the movements or words of the actor (the subject, S) and the reaction of the alter (the object, O). I submit that, in representing an interaction unit of this type, the object must be given the same conceptual status as the subject, that is, our model of the proceeding should include as much formulation of the object's thought and speech as

of the subject's thought and speech. . . . One person's experience of another person has a special quality, quite different from his perception of a piece of cheese, a machine, a mosquito, or even of a dog. It is marked by a recognition of mutuality, of more or less equality, accompanied by some appreciation of the feelings of the other person and some willingness to adjust to them. All this (and a lot more) makes interpersonal proceedings quite different from those in which a person is using some *thing* solely for his own gratification (Murray, 1951, pp. 435–438).

As Thorne (1986) has noted, the shift from the study of individuals to the study of social interaction required a fundamental change in Murray's views of motivation. The concepts of need and press, which had served so well to characterize the themes in stories about pictures, could not accommodate the situationally specific processes of face-to-face encounters. Whenever two people talk to each other or interact in any way, two sets of needs come into play, each of which creates some kind of press for the other, and the situation they are in also creates a press upon them both. This gives rise to the problem of mutual alignment of need and press, of mutual accommodation, and mutual understanding. Murray found a partial solution to the problem in the concept of "need-aim," or goal.

A need, no matter how general, can be satisfied only by aiming at a *particular* target, or at a series of targets, *one at a time*. The particular target as the subject *imagines* it. . . . will be called the aim of the need. 'Aim' is synonymous with 'imaged goal,' 'imaged effect'. . . . The aim might be to eat fish chowder at a restaurant, or to persuade a friend to join the Society for Living, or to write a play about the tribulations of an honest Congressman, or to carry out a series of experiments with turtles to prove that the human mind is aimless (Murray, 1951, p. 461).

In studying social interaction, then, investigators were encouraged to shift attention from individual needs to interpersonal goals—to an understanding of what each person was trying to do to and with the other. Of course, Murray was not the first to appreciate the inherently interpersonal nature of the most significant features of human activities, as Sullivan's work immediately shows. Nor was he the first to emphasize the importance of goals in the cognitive organization of behavior, as Tolman's work reveals. However, Murray was the first to link securely the goal-directed quality of behavior with its fundamentally interpersonal character, and since his time the assertion that goal-directed behavior can only be understood in its interpersonal context has been endorsed and extended by a growing number of psychologists. Kenneth Gergen has written an especially compelling illustration of the absurdity of isolating individual action from its interpersonal context, and of the need to examine interaction rather than action if we are ever to understand goal-directed behavior.

> "We speak of persons as having aggressive motives, altruistic inclinations, playful intentions and so on, as if these were properties of individual selves. However, if my arm is raised above my head there is little that may be said about me as an individual. I am merely a spatiotemporal configuration locked in an otherwise meaningless pose. In contrast, if another person were before me, crouching and grimacing, suddenly it is possible to speak of me as aggressive, oppressive, or ruthless. If the other were a child standing on tiptoes, arms outstretched, his ball lodged in a tree above my head, it would be possible to characterize my pose as helpful or paternal. Additional configurations of the other might yield the conclusion that I was playful, obedient, protective, proud and so on. Note that my action is the same in all circumstances; yet, there is little that may be said of me—to characterize myself—until the relational context is articulated. Similarly, the other person's movements have little bearing on our language of understanding until they are seen within the context of my own. In effect, what we acquire as individualized characteristics—our aggressiveness, playfulness, altruism and the like—are primarily products of the joint configuration. They are derivatives of more holistic units. Intelligibility is thus an outcome of ongoing relational pattern" (Gergen, 1988, p. 46).

Still others have elaborated the interpersonal view conceptually, methodologically, empirically, and practically. Carson (1969) has integrated the early interpersonal psychiatry of Sullivan with the more recent social psychologies of Thibaut, Kelley and others in *Interaction Concepts of Personality*. Hinde (1979) has argued persuasively for development of a "science of relationships" and has sketched the outlines of the science that is needed. Kelley et al. (1983) have developed a conceptual framework and methodological guidelines for the study of close relationships and have delineated the kinds of research that are needed if the vicissitudes of love, power, conflict, and other aspects of close relationships are to be understood. Duck, Perlman, and their colleagues (Duck & Perlman, 1985; Perlman & Duck, 1987) have developed further the conceptions and methods required to study the intricacies of intimate relationships and have added the *Journal of Social and Personal Relationships* to burgeoning libraries devoted to the traditional topics of social psychology. Anchin and Kiesler (1982) have bridged the social psychology of interpersonal behavior and the clinical applications of assessment and treatment in their *Handbook of Interpersonal Psychotherapy*. Benjamin (1974, 1982) and Kiesler (1983, 1986) have refined and extended the taxonomic approach first presented by Leary (1957) into statistically established diagnostic systems that offer many advantages over "official" psychiatric nosologies. Family and marital therapy, inherently interpersonal in conception and conduct, have taken hold in all the professions concerned with mental health: psychiatry, social work, and nursing, as well as clinical psychology. The original family therapy journal, *Family Process,* is now complemented by several others; and the diversity of "schools" of family therapy is nearly as impressive as the range of approaches to individual psychotherapy. In science and in practice, the psychology of interpersonal relationships has developed dramatically over the past quarter century.

Over the same time, cognitive science has attained a conspicuous presence, if not an overpowering dominance, in modern psychology. Unlike the restrictive behaviorisms they helped replace, cognitive formulations clearly allow and usually encourage an emphasis upon goal-directed action. In *Plans and the Structure of Behavior,* Miller, Galanter, and Pribram (1960) showed the importance of plans and strategies in the organization of human activity. In their seminal formulations of cognitive science, Schank and Abelson (1977) have shown how knowledge structures function as people pursue the scripts, plans, goals, and themes of human action. In some recent research, salient conceptions of cognitive science have been extended to an analysis of goal-directed behavior in interpersonal situations (Miller & Read, in press; Read, 1987). Indeed, interdependence theory as formulated by Kelley and Thibaut (1978) centrally assumes goal direction in interpersonal behavior through the concepts of interest and outcome and integrates the motivational and cognitive aspects of personal relationships through the concepts of attribution and transformation (Kelley, 1987).

Conflict is an inescapable issue for investigators concerned with the goal-directed characteristics of interpersonal behavior. When Harold Kelley was asked for current information about his own conceptions and research on interpersonal goal conflict, he replied, "It's difficult to know where to start since everything I do has a close relation to goal conflict" (Kelley, 1987, personal communication). In some of the writer's own research, conflict emerged as the single most important kind of interaction married couples perceived in describing significant interactions in their own relationships (Peterson & Rapinchuk, in press). When two people join in a close relationship they bring their personal goals with them. Sooner or later, in one way or another, the goals of each person are bound to clash with the goals of the other. The reconciliation of goals is one of the most difficult and important problems encountered in any relationship. It is also one of the most difficult and important phenomena for students of human behavior to investigate. In the following pages, I will consider the methods, conceptions, and research that I have found most useful in understanding interpersonal goal conflict. By studying the processes through which conflicts arise and reach their resolutions, the more general field of interpersonal relationships can be illuminated. By approaching the study of goals from an interpersonal perspective, the understanding of goals may be informed.

THE DATA OF INTERPERSONAL GOAL CONFLICT

Suppose we agree that important knowledge might be gained by examining "interpersonal proceedings" (Murray, 1951), "interaction sequences" (Raush, 1965; Peterson, 1979a), "interaction episodes" (Kelley, et al., 1983) or "relational scenarios" (Gergen, 1987) in which goal conflicts are apparent. How can we find out about these? A reasonable starting point is to ask participants for their own accounts. Here is an excerpt from an interview with a married couple. The wife (W) has complained that she feels "hemmed in" by her husband (H). The therapist (T) asks what she means by that.

$W:$ Well, last night for example. I wanted to go out, the way I usually do, to our bridge thing (she regularly played bridge with a group of friends). And you (to Howard) didn't exactly say I couldn't but you sure made it mean for me to go. You left the dishes all to me . . .
$H:$ . . . but I was talking to Alan (their son) . . .
$W:$ I know. I know, and that's OK, but you knew I was late and you could have given me a hand. Alan couldn't . . . wouldn't have minded and then just as I got done throwing the dishes in the dish washer and was getting my coat on you brought up the business about the car . . .
$T:$ What business . . . ?
$W:$ . . . the car wasn't working right and you weren't sure it would get me there.
$H:$ Well it had been stalling a little when I started out from the office and I wanted to warn you.
$W:$ But it got you home all right. Right? And maybe it didn't run just perfectly, but I pumped it a little the way we always do and it took me over to Virginia's house just fine and it got me back just fine—and that was a lousy time for you to bring up stuff about the car unless you really thought it wouldn't move. You acted like you didn't want me to go. And . . . I go out little enough, and for you to resent the few little things I do for my own fun . . .
$H:$ I didn't resent . . .

W: . . . is really crummy.

T: So what about it, Howard? What was going on there?

H: Well, I certainly didn't resent her going. I think that's fine. And I didn't mean to hold her up. I really was worried about the car, and I wanted to warn her . . .

W: But right then? Why didn't you take care of it yourself? If it wasn't running how were you going to get to work in the morning? Why come flying in with a problem like that just when I'm rushing out to do something I want to do? I still think you were blocking my doing, er, blocking my going. Blocking me from doing what I wanted to do.

H: (Softly.) Marilyn, that isn't so. I want you to have a good time out. And I could have helped with the dishes, but Alan and I were talking, about the Yankee game, and I didn't even think about it to tell you the truth. I don't know what to say. I'm sorry.

W: Well you make it tough.

From even so brief an account, the general outlines of the conflict are clear enough. Marilyn wants to spend an enjoyable evening playing bridge with her friends. Howard interferes with her pursuit of that aim. But subtler features also appear. Marilyn says Howard acted as if he didn't want her to go and has evidently inferred that he resents the few little things she does for her own enjoyment. She brought up the episode to illustrate a more general feeling she has about her husband, that he is "hemming her in." Howard, for his part, denies any resentment and says he wants his wife to have a good time with her friends. He seems unaware that he interfered with his wife's aims and offers plenty of good reasons for doing what he did. One need not be a clinician to sense that there is more to this story than meets the eye.

Many conflicts reported by couples in clinical treatment are a good deal more active than the one just described and their interpretation is even more complex. An interaction record (Peterson, 1979a, 1979b) from one couple contains the following account.

We were coming back from an afternoon at my brother's house. Dad and Mom were in the front seat with Dad driving. Carl (husband) and I were in the back seat with Jill (3-year-old daughter) between us. I tried to get Carl to talk, but he refused and attempted to sleep 3 hours home. First, though, because of my attitude he gave me a nasty hand sign and called me some dirty names. Jill would climb on Carl and it made him mad cause I didn't stop her. He then pinched me on the leg hard. Jill continued and he kicked me two separate times. Jill tickled him and he pulled my hair. I yelled 'ouch.' Through the others I continued my attitude until the hair pulling. He told me to knock it off. (He said I put Jill up to tickling him) and I yelled back to him to knock it off. My Dad said, "What's going on

9. INTERPERSONAL GOAL CONFLICT 333

back there?" Carl said, 'We're having a few problems.' After a few minutes my attitude was pleasant again. Since Carl kept pushing Jill away, I told her to stay in front when she wanted in back because Daddy didn't want her back there. He got mad about that."

At the most superficial level, this conflict is simple enough. She wants to talk and he wants to sleep. But where is all the anger coming from? Are we to believe that he gives her a nasty hand sign and calls her dirty names because of her *attitude?* Throughout the episode, each person is interpreting, usually justifying, his or her own action and emotion, and progressively interpreting the action and emotion of the other, often incorrectly. At least it seems fair to say that the perceptions of the two are less then perfectly congruent. Carl's account of the same episode goes as follows:

On the way home I was trying to take a nap. (Much German to do when I got home.) Had I been anyone else in the world she (Janet) would have afforded me the courtesy of keeping Jill from preventing my sleep. Twice I communicated (non-verbally) to her that I did not appreciate her actions (or lack of them). When it got to the point that she encouraged Jill to disturb me *I got Pissed!* I grabbed her by the hair and pulled her head my way a couple feet and informed her that I felt a little attitude rearrangement was in order.

Even with both accounts, however, interpretation of the conflict is incomplete. Why so much anger over so small an incident? What went on before? What are these "attitudes" they both keep talking about? What deeper feelings and beliefs, basic goals perhaps, might be involved?

The accounts written by "average" couples are usually less obscure than those written by people in clinical treatment and their exchanges are typically more straightforward, although the most loving, rational people in the world are perfectly capable of gross expressive and interpretive distortions in their efforts to communicate with one another, and they are certainly not exempt from conflict. Indeed the goal conflicts encountered by people in apparently satisfactory relationships often appear to be as fundamental as those of people in clinical distress. Here is an interaction record written by a wife in a group of couples who claimed to be satisfied with their marriages.

I told Phil I had figured out what I wanted from him . . . I wanted him to approve of me as a homemaker, wife and mother—that that was a legitimate activity as much as being a PhD in English Lit (that he had wanted me to do). . . . We discussed descriptions of a virtuous woman in Proverbs in the Bible where God describes a Christian woman and her activities as a defense for my goals of home-centered activity. (We both take the Bible as a guide to living.) Phil said this was the first time I was able to explain in a logical rather than emotional way, my reasons for being what I am rather than a PhD in English. I was so happy that he could finally understand, and in the light of the Bible . . . he could now *approve* of my choice to be a mother and homemaker.

Psychodynamically oriented clinicians may be skeptical about so sudden a shift in the husband's attitude, and feminists may be galled by so passive a solution to a basic issue in female identity. Yet, as the husband's account confirms, here is a couple who have confronted a fundamental goal conflict, examined their own attitudes and beliefs as squarely as they could, communicated their thoughts and expressed their feelings freely and accurately, and resolved the conflict through common adherence to higher principles. From this account of a single episode and comparison with the two previous accounts, some of the main features of interpersonal goal conflict begin to emerge, and some of the challenges in understanding them begin to grow clear.

A first challenge is to obtain information about the historical and situational context in which the conflicts occur. Without information about antecedents, sensible inference of goal intent is often impossible, and the information required is often distant and obscure. Let us continue the interview with the couple in which the wife felt "hemmed in" by her husband. Howard has just apologized for interfering with his wife's hurried efforts to get to her bridge game, and Marilyn has said "Well you make it tough." A long silence followed. Howard sat quietly in his chair.

H: OK, there was more to it. I don't like it when you go out at night and I have to stay home alone. It spooks me.

T: Spooks you?

H: Yeah, I really feel uncomfortable. I know nothing is going to happen. I mean I *know* nothing is going to happen, but to tell you the truth, I get a little scared. I can't tell you what it is, but I get very uneasy when I'm there alone. I find it very difficult to talk about this. (Another long pause.) Here I am, Mr. Confidence, and I think I've been putting up this front all these years, and everybody thinks I'm in charge but the fact is I get scared . . .

T: . . . when you're home alone.

H: Yes. I get worried about people coming into the house. I know everything is locked . . .

9. INTERPERSONAL GOAL CONFLICT   335

T: Let us understand immediately that logic has nothing to do with this . . .

H: . . . nothing to do with this. The doors are locked. I don't want to turn off all the lights because I'm afraid that. . . . I'll give you an example. I don't want to shut my bedroom door. I keep my bedroom door open.

T: OK.

H: So that I can see out in the hall, see reflections, see shadows, see if anyone is coming up the steps . . .

T: Do you have any images of the kinds of figures who might be entering, or is it just sort of vague . . .

H: They're vague figures these shadows.

T: OK. You hear the sounds—feel a presence, a dangerous presence.

H: Now when I see movies about things like that—*Psycho, The Exorcist.* Oh boy. Those things really get me. I'm a wreck. It's that kind of thing. But Marilyn . . .

W: Yeah—I didn't understand . . .

H: She loves that stuff.

W: But I didn't understand . . .

H: For weeks, I'm nervous after those things. . . . So I have this fear that these things are going to happen to me.

W: I didn't know those things got to you that way.

H: And I have an attic up there too that will throw me off the wall. I don't want to go into Jackie's (daughter) room. Now it's a strange thing. When I'm in a hotel room, pitch black, lights out, I go right to sleep. But in my house its different. I can't understand that.

T: Did you have these fears as a boy?

H: Yeah. I remember. Once we had a fire in the house, in the apartment where we lived. I was alone in the house. All of a sudden fire engines came, and there were fire escapes into my room, and apparently when I was sleeping, I *slept.* All of a sudden there was somebody on the fire escape. Scared the living shit out of me. I didn't know what to do. I was . . .

T: You woke up all of a sudden, and here was this great big . . .

H: Here was this great big man coming through and picking me up and carrying me out.

T: So here's this terrifying, sudden presence . . .

H: Yeah.

T: So were there then fears like this after that?

H: I don't think I even thought about it. I remember coming to the apartment house and I used to be afraid, and I used to look up at the stairway to see if anyone was there. I remember doing it. . . . These things I haven't thought about in years. My God, at least 25 years.

T: And some of these same kinds of fears are with you still?
H: Yeah.
T: Marilyn, did you know about any of this?
W: No, I never . . . he never said anything about that.
H: Mr. Confidence . . .
T: So maybe he isn't just trying to keep you home.
W: (to Howard) I didn't know you felt *that* way.

In this case, an event a quarter of a century earlier, whose cognitive and affective residuals were unclear to the person himself, let alone his wife, not only helped instigate the conflict but led to serious mistakes in perceptions of intent. A confident adult facade concealed the feelings of a frightened child. Fear was mistaken for resentment. A need for comforting company was mistaken for deliberate obstruction. Situations of this kind are commonplace in clinical practice and are also common, if not so frequent, in the exchanges of everyday social experience. Understanding these aspects of interpersonal goal conflict are at once among the most important and the most difficult challenges we face, and some kinds of information are more likely than others to provide the knowledge we seek.

About 10 years ago, I proposed several guidelines for methodology in the study of interpersonal process. Although the ideas expressed at that time have since been elaborated and refined (cf. Kelley, et al., 1983) the basic features of useful method still look about the same to me.

1. The subject of inquiry is the interaction of person with situation . . . . For interpersonal relationships, the dominant features of situations are other people. We deal with person-person interactions.
2. Inquiries are directed toward processes over time, rather than toward states, traits, or any other conditions examined at a single time. This requires study of the sequential relationships among behavioral events, the antecedents of the events, and the consequences of the events.
3. Characterizations of psychological process represent significant natural events as these occur in their natural settings. . . . The more contrived and artificial the conditions of investigation are, the less likely are valid representations of significant natural process to emerge from the investigation. It is exactly those "valid representations of significant natural process" that useful psychological inquiry must provide.
4. The formulations of interaction process include covert as well as overt aspects of behavior. . . . If this condition is accepted, observa-

tion alone becomes an insufficient method for studying interpersonal relationships.
5. Methods for the study of interaction process are multimodal in character. . . . A full range of the methods of behavioral science, namely, observations and records of behavior, verbal inquiry, elicitative procedures, and the experimental management of behavior may all be usefully employed.
6. Methods of inquiry, and the characterizations they are designed to provide, are defined within a reasonably coherent conception of human behavior. . . . All inquiries are guided by some conception, implicit or explicit, that leads the investigator to examine some phenomena rather than others and to frame descriptions of those phenomena in one set of terms instead of another. Since that is the case, it is reasonable to propose that the conceptions guiding any inquiry be stated as clearly as possible as the inquiry begins and then restated as the facts of inquiry suggest.
7. Methods of studying psychological process satisfy at least minimal conditions of psychometric dependability. Most fundamentally, this requires that any descriptive proposition to emerge from an examination be capable of intersubjective test and that appropriate tests show reasonable levels of agreement (Peterson, 1979b, pp. 35–36).

The only notes I am inclined to add at this time concern the limitations of most of the experimental research that still dominates American social psychology and the need to add interpretive modes of inquiry to traditional methods of behavioral science if we are ever to understand the kinds of interpersonal goal conflicts with which this chapter is concerned. Experimental inquiries are valuable, in some regards essential, in examining the implications of psychological theory. The investigations start in theory and they end in theory. They are not necessarily intended to provide generalizable, ecologically valid information about natural events outside the laboratory (cf. Berkowitz & Donnerstein, 1982). If, however, we are interested in learning about natural events, we have to study natural events. As I have already illustrated, the phenomena now under discussion involve long periods of time and complex linkages among events over time. They also involve, possibly as their most important single quality, deep experiences and vigorous expressions of emotion. For ethical reasons, affective responses at the levels involved cannot be instigated in the laboratory. For practical reasons, study of interpersonal processes over long periods of time can rarely be undertaken. The typical *Journal of Personality and Social Psychol-*

ogy experiment, in which strangers, usually college sophomores, interact briefly and dispassionately with one another to test the implications of, say, game theory, cannot possibly tell us what we want to know. Richer information can be gained from narrative accounts, although the interpretation of these is fraught with epistemic peril. The need for a well-articulated discipline of narrative interpretation is clearer to me than it was 10 years ago, although the philosophical foundations for the discipline are only beginning to form (cf. Messer, Sass, & Woolfolk, 1988), and systematic research based on the study of narrative accounts is more a vision than an accomplishment.

CONCEPTIONS OF INTERPERSONAL GOAL CONFLICT

The literatures on interpersonal relationships, goal concepts, and social conflict are all large, and largely independent. Thorough discussion and integration of these fields is obviously beyond the scope of this chapter. Indeed it is not at all clear that the epistemologies, theories, and substantive findings in the separate areas would allow systematic integration at this time. All I attempt in the following section is a summary of some of the main features of a conception of interpersonal goal conflict that has been more fully articulated elsewhere (Kelley, et al., 1983) as amended by more recent conceptual developments proposed by others, and occasionally by further reflection on my own part. The statement is not proposed as an original theory. It is not a theory at all. Rather it is a conceptual framework that may be useful in guiding research, clinical inquiry, and the evolution of coherent theory. The main features of the framework represent the extended collaborative effort of nine participants and were designed to accommodate, or at least to be consistent with, the most plausible theories and the most firmly established empirical knowledge available at the time the conception was formulated.

Action and Interaction

Any interaction between two people involves two chains of events, one for each person, that are causally interconnected. Each person's chain of events is composed of multiple strands, most significantly the cognitive, affective, and behavioral activities that each person experiences and expresses as the interaction proceeds. Within each chain of events, complex causal connections occur continuously. A thought at one moment may be accompanied by an emotion and either simultaneously or later may lead to an observable action. Whenever the action of one person influences the thought, affect, or action of the other, an interaction has occurred.

Interaction and Relationship

An interaction *episode* begins when an act by one person is followed by contingent response on the part of the other, continues as long as reciprocal influence prevails, and ends when direct reciprocal influence ceases, often with physical separation of the participants. Any episode can be broken down into finer units. Many episodes can be divided into identifiable *phases,* such as the agenda-building, arguing, and negotiating phases of conflict resolution that Gottman (1979) has described. Most phases are made up of still smaller units. A single action-reaction unit has been called an interaction *cycle,* and each cycle is made up of the individual *acts* of the people involved. Each act can further be refined into micromomentary moves and expressions, though resolution of an episode only to the level of molar acts is usually sufficient for the study of goal-directed interaction.

On the other side, episodes are often linked temporally by cognitive and affective residues that are carried over from one interaction to another. Rebuff in the morning may bring anger in the evening. As indicated in the preceding section, sensible interpretation of any given episode is often impossible unless the history of previous interactions is known. In close, lasting relationships, frequently repeated interactions usually take on stable, predictable forms. One breakfast routine is much like another. Decision making, love making, conflict resolution, interactions of all kinds, are shaped into regular orders, though no two interactions are exactly alike, and some variation from one episode to another inevitably occurs. The *relationship* between any two people is the total pattern of recurrent interactions that take place between them. Brief episodes are embedded in longer patterns at higher levels. Breunlin and Schwartz (1986) distinguish among face-to-face episodes, longer sequences that are played out for periods from a day to a week, still longer sequences that range from several weeks to a year, and finally patterns of interaction and thought that repeat from generation to generation. They attempt to show how sequences at one level generate and calibrate sequences at other levels. Most family therapists will agree that formulations of this range are needed to accommodate the patterns they see in practice. All researchers will appreciate the formidable difficulties that confront systematic research on issues of such grand scope.

Goals, Interactions, and Relationships

In most interactions, the action chain of each person is directed toward some anticipated outcome, or *goal*. The goal need not be one of simple hedonic gain, nor need the outcome be consciously and accurately foreseen as the interaction proceeds. However, in the ordinary give-and-take exchanges of daily living, each person usually has some idea about the way the interaction might end and values certain outcomes over others. In interdependence theory, the outcome always includes some balance of contributions and rewards of each participant, and these can be portrayed in matrices to show both individual and joint outcomes for those involved in each interaction.

Interactive experiences, like all experiences, are organized in *cognitive-interpretive structures* (Mandler, 1975) that determine the meaning of any event, allow integration of that experience with past experience, and guide action through the current episode, so that, in general, favorable outcomes can be gained and unfavorable outcomes avoided. The interpretive process, however, is complex. Events are restructured and modified by previously established structures, that people often cannot accurately describe and of which they are often unaware. Expectations of future events, including the actions of a relational partner, may have little or no predictive validity. The cognitive-interpretive structures that guide goal-directed interpersonal behavior are more in the nature of "fictions or theories" (Mandler, 1975, p. 52) than veridical representations of social events. Whatever its accuracy or utility may be, however, the cognitive meaning of an event is a decisive guide to the course of action each person pursues as an interaction proceeds. Each situation is interpreted and cognitively *transformed* (Kelley, 1987) according to the relatively stable decision rules that each person has developed over the course of prior interpersonal experience. Cognitive representations of action and interaction allow arrangement of cognitive structures without actually performing further actions. We mull over events of the past and reinterpret them. We anticipate future interactions, imagine scenarios, and rehearse anticipated events to avoid unpleasant surprises and improve chances of favorable outcomes.

Escape from solipsism is provided by a process of disclosure and *social validation*. Social validation, as we conceive it, is essentially the same as the process of consensual validation that the psychiatrist Harry Stack Sullivan described 50 years ago, but our definition is neutral in regard to the surplus implications for personality structure and development that Sullivanian theory entailed. For effective social validation to occur, each person must first of all know what his or her goals, plans, and construals are. This may require a level of insight and integrity that is not easy to attain. Second, each person must express those views and interests to the other. This requires trust, which may also be difficult to attain and is sometimes not justified. The message must be accurately received and understood by the other, but some degree of perceptual alteration and conceptual reorganization in accord with the receiver's own cognitive-interpretive structures and rules of transformation is inevitable. Finally, the receiver must encode a reply, which is subject to all the conditions that surrounded the initial statement. The reply is at the same time an expressive statement and a message for the initiator of the sequence to interpret. The barriers to effective communication are numerous and complex, but to the extent that it occurs effectively, social validation provides the means for correcting the distortions that are bound to arise in solitary rumination. Because of the difficulties inherent in social communication and because of the dangers that await those whose perceptions and construals are incongruent with those of significant others, third parties, such as close friends and counselors, are often brought in as a kind of advisory network. However, there is no way to guarantee that the others' conceptions are any better than one's own, and the risks of "groupthink" (Janis & Mann, 1977), conspiracy theories (Pruitt, 1987) and other errors are ever present.

In social validation and in social interaction generally, the words, gestures, and other actions of one person may influence any combination of the thoughts, affects, and actions of the other. The responses may occur immediately, or through sustained effects on the cognitive and affective components of the action chain of the other, at a later time. The response of one person to the action of another is also an act to which the other may respond in the continuing flow of interaction.

As action sequences are repeated, they are organized in serial order. When the first action in a sequence occurs, the others tend to follow. No matter how long or complex the sequence may be, once a controlling stimulus initiates a sequence, it is likely to continue to its conclusion unless interrupted by some other stimulus. Mandler (1975) has argued that any interruption of an organized action sequence is sufficient to produce emotional arousal. If the organized action sequence is linked with a higher order plan, which is in turn linked with a highly valued goal, affective arousal is likely to be strong.

In interaction sequences, the action of each person proceeds in continual interplay with the action of the other. When the action of one person interrupts the smooth completion of the organized action sequence of the other, some emotion is likely to arise. If action is directed toward a highly valued goal, and the interruption by the other is construed as likely to impede or prevent goal attainment, distress or anger will likely occur. Sometimes, however, the interruptive action of a partner may suggest that the original goal can be exceeded, that an even more favorable outcome can be attained. "Pleasant surprises" lead to joy or delight. Whatever the quality of the affect may be, whether negative or positive, the intensity of arousal is partly determined by the discrepancy between the outcome originally anticipated as the action chain began, and the outcome that is now seen as possible through the following actions of the partner.

Many day-by-day interactions in reasonably congenial relationships are *meshed.* Scripts (cf. Schank & Abelson, 1977) for the action of each person are firmly established, and the action of each person facilitates the action of the other. Husband and wife move through the morning hours, sometimes together, sometimes independently, to prepare breakfast and get the children off to school. In the evening, they work on the monthly bills, and after paying off regular obligations discuss which charities to support. Through many patterned interactions of these kinds, individual goals are attained, and each contributes to the goal attainment of the other.

Goals and the Development of Relationships

So far in this summary, conditions that contribute to relational stability have been emphasized. Relationships also change, however, and changes in goals and goal perceptions are often critically important in determining the courses relationships follow. Five general stages can be distinguished in the development of close relationships: *acquaintance, buildup, continuation, deterioration,* and *ending.* Obviously not all relationships go through all stages.

A great deal of laboratory research has been done on impression formation in the early stages of acquaintance. Among heterosexual couples, appearance, availability, and a wide range of personality traits usually regarded as attractive have been shown to correlate with favorable impressions. The hypothesis that initial images govern subsequent interaction and resist disconfirmation has been frequently tested and generally confirmed in the laboratory but has not been closely examined in natural relationships outside the laboratory. Given availability and sufficiently favorable impressions to encourage further contact, later interactions provide an opportunity for each person to share ideas, interests, and values with the other.

Transitions from casual acquaintance to a stronger relationship are usually marked by successful tests of goal compatibility. George shares his hopes and dreams with Martha. Martha shares her hopes and dreams with George. They find each other sexually attractive. George is headed for medical school, Martha is interested in the law, and the idea of forming a two-profession family is appealing to them. Interactive experiences affect the personal dispositions of each person. Their individual interests and goals change as the relationship develops. In progressively more intimate relationships, each is sympathetic to the other's goals and both find their own goals enlivened, enriched, and supported by the other. These changes, in turn, may lead to changes in environmental conditions. Perhaps George and Martha move in together; and this in its turn changes the frequency, intensity, and diversity of interactions that form the relationship and affect the personal dispositions of the participants. Environmental conditions, relational events, and individual processes feed back upon each other in continuing circular causal loops as the relationship evolves.

In Altman and Taylor's (1973) first major formulation of research and theory on "social penetration," the process of increasing intimacy was tacitly conceived as one of progressively deeper disclosure and openness. In more recent views (Altman, Vinsel & Brown, 1981), relational development is viewed as a dialectical process, continually cycling between superficial and deep contact, between disclosure and privacy. Still earlier, Bolton (1961) had shown that the process was characterized by "advances and retreats along the paths of available alternatives . . . by a tension between open-endedness and closure" (p. 236). In the buildup of interdependence, "progress" is not linear. Not all goals will mesh. The solution of one interpersonal problem often gives rise to another. For these reasons, the developmental trajectory is irregular. The only way to find out about it is to determine the patterns of interaction that define the relationships up to that point. Future trajectories may be extrapolated with greater or lesser confidence at any time, but predictive certainty about the course of human relationships cannot be attained.

The widely investigated but still unsettled controversies over "similarity" and "complementarity" hypotheses in mate selection invite comparable comment. The lay myth that "opposites attract" was quickly laid to rest by early research that showed most married couples to be more alike than different in regard to life goals, interests, values, and personality dispositions, as well as education, economic status, and other sociological variables. The complementarity hypothesis was revived by Winch (1958), however, who argued that both parties in relationships would be best served if the needs of each complemented the needs of the other. Men with strong urges to dominate others would be better off with submissive wives than with equally dominant partners, for example, and the wives would also be better off than with equally submissive husbands.

Despite the superficial plausibility of the argument, the complementarity hypothesis has received scanty empirical confirmation, and the present conception of interpersonal process suggests why. Expression of a "need" can only be understood in its situational context, and different situations require different ways of integrating individual behavior in effective interaction. Levinger (1964) has shown that partners in satisfying marriages show far greater similarity in the socioemotional aspects of their relationship than in task-oriented behavior, whereas specialization rather than mutuality is more common in working together on tasks. Further, the very notion of stable "needs," constant over time and situation, is not tenable. Environmental conditions change, goals change, plans change, and action and interaction designed to satisfy goals change from one situation to another. It is obvious that some complementarities are required for effective social interaction: pitcher and catcher in baseball; buyer and seller in commerce; male and female in heterosexual intercourse. Under time-limited, situation-specific conditions, pairwise complementarities of goals and goal-directed action need to be arranged. More general role complementarities may develop out of repeated patterns of interaction that involve different dispositional expressions over differing classes of environmental conditions. But accurate assessment of relational complementarity requires detailed study of the meshing of situation-specific interaction sequences, as interfered with or as facilitated by the action chain of the interacting other. Intercorrelational studies of generalized traits and needs cannot provide the information required to understand what is going on.

The continuation stage of close relationship is characterized mainly by growing commitment. Stable, mainly satisfying patterns of interaction develop as described in the preceding section. Conflicts inevitably arise, but ways are found to resolve them; and in the happiest of relationships, affection deepens and commitment grows through all the remaining years. Borden and Levinger (in press) have described the transformations of goals and ways of evaluating experiences that take place as partners in long-term relationships shift from self-concern to mutual concern—from an "I" to a "we" orientation. Mere association in a close relationship is bound to require some accommodation of each partner to the discrepant goals of the other. At first, these accommodations are likely to be instigated by particular situations, but as each partner is rewarded by the greater satisfactions that come from cooperative than from self-seeking behavior, initially selfish motives can be transformed into genuinely altruistic concerns for the well-being of the partner. Motivational transformations of these kinds, described by Huesman and Levinger in 1976, are thoroughly incorporated in recent statements of interdependence theory (Kelley & Thibaut, 1978; Kelley, 1987). Borden and Levinger (in press) go beyond the concept of motivational transformation, however, to consider dispositional transformations in which underlying preferences become deeply internalized and generalized beyond the relationship. A person who initially stopped smoking to please a partner may come genuinely to find smoking abhorrent. Changes in personal dispositions of these kinds are independent of the relationship but feed back on the relationship to reduce demands for accommodation and transformation of motives. To the extent that dispositional transformations occur mutually, the goals of the partners will tend to converge, although complete union is limited by the persistently different biological needs and personal goals of the individuals in the relationship.

Other relationships deteriorate, in any of several ways. Some show a replacement of reasonably enjoyable exchanges by more and more frequent conflicts, which may either lead to separation or to the "conflict habituation" pattern that Cuber and Harroff (1965) have described in some long-term marriages. Others drift apart. Satisfactions once gained with a partner lose effect, and satisfactions are sought in other pursuits, often with other partners. Cuber and Harroff describe marriages that have taken this course as "devitalized."

Several conditions, in many combinations, can contribute to deterioration. Environmental conditions may change, as when young couples married in the college years take jobs in another location, enter a new complex of social relationships, and enjoy but also suffer the strains of a different level of income. Personal dispositions may change. A woman who feels content for many years to devote herself to her family may find new, distinctly personal goals emerging when the children leave. Her husband, also content to have his wife devote herself to the family, may find the adjustment difficult and may have to reconsider his own devotion to the personal growth of his wife. Finally, the interaction patterns that define the relationship may change. Gottman (1979) found that married couples were generally less polite to each other than to strangers. The candor that is required for social validation can also lead to rudeness. Several studies comparing "distressed" with "nondistressed" couples show different patterns of reciprocity for the two groups. Couples who get along well reciprocate each other's rewarding behavior but do not so often reciprocate punishing behavior. Distressed couples respond in kind to the other's negative behavior, but their response to compliments, favors, and other positive actions is unpredictable (Gottman, 1979; Jacobson, Waldron, & Moore, 1980). Gottman also found differences in the way distressed and nondistressed partners respond to expressions of problems. Nondistressed partners listened to the problem of the other and engaged in some form of validation to understand the problem more thoroughly. Distressed partners responded by "cross-complaining." "You think you've got a problem? Let me tell you about *my* problem."

The environmental, personal, and interpersonal changes that lead to deterioration may eventually end the relationship, though the process of terminating a relationship is itself complex, and the residuals are likely to carry over into other close relationships the partners may form.

Patterns of Conflict in Close Relationships

Overt conflict is an interpersonal process that occurs whenever the actions of one person interfere with the actions of another. *Conflict of interest* occurs when the goals of one person are incompatible with the goals of another. Pruitt and Rubin emphasize the perceptual and cognitive aspects of conflictual processes. For them "conflict means perceived divergence of interest, or a belief that the parties' current aspirations cannot be achieved simultaneously" (Pruitt & Rubin, 1986, p. 4, italics omitted). The focus entailed by this last emphasis offers a pragmatic advantage over other definitions, since some of the most influential determinants of conflict are perceptual and cognitive, and resolution of conflict is often most effectively achieved by perceptual or cognitive change.

The courses of conflicts can be divided into several stages: initiation, engagement, escalation, conciliation, and settlement. At each stage, the conflict may take any of several turns, depending on the environmental, personal, or interpersonal conditions in effect at that time. One of the tasks of research is to map the alternative courses that conflicts can take and to link the various courses to the causal conditions that determine them. One of the tasks of counselors, mediators, or the participants themselves is to change some of the conditions that lead to undesired outcomes of conflict.

Initiation of Conflict. If overt conflict occurs, some structural conflict of interest is invariably present. The goals of the participants are incongruent in some way. Occasions for conflict increase to the extent that the goals of the participants are incompatible and highly valued. This seems obvious, but the fact is that clear insight into one's own goals and clear perception of the goals of a partner are not easy to attain. When young couples are building a relationship and trying to decide whether they would get along well in marriage, for example, they are often beguiled into believing that they can live together happily because they share many avocational interests; have similar likes and dislikes in art, food, and music; and enjoy discussing their political and religious views. However, the effects of interests, preferences, beliefs, and attitudes in predisposition to conflict are not all straightforward. These conditions will play a part in determining conflict or freedom from conflict just to the extent that they are related to important discrepant or congruent goals in the lives of the people involved.

> A nominal Democrat may marry a nominal Republican and find their political differences a source of mild enjoyment in the games of political debate. If they are professional politicians, however, and their energies and resources are in fact employed in the election of one candidate or another, harmony will be difficult to maintain. (Kelley, et al., 1983, p. 368)

In the course of any conflictual interaction, general predispositions to conflict, especially adherence to deeply held, strongly valued, incongruent goals, can be converted into overt conflict by several kinds of initiating events, among which criticism, perception of an illegitimate demand, rebuff, and cumulative annoyance are particularly common.

Engagement of Conflict. Once overt conflict has been initiated, a decisive turn follows. The major directions are engagement and avoidance. Typically conflicts are engaged when at least one party considers the matter sufficiently important to require action and believes a favorable outcome can be achieved. Avoidance must be mutual and is likely to occur when both parties see the issue either as insufficiently important to outweigh the distress of engagement or as intractable. Although it is commonly assumed that engagement generally leads to more satisfactory outcomes than avoidance, Raush et al. (1974) found some evidently happy married couples who maintained a sense of contentment by systematically denying conflicts that were easily visible to the psychologists who examined them. Pruitt and Rubin (1986) regard deliberate inaction and withdrawal as acceptable strategies for dealing with certain kinds of controversies, especially those in which the perceived feasibility of more productive strategies is limited or lacking. In long-term close relationships, however, it is likely that latent conflicts (Deutsch, 1973) over basic goals will sooner or later become manifest, and it is clear from some systematic research with married couples that the engagement of conflict leads to increased understanding by each spouse of the perceptions of the other (Knudson, Sommers, & Golding, 1980). The most interesting question for researchers to ask is not whether people are generally better off to behave in avoidant or confrontational ways, but how, when, and under what conditions conflicts should be engaged, and how, when, and under what conditions avoidance or deferral is more productive.

If conflict is engaged, it can again take either of two main turns, toward direct negotiation and resolution, or toward escalation. In most ordinary exchanges with other people, settlement can be reached fairly quickly by direct negotiation. Each person states his or her aspiration and proposes means to attain it. Validation is sought and obtained from the other, and a straightforward problem-solving exchange follows. In other cases, the conflict escalates into an impassioned struggle from which rational escape may be difficult or impossible.

Escalation of Conflict

The process of escalation has been carefully examined, in the laboratory and in natural settings as well. Pruitt and Rubin (1986) identify five changes that take place as conflicts intensify. First, attempts by each party to influence the other change from *light* tactics, such as ingratiation and promises, to *heavy* tactics, such as threats, irrevocable commitments, and violence. Second, the perception of the scope and importance of the issue and resources brought to bear in resolving it change from *small* to *large*. Third, *specific* issues are transformed into *general* ones. What began as a simple disagreement over choice of wallpaper for the upstairs hallway spreads to more general issues of control, until the two are arguing about the way they discipline their children and treat their inlaws. Fourth, there is a shift in the aim of the interaction from simply *doing well* for oneself, to *winning* what has become a competitive battle, to *hurting* the other. Every injury must be redeemed by proper vengeance upon the other. Finally, the number of participants in the conflict may be increased from *few* to *many*. Children are triangulated in marital fights. Counselors are manipulated into unwholesome alliances. In intergroup conflicts, the strongest allies available are sought to overpower the opponent.

Pruitt and Rubin (1986) have distinguished three patterns of conflict escalation. In the *aggressor-defender* model, one party, the aggressor, starts with mildly contentious tactics to coerce another party, the defender, into accepting the aggressor's demands. If mild tactics do not work, more forceful actions are brought to bear and are increased until the aggressor either prevails or stops trying. In the *conflict spiral* model, a vicious circle of action and reaction develops. Contentious action by one party, especially threats and abuse, evoke either retaliatory or defensive contention from the other, with each reaction more intense than the action it follows. In the *structural change* model, negative attitudes and negative perceptions of the other grow as contentious exchange proceeds. Conceptions of the other shift from behavioral description to the attribution of deep-seated, long-standing, malevolent dispositions. Acts (you did or said thus and so . . .) are interpreted as signs of traits (you always . . . ; you never . . .) or types (you are a . . .). Once attributions *cum* accusations of these kinds have been expressed, they cannot be easily retracted, and the cognitive-affective residues instilled in both parties are difficult to change.

Some of the main conditions conducive to damaging escalation of conflict are attitudinal and affective in nature. Deutsch's (1973) distinction between cooperative and competitive attitudes is central to an understanding of the process. A person who enters a dispute with genuine interest in the well-being of his or her partner will behave very differently from one who is interested mainly in personal advantage. In the latter case, agendas of self-interest are likely to be concealed, in self-perception as well as interpersonal expression. This condition often adds subtle deceit to blatant coercion, which in turn reduces trust and exacerbates the conflict in all the ways previously described. Couples who are not very fond of each other may stay far enough apart, psychologically and physically, to avoid active engagement in conflict. Those who love one another deeply may care enough about their relationship to confront basic differences, however passionate the process of conflict and resolution may have to be. When the escalating actions of destructive conflict are examined in sequential detail, it is clear that mounting anger lies at the affective core of destructive conflicts, and that experiences and expressions of affection, or at least respect, are central to constructive conflict resolution (Peterson & Rapinchuk, in press).

Intensely bitter conflicts often end in separation. This is not necessarily damaging, at least as an alternative to further verbal abuse or physical violence. A time apart may give people a chance to cool off, review the situation, reappraise their values, and think of better ways to manage their differences. When affection is weak and grievances are stored, however, the separation may do more harm than good. An interaction cycle in which aggression was followed by angry withdrawal was most common in the interaction records of "disturbed" couples in marital therapy. "Satisfied" couples more commonly retaliated against aggression but then stayed on to work their conflicts through to a better resolution (Peterson, 1979a).

Conciliation of Conflict. Seriously intensified conflicts may pause in stalemate, as Pruitt and Rubin have proposed. The battle-weary combatants, having exhausted all their resources for victory through contention, may withdraw from the dispute for a time without yielding, but without any visions either of ways to successful resolution. In close interpersonal conflicts, stalemate is likely to be less prolonged than it is in the more complex, multiply interdependent group, organizational and international conflicts of Pruitt and Rubin's general formulation. In relationships founded on decently positive affectional bonds, stalemate provides some time for anger to subside, reason to return, and for one or both parties to consider conciliatory moves.

In the most common conciliation pattern among the married couples studied by Peterson (1979a), two kinds of action were usually involved. First, the problem was reframed as less important than the relationship. One partner or the other saw that the issue had gotten out of hand and said so to the partner. The value of the relationship and the importance of the immediate problem were put back in perspective. Second, the conciliator acknowledged some personal responsibility for the problem, rather than continuing to blame the other, and in some way expressed willingness to work toward a resolution. Conciliatory moves by one person are often reciprocated. The least that can happen then is a reversal of the process of escalation. Personal attacks, threats, and coercion are replaced by apologies, affection, and reasoned discussion. The best that can happen is that a fundamental difference in the goals and aspirations of the participants is more thoroughly appreciated than before, but commitment to the relationship is preserved and possibly strengthened. Under these conditions, a constructive structural change in the relationship may begin.

Settlement of Conflict

Besides separation, conflict can end in four main ways. The first is *domination*. One partner prevails; the other gives way. The clearest determinants of persistent patterns of domination are differential power and limited interest by the dominant member in the welfare of the other. With the possible exception of clinical masochism, the long-term effects of chronic domination are bound to be damaging to the loser, and even the winner, by securing victory at any cost, has lost the advantages that can flow from a more cooperative relationship.

Many conflicts end in *compromise*. The parties manage some form of problem-solving exchange, but the best solution they can derive is reduced aspiration on both sides. Often, better solutions can be found. Among these are *integrative agreements* (Pruitt & Carnevale, 1980; Pruitt & Rubin, 1986) that reconcile the interests of the participants. The two may agree to abandon limited individual goals for superordinate goals of higher value. They may shift from short-term objectives to concern for long-range outcomes of greater ultimate benefit. They may develop novel alternatives that bypass initial obstructions. All successful conflict resolution requires some mutual interest in the welfare of the partner and some skill in communication and problem solving. Integrative agreements are more satisfactory than domination or compromise but also more difficult to reach. Stubborn insistence on highly valued goals must be accompanied by flexibility in devising means to attain those goals. Creativity and imagination are needed, and the fresh view of a third-party mediator is often helpful. Pruitt & Rubin (1986) suggest several ways—expanding the pie, nonspecific compensation, logrolling, cost cutting, bridging—by which integrative agreements can be reached.

A more lasting outcome of conflict, and clearly the most favorable, is *structural improvement* of the relationship. The general rules for conflict resolution may be changed in constructive ways. Appreciation of the goals of the partner may grow stronger; affection and respect may deepen. Motivational and dispositional transformations may occur. If previously unrecognized or unacknowledged issues are confronted and reconciled, if new patterns of conflict resolution are developed, still other issues may be faced with higher hopes and greater trust than before, and the lasting qualities of the relationship will be improved.

Developmental Patterns of Conflict Management

Important aspects of the engagement and resolution of conflict are best described within a dialectical framework (Altman, Vinsel, & Brown, 1981). Couples reveal their interests and their views to one another more or less thoroughly, try more or less successfully to work through their differences, withdraw, approach, fight, and embrace in cyclical ways. Sometimes conflicts come in bursts. Sometimes revelation of a basic conflict of interest will lead to lengthy withdrawal and fundamental reconsideration of personal goals, mutual goals, personal dispositions of oneself and the other, and of basic commitment to the relationship. No single course of relational development, therefore, can be charted, but the different courses of different relationships, examined over extended periods of time, are likely to show patterned regularities.

The dialectical view is sometimes proposed as an alternative to homeostatic conceptions. The two positions are only inconsistent, however, if the stabilizing features of homeostatic function are emphasized, as in the several forms of balance theory that dominated social psychology a few decades ago. Open-systems models, which include not only equilibrium but novelty and change as outcomes of homeostasis, are consistent with a dialectical view and also with the facts of relational life as we know them.

Kelley et al. (1983) note that two forms of feedback can be seen in the circular loops by which the causal conditions that govern relationships are altered. *Negative feedback* tends to restore the system to a prior state. *Positive feedback* influences the environmental, personal, or interpersonal conditions governing relationships in such ways as to intensify and shift those conditions in the direction of the initial change. Where negative feedback predominates, the relationship tends toward *stability*. Where positive feedback predominates, the relationship tends toward *instability*.

In the preceding section, several general patterns of conflict resolution were described. Although none of these patterns is intrinsically good or bad, some modes of resolution are clearly more effective than others in reconciling basic conflicts of interests and promoting mutually supportive and satisfying relationships in the long run. When considerations of stability and effectiveness are combined, four general developmental patterns of conflict management can be seen. If effective means of conflict resolution have been learned in a stable relationship, *congeniality* results. Agreement is the rule, but the relationship is relatively static in its course. If differences are marked and homeostatically restorative but fundamentally ineffective patterns of resolution, such as withdrawal or unjust domination, are characteristically employed, static patterns of *contention* will be seen. If positive feedback occurs in escalating, destructive conflicts and no effective means of conflict resolution are developed, metastatic deterioration can be expected, and *alienation* will be seen as a result. Finally, if basic conflicts are deeply disclosed and honestly engaged, but constructive modes of conflict resolution are learned so that positive feedback progressively influences the causal conditions governing the relationship, interpersonal *growth* will result. Differences will arise, passionate arguments will be heard, and pain will be felt. But the two learn from each other. They learn more about themselves and the other. Ultimately they learn to carry the interests of the other closer to their hearts as the years go by.

Some Illustrative Research

The formulation of developmental patterns of conflict management proposed here has not been examined empirically, though it is consistent with other formulations of a similar kind. Thus, Cuber and Harroff's (1965) "conflict-habituated" marriages appear similar to our "contentious" relationships, their "passive-congenial" relationships look like our "congenial" ones, their "devitalized" marriages resemble our pattern of "alienation," and their "vital" marriages resemble our pattern of "growth." However, neither the formulation by Cuber and Harroff nor our own is based on the conceptually grounded, epistemically sensitive, multimethodological, longitudinal study of interactional process, which was described early in this chapter, and which is needed to build a coherent body of substantive fact around our conceptual framework. The reasons are clear not far to find. The necessary research is expensive, difficult to design, even more difficult to conduct, imperiled by ethical risk, long delayed in its completion, and uncertain in its outcome. An academic culture that requires immediate production of clear-cut results does not encourage inquiries of the kind we consider most valuable.

Still, investigations of various aspects of interpersonal goal conflict are in progress in many locations. More is known about the topic than was known 20 years ago, and there is reason to hope that still more will be learned in the future. The concept of multilevel, circular causality upon which our formulation is based suggests that many kinds of research on a wide range of issues can all contribute to understanding of interpersonal goal conflict. A schematic outline of our conception of circular causality is shown in Figure 9.1.

The figure suggests that interactions within relationships both affect

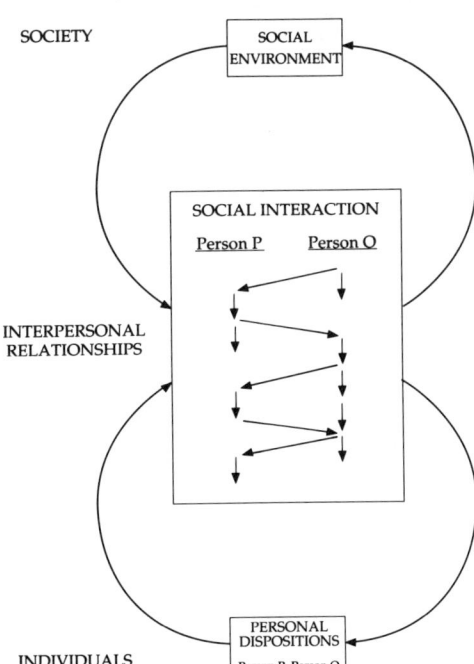

FIG. 9.1 Schematic outline of circular causal linkage among interpersonal relationships, societal conditions, and personal dispositions (adapted from Kelley, et al., 1983, p. 489).

and are affected by environmental conditions. Knowledge developed in the fields of environmental psychology and social ecology (e.g., Bronfenbrenner, 1977; Proshansky, 1976; Stokols & Altman, 1987), therefore, is pertinent to a grasp of interpersonal process. Likewise, social interactions affect and are affected by the personal dispositions of participants. The work of Pervin (1983), Cantor and Mischel (1979), and others on the goals and social perceptions of individuals, therefore, is relevant.

However, social interaction plays a special role in mediating the effects we are all trying to comprehend. Environmental conditions are brought to bear on individuals mainly through interactions with others. Individuals affect societies mainly through interactions with others. Every social revolution in history has taken its form in a small group; the Nazi Brownshirts, the Russian Bolsheviks, the Founding Fathers of the American Revolution. Every societal transformation requires a propitious ecology: the economic injustices that infuriated the Germans after the Treaty of Versailles, the economic and political misery of the working class in Czarist Russia, the economic and political arrogance of the Georgian British toward their American colonies. Every social revolution also requires charismatic individual leadership: Hitler, Lenin, Samuel Adams. But neither societal conditions alone nor charismatic leaders alone transform societies. For that the support and the sustaining power of a small group is required. For the understanding of societal, as well as individual process, the study of social interaction is imperative.

Encyclopedic review of research on interpersonal goal conflict is neither possible nor desirable in a statement of this kind. Rather than attempt a general review, I shall only call attention to several lines of inquiry that are most closely compatible with the methodological and conceptual viewpoint presented here and that seems likely to advance knowledge in areas of particular importance.

Harold Kelley's long career of research on social exchange, attribution, and related topics may already have received more attention than some readers will appreciate. However, the conceptions Kelley developed, largely in partnership with John Thibaut, have had a powerful effect on the field; and the research he continues to conduct blends field study, experimentation, and theoretical integration in an ususually salutary way. Recent research on communal aspects of relationships complement earlier studies of exchange, and the emphasis on transformation in contemporary interdependence theory promises a badly needed link between research on social interaction and research on cognitive process.

Equal risk of overemphasis may arise from further mention of Dean

Pruitt's work; yet Pruitt's program also shows the blend of thoughtful conception, innovative field study, and careful experimentation that seems most productive in this difficult area of inquiry. Examining the dialectical processes of disclosure and privacy maintenance, as Altman and his colleagues have done, is essential not only to understanding social validation, as previously described, but to more general understanding of the ways in which intimate relationships are developed, and inevitable conflicts in those relationships are confronted and resolved. The work of Raush, et al. (1974) remains as one of the few longitudinal studies of conflict and communication in close relationships, though others are in progress. Levinger's (1964; see also Kelley, et al., 1983) program of research, linked as it has been to other aspects of relational development, has contributed not only to factual knowledge about interpersonal conflict but to clear conception of interdependent relationships in general.

Deutsch's (1969, 1973, 1981) long line of research on social conflict has not only contributed to basic scientific knowledge but also has guided useful practical applications in political diplomacy, labor negotiations, and divorce mediation (Kressel, 1985). Gottman's (1979) research is notable not only for the level of rigor he has managed to attain in studying the intricacies of interaction process but also in the practical applicability of the research he and his colleagues have done (Gottman, et al., 1976). To round out summary mention of some of the research programs already noted in the preceding sections, Shank and Abelson's work on the formation of knowledge structures in planful, goal-directed action has not only contributed to cognitive science directly but has provided a coherent operable basis for studying the related processes of social interaction.

Read (1987) has employed a model of causal reasoning based on Schank and Abelson's (1977) formulation to study the way causal scenarios are constructed. Scenarios typically include information about the plans and goals of the actor and help explain the way actions are interrelated in extended sequences of behavior. Miller and Read (in press) have expanded these views in a goal-based model of personality that is then articulated within a general formulation of interpersonal relationships. The goals, plans and strategies, beliefs, and resources of participants form into identifiable configurations that influence, and are influenced by, the social interactions in which people engage. Unique persons are seen to create dynamic, unique relationships, but at the same time prototypically stable configurations may characterize personal dispositions across a range of relationships. The research program that Miller and Read have undertaken is linked on the personal side with the concepts of prototype elaborated by Rosch (1975, 1978), Cantor and

Mischel (1977, 1979), and others. On the environmental side it is linked with the analysis of Argyle, Furnham, & Graham (1981), which emphasizes the rules and roles that govern goal-directed behavior in various situations. So far, Miller and Read have not directly examined issues of conflict in their research, but their conception goes beyond that of Kelley et al. (1983) in its detailed analysis of goals and, therefore, offers added promise as a vehicle for examining interpersonal goal conflict.

Several investigators are examining particular patterns of interpersonal goal conflict. Patterson and his colleagues (Patterson & Reid, 1970; Patterson, 1982) have contributed significantly to understanding coercive family processes. In a typical interaction pattern, conflict arises when a child wants his or her way and the parents want the child to behave in some other way. The child controls the parents by escalating demands until the parents give in. The coercive behavior of the child is reinforced by the yielding of the parents, the compliant behavior of the parent is reinforced by relief from the aversive behavior of the child, and unpleasant but rigidly stable interaction patterns result.

Christensen and his colleagues (Christensen, 1988) have examined several forms of dysfunctional interaction patterns in couples, with special emphasis on the "demand/withdraw" pattern that has been described by Watzlawick, Beavin, and Jackson (1967).

> Suppose a couple have a marital problem in which he contributes passive withdrawal, while her 50 per cent is nagging criticism. In explaining their frustration, the husband will state that withdrawal is his only *defense against* her nagging, while she will label this explanation a gross and willful distortion of what "really" happens in their marriage: namely, that she is critical of him *because* of his passivity. Stripped of all ephemeral and fortuitous elements, their fight consists of a monotonous exchange of the messages "I withdraw because you nag" and "I nag because you withdraw." (p. 56)

So far, Christensen and his colleagues have concentrated on assessing the form and salience of the pattern and demonstrating its association with marital satisfaction (strong inverse correlation), gender of participants (women act more commonly on the demand side; men more often withdraw), and the structure of independence and intimacy needs the partners bring to the relationship (goals of intimacy are more commonly salient among women; goals of independence are usually stronger among men). The authors do not claim to have found reliable clinical solutions to the problem but are moving in that direction. In a cooperative project involving the University of California at Los Angeles and the University of Southern California, Christensen and Margolin (1987) are addressing the issues of conflict and alliance in distressed and nondistressed families. Once investigators move beyond the dyad to larger groups, complexities increase exponentially, but every family therapist knows that these complexities have to be confronted sooner or later if interpersonal goal conflicts are to be more thoroughly understood.

Beginning in complete independence but proceeding upon similar epistemological assumptions and within compatible conceptual frameworks, Kenneth Gergen and I now find ourselves employing complementary procedures to examine nearly identical phenomena that are then described in closely comparable ways. Gergen's research is designed to "elucidate *relational scenarios* in which emotional expressions are embedded, to comprehend the structure of these scenarios, the contexts in which they occur, gender differences in their patterning, and their function in social life" (Gergen, 1987, p. 4). In pilot research, participants have been exposed to hypothetical situations in which a close friend comes to them and expresses one of a variety of emotions (e.g., anger, depression, joy, or affection). The expressions can be contextualized in various ways. Participants are then asked to indicate their probable response. Varying responses can then be employed as expressions that call for further responses, and the search for orderly interdependence in the structure of scenarios can begin. Findings to date show that emotional performances can be reliably identified. When angry expressions are contextualized as blame, for example, three major moves may sensibly follow: remorse, reframing, or reciprocal anger. In one study, these three categories accounted for 90% of the responses and were coded reliably by independent interpreters. Several characteristics of patterned interdependence, such as a progressive narrowing of behavioral options as scenarios reach completion, have been tentatively identified. Computer-based presentation of stimuli and stochastic modelling techniques in analyzing data will be used in future research to chart structural patterns of interdependence within the scenarios and ultimately to define connections with context and function in social life.

In my own research, married couples were asked to write detailed, play-by-play accounts of significant interactions in their daily lives. Participants were asked to describe, independently, the conditions under which the interaction occurred, and to tell what happened then, step-by-step, from start to finish of the episode. We wanted to know who did and said what to whom, how each person felt, and what each person thought or seemed to think, as the interaction proceeded from beginning to end. A complex coding procedure was devised. Early studies showed that major forms of affective expression, cognitive construal, and reciprocal response expectation could be reliably inferred from the reports. Wide differences were found among "satisfied," "average," and "distressed" couples in rates of affective expression and in the frequencies with which various interaction cycles occurred (Peterson, 1979a, 1979b). Some of the findings have already been noted in this chapter.

A later study with a larger number of records showed that four main themes—stress, enjoyment, conflict, and support—were reported in the "significant interactions" of married couples. As mentioned earlier in the chapter, conflictual episodes were reported most frequently, even though no effort was made in recruiting subjects to attract or exclude couples in distress. Records reporting conflicts were divided reliably into those with destructive and constructive outcomes. Cluster analyses showed that nearly all of the statistically interpretable information in our early, laboriously complex coding system was contained in four main forms of affective expression, namely anger, affection, distress, and calm. Widely different courses of affective expression were shown for constructive and destructive conflicts; and sequential analyses, as well as qualitative interpretations, revealed some of the main conditions associated with the anger central to destructive conflicts, and the calm and affection associated with constructive conflict resolution (Peterson & Rapinchuk, in press).

Kenneth Gergen has spent much of his intellectual life in the world of social science. I have spent much of mine in the world of clinical practice. Is it possible that in the kind of work previously described the two can be connected? Many others besides Gergen and me appear to think so (e.g., Anchin & Kiesler, 1982; Carson, 1969; Wachtel, 1977). The kinds of systematic research that seem most promising for the study of interpersonal goal conflict are only beginning. A thorough review of family interaction research published less than 15 years ago showed *no* studies dealing with interaction patterns (Jacob, 1975). We are still examining the dyad for the most part, although every clinician realizes that we must confront the complexities of larger systems to meet the demands of daily practice. Among dyads, married couples have received by far the most attention, in the hopeful presumption that the conceptions and research strategies developed there will be pertinent to the study of other relationships. But conflict also arises among the goals of parents and children, teachers and students, between one world leader and another. The resolution of those conflicts at an interpersonal level is often the key to resolution of conflicts at other levels. We do our research and hope that some of it will be of value. In my view, those values are most likely to be attained if the interpersonal aims of investigators are to inform others who need the knowledge most. If that superordinate goal is firmly maintained, while at the same time we seek creative ways to bridge our differences and complement one another, we have a chance to develop knowledge that is at once conceptually sound, factually accurate, and socially useful.

ACKNOWLEDGMENT

I am indebted to Avril Thorne for calling my attention to this shift in Murray's thinking. I am also grateful to Irwin Altman, Nancy Cantor, Andrew Christensen, Kenneth Gergen, Mavis Hetherington, Harold Kelley, Roger Knudson, Kenneth Kressel, George Levinger, Gayla Margolin, Lawrence Pervin, Dean Pruitt, Stephen Read and Robert L. Weiss for sending me, on my request, materials and ideas on the topic with which this chapter is concerned.

REFERENCES

Altman, I., & Taylor, D. A. (1973). *Social penetration: The development of interpersonal relationships.* New York: Holt, Rinehart & Winston.
Altman, I., Vinsel, A., & Brown, B. A. (1981). Dialectic conceptions in social psychology: An application to social penetration and privacy regulation. *Advances in Experimental Social Psychology, 14,* 108–160.
Anchin, J. C., & Kiesler, D. J. (Eds.). (1982). *Handbook of interpersonal psychotherapy.* New York: Pergamon.
Argyle, M., Furnham, A., & Graham, J. A. (1981). *Social situations.* Cambridge, England: Cambridge University Press.
Benjamin, L. S. (1974). Structural analysis of social behavior. *Psychological Review, 81,* 392–425.
Benjamin, L. S. (1982). Use of structural analysis of social behavior (SASB). In J. C. Anchin & D. J. Kiesler (Eds.), *Handbook of interpersonal psychotherapy.* New York: Pergamon.
Berkowitz, L., & Donnerstein, E. (1982). External validity is more than skin deep: Some answers to criticisms of laboratory experiments. *American Psychologist, 37,* 245–257.
Bolton, C. D. (1961). Mate selection as the development of a relationship. *Marriage and Family Living, 23,* 234–240.
Borden, V. M. H., & Levinger, G. (in press). Interpersonal transformations in intimate relationships. In W. H. Jones & D. Perlman (Eds.), *Advances in personal relationships,* (Vol. 2). Greenwich, CT: JAI Press.
Breunlin, D. C., & Schwartz, R. C. (1986). Sequences: Toward a common denominator of family therapy. *Family Process, 25,* 67–87.
Bronfenbrenner, U. (1977). Toward an experimental ecology of human development. *American Psychologist, 32,* 513–531.
Cantor, N., & Mischel, W. (1979). Prototypes in person perceptions. In L. Berkowitz (Ed.), *Advances in experimental social psychology,* (Vol. 12, pp. 4–53). New York: Academic Press.
Carson, R. C. (1969). *Interaction concepts of personality.* Chicago: Aldine.
Christensen, A. (1988). Dysfunctional interaction patterns in couples. In P. Noller and M. A. Fitzpatrick (Eds.), *Perspectives on marital interaction.* Philadelphia and Clevedon, England: Multilingual Matters Ltd.
Christensen, A., & Margolin, G. (1987). Conflict and alliance in distressed and nondistressed families. Paper presented at Cambridge University Conference on Intrafamilial relationships, Cambridge, England.
Cuber, J. F., & Harroff, P. B. (1965). *The significant Americans: A study of sexual behavior among the affluent.* New York: Appleton-Century-Crofts.
Deutsch, M. (1981). Interdependence and psychological orientation. In V. Derlega & J. L.

Grzelak (Eds.), *Living with other people: Theories and research on cooperation and helping behavior.* New York: Academic Press.

Deutsch, M. (1973). *The resolution of conflict: Constructive and destructive processes.* New Haven: Yale University Press.

Deutsch, M. (1969). Conflicts: Productive and destructive. *Journal of Social Issues, 25,* 7–41.

Duck, S. W., & Perlman, D. (Eds.) (1985). *Understanding personal relationships: An interdisciplinary approach.* London: Sage.

Gergen, K. J. (1988). If persons are texts. In S. B. Messer, L. A. Sass, & R. L. Woolfolk (Eds.), *Hermeneutics and psychological theory: Interpretive perspectives on personality, psychotherapy, and psychopathology* (pp. 28–51). New Brunswick, NJ: Rutgers University Press.

Gergen, K. J. (1987). Exploration of emotional scenarios. Unpublished project description, Swarthmore College, Swarthmore, PA.

Gottman, J. M. (1979). *Marital interaction: Experimental investigations.* New York: Academic Press.

Gottman, J. M., Notarius, C., Gonso, J., & Markman, H. (1976). *A couple's guide to communication.* Champaign, IL: Research Press.

Hinde, R. A. (1979). *Towards understanding relationships.* London: Academic Press.

Jacob, T. (1975). Family interaction in disturbed and normal families: A methodological and substantive review. *Psychological Bulletin, 82,* 33–65.

Jacobson, N. S., Waldron, H., & Moore, D. (1980). Toward a behavioral profile of marital distress. *Journal of Consulting and Clinical Psychology, 48,* 696–703.

Janis, I. L., & Mann, L. (1977). *Decision making: A psychological analysis of conflict, choice, and commitment.* New York: Free Press.

Kelley, H. H. (1987). Interdependence, power, and conflict in interpersonal relations. Paper presented at convention of Western Psychological Association, Long Beach, CA.

Kelley, H. H., Berscheid, E., Christensen, A., Harvey, J. H., Huston, T. L., Levinger, G., McClintock, E., Peplau, L. A., and Peterson, D. R. (1983). *Close relationships.* New York: Freeman.

Kelley, H. H., & Thibaut, J. W. (1978). *Interpersonal relations: A theory of interdependence.* New York: Wiley Interscience.

Kiesler, D. J. (1986). Interpersonal methods of diagnosis and treatment. *Psychiatry, 1,* 1–23.

Kiesler, D. J. (1983). The 1982 interpersonal circle: A taxonomy for complementarity in human transactions. *Psychological Review, 90,* 185–214.

Knudson, R. M., Sommers, A. A., & Golding, S. L. (1980). Interpersonal perception and mode of resolution in marital conflict. *Journal of Personality and Social Psychology, 38,* 751–763.

Kressel, K. (1985). *The process of divorce: How professionals and couples negotiate settlements.* New York: Basic Books.

Leary, T. (1957). *Interpersonal diagnosis of personality.* New York: Ronald.

Levinger, G. (1964). Task and social behavior in marriage. *Sociometry, 27,* 433–448.

Mandler, G. (1975). *Mind and emotion.* New York: Wiley.

Messer, S. B., Sass, L. A., & Woolfolk, R. L. (1988). *Hermeneutics and psychological theory: Interpretive perspectives on personality, psychotherapy, and psychopathology.* New Brunswick, NJ: Rutgers University Press.

Miller, L. C., & Read, S. J. (in press). Why am I telling you this? Self-disclosure in a goal-based model of personality. In V. Derlega & J. Berg (Eds.) *Self disclosure: Theory, research and therapy.* New York: Plenum.

Miller, G. A., Galanter, E., & Pribram, K. H. (1960). *Plans and the structure of behavior.* New York: Holt, Rinehart, & Winston.

Murray, H. A. (1951). Toward a classification of interaction. In T. Parsons & E. A. Shils (Eds.), *Toward a general theory of action.* New York: Harper Torchbooks.

Murray, H. A. (1938). *Explorations in personality.* New York: Oxford University Press.
Patterson, G. R. (1982). *Coercive family process.* Eugene, OR: Castalia.
Patterson, G. R., & Reid, J. B. (1970). Reciprocity and coercion: Two facets of social systems. In C. Neuringer & J. L. Michael (Eds.), *Behavior modification in clinical psychology* (pp. 133–177). New York: Appleton-Century-Crofts.
Perlman, D., & Duck, S. W. (Eds.) (1987). *Intimate relationships: Development, dynamics, and deterioration.* London: Sage.
Pervin, L. A. (1983). The stasis and flow of behavior: Toward a theory of goals. In M. M. Page (Ed.), *Personality: Current theory and research* (pp. 1–53). Lincoln: University of Nebraska Press.
Peterson, D. R. (1979a). Assessing interpersonal relationships by means of interaction records. *Behavioral Assessment, 1,* 221–236.
Peterson, D. R. (1979b). Assessing interpersonal relationships in natural settings. *New Directions for Methodology of Behavioral Science, 2,* 33–54.
Peterson, D. R., & Rapinchuk, J. G. (in press). Patterns of affect in destructive and constructive marital conflicts. *Journal of Personality and Social Psychology.*
Proshansky, H. (1976). Environmental psychology and the real world. *American Psychologist, 31,* 303–310.
Pruitt, D. G. (1987). Conspiracy theory in conflict escalation. In C. F. Graumann, & S. Moscovici (Eds.), *Changing conceptions of conspiracy.* New York: Springer.
Pruitt, D. G., & Carnevale, P. J. D. (1980). The development of integrative agreements in social conflict. In V. Derlega, & J. Grzelak (Eds.), *Living with other people.* New York: Academic Press.
Pruitt, D. G., & Rubin, J. Z. (1986). *Social conflict: Escalation, stalemate, and settlement.* New York: Random House.
Raush, H. L. (1965). Interaction sequences. *Journal of Personality and Social Psychology, 2,* 487–499.
Raush, H. L., Barry, W. A., Hertel, R. K., & Swain, W. A. (1974). *Communication conflict and marriage.* San Francisco: Jossey-Bass.
Read, S. J. (1987). Constructing causal scenarios: a knowledge structure approach to causal reasoning. *Journal of Personality and Social Psychology, 52,* 288–302.
Rosch, E. (1975). Cognitive reference points. *Cognitive Psychology, 7,* 532–547.
Rosch, E. (1978). Principles of categorization. In E. Rosch & B. B. Lloyd (Eds.), *Cognition and categorization.* Hillsdale, NJ: Lawrence Erlbaum Associates.
Schank, R. C., & Abelson, R. P. (1977). *Scripts, plans, goals, and understanding.* Hillsdale, NJ: Lawrence Erlbaum Associates.
Stokols, D., & Altman, I. (Eds.). (1987). *Handbook of environmental Psychology.* New York: Wiley.
Thorne, A. (1986). Toward an interpersonology. Paper presented at convention of American Psychological Association, Washington, DC.
Wachtel, P. L. (1973). *Psychoanalysis and behavior therapy: Toward an integration.* New York: Basic Books.
Wachtel, P. L. (1977). Interaction cycles, unconscious processes, and the person-situation issue. In D. Magnusson & N. S. Endler (Eds.) *Personality at the crossroads: Current issues in interactional psychology.* Hillsdale, NJ: Lawrence Erlbaum Associates.
Watzlawick, P., Beavin, J. H., & Jackson, D. D. (1967). *The pragmatics of human communication.* New York: Norton.
Winch, R. F. (1958). *Mate selection: A study of complementary needs.* New York: Harper & Row.

10 The Role of Goal Categories in the Representation of Social Knowledge

JERZY TRZEBINSKI
University of Warsaw, Poland

The aim of this chapter is to advance and to advocate the idea that categories of social actions and goals are important in the representation of social knowledge. The idea will be elaborated, along with its implications for different areas of social cognition and motivation, and with supportive data. In spite of the fact that existing findings refer primarily to the representation of event knowledge, one of the main objectives of this chapter will be to conceptualize the possible role of goal and action categories in the representation of complex knowledge structures: person knowledge, knowledge about social organization, moral knowledge and self-knowledge.

The idea discussed does not yet form a systematic model of social knowledge organization and function. It is rather a proposition of a theoretical approach that differs from mainstream conceptualizations in social psychology but that can be traced to suggestions and notions rooted sometimes in the beginnings of this discipline. I will attempt to show that the approach has substantial implications and is empirically workable.

The problem of representational forms of an individual's knowledge is a dominant theme in contemporary cognitive psychology, since the shift in its theoretical paradigm in the mid-70s (Brewer & Nakamura, 1984). There is a growing number of refined models and data showing how different representations of knowledge determine processes of understanding and remembering. Until now, the majority of studies on social knowledge have aimed primarily to prove that these knowledge structures are generally "alike" structures modeled by cognitive psychology, and that experimental methods used in this discipline are generally applicable to the social cognition domain (Zajonc, 1980). It might be expected, however, that after this first stage, more thoughtful and carefully planned studies on natural forms of the social knowledge representation will become a major enterprise of social cognition.

These studies will have to take into consideration some distinctive characteristics of social knowledge structure and function. In everyday contexts, the processes of understanding social reality have an intersubjective character: They include different forms of social negotiations on the meaning of ongoing events and facts. A process of understanding is embedded within a given social action network. Fundamentally, we are not "thinkers" but "doers," and this action-rooted character of our mental activity should have an impact on the structure of cognitive processes and knowledge systems that emerge from them. Finally, understanding social reality involves, as inseparable parts, the descriptive and evaluative components. These issues will be addressed in the following presentation.

ACTION-ORIENTED REPRESENTATIONS OF SOCIAL KNOWLEDGE

The idea considered here is that action-oriented representation is an important form in which the human mind organizes knowledge about social reality. According to this idea, an individual's social knowledge is organized mainly within categories of actors, their goals, and conditions and means for the goal realizations. The knowledge organized within these categories is a knowledge about the realities composed of intentional social actions. This knowledge might differ in terms of its abstraction, and it might refer to different domains and aspects of the social reality. It means that the action-oriented representations of social knowledge systems have different structural forms. The simplest ones are representations of knowledge about stereotyped and anchored to a concrete context of events. These representations are modeled in scripts and vignettes concepts by Abelson and Schank (Abelson, 1981; Schank, & Abelson, 1977). The most complex ones might include representations of structures of social actors in terms of interdependences of their goal realizations. The main characteristic of all action-oriented representations is that their contents describe the internal structure of specific action or of main sources and constituents of the action: the actors and their goals.

According to this idea, then, social reality is understood and remembered by an individual, in a natural and most meaningful way, as networks of purposeful actions undertaken by social entities such as persons, groups, social classes, "historical forces," gods, or "evolutionary trends." Just as the natural goal in reading a story is to uncover and to understand the plot of characters' motives and actions, so the natural goal for an observer and a participant of a given fragment of social reality is to understand the particular network of actions and goals staying behind these actions and to identify and understand the potential sources of actions, that is, the actors as carriers of motives, interests, needs, and other intentional forces. The idea advocated here is that action-oriented representations are much more important in regulating thoughts and behaviors in social domains than is commonly recognized now in social psychology. There are enough strong rationales for the hypothesis that not only event knowledge, but also more complex knowledge systems, might be organized within different forms of action-oriented representations.

It seems that there are two preliminary arguments for the action-oriented representation idea. First, if social action is a natural framework for our everyday cognitions and evaluations (Ostrom, 1984), the structure of knowledge that emerges out of such experiences should in some sense be isomorphic to the structure of the action as it is understood by participants. This isomorphism fulfills the economic principle, which is believed to underlie the organization of cognitive structures (Rosch, 1975; Rumelhart, 1984). Action-oriented representation seems to be the best cognitive device to accumulate as well as to apply the knowledge gained while an individual observes or participates in social action. A great variety of findings and common observations show a functional anchoring of mental processes in a social action framework. An individual does not experience the reality as collections of pure entities in the Kantian sense. First of all, they are seen as meaningful elements, backgrounds, and other factors of ongoing actions. Recent examples of such observations are provided by Bruner's studies on knowledge and language development during early social interactions (Bruner & Sherwood, 1982), and by Perret-Clermont's studies on the role of interpersonal activity in understanding processes and cognitive development (Perret-Clermont, 1980). The role of social actions as the roots of cognitive processes and knowledge was stressed from different theoretical positions by classics like Weber, Mead, Znaniecki, Thomas, Wittgenstein, and Vygotsky. Although the problem of the mechanisms involved in this relationship is still an open and challenging one, this line of reasoning argues for the action-oriented representation of social knowledge.

The second rationale for this hypothesis is a common sense experience that two kinds of mental activity—evaluations and motivations on the one side, and cognitive processes on the other—are inseparably interconnected in most cases of our everyday understandings. This common experience says that many, although perhaps not all, evaluations and intentions reflect the "nature" of the situations. It seems then that both evaluations and descriptive cognitions together form units of interpretation of ongoing social facts. If this observation reflects the true character of our everyday understanding, it seems reasonable to expect that knowledge regulating the process of understanding should include, within unified systems, categories directly relevant to evaluative as well as descriptive aspects of experienced reality. Strictly cognitive conceptualizations of knowledge hardly deal with this unitary character of social understanding. However, the action-oriented representations, with goal categories as central elements and with the self represented as an actor, seem to provide the workable bases for intertwined cognitive, evaluative, and motivational processes.

BASIC ASSUMPTIONS

It is now a sound, empirically based assumption that an individual's generic social knowledge is represented in a form of cognitive schemata. Despite some distinctive characteristics, the structure and functioning of social knowledge should be determined by its schematic form of representation.

The main idea proposed here may be stated then in more specific terms: The important portion of generic social knowledge is represented in the form of action-oriented schemata. Different kinds of action-oriented schemata represent different contents of an individual's social knowledge. However, goal categories play a central role in the internal structure of these action-oriented schemata.

The importance of action-oriented forms of schemata was stressed first by contemporary cognitive psychologists and artificial intelligence researchers analyzing text comprehension. The first elaborated model of such representation was presented by Charles Fillmore (1968) in his "case grammar" theory. In this theory, a simple action schema that represents a verb meaning was assumed to be the basic representational form of a whole sentence meaning and as such, the building block of a text comprehension. Fillmore stressed the relational character of an action schema. For example, a schema for a "give" verb consists of specific relations between a giver, a gift, and a recipient's roles, where these roles may be filled by different elements of a sentence and a text.

Because of this relational character, a verb schema can interpret and give a specific integral meaning to a large array of words. The "case grammar" conceptualization was an inspiration for different versions of more elaborated "story grammars" that described mental frames that enabled an individual to comprehend and represent the meaning of a complex test (Kintsch, 1974; Kintsch & van Dijk, 1978). The concept of an action schema was advanced theoretically by cognitive scientists, especially in works of Rumelhart (Rumelhart & Ortony, 1977; Rumelhart, 1984) and Schank and Abelson (1977). Long before the recent shift toward the schema concept, the mental forms of understanding human actions were discussed by Burke in his "Grammar of Motives" (Burke, 1945). He provided a list of basic concepts to describe the content of action representations.

The contemporary conceptualizations did not add substantially new elements to Fillmore's and Burke's descriptions of basic categories of action representation. It is assumed that such representation, in its simplest form, consists of categories of an actor, actor's goal and means, and a scene of the goal realizations. The goal category integrates other categories in a unified mental structure: The goal motivates the actor, determines the possible spectrum of means and objects of realization, and implies the plans. Goals define the actor, which is represented as a source or carrier of the goals. The basic relation integrating the action constituents is the goal-means relation.

In agreement with contemporary theories of cognition, an action-oriented schema can be modeled as an organization of mental procedures to understand reality (Minsky, 1975; Rumelhart, 1984). When activated, these procedures work as specific expectations that initiate and regulate processes of information seeking, interpretation, production of inferences, and memory recollections. These expectations in interaction with incoming stimuli create the understanding of a given situation as a particular instance of an activated schema. In other words, this understanding has a form of instantiation of the schema by a particular configuration of situational characteristics.

Within a schema as an organization of procedures, schema constituents such as categories of an actor, goals, means, and conditions, can be described as subprocedures to understand specific components of a situation. These subprocedures are related functionally in the process of understanding in the sense that the content of specific expectations carried by activation of one subprocedure constrains, or even determines, the content of expectations carried by other subprocedures of a schema, especially when they are activated via top-down processes (e.g., via activation of the former subprocedure).

In action-oriented schemata, goal categories play a dominant role.

When activated, they can influence the content of expectations carried through activation of other subprocedures. Instantiation of goal categories is responsible, in the relatively highest degree, for producing default values, searching for additional data, concentrating on specific aspects of the situational field, and reconstructing memories. Moreover, because other schemata categories are integrated around goal categories by a means-to-goal relation, the instantiation of a goal category seems to be necessary to produce an integrated, "holistic" understanding of a given situation, with all its components and aspects. The change in instantiation of a goal category results in a relatively global and deep change in expectations and interpretations of the situation. It might be said that the dominance of goal categories within an action-oriented schema reveals itself in their strategic role in the top-down component of understanding processes (Rumelhart, 1984; Schank, 1982). The stronger the demand for the top-down processing, the greater the role goal categories play in understanding. When incoming stimuli provide a clear and complete enough set of data constraints on schema generated expectations, the knowledge represented in goal categories, if not activated directly already, may remain operationally "tacit." In the case of a new, complex, or unclear situation, or in the case of unexpected events, the goal categories become activated and generate expectations and reinterpretations in a search for the meaning of a given situation. The category of an actor, as a carrier of specific goals, plays a similarly important role in social understanding, especially in understanding stable patterns of social action.

This general outline of the structure and function of action-oriented schemata and goal categories was inferred from a standard corpus of assumptions and findings on a cognitive schema. On the following pages more specific propositions will be advanced that concern mainly the representation of complex, social knowledge. These propositions were developed through the interaction of "top-down" inferences, from the basic conceptualizations of schemata, with specific, social knowledge-related problems and factual constraints, based on social psychological data and common sense observations.

GOAL CATEGORIES IN THE REPRESENTATION OF EVENT KNOWLEDGE

Two lines of recent research are pertinent to the idea of action-oriented schemata. The first one deals with the representation of event knowledge. The second one tries to investigate if, and in what organizational forms, knowledge about complex social objects, like persons or the self, is represented in action-oriented schemata. The first issue has attracted much more attention. Although this chapter deals mainly with the second problem, as potentially more important for basic topics of social cognition, it is important to discuss first the rich data on event knowledge representation.

The most typical object of study within the first line of research was knowledge about stereotyped, recursive, and rather simple events. Such events usually have obvious content and structure, and time-space boundaries. Typical examples are events studied by Schank and Abelson (1977), Bower (Bower, Black, & Turner, 1979), and by Forgas (1982). The organization of knowledge about such events can be investigated by standard cognitive psychology methodologies, based on response time or false recognition observations. What was probably more important, these relatively simple structures were convenient to simulate in artificial intelligence analyses. The typical problems that were investigated both by psychologists and artificial intelligence researchers included identification of building blocks of the knowledge, its organization (e.g., role of time-order), and the schematic role this knowledge plays in understanding and memory recollection of events.

Generic event knowledge deals with organized sequences of actions involving individuals or groups. Typically, the actions are located within specific time and place boundaries. They have internal structures that might differ in terms of their complexity. They depict both stereotyped interactions within specific scenes, such as "a birthday party," or "visiting a doctor," as well as long-time diversified actions with many participants and with several options, such as "a presidential election." The event knowledge may differ in terms of its concreteness. It may describe particulars of situational background and order of detailed actions. The scripts might contain this kind of knowledge. On the other hand, it might be an abstract knowledge about motives, or plots of motives connecting different persons, without detailed descriptions of interaction patterns or ways of motive gratification. In such a case, the more detailed information has to be inferred from the knowledge on the basis of environmental characteristics and other involved schemata. Such abstract knowledge structures are modeled by the concept of goal (Schank and Abelson, 1977) or by the concept of "thematic organization points" (Schank, 1982).

In the vast literature on event knowledge there is a lack of specific propositions about a taxonomy of this knowledge representation. Such a taxonomy should delineate structures that differ qualitatively and ways they regulate cognitive processes. Models that were proposed until now were motivated by ad hoc emerged problems of text comprehension and computer simulations rather than by an attempt to propose a comprehensive theory of event knowledge structures. In spite of all these limitations, the literature on event knowledge provides broad and empirically based insights into the structure and functioning of this kind of knowledge.

The prevailing data come from studies on comprehension and memory of stories with a social content, and from studies on processing of everyday events, described verbally, presented on video, or evoked from memory. Generally, the data strongly suggest that generic event knowledge is represented basically in the form of a schema that includes, as central elements, categories of goals; the actors, as goal carriers or sources; subordinated categories of plans or subgoals; and means and conditions of goal activation and realization. This representation may be called an event schema. In spite of how concrete knowledge is represented, it is organized around the mechanism of an event: around a goal with specified or implied actions pursuing the goal. The following data elaborate on this assumption.

Goals and subgoals of individuals interacting and creating an event seem to delineate "phenomenological" boundaries of the event and boundaries between its internal constituents. The subjective beginning of an event normally means an emergence of conditions that activate, or modify a goal, or change ways it is pursued. The subjective end of an event normally means resolution of action initiated for former conditions (Newtson, 1976). Individuals from a given culture overwhelmingly agree on the beginning, the end, and the internal structure of common events (Bower, Black, & Turner, 1979; Barsalow & Sewell, 1984). Event constituents that are most commonly listed, and jointly evaluated as most important, are main characters' goals and actions pursuing the goals (Bower, et al., 1979). The main action that pursues the central goal of an event is used most commonly as an equivalent name for the whole event (Galambos & Rips, 1982). This confirms the assumption that an event is understood naturally as a goal initiation and realization. It means, then, that event schema categories provide the meaningful frame to identify and to interpret social events.

There is a great variety of data on how categories of goals and their subgoals regulate processes of understanding and remembering social events. Information that leads to instantiation of a particular goal category, that is information about individuals' motives, interest, etc., can have a decisive effect on processing social input. If such information is easily detected, or if it is at the beginning, instead of the end of the information flow, the event is understood or understood better, and therefore is better remembered (Owens, Bower, & Black, 1979; Lichtenstein & Brewer, 1980). If goal-means connections in a story are explicit rather than implicit, memory for a test improves significantly (Bower, et al., 1979; Black & Bern, 1981; Haberland & Bringham, 1978; Mandler & Johnson, 1977). How fast a story is read depends positively on how easily the goal-means relations between episodes can be detected (Seifert, Robertson & Black, 1982; Smith & Collins, 1981). In a recognition test for a text memory, a statement is recognized faster, and more often, when it is primed by a statement about a relevant goal link, instead of by a statement with a similar term (Abbot & Black, 1980).

Instantiation of an appropriate goal category results in selectivity in processing event information. Statements about story episodes that form a main line of goal realization are better remembered than statements depicting episodes that are more marginal (Trabasso, Seco, & van der Broek, 1984). Statements depicting story episodes that are not components of other episodes and either introduce a character realizing his or her main goal, or form a sequence that leads from the beginning to the end of the event, are better recalled and judged as more important than other statements of the story (Omanson, 1982). Interruptions and inadequacies in events described in a story are remembered differently depending on their relation to the main goal: Those that block the goal realization are remembered better than others (Bower et al., 1979; Graesser, 1981). When an event ends in failure, conditions of the main goal activation and realization are the first objects to be inquired about by an observer who tries to explain the failure (Leddo & Abelson, 1986).

The main goals in a story are better recalled than their subgoals; the more distant a subgoal is in a goal-means network, the worse is its memory in a free recall task (Black & Bower, 1980; Thorndyke, 1977). Priming by story episodes increase free-recall of main goals, rather than episodes subsequent in time-order (Galambos & Rips, 1982; Nottenburg & Shoben, 1980). This does not mean that individuals are not able to recollect a temporal sequence of story episodes when it is needed (Barsalow & Sewell, 1984; Bower et al., 1979). However, the way such episodic sequences are identified and remembered depends on the presence and content of goal-relevant information. When a text to be memorized includes randomly mixed descriptions of two independent episode networks, these networks are regrouped as independent clusters in a free recall (Mandler, 1978).

Event schema and its goal categories are responsible for specific biases in information processing. The more directly information is implied by the main goal in a story, the more likely this information is to be falsely recognized (Abbott & Black, 1980; Bower et al., 1979). In the case of goal-related information, the amount of false recognitions does not depend on the number of goal implications mentioned in the text. However, in the case of information relevant to marginal goals in the story, the number of false recognitions depends positively on the number of implications of these goals in the text (Walker & Yekovich, 1984). This finding indicates that the categories pertinent to the main goals, in contrast to the marginal goals, are activated during text comprehension and regulate this process via top-down expectations.

If goal categories with their means-to-goal links affect strongly the understanding and remembering of social stories and events, it is not a surprise that when different goal categories are activated to frame the same incoming stimuli, the situation is understood differently, in a way that is relevant to the content of each goal category (Bartlett, 1932: Bower, 1978; Zadny & Gerard, 1974).

Several data confirm the hypothesis that cognitive building blocks in understanding events and stories are episodes involving realization of subgoals to the main goal. Such a subgoal-realization episode forms an independent unit in memory: number of actions within an episode affects remembering of these actions but has no effect on remembering of actions from other episodes of the story (Black & Bower, 1980). How detailed is the perception of such episodes depends on predictability of an ongoing event within a given schema frame. Disturbances and unexpected facts within a particular event's component results in emergence of more detailed and more atomistic units of interpretation. This observation applies to situations where somebody is observing an event, as well as taking part in an event as the agent (Newtson, 1976; Newtson, Enquist, & Bois, 1977; Wegner & Vallacher, 1986). No matter how detailed the building blocks of an event interpretation, they are organized around subgoals of a main goal. When reading sentences in a story, the longest time is taken to read sentences that open and end story episodes. The content of these sentences deals with conditions or indicators of goal instantiation and with results of actions pursuing these subgoals (Haberland, 1980).

There is no such extensive research on more complex event knowledge. It might be assumed, in accordance with Schank and Abelson's analyses (Abelson, 1976, 1981; Schank, 1982), that in the case of knowledge about events less situationally anchored and more open in terms of optional plans and strategies, the dominant role of goal categories in understanding, projecting or remembering should be more spectacular, because of stronger demands for top-down processing. Some data are relevant to more abstract event schema. In the Reiser, Black, and Lehnert (1982) study, the subjects used general plots of goals and plans as categorization principles when asked to categorize stories. In a study by Seifert and Black (1983), subjects were confronted with several stories and asked to create for each story, their own, similar one. The story written by subjects were similar in terms of general plot of goals. It is not clear, however, if the subjects' ability to abstract general patterns of goals, and then to use them as a production device, reflects the social knowledge structure, as the authors suggest, or rather an ability to think abstractly under task demand. In six experiments reported by Seifert, Abelson, and McKoon (1986) there were no indications that subjects spontaneously used more abstract action schemata, but they used this abstract principle when it was suggested in the instructions.

The growing number of data confirm, then, diverse implications of the assumption that event schemata represent an individual's knowledge that regulates understanding and remembering information on social activities and situations. However, there is a lack of a theory and systematic studies on qualitatively different types of event schemata. Also, there are no significant data or conceptualizations on the development of event schemata. The exception is an important work of Nelson (1986) on the structure of event schemata among young children. One possible reason why developmental questions do not attract more attention is a close relationship between the majority of the preceding studies and the artificial intelligence paradigm. A weak point of this paradigm is that it does not provide a conceptual framework to analyze natural, content-specific mechanisms of knowledge formation. Only already formed, and structurally stabilized packages of human knowledge are, and perhaps can be simulated on a computer.

Another important issue that should be addressed in future research are conditions of self-involvement. Event schemata, as well as other forms of action-oriented schemata, include knowledge on rules under which the self begins to be preoccupied with a particular goal and enacts specific plans and behaviors. It is this topic that links action-oriented schemata to mechanisms of motivation. Except for the interesting experiments by Langer on reactions to requests for help (Langer & Abelson, 1972; Langer, Blank & Chanowitz, 1978), there are no other data directly pertinent to this crucial problem.

GOAL CATEGORIES IN THE REPRESENTATION OF PERSON KNOWLEDGE

Our common observations, as well as empirical data, suggest convincingly that, besides events, other entities naturally identified in social reality are people. People are obviously independent units of our interpretations, predictions, and our memories; and, therefore, our knowledge systems should be organized, among others, around persons—particular individuals, classes of individuals, or humans in general.

Some recent data provide simple but strong arguments that knowledge structures are naturally organized around persons. For instance, Pryor and Ostrom (1981) have shown that if the input information can be referred to a familiar person, memory for the input is much better then when the input has no such personal reference. Similarly, Srull (1983) found that the same behavioral descriptions are better remembered when they are outlined as characteristics of some person, than when there is no such personal outline.

How is person knowledge represented? In particular, what is the role of goal and action categories in representation of person knowledge? In contrast to event knowledge, this topic is rarely addressed directly. Classical studies on knowledge structures relate to how we form person impressions, but they lack detailed inquiries about the internal structure and function of that knowledge system. The first systematic attempt to study person knowledge is known as the "implicit personality theory" approach (Schneider, 1973). Within this framework, person knowledge seems to consist of psychological trait dimensions that implicate each other to a different extent. The studies were concerned almost exclusively with formal characteristics of these interdependencies (e.g., their complexity, or centrality of a dimension). One of several weak points of this approach was a simplistic, nonstructural notion of knowledge, and not surprisingly inability to produce assumptions on how these knowledge structures regulate cognitive processes, not to mention behavior.

More recently, there was a series of studies on the influence of processing set on the organization of personal input data (Hastie, Park, & Weber, 1984; Wyer, & Gordon, 1984). The objective of these studies was to identify natural ways an individual stores personal information in different task contexts. However, the obtained data do not provide for statements of consistent relationships. More important, it is not clear what could be responsible, or in what degree, for the observed differences between processing tasks: the structure of the task together with the provided material or the structure of knowledge that regulates processing. More interesting data were collected in studies on the content of personal knowledge in naturalistic situations (Cantor, Mischel, & Schwartz, 1982). These data will be discussed later.

In general, the scattered findings do not provide convincing and consistent hints and constraints on our conceptualizations of the internal structure of personal knowledge. After reviewing the literature, Wyer and Gordon (1984) suggest that the obtained data do not prove a schematic form of person knowledge representation. They insist that the knowledge we use to form a person impression, at least on a basis of abstract personality traits, might be organized rather within semantic networks of psychological terms, or by simple evaluative criteria.

However, it might be argued that some recent findings indicate clearly the schematic representation of person knowledge and, more important, they suggest the action-oriented character of this representation. For example, some studies show that person knowledge is strongly intertwined with knowledge about social situations typical for the persons. In naturalistic studies by Cantor et al. (1982) subjects were asked to imagine typical players of everyday roles, these players in situations typical for them, or the situations themselves. Time of formation of such images and number and content of information in descriptions of the images were recorded. It appeared that images of a role player in situation were faster to form than images of a role player "as such." Images of situations were fastest to form and included the greatest amount of information, but a great part of this information consisted of psychological characteristics of persons participating in these situations.

Data from a study by Zuroff (1982) support these observations. Results of Zuroff's study indicate that the more familiar one is with a particular person, the more "interactionist" is one's knowledge about this person; that is, the target's traits are more likely to be perceived as anchored, in specific ways, to concrete situations rather than as universal dispositions.

Some data on the role of a processing set in person information processing can be interpreted as supportive of the preceding conclusions. In Hoffman, Mischel, and Mazze's study, the subjects processed descriptions of a person's activity in two rather naturalistic contexts (instruction to remember the input, or to empathize with the target), and in two rather unrealistic contexts (instruction to image the target's "personality", or to predict the target's behavior "five years ahead"). The subjects were asked to categorize the descriptions. In the first two conditions they organized the input according to the target's main goals involved in the activity, while in the last two conditions they organized the input into abstract trait categories. The input was remembered better by other subjects when it was organized into goal categories by the memory task subjects. Results from other experiments suggest that under contextually nonspecific or difficult conditions (e.g., in some impression set conditions), trait organization of impression formation is regulated by normative, and perhaps semantic criteria of traits or trait-terms interdependencies (Cohen & Ebbesen, 1979; D'Andrade, 1965), or by evaluative, good-bad criteria (Rosenberg & Sedlak, 1972). Although the findings do not provide clear suggestions as to the conditions of trait versus goal category processing, they support Cantor et al. and Zuroff's general observations. In real life situations, individuals spontaneously organize personal input around a person's goal categories, and this form of organization seems to be functional to situational demands.

Taken together the preceding data seem to indicate that person knowledge describes personal dispositions and goals in interaction with situations typical for the person's social environment. The more organized or schematic this knowledge, the more situation and behavior-related its content. In opposition to the old assumptions, it is not a knowledge about personal traits, whatever their organization could be.

If person knowledge, at least an important part of it, consists of both situational and psychological content, what does its internal organization look like? It will be argued below that person knowledge could be represented in some form of action-oriented schemata, the actor schemata.

Person Knowledge Within Actor Schemata

It might be assumed that when a given individual is playing a given role repetitively, or within a long time frame, a generic knowledge package referring specifically to this individual develops. This knowledge system is represented in an actor schema. The internal structure of an actor schema reflects the action-oriented character of its roots and ways that it functions. The dominant elements of this schema are the actor's goals categories: The actor is described as a relatively permanent carrier of particular goals. These goals usually form a pattern: They may be interdependent in their activation and fulfillment and in their strategies of realization. They may be organized in hierarchies of importance or as conflicting forces. Mythologies and religions, as well as literature, provide a diversified panorama of prototypical characters defined primarily by goals they carry and realize. The assumption here is that goals or patterns of goals are basic building blocks of our common sense knowledge about people. Other elements of an actor schema are categories of attributes identifying a person as carrying the actor's goals (e.g., social status attributes), conditions that activate the goal-related actions, conditions (like specific inner dispositions) that regulate ways and chances of goal realization, and specific strategies of these realizations, including strategies of interaction with partners.

Certainly, these elements are interrelated and form a system, with subsystems and options. A person knowledge package is represented usually in a complex schema. This schema may include detailed relations (e.g., between parameters of different conditions, strategies undertaken and results of a given goal realization). Also, there are certainly intraindividual and interindividual differences in terms of how complex and how organized such packages of person knowledge are. However, considering the scarcity of pertinent data, it would be too early to propose any elaborate model describing these complexities and differences.

Within an actor's schema, the actor's partners are represented in categories subordinate to the main actor's goals. They are described, for instance, as collaborators or antagonists. Also, their behaviors and dispositions, including their goals, are represented within categories of conditions and as means to the main actor's goals activation and realization. Generally, within a given actor schema, other people and social objects are represented instrumentally to the main actor's goal and possible strategies.

One consequence of the proposed assumptions is that our person knowledge, at least in modern societies, is pluralistic. We do not usually possess one universal "implicit personality theory" that applies to a particular person, or a class of them. Person knowledge, because of its roots in different networks of social actions, is organized within different sets of social actors schemata. There might be family life, professional life, or peer group life schemata of actors; and they may apply to the same person as alternative cognitive frames to understand him or her. It is a matter of empirical study to differentiate social backgrounds of actor schemata, and it is a challenge for future studies to describe the mechanisms of actor schemata development on the basis of different social contexts.

Both event schema and actor schema have an action-oriented structure, with dominant categories of goals as sources of action; however, they differ. Knowledge represented in an event schema describes social reality as an ordered, pragmatic stream of goal-generated episodes pursuing the goals. Knowledge represented in an actor schema describes social reality in terms of specified carriers of goals, where these goals, under specified conditions, might generate plans, then actions. It is not a linear description of reality but a description in terms of relatively stable agencies that generate social actions.

Goal Categories in the Representation of General Knowledge about Persons

Two kinds of person knowledge systems are organized within the actor schemata. The *general person knowledge* refers to categories of persons (e.g., to a father as a member of a family, or to a specific social role, like a teacher). An *individualized person knowledge* refers to single, concrete individual—to my father, or to my math teacher.

General person knowledge concerns humans in general or specific categories of individuals. This knowledge is organized within general actor schemata. The actor's goal categories, as was assumed already, are dominant building blocks of such schemata, and they might have a least two forms. In the first form, they prescribe an actor who carries specific goals as answers for specific life demands, or situational demands. So, the goals are prescribed in this form as stemming from a specific position of an actor in the social environment. Examples are role schemata, like "a leader," or "a father" and schemata of actors in short-term contexts, like "a guest." Life and situational demands usually delineate a spectrum of possible actor's goals, where some of them are more prototypical than others. The knowledge about relations between these different goal configurations, related dispositions and conditions and possible ways of demands fulfillment is the most important content in the general actor schemata. Our knowledge about "a father" category that depicts a class of individuals in a family life include a spectrum of possible answers—in goal terms—for such family life demands as child rearing. This knowledge might describe psychological dispositions that influence or determine the pattern of demand-relevant motives, interests, needs, specific ways of pursuing them, and chances of their realization.

The second form of a general person knowledge refers to categories of individuals who carry specific leit-motives, or patterns of them. The individuals, themselves, not social demands, are primal sources of goals here. Leit-motive is a basic goal or pattern of homogeneous goals that can be filled with specific values and might have concrete additional features in each individual case. Examples are actor schemata for "a revolutionist," or "a playboy" concept.

The concept of a role actor schema reminds one of Schank and Abelson's (1977) early conceptualization of a thema category. Both role and leit-motive actor schema are psychological counterparts of sociological role concepts, but they also differ from them significantly. First, they are cognitive schemata, not sets of social expectations or internalized norms and standards. As cognitive schemata, they possess the distinctive features of these mental structures: (a) They are active procedures to understand and memorize specific aspects of social reality; (b) they include prototypical value configurations; and (c) they represent packages of knowledge with hierarchically organized internal structures. Also, there are no obvious isomorphic relationships between contents of role-relevant social expectations and generalized knowledge about person categories. There may be idiosyncratic variances in general actor schemata among individuals. However, they should be coordinated in some way and thus enable members of a given group to cooperate in a manner predictable for each other.

A good case to observe the function of a generalized person knowledge structure is impression formation of an unfamiliar person. It is a clear example of how schema generated, top-down processes affect an interpretation of personal data. In studies by Trzebinski and Richards (1986), it was assumed that if goal categories are dominant in an actor schema, the earlier and more completely these categories were instantiated by person characteristics, the more complete and subjectively certain would be the processes of top-down activation of specific expectations and default values to interpret and organize the input into a global impression. It was assumed further that, if an input included personal characteristics directly relevant to the goal categories of a given actor schema (i.e., description of a target's motives, interests, etc.), the instantiation of goal categories should be faster and more complete and should lead, therefore, to more elaborate and meaningful impressions than in the case of characteristics not directly relevant to goal categories (e.g., related to means-to-goal categories, such as description of target's abilities, experiences, disadvantages, etc.). Memory for an input depends on an elaboration of the corresponding understanding, so it was expected that in the first case the input would be better remembered than in the second case.

Female subjects were provided with characteristics of several women in the form of short sentences. These sentences differed in two ways: Some referred to women in family life situations and others to women in professional life situations. Within these two categories some sentences described women's goals (e.g., what she cared about), and some described women's capabilities and devices to realize the goals. These sentences were selected after a pilot study aimed to provide lists of common attributes of typical women in family or professional life contexts. The sentences depicting goals versus means differed only by a short phrase referring a given attribute to a goal or to an ability category (e.g., "striving to keep marriage intact" or "learned how to keep marriage intact").

In the first study, a subject was asked to press a button if she felt that she had a general impression of the target woman after reading the provided information. After that, she was asked to evaluate how confident she was that her impression accurately fit the real person. Finally, she was asked to describe the content of the impression. Observed were subjective time of impression formation, confidence in impression, and number of independent units of information in an impression description. In the second study, the subjects were asked to recall the provided characteristics. In both studies half of the subjects were unobtrusively exposed to family terms, and half were exposed to nonsocial terms. The expectation was that the goal-related characteristics of the target woman would facilitate top-down processing of the input, primarily when it was congruent in content with cognitive schema active at the moment. This condition should be met in the family priming and family characteristic case. The family priming should activate the representation of family life, which would function as a cognitive template that provides a basis for structuring impressions of the target. The schema of a mother/wife actor within this representation should be the most likely category to organize processing of the woman's family characteristics. If the mother/wife goal categories are dominant within this schema, the woman's goal-related input characteristics, as opposed to means-related ones, were expected then to result in a more elaborate and confident impression and in a better memory for the input.

The results for the number of information units in subjects' impressions and for subjects' confidence in their impressions are presented in Figures 10.1 and 10.2.

It appears that, after family as opposed to neutral priming, there was much more information in the impression descriptions based on family goal than family means-to-goal-related characteristics. Also, family priming was followed by more confident impressions based on family goals rather than means-to-goal-related characteristics. The data indicated also that, after family priming, but not after neutral priming, family goal-related characteristics were better remembered than family means-to-goals ones. There were no differences in impression formation time. However, there was no clear expectation about these data. The initial structuring processes should be easier and so take less time in the case of goal-related characteristics and priming-input congruence but activated top-down processes, because of their greater elaboration, could take more time.

It is worthwhile to note that the important role priming has played in the observed relationships supports strongly the interpretation of the data in schemata terms. It seems that it was a goal-centered schema that was primed and that interacted differently with the input depending both on the content-congruence and goal relevance of it and thus produced different results in person impression and memory.

If goals categories are dominant in actor schemata, they should play a decisive role not only in person impression formation but also in inferences generated on the basis of input personal characteristics. An actor schema plays a double role in such a case: It interprets and organizes the input into a meaningful person impression, and then, during inference phase, it reinterprets and elaborates the initially re-

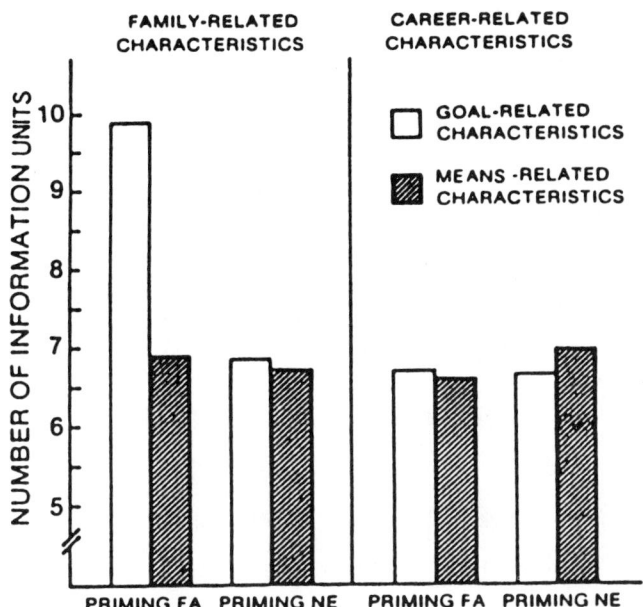

FIG. 10.1 Number of information units in subjects' impression description as a function of content and goal relatedness of input person characteristics and priming (FA = family, NE = neutral). (From Trzebinski, J., & Richards, K. (1986). The role of goal categories in person impression. *Journal of Experimental Social Psychology, 22,* 216–227. Copyright, 1986 by Academic Press Inc., and reproduced by permission).

membered impressions, on the basis of schema driven top-down processes. If actor goal categories are dominant in both of these processes then, as the first studies confirmed, the personal input is selected and interpreted primarily in terms of how well and in what characteristic ways the person realizes the constituent goals of the relevant actor schema. Further, instantiated goal categories are most likely to serve as a strategic data base for the most meaningful and far-reaching top-down inferences. In that way, goal categories significantly determine the spontaneous or required expectations, evaluations, etc. about a given person.

It might be expected, therefore, that the more closely required inferences are related to the main goals of the actor schema instantiated by the target person, the faster and with more certainty these inferences should be produced. The assumption that required inferences are faster when the content of a representation of a target matches the content of the inferences is supported by standard findings in studies on cognition (e.g., Rosch, 1975) and social cognition (e.g., Taylor & Fiske, 1981).

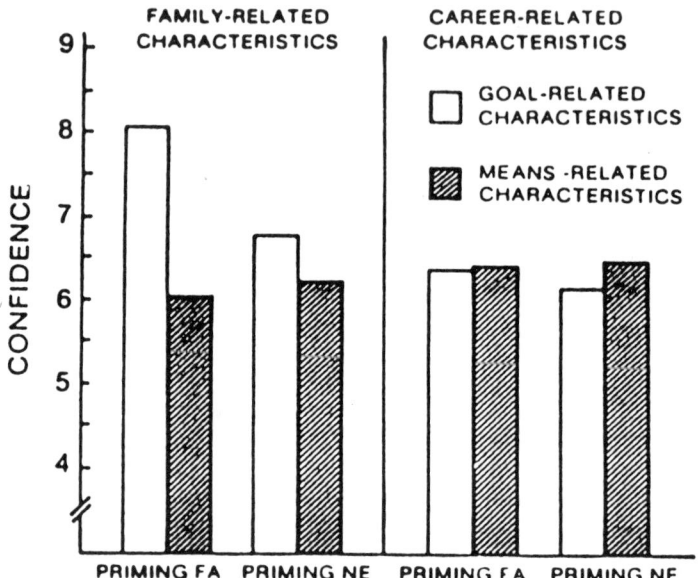

FIG. 10.2 Confidence in impression (on a 10-point scale where higher scores indicate more confidence) as a function of content and goal relatedness of input person characteristic and priming (FA = family, NE = neutral). (From Trzebinski, J., & Richards, K. (1986). The role of goal categories in person impression. *Journal of Experimental Social Psychology, 22,* 216–227. Copyright, 1986 by Academic Press Inc., and reproduced by permission).

In an experiment by Trzebinski, McGlynn, Gray, and Tubbs (1985) subjects were unobtrusively primed by family life cue-terms, professional life cue-terms, or by socially unspecific terms. Next, each subject studied a list of arbitrary personality trait adjectives that were said to describe a 30-year-old woman. Trait terms on each list differed randomly. Finally, subjects were asked to make inferences about the woman by pressing as fast as possible a button to indicate whether statements presented successively on a screen applied to the target woman "more" or "less" than to the "typical, American 30-year-old woman." They were informed that their responses would be timed and checked for accuracy against the actual data about the target.

The presented statements, and, therefore, the required answers differed in two ways: They referred to a mother/wife role or a career woman role, and they referred to goals that were fundamental, important, or peripheral (but all independently evaluated as characteristic to the same, high degree) for the mother/wife or the career woman role. Before exposure to the input, half of the subjects were asked to form an

10. THE ROLE OF GOAL CATEGORIES

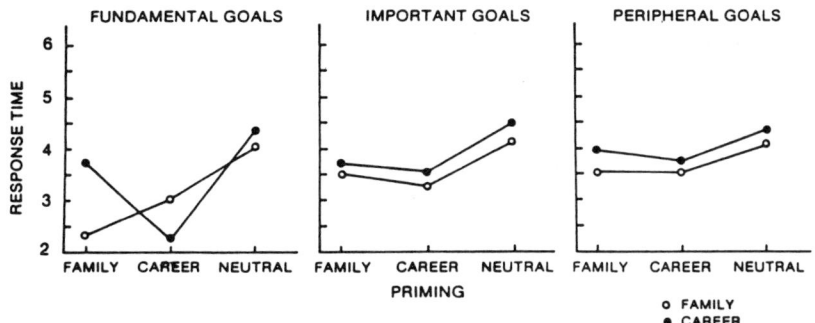

FIG. 10.3 Mean response time in seconds in impression processing set as a function of question content, (family or career) question goal-relevance, and priming. (From Trzebinski, J., McGlynn, R., Gray, G., & Tubbs, D. (1985). The role of categories of an actor's goal in organizing inferences about a person. *Journal of Personality and Social Psychology, 48*(6), 1387–1397. Copyright, 1985 by the American Psychological Association Inc., and reproduced by permission).

impression of the woman, another half were asked to remember correctly the terms presented.

The dependent variables were response time and subjective confidence for answers to the questions in a 2 × 3 × 2 × 3 experimental design with the between-subjects variables being processing set and priming, and the within-subjects variables being question content and question goal relevance. The data for response time and confidence, for the impression processing set are presented in Figures 10.3 and 10.4.

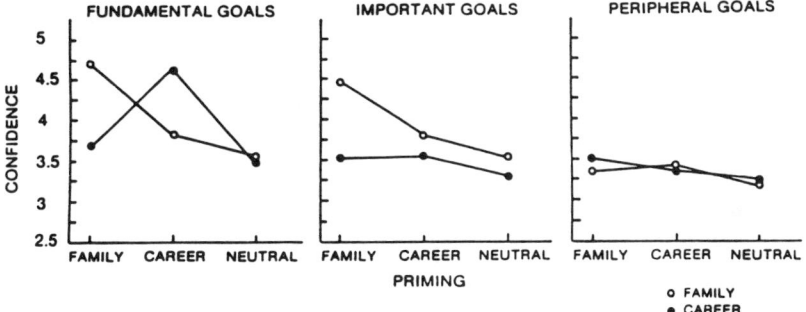

FIG. 10.4. Mean subjective confidence in own impressions, in impression processing set, as a function of question content (family or career), question goal-relevance, and priming. (From Trzebinski, J., McGlynn, R., Gray, G., & Tubbs, D. (1985). The role of categories of an actor's goal in organizing inferences about a person. *Journal of Personality and Social Psychology, 48*(6), 1387–1397. Copyright, 1985 by the Americam Psychological Association Inc., and reproduced by permission).

As predicted, the data indicated that the inferences were made fastest and were most confident when questions congruent in content with priming concerned fundamental goals and when subjects had an impression set. There were no goal-relevant differences after neutral priming or in memory set. Again, the important role of the priming factor in producing the observed differences indicates that the structure of primed schemata, rather than situational factors (e.g., goal-relevancy effect), determined the character of inference processes. Inferences about a person appear to be more certain and easier to make when they are congruent in content with the main goal categories of active, relevant actor schema.

Goal Categories in Representation of Knowledge about Specific Individuals

Knowledge that operated in processes observed in the preceding studies was undoubtedly general. It relates to specific categories of people, not to a single, concrete person. This generalized person knowledge regulates our understanding and memory of an unfamiliar person, as well as, perhaps, thinking on more abstract issues. Has individualized person knowledge the same actor-oriented character as the generalized knowledge?

There are two premises for a positive answer. First, in the formation of person-specific knowledge, an appropriate general actor schema should provide initially a frame to structure the incoming personal stimuli. This general schema regulates the contents of impressions, inferences, and memories we have on the person and, as a result, the developed person knowledge should reveal the global characteristics of the general actor schema. This pattern schema generation mechanism of knowledge development was suggested by Rumelhart (1984).

Second, we understand the given person in the framework of context and content-specific social actions, where these actions are understood on the bases of appropriate action-oriented schema (e.g., specific event schema). It gives specific action-related contexts for our understanding of the target person. Working in concordance, general actor schema and relevant action contexts should structure development of specific person knowledge into an individualized actor schema. Once individualized person knowledge systems are formed, there is obviously a mutual influence of generalized and individualized person knowledge systems during their future development.

The hypothesis about an actor schema as a possible representation of knowledge about a particular individual was addressed in a study by

Trzebinski (1985). The object of this study was representation of knowledge about psychological traits of familiar persons. These knowledge systems were assumed to be organized within means-to-goal categories of particular actor schemata relevant to these persons. Thus, knowledge about internal dispositions of the person should facilitate, allow, disturb, or make impossible attainment of his or her goals as the specific actor, and should determine the ways of attainment of these goals.

The knowledge about these particular actor's goals and psychological means and conditions for their attainment develop during long-term experiences with the person, within a given social context, and on the basis of context-dependent, action-oriented schemata. Such knowledge regulates ways we interpret this person in sequences of emerging episodes or within more global contexts. It determines out attention for selective information about this person, including her or his own communications. This knowledge, therefore, regulates the ways we understand and recollect memories about this person.

The second, related assumption addressed in this study concerned the polymorphic structure of knowledge about a single person and, therefore, the alternative ways we can understand the same person. If single person knowledge develops within a particular social context, and on the basis of context relevant general person schemata, then if we become familiar with a person in different contexts, of broad and sustained enough networks of social actions, different actor schemata might develop. When activated, they would regulate the different ways we understand a given person.

The teenaged female subjects were asked to rate specified familiar persons (e.g., mother, best friend) on a provided list of trait dimensions. The dimensions were selected after a pilot study as most often chosen to describe familiars. Two sets of dimensions were then identified on the basis of independent evaluation by judges from the studied population: dimensions related to psychological traits, the presence or absence of which were important for attainment of family actors' goals, and dimensions related to traits important in the same sense to peer (partnership) life goals.

To delineate the role person knowledge plays in such descriptions, the following manipulations were applied. First, before ratings, the subjects were randomly primed by family cue-terms, peer relations cue-terms, or they were not primed. Second, after familiars' roles were individually named by each subject, and the task was presented, but before ratings were started, half of the subjects completed a free-sorting task to make them concentrate more on the psychological characteristics of the familiars. Finally, one week after the ratings were made, the subjects filled out a test measuring interval consistency of judgments about relationships between family actors' goals and peer group actors' goals.

The main dependent variable was variability in ratings on a dimension, interpreted as a measure of cognitive elaboration of person description on a given dimension. The hypothesis was that, depending on priming, the most variable ratings of familiars would be made on dimensions instrumentally related to family or peer actors' goals. Moreover, it was expected that this effect would be stronger after previous concentration on targets and, in the case of subjects with relatively consistent judgments, on family goals or peer goals respectively. The rationale for the last two predictions was as follows. The concentration would make it possible to activate and elaborate more memories and general judgments and evaluations based on active knowledge structures about a particular familiar person. The subsequent ratings should then reflect more clearly the content of this knowledge, for instance the assumed goal-related character of this knowledge. Because the interval consistency of goal-related judgments might reflect the more developed structure of actor schemata within a given social context (family or peer-life), subjects with more consistent judgments were expected to reveal more strongly the goal instrumentality effect. The results are presented in Figure 10.5.

The data confirm expectations about goal-instrumental and content-dependent selectivity in the elaboration of description of familiar persons. The fact that this selectivity was higher after concentration on the targets, before descriptions took place, reinforces the assumption that it was determined by a single person knowledge system rather than by generalized person knowledge. Concentration on a single, concrete person should activate thoughts and memories related directly to him or her. Therefore, if it were a general action-related knowledge rather than an individualized one that was primed and then regulated person description, the expected goal-related selectivity would be reduced rather than enhanced after concentration on particular, familiar persons. The results are the opposite and suggest that there were single person knowledge systems primed and then operating. It appears that the internal organization of this individualized personal knowledge is goal-oriented with psychological dispositions represented as means and conditions for the goals. The closer the content of a person description (e.g., in the form of required dimension ratings) to the activated means and conditions categories, the easier to make and more elaborate the description.

The data are also congruent with the assumption of alternative knowledge systems that may refer to a single familiar person. These data contradict the presupposition of universalistic person-relared knowl-

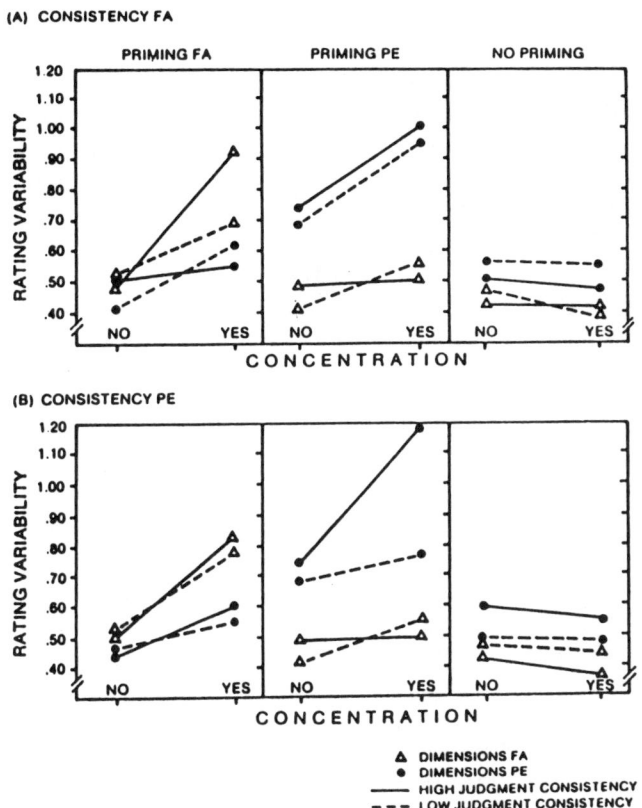

FIG. 10.5 Level of person rating variability as a function of priming (FA = family vs PE = peer vs No priming), previous concentration, dimension content (FA = instrumental to family goals, PE = instrumental to peer goals), and judgment consistency (a) FA (for family goals), and (b) PE (for peer goals). (From Trzebinski, J. (1985). Action-oriented representation of implicit personality theories. *Journal of Personality and Social Psychology, 48*(5), 1266–1278. Copyright, 1985 by the American Psychological Association Inc., and reproduced by permission).

edge systems. It seems that in a pluralistic social reality, we possess alternative action-oriented packages of knowledge about a particular person which, depending on context, can differentially structure our impressions of this person. It appeared in this study that for 17-year-old girls, family and partnership social contexts have provided the basis for two alternative sets of individualized cognitive frames to understand the same close familiars. Probably, for these persons, these social worlds were universalistic enough and independent enough to structure meaningfully experiences with these people in different ways. Although the mechanisms involved in the development of such knowledge systems and the structure of these systems were far beyond the scope of this study, the findings provide a rather clear argument for the action-oriented and plymorphic character of individualized person knowledge.

Taken together, the data from these studies confirm several expectations implied by the assumption about actor schemata as a representation of person knowledge. These confirmations are provided by studies of different aspects of person information processing: organizing input data, making required inferences based on initial data, memory for the input, and interpretation of familiar people on provided dimensions. It is worthwhile to note also the diversity of personal contents involved in the studied processes: They deal with motives and abilities, as well as abstract psychological traits. All of these results seem to indicate the importance of an actor schema as a flexible and context-bounded organization of both general and individualized knowledge about people.

Actor schemata are not the only possible mental structures to store and to interpret personal information. Another way to view the presented data and other findings on person memory and perception is that they seem to identify some conditions under which different forms of knowledge structures become activated and regulate person understanding.

It seems that actor schemata, as well as other action-oriented schemata, are activated by conditions that specify clearly enough the real-life social context. The action-oriented schemata, as was argued, are content and context specific, and anchored developmentally and functionally to natural niches of an individual's social life. The less contextually-bounded a specific task, the more likely other structures, at least temporarily, will provide the basis for understanding processes. They may include some context-independent, general heuristics, like evaluative criteria in person understanding. There are data indicating the central role of an evaluative factor in organizing person impression in nonnaturalistic, abstract settings (Hartwick, 1982; Rosenberg & Sedlak, 1972).

Another possible cognitive device in such nonnaturalistic tasks is semantic associations among language terms depicting the realm of interpersonal experiences. There are clear indications that in abstract "personality" descriptions without meaningful context, semantic links between psychological traits play a significant role (D'Andrade, 1965; Wyer & Gordon, 1982; Smith & Kihlstrom, 1987). Probably, there are other possible cognitive frames to structure experiences with people, such as formalized "school" knowledge systems, like naive versions of scientific psychological assumptions or ethical and legal codes. It is likely that none of these knowledge structures has a schematic form of representation, as Wyer and Gordon (1984) suggest.

GOAL CATEGORIES IN THE REPRESENTATION OF KNOWLEDGE ABOUT SOCIAL ORGANIZATION

The previous data support the assumption that persons can be represented cognitively as actors within specific social action networks. Therefore, to understand others, an individual has to understand social action environments within which these others activate their goals and pursue them. One form of knowledge about this environment is event knowledge represented in event schemata. Probably it is developmentally the first kind of organization of an individual's social knowledge (Nelson, 1986).

However, the social reality, as understood by an individual, consists not only of single persons involved in undergoing social events and interacting within their contexts. As common sense suggests, social reality is populated also by social organizations: different groups like family or a peer clique, institutions like a school or a hospital, and macro-social structures like a nation or a power elite. Through our life we develop and elaborate knowledge about different organizations of persons and groups interrelated in some stable ways.

Surprisingly, there are almost no empirical data on how an individual's knowledge about structures of social relationships that constitute social organization are represented. Social psychological studies concentrate primarily not on an individual's knowledge about social organization but on one's knowledge about an assembly of persons who share specific attributes ("rich," "catholics," e.g., studies of social comparison), or who believe that they "form the group" ("we catholics," e.g., studies on social categorization or social identity processes).

A Social Unit Schema

It will be proposed here, that the individual's knowledge about social organizations may be represented in a specific form of action-oriented schema: a schema unit of actors (i.e., unit schema). Knowledge organized within a unit schema is about stable patterns of interdependencies among persons, or groups constituting a given social organization. Persons and groups are modeled as carriers of specific goals that are autonomous, that is, irreducible to means-to-another actor's goal, as in actor schemata. Within a unit schema, actor's goals, being autonomous, are interdependent in the sense that realization of goals of one actor affects ways and chances of realization of goals of another actor. Knowledge about an actor's goal interdependencies constitute an important content of a unit schema.

The interdependencies exist, primarily, between ways of realization and fulfillment of a given actor's goal and chances and ways of realization of another actor's goal. There are also other possible forms of dependencies between actors realizing their goals, and these dependencies may determine goals activation, interruption, termination, change, etc. In addition, these dependencies may generate their own specific goals regulating interpersonal behavior and attitudes within a group.

Microsociological and ethnomethodological field studies on family, peer groups, and institutional life provide a great amount of descriptive data that might illustrate how individuals understand social structures as interdependencies between actors pursuing their own goals (Garfinkel, 1967; Goffman, 1959). Studies by Wilson and Mulhall (1983) on understanding relations among members of families of alcoholics, seem to indicate that knowledge about the structure of an important group one belongs to may differ among group members, and that these differences may be related in a meaningful way to their behaviors. Data from Wyer and Gordon's (1984) study suggest that such knowledge could have a schematic representation because it seems to affect, in a schematic way, the memory for inconsistencies in intergroup relations.

However, the data are too indirect and too unsystematic to provide insight into the structural forms and functions of knowledge about social organizations. What is needed are clearly interpretable evidences of the particular role an individual's knowledge about interdependencies within social organization play in his or her understanding processes.

Moral Knowledge Within Unit Schemata

Relations between an individual's knowledge about the structure of a family and "everyday" moral judgements on family related matters were analyzed in studies by Trzebinski and Najda (1987). These studies were based on several assumptions about the organization and function of unit schemata. First, it was assumed that in a unit schema, actor's goals differ in how strongly their fulfillments positively affect the chances of other actors' goal fulfillments. The more the goals of other actors are positively and directly affected by the fulfillment of a given goal (i.e., the more important for a unit is this goal), the more positively valued will be actions aimed to this goal realization. Consequently, if goals pursued by two persons are in conflict, then actions, plans, interactions, etc. related to one's own categories of important goals are more likely to be evaluated as more justifiable, or "moral" than the actions, plans etc., stimulated by the goals of the other actor. It also can be expected that somebody's help in realization of important goals will seem more natural and "obvious" and, therefore, less rewarded by a group but more condemned if not undertaken. In an individual's knowledge, the goal importance hierarchy is a stable characteristic of a given social structure (e.g., a family). Therefore, from an individual's perspective, realization of an important goal, no matter its actual consequences or circumstances, deserves more than other goal realizations in terms of help or final outcome.

A special method has been developed for the analysis of goal interdependence within a group (Trzebinski & Najda, 1987). First, after a pilot study, a poll of motives, interests, and needs was collected that, according to common knowledge of the studied population, characterize family figures. In another pilot study, subjects were asked to decide, on the grounds of their own memories and knowledge, to what degree each goal from provided pairs of goals carried out by different family figures, depends on the other for its realization. The obtained data were submitted to network analysis. Network analysis is used to study relations among constituents of social or economic organizations and processes (Burt, 1982). In this study, the network analysis served to explore the internal structure of a family as represented by an individual (Krackhardt, 1987). It should be stressed that the measure of structural goal importance was based on the subject's descriptive, not evaluative, statements about "a typical family" and that the measure had an analytical character. The goal importance scores were products of reconstruction of the knowledge base for the preceding statements. Network analysis has provided, among other things, scores for the structural importance of each family actor's goal.

Data from additional studies (Trzebinski, 1986) indicate that different structural measures obtained by this method correlate substantially with external indicators of family knowledge content. For instance, it has appeared that knowledge about a "typical family" structure of goal interdependencies, as measured by this method, differ in meaningful ways between teenagers from full versus single parent families, between women occupying different family roles, and between individuals from different age groups. A positive correlation was also found between complexity scores of represented family interdependencies and ability for interpersonal decentration (Feffer, 1959).

In the three studies on "everyday" moral judgments, 18-year-old subjects were provided with descriptions of typical conflicts between a mother/wife figure, and a father/husband figure, or with descriptions of pairs of typical activities of these two family figures. Goals involved in each conflict or each pair of activities differed in their importance. The goal importance was based on scores obtained after the pilot study, with an assumption that the main features of family knowledge were shared among members of the studied population. The studies differed in terms of content and complexity of presented conflicts. Moreover, in the third study subjects were asked to generate their own best examples of actions pursuing the provided family goals. The subjects were asked to evaluate which motive or action in a conflict was more justifiable.

In agreement with expectations, the data indicated that the more structurally important the goal, the more likely it will be perceived as justifiable in family conflicts. This goal importance effect appeared to be independent of the effects of identification with the same sexed parent and of magnitude of empathy evoked by the person involved in a conflict.

It might be argued, then, that an individual's knowledge about structural interdependencies between goals of group members may contain some kind of moral knowledge that refers to this group's problems. This knowledge may regulate an individual's judgments on what is just or unjust, normal or abnormal in the interpersonal relations. Such knowledge might provide some moral algebra for evaluation of personal responsibilities, contributions, blame, compensations, etc. Moreover, because a given unit schema organizes knowledge about patterns of coexistence and interaction of goals, and means-to-goals within a group, it also provides specific frames to understand mechanisms and contents of social conflicts, distribution dilemmas, and prosocial and antisocial behaviors. Different aspects of moral knowledge organized within unit schemata are content and context specific. In heterogeneous modern societies, the moral algebra an individual possesses can be polymorphic in the same sense as are representations of person knowledge.

Lerner's "belief in a just world" hypothesis (Lerner, 1977, 1984) may be interpreted within the proposed conceptualization. Knowledge about a just world could be represented in the event or actor schemata. As mentioned, an important part of such schemata models relations between specific values of means and condition categories, and values of results of goal realization. These schemata relations describe the "nature" of the social reality from an individual perspective. They enable an individual to evaluate if "people get what they deserve," or "deserve what they get." If an individual can interpret events or a life path of a familiar person as matching the prescribed relations between values of the action categories, the events and facts are seen as "natural," the "predictable," and fundamentally "just." If an interpretation cannot reach an appropriate match, an individual looks for explanations that would reinstate the image of a "just reality" or may try to intervene or support intervention in the ongoing events to reshape them into a "just" order.

The assumption of event and actor schemata as representations for a "just world" concept may stimulate some elaborations of Lerner's hypothesis. The total structure of social events, as interpreted by a given schemata, should determine someone's way of construing explanations of a given fact and evaluations of how just it is, or how to deal with its injustice. Generally speaking, the feeling of justice or injustice should be related in systematic ways to broader processes of social understanding that operate within a frame of action-oriented schemata.

When social knowledge is represented within a unit schema, the content of a "just world" belief changes substantially. What counts in such a case is not a balance between "inputs" and "outputs" of individual's actions, but a balance between the role of an actor's goal in a stable network of group goals interdependence at one side, and the value of actions pursuing the goal against values of other actions taking place in a group at the other side. The justice notion has a more social character; it refers to relative social merits of actors' goal fulfillments.

Unit Schemata and Understanding Others

Three basic forms of social knowledge representation regulate the ways we understand others: schemata of events, actors, and units of actor.

In the event, schemata people are represented as actors in particular social actions. Event actors are mainly understood in terms of goals they bring to the event and in terms of conditions they create for actions of other participants in the event. For instance, in "a visiting doctor" script (Schank & Abelson, 1977), "a doctor" and "a client" categories are described primarily as carriers of specific goals and concrete plans that create an ordered flow of particular episodes. These categories do not include knowledge about stable patterns of goals, plans, and relevant dispositions that create potentialities for networks of institutionalized health-care-related events. Having only a collection of event schemata we cannot understand or predict emerging conflicts or changes within a given social context.

More powerful devices to understand complexities and dynamisms of the social reality are provided by actor schemata. Social knowledge represented in these schemata concerns particular actors, events, and relevant goals and plans. Knowledge about a hospital may be represented in that case in terms of sequences of intertwined events (e.g., an admission or operation), and in terms of the main actors (e.g., a doctor or a nurse) having specific patterns of goals, plans, and related dispositions.

Knowledge about an actor's goal repertoires enable an individual to understand more deeply possible alternative plans and actions, the probabilities and contents of conflicts, and changes. However, within this schemata there is a lack of knowledge about stable interdependencies between actor's goals. Therefore, the understanding of changes, conflicts, possible alternatives is still restricted because it is tied to a perspective of a particular actor. Moreover, when a particular actor schema is activated, the partners of a person who instantiated this schema are understood instrumentally—in terms of means and conditions to the main actor's goals. The partner's goals are conceived as specific conditions, facilitating the handicapping of the main actor's goals. This aspect of instrumental person understanding is illustrated in the study of Wegner and Giuliano (1983), where the subjects read a story about interacting characters from the point of view of one specified character. It appears that they remembered goals of the central character much better than the goals of others, but they remembered quite well those facts about others that created conditions for realizing the central character's goals.

Knowledge about interdependencies between actors as carriers of autonomous sets of goals is organized within a unit schema. This kind of schemata predisposes an individual to understand persons in a noninstrumental way as independent, yet interrelated, participants of events. Unit schema is a device to understand the moral merits of actors' motives and actions and to understand fully individual's personalities and deep mechanisms of social interaction.

Understanding other people and social events depends not only on content, but also on representational forms of activated social knowledge. Further considerations of this problem require analyses of conditions and mechanisms involved in the development and situational activation of these different forms.

GOAL CATEGORIES IN THE REPRESENTATION OF SELF-KNOWLEDGE

Several recent investigations of self-knowledge and self-understanding differ significantly in theoretical assumptions and methodologies from the old view of the self as a unified collection of context-independent traits or attributes (Greenwald & Pratkanis, 1984). The new conceptualizations stress the inherently motivational character of the self-knowledge, pluralism of its content and structure and the social character of self understanding processes (Cantor, this volume; Cantor, Markus, Niedenthal & Nurius, 1986; Gergen & Gergen, 1983; Markus, this volume; Markus & Nurius, 1983).

Self-Knowledge in Action-Oriented Schemata

Consideration of action-oriented representations of social knowledge provides a model of self-knowledge that seems compatible with these recent propositions. It is argued that self-knowledge is represented within action-oriented schemata that generate motivational processes and behavioral decisions as natural aspects of their functioning. Self-knowledge can be organized within each of the three forms of schemata discussed. Within each of these schemata the self-knowledge is about a context-related pattern of goals and about related means and conditions, both in terms of psychological dispositions and situational factors, including reactions of partners. In each of these cases, the self is represented as a particular actor in a particular action network: as an event actor, a main actor, or as an actor belonging to and creating a particular social unit.

Self-knowledge might be organized within an event schema, for instance, as a "me-in-a-party." Such knowledge can differ in complexity and abstractness, but in each case its content is bounded to the characteristics of events represented in a schema. An important part of this knowledge, as well as self-knowledge organized within another action-oriented schemata, prescribes conditions of entering into a social situation as a participant of a given event. The behavioral consequences of this component of self-knowledge seem to be illustrated by the studies of Langer (Langer & Abelson, 1972; Langer et al., 1978). The pathological implications of a lack of this knowledge, in the case of everyday activities, can be inferred from data provided by Kuhl and Helle (1984).

Self-knowledge organized within event schemata enables an individual to plan specific routes of involvements in social situations; to construe specific aspirations; and to interact in specific ways with partners. This self-knowledge is tied to event contexts and might not be integrated within more abstract structures until different social actions being the roots for these knowledge systems become integrated themselves and until more complex event schemata develop. Probably, the event self-knowledge is the first form of the self-concept in young children because for them the social reality means streams of repetitive events (Nelson, 1986).

More integrative and abstract self-knowledge is organized within the actor schemata. They are developed in contexts of complex social action networks, such as family life or professional life, in which an individual is involved more permanently. As in the case of the person knowledge, these systems of self-knowledge are relatively abstracted from sequences of concrete events and are organized around patterns of personal goals rather than around the structure of actions. This knowledge is action-oriented, however, in the sense that it describes the self as a carrier of specific goals that implicate, more or less directly, particular sets of plans, behavioral strategies, and interpersonal activities which, under prescribed circumstances, construe the reality of concrete social actions. This kind of self-knowledge differs from the individualized person knowledge mainly because it includes more references to emotional, sensomotoric, and, most importantly, decisional experiences. Also, it is more elaborate in terms of situation conditions and means for achievement of personal goals.

Most integrated systems of self-knowledge are represented within unit schemata that organize knowledge about such important social life settings as a family, close partners, or a work team. These self-knowledge systems are inseparably tied with knowledge about respective partners and about goal interdependencies that relate the self and the partners within social units. Each of the proposed forms of self-knowledge implicates close relationships between self attributes and partner's attributes, but in the case of unit schemata, these relationships become important structural components of an individual's knowledge system. Within a unit schema, the self-knowledge of a mother is structurally related to her knowledge about her children and husband. This knowledge forms one organization depicting interdependent goals, related psychological traits of the family members, their interconnected behavioral strategies, and patterns of interactions. It is impossible to change the relevant self-knowledge without changing the knowledge about important partners, and vice versa. The embededness of self-knowledge within more global knowledge of an important social group is illustrated by the clinical observations of family therapists working with a "structural family approach" (Minuchin, 1974; Minuchin & Fishman, 1981).

Self-knowledge within the event, actor, and unit schemata may differ in terms of individualization. At one extreme, the self may be depicted as a particular actor participating in a given sort of social event. The self here enacts generally prescribed motives and activities, in the same sense that others might. Within these general prescriptions, there are some specific individual variants, referring to the self or to another individual, respectively. However, the structure and basic content of the self-knowledge is determined by generalized schemata.

At the other extreme, there might be self-knowledge with a highly idiosyncratic structure that describes the self as an actor involved in solving a particular historically located problem. The self-problem is described in terms of initial goals the self carries and challenges or obstacles for these goal realizations which have to be overcome. For instance, the self-as-a-tennis-player would describe a very personal history of an individual's goals and challenging plots of events that lead to a distinctive history of becoming a particular tennis player. The knowledge about our related activities, their development, or one partner's attitudes are integral parts of this self-knowledge. Particular episodes of enactment of such self-as-an-actor schema are understood in connection to each other, as parts of one, personal scenario. In contrast, episodes interpreted by less individualized self-knowledge systems are understood rather as successive, repetitive enactments of a general "theme."

The assumption that a problem schema (Rumelhart & Ortony, 1977) could be a representational form of idiosyncratic self-knowledge reminds one of Adler's concept of life goals (Adler, 1927; Adler, 1929). According to Adler, long-term life goals are established when children are confronted with handicaps, usually physical in nature, when striving to be like partners or older siblings. The style of life is shaped by specific configurations of social comparisons, the kinds of handicaps experienced, and the specific strategies of overcompensations that are learned.

Recently, the problem-related character of self-knowledge was suggested by Csikszentmihaly and Beattie (1979) who, similar to Adler, located the beginning of the self-problem in early childhood. Csikszentmihaly provided clinical data indicating that individuals can easily produce detailed descriptions of problem-centered personal histories, and that the character of these histories has some external validation. Gergens' notion of self-narratives, which will be discussed later, might also suggest that our self-knowledge can be organized in a form of specific problems we overcome through our life (Gergen & Gergen, 1983).

The assumption of idiosyncratic self-knowledge does not mean that it is impossible to analyze the structure, functioning, and development of these knowledge systems in terms of general regularities, in the same ways as other knowledge structures are analyzed. Idiosyncratic self-knowledge develops within a given social action context and obviously shares common characteristics with other action-oriented knowledge systems. This kind of self-knowledge, however, is perhaps most integrative and sustained and most difficult to change among other self-knowledge systems.

The preceding considerations stress again the polymorphic character of self-knowledge. This knowledge is organized within cognitive systems that differ not only in terms of anchoring to specific social actions, but also in terms of different schematic forms. However, how polymorphic the self is depends on the kind of social organization in which an individual is involved. More specifically, the structure of self-knowledge depends on the character of social action networks that create social environments for an individual. Neither polymorphic nor homomorphic structure of self-knowledge is an imminent characteristic of the individual's mind.

Self-Knowledge and Motivation

Action-oriented representations of self-knowledge regulate directly an individual's motivations and social behavior. Two kinds of motivational mechanisms are built into these representations. The first one produces task-oriented self-motivations; the second one produces ego-oriented motivations.

The first mechanism is based on a set of personal goals that constitute a dominant component of all forms of self-knowledge representation. When conditions of goal activation are instantiated by characteristics of a social context, these goal categories begin to regulate an individual's understanding and planning of activity. The activated goals and means-to goal categories generate and monitor an individual's decisions and actual behavior aimed toward fulfillment of the goals. Depending on the character of self-schemata and corresponding goal categories, these motivational processes and the resulting behavior may differ in terms of time-space frame, flexibility, and complexity. Examples of such self-generated task motivations are "responsible and fair" doctor caring for his patients' health, a piano player training his hands, and a husband striving to improve the quality of his family's house. In all these cases, if there are self-goal generated motives, they are experienced phenomenologically as natural imperatives that emanate from the organization of the world we live in and our place in this world.

This kind of task-oriented motivation does not attract much attention from social psychologists. The conceptualization seems similar to sociological concepts of roles, and role enactments, as motivational forces of social behavior. However, as was noted already, the concept of action-oriented schemata differs in many ways from that of social role. Cantor's concept of life tasks might be conceptually closer (Cantor, this volume; Niedenthal, Cantor & Kihlstrom, 1985). Descriptive data on students' self-related tasks suggest an important feature of this kind of motivation: Motivationally driven cognitive processes concern characteristics of the environment pertinent to task accomplishment rather than characteristics of the doer's self (Neidenthal et al., 1985). The proposed conceptualizations are also related in a general sense to Adler's concepts of life goals, life style, and the creative self (Adler, 1927, 1929).

The second kind of self-related motivations concerns the content of an individual's notion of the self. These motivation processes, which might be called ego-centered, have been studied rather intensively by personality and social psychologists. Within the presented theoretical framework, these processes are activated whenever an individual meets problems with an instantiation of the self-as-an-actor schemata within a context of ongoing social actions. There are two kinds of such problems. The first one deals with the issue of an actor's identification. An individual is confronted here with a lack of social support, or lack of other external evidences, for being the specific kind of actor he expected to be, according to his understanding of the social context. This lack of social support or other external evidence concerns specified, "definitional" attributes, and makes it disputable, or even impossible, to enter relevant social actions as a participant. Phenomenologically, it is experienced as a lack of self-identity within a given social context. An individual is thus motivated to define or to protect his or her identity within a framework of relevant, action-oriented schemata, and before his or her partner's audience. The antecedents and the process of identity building, as well as its social consequences, are described in the self-completion theory of Wicklund and Gollowitzer (1982).

The second kind of ego-centered motivation is actualized when input data, such as social appraisals that refer to an individual's ways of pursuing goals and to their outcomes, does not fit with the goal-means-outcome relations prescribed in an individual's relevant action schemata. An individual's own contributions to the goal fulfillments, or the group merits of his or her goal fulfilments, are questioned, seen as invalid, or are unclear. In the first case, the individual's outcomes are seen as unjust; in the second case, his or her actions or motives are seen as less morally legitimate than those of other participants. An individual is urged in such cases to defend and maintain, or perhaps to increase, the positive amount of his contributions or social merits. This urge emanates from pure understanding processes, which are regulated by the relevant action-oriented schemata. An individual thus defends his beliefs, in the "nature of matters" in question, and negotiates them with partners, or accumulates confirming evidences (e.g., through his own activities). In cases of "socially adapted" people, in contrast to others, such as depressives, the content of self-schemata normally produces interpretations more favorable for themselves than "objective interpretations," that is, partners' interpretations. So, as many social psychologists suggest, we are very often engaged in striving to defend and to increase the moral value of our actions, as well as justifiability of our successes and unjustifiability of our failures. The conceptualizations developed by Stryker (1983), Backman (1983), and Schlenker (1982; this volume), and the data collected by them similarly describe aspects of ego-centered motivations and their consequences for social behavior.

The strivings to be fair and morally worthwhile, as well as the striving to be a particular, unquestionable actor within a context meaningful for us, are motives underlying our social life. Often both motives coexist and regulate jointly an individual's behavior. Even if they have different mechanisms, they both are based on action-oriented schemata of self-knowledge that determine the way we perceive social scenes and our role in them.

The task-centered and ego-centered motives are not the only motives based on action-oriented schemata. There are two other classes of motives generated by other social knowledge systems. The first kind of motive is generated when important constituents of activated schema cannot be instantiated by situational characteristics. An individual is thus unable to define a goal, basic actors, or other crucial elements of an ongoing event or is unable to understand a person or a group as a carrier of potentially important goals. Under such conditions, a motivation to understand the social situation is activated and dominates the individual's mental activity and behavior. Usually, it is a group that is engaged in searching for a meaning of ongoing important events. This kind of meaning or identity seeking social motivation is investigated most intensively, on a descriptive level, by ethnomethodologists and symbolic interactionists (Garfinkel, 1967).

Another important kind of motive is based on the goal-means-outcome relation prescribed within an action-oriented schema. If social events fit well with these schemata relations, in terms of participants contributions and results, or in terms of social appreciation, the events, like social conflicts with their resolutions, are valued as "fair," "just," or "morally right." If a created interpretation does not provide such a fit, the relevant aspects of events, and relevant participants, are valued as "unjust," "unfair," "morally condemned," etc. These evaluations can, under some conditions, provoke an observer's action, or support action aimed to restore the "proper" and "natural" order. An observer's action is undertaken when, within his or her schemata operating at the time, the observer may fill an appropriate role, environmental support exists for enactment of this role, and enough clear strategies exist for pursuing actions within this role. The possibility of social knowledge-based, but not self-centered, motives was proposed and analyzed by Reykowski (1984) in his studies of helping behavior.

Self-Understanding Processes

Our active involvements in social processes are regulated interchangeably by task-centered and ego-centered self-motives. Under appropriate conditions of self-involvement, self-goal categories are activated and an individual's behavior and mental processes are organized toward accomplishment of the task implied by these activated goals. An individual's attention is preoccupied with the task problems (e.g., with situational, relevant factors). When, in the context of given self-goals activation, problem with the self emerges, a shift from task-centered to ego-centered self motivation occurs, with accompanying shifts in mental processes and behavior. An individual becomes preoccupied with self-definitions and self-accomplishments, not with the task itself. It is worthwhile to stress, however, that in both cases of self-motives, the problems, strivings, and outcomes are understood by an individual as emerging from the "nature" of the world, and from the urge for a "truth" about this world.

Concentration on self-related problems leads to the development of specific contents and forms of self-understanding and self-presentation processes, and to specific egocentric social behaviors. Recently, Wicklund (1986) argued convincingly that these processes, as well as self-knowledge systems based on them, are effects of a person's incompetence in dealing with environmental demands. Accordingly, this self-knowledge is a result of maladjustment rather than a basis or indicator of social effectiveness.

However, not only incompetence may concentrate our mental resources on the self. When we meet new, long distance, or difficult demands for ourselves, some aspects of the self-as-an actor may have to be clarified, changed, or developed. This requires preoccupation with self-related problems and elaboration of new systems of self-knowledge. Examples of such demands are getting a first job, divorce, birth of the first child, new opportunity for a professional career, etc. In such cases, self-understanding processes are healthy answers for new experiences. They mediate changes in self-as-an-actor schema, and they prepare an individual to undertake more smoothly new task-centered self-motives. Moreover, task-centered motives may refer directly to specific attributes of the self, as in cases of a piano player or a drama actor who is engaged in training personal skills and dispositions as important elements of professional objectives. Self-understanding processes might thus become salient constituents of such task motivations.

Whatever the reasons, self-understanding processes are regulated by action-oriented self-schemata that interpret ongoing social situations. The self-understanding processes primarily have a form of self-narrative. Self-narratives, as proposed recently by Gergen and Gergen (1983, 1984), are self-generated, conscious explanations and accounts of one's own position in a stream of ongoing events. They take the form of a story with the self as a main, or one of the main, actors, a story that describes the self's goals, related demands, difficulties, history of overcoming these problems, and plans for possible future development. Self-narratives seem to be natural forms of self-understanding, if it is true that important parts of self-knowledge are represented in action-oriented schemata because instantiations of such schemata mean interpretation of the environment in terms of social actions. Self-narratives are social in nature; they usually depict the self interacting with specified other partners but also are created and maintained jointly by all these partners during social communication processes and within a given social action network. Self-narratives of interacting partners depend on their mutual efforts to maintain specific concepts of themselves, the group, and the social background (Gergen & Gergen, 1983).

An important part of a self-narrative is generation of expectations and plans about possible actions and outcomes, (e.g., in terms of one's own attributes, possible social reactions for one's accomplishments, etc). This aspect of self-understanding processes was discussed and studied by Markus and her colleagues, within a compatible theoretical framework of the "possible self" (Markus, this volume; Markus & Nurius, 1983). Preliminary data indicate the richness and ease with which individuals make "possible self" expectations. These processes play the same important role in self-motivation as "mental experimentation" on possible states and events play in every process of problem solving and decision making. Through imagining possible scenarios for different strategies of goal realizations, and for possible developments of present self-involving events, "possible self" reasonings regulate the course of an individual's behavior.

Self-narratives, which are conscious and very often negotiated socially, are not the only, or usually even not most important, implications of activation of self-knowledge. Especially when we are not concentrated on self-related problems but pursue task-oriented self-motives, our self-knowledge still regulates our behavior as a "tacit knowledge." The "tacit" role knowledge plays in understanding processes is a natural aspect of schema functioning. When activated, a given knowledge structure regulates the total content of our understanding and behavior but only the

10. THE ROLE OF GOAL CATEGORIES

most problematic aspects of information processing takes the form of consciously controlled processes (Bargh, 1984). The rest of the components of this processing are regulated by "tacit" knowledge or, speaking properly, are regulated "tacitly" (i.e., automatically) by the active knowledge structure. This "tacit" role of action-oriented self-knowledge reveals itself, for instance, in the level of aspiration we spontaneously choose, in the kind of social interactions we enter, and in the kinds of explanations for our failures and successes we automatically look for and believe in.

CONCLUSIONS

The proposed assumptions concerning action-oriented representations of social knowledge can be related to theoretical traditions and recent conceptualizations and empirical studies. However, the mainstream of social psychological thinking about social knowledge representations, although usually not fully verbalized, seems to be based on different ideas. It may be useful to clarify the presented standpoint by contrasting it with this more traditional and prevailing view.

It seems that mainstream conceptualizations in social psychology are based on a general idea of the object oriented character of social knowledge. This assumption states that social knowledge is represented basically as knowledge about a collection of social objects, such as specific persons and their categories, social groups, or selves. Along with the empiricist tradition, it is assumed further that if there is one object "in reality," there is one knowledge system related to this object in an individual's mind. For instance, because there is one "physical me," each individual must possess an universal, single self-knowledge system. Because these social objects may play different roles in different social contexts, formation of universal knowledge system about a given object or class of objects means the extraction of its context-free attributes into a meaningful unit of knowledge. Obviously, the rules of organization of these attributes into a coherent structure themselves have to be context-independent.

The basic idea, then, is that the dominant knowledge structures have the form of universalistic "private theories" about people, social roles, the self, and also abstracted ideas, and that these "theories" have content and context independent structure, that is, they consist primarily of abstracted attributes connected by some simple links (e.g., association links). The intellectual and empirical models for this kind of reasoning might be provided, among others, by traditional general or cognitive psychology, for instance by studies on the formation and structure of artificial perceptual concepts, or by earlier associationistic models of memory organization (Gardner, 1985).

The assumption of an object-oriented representation was at the forefront in studies on attitudes. What had been conceived as naturally developed attitudes were cognitive systems, loosely connected with contextual constraints, and organized around "really existed" objects. In fact, the existence of such "objects" was taken for granted, as obvious, when "attitudes" towards them were studied. The assumed internal organization of an attitude was content-independent. For example, in typical handbooks, the attitude structure is described as consisting of relatively independent cognitive, motivational, and behavioral components. Similarly, until some recent conceptualizations (e.g., Markus, Cantor), mainstream work on self-knowledge was based on the assumption that, because there is one "real" object, a self, only one self-knowledge system develops. This abstracted knowledge is organized within content and context independent categories (e.g., physical, social, and psychological self or social-self and collective-self) that might be characterized on abstract dimensions (e.g., congruence between ideal and real self). These conceptualizations of the self have an old tradition (e.g., see James, 1890; Rogers, 1959), and seem to be widely accepted (see review: Wylie, 1974, 1978), including recently (Greenwald & Pratkanis, 1984).

The idea that dominant knowledge structures are object-oriented may have restricted heuristic power. Relatively little knowledge has been accumulated within this paradigm, in spite of long-term efforts about the content-dependent characteristics of knowledge representations and about the regulative functions of these representations for mental processes and social behavior. A good example is the weak predictive power of theories on "object-related" attitudes or other mental categories such as self-knowledge. As Kiesler and Munson wrote, "The most common tack to increase the predictability of behavior from attitude has been the 'other variable' approach" (Kiesler & Munson, 1975, pp. 417–418; Cialdini, Petty, & Cacioppo, 1981, pp. 368–372). But this advice means that the theories of attitudes themselves are not very useful in explaining and predicting an individual's social behavior. Another example is the lack of important evidence of a relationship between the content of assumed object-oriented "implicated personality theories" and an individual's social behavior, an intuitively surprising fact.

It is not the objective of the preceding remarks to criticize the assumptions of nonaction-oriented representations of social knowledge. Rather, the overall aim of this chapter is to provide the preliminaries that may promote greater interest in, and more systematic studies of action- and goal-oriented representations of knowledge.

The present conceptualizations are uneven in the level of their elaboration and their empirical basis. In particular, the proposals on self-knowledge, on the action-oriented bases for motivation, and on the structure of unit schemata, need more direct empirical data and subsequently more systematic clarification. However, in spite of the very tentative character of the idea at the present time, it allows us to delineate challenging new questions worth investigating.

One set of such important questions deals with the development of action-oriented knowledge systems. As was mentioned, even most advanced studies on event knowledge do not touch this problem very often, probably because the computer simulation paradigm of these studies did not provide useful conceptualizations. The relations between the real structure of social actions, including stable patterns of interdependencies within a group, on one hand, and the development and changes of an individual's knowledge about the social reality on the other is an important topic according to present ideas. There is an old tradition of dealing with the problem, including, first of all, Vygotsky's works. The role an individual plays within these action networks and the social perspectives an individual takes during these interactions should affect the development and structure of his or her knowledge. (Doise & Mackie, 1982; Hinde, Perret-Clermont & Stevenson-Hinde, 1985; Perret-Clermont, 1980). It is a classical topic in sociology and social psychology and within the proposed model, it can potentially be readdressed with new insight.

It is widely recognized now that understanding complex social issues, like self-identity, or moral accounts, takes place naturally during processes of social negotiations. Two problems are implicated by this fact. First, the action-oriented schemata an individual brings to these processes have to provide cognitive procedures to interpret and creatively participate in the social construction of understanding. Second if social experiences are mediated by social negotiation processes, so action-oriented schemata based on these experiences should reflect, in their internal structure, these aspects of the social input. Some initial studies on the relationships between structure of communication process and the character of developed knowledge were done by Zajonc (1960), and more recently by Higgins and collaborators (Higgins, McCann, & Fondacaro, 1982).

The advocated assumptions stress the diversity of internal structures of action-oriented schemata. Also, there are specific structural constituents and parameters of these different forms. The modern theory of schemata provides hypotheses concerning functionally important variables characterizing the structure of the knowledge systems. This accent on possible structural variety and its functional implications can stimulate hypotheses on individual differences. Depending on personal histories of involvement in social action networks and the structure of resulting knowledge systems, individuals will differ characteristically in the ways they interpret and evaluate others, the ways they explain and forecast their own fate, or the ways they adjust to and participate in ongoing events. The proposed assumptions, which accentuate the structural diversity and procedural character of action-oriented schemta, and the motivational component of schemta functioning, could be applied potentially to analyze personality and clinical psychology issues.

There are, finally, some methodological recommendations. If social knowledge is organized within action-oriented schemata that are highly content-and context-specific, and polymorphic in structure, then the appropriate framework to analyze this knowledge is the natural, real-life problems of the individual. Moreover, attention should be given to a wide spectrum of qualitatively different classes of such problems. It does not mean neglecting theoretical investigations of the universal principles underlying this knowledge nor neglecting laboratory experimentations. Rather, it is a recommendation of the particular frame within which models of social knowledge should be constructed and empirical observations should be performed.

REFERENCES

Abbott, V., & Black, J. B. (1980). *The representation of scripts in memory.* (Tech. Rep. No. 5). New Haven, CT: Yale University, Cognitive Science Program.

Abelson, R. (1976). Script processing in attitude formation and decision making. In J. Carroll, & J. Payne (Eds.), *Cognition and social behavior* (pp. 33–45). Hillsdale, NJ: Lawrence Erlbaum Associates.

Abelson, R. (1981). The psychological status of the script concept. *American Psychologist, 36,* 715–729.

Adler, A. (1927). *Practice and theory of individual psychology.* New York: Harcourt.

Adler, A. (1929). *The science of living.* New York: Greenberg.

Backman, C. (1983). Toward an interdisciplinary social psychology. In L. Berkowitz (Ed.), *Advances in experimental social psychology* (Vol. 16), (pp. 220–262). New York: Academic Press.

Bargh, J. (1984). Automatic and conscious processing of social information. In R. Wyer, & T. Srull (Eds.), *Handbook of social cognition* (Vol. 2) (pp. 1–44). Hillsdale, NJ: Lawrence Erlbaum Associates

Barsalow, L., & Sewell, R. (1984). *Contrasting the representation of scripts and categories.* Unpublished manuscript.

Bartlett, F. C. (1932). *Remembering: A study in experimental and social psychology.* London: Cambridge University Press.

Black, J. B., & Bern, H. (1981). Causal coherence and memory for events in narratives. *Journal of Verbal Learning and Verbal Behavior, 20,* 267–275.

Black, J. B., & Bower, G. H. (1980). Story understanding as problem-solving. *Poetics, 9,* 223–250.

Bower, G. H. (1978). Experiments in story comprehension and recall. *Discourse Processes, 1,* 211–232.
Bower, G., Black, J. B., & Turner T. (1979). Scripts in memory for text. *Cognitive Psychology, 11,* 177–220.
Brewer, W., & Nakamura, G. (1984). The nature and functions of schemas. In R. Wyer, & T. Srull (Eds.), *Handbook of social cognition.* (Vol. 1) (pp. 119–160). Hillsdale, NJ: Lawrence Erlbaum Associates.
Bruner, J., & Sherwood, V. (1982). Thought, language and interaction in infancy. In J. Forgas (Ed.), *Social cognition: Perspectives on everyday understanding* (pp. 75–96). London: Academic Press.
Burke, K. (1945). *A grammar of motives.* New York: Prentice-Hall.
Burt, R. S. (1982). *Toward a structural theory of action: Network models of social structure.* New York: Academic Press.
Cantor, N., Mischel, W., & Schwartz, J. (1982). A prototype analysis of psychological situations. *Cognitive Psychology, 14,* 45–77.
Cantor, N., Markus, H., Niedenthal, P., & Nurius, P. (1986). On motivation and the self-concept. In R. Sorrentino, & E. Higgins (Eds.), *Handbook of motivation and cognition* (pp. 96–121). New York: The Guilford Press.
Cialdini, R., Petty, R., & Caccioppo, J. (1981). Attitude and attitude change. *Annual Review of Psychology, 32,* 357–404.
Csikszentmihalyi, M., & Beattie, O. (1979). Life themes: A theoretical and empirical exploration of their origins and effects. *Journal of Humanistic Psychology, 19,* 45–77.
Cohen, C. E., & Ebbesen, E. (1979). Observational goals and schema activation: A theoretical framework for behavior perception. *Journal of Experimental Social Psychology, 15,* 305–329.
D'Andrade, R. G. (1965). Trait psychology and componental analysis. *American Anthropologist, 67,* 215–278.
Doise, W., & Mackie, D. (1982). On the social nature of cognition. In J. Forgas (Ed.), *Social cognition: Perspectives on everyday understanding* (pp. 101–137). London: Academic Press.
Feffer, M. (1959). The cognitive implications of role taking behavior. *Journal of Personality, 27,* 152–168.
Fillmore, C. (1968). The case for case. In E. Bach, & R. Harms (Eds.), *Universals in linguistic theory* (pp. 1–90). New York: Holt, Rinehart, Winston.
Forgas, J. P. (1982). Episode cognition: Internal representation of interaction routines. In L. Berkowitz (Ed.), *Advances in Experimental social psychology* (Vol. 15) 59–103. New York: Academic Press.
Galambos, J. A., & Rips, L. J. (1982). Memory for routines. *Journal of Verbal Learning and Verbal Behavior, 21,* 260–281.
Gardner, H. (1985). *The mind's new science: A history of the cognitive revolution.* New York: Basic Books.
Gergen, K. J. & Gergen, M. M. (1983). Narratives of the self. In K. Scheibe, & T. Sarbin (Eds.), *Studies in social identity* (pp. 121–140). New York: Praeger.
Gergen, M. M., & Gergen, K. J. (1984). The social construction of narrative accounts. In K. Gergen, & M. Gergen (Eds.), *Historical social psychology* (pp. 173–190). Hillsdale, NJ: Lawrence Erlbaum Associates.
Garfinkel, H. (1967). *Studies in ethnomethodology.* Englewood Cliffs, NJ: Prentice-Hall
Goffman, E. (1959). *The presentation of self in everyday life.* New York: Doubleday.
Graesser, A. C. (1981). *Prose comprehension beyond the world.* New York: Springer-Verlag.
Greenwald, A., & Pratkanis, A. (1984). The self. In R. S. Wyer & T. K. Srull (Eds.), *Handbook of social cognition* (pp. 129–178). Hillsdale, NJ: Lawrence Erlbaum Associates.

Haberland, K. (1980). Story grammar and reading time of story constituents. *Poetics, 9,* 99–116.
Haberland, T. K., & Bringham, H. (1978). Verbs contribute to the coherence of brief narratives: Reading related and unrelated sentence triples. *Journal of Verbal Learning and Verbal Behavior, 17,* 419–426.
Hartwick, J. (1979). Memory for trait information: A signal detection analysis. *Journal of Experimental Social Psychology, 15,* 533–552.
Hastie, R., Park, B., & Weber, R. (1984). Social memory. In R. Wyer, & T. Srull (Eds). *Handbook of social cognition.* (vol. 2), 151–212, Hillsdale, NJ: Lawrence Erlbaum Associates.
Higgins, E. T., McCann, C., Fondacaro, R. (1982). The "communication game": Goal-directed encoding and cognitive consequences. *Social Cognition, 1,* 21–37.
Hinde, R., Perret-Clermont, A., & Stevenson-Hinde, J. (Eds.). (1985). *Social relationships and cognitive development.* Oxford: Clarendon Press.
Hoffman, C., Mischel, W., & Mazze, K. (1981). The role of purpose in the organization of information and behavior: Trait-based versus goal-based categories in person cognition. *Journal of Personality and Social Psychology, 40,* 211–225.
James, W. (1890). *The principles of psychology.* New York: Holt.
Kiesler, C. A., & Munson, P. A. (1975). Attitudes and opinions. In M. Rosenzweig, & L. Porter (Eds.), *Annual reviews of psychology.* 415–456. Palo Alto., CA: Annual Reviews Inc.
Kintsch, W. (1974). *The representation of meaning in memory.* Hillsdale, NJ: Lawrence Erlbaum Associates.
Kintsch, W., & van Dijk, T. (1978). Toward a model of text comprehension and production. *Psychological Review, 85,* 363–394.
Krackhardt, D. (1987). Cognitive social structures. *Social Network,g,* 109–134.
Kuhl, J., & Helle, P. *Motivational and volitional determinants of depression: The degenerated-intention hypothesis.* Unpublished manuscript.
Langer, E., & Abelson, R. (1972). The semantics of asking a favor: How to succeed in getting help without really trying. *Journal of Personality and Social Psychology, 24,* 26–32.
Langer, E., Blank, A., & Chanowitz, B. (1978). The mindlessness of ostensibly thoughtful action. *Journal of Personality and Social Psychology, 36,* 635–642.
Leddo, J., & Abelson, R. (1986). The nature of explanations. In J. Galambos, R. Abelson, & J. Black (Eds.), *Knowledge structures.* 103–122 Hillsdale, NJ: Lawrence Erlbaum Associates
Lerner, M. (1977). The justice motive in social behavior: Some hypotheses as to its origins and forms. *Journal of Personality, 45,* 1–52.
Lerner, M. (1984). *The belief in a just world: A fundamental delusion.* New York: Plenum Press.
Lichtenstein, E. H., & Brewer, W. F. (1980). Memory for goal directed events. *Cognitive Psychology, 12,* 412–445.
Mandler, J. M. (1978). A code in the node: The use of story schemas in retrieval. *Discourse Processes, 1,* 14–35.
Mandler, J. M., & Johnson, N. S. (1977). Remembrance of things parsed: Strong structure and recall. *Cognitive Psychology, 9,* 111–151.
Markus, H., & Nurius, P. (1986). *Possible selves. American Psychologist, 41,* 954-969.
Markus, H. (this volume). *Goals and possible selves.*
Minsky, M. (1975). A framework for representing knowledge. In P. Winston (Ed.), *The psychology of computer vision* (pp. 211–277). New York: McGraw-Hill.
Minuchin, S. (1974). *Families and family therapy.* Cambridge, MA: Harvard University Press.
Minuchin, S., & Fishman, H. L. (1981). *Family therapy techniques.* Cambridge, MA: Harvard University Press.

Nelson, K. (1986). *Event knowledge: Structure and function in development.* Hillsdale, NJ: Lawrence Erlbaum Associates.
Newtson, D. (1976). Foundation of attribution: The perception of ongoing behavior. In J. Harvey, W. Ickes, & R. Kidd (Eds.), *New directions in attribution research* (Vol. 1), (pp. 223–248). Hillsdale, NJ: Lawrence Erlbaum Associates.
Newtson, D. A., Enquist, G., & Bois, J. (1977). The objective basis of behavior units. *Journal of Personality and Social Psychology, 35,* 847–862.
Niedenthal, P., Cantor, N., & Kihlstrom, J. (1985). Prototype-matching: A strategy for social decision-making. *Journal of Personality and Social Psychology, 48,* 575–584.
Nottenberg, G., & Shoben, E. J. (1980). Scripts as linear orders. *Journal of Experimental Social Psychology, 16,* 329–347.
Omanson, R. (1982). The relation between centrality and story category variability. *Journal of Verbal Learning and Verbal Behavior, 21,* 326–337.
Ostrom, T. (1984). The sovereignty of social cognition. In R. Wyer, & T. Srull (Eds.), *Handbook of social cognition* (Vol. 1) (pp. 1–38). Hillsdale, NJ: Lawrence Erlbaum Associates
Owens, J., Bower, G, & Black, J. (1979). The "soap opera" effect in strong memory. *Memory and Cognition, 7,* 185–191.
Perret-Clermont, A. N. (1980). *Social Interaction and cognitive development in children.* London: Academic Press.
Pryor, J. P., & Ostrom, T. (1981). The cognitive organization of social information: A converging-operations approach *Journal of Personality and Social Psychology, 41,* 628–641.
Reiser, B. J., Black, J., & Lehnert, W. L. (1982. *Thematic knowledge structures in the understanding and generation of narratives.* (Tech. Rep. No. 16). New Haven, CT: Yale University, Cognitive Science Program.
Reykowski, J. (1984). Spatial organization of a cognitive system and intrinsic prosocial motivation. In E. Staub, D. Bar-Tel, J. Karylowski, & J. Reykowski (Eds.), *Development and maintenance of prosocial behavior* (pp. 51–76). New York: Plenum Press.
Rogers, C. (1959). A theory of therapy, personality, and interpersonal relationships, as developed in the client-centered framework. In S. Koch (Ed.), *Psychology: A Science* (Vol. 3). 184–256. New York: McGraw-Hill.
Rosch, E. (1975). Cognitive representation of semantic categories. *Journal of Experimental Psychology: General, 104,* 192–233.
Rosenberg, S., & Sedlak, A. (1972). Structural representations of implicit personality theory. In L. Berkowitz (Ed.), *Advances in Experimental Social Psychology* (Vol. 6) (pp. 235–297). New York: Academic Press.
Rumelhart, D. (1984). Schema in social cognition. In R. Wyer, & T. Srull (Eds.), *Handbook of social cognition* (Vol. 1) (pp. 161–188). Hillsdale, NJ: Lawrence Erlbaum Associates.
Rumelhart, D., & Ortony, A. (1977). The representation of knowledge in memory. In R. C. Anderson, R. Spiro, & W. Montaque (Eds.), *Schooling and the acquisition of knowledge* (pp. 99–135). Hillsdale, NJ: Lawrence Erlbaum Associates.
Schank, R. (1982). *Dynamic memory: A theory of reminding and learning in computers and people.* New York: Cambridge University Press.
Schank, R., & Abelson, R. (1977). *Scripts, plans, goals and understanding.* Hillsdale, NJ: Lawrence Erlbaum Associates.
Schlenker, B. (1982). Translating actions into attitudes: An identity-analytic approach to the explanation of social conduct. In L. Berkowitz (Ed.), *Advances in experimental social psychology* (Vol. 15), (pp. 194–248). New York: Academic Press.
Schneider, D. (1973). Implicit personality theory: A review. *Psychological Bulletin, 79,* 294–309.

Seifert, C., & Black, J. (1983). Thematic connections between episodes. *Proceedings of the Fifth Annual Conference of the Cognitive Science Society.* Rochester, NY.
Seifert, C., & Abelson, R., & McKoon, R. (1986). The role of thematic knowledge structures in reminding. In J. Galambos, R. Abelson, & J. Black (Eds.), *Knowledge structures (pp. 185–210).* Hillsdale, NJ: Lawrence Erlbaum Associates.
Seifert, C. Robertson, S., & Black, J. (1982). *On-line processing of pragmatic inferences* (Tech. Rep. No. 15). New Haven, CT: Yale University.
Smith, E. E., & Collins, A. (1981). Use of goal-plan knowledge in understanding stories. *Proceedings of the Third Conference of the Cognitive Science Society.* Berkeley, CA.
Srull, T. (1983). Organizational and retrieval processes in memory: A examination of processing objectives, presentation formats, and the possible role of self-generated retrieval cues. *Journal of Personality and Social Psychology, 44,* 1157–1170.
Stryker, S. (1983). Social Psychology from the standpoint of a structural symbolic interactionism: Toward an interdisciplinary social psychology. In L. Berkowitz (Ed.), *Advances in experimental social psychology* (Vol. 16) (pp. 181–219). New York: Academic Press.
Taylor, S. E. & Fiske, S. T. (1981). Getting inside the head: Methodologies for process analysis in attribution and social cognition. In J. H. Harvey, W. Ickes & R. F. Kidd (Eds.) *New Directions in Attribution Research* (Vol. 3) 459–524. Hillsdale, NJ: Lawrence Erlbaum Associates.
Thorndyke, P. (1977). Cognitive structures in comprehension and memory of narrative discourse. *Cognitive Psychology, 9,* 77–110.
Trabasso, T., Secco, T., & van der Broek, P. (1984). Causal cohesion and story coherence. In N. Mandell, N. Stein, & T. Trabasso (Eds.), *Learning and comprehension of text* (pp. 93–122). Hillsdale, NJ: Lawrence Erlbaum Associates.
Trzebinski, J. (1985). Action-oriented representations of implicit personality theories. *Journal of Personality and Social Psychology, 48,* 1266–1278.
Trzebinski, J. (1986). *Network analysis in studies of action-oriented schemata* (Tech. Rep.). Warsaw: Polish Academy of Sciences.
Trzebinski, J., McGlynn, R., Gray, G., & Tubbs, D. (1985). The role of categories of an actor's goals in organizing inference about a person. *Journal of Personality and Social Psychology, 48,* 1387–1397.
Trzebinski, J., & Najda, M. (1987). *Social unit schema and moral reasoning.* Unpublished manuscript, University of Warsaw.
Trzebinski, J., & Richards, K. (1986). The role of goal categories in person impression. *Journal of Experimental Social Psychology, 22,* 216–227.
Walker, C. H., & Yekovich, F. (1984). Script-based inferences: Effects of text and knowledge variables on recognition memory. *Journal of Verbal Learning and Verbal Behavior, 23,* 357–370.
Wegner, D., & Giuliano, T. (1983). Social awareness in story comprehension. *Social Cognition, 2,* 1–17.
Wegner, D., & Vallacher, R. (1986). Action identification. In R. Sorrentino, & E. T. Higgins (Eds.), *Handbook of motivation and cognition* (pp. 550–582). New York: The Guilford Press.
Wicklund, R. (1986). Orientation to the environment versus preoccupation with human potential. In R. Sorrentino, & E. T. Higgins (Eds.), *Handbook of motivation and cognition* (pp. 64–95). New York: Guildford Press.
Wicklund, R., & Gollowitzer, P. (1982). *Symbolic self-completion.* Hillsdale, NJ: Lawrence Erlbaum Associates.
Wilson, C., & Mulhall, D. (1983). Describing relationships in families with alcohol problems. *British Journal of Addiction, 78,* 181–191.

Wyer, R., & Gordon, S. (1982). The recall of information about persons and groups. *Journal of Experimental Social Psychology, 18,* 128–164.

Wyer, R., & Gordon, S. (1984). The cognitive representation of social information. In R. Wyer, & T. Srull (Eds.), *Handbook of social cognition* (Vol. 2) (pp. 73–144). Hillsdale, NJ: Lawrence Erlbaum Associates.

Wylie, R. (1974, 1978). *The self concept* (Vols. 1 & 2). Lincoln, NE: University of Nebraska Press.

Vygotsky, L. S. (1978). *Mind in society.* Cambridge: Harvard University Press.

Zadny, J., & Gerard, H. B. (1974). Attributed intentions and information selectivity. *Journal of Experimental Psychology, 10,* 34–52.

Zajonc, R. B. (1960). The process of cognitive tuning in communication. *Journal of Abnormal and Social Psychology 61,* 159–167.

Zajonc, R. B. (1980). Cognition and social cognition: A historical perspective. In L. Festinger (Ed.), *Four decades of social psychology* (pp. 54–81). New York: Oxford University Press.

Zuroff, D. (1982). Person, situation, and person-by-situation interaction components in person perception. *Journal of Psychology, 50,* 1–14.

11 Inter-Personalism: Toward a Goal-Based Theory of Persons in Relationships[1]

STEPHEN JOHN READ
University of Southern California

LYNN CAROL MILLER
Scripps College
and Claremont Graduate School

Recently, we experienced an event that we found ourselves mulling over for days. These reflections altered our initial interpretation of the event and raised new questions for us concerning the nature of social interactions. Let us share this event with you.

Two women, one in her 60s and the other in her 80s, stood at the baggage carousel area of a major airport ready to retrieve their luggage. Within a few moments a well-dressed man in his 50s appeared behind them. After the carousel began to move and baggage came down the chute, the man spotted his luggage and pushed through the women quickly to grab his luggage before it moved away from him down the carousel. Noticing that one lady had nearly lost her balance and that both women looked upset, the man commented "I don't want to hurt anyone but I have to get my luggage." One lady suggested, in an obviously annoyed voice, that he "just forget about getting his luggage for now." The man seemed incredulous that she should suggest this, "what do you mean, forget it?" he said. Then, he pushed into these women again, this time uttering no excuses and expressing no apparent remorse. Finally, he retrieved all of his luggage, which he piled on a nearby rented cart where his companion (presumably his wife) stood. Upon questioning the two elderly women about this incident, one com-

---

[1]This project was supported in part by a grant from the National Institute of Mental Health (MH39510-03) to the second author and a grant from the National Science Foundation (BNS-8406262) to the first author.

mented that she had arrived early for a "good spot" to pick out her luggage and she was entitled to her space by the chute. She "certainly wasn't about to let a bully like that make her give up her spot" . . . "some men just think they can just use brute force to push women around and that women should just move out of their way" . . . he was a very "hostile and rude man" and "I'm sure glad I'm not married to a man like that" . . . . "I wouldn't take someone like that for one minute!"

This encounter, although brief, raises a number of questions about each of the characters. Here were three strangers well dressed older adults (a man over 50 and two women over 60), within minutes involved in a very negative public exchange. What were their goals? Why did their interpersonal goals conflict? Why did they do what they did? How did they perceive what was happening? And how did these perceptions influence the nature of their behavioral interaction and their subsequent inferences about each other? In short, how did these unique individuals come together in this context to create a negative behavioral sequence and a unique relationship (however brief).

Inter-personalism, a goal-based theory of persons in relationships, is one attempt to address some of these issues. In this chapter we suggest that goal-based structures (e.g., goals, plans, resources, and beliefs) provide a common language for a theory incorporating not only a model of persons and situations, but also a model of how we perceive our partner and understand our relationships in varying contexts and over time. We suggest that individual differences among people can be conceptualized in terms of configurations of their goals, plans, resources, and beliefs. What's more, situations can be conceptualized in a parallel manner, in terms of the goals they afford, the rules and roles that govern behavior in them, and the resources they make available. As a result person-person interactions can be analyzed as the interplay among the goals, plans, resources, and beliefs of the members of the interaction. And person-situation interactions can be analyzed as the interplay between the goals, plans, resources, and beliefs of the person and the parallel structures in the situation.

In the first part of the paper we outline how goal-based structures provide a model of persons, as well as a model of situations. Next we describe a model of person perception that relies on similar goal-based structures for the understanding of behavior and that seems especially appropriate for illuminating how people interpret ongoing sequences of behavior, including interpersonal interactions. With Trzebinski (this volume) we feel that such goal-based structures are particularly suited for representing the nature of people and their social interactions. In the final part of the paper, we outline how the models of persons, situations and person perception can be integrated to form a general account of the planning and coordination of interpersonal interactions.

GENERAL FRAMEWORK

How might we develop a comprehensive model of persons, situations, and relationships? Somewhere along the way, all of us learned that we cannot add "apples" and "oranges;" we need to come up with a common language (e.g., pieces of fruit) before we can proceed. In a similar way, we cannot add 1/2 and 2/5 until we find the "common denominator" with which to express both fractions in the same "units" (e.g., 5/10; 4/10) so that they can be added. As this suggests, one way to find common "units" (as in the case of the fraction problem) involves going to smaller units of analysis (e.g., tenths are a smaller unit than halves or fifths).

Our task, then, in developing a comprehensive model of persons, relationships, and situations may be to specify the set of "units" or a common language (or common denominator) that allows us to understand in detail the processes by which persons, situations, and relationships influence one another. One possibility for such units, frequently suggested over the years, involves various goal-based structures.

Goal-Based Structures

A long tradition in personality psychology suggests that goals or related concepts (e.g. needs, motives, goals, instincts) and plans are important in understanding persons (e.g., Adler, 1964; Allport, 1937; Cantor & Kihlstrom, 1985; Murray, 1938; Mischel, 1973, 1977; Pervin, 1983). Regarding resources, Allport (1937) among others emphasized the role of "innate individual equipment" and "adaptive mechanisms" (p. 108) that individuals can use to accomplish their goals. We refer to these as "resources." And, beliefs (or attitudes) have been considered important facets of personality. Allport (1937) for example, noted that

> both *attitude* and *trait* are indispensable concepts. Between them they cover virtually every type of disposition with which the psychology of personality concerns itself. Ordinarily, *attitude* should be employed when the disposition is bound to an object or value, that is to say, when it is aroused by a well-defined class of stimuli, and when the individual feels toward these stimuli a definite attraction or repulsion." (p. 294)

Furthermore, in considering structures for understanding social behavior, a number of cognitive and social theorists (e.g., Miller, Galanter,

& Pribram, 1960; Schank & Abelson, 1977; and Wilensky, 1983) have argued that social interaction can be analyzed in terms of people's goals and the plans and strategies necessary to achieve those goals. Implicit (and sometimes explicit) in their analyses are concerns about an individual's beliefs as they relate to these goals and strategies, and the resources necessary to carry out the plans and attain these goals.

These analyses of persons and social interaction suggest a common language of goal-based, mediating structures. In the following we elaborate a theory in which we suggest that stable individual differences can be viewed as chronic configurations of the individual's goals, plans, resources, and beliefs. We also suggest how similar structures can be used to describe situations and relationships and to understand the behavioral sequences of persons (in unique relationships) in varying situations. Let us consider each of these structures for a "common language" in greater detail.

Goals

For our present purposes a goal is, quite simply, something which the individual desires or wants to attain because it is rewarding in its own right. Among the wide range of possible goals are basic biological needs, such as food, sleep, and sex; social needs such as companionship, respect, love, and success; and more abstract needs or goals, such as truth and justice. Examples of goals particularly relevant to relationships may include impressing another, understanding oneself and others, making friends, having an intimate relationship, and avoiding rejection and ridicule. Most of the time, we may not be "consciously" aware of these goals or their activation. But, individuals may be more or less consciously *aware* of various beliefs, standards, and goals depending upon the situation (Duval & Wicklund, 1972), and their ability to reach their goals. Furthermore, individuals clearly differ in the extent to which they may be chronically *aware* of their thoughts, feelings, and motives (Carver & Scheier, 1981).

Plans and Strategies

Plans are organized sequences of behavior aimed at the attainment of some end goal or set of goals. Oftentimes, a given plan is composed of several subsequences or subplans linked together into an overall plan in order to attain the goals in a particular situation. Such plans can contain considerable detail. For example, a plan to disclose something personal

11. INTER-PERSONALISM

to another would include what to disclose (and not disclose) about oneself, the way one would go about disclosing it, when and where it would be disclosed, and how it is likely to be construed as the interaction unfolds. Often an individual may have a hierarchy of possible plans and strategies. The use of a particular strategy probably depends upon a variety of factors including one's perception of the context, the rapidity with which such a choice must be made, expectations (based on experience or simulations) of probable success associated with a strategy, and the probable impact of the strategy. In addition, as Mandler (1975) points out, higher order plans involve organized sequences of behaviors that can be fairly "automatic" or relatively "unconscious." Berscheid (1983) gives the following excellent example:

> For many people the early-morning rising and breakfast routine is a highly organized action sequence. Triggered by the alarm clock, for example, Joan gets up, puts on her robe, yells at Johnny to get up, stumbles downstairs, makes the coffee, yells at Johnny to get up again, waits to hear his feet land on the floor, unloads the dishwasher, puts plates on the table, and so forth. The sequence has been performed so many times in the past, in just that invariant order and with each response in the intrachain sequence of activities serving as the stimulus for the next, that she can do it in her sleep—and often does. . . . Many organized action sequences are part of higher-order plans that are in the process of execution . . . Joan's highly organized morning routine, for example, may be part of several of her higher-order plans, including seeing to it that Johnny gets an education and arrives at school on time, as well as preserving her marriage to a man who believes a good wife and mother always provides a hardy breakfast for her family. Higher-order plans, then, are response sequences initiated and in some state of completion. (pp. 150–151)

Beliefs

An individual's beliefs about the world are apt to affect what goals and strategies are chosen, how they are implemented, and what inferences are made about one's own and others' behavior. There are beliefs (ends-beliefs) that may relate more to goals per se, such as "having people like me is rewarding," whereas other beliefs, such as "disclosing about myself is a good way to get others to like and pay attention to me," are beliefs about the strategies or plans an individual would adopt to reach his goals (these will be referred to as means-beliefs). Beliefs may involve evaluations of the morality as well as effectiveness of various plans. And, beliefs may involve inferences about the characteristics and likely behavior of social objects generally (e.g., "people are basically worthwhile and trustworthy") and particular relationships with others ("if I tell her this, she'll continue talking to me") that may influence one's behavior and set one apart from others. Some beliefs individuals may have such as, "I must be loved and adored by my spouse and it would be horrible if such love was not forthcoming," have been described as illogical (Ellis & Harper, 1977). Individuals may often be unaware of the extent to which their beliefs may influence their responses (Ellis & Harper, 1977).

Resources

Most plans carry with them numerous conditions that must be satisfied for the plan's successful completion. Some of these conditions simply depend on the particular state of the world and are beyond the control of the individual trying to enact the plan. However, most of the time, plans require certain resources to carry them out.

Surprisingly little is known (Miller & Berg, 1984; Wilensky, 1983) about the role and nature of perceived and actual resources in influencing the successful completion and coordination of plans. Foa and Foa (1974) have suggested six general classes of resources: money, goods, services, love, status, and information and have shown that the resources available (similar or dissimilar to the ones that subjects had been deprived of) to carry out plans (e.g., retaliation) influenced the intensity and duration of affect (e.g., hostility) subjects expressed. Foa and Foa's (1974) work, however, seems aimed at addressing the question, "What resources do I have that others want?"

On the other hand, Wilensky (1983) addressed the question, "What resources enable plans?" For Wilensky these included such resources as (a) time (a resource required for all plans and, therefore, apt to be a source of goal conflict), (b) consumable function objects (e.g. money), (c) nonconsumable function objects (a stove that once used can be used again), and (d) abilities (e.g., strength, speed, intellect, stamina, etc.). Because the availability of resources would seem to greatly affect what plans are enacted to fulfill which goals, a more detailed taxonomy of resources and a more thorough examination of the properties of resources might prove useful.

Towards that end we would like to suggest that there are three general sources of resources: resources that the individual has access to individually, resources that are afforded by situations that we find ourselves in, and resources provided through our interassociations with others in relationships. Different sources provide some overlapping and distinct types of resources.

Personal Resources. Personal resources include the following:

1. Cognitive Resources. These include cognitive tools and skills (e.g., analytic, integrative, improvisational, problem solving, planning, and self-regulatory), attributes (e.g., speed of processing, reflectivity-impulsivity, vividness of imagery), devices individuals may use to call up and actively alter their affective, motivational, physical, or attentional state. Also included here are meta-cognitive skills (skills for thinking about or monitoring one's thinking).

2. Knowledge. Cantor & Kihlstrom (1985) argue that knowledge bases are important in understanding persons. We would concur, arguing that knowledge bases are a critical resource individuals call upon in developing plans to achieve goals. Such knowledge can be categorized as declarative (facts concerning the social and physical world) or procedural (procedures, skills, and rules for operating on declarative knowledge).

3. Specialized Talents and Abilities. These include musical, artistic, or physical and mechanical abilities.

4. Physical Attributes and Physical Functioning. These resources include body build, agility, and physical attractiveness, size and strength, physical condition and health, energy level, sexual attributes and functions, and sensory capacities.

5. Social, Expressive and Communicative Skills. Included here would be "social intelligence." Allport (1937) noted that

> there is no doubt that social intelligence is a generalized trait. Entirely different types of behavior may be called for depending on circumstance, and a flexibility in shifting from one to the other is the very essence of the trait. . . . Social intelligence is not a matter of performing one act on all occasions, but of varying (even reversing) behavior to accord with circumstances, appreciating and doing what is required by social circumstances . . . If any trait depends upon experience and training, social intelligence does so. The skillfull hostess, high in social intelligence, has *learned* how to make people feel at home, to anticipate their needs, to draw them out in conversation, and how to be present-minded when minor social catastrophes occur. (p. 426)

A new, but overlapping concept of individual differences in "social intelligence" and its importance for person structures has more recently been developed by Cantor and Kihlstrom (1985) who suggest that personality may be construed in terms of individual differences in the mental structures and processes that guide social interaction. This repertoire of *social intelligence* is stored in memory as organized knowledge. This knowledge, in turn, forms the structural basis for personality [e.g., declarative-semantic, declarative-episodic, and procedural knowledge structures]. (p. 18)

6. *Coping Skills and "Inner" Resources.* These include for example, "ego resiliency" or the general ability to effectively adapt to changing contingencies (Block, 1982). Also included would be such things as "spiritual resources" that the individual can call upon to more effectively cope and reach personal goals.

7. *Position and Status.* This includes professional status, reputation (financial, professional, social), social class, and social status.

8. *Possessions.* Possessions include money and goods, as well as "possession extenders" (e.g., credit lines, credit cards).

9. *Time.* This resource is perhaps the most valuable of all because it is required by almost any action. Still individuals can maximize their time by accomplishing multiple goals within the same time frame (see Wilensky, 1983 for an extended discussion) and using resources to "buy time" (e.g., pay money to get somewhere faster, use someone else's services to free one's own time, etc.).

Resources Afforded by the Nature of the Situation. In addition to personal resources, there are *resources afforded by the nature of the situation* that we find ourselves in (Argyle, Furnham, & Graham, 1981; Baron & Boudreau, 1987; Murray, 1938). Situations by their physical nature (e.g., architecture, physical layout of obstacles) or socially prescribed nature (e.g., norms, rules, roles) vary in the extent and nature of three resources that may be typically afforded:

1. Situations allow us *access to people* that may be important in enacting various goals. For example, wanting "to impress others" requires having "others" to impress. Although achieving that goal is possible in almost any imaginable social situation, the mode of expression is apt to differ dramatically. Impressing someone in most "church situations" is more likely to be expressed by what one wears than what one says. On the other hand, we may choose situations (e.g., gym, tennis courts, debate competition, intellectual discussion group) where we know we will have others around to

impress with our ability (Swann, 1987). As situations differ so too does the nature of our access to others.
2. Situations also afford access to *objects* (e.g., tennis courts, athletic equipment) that are needed to enable plans to achieve goals.
3. Situations also afford access to *experiences* whereby, for example, our state is changed (we take a walk in the woods to relax), or other goals are enabled (so we can clear our heads, avoid the distractions at home, or get on with writing a manuscript).

What the environment is perceived as affording may depend on the overall physical and social resources within a location at a particular time. And, how we see a situation in terms of the resources it affords may greatly depend on what our present goals and needs are (Baron & Boudreau, 1987).

Relational Resources. Relational resources include such things as

1. *Cognitive resources,* such as transactional memories (Wegner, Guiliano, & Hertel, 1985), in which couples' knowledge bases together are greater than the sum of their parts, and where the rational memories themselves may serve as a resource to call upon as a source of comfort, or to alter one's affective or motivational state.
2. *Material resources,* including for example, a home that couples can afford only by combining their financial resources,
3. *Physical and psychological resources,* including for example, the quality of the couple's sex life.
4. *Affective resources,* including mutual love and shared understandings as a combined resource.
5. *Support* (professional and social) networks afforded by one's relationships that afford access to emotional, physical, financial, and professional support.

There are a variety of connections among personal, relational and situational resources. For example, personal resources (e.g., money) allow access to situational resources (e.g., a gym) that may afford opportunities to "work out" and improve one's physical appearance (a personal resource) and enhance one's opportunities for meeting friends (a relational resource), which may in turn enhance other personal resources (access to information about a job) that could enhance one's material net worth (personal resource) and so forth. Situations may afford multiple resources, some of which serve as the basis for entering situations and some of which make salient other goals once we are in those situations

There is obviously much that we do not know about the qualities of different resources that would greatly affect when individuals will enact certain plans and how their ability to enact plans will depend upon changing properties of their store of personal, relational, and situational resources. Furthermore, it seems likely that even among personal resources, many resources are not "permanent." Some are "consumable," others perishable; and there are overall constraints on the use of particular resources that make it possible to enact plans sometimes, but not always.

For example, Wilensky (1983) has specified three types of "consumability" of resources: physical consumption (in which the object fails to exist or exists in an altered form without the desired properties), social consumption (where control is shifted from the planner to another), and "continuous enablement consumption" (in which the object must remain continuously applied in one location making it unavailable for use elsewhere). Additional distinctions regarding the level of usability and "consumability" of resources could be made. For example, some resources such as energy are "rechargeable" with appropriate action (e.g., a good night's sleep). Some resources (e.g., food, physical attractiveness) may have "peak" periods during which their "value" is highest and they may in some sense be "perishable."

Some resources need "maintenance work" to remain useful (e.g., social networks, physical fitness level). Some resources may be candidates for "hard wiring" (e.g., energy level [activity level], reflectivity [impulsivity], intellectual abilities, arousability [emotionality]). And, some resources may be more "primary" (e.g., intellectual competencies) because although they can generate more "secondary" resources (e.g., plans for earning money) they themselves can not be generated by other resources. The nature of such resource differences may provide important clues to consistencies in behavior across situations and over time. Furthermore, knowledge of resource relations may allow us to examine how individuals deal with goal conflict. For example, some resources (money) may allow us access to another person's resources (another's time and service) so that we can more effectively accomplish more goals within a limited time frame and reduce what would otherwise be apparent goal conflicts.

Goal-Based Configurations and Behavior

Although people may have a large repertoire of goals, the salience of these goals in social interaction is apt to vary depending on the context and the nature of their interpersonal relationship. Activating a goal or set of goals is apt also to activate a consideration of plans, strategies, and beliefs associated with the goals and plans, and an assessment of resources needed to carry out the plans to attain the goals. For any given individual, at a given time, some goals and goal-configurations are apt to be more salient than others. It is expected that the hierarchies and relationships among this complex of activated goal configurations and the nature of the constraints on behavior imposed by the context and the interpretation of responses from ongoing interactions would affect the content, style and timing of plans, strategies, and behavioral sequences that are executed.

At the same time, resources afforded by situations or relationships may make new goals or plans salient or activate portions of belief systems. These new goals may be so immediately salient that they supplant other goals or they may be integrated with other prevailing goals of the person in different ways depending on the goal relationships involved. Because the interrelations among goals are apt to be important in considering which plans are enacted, we turn to a discussion of the relationships among goals, first at the intrapersonal and then at the interpersonal level.

Intrapersonal Goal Relations. Wilensky (1983) has argued that there are two types of goal relations at the level of the individual. "Goal conflict" involves goals at the intrapersonal level (within the individual) that are negatively related (e.g., in opposition to one another). Goals may be negatively related to one another because of a variety of reasons: (a) resource limitations, such as not having enough time to carry out all of one's plans, restrictions on material resources, and limitations on abilities or skills needed to carry out one's plans; (b) state limitations (e.g., we can't physically be in two places at the same time); and (c) preservation goals and limitations (e.g., engaging in disclosing in order to be close to another endangers another goal, being viewed positively). Wilensky (1983) argues that when people are faced with negative goal relations, they typically try to circumvent them either by figuring out a new plan that will allow them to attain all their goals, or by determining which goals are most important and focusing on achieving those, abandoning the others.

In coming up with a new plan, people can do one of the following: (a) find a new plan without the problems of the first; thus, for example if the first plan failed because of a resource limitation, find a plan that doesn't require the same resource; or (b) remove the reason for the negative goal relation. If the original plan failed for lack of a resource, such as money, one possibility is first to try to get more of the resource and then retry the old plan.

Fortunately, goals are not always negatively related. Some goals are unrelated to one another, and others involve what Wilensky (1983) describes as "goal overlap." These are goals at the intrapersonal level that are consistent with one another, for example, because they can be achieved by the same plan or because they can be achieved more easily together than apart.

Interpersonal Goal Relations. The relations among the goals of the members of an interaction are also important for understanding their behavior. Wilensky's (1983) analysis suggests that there are two kinds of interpersonal goal relations: (a) goal competition, in which individuals' goals are negatively related to one another, and (b) goal concord in which individuals' goals are positively related, for example because they both possess the same goal, or each individual's goals facilitate the other's.

Wilensky (1983) outlines three classes of reason why goals may be negatively related to one other. One is resource limitations (e.g., time, knowledge, materials, abilities). For example, consider a couple in which the wife wishes that her husband would be more open about his feelings. But the husband has never really thought about his feelings and lacks the ability to "get in touch" with what he is really experiencing.

Goals may also be negatively related because achieving them would require us to be in two mutually exclusive states. For instance, it is illegal to be married to two different people at the same. Finally, goals may be negatively related because achieving one goal threatens a goal we have already achieved, thus creating a preservation goal (Schank & Abelson, 1977; Wilensky, 1983). For instance, a woman who is married may think it a good idea to date other men until she realizes that doing so would threaten the happiness of her marriage.

In our discussion of intrapersonal goal conflict, we noted that one way to deal with it is to change a plan. In interpersonal relations, however, we cannot typically make a unilateral change in an ongoing plan, but we can try to get the other member of the relationship to change or abandon his or her goals. There are a number of ways we could do this, such as persuasion, negotiation, or perhaps even the use of force. A variation on this would be to get our partner to postpone the achievement of his or her goals to a later time.

Fortunately, people often possess similar goals. Oftentimes, these goals may be achieved more quickly or with less effort than by either individual working alone. In other cases, achievement of the goals may be possible only if they both work together. But, having similar goals does not always lead to positive goal relations. If both members of a couple wanted the last soda in the refrigerator, this would not lead to a positive goal relation. Moreover, people sometimes have quite different goals, but the same plan, which requires action by both members, can be used to achieve both goals at the same time.

Goal relations may change over the course of a relationship. Kelley (1979) has argued that as relationships develop, motives are often transformed from more individualistic ones to ones centered on the outcome of the dyad. For example, members of a dyad may shift from trying to maximize individual outcomes to trying to maximize the outcomes of the dyad.

Also, one member of a couple may have a higher order goal about the other such that achievement of a wide range of different goals by the partner will satisfy that goal. For instance, if one member has the goal of making the other happy, there are a number of different things the other person can do that would be consistent with that goal.

Other factors that contribute to positive goal-based relations are

1. Similar beliefs about other people and the world. For example, even when two individuals share the same compatible goals, if one individual uses a strategy that the other individual views as morally unacceptable, there is apt to be conflict.
2. Use of similar strategies, both in terms of style and content. Generally, if our partner uses a strategy that we would use to accomplish the same goal, we are apt to understand what our partner is trying to do and to more accurately predict their behavior. Whether the strategies are similar or not, if the behavioral enactments in our strategies easily "mesh" with the behavioral enactments in our partner's strategies (Kelly et al., 1983), there is less apt to be an interruption in an ongoing sequence that might lead to negative affect (Berscheid, 1983). Furthermore, as a couple's behavioral sequences become "meshed" (Kelley et al., 1983), each member's behavior may play a major role in the other's plans, helping to facilitate partner and relationship goals.
3. Similar and complementary resources. Complementary skills, abilities, and knowledge, may allow one individual to fill in a gap left by the other. Similar skills (e.g., cognitive abilities) are often needed to meet important needs of the partners (e.g., to have a mutually intellectually stimulating conversation).

Some individuals may have a great deal of difficulty developing plans that involve apparently conflicting (or at least noncomplementary) goals because they have a deficit in cognitive skills necessary for successful integrations, they cannot come up with such a plan and strategies fast enough, or one isn't available in their repertoire, or both. Presumably, over the course of development, children become better at integrating conflicting goals and employing strategies (from ever increasing repertoires) that most effectively meet their composite of available (salient) goals in a given situation. Even so, there may be marked individual differences, with some adults continuing to have difficulty integrating goals (especially those that involve conflicts) and changing plans to reflect these integrations. Problems with such integrations may lead to intrapersonal and interpersonal goal conflicts.

We are reminded of the man at the baggage carousel in the airport who kept pushing the elderly women in the process of getting his luggage. Perhaps he had deficits in his skills for modifying his plan so as to both not hurt the women and still get his luggage.

This analysis of goal relations suggests that if we wish to predict which plan an individual is apt to execute, we first need to know that individual's goals, the relations among them, and the individual's resources for goal integration and plan generation. We will also need to know what factors will facilitate or interfere with the likelihood of enacting a particular plan (e.g., knowledge of the plan, resources for enacting plans of action, beliefs about various plans). Finally, we also need to know something about the goals, plans, resources, and beliefs of any individuals with whom they are interacting.

Linkages. Although individuals may have a variety of goals, plans, resources and beliefs that may be interassociated, the nature and strength of these linkages presumably play a major role in determining what strategies are actually enacted in social interaction. For example, individuals may have a well worked out plan for getting attention (e.g., play the class clown) but not think of using that plan for obtaining other goals or subgoals (e.g., making money) even though they could (e.g., playing the clown in a nightclub act could make one money). An interesting question then becomes how strong are the linkages among the goals, plans, resources, and beliefs of individuals. To what extent does an element from one category (e.g., a specific goal, a specific resource, a specific strategy, or belief) call up linkages to specific members of other categories?

An additional question concerns linkages among different elements within a category. For example, let us consider two goals and their relationship. Imagine an individual who finds that when the goal of being assertive is salient, a second goal (do not alienate/hurt others) is called up. Such a linkage might come about through repeatedly discovering that when strategies are engaged in that effectively meet both goals concurrently, others are more responsive to one's needs and requests.

It also seems likely that the presence *and* absence of various resources may affect the development of other goal-based structures. For example, individuals who have a variety of abilities are especially likely to find that using those resources is rewarding, enhancing the importance of goals associated with those resources. Or, not having resources may influence which alternative goals and plans one enacts and may also influence one's belief system. For example, we have probably all known people who believe that in close relationships there are "winners and losers." It is tempting to wonder whether such beliefs are particularly prevalent among couples who have difficulty integrating intrapersonal and interpersonal conflicting goals and who may have trouble seeing alternative strategies for conflict resolution (e.g., creative goal integrations that maximally meet the needs of both individuals).

The goal-based structures that we have outlined here (goals, plans, resources, and beliefs) are like "building blocks" with which to build a variety of structures, including structures for thinking about persons, situations, and relationships. Next we consider some of these different types of structures.

PERSON STRUCTURES

Idiographic Configurations

We would expect that for most individuals some higher order goals form a stable core. We have argued (Miller & Read, 1987; Miller & Read, in press) that most stable individual differences can be viewed as chronic configurations of (a) an individual's goals, (b) the plans and strategies for attaining those goals, (c) the resources required for successfully carrying out the plans, and (d) beliefs about the world that affect the execution of their plans. Similar arguments concerning the importance of one or more of these components have been made by Allston (1970, 1975) and Carbonnell (1979). Pervin (1983) and Mischel (1973) have also argued for the importance of plans and goals in understanding individual differences. Obviously the exact complex chronic configurations of goals, plans, resources, and beliefs are apt to be unique and idiographic for different individuals.

Traits

We argue that although many of these chronic configurations are idiosyncratic, some configurations are shared as "fuzzy sets" (Rosch, 1975; 1978) by a large number of people and as a result are apt to be recognized with a trait label. An individual's configurations may differ in how prototypical (Rosch, 1975, 1978; Rosch & Mervis, 1975) they are of a particular trait, with configurations varying in their similarity to the central members or prototypes of the category. Thus, we are adopting a prototype notion of traits (Buss & Craik, 1983, 1984; Cantor & Mischel, 1977, 1979), in which these configurations may share a "family resemblance" (Rosch & Mervis, 1975) to each other and so form a coherent set, even though they may differ in their similarity to the central members of the category. Our approach, however, differs from previous approaches that have examined the prototypicality of traits. First, we view the concept "trait" from an interactional perspective, and we are concerned with traits as mediating systems for behavior (Magnusson & Endler, 1977) unlike Buss and for Craik (1983, 1984) who view traits as summary statements, without making any assumptions about latent causal structures. Second, in contrast to previous approaches (Buss & Craik, 1983, 1984; Cantor & Mischel, 1977, 1979) we are concerned with the configuration and organization of components or "units" (e.g., goals, plans, resources, and beliefs) that make up structures that may prototypically be viewed as traits. Third, we are interested in how individuals cluster particular enactments (behaviors) by the functions or goals that those enactments serve rather than on the basis of mere surface behavioral similarity (Barsalou, 1985). We elaborate this point later.

For a concrete example of how such a configuration can be viewed as a trait, let's consider Alan. Alan very much wants and likes to be with people, engages in various plans and behaviors to interact with them, possesses the skills and resources to successfully interact with them, and has certain beliefs and knowledge that are instrumental to carrying out his plans. In terms of the present model, Alan has a chronic configuration of goals, plans, resources, and beliefs that might best be described by the trait sociable. An example is given in Figure 11.1A.

To be called sociable, Alan presumably has to have the goal of wanting to be with people. Further, a truly sociable individual should be able to successfully carry out various plans for social interaction. An individual who is not able to interact successfully (e.g., achieve his or her goal to be with others) would probably not be considered sociable but instead may be chronically lonely. Figure 11.1 contrasts sociability with chronic loneliness. As can be seen, the sociable person and the lonely person may have very similar goals. However, because their beliefs,

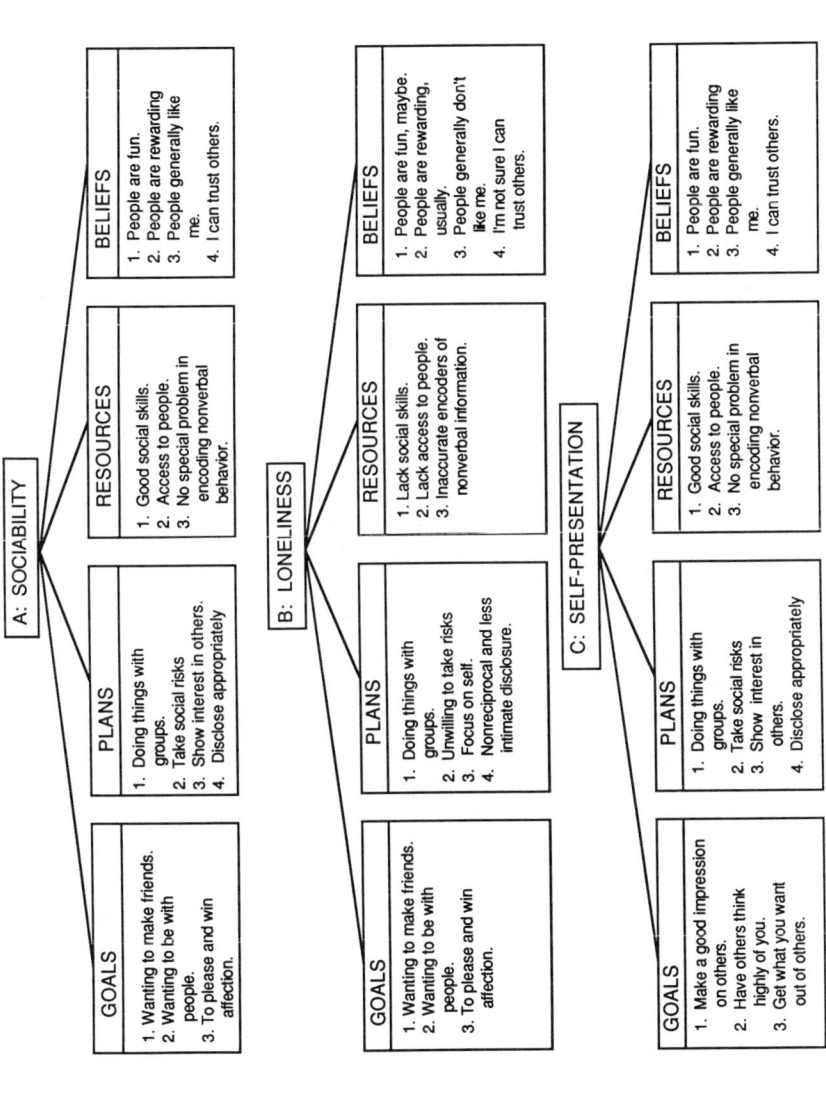

FIG. 11.1 A comparison of sociability, loneliness and self-presentation. From Miller, L. C., & Read, S. J. (1987). Why am I telling you this? Self-disclosure in a goal-based model of personality. In V. Derlega & J. H. Berg (Eds.), *Self-disclosure: Theory, research and therapy*. New York: Plenum Publishing Corporation. Reprinted with permission of the publisher.

strategies, and resources differ considerably, we would expect only one of these individuals to be construed as falling on the high end of the sociability dimension.

Likewise, individuals may have similar strategies but associate these strategies with the attainment of different goals. Thus, one individual, Ellen may be quite likely to self-disclose intimate information about herself when she is trying to impress others, whereas another person, Alan, may typically self-disclose only when he is trying to make new friends. Given a chronic configuration of Ellen's goals, strategies, beliefs, and resources, as indicated in Figure 11.1c, the trait "positive self-presenter" might be a more useful way to describe Ellen's constellation of goals and strategies, whereas Alan's constellation of goals and strategies might be better summarized (see Figure 11.1A) as involving "sociability" (Cheek & Buss, 1981), or "need for affiliation" (Murray, 1938). In short, although both Ellen and Alan may have similar, overlapping strategies, because these strategies are associated with different chronic goals, Alan and Ellen could be said to possess different traits. (This suggests that individuals who are attempting to make inferences about others' traits on the basis of limited observations may often have difficulty. We discuss this problem further in the portion of this manuscript concerned with "perceiving and understanding others").

Goal Relations and Traits. As suggested earlier, in considering the probability of a particular plan being executed, researchers should consider an individuals's goals, plans for enactment, resources pertinent to enactment, and beliefs relevant to the goals and plans. By considering these goal structures as components of traits, researchers should be better able to understand why expected behaviors do not consistently occur (e.g., a resource was unavailable) and why and when we might expect behavioral change (e.g., a person develops new social skills or learns alternative strategies to more effectively enact a behavior critical to a plan). In addition, it is critical for researchers to consider how relations among goals may influence plan execution. For example, one individual may want to be intimate to establish a close relationship while simultaneously avoiding rejection. He may want to disclose his fears but considers this too "risky." Instead, he engages in a more moderate, compromise behavior (listening) that satisfies these multiple goals to some extent but that may not be the most effective strategy for either goal by itself. By viewing traits in terms of goal structures, researchers may have a more useful language for understanding those factors that affect the nature, frequency, and perceived coherence and consistency of behaviors.

Additional Organizational Frameworks

There are a variety of possible ways to organize information about people. For example, we may use categories, such as mother, that have "radial structures" (Lakoff, 1987), in which there is a central case and variations on it that one could not predict using general rules, but which are nevertheless consistent with it (e.g., stepmother, adoptive mother, natural mother, foster mother, surrogate mother, unwed mother, and so forth). And, these variations may refer to different "models" of mother (e.g., birth model, genetic model, nurturance model, marital model, genealogical model). But, when we consider how one would act out the *role* of being a mother we are probably likely to consider the model of mother Lakoff (1987) refers to as the "nurturance model" or the "female adult who nurtures and raises a child" (p. 74). In a similar way, we may think of the trait "extrovert" as a radial category in which there are a variety of "models" of extroverts involving a variety of goals (e.g., attention, recognition, control, to make a positive impression, to get ahead, etc.) that are associated with different extrovert stereotypes (e.g., politician, clown, bully, brain, guru, neurotic) as suggested by recent work examining the relationship between traits and social stereotypes (Cantor & Mischel, 1979; Andersen & Klatzky, 1987).

Furthermore, we may have a variety of additional cognitive structures for organizing person information. Such possibilities include "possible selves" (Markus & Nurius, 1986) that can be viewed as the cognitive manifestation of enduring goals, aspirations, motives, fears, and threats. Possible selves provide the specific self-relevant form, meaning, organization, and direction to these dynamics. As such, they provide the essential link between the self-concept and motivation" (p. 954).

This is a distinct and interesting concept because of the emphasis on the possibilities for the future. Although very useful, one is reminded of Allport's (1937) concern in describing "multiple selves" (p. 146) when he wrote

> The case for the existence of separate and distinct selves is easy to exaggerate.... No one, as William James remarked, can at one time be a bon vivant, a philosopher, a tone poet, a lady-killer, and a saint; such diverse integrations could not keep house together in the same tenement of clay. Even if these phases *succeeded* one another in the course of life the picture would still be one of pathological disunity (p. 147).

Thus, the ways and extent to which such "possible selves" are integrated would seem to be an important question, which we consider in a later section of this chapter.

A variety of other goal-based structures are possible. Some examples include the use of personal strivings (Emmons, 1986), role themes, interpersonal themes and life themes (Schank & Abelson, 1977), and life tasks (Cantor, Norem, Niedenthal, Langston, & Brower, 1987) to organize information about self and other people in situations. Such structures may also be used to explain our own or other's actions and reactions and make predictions about future interactions and outcomes.

It also seems likely that there are goal-based mechanisms by which the self evaluates itself and stores memories concerning such evaluations. Such self-esteem evaluations, given the present model, may greatly depend on whether individuals feel that they have the resources and opportunities to accomplish the goals that they wish to achieve, whether the resources they lack are ones they can accrue and that they will have the resources to accrue, and whether they have made the most of those resources that they have had access to in the past. Similarly, our evaluations of other people might involve similar mechanisms.

Integration and Coherence of Persons

One important issue regarding person structures is the extent to which these structures are isolated, fragmented, or part of more or less integrated selves. There are likely to be individual differences in the extent, strength and nature of the linkages among various self structures and how these are tied to general models and processes for understanding others and relationships. These differences might be tied to changes with age and critical "milestones" in one's life, such as marriage or retirement. The adolescent and college years especially may be those during which individuals try out a variety of possibilities and where integrations may be less likely and more limited in scope.

A variety of factors may influence the probability that individuals will develop more integrated "selves." For example, individuals who score high on the self-consciousness scale (Fenigstein, Scheier, & Buss, 1975) report being more aware of their thoughts, feelings, and motives. Chronically focusing on these various facets of self at a meta level would appear to increase the possibilities of individuals taking an active role in developing a more integrated model of self. In fact, such individuals have been shown to be better at predicting their own behavior (Turner & Peterson, 1977). Interestingly enough, Allport (1937) noted that

> while differentiation and integration [of personality] are under way there develop gradually an important core of *self-consciousness*. Perhaps nothing

contributes to the unity of personality as much as this subjective point of reference, by virtue of which the individual feels that there is coherence between his memories of the past and his plans for the future ... in order to bind the past with the future, memory must be supplemented by *imagination,* another unifying capacity of the self. With its aid the human being may plan his life when he is young, and spend years of concerted effort in pursuit of his chosen goals. (p. 345).

Individuals, then, who are more self-aware may be more likely to use a collection of metacognitive skills (Dorner, 1985; Kluwe & Friedrichsen, 1985) in integrating their goals and in planning their future actions.

Relational Structures

The person structures that individuals use in organizing self information are also apt to be used in thinking about others (Markus & Smith, 1981), as well as thinking about our relationships with others. And just as we may think of "possible selves" (Markus & Nurius, 1986), we may also think of "possible others" and "possible relationships" that we may conjure up when we meet another (we may project what a relationship might be like between us). Or, our past relationships may be used as a framework for guiding relationship choice in present relationships (Read, Collins, & Miller, 1988) and possible future relationships. Or, we may think about our present relationships and compare them with relationships that we have had in the past and relationships we might have in the future (Rusbult, 1983) in making judgments about current relationship satisfaction.

Individuals may base their projections of what a relationship might be like with someone, at least in part, on the resources that they perceive that the other has and how those resources would be likely to mesh with one's own and afford the accomplishment of various personal and interpersonal goals (e.g., marrying someone with whom one might have frequent intellectually stimulating conversations, buy a home, have children, etc.). In doing so, individuals probably attempt to take into account whether the other's goals and plans (for resource use and allocation) are likely to mesh with or conflict with one's own, whether present and possible future goal integration is possible (e.g., will it be possible for us to negotiate two careers in the future?), whether one's personal resources will be depleted or enhanced by one's relationship with another, and how such "possible relationships" might change—how we view ourselves and our own personal possibilities.

SITUATIONAL STRUCTURES

The preceding analysis of persons provides a major part of an explicit conceptual framework for a general goal based model of inter-personalism. One missing piece, however, is a specification of the features of social situations. This missing piece is provided by Argyle et al.'s (1981) analysis of situations. Several of the major aspects of situations that they identify have a parallel in our analysis of traits. First, the chief component of a situation is the goals whose satisfaction it affords. Second, situations have associated with them rules governing the appropriateness of behavior in that situation. Third, different situations have different roles that people can fill. Each role specifies particular behaviors that are appropriate for people filling those roles. The rules and roles associated with situations make certain kinds of plans more salient, while at the same time restricting other kinds of plans. Fourth, situations often provide or make available resources and objects that are important to carrying out different plans. Finally, associated with any given situation are elements and sequences of behavior that can be used to attain goals within that situation.

Thus, both personality and situation can be analyzed in a common language. As a result, it becomes much easier to specify precisely what the interaction should be between any given situation and any given person. For instance, we have argued that central to most traits is a goal, and central to Argyle et al.'s conception of a situation is the goals whose satisfaction it affords. Thus, the behavior of individuals in any given situation should depend on the degree and type of match between the goals of the individuals and the goals whose satisfaction is afforded by the situation. Although the goals afforded by the situation are important, the behavior of an individual should also depend on the degree and type of match between the plans and resources in the individual's repertoire and the plans of action appropriate for attaining the goals of that situation. Individuals often possess a number of different ways for attaining a particular goal. The situation should affect which, if any, of these plans are chosen and how smoothly and effectively chosen plans are enacted.

Analyzing traits and situations in this way provides an explicit conceptual framework for the analysis of person-situation interactions. We can think of them in terms of the interplay between the goals, plans, resources and beliefs of the individual and the goals, plans, resources, and rules and roles associated with the situation.

This approach bears a strong similarity to Murray's (1938) attempt to characterize person and situation in a common language. Murray referred to characteristics of the individual that directed behavior as needs, while referring to aspects of the situation that activated those needs as press. Thus, if an individual had a need for achievement or a need for affiliation, the situation would be characterized in terms of its press for achievement or its press for affiliation. However, the present formulation goes beyond Murray in its emphasis on the additional components of plans, resources, and beliefs and the way in which these additional characteristics of person and situation also interact.

Inter-personalism also makes it quite easy to analyze person-person interactions in terms of how the goals, plans, resources and beliefs of each member of a dyad are affected by the perceived goals, plans, resources and beliefs of the other. Because the perception and understanding of the other is central to analyzing person-person interactions, we need a model of how people understand others. The following model of person perception and attribution seems particularly appropriate for dyadic interactions.

PERCEIVING AND UNDERSTANDING OTHERS

Understanding the Meaning of Actions

How do we make sense of our partner's behavior in our ongoing interactions with her or him? Perhaps the best place to start in answering this question is to look at the structure of the behavioral sequences we are trying to understand. Awareness of this structure provides insight into the task facing us when we try to understand a behavioral sequence.

Behavioral episodes have a general form consisting of four components: (a) the goal of the sequence, (b) the factors that instigated the goal, (c) the behaviors that make up a plan aimed toward the achievement of that goal, and (d) the outcome of the sequence (e.g., Miller et al., 1960; Schank & Abelson, 1977). Such behavioral episodes take place in specific physical settings and involve both the actors who carry out the actions and various objects that are necessary to the actions.

That behavioral episodes have this form suggests that understanding a behavioral sequence requires people to determine what plan the individual actions form, the goals of that plan, the factors that instigated the goals and precisely how that plan would achieve those goals (Read, 1987). Basically, people must figure out how everything fits together into a coherent scenario or story. The information necessary to create this scenario is rarely explicit. Instead, to tie the events together numerous inferences must be made, relying both on information available in the context and on detailed knowledge about the social and physical worlds. In line with Trzebinski (this volume) and others (Schank &

Abelson, 1977), we argue that much of this knowledge is in terms of action-oriented schemata that represent the goals and plans of people.

Before considering how individuals create such scenarios or stories, we will discuss some of the detailed social knowledge that individuals use. Then we will examine the steps that perceivers go through in comprehending particular interactions and forming coherent understandings of interactions, other people, and relationships.

The same knowledge that we use to plan our own behavior is also used to understand other people's behavior (also see Wilensky, 1983). For instance, our knowledge of goals and the plans needed to achieve them is used both to plan our behavior and to understand and explain other's behavior. Next we outline some of the numerous forms of knowledge that people possess and how they may be used to interpret an interaction partner's behavior. We start by discussing knowledge that is culturally shared and then discuss more idiographic types of knowledge. Although our discussion is restricted to social knowledge, clearly physical knowledge is also important.

Sources of Culturally Shared Social Knowledge

Social Norms, Rules, and Maxims. These structures prescribe what one ought to do in a social interaction (norms and rules) and the assumptions (maxims) that individuals in a given culture subscribe to (cf. McLaughlin, 1984 for a fascinating review). Some are tied to specific situations, and others apply across all social situations. As Argyle et al. (1981) have pointed out, most situations possess rules governing the appropriateness of behavior in that specific context. On the other hand, rules, such as those governing what is moral and ethical behavior, tend to apply across all situations. In addition to guiding our behavior, knowledge of these rules is crucial in the understanding of behavior.

One interesting class of rules that apply across situations are those regulating conversation (reviewed in McLaughlin, 1984). For example, Grice (1975) suggests that there are a number of general maxims that if followed tend to result in a "cooperative contribution" (McLaughlin, 1984). Among these are "The maxim of quantity"—be as informative as is required but do not give unnecessary information, and "The maxim of relation"—make sure your contribution is relevant to the purpose of the exchange. When violations occur, conversants will try to infer a reason why (Grice, 1975). As a result people can sometimes use deliberate violations of the maxims to convey information. For instance, Grice (1975, cited in Clark, 1985, p. 191) gives the example of the following letter of recommendation for a philosophy job: "Dear Sir, Mr. X's command of English is excellent, and his attendance at tutorials has been regular. Yours, etc." The writer is violating the maxim of quantity by giving much less information than is required for a letter of recommendation and may be violating the maxim of relation by giving information that does not seem strictly relevant to the purpose of the letter. Because we assume that the writer is aware of these maxims, we infer that there is a purpose to this violation which is to convey, indirectly, that the candidate lacks the necessary skills. Thus, structures, such as norms, rules, and maxims, provide members of a culture with a background of what is "normal" or "expected" against which to predict and understand behavior and to make inferences about why violations occur.

Scripts, Plans, Goals, and Themes. Schank and Abelson (1977) have analyzed a number of types of social knowledge, focusing primarily on knowledge about the plans and goals of individuals (see Read, 1987 for a summary). Evidence that such goal-oriented structures are extremely important in comprehending behavior has been reviewed by Black, Galambos, and Read (1984), Galambos, Abelson, and Black (1986), and Trzebinski (this volume).

Scripts are representations of stereotyped or routinized action sequences (e.g., going on a first date; going camping) that provide information about a number of different characteristics of the action such as (a) its typical goals, (b) the actors and roles found in that context, (c) objects and instruments that play an important role in behavior in that script, (d) the context in which the script is typically enacted, (e) conditions that must be fulfilled to enact the script, and (f) the sequence of actions that constitute the script. Such knowledge makes important contributions to our understanding of behavioral sequences. For instance, if we recognize that a particular sequence in a bar is the "pick up script" we can make inferences about the likely goals of the individuals in that script and can make predictions about possible directions the interaction may take.

When knowledge of more concrete, stereotyped action sequences is unavailable, we can still understand people's actions using our knowledge of plans. These tend to be more abstract and general than scripts and are far less likely to be tied to specific situational contexts. For instance, a general plan may be to gain control of an object. Associated with that would be more specific plans for different ways of gaining control of objects, such as ask someone or take by force. Such plans are less concrete and specific than scripts. Nevertheless they provide the same kinds of knowledge, such as the goals of the sequence, typical objects, and people, that play a role in the plan and the conditions necessary for successfully carrying it out.

Understanding others also depends on detailed knowledge of possible goals. Associated with different goals is information, such as the conditions that initiate them and plans that can be used to achieve them. Since we know what goals are likely to be active in response to what factors, knowledge of the conditions to which an individual is responding often allows us to make inferences about goals they might have. And because goals are often associated with particular plans and scripts, recognition of a particular sequence as a specific plan or script provides some clues as to the individual's goals.

Knowledge about an individual's goals often comes from knowing their roles and their interpersonal relationships. These "themes" (Schank & Abelson, 1977) provide information about the expected characteristics of people in particular roles, such as the behaviors they enact, their goals, and the conditions that initiate these goals. Role themes also provide information about the likely behavior of people who interact with the role member. For instance, knowing that someone is a mother, a boyfriend, a husband, or a wife provides some expectations about the possible behavior of people who interact with them in complementary roles. Schank and Abelson (1977) also suggest that our behavior is often organized by "life themes," which are general patterns of goals that apply across a variety of contexts.

Traits and Social Stereotypes. Social stereotypes triggered by gender, race, physical appearance, clothing, mannerisms, etc., play a crucial role in social inference (Cantor & Mischel, 1979; Hamilton, 1981). They carry with them beliefs about such things as the typical behaviors, goals, interests, and traits of the individuals who fit these stereotypes. Stereotypes should be particularly influential in the early parts of a social interaction, when other kinds of information are scarce.

Earlier (see also Miller & Read, 1987) we argued that traits can frequently be viewed as chronic configurations of goals, plans, resources, and beliefs. Therefore, trait information can often be used to make inferences about an individual's goals, plans, resources, and beliefs. Conversely, people can make inferences from an individual's behavior in a particular context to likely configurations of goals, plans, resources, and beliefs. Frequently, this information can, in turn, be used to make trait attributions.

How do people make inferences from behaviors to traits? In interactions, individuals receive an *array* of information about others, frequently including long sequences of behavior made up of numerous individual actions. Perceivers, we would suggest, try to make coherent inferences from this array, even trying to "fit together" information that, at least on the surface, seems incongruent. Part of this task is ascertaining which behaviors constitute which plans and how these plans might be organized to achieve different hierarchies and configurations of goals. That is, perceivers try to figure out the goals, plans, resources, and beliefs of the target. If desired, this can then be used to make inferences about an individual's traits because traits are apt to be organized in terms of chronic configurations of these four components. However, this does not mean that people always automatically make trait inferences. Hoffman, Mischel, and Baer (1984) have demonstrated that people are more likely to use global trait descriptions and to be influenced by their implicit personality theories when they think that they will be communicating with someone else about the target individual. In the absence of a communicative intent, people are less likely to make global trait inferences.

Behaviors vary in how quickly and easily they lead to trait inferences about another. A behavior that is highly prototypical (Buss & Craik, 1983; 1984) of a trait leads to quicker and more confident attributions of the trait than does a less prototypical one (Cantor & Mischel, 1979). In addition, Reeder and Brewer (1979) have argued that some trait inferences are asymmetrical. For example, we are more willing to infer that someone is intelligent from one intelligent behavior than we are to infer that someone is stupid from one stupid behavior.

Interestingly, Buss and Craik (1983, 1984) have noted that behaviors prototypical of a trait are frequently not topographically similar, suggesting that what makes these behaviors prototypical is *not* similarity among members of a category. However, if the category membership of behaviors is not based on similarity to other exemplars of the category, then what does define category membership? Recent work by Barsalou (1985) leads us to suggest one possible basis for membership in trait categories. He has argued that for some kinds of categories, among them what he calls goal-based categories, typicality judgments are based on the extent to which the category member fits an ideal. One kind of ideal is defined by the goal of the category. We have argued that goals are a central part of most traits. Thus, for traits, typicality of a category member or trait-related behavior may be based, at least to some extent, on the degree to which the behavior achieves the goal of the trait. Thus, we decide whether a behavior is aggressive, at least partially on whether it succeeds in hurting someone and we decide whether a behavior is affiliative on the basis of whether it brings us closer to someone.

Consistent with this argument, Murphy and Medin (1985) have observed that simple similarity among exemplars of a category is only rarely a sufficient explanation of the coherence of a category. They strongly argue that the conceptual coherence of a category depends on a theory, frequently a causal theory, that organizes it. We suggest that configurations of goals and their related plans, resources, and beliefs provide a causal theory that supplies the basis for coherence for many traits.

If the prototypicality of a behavior depends on the extent to which it achieves a goal, then even *single behaviors* that may be prototypical and diagnostic in isolation need to be understood in the context of the goals of the ongoing interaction and the relationships among individuals, to form a coherent understanding of the interaction. The meaning of individual actions can change drastically as a function of their context (e.g., Read, Druian, & Miller, 1987). Although individuals may make confident initial trait inferences based on single prototypical or diagnostic behaviors, these may be vulnerable to change if they are not embedded in a rich, coherent, supporting array.

Self Schemas, Other Schemas, and Mental Models. Self-schemata and self-concepts play an important role in person perception (Markus & Smith, 1981) and interpersonal processes (Swann, 1983, 1987). What we believe or know to be our characteristics often seems to affect our perceptions of others and their behavior toward us. For instance, a rich woman probably responds differently to people's friendly overtures than someone who is middle-class. She will have explanations for why others befriend her (e.g., her money, her connections) that the middle-class woman would not. And since she has more potential explanations she may have greater difficulty differentiating among them (Jones & Davis, 1965; Kelley, 1971).

Other sources of knowledge are "mental models" of what people in general are like and what relationships are like (Bowlby, 1973; Collins & Read, 1987; Hazan & Shaver, 1987). These mental models are presumably based on our interactions with other people, in particular our parents (cf. Waring, 1987). And these models should affect our inferences about other's actions. If we think people are trustworthy, we will tend to make different inferences about someone's goals than if we tend to think that people can't be trusted. Or, if we think that marriage is typically an exploitative relationship we will tend to interpret our spouse's actions as attempts to take advantage of us.

Assumptions About Other's Meta-Cognitive Abilities. People possess meta-cognitive abilities and self-regulatory skills (e.g., Dorner, 1985; Kluwe &

Friedrichsen, 1985; Kuhl, 1985), such as the ability to delay gratification, to project the consequences of one's actions, or to try to integrate multiple goals. It seems likely that assumptions about people's possessions of these skills play an important role in social inference.

For instance, we assume that adults are more able to project the consequences of their actions than are children. Thus, because foreseeability is a major component of judgments of responsibility and intentionality (e.g., Fincham & Jaspers, 1980; Heider, 1958), we judge adults as more responsible for the consequences of their behavior and are more likely to ascribe intentions to them. Yet if some adults lack the ability to project the consequences of their actions we may erroneously ascribe an intention to them. Or, if someone lacks the skills to try to integrate their goals with someone else's, we may attribute selfish intentions to them, when in reality they lack some necessary skills.

For example, recall the beginning of the chapter and the example of the man in the airport trying to get his luggage and nearly trampling a 60-year-old woman. We initially assumed that the man was somewhat rude and hostile because he seemed aware that someone might get hurt and there were easily available alternative courses of action such as going to the other side of the carousel where there was ample room. We assumed that this man (as an adult) was capable of combining two goals and generating new plans to come up with a solution that adequately satisfied both, especially since the new plan was so obvious to outside observers.

But what if our assumption was wrong? Unfortunately, some people, perhaps like the man in our airport experience, may have difficulty combining their own intrapersonal goals (e.g., getting one's own luggage and avoiding harming others) and/or combining their goals with those of another where conflict may arise. Such an individual could clearly be concerned about hurting others (as this man stated) but simply have no idea how to implement this, given his other conflicting goals. Such a man might easily view hurting others in such a context as the outcome of situational constraints ("the women were in the way when I went to get my luggage—they didn't move when they saw me coming").

Sources of Idiographic Knowledge

In the preceding discussion, we have considered shared social knowledge. However, we all possess types of knowledge that are unique to us. This knowledge, too, is important in the perception and understanding of behavior.

Mental Models of Unique Relationships. During an interaction and indeed during the course of a relationship, people develop mental models of both their interaction partner and the relationship itself (Park, 1986). These mental models are causal models that represent the characteristics of the persons, such as their goals, plans, resources, and beliefs, as well as representing the relations among these elements. In particular, they represent the causal and goal-based relations among elements. These models are dynamic representations that are continually updated in response to new information. Furthermore, because they are causal models they can be "run" so that we can use our model of a person to simulate how they might respond to some action of ours. Thus, these models can be used to guide our interactions with the individual and to predict and explain behavior.

This conception of mental model is adapted from work on mental models in cognitive psychology (e.g., Gentner & Stevens, 1983; Johnson-Laird, 1983). Work on mental models of physical systems has demonstrated that people have detailed models of physical systems that contain the objects in a given domain, their characteristics, and their causal interactions with one another. These models are used by individuals to understand and predict the behavior of such physical systems. They can be "run" so that people can simulate the changes in the physical system across time in response to changes in inputs to the system. Although the elements making up models of persons will differ from models of things such as a steam engine, many of the general principles and the ways in which people use such models should be similar. As Pennington and Hastie (1986) observe, models of such causal systems play an important role in a number of domains, such as jury decision making, medical diagnosis, and foreign policy decision making.

How do people create such models? Individuals entering relationships make inferences about the likely goals, beliefs, plans, and resources of the other and gradually start developing a model of their partner and a model of their unique relationship with each other by combining their own goals, plans, resources, and beliefs with their perception of their partner's. This is modified and elaborated as the relationship progresses, with more concrete and detailed information added and additional connections made among their own goal-based structures and those of their partner. Some of these inter-connections involve discovering goals, strategies, and beliefs that the other may not view positively or that may be incompatible with the other's goals, strategies, and beliefs. Among the numerous possible responses to this discovery will be attempting either to work out a unique understanding of these differences, or identifying incompatible structures. For example, imagine that we discover in a developing relationship that in order to get "a word in edgewise" we need to violate a rule about interrupting another (which we may believe indicates rudeness, but which does not seem to be how our partner interprets interruptions). One approach may be to modify who we apply this belief to, whereas another may be to deactivate it completely. Unfortunately, people may often have difficulty "working through" such incompatible structures. Therefore, learning to understand and articulate beliefs, feelings, and motives within one's relationships may be critical to satisfaction in close relationships such as marriage (cf. Waring, 1987 for a discussion of cognitive restructuring of disclosure in marital therapy).

In developing a relationship, partners may be able to try out new strategies that they would not have been comfortable with previously. And, partners may discover how their unique relationships allow them to achieve goals that previously were out of reach. For example, individuals may possess resources they previously lacked that enable them to achieve personal as well as interpersonal goals. Or, an individual's perceptions that a partner is "accepting" may reduce the salience of some goals (e.g., avoid rejection), enabling the individual to more effectively enact plans to reach other, previously blocked goals (e.g., enhanced intimacy). In short, we would argue that individuals develop mental models of relationships that affect the activation, deactivation, and creation of goal-based structures guiding behavior in relationships.

Analogies to Specific Situations. In addition to our mental models of other people and relationships we also possess a rich set of memories about our experiences. Because our representation of these events are presumably structured in terms of the plans and goals of the interactants, this information should be available for understanding and explaining behavior. For instance, many of us have found ourselves saying something like, "Oh, I know why George is upset. He's acting just like he did the last time Martha walked out on him." Or, "I know why George is so upset. He's acting just like Jeff did when his wife walked out on him." In both cases we are using an analogy to a previous experience to explain someone's behavior. We should be particularly likely to use specific experiences when more general knowledge does not seem particularly applicable or when a particular experience provides an especially good fit. Read and Jones (1988) have demonstrated that when people were asked to explain a woman's suicide they would use an analogy to a previous case study of a suicide. Read and Cesa (1988) found that people would often explain the violation of an expectation by an analogy to a similar event they had learned about previously.

Developing Models of the Interaction, Our Partner, Our Relationship

How might we use this knowledge to understand an interaction? In the following discussion, we outline one possible model. Understanding a dyadic interaction is very similar to what happens when we read a short story or novel. As we progress we build a representation of the sequence of events. New information is integrated with the preexisting representation. We continually build and add to our model of the characters and the sequence of events (Read, 1987).

We assume that relevant knowledge is activated through a spreading activation process (e.g., Anderson, 1983; Collins & Loftus, 1975). Input activates relevant knowledge and activation then spreads to related structures. The greater the activation of a structure, the more likely it is to be used to interpret information. Structures that are used in comprehension receive additional activation, but those that are not decay.

Initially, we categorize people (e.g., gender, race or role) and the situation we are presented with, activating a set of knowledge structures. As the interaction proceeds, additional knowledge structures are activated and subsequent actions are interpreted within the context of previous actions and connected to our current scenario. New actions are connected to the existing scenario as follows: (a) We examine whether this action could be part of a plan or causal sequence suggested by our current scenario. If so, the action is connected to the scenario and it is at least partially explained. (b) If we fail to connect the action to our scenario, we then search general world knowledge for a plan of which it may be a part that can be connected to the existing scenario. (c) This new plan or sequence may generate expectations and be used to interpret subsequent input. (d) If the action is part of a plan, we try to identify its goal. (e) Once identified, we examine whether the goal is merely part of a larger plan or whether it is an end in itself. (f) If the latter, we try to identify its source, such as an interpersonal role, a personal relationship, or some occurrence that instigated the goal. We see if this information "fits" with other information or if it is discrepant from our existing mental models and representations of this person, the roles they are apt to enact, and/or their relationships with others. This model assumes that there are multiple knowledge structures active at the same time and that oftentimes interpreting a sequence requires people to integrate these multiple sources of knowledge.

Several principles probably govern how people arrive at a coherent understanding of the dyadic interaction, of the persons in the context of the interaction, and the unique relationships of those individuals. Theorists (for a summary see Wilensky, 1983) have identified a number of principles, or metarules, of story comprehension that should also affect people's representations of social interactions (Read, 1987). They should apply as well to people's representations and developing models of persons. For example, the *principle of exhaustion* says that people should pick the interpretation accounting for the most data. Thus, the observer must attempt to develop a representation that takes into account the total array of sequences of actions (not just single behaviors), the characteristics of the situation, and the perceived attributes and stylistic facets of the person. Doing this often requires testing out "alternative explanations and models" concerning this person and relationship.

Another metarule, the *principle of parsimony*, suggests that one's interpretation should maximize the connections among events. For instance, if one interpretation of a sequence is of two unrelated plans and the second interpretation is of two plans that are part of a broader plan, people should choose the second interpretation. To make this more concrete, let's consider the following behavioral sequence:

1. Mary congratulates Ellen, saying she's just heard from Bill the happy news that he's going to propose to Ellen. Ellen is delighted and goes off to plan the wedding.
2. An hour later, Mary tells Bill she's crazy about him and she'll agree to his proposal if they elope immediately. Bill embraces Mary.

From the first behavioral sequence alone, we should infer that Mary is trying to be friendly and helpful. From the second sequence alone, we should infer that Mary is trying to enhance commitment and get Bill to marry her. However, from the entire behavioral sequence we should infer that Mary is trying to hurt Ellen. Read and Marcus (1988) have shown that this is precisely what people do.

Note several interesting things about this example. First, the last interpretation would be improbable if we were not trying to find a parsimonious explanation maximizing the connections among inputs. Second, the individual behaviors by themselves do not seem prototypical of possible negative traits (e.g., hostile, manipulative, aggressive). Yet the whole sequence taken together strongly suggests such traits. This goes back to our earlier point that the trait assigned to a behavior is not solely dependent on the prototypicality of the isolated behavior, but rather depends on the meaning of the behavior in context. Third, this example suggests that when our interaction partners use indirect or deceptive strategies or strategies that involve "hidden goals, developing coherent interpretations of behavior and models of persons may require much more extensive information.

Explaining the Unexpected

Up to this point we have focused on the explanation and understanding of expected behavior. However, it frequently happens in social interaction that our expectations of what should happen are violated. Because the successful coordination of behavior depends on understanding what is going on, it becomes quite important to understand why our expectation failed or was violated. As Wilensky (1983) and others have argued, developing an explanation for an unexpected event is a critical component of diagnosing what went wrong and, therefore, what, if anything, can be done about it. For instance, if the reason for the unexpected event is that we had initially misidentified our partner's goal, coming up with that explanation would be a first step toward figuring out what their goal actually is and then modifying our behavior appropriately.

How might people go about explaining unexpected events? Suppose that someone is part way through an interaction when something unexpected happens. At this point a great deal of information is activated: their representation of the interaction so far, their mental model of this specific person, their model of themselves, their mental model of people in general, information about the situation, and much of the other knowledge that might have been activated in order to comprehend the interaction. Clearly not all of these sources of information are equally likely to be active. For example, those sources that are currently important to comprehension or that were recently used will be more active than those used in the beginning of the interaction.

Any of these active structures could be the source of the expectation that is violated. The source of the violated expectation should be an important piece of information in generating the explanation for the violation. There are a number of possible sources for the violated expectation and thus a number of different ways in which an event could be unexpected.

1. Violate what is typical or acceptable behavior for a given situation
2. Violate our expectations about the nature of the situation. We might show up for a party in shorts and sneakers, only to find every one else in formal evening wear.
3. Violate our model of ourself
4. Violate our expectancies of what people are like in general
5. Violate expectations based on knowledge of social stereotypes or roles

6. Contradict some aspect of our model of our partner, such as what we think his or her goals and typical plans are
7. Contradict some aspect of our model of our relationship with our partner
8. Be incompatible with a particular interpretation of a sequence of behaviors. Many an eager man has been jolted by a sisterly kiss on the cheek and a door quickly closing in his face at the end of an evening.

Now how do people explain such unexpected events? There are several possible ways in which people may generate an explanation. One possible source is the retrieval of explanations of previous expectation violations that have been stored in memory. Abelson and Lalljee (in press) and Schank (1986) argue that for some types of expectation failures, such as those that occur with some frequency (e.g., unexpected deaths), people come to develop stereotyped explanations that can be retrieved from memory and applied in the present situation. These stereotyped explanations have been termed explanation patterns (Schank, 1986) or explanation prototypes (Abelson & Lalljee, in press).

A primary memory index to these explanation patterns is the anomaly or failure they explain. Although Abelson and Lalljee (in press) argue that explanation prototypes are indexed in terms of failures or chronic difficulties in goal attainments, there are numerous sources of expectations and subsequent failures, not all of them having to do with failures of goal attainment. Thus, we would make the more general suggestion that one of the primary indices that can be used to retrieve explanation patterns is the source of the violated expectation.

Once the unexpected event has been noticed, people will try to retrieve an explanation for the expectation violation (Schank, 1982, 1986). All the currently active information, including the event that violated the expectation, provide possible retrieval cues into memory for possible explanations. However, the information that was the source of the violated expectation and the associated failure should provide a particularly important index into memory. For instance, if the source of the expectation was your model of the person, then you should preferentially search what you know about the person. On the other hand, if the source of the expectation was situational knowledge, then you might preferentially search what you know about the situation.

Explanation patterns have stored with them a stereotyped sequence, very much like a script, that explains how the anomalous event came about. Thus, if people can retrieve the appropriate pattern they can diagnose the problem that led to the expectation failure.

Many of these explanation patterns should be widely shared. However, over the course of any long-term relationship, we should develop explanation patterns that are specific to that relationship, in response to its unique problems and concerns. This suggests several interesting possibilities. First, to the extent that people develop appropriate explanation patterns they should be particularly quick to notice and diagnose problems in their interactions. However, if they fail to develop such patterns they will have trouble accurately diagnosing problems. Second, people could develop dysfunctional explanation patterns that lead them to misdiagnose their interactions. For example, work on attributions in close relationships (as reviewed by Fincham & Bradbury, 1987; Fletcher, Fincham, Cramer, & Heron, 1987; Sillars, 1985) demonstrates that members of dissatisfied couples attribute positive behaviors by their partner to factors external to the partner, while attributing negative behaviors by their partner to internal factors. Although such a pattern may be veridical, it is interesting to speculate that in some cases such patterns may be inaccurate and may be highly dysfunctional, helping to maintain negative interaction patterns. A third possibility that might contribute to problems in relationships is that one or both members of a couple may not have learned a pattern that most members of a culture know for diagnosing problems in interactions.

Sometimes retrieved explanations seem almost appropriate but do not quite fit the details of the case. Schank (1986) provides an extensive discussion of how people can actively modify explanation patterns to make them more appropriate.

In addition to these stereotyped patterns, a second possible source of explanations is being reminded of specific instances in which similar expectations failed (Read & Cesa, 1988; Schank, 1982). Read and Cesa (1988) have shown that people are reminded of such analogous expectation failures and will use explanations from previous failures to explain a present failure. This process of reminding may provide the basis for the development of the more general explanation patterns discussed earlier (Schank, 1986). Remindings of such previous expectation failures allow us to compare multiple specific instances in which similar expectations failed and attempt to ascertain whether there is an underlying pattern that can capture the commonalities among the events.

An alternative possibility for how people explain unexpected events does not rely on retrieval of explanations from memory, but instead suggests that people engage in a process of analysis, comparing what actually happened with the assumed causal background of what usually happens in that situation (Einhorn & Hogarth, 1986; Kahneman &

Miller, 1986; Lalljee & Abelson, 1983; Mackie, 1974). The common thread to these different analyses is that by comparing what actually happened to what usually happens (the assumed causal background) people will be able to identify those deviations from normality that are responsible for the unexpected outcome. Clearly, such an analysis does not depend on retrieving explanations from memory.

Part of the assumed causal background for an event will be the knowledge that is activated during the comprehension of the sequence. This suggests that different people may have different causal backgrounds activated for the same event. For instance, if we know someone well our mental model of them should be an extremely important part of the causal background, and our models of people in general should be relatively less important. However, if we do not know someone at all, then our model of people in general should be the primary causal background. Our mental model of them can play no role.

Because different causal backgrounds are spontaneously available, we may come up with very different explanations for the same behavior. Again consider the man in the airport. Presumably when the 60-year-old woman explained the man's behavior, her assumed causal background was the typical behavior of adult males. After all, she had never met this man before. Against that background his behavior was very atypical, and the question that would immediately come to mind was, "How does this man differ from other adult males his age?" "Well, given that his behavior was rude and hostile he must be a fairly hostile person." But now consider his wife. Because she presumably knows her husband well, her assumed background would be how *he* normally behaves, not how men in general behave. If we assume that his behavior in the airport was very different from what his wife was used to, then the question that would occur to her is, "How does this situation differ from the ones in which he behaves more normally?" One possibility would be to focus on the behavior of the two older women because they represent a potential difference from the normal causal background.

When someone with whom we are interacting behaves in an unexpected way, there are innumerable explanations specific to the concrete details of the situation. However, two major classes of explanation worth noting are the possibility that the partner has different goals than we thought or that they are having problems enacting plans (Lalljee & Abelson, 1983). When something unexpected happens, people consider the following possibilities (among others):

1. What the partner is doing is really quite consistent with what we know to be their goals, but their plan was misidentified. Once we

realize what they are doing, we see that it actually fits quite nicely with our model of them.

2. We were, in fact, mistaken about the other's goals. We may have attributed to them goals they do not actually possess or that have already been satisfied, or we may have failed to realize that they also possess additional goals that override or affect the first set. To explain their behavior we must identify their actual goals.

3. The other does possess the goals that we attributed to them but cannot carry out the necessary plans. They may lack a necessary resource, not know how to carry out the plan, or environmental factors may block plan enactment. Here we must explain what could be keeping them from enacting the plan.

4. One's partner may possess the hypothesized goal but not share the beliefs about ways to achieve that goal. For example, the two authors of this paper differ considerably on the meaning associated with different kinds of gifts.

5. Our partner misidentified our goal. We have all been in the midst of an interaction that is going badly when our partner says something like, "I thought you wanted X. I was just trying to help." To which you reply, "What made you think that?" Here our partner's goal has been to help us attain our goal, only to discover that they had misidentified the goal we wanted.

Whether we retrieve or generate an explanation, we may entertain multiple possibilities. From among these we must choose the most plausible or adequate. Several factors go into this judgment. First, it is probably the case that the more important it is that the explanation be correct, the higher the criteria for an adequate explanation. Second, adequacy should depend on the meta-rules we have outlined previously. Third, an adequate explanation should be consistent with known facts of physical causality and as far as possible should be consistent with what we know about this person and people in general.

While to some extent different processes are involved in explaining expected and unexpected behavior, clearly they also share many processes. To a large degree the explanation of unexpected behavior is embedded in the processes used for explaining expected events. For example, noticing that something is unexpected and then trying to retrieve an explanation depend heavily on the processes involved in understanding expected events.

INTER-PERSONALISM IN PROCESS: THE PLANNING AND COORDINATION OF BEHAVIOR

Now that we have outlined the components of the model, let us examine the roles they play in the planning and coordination of behavior in an ongoing interaction. As suggested in the flowchart in Figure 11.2, each member of the dyad brings to the interaction a unique set of goals, plans, resources, and beliefs. Some of these are chronic configurations that may be prototypically described as traits. Other possible organizations are Cantor's "life tasks" (e.g., Cantor et al., 1987) and Markus' "possible selves" (e.g., Markus & Nurius, 1986). The goals are organized in a partial hierarchy, with some goals being chronically more salient and important than others.

Individuals entering an interaction continually monitor both the external environment and their internal states. This monitoring has several results, one of which is a change in the activation of goals. Their importance may increase or decrease with changes in both internal and external factors.

In a dyadic interaction an individual's salient goals should be affected by the perceived goals, plans, resources, and beliefs of their partner. For instance, an individual who has the goal of establishing close friendships but who chronically has a goal of avoiding rejection may typically not disclose very much about herself except when she is with a colleague who is especially accepting and supportive. Here fear of rejection may be sufficiently reduced in salience that the typically low disclosing person "opens up" (See Miller, Berg, & Archer, 1983 for research consistent with this possibility). Salience can be further affected by the situation, since different situations afford the satisfaction of different goals, and different situations vary in whether they present a threat to one's goals (e.g., office meeting vs. tea at a cozy kitchen table).

Obviously, people do not wear signs listing their goals, plans, resources, and beliefs. Instead, we must figure them out. Doing this requires the use of detailed social and physical knowledge to create a detailed scenario that represents how the individual's actions fit together into a coherent plan aimed toward the attainment of some goal or set of goals. Earlier in this chapter, we outlined a model of how people may do this. Thus, attributional processes play a central role in dyadic interactions (Kelley, 1979; Kelley et al., 1983; Sillars, 1985).

Our goals may also be activated by a perceived discrepancy between what we wish to be and what is. For example, if a friend's behavior indicates that his view of us differs from our own, this may threaten our

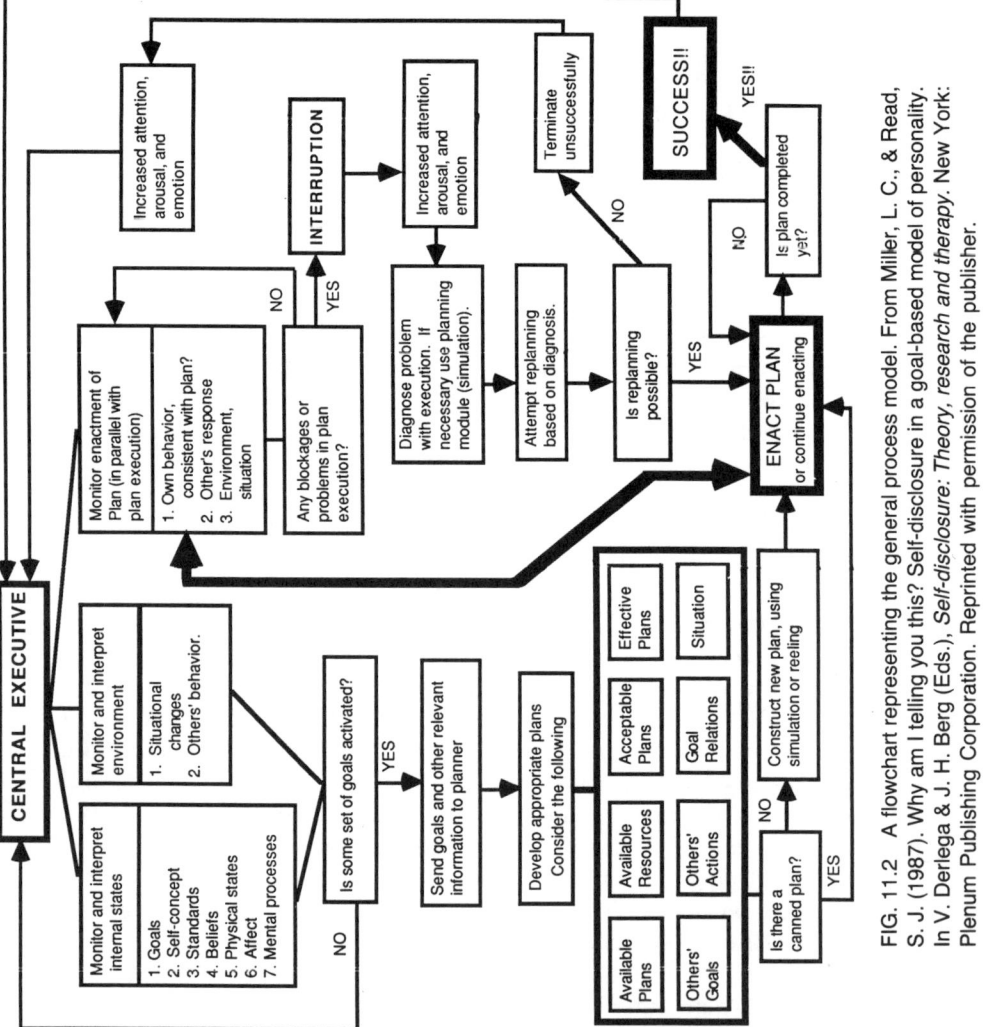

FIG. 11.2 A flowchart representing the general process model. From Miller, L. C., & Read, S. J. (1987). Why am I telling you this? Self-disclosure in a goal-based model of personality. In V. Derlega & J. H. Berg (Eds.), *Self-disclosure: Theory, research and therapy*. New York: Plenum Publishing Corporation. Reprinted with permission of the publisher.

self-concept and motivate us to reassert our own self view (Swann, 1983; 1987; Swann & Read, 1981a, 1981b). Or, noticing that we have failed to live up to our standards for behavior may motivate us to meet those standards (Duval & Wicklund, 1972).

The chronic importance of a goal may also affect the likelihood of its activation, with more important goals more likely to be activated. For instance, people may selectively encode features that are relevant to chronic, important goals. Higgins and King (1981) (see also Bargh, 1984) argue that the interpretation of social stimuli is affected by both chronic and temporary differences in the accessibility of relevant constructs. Postman, Bruner, & McGinnies (1948) (cited in Bargh & Pratto, 1986) showed that the importance of various abstract social values, such as discovery of truth or aesthetics, affected people's recognition threshold for words related to those values.

When we really want to become closer to someone, we may be particularly vigilant for a behavior to which we can respond, a request that we can fulfill, or a way in which we can better meet their needs. Baron and Boudreau (1987) suggest that differences in people's needs may lead them to become perceptually attuned to different affordances in the environment, even to the extent of developing dysfunctional attunements where they miss what is there and overemphasize things that may be only marginally present.

Also, Cantor and Kihlstrom (1985), in their discussion of social intelligence, point out that work on expertise (e.g., Chi, Glaser, & Rees, 1982) demonstrates that experts in a domain categorize the world differently and often make distinctions different from those made by people who are less expert. In a very real sense, experts may see different things than the novice does (Chase & Simon, 1973). As a result, people with different levels of expertise in a particular social environment (which may be a result of differences in chronic goals) may perceive very different characteristics of people and their environment.

Thus, the importance of a goal in a given situation is a function of (a) its chronic salience or importance to the individual, (b) the individual's sensitivity to characteristics relevant to his or her goals, and (c) the extent to which it has been activated by aspects of the particular context, including other people. Perceived characteristics of one's interaction partner and the situation then may change the configuration and hierarchy of goals guiding behavior. This is a crucial point, for it argues that even if there are strong and consistent individual differences in these chronic configurations, an individual's behavior in any given interaction can be only partially predicted by knowledge of that individual's traits and idiosyncratic configurations of goals, plans, resources, and beliefs. Greater predictability seems likely only when we simultaneously consider how one such unique individual interacts with another within a specific situation (Miller & Kenny, 1986; Miller, 1988; Thorne, 1987).

However, it is important to bear in mind that people do not simply find themselves in particular situations, interacting with random strangers. As a number of authors have argued (e.g., Allport, 1937; Snyder & Ickes, 1985; Swann, 1987; Wachtel, 1973), many times people actively choose both situations and interaction partners; and these choices are frequently based on consistency with their own personalities. Emmons, Diener, and Larsen (1986) have shown that people spend more time in situations that "fit" their personalities and that their affective response to the situations could sometimes be predicted by the degree of "fit."

Once some goal or set of goals is activated, we must decide what to do. As can be seen from the model in Figure 11.2, knowledge of our own goals and relevant additional information, such as our perception of the goals and characteristics of our interaction partner and knowledge about the situation, is used to develop an appropriate plan.

To develop a plan, we must consider numerous factors. First, we must assess the relations among our own goals and actions and their relation to the possible goals and actions of those with whom we are interacting. If we have multiple goals we must consider various relations among them, such as which are most important and which conflict with each other, as well as the relation of our goals to our partner's goals, such as which might compete and which might possibly be achieved by the same plan. In the sections on intrapersonal and interpersonal goal relations we have discussed many of these issues in more detail. Thus, the plan we develop depends on how it fits with our goals, as well as how we think it fits with the possible goals and plans of our partner. Whether we can effectively carry out our plan typically depends on cooperation from our partner. Thus, the success of our plan partially depends on the accuracy with which we perceive our partner's goals and plans.

Second, we need to consider what we know about our situation. For instance, what goals does it easily afford (Argyle et al., 1981; Baron & Boudreau, 1987), what goals might it threaten, and what are the rules and roles associated with it? Third, we must look at the plans we know, and whether they are available in this particular situation, with this particular partner. Fourth, we then need to know whether these are likely to be effective in achieving our goals, and whether they are socially and morally acceptable. Finally, we need to assess whether we possess the resources necessary to carry out possible plans. If we do possess the resources, but they are limited, we need to decide whether the benefits of attaining our goals are worth the expenditure of resources, such as time, money, effort, etc.

Our perceptions of these various factors will affect the likelihood that a particular goal will guide behavior. If people decide they lack the resources, if they find they cannot resolve the conflict between their goals and their partner's, or for some other reason cannot come up with a plan that is likely to be successful, they may give up on some goals and focus on others.

People's expectancies about likely outcomes and the reactions of others play an important role in many parts of the planning process. For instance, an individual's expectancies influence which particular plan components are chosen and even whether a developed plan will be enacted. Essentially, we consider the probability of success of various courses of action and the associated costs and benefits of each course. In this sense, the present model is related to the class of expectancy-value models (See Feather, 1982, for a useful compendium of these approaches).

On what are these expectancies based? Earlier we argued that people build mental models of other people and use such models to simulate their behavior. People also build models of the current interaction and use that to predict the direction in which it is progressing. Thus, in a dyadic interaction, our expectancies about the interaction are based on our mental model of ourselves, our partner, our relationship, and our model of the current interaction. Also, to the extent that our mental models are based on more general knowledge, this also can influence our expectancies.

The plans that people develop vary widely in how specific and detailed they are. Some may have filled in every detail, while others may furnish only broad strategic directions. The degree of specificity may be both an individual difference (e.g., Frese, Stewart, & Hannover, 1987), as well as a response to the nature and importance of the situation.

At one level, the planning process can be viewed in terms of an analysis of person-person and person-situation interactions. The actor is trying to integrate his or her goals, plans, resources, and beliefs with those of the other member of the dyad and at the same time with the goals, plans, roles, and rules associated with the particular social situation. Thus, an individual's behavior is going to be influenced both by their interaction partner and by the situation they are in (Miller & Kenny, 1986; Miller, 1988; Thorne, 1987).

If we are fortunate, a canned plan or script (Schank & Abelson, 1977) may already exist, and we will not need to spend very much time in the planning process. We can just take the script and act it out. However, frequently we do not have such canned plans available and must spend time developing them. How do people develop such plans? Although social psychologists have not focused much attention on this issue, recently social planning has been a growing target of research interest (e.g., Kluwe & Friedrichsen, 1985; Dorner, 1985; Kuhl, 1985). Also, Wilensky (1983) has recently presented a detailed model of social planning from an artificial intelligence perspective.

One way to develop plans is to mentally simulate the enactment of a possible plan or sequence of plans (Nuttin, 1984; Wilensky, 1983), mentally trying out different plans or parts of plans, seeing how they fit together, seeing what role one's partner will play in these plans, and simulating how both people and the environment will respond to those plans. Such simulations are often useful in identifying potential problems, such as undesirable interactions between components of a plan, or unfavorable reactions from other people. Wilensky (1983) provides a detailed treatment of many of these issues.

Clearly, success in developing such plans depends on people's knowledge of appropriate plan components (Schank & Abelson, 1977; Wilensky, 1983) that can be combined to form larger units. In addition, a number of different meta-cognitive skills are involved in successful planning (Dorner, 1985; Kluwe & Friedrichsen, 1985). Meta-cognitive skills are essentially a set of skills for thinking about or monitoring one's thinking. The extent to which people are able to develop successful plans should depend on the expertise with which these skills are employed.

Kluwe and Friedrichsen (1985) divide meta-cognition into two areas: (a) declarative knowledge about cognitive processes, such as, "Difficult problems require many resources and a long time;" and (b) procedural knowledge, which is procedures that can be used to evaluate and control one's thinking. Some of the different meta-cognitive procedures they discuss are monitoring and evaluating the progress of the solution process, making deliberate decisions about the allocation of resources to different subproblems, and identification and development of the nature of the problem.

Application of many of these meta-cognitive strategies depends on an individual paying attention to his or her own thought processes. This suggests that the greater the degree to which an individual focuses internally on his or her own mental processes (e.g., Carver & Scheier, 1981; Duval & Wicklund, 1972) and thus focuses on this simulation and its development, the more complete and adequate the planning process should be. Kluwe and Friedrichsen (1985) reviewed several studies that indicate that one characteristic of good problem solvers and planners is that they more often monitor and evaluate their problem solving activity than do poor planners. And Dorner (1985) provides evidence that ". . . just instructing the experimental subjects to critically analyze their own way of thinking from time to time results in a distinct and statistically significant improvement of thinking. . . ." (p. 232).

Kuhl (1985) notes that simply forming an intention is not sufficient to ensure that it will be carried out. For example, changes in both the external and internal environment may give rise to goals that conflict with our current intention and could deflect us from it. If we are to succeed in carrying out our intention we must protect it. Thus, self-regulatory actions become important for protecting the current intention and making sure that it becomes actualized in behavior.

Kuhl (1985) also identifies two different orientations that people may take when trying to develop and enact an intention. In action orientation an individual's attention is focused on a fully developed plan and its enactment. However, in state orientation individuals are focused on a particular internal or external state, for example, they may focus only on the goal, to the exclusion of developing a plan, or they may continually focus on past failure and not on how to overcome the failure. People who are action oriented should be more successful in carrying out an intention.

During enactment of a plan we continually monitor our performance, the responses of our interaction partner, and the nature of the situation. At the same time, we are continually updating our model of our partner's characteristics, goals, and the reasons for their actions. We are also updating our models of the situation and the interaction. All during this process we are gathering new information about what our partner and the situation afford for social interaction. As Baron and Boudreau (1987) argue, many times characteristics of people and objects are revealed only through our interactions with them. For example, many characteristics of people, such as their goals and beliefs, can only be perceived when we see how they respond to our actions or someone else's. Perception and action have a reciprocal relation with each other (Baron & Boudreau, 1987), with perception affecting action and the results of action affecting perception. The results of this cycle can thus modify our current plans and the goals guiding our behavior. Consider the following example in which one such interaction evolves.

Ellen starts out liking her partner, Tom, and desires to become more intimate with him; she decides to disclose some personal feelings to him. However, he doesn't seem responsive to these initial disclosures and she perceives that he has become more distant. So, Ellen becomes more distant in turn, and Tom perceives that Ellen doesn't like him. Because his self-concept involves perceiving himself as likable (cf. Swann, 1983, 1987 for research addressing this issue) Tom becomes extremely friendly. Ellen responds positively, but she is wary of becoming too intimate.

Meanwhile, Tom decides that Ellen is a friendly person and begins to feel that he can "open up" to her. Since he does desire to become more intimate and close with someone, he decides to tell her something moderately intimate about himself. Because Ellen responds warmly to this, Tom feels more relaxed and less concerned about "making a fool of himself."

Most plans in social interaction require a coordinated response from our partner. Whether we are gossiping, going on a date, or negotiating a business deal, successfully carrying out our plan typically requires certain responses from our partner. Thus, we must monitor their behavior to see whether and how it fits into our plans. Does it fit or facilitate our plan, is it a slight variation that can be handled with minimal adjustment, or is it a more major deviation, perhaps something that will totally block our plan? The answers tell us what modifications, if any, must be made.

At the same time, our interaction partner has his or her own set of goals and corresponding plans and will be trying to enact those plans. Thus, interactions are a continuing process of negotiation between both partners as each tries to let the other know what he wants and tries to constrain the other's behavior so it fits one's own plan (Carson, 1969; McClintock, 1983). Each individual says and does things to carry out his or her own plan and hopes that the other responds in line with the offered behavior. The other person, by his or her response, indicates whether the person is willing to go along or not. Carson (1969) presents a particularly insightful analysis of such coordination and the negotiation that supports it. In a similar vein, Berscheid (1985) and Kelley et al. (1983) have argued that one can analyze the level of compatibility in relationships in terms of the extent to which the behavioral sequences of each member of the dyad facilitate or interfere with the behavioral sequences of the other member. There are a number of different reasons why coordination may be difficult or may even fail. Among them are such things as competing goals, misunderstanding of what the other is trying to do, and lack of the skills or resources necessary to carry out one's part.

Problems during the enactment of our plans produce an interruption (Mandler, 1975), which increases both our attention to what is happening and our arousal and emotional responses. Interruptions can occur at both the cognitive level, with the violation of an expectancy, and at the behavioral level with the blockage of a behavioral sequence. The severity of an interruption or discrepancy at the cognitive level is at least partially a function of the degree of disconfirmation of the expectancy and its importance. The severity of an interruption at the behavioral level is a function of the extent to which the ongoing goals or plans are blocked and the importance of the blocked goals. Slight deviations from a plan create only minor interruptions and arousal, whereas major threats to a plan's success should create high levels of arousal and strong emotional responses. This is especially likely, when we have few good alternative plans, and the plans are critical to important goals. Berscheid (1983) has argued that such interruptions are an important source of emotion in close relationships. Other authors (e.g., Roseman, 1984) have also discussed emotional reactions in terms of the satisfaction or failure of goal attainment.

An interruption, if serious enough, leads us to explain the problem and throws us into a replanning mode where we use our explanation to come up with a new plan that can overcome the source of the interruption. In nonstereotyped social interaction, such replanning occurs continually as we attempt to adjust our behavior to our partner. In the example of Ellen and Tom, Ellen had to do some replanning when her initial disclosure to Tom was not met with as responsive a reply as Ellen expected. Although, as in Ellen and Tom's case, the required replanning is usually relatively minor, sometimes major replanning is required.

Attempts to deal with problems in plans are highly dependent on our explanation for the problems (Wilensky, 1983). Identifying what went wrong is the first step toward trying to change it. Earlier we outlined how people might deal with unexpected outcomes, some of the possible explanations, and how this process is affected by different kinds of knowledge. For example, the explanation will depend on individuals' belief systems. Consider a depressive or lonely person who receives the type of rebuff that Ellen initially may have received from Tom. Instead of changing gears as she did, she might have decided that Tom was really rejecting her because she was not a likable person. Also, different people will undoubtedly bring to bear different background knowledge in understanding what is going on. And some people may have better learned a library of explanation patterns, some based on general cultural knowledge and some based on experience in the specific relationship. Some people's belief systems and attributional styles may prevent them from easily replanning and initiating a new plan that will enable them to reach their goals. Thus, to the extent that replanning and "repairing" interaction sequences is dependent on an accurate explanation, the adequacy of the "repair" will be affected by differences in explanation.

If replanning is possible, we should proceed to enact the new plan. However, if replanning is impossible or impractical, we will stop, having failed to attain our goals.

Although the current presentation sometimes makes it sound as if the planning and coordination of dyadic interactions is a linear, sequential process, it is clear that it is actually cyclical, with a continuing interplay among all parts of the process. People's goals are continually responding to new information and their plans are continuously changing in reaction to their interaction partners' behavior and the nature of the situation.

ISSUES: IMPLICATIONS OF THIS APPROACH

At first blush, inter-personalism, as a theory of personality, may seem both "familiar" and "radical." It is radical in that unlike some nomethetic approaches to describing personality, this framework addresses processes as well as structures of personality and can accommodate both an "idiographic" and a "nomothetic" understanding of persons. It is familiar in that inter-personalism finds the concept "trait" a very useful person structure, not one that should be abandoned by personologists. Inter-personalism is a truly interactional theory, in which traits can be viewed as "a certain aspect of the mediating system's way of selecting, interpreting, and treating information as a basis for coherent behavior across situations" (Magnusson & Endler, 1977, p. 17). As such, it blends well with a venerable tradition in personality in which traits (Allport, 1937) were viewed as explanatory concepts.

Theoretical Connections

For personologists the framework presented here may seem like a wedding of a variety of historical, as well as current, theoretical approaches to personality. For example, Allport (1929) noted that the "only really significant congruences in personality must be sought in the sphere of conation. It is the striving of a man which binds together the traits, and which shows how essentially harmonious they are in their determination of his behavior" (p. 14).
And, in advocating a dynamic theory, Allport (1938) noted that his theory of personality

> breaks with the nomothetic tradition completely, and regards motives as personalized systems of tensions, in which the core of impulse is not to be divorced from the images, ideas of goal, past experience, capacities, and style of conduct employed in obtaining the goal. The whole system is integral . . . Only individualized patterns of motives have the capacity to select stimuli, to control and direct segmental tensions, to initiate responses and to render them equivalent, in ways that are consistent with, and characteristic of, the person himself. (pp. 320–321)

Murray's (1938) theory of personality focused on needs (e.g., need for dominance, affiliation, achievement). Such needs were viewed as constructs which stand

> for a force . . . which organizes perception, apperception, intellection, conation and action in such a way as to transform in a certain direction an existing, unsatisfying situation. A need is sometimes provoked, directly by internal processes of a certain kind . . . but, more frequently . . . by the occurrence of one of a few commonly effective press (or by anticipatory images of such a press). Thus, it manifests itself by leading the organism to search for or to avoid encountering or, when encountered, to attend and respond to certain kinds of press. It may even engender illusory perceptions and delusory apperceptions . . . Each need is characteristically accompanied by a particular feeling or emotion and tends to use certain modes (subneeds and actones) to further its trend. It may be weak or intense, momentary or enduring. But, usually it persists and gives rise to a certain course of overt behavior (or fantasy), which (if the organism is competent and external opposition not insurmountable) changes the initiating circumstance in such a way as to bring about an end situation which stills (appeases or satisfies) the organism. (p. 124)

According to Murray, "every need is associated with traces (or images) representing movements, pathways, agencies, goal objects, which, taken together, constitute a *need integrate*" (Murray, 1936, p. 37 as cited in Allport, 1937). And, Allport (1937) felt that "this conception of a need integrate is a great improvement over the skeleton need. It fulfills well our demand for a unit of analysis that is concrete, life-like, and personal, provided only that the need integrate is understood to be not merely a momentary organization but a mental structure that endures and is a constant characteristic of the person." (pp. 241–242)

But, how does inter-personalism take us beyond Allport and Murray? Inter-personalism starts with a variety of goal-based structures: "building blocks" for persons. These "blocks" can be configured to represent a variety of person structures—some stable, some not. Some of these "building blocks" can be thought of as "loosely associated," whereas others are linked. Such structural components provide a language (e.g. goals, plans, resources, and beliefs) that allows us to bring the more typically salient "blocks" of a person together with the "blocks" made salient for that person by the situation (e.g., goals, resources, norms activated) and their relationships (e.g., goals, plans, resources, beliefs of others) to build the "interaction" of these persons in this place at this time. Goal-based structures provide a "common denominator" that allows an analysis of the meshing of "structures" difficult to achieve at a higher (more abstract) level of analysis (e.g., traits).

With this goal-based language of persons and situations and an explicit process model regarding the activation and enactment of these structures, the theory moves us beyond Allport and Murray. As Zuroff (1986) pointed out, Allport, although well aware of the effects of people on situations, did not clearly articulate the processes by which situations affect people.

> [Allport] repeatedly referred to the immediate situation as "arousing" various traits, but he failed to explicate how the arousal took place; arousal remained essentially a neurophysiological metaphor. . . . It should be emphasized, however, that there is nothing in Allport's account that is inconsistent with a process theory of the effects of the immediate situation; the problem, rather, is that he was unable to develop an explicit theory of such interactions. (p. 995)

Inter-personalism provides the language and the processes by which to explain such dynamic interactions: It can explain changes in persons caused by situations, as well as explicating stability and coherence of person structures. The model also opens a door for thinking about how stable and coherent patterns of individual structures develop. For example, initial ("hard-wired") differences in both resources (e.g., competencies, energy levels, attentional levels) and "rudimentary" goals (e.g., social stimulation, food, etc.) might lead to individual differences in the development of different stable configurations over time. And, part of the socialization process may involve children developing the skills necessary to generate more differentiated strategies in response to multiple concurrent goals. Thus, the rudiments of a model of development and the processes by which change occurs are also suggested in the present theory.

The emphasis on goals and plans has historically resurfaced again and again in personality theory. For example, Adler (1964) said "We cannot think, feel, will, or act without the perception of some goal . . . Every psychic phenomenon, if it is to give us any understanding of a person, can only be grasped and understood if regarded as a preparation for some goal" (pp. 68–69). And, more recently the emphasis on goals and plans in discussing personality has, if anything been heightened (cf. Allston, 1970, 1975: Cantor & Kihlstrom, 1985; Carbonnell, 1979; Carson, 1969; Mischel, 1973, 1977, Pervin, 1983). These themes in personality seem to mesh naturally with concurrently emerging concerns in social cognition and cognitive science (Galambos et al., 1986; Read, 1987; Wilensky, 1983).

One thing becomes clear in considering personality historically. We need to carefully examine and deal with the theories, controversies, and personality issues of our past if we are to move beyond them for the future. Next, we consider some of these personality issues as they relate to the inter-personalism approach.

Nomothetic and Idiographic

Inter-personalism accommodates a variety of ways of thinking about persons, both nomothetically and idiographically. That is, we could presumably determine which configuration of goals, strategies, beliefs, and resources most people would refer to as prototypically involving "sociability" (e.g., a nomothetic perspective). And, we can consider how individual differences in prototypicality (e.g., in terms of resources or in terms of goals) might lead to very different explanations and predictions regarding future behavior. We can also examine the exact unique (idiographic) set of goals (and their organization and salience), strategies, resources, and beliefs for any particular individual. In so doing, because we are examining these components, it becomes easier to attempt to mesh relevant goals from one configuration with other salient structures (e.g., other goals chronically salient or even those made salient by situations or relationships) and examine how such multiple goals (rather than single goals alone) might change which particular plans are activated. Which plans are enacted will depend on whether the individual can integrate this set of goals (presumably affected by the nature of the goal relations and the competencies the individual has for goal integration) and whether the resources necessary for generated plans are available for their enactment. Beliefs relevant to the activated goals and relevant to the particular situation (e.g., what is appropriate or normative) would presumably also affect which plan is enacted.

Stability and Consistency

The present approach also provides us with a unique framework to examine how and when some configurations may be more unstable (e.g., loneliness) than others (e.g., sociability). That is, loneliness probably involves a set of goals that the individual is unable to achieve because of difficulties relating to plans, resources, and/or beliefs. Change would seem likely to occur because there is incompatibility among these structures: Either the individual will work toward developing plans, resources, and beliefs that are more compatible with effectively reaching the goals, or the importance of the goals for the person may change (e.g., a person decides to concentrate on professional goals). In contrast, a sociable individual may have the same set of goals (as the lonely person) but different, more effective and compatible structures for goal attainment. To the extent that individuals have developed effective plans, have resources to enable them, and a set of beliefs compatible with those structures in achieving their goals, the configuration is more apt to be a stable one.

Similarly, because situations and relationships afford different resources (as well as make salient different goals and norms), behavior over situations is apt to vary, in part, as the viability of different plans (and goals) changes. In addition to their role in "filling in" missing pieces in goal-based configurations, situational factors may also increase the overall array of goals and information that individuals need to consider and integrate into viable plans. The way that these multiple concerns and task demands are integrated will depend on a variety of person factors (e.g., coping skills; competencies, including integration competency; other resources; and repertoires of strategies), but in general, the more complex the situation and the more the individual must act quickly the less well the chosen enactment will integrate multiple goals. To the extent that one of the goals not integrated in a particular enactment frequently is incorporated into enactments in other (less complex) situations, behavior (with respect to that particular goal) will be inconsistent from one specific situation to another.

Units and Level of Analysis

We would argue that goal-based structures provide the needed level of analysis to understand how "traits" influence behavior and how persons interact with situations and others. Although earlier personality psychologists (Allport, 1937; Carson, 1969; Murray, 1938) realized that understanding the behavior of individuals required examining the role of the situation, a good common language for describing the interaction of person and situation remained elusive. The present model moves us closer to such a common language, a language in which the "units" most appropriate for examining such interactions may be goal-based structures. These units provide a language sufficiently detailed that it readily accommodates the computer simulation of persons (Wilensky, 1983) while at the same time we may move from these units to more abstract levels of analysis (e.g., traits).

Self and Personality

The present model suggests a way in which various aspects of the self (e.g., self-awareness and self-concept) may be associated with the activation of various goals, strategies, resources, and beliefs. Thus, for example, although usually most individuals may be relatively unaware of the goals that are salient to them, some individuals, those high in private self-consciousness (Carver & Scheier, 1981), would presumably be more aware of their goals, beliefs, affective reactions, plans, and resources than others. In addition, the present model specifies that the self-concept often plays an important role in initiating goals and specifying strategies of action (also see Markus & Nurius, 1986). Thus, the role of the self-concept within a general model of personality is more apparent.

Personality and Relationships

Inter-personalism also suggests how we can study the various facets of persons and relationships within a general process model of interpersonal interaction. The theory emphasizes the importance of understanding persons in detail (and their goal-based configurations) in order to understand the unique relationships that emerge among unique persons over time. As such, the theory is compatible with theories concerned with analyzing causal sequences in behavioral interactions. For example, consider the causal chain analysis presented by Kelley et al. (1983). They acknowledge that dyadic relationships can be analyzed at many levels, including the level of goals and plans. And, although their analysis focuses primarily on the level of causal relations among behaviors and does not examine, in detail, the level of goals and plans, the connections are there.

Furthermore, inter-personalism also suggests how individuals develop models of their present (and past and "possible") relationships that guide their dyadic interactions and enable individuals to explain and predict their present and future interactions. Thus, inter-personalism opens a door to an idiographic approach to understanding the rich fabric and dynamics of particular relationships that is compatible with both a language of persons who make up these relationships (Miller & Read, 1987) and a language of situations (Argyle et al., 1981) in which these relationships occur. By looking at the unique organization of goal-based structures of persons we may better understand not only intrapersonal and interpersonal conflicts but develop coherent models of persons and how persons mesh with other persons and situations. In fact, the goal of understanding *coherence* (beyond consistency) is the primary goal of this interactional model.

Coherence: Beyond Consistency

One of the authors routinely asks her personality students, "Is your behavior consistent across situations or is it specific to the particular situation you are in?" A typical reply is, "Well, of course my behavior is different in different situations! But, I'm still the same person, and I could certainly tell you what I'm generally like. And, if you knew me, it would all seem to go together and make sense." In some respects, this response is both at the heart of the person-situation "consistency" controversy that has remained with us in personality for decades (Epstein & O'Brien, 1985; Magnusson & Endler, 1977; Mischel & Peake, 1982; Mischel, 1984; Pervin, 1983) and also suggests where we need to go in the future. First, as the dust settles, it appears that behavior, as our students seem to suggest, "is simultaneously situationally specific and unstable at the individual level and general and stable at the aggregate level" (Epstein & O'Brien, 1985, p. 533). Second, it also appears that people, like our student, do not expect to find cross-situational consistency at the individual level (Epstein & Teraspulsky, 1986; Wright & Mischel, 1987).

If people are not preoccupied with looking for cross-situational consistencies at the individual level, what are they doing? We would argue that people—including our student in our example—are, in a variety of different ways, looking for *coherence,* or how it "all fits together." In doing so, individuals may use a variety of strategies, including using average or typical examples, extreme examples, broad response categories (traits), broad situational categories, and cross-situational and cross-modal responses (Epstein & Teraspulsky, 1986). Although information about cross-situational consistencies may be used by individuals in making inferences about how someone's behavior "fits together", it is but one class of information in an array of information that individuals would appear to need to develop coherent models of extended behavioral sequences of other persons, of themselves, and of their relationships with others. But, as the present theoretical approach suggests, the knowledge structures used and the process of developing such "models" may be quite complex.

Just as we would argue that individuals are trying to develop coherent "models," we would also argue that our goal in personality should be to develop coherent models of persons. Our task, it would seem, is to understand the "mediating system's way of selecting, interpreting, and treating information as a basis for coherent behavior across situations" (Magnusson & Endler, 1977, page 17). In 1964, Gordon Allport in describing open systems in personality theory noted

> For now the open question becomes: what makes the system hang together in any one person? Let me repeat this question, for it is the one that more than any other has haunted me over the years: *What makes the system cohere in any one person?* That this problem is pivotal, urgent, and relatively neglected will be recognized by open-system theorists even while it is downgraded and evaded by those who prefer their systems semi-closed. (Allport, 1964, p. 163)

We would argue, that as we approach the 21st century, it is towards this search—towards understanding *coherence*—that personologists should now direct their energies.

REFERENCES

Abelson, R. P., & Lalljee, M. (in press). Knowledge structures and causal explanation. In D. Hilton (Ed.), *Contemporary science and natural explanation: Commonsense conceptions of causality*. London: Harvester Press.

Adler, A. (1964). Individual psychology, its assumptions and its results. In H. M. Ruitenbeek (Ed.), *Varieties of personality theory*. (pp. 65–79). New York: E. P. Dutton & Co.

Allport, G. W. (1929). The study of personality by the intuitive method. *Journal of Abnormal and Social Psychology, 24*, 14–27.

Allport, G. W. (1937). *Personality: A psychological interpretation*. New York: Henry Holt.

Allport, G. W. (1964). The open system in personality theory. In H. M. Ruitenbeek (Ed.), *Varieties of personality theory*. (pp. 149–166). New York: E. P. Dutton & Co.

Allston, W. P. (1970). Toward a logical geography of personality: Traits and deeper lying personality characteristics. In H. D. Krefer & M. K. Munitz (Eds.), *Mind, science and history*. (pp. 59–92). Albany, NY: SUNY Press.

Allston, W. P. (1975). Traits, consistency and conceptual alternatives for personality theory. *Journal for the Theory of Social Behaviour, 5*, 17–48.

Andersen, S. M., & Klatzky, R. L. (1987). Traits and social stereotypes: Levels of categorization in person perception. *Journal of Personality and Social Psychology, 53*, 235–246.

Anderson, J. R. (1983). *The architecture of cognition*. Cambridge, MA: Harvard University Press.

Argyle, M., Furnham, A. & Graham, J. A. (1981). *Social situations*. Cambridge, England: Cambridge University Press.

Bargh, J. A. (1984). Automatic and conscious processing of social information. In R. S. Wyer, Jr., & T. K. Srull (Eds.), *Handbook of social cognition*. (Vol. 3, pp. 1–43). Hillsdale, NJ: Lawrence Erlbaum Associates.

Bargh, J. A., & Pratto, F. (1986). Individual construct accessibility and perceptual selection. *Journal of Experimental Social Psychology, 22*, 293–311.

Baron, R. M., & Boudreau, L. A. (1987). An ecological perspective on integrating personality and social psychology. *Journal of Personality and Social Psychology, 53,* 1222–1228.

Barsalou, L. W. (1985). Ideals, central tendency, and frequency of instantiation as determinants of graded structure in categories. *Journal of Experimental Psychology: Learning, Memory, and Cognition, 11,* 629–654.

Berscheid, E. (1983). Emotion. In H. H. Kelley et al. (Eds.), *Close Relationships.* (pp. 110–168). New York: W. H. Freeman.

Berscheid, E. (1985). Compatibility, Interdependence, and Emotion. In W. Ickes (Ed.), *Compatible and Incompatible relationships.* (pp. 143–161). New York: Springer-Verlag.

Black, J. B., Galambos, J. A., & Read, S. J. (1984). Comprehending stories and social situations. In R. S. Wyer, Jr., & T. K. Srull (Eds.), *Handbook of social cognition* (Vol. 3, pp. 45–86). Hillsdale, NJ: Lawrence Erlbaum Associates.

Block, J. (1982). Assimilation, accommodation, and the dynamics of personality development. *Child Development, 53,* 281–295.

Bowlby, J. (1973). *Attachment and loss: Vol. 2. Separation: Anxiety and anger.* New York: Basic Books.

Buss, D. M., & Craik, K. H. (1983). The act frequency approach to personality. *Psychological Review, 90,* 105–126.

Buss, D. M., & Craik, K. H. (1984). Acts, dispositions, and personality. *Progress in Experimental Personality Research, 13,* 241–301.

Cantor, N., & Kihlstrom, J. F. (1985). Social intelligence: The cognitive basis of personality. In P. Shaver (Ed.), *Review of Personality and Social Psychology.* (Vol. 6, pp. 15–33). Beverly Hills, CA: Sage.

Cantor, N., & Mischel, W. (1977). Traits as prototypes: Effects on recognition memory. *Journal of Personality and Social Psychology, 35,* 38–48.

Cantor, N., & Mischel, W. (1979). Prototypes in person perception. In L. Berkowitz (Ed.), *Advances in experimental social psychology.* (Vol. 12, pp. 3–52). New York: Academic Press.

Cantor, N., Norem, J. K., Niedenthal, P. M., Langston, C. A., & Brower, A. M. (1987). Life tasks, self-concept ideals, and cognitive strategies in a life transition. *Journal of Personality and Social Psychology, 53,* 1178–1191.

Carbonnell, J. G. (1979). Subjective understanding: Computer models of belief systems. *Computer science technical report 150,* Doctoral Dissertation, Yale University.

Carson, R. C. (1969). *Interaction concepts of personality.* Chicago: Aldine Publishing.

Carver, C. S., & Scheier, M. F. (1981). *Attention and self-regulation: A control-theory approach to human behavior.* New York: Springer-Verlag.

Chase, W. G., & Simon, H. A. (1973). Perception in chess. *Cognitive Psychology, 4,* 55–81.

Cheek, J. M., & Buss, A. H. (1981). Shyness and sociability. *Journal of Personality and Social Psychology, 41,* 330–337.

Chi, M. T. H., Glaser, R., & Rees, E. (1982). Expertise in problem solving. In R. J. Sternberg (Ed.). *Advances in the psychology of human intelligence.* (Vol. 1, pp. 7–76). Hillsdale, NJ: Lawrence Erlbaum Associates.

Clark, H. H. (1985). Language use and language users. In G. Lindzey & E. Aronson (Eds.), *The handbook of social psychology.* (Vol. 2, pp. 179–231). New York: Random House.

Collins, A. M., & Loftus, E. F. (1975). A spreading activation theory of semantic processing. *Psychological Review, 82,* 407–428.

Collins, N. L., & Read, S. J. (1987). *Early attachment experience and adult romantic love: Continuities in social relationships from childhood to adulthood.* Unpublished manuscript, University of Southern California.

Dorner, D. (1985). Thinking and the organization of action. In J. Kuhl & J. Beckmann (Eds.), *Action control: From cognition to behavior.* (pp. 219–235). Berlin, Germany: Springer-Verlag.

Duval, S., & Wicklund, R. A. (1972). *A theory of objective self-awareness.* New York: Academic Press.
Einhorn, H. J., & Hogarth, R. M. (1986). Judging probable cause. *Psychological Bulletin, 99,* 3–19.
Ellis, A., & Harper, R. (1977). *A guide to successful marriage.* Los Angeles: Wilshire.
Emmons, R. A. (1986). Personal strivings: An approach to personality and subjective well-being. *Journal of Personality and Social Psychology, 51,* 1058–1068.
Emmons, R. A., Diener, E., & Larsen, R. J. (1986). Choice and avoidance of everyday situations and affect congruence: Two models of reciprocal interactionism. *Journal of Personality and Social Psychology, 51,* 815–826.
Epstein, S., & O'Brien, E. J. (1985). The person-situation debate in historical and current perspective. *Psychological Bulletin, 98,* 513–537.
Epstein, S., & Teraspulsky, L. (1986). Perception of cross-situational consistency. *Journal of Personality and Social Psychology, 50,* 1152–1160.
Feather, N. T. (Ed.). (1982). *Expectations and actions: Expectancy-value models in psychology.* Hillsdale, NJ: Lawrence Erlbaum Associates.
Fenigstein, A., Scheier, M. F., & Buss, A. H. (1975). Public and private self-consciousness: Assessment and theory. *Journal of Consulting and Clinical Psychology, 43,* 522–527.
Fincham, F. D., & Bradbury, T. N. (1987). Cognitive processes and conflict in close relationships: An attribution-efficacy model. *Journal of Personality and Social Psychology, 53,* 1106–1118.
Fincham, F. D., & Jaspars, J. M. (1980). Attribution of responsibility: From man the scientist to man as lawyer. In L. Berkowitz (Ed.). *Advances in experimental social psychology* (Vol. 13, pp. 81–138). New York: Academic Press.
Fletcher, G. J. O., Fincham, F. D., Cramer, L., & Heron, N. (1987). The role of attributions in the development of dating relationships. *Journal of Personality and Social Psychology, 53,* 481–489.
Foa, E. B., & Foa, U. G. (1974). *Societal structures of the mind.* Springfield, IL: Thomas.
Frese, M., Stewart, J., & Hannover, B. (1987). Goal orientation and planfulness: Action styles as personality concepts. *Journal of Personality and Social Psychology, 52,* 1182–1194.
Galambos, J. A., Abelson, R. P., & Black, J. B. (1986). *Knowledge structures.* Hillsdale, NJ: Lawrence Erlbaum Associates.
Gentner, D., & Stevens, A. (1983). *Mental models.* Hillsdale, NJ: Lawrence Erlbaum Associates.
Grice, H. P. (1975). Logic and conversation. In P. Cole & J. L. Morgan (Eds.), *Syntax and semantics, Vol. 3: Speech acts* (pp. 83–106). New York: Academic Press.
Hamilton, D. L. (1981). (Ed.). *Cognitive processes in stereotyping and intergroup behavior.* Hillsdale, NJ: Lawrence Erlbaum Associates.
Hazan, C., & Shaver, P. (1987). Romantic love conceptualized as an attachment process. *Journal of Personality and Social Psychology, 52,* 511–524
Heider, F. (1958). *The psychology of interpersonal relations.* New York: Wiley.
Higgins, E. T., & King, G. (1981). Accessibility of social constructs: Information-processing consequences of individual and contextual variability. In N. Cantor & J. F. Kihlstrom (Eds.), *Personality, cognition, and social interaction* (pp. 69–121). Hillsdale, NJ: Lawrence Erlbaum Associates.
Hoffman, C., Mischel, W., & Baer, J. S. (1984). Language and person cognition: Effects of communicative set on trait attribution. *Journal of Personality and Social Psychology, 46,* 1029–1043.
Johnson-Laird, P. N. (1983). *Mental models.* Cambridge, MA.: Harvard University Press.
Jones, E. E., & Davis, K. E. (1965). From acts to dispositions: The attribution process in

person perception. In L. Berkowitz (Ed.), *Advances in experimental social psychology* (Vol. 2, pp. 219–267). New York: Academic Press.

Kahneman, D., & Miller, D. T. (1986). Norm theory: Comparing reality to its alternatives. *Psychological Review, 93,* 136–153.

Kelley, H. H. (1971). Attribution in social interaction. In E. E. Jones, D. E. Kanouse, H. H. Kelley, R. E. Nisbett, S. Valins, & B. Weiner (Eds.), *Attribution: Perceiving the causes of behavior* (pp. 1–26). Morristown, NJ: General Learning Press.

Kelley, H. H., (1979). *Personal relationships: Their structures and processes.* Hillsdale, NJ: Lawrence Erlbaum Associates.

Kelley, H. H., Berscheid, E., Christensen, A., Harvey, J. H., Huston, T. L., Levinger, G., McClintock, E., Peplau, L. A., & Peterson, D. R. (Eds.). (1983). *Close Relationships.* New York: W. H. Freeman.

Kluwe, R. H., & Friedrichsen, G. (1985). Mechanisms of control and regulation in problem solving. In J. Kuhl & J. Beckmann (Eds.), *Action control: From cognition to behavior.* (pp. 183–218). Berlin, Germany: Springer-Verlag.

Kuhl, J. (1985). Volitional mediators of cognition-behavior consistency: Self-regulatory processes and action versus state orientations. In J. Kuhl & J. Beckmann (Eds.), *Action control: From cognition to behavior.* (pp. 101–128). Berlin, Germany: Springer-Verlag.

Lakoff, G. (1987). *Women, fire, and dangerous things: What categories reveal about the mind.* Chicago: University of Chicago Press.

Lalljee, M., & Abelson, R. P. (1983). The organization of explanations. In M. Hewstone (Ed.), *Attribution theory: Social and functional extensions.* (pp. 65–80). Oxford: Blackwell.

McClintock, E. (1983). Interaction. In H. H. Kelley et al. (Eds.), *Close Relationships.* (pp. 68–109). New York: W. H. Freeman.

Mackie, J. L. (1974). *Cement of the universe.* London: Oxford University Press.

McLaughlin, M. L. (1984). *Conversation: How talk is organized.* Beverly Hills, CA: Sage.

Magnusson, D., & Endler, N. S. (1977). Interactional psychology: Present status and future prospects. In D. Magnusson & N. S. Endler (Eds.), *Personality at the crossroads.* (pp. 3–31). Hillsdale, NJ: Lawrence Erlbaum Associates.

Mandler, G. (1975). *Mind and emotion.* New York: Wiley, 1975.

Markus, H., & Nurius, P. (1986). Possible selves. *American Psychologist, 41,* 954–969.

Markus, H., & Smith, J. (1981). The influence of self-schemata on the perception of others. In N. Cantor & J. F. Kihlstrom (Eds.), *Personality, cognition, and social interaction.* (pp. 233–262). Hillsdale, NJ: Lawrence Erlbaum Associates.

Miller, G. A., Galanter, E., & Pribram, K. H. (1960). *Plans and the structure of behavior.* New York: Holt, Rinehart, & Winston.

Miller, L. C., & Berg, J. H. (1984). Selectivity and urgency in interpersonal exchange. In V. Derlega (Ed.). *Communication, intimacy, and close relationships.* (pp. 161–205). New York: Academic Press.

Miller, L. C., Berg, J. H., & Archer, R. L. (1983). Openers: Individuals who elicit intimate self-disclosure. *Journal of Personality and Social Psychology, 44,* 1234–1244.

Miller, L. C., & Kenny, D. A. (1986). Reciprocity of self-disclosure at the individual and dyadic levels: A social relations analysis. *Journal of Personality and Social Psychology, 50,* 713–719.

Miller, L. C. (1988). *Disclosure-liking effects at the individual and dyadic level: A social relations analysis.* Unpublished manuscript, Scripps College, Claremont, CA.

Miller, L. C., & Read, S. J. (1987). Why am I telling you this? Self-disclosure in a goal-based model of personality. In V. J. Derlega & J. Berg (Eds.), *Self-disclosure: Theory, research, and therapy.* (pp. 35–58). New York: Plenum.

Miller, L. C., & Read, S. J. (in press). Inter-personalism: Understanding persons in relationships. In W. H. Jones & D. Perlman (Eds.), *Perspectives in interpersonal behavior and relationships.* (Vol. 2). Greenwich, CT: JAI Press.

Mischel, W. (1973). Toward a cognitive social learning reconceptualization of personality. *Psychological Review, 80,* 252–283.

Mischel, W. (1977). On the future of personality measurement. *American Psychologist, 32,* 246–254.

Mischel, W. (1984). Convergences and challenges in the search for consistency. *American Psychologist, 39,* 351–364.

Mischel, W., & Peake, P. K. (1982). Beyond deja vu in the search for cross-situational consistency. *Psychological Review, 89,* 730–755.

Murphy, G. L., & Medin, D. L. (1985). The role of theories in conceptual coherence. *Psychological Review, 92,* 289–316.

Murray, H. (1938). *Explorations in personality.* New York: Oxford University Press.

Nuttin, J. (1984). *Motivation, planning, and action: A relational theory of behavioral dynamics.* Hillsdale, NJ: Lawrence Erlbaum Associates.

Park, B. (1986). A method for studying the development of impressions of real people. *Journal of Personality and Social Psychology, 51,* 907–917.

Pennington, N., & Hastie, R. (1986). Evidence evaluation in complex decision making. *Journal of Personality and Social Psychology, 51,* 242–248.

Pervin, L. A. (1983). The stasis and flow of behavior: Toward a theory of goals, In M. M. Page (Ed.), *Nebraska Symposium on Motivation 1982.* (pp. 1–53). Lincoln, NE: University of Nebraska Press.

Postman, L., Bruner, J. S., & McGinnies, E. (1948). Personal values as selective factors in perception. *Journal of Abnormal and Social Psychology, 43,* 142–154.

Read, S. J. (1987). Constructing causal scenarios: A knowledge structure approach to causal reasoning. *Journal of Personality and Social Psychology, 52,* 288–302.

Read, S. J., & Cesa, I. (1988). *The role of failed expectations in analogical reasoning and explanation.* Unpublished manuscript, University of Southern California, Los Angeles, CA.

Read, S. J., Collins, N. L., & Miller, L. C. (1988). *The relationship of attachment style and parental behavior to partner choice in dating couples.* Unpublished manuscript, University of Southern California, Los Angeles, CA.

Read, S. J., Druian, P. R., & Miller, L. C. (1987). *The role of causal sequence in the meaning of actions.* Unpublished manuscript, University of Southern California, Los Angeles, CA.

Read, S. J., & Jones, D. K. (1988). *Factors affecting the use of abstract analogies in the prediction and explanation of suicidal behavior.* Unpublished manuscript, University of Southern California, Los Angeles, CA.

Read, S. J., & Marcus, A. (1988). *Metarules in the construction of causal explanations.* Unpublished manuscript, University of Southern California, Los Angeles, CA.

Reeder, G. D., & Brewer, M. B. (1979). A schematic model of dispositional attribution in interpersonal perception. *Psychological Review, 86,* 61–79.

Rosch, E. (1975). Cognitive reference points. *Cognitive Psychology, 7,* 532–547.

Rosch, E. (1978). Principles of categorization. In E. Rosch & B. B. Lloyd (Eds.), *Cognition and categorization* (pp. 27–48). Hillsdale, NJ: Lawrence Erlbaum Associates.

Rosch, E., & Mervis, C. B. (1975). Family resemblances: Studies in the internal structure of categories. *Cognitive Psychology, 7,* 573–605.

Roseman, I. J. (1984). Cognitive determinants of emotion: A structural theory. In P. Shaver (Ed.), *Review of personality and social psychology* (Vol. 5, pp. 11–36). Beverly Hills, CA: Sage.

Rusbult, C. E. (1983). A longitudinal test of the investment model: The development (and deterioration) of satisfaction and commitment in heterosexual involvement. *Journal of Personality and Social Psychology, 45,* 101–117.

Schank, R. C. (1982). *Dynamic memory: A theory of reminding and learning in computers and people.* Cambridge, England: Cambridge University Press.

Schank, R. C. (1986). *Explanation patterns: Understanding mechanically and creatively.* Hillsdale, NJ: Lawrence Erlbaum Associates.

Schank, R. C., & Abelson, R. P. (1977). *Scripts, plans, goals, and understanding.* Hillsdale, NJ: Lawrence Erlbaum Associates.

Sillars, A. L. (1985). Interpersonal perception in relationships. In W. Ickes (Ed.), *Compatible and incompatible relationships.* (pp. 277–305). New York: Springer-Verlag.

Snyder, M., & Ickes, W. (1985). Personality and social behavior. In G. Lindzey & E. Aronson (Eds.), *The Handbook of social psychology,* (Vol. 2, pp. 883–947). New York: Random House.

Swann, W. B., Jr. (1983). Self-verification: Bringing social reality into harmony with the self. In J. Suls & A. G. Greenwald (Eds.), *Psychological perspectives on the self.* (Vol. 2, pp. 33–66). Hillsdale, NJ: Lawrence Erlbaum Associates.

Swann, W. B., Jr. (1987). Identity Negotiation: Where two roads meet. *Journal of Personality and Social Psychology, 53,* 1038–1051.

Swann, W. B., & Read, S. J. (1981a). Self-verification processes: How we sustain our self-perceptions. *Journal of Experimental Social Psychology, 17,* 351–372.

Swann, W. B., & Read, S. J. (1981b). Acquiring self-knowledge: The search for feedback that fits. *Journal of Personality and Social Psychology, 41,* 1119–1128.

Thorne, A. (1987). The press of personality: A study of conversations between introverts and extraverts. *Journal of Personality and Social Psychology, 53,* 718–726.

Turner, R. G., & Peterson, M. (1977). Public and private self-consciousness and emotional expressivity. *Journal of Consulting and Clinical Psychology, 45,* 490–491.

Wachtel, P. L. (1973). Psychodynamics, behavior therapy, and the implacable experimenter: An inquiry into the consistency of personality. *Journal of Abnormal Psychology, 82,* 324–334.

Waring, E. M. (1987). Self-disclosure in cognitive marital therapy. In V. J. Derlega & J. H. Berg (Eds.), *Self-disclosure: Theory, research, and therapy* (pp. 283–301). New York: Plenum.

Wegner, D. M., Giuliano, T., & Hertel, P. T. (1985). Cognitive interdependence in close relationships. In W. Ickes (Ed.), *Compatible and incompatible relationships.* (pp. 253–276). New York: Springer-Verlag.

Wilensky, R. (1983). *Planning and understanding: A computational approach to human reasoning.* Reading, MA.: Addison-Wesley.

Wright, J. C., & Mischel, W. (1987). A conditional approach to dispositional constructs: The local predictability of social behavior. *Journal of Personality and Social Psychology, 53,* 1159–1177.

Zuroff, D. C. (1986). Was Gordon Allport a trait theorist? *Journal of Personality and Social Psychology, 51,* 993–1000.

12 Goals Concepts: Themes, Issues, and Questions

LAWRENCE A. PERVIN
Rutgers University

The chapters in this volume give testimony to the growing interest in the concept of goals and to the widened acceptance of a purposive view of behavior. At the same time, it is clear that complex questions remain. Some of these border on the philosophical and perhaps cannot be answered by psychologists, whereas others are of fundamental import to psychologists and can hardly be ignored. In this concluding chapter let us consider some of these questions and issues.

THE GOALS CONCEPT: DEFINITION AND ESSENTIAL FEATURES

The concept of a goal clearly is distinct from other motivational and personality concepts present in the field, such as needs, traits, skills, values, and the self. The goal concept departs from a biologically based view of motivation, though biological factors can influence goals. The goal concept suggests a more motivational view of the person than that suggested by the trait concept, though clusters of goals and plans may be expressed in traits. Depending on the definition of values, goals and values would appear to have similar properties, though it may be suggested that one could have goals that are not values (e.g., something that is "desired" but not "valued") and values that are not goals (e.g., a value that does not have any motivating properties for the person). In addition, the concept of goals would appear to be more directly tied to such concepts of action as plans, strategies, beliefs, and self-regulation than is true for the belief concept. As many of the contributors suggest, goals and the self are intimately linked to one another in the person. Goals contribute to the definition of the self and are expressed through self-directed action. At the same time, self-knowledge and self-efficacy beliefs influence goal-directed action. Finally, the concept of skills would appear to have more to do with the perceived potential for development and implementation of plans and strategies than with the motivational properties of goals, though the perception of one's skills and resources influences the strength and direction of purposive behavior.

A goal may be defined as a mental image or other end point representation associated with affect toward which action may be directed. Goals have both cognitive and affective features. The cognitive features may be very general or very detailed, and the affective features may be weak or intense, positive or negative. By virtue of these cognitive and affective components, goals play a major role in the activation and organization of action, though whether a goal is translated into action depends on a variety of internal and perceived external considerations. As emphasized by McDougall and Tolman, goal-directed action is characterized by a persistence until quality and by a plasticity of means-ends relationships. As part of the latter, goal-directed action is characterized by the utilization of feedback information so as to keep action directed toward the represented end point. Goal-directed action is both focused (directed) and organized.

Within the preceding context, it may be observed that a number of fundamental questions remain unanswered. For example, we can briefly consider the following:

1. How are goals acquired? The basis upon which goals are acquired has all too frequently been neglected by psychologists. This is not a problem for those working in the area of artificial intelligence since it is the investigator who defines the goal. However, it is a critical question for motivation psychologists. In essence the question here is what gives goals their motivating quality. The most common response to this question is the association of goals with affect (Klinger, 1977; McClelland, 1961; McDougall, 1908; Mowrer, 1960; Pervin, 1983; Tomkins, 1970; Young, 1961). In other cases the role of affect is not specifically stated but is implicit in the discussion of the relation of goals to motivation. Thus, for example, both Mischel (1973) and Bandura (1986) do not specifically emphasize the role of affect in motivation but do talk about self-evaluative responses (e.g., pride and disappointment) to meeting performance standards.

12. GOAL CONCEPTS   **475**

Addressing the issue of the development of goals involves not only how goals are acquired, but also how they may be relinquished or become functionally autonomous from one another (Allport, 1961). Further, since ordinarily we are considering goal systems rather than single goals, attention must be given to how goals become interrelated and organized in some hierarchical fashion. Thus, there is the task of understanding the developing complexity of the goal system in terms of number of goals, interconnections among goals, and plans and strategies developed to obtain goals.

2. Are goals conscious? The contributors to this volume take a variety of stands on the issue. Some suggest that goals are conscious, but others suggest that goals need not be conscious or can be unavailable to awareness. Such diversity of view is representative of others who have addressed the issue. Thus, Boden (1972) argues that purposive behavior involves consciousness, whereas Brody (1983) argues that consciousness may be important but not necessary for goal-directed action. Heider (1958) included unconscious intention within the realm of personal causality and Miller, Galanter, & Pribram (1960) indicated that they were willing to tolerate unconscious intentions. In sum, most psychologists would appear to suggest that the organism may or may not be conscious of its goals and intentions (Woodfield, 1976).

Provision for the lack of awareness of goals, of course, greatly complicates the issue of assessment. The contributors to this volume suggest a variety of measures for goals: verbal self-report, fantasy, experience sampling, and observational analysis. Whereas in some cases individuals may be able to report their goals, in other cases extended behavioral observation may be required. Even here there is the potential problem that a person may have an important goal that is rarely tied to action or is tied to action in complex ways. As suggested by the principles of equipotentiality and equifinality, the same goal can lead to varied behaviors and the same behavior can be expressive of multiple goals at one time or of different goals at different times.

3. Is all action goal-directed? Not all action would appear to be goal-directed. Illustrations of nonpurposive action would be reflex movements and purely habitual responses. Although the suggested criteria for goal-directed action will apply for most cases, in fact it is difficult to define necessary and sufficient criteria that will hold for all cases (Woodfield, 1976). Further, it is useful to maintain the distinction between goal-directed action and such other concepts as intention, volition, and will (Libet, 1985).

4. Is goal-directed action present in machines, plants, nonhuman species, and children? Some of the action of machines, plants, and nonhuman animals would appear to have the goal-directed action qualities of persistence, plasticity, and the utilization of feedback information. Although a mental image would not be present in all cases, some other representation of the end point would be stored in the system. The affective component of goals, of course, would be limited to animals. Griffin (1978) suggested that animals have mental images of objects, events, and remote relationships, as well as self-awareness and intention. Similarly, Hebb (1978) suggested that other animals besides humans have conscious representational processes and intention. And, in accord with this, Premack and Woodruff (1978) suggest that chimpanzees attribute wants, purposes, and affective attitudes to others.

Piaget (1952) distinguished between goal-directed behavior and intentional behavior. He suggested that at about the age of 8 or 9 months the child begins to coordinate previously independent schemata so that new combinations of actions are used to reach ends. Such utilization of schemata is seen as reflecting consciousness of a desire and intention but not the characteristics of intentional behavior that take place at later stages of the development of intelligence. In the latter case, the child reflects upon and develops a plan in the absence of external events. In sum, for Piaget, children are capable of goal-directed action before they are capable of intentional behavior, the latter involving the establishment of goals in the absence of external stimuli, as well as the development of new schemata through active exploration.

GOAL SYSTEMS, THE DYNAMICS OF GOAL SYSTEM FUNCTIONING, AND WILL

An important theme throughout these chapters has been that of goals as organized into a system; that is, there is a hierarchical organization of goals and subgoals, superordinate goals and subordinate goals. At the same time, the suggestion that goals are organized does not suggest a fixed structure. Goals are organized into a system that is capable of change according to context as well as capable of change over time. A central issue for personality, emphasized so well by Allport (1961), concerns the organization of goal systems, that is, how the person is able to maintain stability in goal system functioning while remaining flexible to meet changing internal and external demands.

The concept of a goal system leads to a focus on relations among parts. Goals are potentially irrelevant to one another, compatible with one another, or in conflict with one another. Similar issues arise in considering the relations between goals of individuals in an interpersonal or group setting.

The dynamics of goals system functioning involves the organization and integration of goals, the development of plans and the acquisition of skills to implement plans, and the development of strategies for the simultaneous achievement of multiple goals and the adaptive sequencing of goals that cannot be achieved simultaneously. The dynamics of goal system functioning involves a cognitive assessment of the importance of various goals, the difficulty of achieving goals, the availability of internal resources and external affordances (Baron & Boudreau, 1987), and the potential for "satisficing" goals if not fully achieving them. Although related to expectancy-value theory, what is suggested is a much more complex operation involving multiple goals, beliefs about the self, the task of sequencing, and the utilization of feedback. At the same time, it is not suggested that decisions concerning goal system functioning are completely rational or optimal.

An issue worthy of note here is whether it is goals per se that are motivating or the movement toward or away from them that is motivating. Some goals theorists suggest that it is affect associated with the goal image that is motivating, whereas others reject this view and instead emphasize the evaluative response associated with knowledge of performance. Allport (1937) appeared to take the latter view in his suggestion that "the attainment of unity depends more upon knowing what one wants than upon getting it. It is the striving towards the known goal that confers unity, not the successful arrival" (p. 350). Or, consider the suggestion by Cantor and Kihlstrom (1987), in tune with the view expressed by Bandura, that "the paradox of goal-setting is that people are often less intrigued or impressed with an end-state the closer they come actually to achieving it" (p. 179).

Recently, action psychologists have been concerned with the question of how the organism goes from image to action (Frese & Sabini, 1985; Kuhl & Beckman, 1985). Continuing with the action process, there is the question of the organism's response to interruption of the action (Mandler, 1975), to perceived threat (Paterson & Neufeld, 1987), and to failure. A number of the contributors point to the health implications of conflict and stress within the system and raise the important question of determinants of the response to failure—greater effort, depression, goal modification, etc.

Of considerable importance to our understanding of goal system functioning are occasions of disturbance in the sense of will or volition, either in terms of the person being blocked from taking action or feeling compelled to take action (Shapiro, 1981). Virtually every person experiences some such "compulsion" or "inhibition." Yet, the determinants of such disturbances in volitional goal system functioning are poorly understood.

GOALS AND SOCIAL COGNITION

Social cognition is motivated cognition. Goals influence the selection, organization, and retrieval of information. According to the contributors, the very structure of social knowledge, including self-knowledge, is tied to goals and related concepts. To a very great extent, one's own actions, as well as those of others, are interpreted and anticipated in goals terms.

As indicated in the introduction, goals concepts have been viewed as basic organizing categories within an artificial intelligence framework. Yet, much of the person perception or implicit personality theory literature has emphasized trait conceptions of peronality. The difference here is partly due to historical factors, but the interesting question remains concerning the relation between goal and trait conceptions of personality or, indeed, other ways people may have of processing social information. One would expect people to use differing categories depending on the information available to them and the task at hand. However, in fact little research has investigated this question (Hoffman, Mischel, & Mazze, 1981).

From a developmental standpoint, one can consider the comparative development of goal and trait categories as ways of processing person information, as well as the varying occasions upon which each is used. Such an analysis could perhaps parallel developing interest in the field of personality concerning relations between goal (need, motive) and trait concepts.

CONCLUSION

The contributions to this volume express the vigor of the field. While advancing knowledge, they help to focus attention to issues that remain and new problems to be addressed. I believe that they get to the very heart of what personality and social psychology are about.

REFERENCES

Allport, G. W. (1937). *Personality: A psychological interpretation.* New York: Holt, Rinehart, & Winston.
Allport, G. W. (1961). *Pattern and growth in personality.* New York: Holt, Rinehart, & Winston.

Bandura, A. (1986). *Social foundations of thought and action: A social cognitive theory.* Englewood Cliffs, NJ: Prentice-Hall.
Baron, R. M., & Boudreau, L. A. (1987). An ecological perspective on integrating personality and social psychology. *Journal of Personality and Social Psychology, 53,* 1222–1228.
Boden, M. A. (1972). *Purposive explanation in psychology.* Cambridge: Harvard University Press.
Brody, N. (1983). *Human motivation: Commentary on goal-directed action.* New York: Academic Press.
Cantor, N., & Kihlstrom, J. F. (1987). *Personality and social intelligence.* Englewood Cliffs, NJ: Prentice-Hall.
Frese, M., & Sabini, J. (Eds.). (1985). *Goal directed behavior: The concept of action in psychology.* Hillsdale, NJ: Lawrence Erlbaum Associates.
Griffin, D. R. (1978). Prospects for a cognitive ethology. *Behavioral and Brain Sciences, 1,* 527–538.
Hebb, D. O. (1978). Behavioral evidence of thought and consciousness. *Behavioral and Brain Sciences, 1,* 577.
Heider, F. (1958). *The psychology of interpersonal relations.* New York: Wiley.
Hoffman, C., Mischel, W., & Mazze, K. (1981). The role of purpose in the organization of information about behavior: Trait-based versus goal-based categories in person cognition. *Journal of Personality and Social Psychology, 40,* 211–225.
Klinger, E. (1977). *Meaning and void: Inner experience and the incentives in people's lives.* Minneapolis: University of Minnesota Press.
Kuhl, J., & Beckman, J. (Eds.). (1985). *Action control: From cognition to behavior.* Berlin: Springer-Verlag.
Libet, B. (1985). Unconscious cerebral initiative and the role of conscious will in voluntary action. *Behavioral and Brain Sciences, 8,* 529–566.
Mandler, G. (1975). *Mind and emotion.* New York: Wiley.
McClelland, D. C. (1961). *The achieving society.* Princeton, NJ: Van Nostrand.
McDougall, W. (1908). *An introduction to social psychology.* London: Methuen.
Miller, G. A., Galanter, E., & Pribram, K. (1960). *Plans and the structure of behavior.* New York: Holt.
Mischel, W. (1973). Toward a cognitive social learning reconceptualization of personality. *Psychological Review, 80,* 252–283.
Mowrer, O. H. (1960). *Learning theory and the symbolic processes.* New York: Wiley.
Paterson, R. J., & Neufeld, R. W. J. (1987). Clear danger: Situational determinants of the appraisal of threat. *Psychological Bulletin, 101,* 404–416.
Pervin, L. A. (1983). The stasis and flow of behavior: Toward a theory of goals. In M. Page (Ed.), *Personality: Current theory and research* (pp. 1–53). Lincoln: University of Nebraska Press.
Piaget, J. (1952). *The origins of intelligence in children.* New York: International Universities Press.
Premack, D., & Woodruff, G. (1978). Does the chimpanzee have a theory of mind? *Behavioral and Brain Sciences, 1,* 515–526.
Shapiro, D. (1981). *Autonomy and rigid character.* New York: Basic Books.
Tomkins, S. S. (1970). Affects are the primary motivational system. In M.B. Arnold (Ed.), *Feelings and emotions: The Loyola symposium* (pp. 101–110). New York: Academic Press.
Woodfield, A. (1976). *Teleology.* Cambridge: Cambridge University Press.
Young, P. T. (1961). *Motivation and emotion.* New York: Wiley.

Author Index

A

Abbott, V., 371, *406*
Abel, M., 25, *79*
Abelson, R. P., 12, *16*, 94, *125*, 195, 209, 217, *240*, 247, *282*, *287*, 330, 342, 355, *361*, 364, 367, 369, 371, 372, 373, 378, 393, 395, *406*, *408*, *409*, *410*, 416, 424, 432, 435–38, 447, 449, 455, 456, 462, *467*, *469*, *470*, *472*
Abrams, K., 61, 62, *79*
Abramson, L. Y., 41, *78*
Ach, 8, 234
Achtenberg, J., 232, *237*
Ackerman, A., 233, *241*
Acksen, B., 265, *284*
Adams, J. S., 294, *321*
Adler, A., 4, *12*, 118, 119, *121*, 130, *163*, 397, 399, *406*, 415, 462, *467*
Adler, S., 313, *326*
Adrian, N., 308, *321*
Agustsdottir, S., 267, *287*
Ajzen, I., 312, *321*
Alderfer, C. P., 292, 293, 298, *321*
Alexander, C. N., Jr., 245, 246, 251, *282*
Alexander, Y., 67, *83*
Alicke, M. D., 268, *282*
Alker, H. A., 113, *121*
Allen, A., 249, *283*

Allen, V. L., 259, *287*
Alloy, L. B., 41, *78*
Allport, F. H., 5, 8, *13*, 87, 91, *121*, *123*, *125*
Allport, G. W., 5, 6, 8, *13*, 90, 92, 95, *121*, 216, *237*, 255, *282*, 415, 419, 431, 432, 454, 460, 461, 462, 464, *467*, 475, 476, 477, *478*
Allston, W. P., 427, 462, *467*
Alston, W. P., 112, 113, *121*, *122*
Altman, I., 343, 351, 354, 355, *359*, *361*
Anchin, J. C., 329, 358, *359*
Andersen, S. M., 431, *467*
Anderson, C. A., 229, *237*, *240*
Anderson, J. R., 11, *13*, 129, *163*, 444, *467*
Annear, W. C., 233, *237*
Ansbacher, H. L., 4, *13*, 215, *237*
Ansbacher, R. R., 4, *13*, 215, *237*
Appelman, A. J., 256, *282*
Appley, M. H., 189, *208*
Arad, R., 306, 309, *322*
Archer, R. L., 451, *470*
Argyle, M., 11, *13*, *14*, 356, *359*, 420, 434, 436, 454, 465, *467*
Aristotle, 8
Arkin, R. M., 256, 262, 276, 279, *282*, *290*
Arkowitz, H., 41, *81*, 264, *282*, *284*
Arnold, L., 155, *164*

481

Aronoff, J., 97, 118, 119, 120, *122*
Aronson, E., 256, 268, *286*
Arvey, R. D., 58, *78*
Atkinson, J. W., 6, 8, *13*, 22, *78*, 85, *122*, 216–19, *237, 239*
Avener, M., 231, 234, *239*

B

Backman, C., 400, *406*
Baer, J. S., 439, *469*
Bailey, T., 31, 51, *84*
Bakan, D., 108, *122*
Baldes, J. J., 311, *323*
Baldwin, M. W., 248, 252, *282*
Baltes, P. B., 128, 131, *163*
Bandura, A., 3, 8, 9, *13*, 19, 21, 27, 28, 29, 31–35, 37–41, 43–49, 51–57, 59, 61, 62, 64, 65, 66, 70–73, 75, 76, *78, 79, 84*, 127, 131, 132, 151, 159, *163*, 215, 217, 218, 219, *237*, 244, 251, 256, 266, 275, 278, *282*, 297, 307, 311, *321*, 474, 477, *479*
Bandura, M. M., 21, 49, *79*
Banjamin, L. S., *359*
Barden, R. C., 230, *237, 239*
Bargh, J. A., 403, *406*, 453, *467*
Barling, J., 25, *79*
Barnes, R. D., 256, *285*
Barnes, V. E., 50, *79*
Baron, A., 297, *323*
Baron, R. M., 11, *15*, 420, 421, 453, 454, 457, *467*, 477, *479*
Barry, W. A., 347, 355, *361*
Barsalou, L. W., 11, *13*, 428, 439, *468*
Barsalow, L., 370, 371, *406*
Barta, S. G., 89, 90, 98, 101, *124*, 228, *239*
Bartlem, C. S., 308, *321*
Bartlett, F. C., 372, *406*
Barton, R., 41, *82*
Barwick, K. D., 297, 304, *323*
Battle, E. S., 230, *237*
Baumeister, R. F., 107, *122*, 152, 155, 160, *163*, 250, 251, 255, 258, 262, 263, 266, 268, *282*
Baumgardner, A. H., 266, *283*
Beach, L. R., 50, *79*
Bealls, S. K., 105, *125*
Beaman, A. L., 67, 68, *80*
Beattie, O., 397, *407*
Beattie, R., 25, *79*

Beavin, J. H., 356, *361*
Beck, A. T., 59, *82*
Beck, K. H., 24, *79*
Becker, G., 259, *283*
Becker, L. J., 27, *79*, 304, *321*
Becker, W. S., 292, *323*
Beckmann, J., 8, *15*, 127, *165*, 223, 228, 229, 234, *239*, 477, *479*
Behling, O., 23, *79*
Belanger, D., 190, *207*
Bell, C. H., Jr., 47, *84*
Bem, D. J., 249, 277, *283*
Benjamin, L. S., *359*
Benjamin, L. T., Jr., 1, *13, 329*
Bennis, W., 317, *321*
Berg, J. H., 418, 451, *470*
Berglas, S., 131, 161, *163, 164*, 230, *237*, 267, *285*
Berkowitz, L., 337, *359*
Berlyne, D., 6, *13*
Bern, H., 371, *406*
Berndt, E. G., 11, *13*
Berndt, T. J., 11, *13*
Berscheid, E., 244, 274, *283*, 329, 331, 336, 338, 347, 352, 353, 355, 356, *360*, 417, 425, 451, 458, 459, 465, *468, 470*
Betz, N. E., 24, *79*
Biggs, D. A., 264, *283*
Binder, D. M., 264, *283*
Bindra, D., 6, *13*
Biner, P. M., 184, 186, 204, *207, 208*
Binik, Y. M., 63, *80*
Birch, D., 85, *122*
Bird, E. I., 235, *237*
Black, J. B., 369, 370–71, 372, *406, 407, 409, 410*, 437, 462, *468, 469*
Blaney, P. H., 230, *237*
Blank, A., 373, 395, *408*
Blaustein, E. H., 155, *164*
Block, J., 113, *122*, 135, 139, *163*, 420, *468*
Bobko, P., 41, 43, *82*, 307, *324*
Boden, M. A., 2, 7, *13*, 475, *479*
Bois, J., 372, *409*
Bok, S., 76, *79*
Bolinger, D., 68, *79*
Bolton, C. D., 343, *359*
Bolton, W., 10, *15*

AUTHOR INDEX

Bonoma, T. V., 244, 262, *289*
Booth-Kewley, S., 106, *123*, 223, *238*
Borden, V. M. H., 344–45, *359*
Boudreau, L. A., 420, 421, 453, 454, 457, *467*, 477, *479*
Bower, G. H., 63, 64, *79, 81*, 369, 370–71, 372, *406, 407, 409*
Bowlby, J., 440, *468*
Bradbury, T. N., 448, *469*
Bramwell, A., 180, 186, 204, *210*
Brandt, R. B., 23, *79*
Breckler, S. J., 116, *122*, 248, 251, 252, 256, *284*
Brehm, J. W., 146, 150, 160, 169, 175–82, 204, *207, 208, 209, 210*
Breunlin, D. C., 339, *359*
Brewer, M. B., 439, *471*
Brewer, W. F., 363, 370, *407, 408*
Brewin, T. B., 233, *237*
Brickman, P., 230, *241*
Bridwell, L. G., 292, *326*
Briggs, J., 63, *80*
Briggs, S. R., 248, 279, *283*
Brim, O. G., Jr., 53, *81*
Bringham, H., 371, *408*
Broadbent, D., 7, *13*
Brock, T. C., 71, *79*, 265, *283*
Brody, N., 2, *13*, 475, *479*
Bronfenbrenner, U., 354, *359*
Brower, A. M., 90, *122*, 129–33, 136, 140, 147, 148, 152, 157, 161, *163, 164*, 432, 451, *468*
Brown, B. A., 343, 351, *359*
Brown, D. R., 155, *164*
Brown, I., Jr., 29, *80*
Brown, J., 160, *166*
Brown, J. D., 255, *289*
Brownlee, E. A., 266, *283*
Bruner, J. S., 2, 11, *13*, 365, *407*, 453, *471*
Bryan, J. F., 43, 59, *80, 82*, 304, 310, 313, *324*
Bryant, J., 196, 197, *208*
Buck, R. W., 106, *122*
Burch, R. W., 106, *122*
Burger, J. M., 215, *237*, 256, *282*
Burke, K., 367, *407*
Burns, G. L., 8, *16*
Burt, R. S., 391, *407*
Bushman, B. J., 182, 193, 195, 196, *210*

Buss, A. H., 71, *79*, 248, 265, 279, *283*, 430, 432, *468, 469*
Buss, D. M., 87, 88, 111, 112, 113, 120, *122*, 428, 439, *468*
Butzin, C. A., 11, *13*

C

Cacioppo, J. T., 180–81, *208*, 273, *287*, 404, *407*
Campbell, A., 102, *122*
Campbell, J. P., 156, *166*, 292, 293, 295, 308, 320, *321*
Campion, M. A., 33, *80*
Canavan-Gumpert, D., 265, *286*
Cantor, J. R., 196, 197, *208*
Cantor, N., 9, 11, *13, 16*, 87, 90, 116, 120, *122*, 127, 129–34, 136, 139, 140, 141, 144, 146–53, 155–61, *163, 164, 165*, 169, 216, 223, 231, *237, 239*, 250, *283*, 354–56, *359*, 374, 375, 395, 398, 399, 404, *407, 409*, 415, 419, 428, 431, 432, 438, 439, 451, 453, 462, *468*, 477, *479*
Carbonell, J. G., 11, *13*, 427, 462, *468*
Carlsmith, J. S., 174, *208*
Carnevale, P. J. D., 350, *361*
Carpenter, K. M., 229, *238*
Carpentieri, A. M., 162, *164*
Carroll, J. S., 11, *13*
Carson, R. C., 247, 259, *283*, 329, 358, *359*, 458, 462, 464, *468*
Cartledge, N. D., 44, 45, *82, 83*, 304, 319, *324*
Carver, C. S., 8, *13*, 36, *37, 80, 83*, 94, 95, 117, *122*, 160, 161, *164, 166*, 223, 228, 230, *237*, 249, 251, 252, 274, 275, 279, *283*, 416, 456, 465, *468*
Caspi, A., 147, 162, *164*
Cella, A., 308, *321*
Cervone, D., 3, 27–30, 33, 34, 35, 37, 38, 39, 41, 43, 45, 48, 59, *79, 80, 83*, 307, *321*
Cesa, I., 443, 448, *471*
Chah, D., 301, 318, *324*
Chaiken, S., 259, *284*
Champlin, T. S., 76, *80*
Chance, J. F., 215, *240*
Chanowitz, B., 373, 395, *408*
Chaplin, W., 41, *82*

Chase, W. G., 453, *468*
Cheek, J. M., 162, *164*, 251, 253, 260, *283, 285,* 430, *468*
Chi, M. T. H., 453, *468*
Christensen, A., 329, 331, 336, 338, 347, 352, 353, 355, 356, *359, 360,* 425, 451, 458, 465, *470*
Christensen-Szalanski, J. J., 50, *79*
Cialdini, R. B., 229, *238,* 256, 271, *283, 287,* 404, *407*
Ciminero, A. R., 60, *80*
Clark, H. H., 436, *468*
Clark, L. F., 11, *14*
Clark, R. A., 216, *239*
Cocc, L., 308, *321*
Cofer, C. N., 1, 6, *13,* 189, *208*
Cohen, C. E., 11, *13,* 375, *407*
Cohen, S., 133, 134, 135, *164*
Cole, J. D., 159, *164*
Collins, A. M., 371, *410,* 444, *468*
Collins, C., 188, *208*
Collins, J. L., 22, 45, *80*
Collins, N. L., 433, 440, *468, 471*
Collins, R. L., 161, *166*
Comstock, C., 67, *84*
Contrada, R. J., 182, 183, 184, 188, *208, 210,* 231, *241*
Converse, P. E., 102, *122*
Cooley, C. H., 251, *283*
Cooper, J., 273, *284*
Corbin, C. B., 233–34, *237*
Costa, J., 249, *286*
Costa, P. T., 103, *122*
Costanzo, P. B., 265, *290*
Cousins, E., 43, *82*
Covington, M. V., 20, 21, *80,* 231, *237*
Cox, P. D., 21, 22, *84*
Craik, K. H., 88, 112, 113, 120, *122,* 428, 439, *468*
Cramer, L., 448, *469*
Creighton, J., 233, *240*
Crutcher, B., 180, *210*
Csikszentmihalyi, M., 33, *80,* 102, *124,* 147, *164,* 223, *237,* 397, *407*
Cuber, J. F., 345, 352, 353, *359*
Cunningham, A. J., 233, *237*
Curtis, M. I., 59, *83,* 313, *325*
Cutrona, C. E., 63, *80,* 147, *164*

D

D'Andrade, R. G., 375, 388, *407*

Darley, J. M., 11, *14*
Dattel, M., 63, *80*
Davidson, R. J., 104, *125*
Davies, F. W., 59, *80*
Davis, D., 265, *283*
Davis, K. E., 11, *14,* 440, *469*
Debus, R. L., 21, *82*
deCharms, R., 215, *238*
Deci, E. L., 215, *238*
Denney, N., 128, *164*
DePaulo, B. M., 263, *283*
Dermer, M., 244, 274, *283*
Deutsch, M., 347, 349, 355, *359, 360*
Devins, G. M., 63, *80*
Dewhirst, H. D., 58, *78*
Diederichs, P., 232, 233, *240*
Diener, E., 67, 68, 70, *80,* 88, 102, 103, 109, 110, 111, 116, *122, 123, 124,* 454, *469*
Diggory, J. C., 59, *82*
DiMatteo, M. R., 107, *123*
Dineen, J., 67, 68, *80*
Dittman-Kohli, F., 131, *163*
Dixon, R. A., 131, *163*
Dlugolecki, D., 267, *283*
Dodge, K. A., 159, *164*
Dodson, J. D., 184, *210*
Doise, W., 405, *407*
Dollard, J., 263, *283*
Donnerstein, E., 337, *359*
Doob, A. N., 260, *285*
Dorner, D., 433, 440, 456, *468*
Dossett, D. L., 297, 304, 308, *321, 323*
Dozier, M., 11, *13*
Druian, P. R., 440, *471*
Dubbert, P. M., 48, *80*
Duck, S. W., 329, *360, 361*
Duncan, S. W., 230, *237*
Dunnette, M. D., 295, 308, 312, 320, *321*
Duval, S., 416, 453, 456, *469*
Dweck, C. S., 8, 9, 10, *14,* 21, 49, 50, *79, 80*

E

Eagly, A. H., 259, 265, *284*
Earley, P. C., 306, 307, 309, 314, 315, 318, *322*
Easterbrook, J. A., 232, *238*
Ebbesen, E. B., 11, *13,* 250, *287,* 375, *407*

AUTHOR INDEX

Eder, S., 155, *164*
Edmister, R. O., 317, *322*
Effrein, E. A., 267, *284*
Einhorn, H. J., 448, *469*
Elliott, E. S., 21, 49, 50, *80*
Elliott, R., 181, 190, 196, *208*
Ellis, A., 117, *122*, 418, *469*
Elting, E., 188, *208*
Emmons, R. A., 10, *14, 64,* 87, 88, 96, 98, 99, 102, 103, 104, 106–11, 113, 116, *122, 123, 124,* 127, 130, 159, 217, *238,* 432, 454, *469*
Endler, N. S., 460, 466, 467, *470*
Endresen, K., 67, 68, *80*
Engler, N. S., 428, *470*
Enquist, G., 372, *409*
Epstein, S., 104, 118, 119, *123,* 245, *284,* 466, *469*
Erez, M., 43, *80,* 305, 306, 308, 309, 314, 315, 319, *322, 323, 324*
Erffmeyer, E. S., 228, *238*
Erickson, B., 260, *284*
Erikson, E. H., 108, *123,* 130, 146, *164,* 246, *284*
Esqueda, L. S., 185, *208*
Eulberg, J. R., 320, *325*
Evenbeck, C., 271, *283*

F

Falender, V. J., 267, *284*
Fazio, R. H., 11, *14,* 267, 273, *284*
Feather, N. T., 23, *81,* 216, 218, 230, *238,* 256, 266, 278, *284,* 455, *469*
Feffer, M., 391, *407*
Feldman, S. M., 190, *207*
Feltz, D. L., 228, 234, 235, *238*
Fenichel, O., 202, *208*
Fenigstein, A., 275, *284,* 432, *469*
Festinger, L., 42, *81,* 314, *322*
Fillmore, C., 366, 367, *407*
Fincham, F. D., 441, 448, *469*
Fingarette, H., 71, 77
Finke, R. A., 234, *238*
Fishbein, M., 22, *81,* 217, *238,* 312, *321*
Fisher, A. E., 190, *208*
Fisher, C. D., 314, *322*
Fishman, H. L., 396, *408*
Fiske, S. T., 381, *410*
Fletcher, G. J. O., 448, *469*
Floor, E., 104, *125*
Foa, E. B., 418, *469*

Foa, U. G., 418, *469*
Fondacaro, R., 405, *408*
Foote, N. N., 244, 259, *284*
Ford, C. E., 169, 185, *208*
Ford, D. H., 98, 101, *125*
Ford, M. E., 230, *239*
Forgas, J. P., *407*
Forward, J., 314, *322*
Fossum, J. A., 295, *323*
Fowler, P. C., 27, *84*
Fowles, D. C., 190, *208, 209*
Frankenhaeuser, M., 184, *208*
Fraser, S. C., 67, 68, *80*
Frayne, C., 317, 318, *322, 323*
Frederick, E., 41, *82,* 307, *324*
Frederiksen, N., 91, *123*
French, J. R. P., 308, *321, 322, 323, 325*
Frese, M., 2, 3, 4, 8, *14,* 87, 88, 91, *123,* 455, *469,* 477, *479*
Freud, S., 8, 104, 255, *284*
Frey, D., 264, 267, 274, 275, *284, 290*
Friedman, H. S., 106, 107, *123,* 223, *238*
Friedrichsen, G., 433, 440–41, 456, *470*
Fromson, M. E., 70, 71, 73, 75, *79*
Fultz, J., 184, *208*
Furnham, A., 10, 11, *13, 14, 15,* 356, *359,* 420, 434, 436, 454, 465, 467

G

Gaebelein, C. J., 181, 194, *209*
Gagne, R. M., 129, *164*
Gaines, B., 270, 271, *289*
Galambos, J. A., 370, 371, *407,* 437, 462, *468, 469*
Galanter, E., 6, *15,* 247, 287, 330, *360,* 416, 435, *470,* 475, *479*
Gambino, R., 67, *81*
Garber, J., 60, *81,* 230, *237*
Gardner, H., 404, *407*
Garfinkel, H., 390, 400, *407*
Garland, H., 43, 44, *81*
Gedo, J. E., 8, 9, *14*
Gentner, D., 442, *469*
Gerard, H. B., 372, *411*
Gergen, K. J., 244, 248, 252, 260, 262, 263, 267, *284,* 287, 328, 329, 331, 357, 358, *360,* 395, 397, 402, *407*
Gergen, M. M., 395, 397, 402, *407*

Gewirtz, J. L., 65, *82*
Gibbons, R., 32, *82*
Gibson, J. T., 73, *81*
Gist, M. E., 313, *326*
Giuliano, T., 11, *16*, 394, *410*, 421, *472*
Glaser, R., 453, *468*
Glasgow, R. E., 25, 41, *81*, 264, *284*
Glass, D. C., 182, 188, *208*
Godding, P. R., 25, *81*
Goffman, E., 244, 245, 262, 263, *284*, 390, *407*
Goldberg, A., 9, *14*
Goldberg, L. R., 11, *14*
Goldfried, M. R., 131, *164*, *166*
Golding, S. L., 347, *360*
Goldman, H. J., 256, *288*
Golin, S., 59, *81*
Gollwitzer, P. M., 216, *238*, 260, *290*, 399, *410*
Gonso, J., 355, *360*
Gooding, R. Z., 309, *326*
Gordon, S., 374, 388, 389, 390, *411*
Gorman, P., 63, *80*
Gottman, J. M., 339, 345, 355, *360*
Gould, D., 29, 30, 31, *84*, 235, *241*
Graesser, A. C., 11, *14*, 371, *407*
Graham, J. A., 11, *13*, *14*, 356, *359*, 420, 434, 436, 454, 465, *467*
Grant, L., 155, *164*
Gray, G., 250, *290*, 382, 383, *410*
Graziano, W., 244, 274, *283*
Green, G., 295, *322*
Greenberg, C. L., 308, *321*
Greenberg, J., 169, 175, 177, 178, 179, *207*, 255, 256, 268, 275, 279, *284*, *287*
Greenwald, A. G., 116, *122*, *123*, 245, 248, 251, 252, 255, 256, 276, *284*, 394, 404, *407*
Gregorich, S., 187, 188, 204, *210*
Gregory, W. L., 229, *238*
Gregory, W. S., 91, 101, 119, *123*
Grice, H. P., 436, *469*
Griffin, D. R., 476, *479*
Griffin, J. J., 270, 271, *289*
Grignolo, A., 181, 194, *209*
Gumpert, P., 265, *286*
Gunn, T. P., 21, 22, *84*
Gurin, P., 53, *81*

H

Haberland, K., 372, *408*
Haberland, T. K., 371, *408*
Hackett, G., 24, *79*
Hadari, D., 63, *83*
Hagerman, S., 59, *81*
Hahn, W. W., 190, 191, *208*
Haight, M. R., 76, 77, *81*
Haith, M. M., 11, *15*
Halberstadt, A. G., 108, *123*
Hall, E. G., 228, *238*
Hallam, J. R., 256, *288*
Hamilton, D. L., 266, *282*, 438, *469*
Hamner, E. P., 297, *322*
Hamner, W. C., 297, *322*
Hampson, S. E., 11, *14*
Handelsman, M. M., 230, *240*
Hannover, B., 4, *14*, 455, *469*
Harackiewicz, J. M., 47, *82*
Haritos-Fatouros, M., 73, *81*
Haroff, P. B., *359*
Harper, R. A., 117, *122*, 418, *469*
Harre, R., 246, 247, *285*
Harris, B., 256, *285*
Harrison, S., 301, 318, *324*
Harroff, 345, 352, 353
Harter, S., 215, 219, *238*
Hartwick, J., 388, *408*
Harvey, J. H., 256, *285*, 329, 331, 336, 338, 347, 352, 353, 355, 356, *360*, 425, 451, 458, 465, *470*
Harvey, S. H., 188, *209*
Hassett, J., 181, *208*
Hastie, R., 11, *13*, 374, *408*, 442, *471*
Haythornthwaite, J., 185, *208*
Hazan, C., 440, *469*
Healy, J., Jr., 130, *166*
Heaton, A., 193, 195, 196, *210*
Hebb, D. O., 476, *479*
Heider, F., 10, *14*, 219, *238*, 441, *469*, 475, *479*
Helle, P., 395, *408*
Hempel, C. G., 261, *285*
Hemsley, G. D., 260, *285*
Heneman, H. G., III, 23, *84*
Henne, D., 292, 293, 318, *324*
Herman, C. P., 256, 271, *283*
Herman, S. J., 71, *83*
Hernandez, 197
Heron, N., 448, *469*

Hertel, P. T., 421, *472*
Hertel, R. K., 347, 355, *361*
Hewitt, J. P., 246, *285*
Higgins, E. T., 10, *14*, 87, 116, 120, *123*, *125*, 127, 129, 134, 139, 146, 147, 160, *164*, *166*, 216, *240*, 251, *289*, 405, *408*, 453
Hill, C. A., 274, 275, *289*
Hill, M. G., 279, *285*
Hill, T., 184, *208*
Hinde, R. A., 329, *360*, 405, *408*
Hines, P., 264, *282*
Hobbes, T., 264, *285*
Hochschild, A., 108, *123*
Hoffer, J. L., 194, *209*
Hoffman, C., 11, *14*, 375, *408*, 439, *469*, 478, *479*
Hogan, R., *83*, 114, 118, 120, *123*, 249, 251, 253, 260, 280, *285*
Hogarth, R. M., 50, *81*, 448, *469*
Hogg, E., 264, *286*
Holahan, C. J., 63, *81*
Holahan, C. K., 63, *81*
Holland, J. L., 264, *285*
Hollenbeck, J. R., 219, *238*, 307, 314, *322*
Hollon, S. D., 60, *81*, 162, *164*
Holmes, C., 264, *286*
Holmes, D. S., 189, 190, *209*
Holmes, J. G., 11, *16*, 248, 252, *282*
Holt, E. B., 5
Hormuth, S., 102, *123*, 161, *164*
Horney, K., 255, *285*
Horowitz, M. J., 235, *238*
Houston, B. K., 188, 190, *208*
Huber, V. L., 316, *322*
Huesman, 344
Hulin, C. L., 306, 309, *322*
Hull, C. L., 3, 5, *14*
Hummel, M., 232, 233, *240*
Humphrey, L. L., 48, *82*
Hunter, J. E., 318, 319, 320, *322*
Huston, T. L., 329, 331, 336, 338, 347, 352, 353, 355, 356, *360*, 425, 451, 458, 465, *470*
Hutcheson, J. S., 194, *209*
Hyland, M. E., 10, *14*, 94, *124*

I

Ickes, W., 90, *125*, 454, *472*
Ilgen, D. R., 314, *322*

Ingram, R. E., 162, *164*
Inouye, D. K., 29, *80*
Irwin, F. W., 8, *14*
Isecke, W., 188, *208*
Isen, A. M., 230, *238*, 250, *285*
Isher, A. E., *209*
Ivancevich, J., 308
Ivie, R. L., 77, *81*
Izard, C. E., 261, *285*

J

Jackson, A., 29, 30, 31, *84*, 235, *241*
Jackson, D. D., 356, *361*
Jackson, D. N., 314, *323*
Jacob, T., 358, *360*
Jacobs, B., 29, 31, 32, *81*
Jacobson, N. S., 345, *360*
James, W., 2, 3, 8, *14*, 214, *238*, 246, 253–55, 271, *285*, 404, *408*
Janis, I. L., 341, *360*
Jaspars, J. M. F., 1, *16*, 441, *469*
Jecker, J. D., 177, *208*
Jeffery, K. M., 250, *285*
Jellison, J. M., 262, *285*
Jemmott, J. B., 104, *124*, *125*
Jensen, M. C., 317, *323*
Jensen, M. R., 106, *124*
Jobe, L. D., 46, *81*
Johanson, G., 184, *208*
John, O. P., 11, *14*
Johnson, B. C., 260, *284*
Johnson, H. J., 188, *208*
Johnson, K., 234, 235, *239*
Johnson, N. S., 371, *408*
Johnson-Laird, P. N., 442, *469*
Jones, D. K., 443, *471*
Jones, E. E., 11, *14*, 131, 161, *163*, *164*, 230, *237*, 250, 251, 257, 258, 262, 263, 267, 271, 279, *282*, *284*, *285*, 440, *469*
Jones, J. G., 264, *283*
Jones, M. R., 1, *13*
Jones, S. C., 255, 256, 264, 268, *285*, *286*

K

Kagan, J., 11, *15*
Kahneman, D., 184, *209*, 229, *238*, 296, *323*, 449, *470*
Kakuyama, T., 58, *82*, 306, *324*

Kamarick, T., 133, 134, 135, *164*
Kanfer, F. H., 36, 59, *81*, 117, *124*, 309, 317, *322*, *323*
Kanfer, R., 59, *81*, 306, 307, 318, *322*
Kanouse, D. E., 265, *286*
Karren, R. J., 26, 43, 52, *83*, 300, 301, 302, 304, 305, 309, *324*
Kaufman, A., 297, *323*
Kavanagh, D. J., 63, 64, *81*
Kay, E., 308, *322*, *323*, *325*
Keefer, K. E., 264, *286*
Kehoe, K., 188, *208*
Kelley, C. L., 180, 186, 204, *210*
Kelley, H., 329, 330, 331, 336, 338, 340, 344, 347, 352–56, *360*, 425, 440, 451, 458, 465, *470*
Kelly, G. A., 7, *14*
Kelman, H. C., 67, 70, *81*
Kendall, L. M., 59, *82*, 313, *324*
Kennedy, C. W., 295, *323*
Kenny, D. A., 454, 455, *470*
Kenrick, D. T., 88, *124*
Kent, G., 32, *82*
Kiesler, C. A., 404, *408*
Kiesler, D. J., 329, 358, *359*, *360*
Kihlstrom, J. F., 9, *13*, 87, 90, 116, 120, *122*, 127, 130, 132, 149, 151, 153, 156, 157, 159, 161, 162, *163*, *164*, *165*, 216, 223, *237*, 388, 398, 399, *409*, 415, 419, 453, 462, *468*, 477, *479*
King, G. A., 8, *14*, 453
King, L. A., 10, *14*, 102, 104, 106–9, *123*
Kintsch, W., 367, *408*
Kirker, W. S., 256, *287*
Kirschenbaum, D. S., 48, *82*
Klatzky, R. L., 431, *467*
Kleck, R. E., 106, *124*
Klein, H. J., 307, 314, *322*
Klein, R., 10, *14*, 129, 134, 139, *164*
Klinger, E., 8, *15*, 89, 90, 98, 101, 102, 120, *124*, 130, 149, 160, *165*, 217, 228, *238*, *239*, 474, *479*
Kluwe, R. H., 433, 440–41, 456, *470*
Knerr, C. S., 45, *82*
Knudson, R. M., 347, *360*
Koeppel, J., 304, 319, *324*
Kohler, W., 5, 8, *15*
Komaki, J. L., 297, 304, *323*
Kopp, R., 297, *323*

Korn, E. R., 234, 235, *239*
Korn, H., 90, *122*
Kotter, J. P., 317, *323*
Kozlowski, L. T., 256, *283*
Krackhardt, D., 391, *408*
Krakoff, L. R., 188, *208*
Krantz, D. S., 188, *208*
Kratzer, P., 232, 233, *240*
Kressel, K., 355, *360*
Krohne, H. W., 222, *239*
Kuhl, J., 8, *15*, 127, 132, 139, 145, 161, *165*, 223, 228, 229, 234, *239*, 395, *408*, 441, 456, 457, *470*, 477, *479*
Kuhn, T. S., 298, *323*
Kuiper, N. A., 256, *287*
Kun, A., 21, *82*
Kunda, Z., 213, *239*
Kurtines, W. M., 65, *82*

L

Laird, J. D., 261, *286*
Lakatos, I., 261, *286*
Lakoff, G., 431, *470*
Lalljee, M., 447, 449, *467*, *470*
Lamiell, J. T., 112, *124*
Landers, D. M., 228, 234, 235, *238*
Landy, F. J., 292, *323*
Langer, A. W., 181, 194, *209*
Langer, E. J., 195, *209*, 247, 271, *286*, 373, 395, *408*
Langer, E. S., 215, *240*
Langston, C. A., 90, *122*, 129–33, 136, 140, 144, 147, 148, 152, 155, 157, 158, 161, *164*, *165*, 432, 451, *468*
Lanzetta, J. T., 106, *124*
LaPorte, R. E., 310, *323*
LaPrelle, J., 275, *287*
Larsen, R. J., 88, 102, 109, 110, 111, *122*, *123*, *124*, 161, *165*, 454, *469*
Larson, R., 102, *124*, 147, *164*
Lassiter, G. D., 263, *283*
Latham, G. P., 26, *39*, 43, 47, 52, 58, *81*, *82*, 85, 218, 228, 266, *286*, 297, 298, 300–315, 317, 318, *322*, *323*, *324*, *325*
Launier, R., 32, *81*
Laux, L., 222, *239*
Lawler, E. E., 295, 308, 320, *321*, *325*
Lawrence, E. C., 27, *84*

AUTHOR INDEX

Lazarus, R. S., 32, *81*
Leana, C. R., 309, *325*
Leary, M. R., 244, 252, 256, 263, 264, 265, 275, 277, 278, 279, *288*
Leary, T., 330, *360*
Lechleiter, S. L., 188, *209*
Lecky, P., 104, *124*
Leddo, J., 371, *408*
Lee, C., 25, 41, *81, 82*, 307, 313, *324, 326*
Lee, T. W., 26, *82*, 301, 302, 303, 308, 311, 312, *323*
Lefcourt, H. M., 215, *239*, 264, *286*
Lehnert, W. L., 372, *409*
Lepper, M. R., 229, *237*
Lerner, M. J., 75, *81*, 392, 393, *408*
Levi, A., 243, 268, 276, *289*
Levine, S., 102, 109, 110, *122*
Levinger, G., 329, 331, 336, 338, 344–45, 347, 352, 353, 355, 356, *359, 360*, 425, 451, 458, 465, *470*
Levinson, D. J., 130, 156, *165*
Levitt, K., 256, *287*
Levy, A., 256, 271, *283*
Lewin, K., 5, 8, *15*, 87, 215, *239*, 299, 307, 308, *324*
Lewinsohn, P. M., 41, *82*
Libet, B., 475, *479*
Lichtenstein, E. H., 264, *282*, 370, *408*
Light, K. C., 181, 194, *209*
Lind, E. A., 260, *284*
Linville, P. W., 109, 110, 111, *124*, 155, *165*
Little, B. R., 8, *15*, 87, 89, 90, 98, 120, *124, 125*, 129, 130, 134–37, 149, *165*, 214, 217, *239*
Locke, E. A., 26, *39*, 41, 43, 44, 45, 52, 59, *80, 82, 83, 85*, 218, 228, *239*, 266, *286*, 292, 293, 297–302, 304–10, 312–19, *321, 322, 323, 324, 326*
Loeb, A., 59, *82*
Loftus, E. F., 444, *468*
Lord, R. G., 33, *80*
Lorge, I., 264, *286*
Lowell, E. L., 216, *239*
Lund, A. K., 24, *79*
Lundberg, U., 184, *208*
Lundgren, D. C., 260, *286*
Lustgarten, N., 301, 318, *324*
Lyman, S. M., 259, *288*

M

McAdams, D. P., 87, 88, 89, 94, 95, 100, 198, 120, *125*
McArthur, L. Z., 11, *15*
McCall, G. J., 247, 255, *286*
McCann, C., 405, *408*
McCaul, K., 189, 190, *209*
McClelland, D. C., 6, 8, *15*, 87, 88, 95, 100, 104, 112, 113, 114, 120, *125*, 216, *239*, 474, *479*
McClintock, C. G., 259, *283*
McClintock, E., 329, 331, 336, 338, 347, 352, 353, 355, 356, *360*, 425, 451, 458, 465, *470*
McCloskey, B., 63, *80*
McCown, N. E., 256, *288*
McCrae, R. R., 103, *122*, 249, *286*
McCubbin, J. A., 181, 194, *209*
McDonald, D. G., 190, 191, *208*
McDougall, W., 3, 4, 5, 8, *15*, 215, *239*, 474, *479*
MacFarlane, S., 88, *124*
McFarlin, D. B., 217, *240*
McGinnies, E., 453, *471*
McGlynn, R. P., 250, *290*, 382, 383, *410*
McGovern, K., 264, *282*
Mackay, D. G., 234, 235, *239*
Mackie, D., 405, *407*
Mackie, J. L., 449, *470*
McKillop, K. J., Jr., 266, *286*
McKoon, R., 373, *410*
McLaughlin, M. L., 436, *470*
MacLeod, R. B., 211, *239*
McMullin, D. J., 47, *83*
Maddi, S. R., 118, *124*
Maddux, J. E., 63, *84*
Magnusson, D., 428, 460, 466, 467, *470*
Mahoney, M. J., 231, 234, *239*
Makus, H., *239*
Malett, S. D., 48, *82*
Mancuso, J. C., 120, *124*
Manderlink, G., 47, *82*
Mandler, G., 340, 341, *360*, 417, 458, *470*, 477, *479*
Mandler, J. M., 371, *408*
Mann, L., 341, *360*
Manstead, A. R. S., 11, *16*, 243, *289*
Mantell, D. M., 69, *82*
Manuck, S. B., 188, *209*
Maracek, J., 266, *286*

March, J. G., 296, *324*
Marcia, J. E., 147, *165*
Marcus, A., 445, *471*
Margolin, G., 356, *359*
Markman, H., 355, *360*
Markus, H., 4, 9, *15*, 94, 116, *124*, 127, 129, 131, 156, *164*, *165*, 212–13, 220, 223, 224, 225, 227, *239*, *240*, 244, 245, 246, 255, 256, *286*, 395, 402, 404, *407*, *408*, 431, 433, 440, 451, 465, *470*
Martin, C. L., 151, 153, 159, 161, *165*
Martindale, C., 94, 95, *125*
Mascolo, M. F., 120, *124*
Maslow, A. H., 118, *125*, 292, 298, *324*
Masters, J. C., 230, *237*, *239*
Matsui, T., 44, 58, *82*, *83*, 306, *324*
Matthews-Simonton, S., 233, *240*
Maxeiner, M. E., 89, 90, 98, 101, *124*, 228, *239*
Mazze, K., 11, *14*, 375, *408*, 478, *479*
Mead, G. H., 251, *286*, 365
Means, B., 230, *238*
Meckling, W. H., 317, *323*
Medin, D. L., 11, *15*, 440, *471*
Meichenbaum, D. H., 32, *83*
Meiselas, L., 155, *164*
Melburg, V., 256, *287*
Melchior, L. A., 162, *164*
Mento, A. J., 26, 43, 44, 52, *83*, *85*, 300, 301, 302, 304, 305, 307, 309, *324*, *326*
Mermelstein, R., 133, 134, 135, *164*
Mervis, C. B., 428, *471*
Messer, S. B., 338, *360*
Mettee, D. R., 256, 266, 268, *286*
Meyer, H. H., 308, *322*, *323*, *325*
Milgram, S., 68, 69, 71, 72, *83*
Miller, A. T., 21, *83*
Miller, D. T., 75, *81*, 266, *286*, 449, *470*
Miller, G. A., 6, *15*, 247, *287*, 330, *360*, 416, 435, *470*, 475, *479*
Miller, L. C., 330, 355, 356, *360*, 418, 427, 429, 433, 438, 440, 451, 452, 454, 455, 465, *470*, *471*
Miller, N. E., 202, *209*, 227, *239*
Miller, R. S., 256, 264, *287*, *288*
Mills, C. W., 259, *287*
Miner, J. B., 292, 298, *325*
Minsky, M., 367, *408*

Minuchin, S., 396, *408*
Mischel, W., 8, 9, 11, *14*, *15*, 41, *82*, 88, 114, *125*, 159, 161, *167*, 250, *283*, *285*, *287*, 354, 355–56, *359*, 374, 375, *407*, *408*, 415, 427, 428, 431, 438, 439, 462, 466, *468*, *469*, *471*, *472*, 474, 478, *479*
Mitchell, T. R., 23, 47, *83*, *84*, 292, 295, 297, 304, *323*, *325*
Mizuguchi, R., 44, *83*
Mobley, W. H., 299, *325*
Monson, T., 244, 274, *283*
Montello, D. R., 88, *124*
Mook, D. G., 8, *15*, 216, *239*
Moore, D., 345, *360*
Moore, E., 147, 160, *165*
Moore, M. J., 11, *15*
Moos, R. H., 135, 140, 141, 152, *165*
Morgan, M., 46, *83*
Morse, N. C., 91, *125*
Morse, S., 248, 252, *287*
Mossholder, K. W., 46, *83*
Mowday, R. T., 294, *325*
Mowrer, O. H., 474, *479*
Mulhall, D., 390, *410*
Muller, E. N., 41, *83*
Munson, P. A., 404, *408*
Murphy, G. L., 11, *15*, 440, *471*
Murray, D. M., 260, *290*
Murray, H. A., 8, *15*, 87, 89, 95, *125*, 327, 328, 331, *360*, *361*, 415, 420, 430, 434, 435, 461, 462, 464, *471*
Musgrave, R. S., 91, *125*
Mynatt, C., 71, *83*

N

Najda, M., 390, 391, *410*
Nakamura, G., 363, *407*
Nanus, B., 317, *321*
Nasby, W., 162, *165*
Nath, R., 310, *323*
Neal, K. S., 188, *209*
Neale, M. A., 316, *322*
Neisser, U., 213, *239*
Nelson, K., 373, 389, 395, *409*
Nemeth, C. J., 260, *287*
Neufeld, R. W. J., 10, *15*, 477, *479*
Newell, A., 6, *15*
Newtson, D. A., 370, 372, *409*
Nezlek, 134
Nicholls, J. G., 21, 49, *83*, 217, *239*

AUTHOR INDEX

Nichols, R. C., 264, *285*
Niedenthal, P., 90, *122*, 129–33, 136, 140, 147, 148, 152, 157, 161, *164*, 395, 398, 399, *407*, *409*, 432, 451, *468*
Nigro, G. N., 234, *239*
Nisbett, R. E., 97, *125*
Norem, J. K., 90, *122*, 129–34, 136, 138–41, 147, 148, 151, 152, 155, 157, 158, 161, *164*, *165*, 231, *239*, 432, 451, *468*
Norman, N., 245, 250, 262, *289*
Notarius, C., 355, *360*
Nottenberg, G., 371, *409*
Nurius, P., 4, 9, *15*, 94, *124*, 129, *164*, 212, 213, *239*, 244, 246, 255, *286*, 395, 402, *407*, *408*, 431, 433, 451, 465, *470*
Nuttin, J., 8, *15*, 216, *240*, 456, *471*

O

Oatley, K., 10, *15*
O'Barr, W. M., 260, *284*
O'Brien, E. J., 466, *469*
Obrist, P. A., 181, 194, *209*
O'Connor, E. J., 314, 320, *325*
Offerman, G., 232, 233, *240*
Okada, A., 44, 58, *82*, *83*
Olian-Gottlieb, J. D., 23, *84*
Omanson, R., 371, *409*
Omelich, C. L., 20, 21, *80*
Onglatco, M. L. U., 306, *324*
Ordiorne, G. S., 299, *325*
Ordman, A. M., 48, *82*
Orlick, T., 234, *240*
Ortony, A., 367, 397, *409*
Oscar, G., 63, *80*
Ostrom, T., 365, 374, *409*
Ostrow, A. C., 58, *83*
Owens, J., 370, *409*
Oyserman, D., 223, 224, 225, 227, *240*

P

Pack, S. J., 262, *290*
Padawer, W., 131, *164*
Palys, T. S., 89, *125*
Panzarella, R., 69, *82*
Park, B., 374, *408*, 442, *471*
Parsons, J., 146, 147, *164*
Pascale, L., 233, *241*

Patane, M. J., 183, 184, *210*, 231, *241*
Paterson, R. J., 10, *15*, 477, *479*
Patterson, G. R., 356, *361*
Paulhus, D. L., 151, 153, 159, 161, *165*, 256, *287*
Payne, J. W., 11, *13*
Peake, P. K., 29, 30, *80*, *83*, 466, *471*
Pennebaker, J. W., 105–8, *125*
Pennington, N., 442, *471*
Peplau, L. A., 329, 331, 336, 338, 347, 352, 353, 355, 356, *360*, 425, 451, 458, 465, *470*
Perlman, D., 329, *360*, *361*
Perret-Clermont, A. N., 365, 405, *408*, *409*
Perry, B. C., 322
Pervin, L. A., 1, 7, 8, 10, *15*, 88, 91, 101, 104, 113, 119, 120, *125*, 127, 131, 132, *165*, *166*, 216, *240*, 354, *361*, 415, 427, 462, 466, *471*, 474, *479*
Peters, L. H., 314, 320, *325*
Peterson, C., 161, *166*
Peterson, D., 11, *15*
Peterson, D. R., 329–32, 336, 337, 338, 347, 349, 350, 352, 353, 355, 356, 358, *360*, *361*, 425, 451, 458, 465, *470*
Peterson, M., 432, *472*
Petty, R. E., 180–81, *208*, 256, 273, *283*, *287*, 404, *407*
Pfeffer, J., 292, 293, *325*
Phares, E. J., 215, *240*
Piaget, J., 476, *479*
Pierce, C. S., 253, *287*
Pinder, C. C., 292, 294, 296, 298, 312, *325*
Pine, H. A., 264, *286*
Pittman, T. S., 11, *14*, 250, 251, 257, 279, *285*
Platt, J. R., 309, *325*
Plutchik, R., 130, *166*
Pommer, W., 232, 233, *240*
Porkert, M., 232, *240*
Porter, L. W., 292, 295, 314, *325*, *326*
Postman, L., 453, *471*
Powers, W. T., 7, 9, *15*, 94, 95, *125*
Pratkanis, A. R., 245, 256, *284*, 394, 404, *407*
Pratto, F., 453, *467*
Predmore, S. C., 260, 270, 271, *289*

Premack, D., 476, *479*
Prentice-Dunn, S., 29, 31, 32, *81*
Pribram, K. H., 6, *15*, 247, *287*, 330, *360*, 416, 435, *470*, 475, *479*
Prince, L., 107, *123*
Pritchard, R. D., 59, *83*, 292, 293, 295, 313, *321*, *325*
Proshansky, H., 354, *361*
Pruitt, D. G., 341, 346–51, 354, *361*
Pryor, J. P., 374, *409*
Pyszczynski, T. A., 181, *207*, 255, 256, 268, 275, 279, *284*, *287*

R

Rabink, A. I., 97, *125*
Rakestaw, T. L., 314, *325*
Rank, O., 215, *240*
Rapinchuk, J. G., 330, 349, 358, *361*
Rapoport, D. C., 67, *83*
Raulin, M. L., 107, *125*
Raush, H. L., 331, 347, 355, *361*
Rawana, E., 233, *241*
Raynor, J. O., 8, *13*, 217, *240*
Read, S. J., 11, *15*, 275, *289*, 330, 355, 356, *360*, *361*, 427, 429, 433, 435, 437, 438, 440, 443, 444, 445, 448, 452, 453, 462, 465, *468*, *470*, *471*, *472*
Reeder, G. D., 439, *471*
Rees, E., 453, *468*
Rehm, L. P., 59, *83*
Reich, J. W., 146, *166*
Reid, J. B., 356, *361*
Reis, 134
Reiser, B. J., 372, *409*
Relich, J. D., 21, *82*
Rempel, J. K., 11, *16*
Reykowski, J., 401, *409*
Rhodes, S. R., 299, *326*
Rhodewalt, F., 267, *285*, *287*
Rice, J. M., 21, 22, *84*
Richards, K., 379, 381, 382, *410*
Richardson, A., 234, *240*
Richardson, K. D., 256, *287*
Riecken, H. W., 11, *16*
Riess, M., 256, *287*
Riggio, R., 107, *123*
Rips, L. J., 370, 371, *407*
Roberson, B. F., 191, 192, *209*
Robertson, S., 371, *410*
Robins, C., 131, *164*

Rodgers, W. L., 102, *122*
Rodin, J., 160, *166*, 215, *240*
Rogers, C. R., 255, *287*, 404, *409*
Rogers, R. W., 29, 31, 32, *81*
Rogers, S. L., 267, 276, *289*
Rogers, T. B., 256, *287*
Rokeach, M., 95, 96, *125*
Rosch, E., 355, *361*, 365, 381, *409*, 428, *471*
Roseman, I. J., 459, *471*
Rosenbaum, M., 63, *83*
Rosenberg, M., 244, 255, 260, *287*
Rosenberg, S., 375, 388, *409*
Rosenblatt, A. D., 8, *16*
Rosenfeld, P., 256, *287*
Rosenfield, D., 256, 276, *289*
Ross, L., 229, *237*
Rotter, J. B., 6, *16*, 22, *83*, 215, *240*
Rubin, J. Z., 346–51, *361*
Rudd, J., 251, *282*
Rumelhart, D., 365, 367, 368, 384, 397, *409*
Rusbult, C. E., 433, *471*
Ruvolo, A., 220, *240*
Ryan, E. D., *40*, 234
Ryan, R. M., 215, 228, 234, *238*
Ryan, T. A., 2, *16*, 42, *83*, 299, 312, *325*
Ryff, C. D., 147, 162, *166*

S

Saari, L. M., 26, *39*, 43, 52, *82*, 218, 228, 266, *286*, 297, 300, 302, 305, 306, 307, 313, 314, 318, *323*, *324*, *325*
Sabini, J., 2, 3, 8, *14*, 87, 88, 91, *123*, 477, *479*
Salancik, G. R., 292, 314, *325*
Sales, S. M., 310, *325*
Salovey, P., 160, *166*
Sandner, D. F., 232, *240*
Sanford, N., 67, *84*, 113, *125*
Sarason, I. G., 32, *84*, 222, 231, *240*
Sarbin, T. R., 259, *287*
Saron, C., 104, *125*
Sass, L. A., 338, *360*
Schachter, S., 203, *209*
Schafer, R., 8, *16*
Schank, R. C., 12, *16*, 94, *125*, 217, *240*, 247, *287*, 330, 342, 355, *361*, 364, 367, 368, 369, 372, 378, 393,

AUTHOR INDEX

409, 416, 424, 432, 435–38, 447, 448, 455, 456, *472*
Scheier, M. F., 8, *13*, 36, *37*, *80*, *83*, 94, 95, 117, *122*, 160, 161, *164*, *166*, 223, 228, 230, *237*, 249, 251, 252, *283*, 416, 432, 456, 465, *468*, *469*
Scher, S., 152, 155, 160, *163*
Schlenker, B. R., 11, *16*, 216, 219, *240*, 244, 245, 246, 248–67, 269, 271–79, *283*, *286*, *287*, *288*, *289*, *290*, 400, *409*
Schlenker, P. A., 256, *288*
Schmidt, C. F., 11, *16*, 97, *125*
Schneider, D., 374, *409*
Schoeneman, T. J., 260, *289*
Schunk, D. H., 21, 22, 29, 44–49, *79*, *84*
Schwab, D. P., 23, *84*
Schwartz, J., 374, 375, *407*
Schwartz, J. L., 59, *84*
Schwartz, R. C., 339, *359*
Schweiger, D. M., 308, 309, *324*, *325*
Scott, L. R., 297, 304, *323*
Scott, M. B., 259, *288*
Secco, T., 371, *410*
Sedlak, A., 11, 375, 388, *409*
Seifert, C., 371, 372, 373, *410*
Seligman, M., 161, *166*
Sentis, K., 212–13, *239*, 245, *286*
Sewell, R., 370, 371, *406*
Shantz, C. U., 11, *16*
Shapiro, D., 181, *209*, 477, *479*
Shaver, P., 440, *469*
Shaw, J. C., 6, *15*
Shaw, K. N., 26, *39*, 43, 52, *82*, 218, 228, 266, *286*, 300, 302, 305, 306, 307, 313, 318, *324*
Sherman, R. T., 229, *240*
Sherwood, V., 365, *407*
Shoben, E. J., 371, *409*
Showers, C., 11, *16*
Shrauger, J. S., 260, 264, 268, 270, 271, *288*, *289*
Silka, L., 169, 175, 177–80, *207*, *210*
Sillars, A. L., 448, 451, *472*
Silver, M., 2, 3, 7, *16*
Silverman, V., 60, *81*
Simmons, J. F., 247, 255, *286*
Simon, H. A., 2, 6, *15*, *16*, 23, *84*, 296, *324*, *326*, 453, *468*
Simon, K. M., 48, 59, 60, *79*, *84*

Simons, J., *40*, 228, 234
Simonton, O. C., 233, *240*
Singer, J. L., 88, 101, *125*, 203, *209*
Skelton, J. A., 267, *285*
Skinner, B. F., 5, 7, *16*, 297, *326*
Skokan, L. A., 161, *166*
Sloan, T., 280, *285*
Smith, E. E., 371, 388, *410*
Smith, J., 433, 440, *470*
Smith, T. W., 230, *240*
Snyder, C. R., 131, *166*, 230, *240*, 251, 276, *289*
Snyder, M. L., 90, *125*, 162, *166*, 250, 253, 256, 260, 276, *289*, 454, *472*
Solomon, H., 264, *286*
Solomon, R. S., 91, *125*
Solomon, S., 169, 175, 177–80, 189, 190, *207*, *209*, *210*, 255, 256, 268, *284*
Somers, R. L., 316, *324*
Sommers, A. A., 347, *360*
Sorrentino, R. M., 8, *14*, 87, 120, *125*, 127, *166*, 216, *240*
Spence, K. W., 232, *240*
Spivak, K. R., 134, 135, 267, 276, *289*
Srull, T. K., 10, 11, *16*, *17*, 120, *125*, 374, *410*
Staats, A. W., 8, *16*
Stanley, M. A., 63, *84*
Starke, F. A., 23, *79*
Staub, E., 217, *241*
Steel, R. P., 26, 43, 52, *83*, 300, 301, 302, 304, 305, 309, *324*
Steers, R. M., 292, 299, 314, *326*
Steffen, J. J., 47, *83*
Steingarten, K. A., 60, *80*
Steinhilder, 266, *282*
Stephan, W. G., 256, 276, *289*
Stern, J. A., 190, 191, *208*
Stern, M. J., 233, *241*
Stern, W., 4
Sternberg, R. J., 127, 128, 131, *166*
Stevens, A., 442, *469*
Stevenson-Hinde, J., 405, *408*
Stewart, A., 130, *166*
Stewart, A. J., 89, 95, 100, *125*
Stewart, J., 4, *14*, 455, *469*
Stokols, D., 11, *16*, 354, *361*
Stoll, B. A., 233, *241*
Stone, J. I., 263, *283*
Strang, H. R., 27, *84*

Strauman, T. J., 10, *14*, 129, 134, 139, 160, *164*, *166*
Strowig, R. W., 264, *283*
Struther, S., 264, *286*
Stryker, S., 400, *410*
Stucky, R. J., 251, *289*
Sullivan, H. S., 328, 329, 340
Surwit, R. S., 181, *209*
Swann, W. B., Jr., 156, 162, *166*, 249, 260, 268, 270, 271, 274, 275, *289*, 347, 355, *361*, 421, 440, 453, 454, 457, *472*

T

Tannenbaum, A. S., 91, *125*
Tavris, C., 108, *125*
Taylor, D. A., 343, *359*
Taylor, F. W., 299, 306, *326*
Taylor, M. S., 313, 314, *322*, *326*
Taylor, S. E., 160, 161, *166*, 255, *289*, 381, *410*
Tedeschi, J. T., 244, 245, 250, 251, 256, 258, 262, *287*, *289*
Tellegen, A., 103, *125*
Teller, E. S., 181, 194, *209*
Teraspulsky, L., 466, *469*
Terborg, J. R., 310, 311, *326*
Terrill, F., 59, *81*
Tesser, A., 156, *166*
Tetlock, P. E., 11, *16*, 243, 262, 268, 274, 275, 276, *289*
Thibaut, J. W., 11, *14*, *16*, 329, 330, 344, 354, *360*
Thickstun, J. T., 8, *16*
Thomas, 365
Thorndyke, P., 371, *410*
Thorne, A., 328, *361*, 454, 455, *472*
Tice, D. M., 107, *122*, 266, *282*
Tilker, H. A., 68, 69, *84*
Tinsley, K. J., 264, *283*
Toi, M., 176, *209*, *210*
Tolman, E. C., 3, 5, 8, *16*, 328, 474
Tomarken, A. J., 48, *82*
Tomkins, S. S., 111, 118, 120, *125*, 261, *289*, 474, *479*
Tompkins, S. S.,
Trabasso, T., 371, *410*
Tranel, D. T., 190, *208*, *209*
Trope, Y., 268, *290*
Troutman, B. R., 63, *80*
Trudeau, J. V., 249, *290*

Trzebinski, J., 11, *16*, 127, 236, 250, *290*, 379, 381, 382, 383, 385, 387, 390, 391, *410*, 414, 435
Tubbs, D., 250, *290*, 382, 383, *410*
Tubbs, M. E., 300, 301, 302, 304, 305, 309, *326*
Turner, R. G., 432, *472*
Turner, R. H., 255, *290*
Turner, T., 369, 370–71, *407*
Tuthill, R., 59, *82*
Tversky, A., 229, *238*, 296, *323*, *326*

U

Umstot, D. D., 47, *84*
Underwood, B., 70, 71, 73, 75, *79*
Ungar, S., 258, 264, *290*
Uykl, G. A., *81*

V

Vallacher, R. R., 94, 111, 114, 115, 117, *121*, *125*, 372, *410*
Van de Geer, J. P., 1, *16*
van der Broek, P., 371, *410*
van Dijk, T., 367, *408*
Verbugge, 135
Veroff, J., 128, 129, 146, 147, 162, *166*
Vinsel, A., 343, 351, *359*
Viscusi, D., 41, *78*
Vogel-Sprott, M., 233, *237*, *241*
Volpert, W., 234, *241*
Vought, C., 173, 174, 175, 181, *207*, *209*
Vroom, V. H., 22, 24, *84*, 170, *209*, 217, *241*, 295, 307, *326*
Vygotsky, L. S., 365, 405, *411*

W

Wachtel, P. L., 358, *361*, 454, *472*
Wadsworth, M. W., 98, 101, *125*
Wagner, J. A., 309, *326*
Wahba, M. A., 292, *326*
Waldron, H., 345, *360*
Walker, C. H., 372, *410*
Walker, R., 21, *82*
Waring, E. M., 440, 443, *472*
Watson, D., 103, *125*
Watson, J. B., 3, *16*
Watson, N., 25, *84*
Watzlawick, P., 356, *361*
Weary, G., 256, 262, 276, 279, 285, *290*

AUTHOR INDEX

Weary-Bradley, G., 256, 262, 276, *290*
Weber, R., 365, 374, *408*
Webster, R., 233, *241*
Weeks, J. L., 197, 202, *209*
Wegner, D. M., 11, *16,* 94, 111, 114, 115, 117, *125,* 372, 394, 395, *410,* 421, *472*
Weick, K. E., 295, 308, 320, *321*
Weigold, M. F., 274, *288*
Weinberg, R. S., 29, 30, 31, *84,* 235, *241*
Weiner, B., 20, *84,* 101, *125,* 189, *209*
Weiss, H. A., 313, *326*
Weiss, H. M., 314, *325*
Wells, G. L., 260, *290*
Wheeler, K. G., 24, *84,* 134
White, B. J., 295, *323*
White, J., 40, *84*
White, P., 250, *289*
White, R. W., 6, *16,* 215, 219, *241*
Wicklund, R. A., 177, *209,* 216, *238,* 260, *290,* 399, 401, *410,* 416, 453, 456, *469*
Wiener, N., 7, *17*
Wilensky, R., 416, 418, 422, 423, 424, 436, 444, 446, 456, 459, 462, 464, *472*
Wiley, M. G., 245, 246, 251, *282*
Williams, C. R., 219, *238,* 307, *322*
Williams, J., 279, *285*
Williams, R. B., 181, *209*
Williams, S. L., 25, 33, *84*
Wilson, C., 390, *410*
Wilson, G. T., 48, *80*
Wilson, J. P., 118, 119, 120, *122*
Wilson, T. D., 97, *125*
Winch, R. F., 343, *361*
Wine, J., 231, *241*
Winer, B. J., 195, *209*
Winfrey, L. L., *166*
Winter, D., 89, 95, 100, *125*
Witt, T. R., 265, *290*
Wittgenstein, ., 365
Wood, R. E., 31, 44, 51–57, *79, 84, 85,* 307, 320, *326*

Woodfield, A., *17,* 475, *479*
Woodruff, G., 476, *479*
Woolfolk, R. L., 338, *360*
Wortman, C. B., 250, 251, 262, 265, 271, *285, 290*
Wright, J. C., 159, 161, *167,* 466, *472*
Wright, R. A., 169, 175–88, 193, 195, 196, 197, 202, 204, 205, *207, 208, 209, 210,* 231, *241*
Wundt, W. M., 214, *241*
Wurf, E., 116, *124,* 157, *167*
Wyer, R. S., Jr., 10, 11, *16, 17,* 120, *125,* 274, *290,* 374, 388, 389, 390, *411*
Wylie, R., 404, *411*

Y

Yates, B. T., 59, *80*
Yekovich, F., 372, *410*
Yerkes, R. M., 184, *210*
Young, P. T., 8, *17,* 474, *479*
Yukl, G. A., 47, 58, *85*

Z

Zadny, J., 372, *411*
Zajonc, R. B., 213, 230, *239, 241,* 270, *290,* 364, 405, *411*
Zander, A., 314, *322*
Zanna, M. P., 11, *16,* 262, 273, *284, 290*
Zautra, A. J., 146, *166*
Zecker, S. G., 234, *241*
Zeiss, A. M., 59, *81*
Zeiss, A. R., 250, *287*
Zidon, I., 43, *80,* 306, *322*
Zillmann, D., 196, 197, 203, *208, 210*
Zimbardo, P. G., 70, *85,* 158, *167*
Zirkel, S., 146, 150, 160, 169
Zlotogorski, Z., 97, *125*
Znaniecki, 365
Zubritzky, E., 43, *82*

Subject Index

A

Ability(ies)
  attributions, 21, 22
  performance and, 308
  specialized, 419
Accomplishments, organizational, 50–57
Accounting in self-identification, 276–77
Achievement motivation, 20–22, 58–59
Acquaintance stage of relationship, 342
ACT, 107–8
Act frequency approach, 112, 113, 120
Action identification theory, 111, 117
  personal striving and, 114–16
Action-oriented schemata, 364–68
  self-knowledge in, 395–98
Actions, understanding meaning of, 435–36
"Active" self-identification, 271–81
Actor schemata, 388, 393, 396, 397, 399
  person knowledge within, 376–77
Actual motivation. *See* Energization model
AEQ, 107–8
Affect
  desired self-identification and, 270–71
  goal discrepancies and, 59–64
  possible selves and, 230–31
Affect Intensity Measure (AIM), 110

Affective Communication Test (ACT), 107–8
Affective priming theory, 63
Affective reactivity, 109–11
Affective resources, 421
Aggressor-defender model, 348
Agreements, integrative, to settle conflicts, 350–51
AIM, 110
Alienation, relational, 352
Ambivalence, 103–8
Ambivalence Over Expressing Emotion Questionnaire (AEQ), 107–8
Anticipation, 180–85, 213
Anxiety, 231
Arousal, anticipatory, 180–85
Arousal-regulation theory, 109–10, 111
Arousal transfer model, 203
Artificial intelligence, 366, 373, 456
Ascriptive components of act identities, 115
Aspirational standards, 42, 58–59
Attitudes, 404, 415, 417–18
Attraction, energization and, 176–77
Attractiveness, goal, 169–210
  perceptions of, 173–80
Attributes, physical, 419
Attribution(s)
  ability, 21, 22
  of blame, 75–76

Attribution(s) "cont."
  causal, 19, 20–22
  effort, 21–22
  performance and, 267
Attribution theory, 10, 20–22
Audiences, self-identifications and, 250–52
Authority, legitimate, 68–69, 306, 318
Autobiographical frameworks of life tasks, 151, 153, 158
Avoidance, 177–80, 182, 186–87, 192, 202, 347–48

B

Bargaining, goal setting and, 316
Behavior
  change in, 458
  goal-based configurations and, 422–27
  planning and coordination of, 451–60
  possible selves and control of, 223–24
  purposive, 3–4, 5, 7
Behavioral consistency, 113–14
Behavioral sequences, 435–36
Behaviorism, 3
Behavior modification, organizational, 297
"Belief in a just world" hypothesis, 392–93
Beliefs, 417–18
Blame
  attribution of, 75–76
  self-censure and, 77
Build-up stage of relationship, 342–43

C

Case grammar theory, 366–67
Causal attributions, 19, 20–22
Causation, personal, 215
Challenge, goal, 60
Character and Personality (Allport), 91
Cognition
  self-identification and, 270–75
  social, 381
  goals and, 10–12
Cognitive consequences of possible selves, 228–30
Cognitive-interpretive structures, 340, 341
Cognitive motivators, 217
  forms of, 19–20

Cognitive priming theory, 63
Cognitive processes, 365, 366. *See also* Goal categories; Knowledge
Cognitive psychology, 363, 364
Cognitive resources, 419, 421
Cognitive structures, 365. *See also* Schemata
Cognitive theories, 330, 367
  history of, 1–12
Cognized goals, 19
Coherence of persons, 432–33
Commitment, goal, 305–7, 311, 314, 318
Communicative skills, 419–20
Compatibility, build-up stage of relationship and, 342–43
"Complementarity" hypothesis of mate selection, 343–44
Complexity
  goal, 299, 318
  task, 314
Compromise, conflict settlement by, 350
Conflict
  goal, 299–300, 318. *See also* Interpersonal goal conflict
  of interest, 346, 351
  management of, 351–52
  marital, 330, 331–36, 345–50, 356–58
  resolution of, 339, 349–52, 358
  spiral model of, 348
  among strivings and well-being, 103–8
Congeniality, relational, 352
Consistency
  behavioral, 113–14
  in inter-personalism, 463–64
Conspiracy theories, 341
Constraints, social, 132, 139, 141–45, 158, 162
Contentious relationships, 352
Context, social intelligence framework and, 153–57
Continuation stage of relationship, 342, 344–45
Control of environment, 215
  self-identification and, 244
Coordination of behavior, 451–60
Coping skills, 420
Creative self, 399
Cultural values, goal setting and, 315

SUBJECT INDEX   **499**

Current concern concept, 88, 89, 90, 120–21, 217

D

Decentration, interpersonal, 391
Decision making, 50–57
  group, 70
  participative (PDM), 308–10, 315
Defensive pessimism, 132, 139, 140–41, 145, 152, 153–54, 157–58, 161, 231
Dehumanization, 72–75
Delinquency, possible selves and, 224–27
Depression, self-efficacy beliefs and, 59–64
Desired identity images, 253–71
  believability of, 257–61
  beneficiality of, 255–57
  cognition and affect in, 270–71
  in context, 261–65
  motive for, 268–70
  positivity vs., 265–66
  response bias vs. private belief in, 266–68
Deterioration stage of relationship, 342, 345
Difficulty, goal, 299–304, 318
Diffusion of responsibility, 70, 71
Dimensions of goals, 98–99
Direction of activities, 310
Disengagement
  of internal standards, 66–67
  in life tasks, 161
  of self-sanctions and self-deception, 76–78
Displacement of responsibility, 68–70
Dispositional transformations, 345, 351
Dispositions, personal, 95. *See also* Personal strivings
Disregard of consequences, 70–72
Dissonance, 177
Distal goals, 44, 45–48
Distortion of consequences, 70–72
Doer's self, 399
Domination, conflict settlement by, 350
Drive, 4, 6

E

Effectance motivation, 215

Effectiveness, goal, 236
  possible selves and, 218–19
Effort
  attributions, 21–22
  performance and, 24–25
Egocentrism, 275
Ego tasks, 116
Emotional expression, conflict over well-being and, 106–8
Ending stage of relationship, 342
Energization model, 169–210, 310
  functional significance, 203–4
  goal valence and, 173–80, 196–98
  interpersonal attraction and, 176–77
  potential motivation and, 170–73, 185–96, 199–203
    motivation vs., 200–203
    subjective effects and, 203–6
  relationships in, 189–98, 204–6
  task difficulty and, 173–85, 207
Engagement in life tasks, 161
Environmental change, 53–57
  self-efficacy beliefs and, 55–57
Environmental factors in interpersonal relationships, 354, 356
Equity theory, 294–95
ERG theory, 293
Euphemistic labeling, 67–68
Evaluation of conduct, 253
Event knowledge, 368–73, 389, 405
Event schemata, 370, 371–73, 377
Exhaustion principle, 445
Expectancy-value theory, 22–26, 43–44, 102–3, 217–18, 295–97, 307, 318, 455
Expectations, outcome
  performance separated from, 218
  self-identification and, 245, 277–79
  violation of, 446–50, 458
Experience, life task, 138–39
Experience sampling method, 102
Explanations
  identity-relevant, 276–77
  patterns of, 446–50
Explorations in Personality (Murray), 327
Expressiveness, self-presentation vs., 279–81
Expressive skills, 419–20
External incentives, 58–59

F

Factor analytic techniques, 136–37
Family Environment Scale, 140, 152
Family Process (journal), 330
Feedback, 155, 156, 275
  job performance and, 304–5, 319
  negative, 36–39
  performance, 27–28
  in relationships, 352
Feedforward control, 38
Financial tasks, goal setting and, 317
Functioning, physical, 419

G

General person knowledge, 377–84
Generic goal orientations, 49–50
Gestalt psychology, 5, 299
Goal attractiveness, 169–210
  perceptions of, 173–80
Goal categories
  in event knowledge, 368–73
  in person knowledge, 373–89
    within actor schemata, 376–77
    general knowledge, 377–84
    individualized, 384–89
  role of, 367–68, 371–72
  in self-knowledge, 394–403
  in social organizational knowledge, 389–94
Goal challenge, 43–44, 60
Goal commitment, 305–7, 311, 314, 318
Goal compatibility, build-up stage of relationship and, 342–43
Goal complexity, 299, 318
Goal conflicts, 299–300, 318, 418, 423, 424–26. *See also* Interpersonal goal conflict
Goal difficulty, 299–304, 318
Goal-directed behavior, 2, 8, 91, 96, 213, 214–17. *See also* Self-identification
  cognitive science on, 330
  interpersonal character of, 328–29
  possible selves and, 219
Goal discrepancy(ies), 33–36, 451
  affective consequences of, 59–64
  performance and, 33
  self-efficacy and, 40–42
  students and, 61–62
Goal effectiveness, 236
  possible selves and, 218–19

Goal orientation, generic, 49–50
Goal proximity, 44–48
  performance and, 48
  planning vs., 47
Goal relations, 430, 454
  interpersonal, 424–26
  intrapersonal, 423–24, 441
Goals, 1–12
  hierarchical structure of, 7–8, 44, 48–49
  historical overview, 2–7
  motivation and, 7–10
  social cognition and, 10–12
Goal setting, 297–321. *See also* Job performance
  bargaining research and, 316
  complex financial tasks and, 317
  critique of, 311–12
  cultural values and, 315
  leadership and, 316–17
  origins and concepts of theory of, 299
  participation in, 308–10
  process of, 318–20
  self-efficacy beliefs and, 307
  self-management and, 317–18
Goal Setting: A Motivational Technique That Works (Locke & Latham), 298
Goal specificity, 42–43, 299–304, 318
Goal valence, energization and, 173–80, 196–98
"Grammar of Motives" (Burke), 367
Group(s)
  performance in, 52–53
  pressure, 306–7, 318
Groupthink, 341
Growth, interpersonal, 352

H

Handbook of Interpersonal Psychotherapy (Anchin & Kiesler), 329
Health, global measures of, 158–60
Hierarchical structure of goal systems, 7–8, 44, 48–49
Honors Project study, 132–45
Hormic psychology, 3

I

Ideal self, 255
Identity(ies), 244–46. *See also* Self-concept(s); Self-identification

SUBJECT INDEX   **501**

lost, grappling with, 150–51
Identity images, 246, 253. *See also* Desired identity images
   functions of, 253
Idiographic configurations of person structures, 427
Idiographic knowledge, 441–44
Idiographic-nomothetic properties, 88–91, 95, 98, 100, 460, 463
Idiographic properties of inter-personalism, 463
Idiomotives, 95. *See also* Personal strivings
Image-outcome relationship, 253
Imagery, mental, 220, 228, 233–35, 375
Imagination, 433
Imago, 88, 89, 95
Implicit personality theory, 374, 377
Impression formation, 379–84
Incentives, 307
   external, 58–59
   monetary, job performance and, 312–13
Independence, grappling with, 150–51
Individualized person knowledge, 377, 384–89
Inferences, trait, 438–40
Information, organizational structure of, 253
Information processing. *See also* Goal categories; Knowledge
   active self-identification and, 272–73
   intensified, 274–75
Inner resources, 420
Instability, relational, 352
Integration of persons, 432–33
Integrative agreements to settle conflicts, 350–51
Intelligence
   artificial, 366, 373, 456
   as incremental skill, 49
   social, 419–20, 453
   as stable entity, 49–50
Interaction, social, 328, 338–42, 365, 426, 434–35, 458, 465. *See also* Interpersonal goal conflict; Interpersonalism
Interaction Concepts of Personality, 329
Interaction models, 444–45
   developing, 444–45
Interdependence theory, 330, 340, 344, 354

Interest, conflict of, 346, 351
Interpersonal decentration, 391
Interpersonal goal conflict, 327–62. *See also* Inter-personalism
   action and interaction in, 338–39
   conciliation of, 349–50
   data of, 331–38
   engagement of, 347–48
   escalation of, 348–50
   initiation of, 346–47
   interaction episode in, 338–42
   management of, 351–52
   overt, 346–47
   relationship and, 339, 340–446
   research review, 352–58
   settlement of, 350–51
Interpersonal goal relations, 424–26
Interpersonal growth, 352
Inter-personalism, 413–79
   consistency in, 463–64
   critique of, 460–67
   goal-based structures, 415–27
      behavior and, 422–27
      beliefs, 417–18
      goals, 415, 416
      plans and strategies, 415, 416–17
      resources, 415, 418–22
   nomothetic and idiographic properties of, 427, 441–44, 463
   perceiving and understanding others, 435–50
      culturally shared knowledge and, 436–41
      explaining the unexpected and, 446–50
      idiographic knowledge and, 441–44
      interaction models and, 444–45
      meaning of actions and, 435–36
   personality and, 465–66
   person structures, 427–33
      idiographic configurations, 427
      integration and coherence of persons and, 432–33
      interpersonal themes, 432
      life tasks, 432
      life themes, 432
      personal strivings, 432
      possible selves, 431
      radical structures, 431
      relational structures, 433
      roles themes, 432
      traits, 428–30

planning and coordination of behavior, 451–60
self and, 465
situational structures, 434–35
stability in, 463–64
theoretical connections in, 460–63
Interpersonal relationships, 269, 339
environmental factors in, 354, 356
methodology for study of, 336–37
stages of, 342–46
Interpretational filter, identity images as, 253
Interpretive-cognitive structures, 340, 341
Intrapersonal goal relations, 423–24, 441
Intrinsic motivation, 215

J

Job performance, 291–326. *See also* Goal setting
ability and, 308
feedback and, 304–5, 319
goal commitment and, 305–7, 314
goals and, 300–301
individual differences in, 313–14
monetary incentives and, 312–13
self-efficacy beliefs and, 307
task complexity and, 307, 320
task strategies and, 314–15
Journal of Personality and Social Psychology, 337–38
Journal of Social and Personal Relationships, 329
Justification, moral, 67

K

Knowledge, 419
culturally shared, 436–41
event, 368–73, 389, 405
idiographic, 441–44
moral, 390–93
organization of, 364–68
person, 392, 396, 447
  leit-motives of, 378
  polymorphic structure of, 385
situational, 447, 454
social, 436–41, 451
social organization, 389–94
tacit, 402–3

L

Labeling, euphemistic, 67–68
Leadership, goal setting and, 316–17
Legitimate authority, 68–69, 306, 318
Leit-motives of person knowledge, 378
Life goals, 397, 399
Life style, 399
Life tasks, 88, 90, 120–21, 127–68, 216–17, 398, 432, 451
appraisals of, 148–49
definition of, 130–31
engagement and disengagement in, 161
experience from, 138–39
goals and, 129–32
Honors Project study, 132–45
interpretive contexts for, 145–53
social intelligence framework, 145–62
  autobiographical frameworks, 151, 153, 158
  complex pragmatics of problem solving, 157–58
  context sensitivity, 153–57
  evaluation of, 158–62
  independence and lost identities, 150–51
  normative framework, 147–49, 154–55
  personal frameworks, 149–50
strategies for, 129–32, 139, 140–45
of students, 133–38
students' selves and, 139–40
Life themes, 217, 432, 437–38
Linkages, 426–27
Loneliness, 428–30

M

Management
of interpersonal goal conflict, 351–52
by objectives, 299
scientific, 299
self-, 317–18
Managers, self-regulation by, 51–57
Marital conflict, 330, 331–36, 345–50, 356–58. *See also* Interpersonal goal conflict
Material resources, 421
Mate selection, "similarity" vs. "complementarity" hypotheses of, 343–44

Maxims, 436–37
Memory, transactional, 421
Mental models, 440, 449, 455, 466
  of unique relationships, 442–43
Meta-cognitive processes, 456
  of others, 440–41
Models
  interaction, developing, 444–45
  mental, 440, 449, 455, 466
    of unique relationships, 442–43
Money, job performance and, 312–13
Morale, 215
Moral knowledge, 390–93
Moral standards, self-regulation of motivation through, 64–78
  advantageous comparison, 68
  attribution of blame, 75–76
  dehumanization, 72–75
  diffusion of responsibility, 70
  disengagement of self-sanctions and self-deception, 76–78
  displacement of responsibility, 68–70
  disregard or distortion of consequences, 70–72
  euphemistic labeling, 67–68
  moral justification, 67
  selective activation and disengagement of internal standards, 66–67
Motivation. *See also* Goal-directed behavior; Personal strivings; Self-regulation
  to boost self-esteem, 255–57
  conceptions of, 88–91
    attribution theory, 20–22
    classic theories, 216, 217–18
    current concern, 88, 89, 90, 120–21
    imago, 88
    life task, 88, 90, 120–21
    motive disposition/social motive, 88
    nomothetic-idiographic, 88–91, 95, 98, 100
    personal project, 88, 89–90, 120–21
  effectance, 215
  ego-centered, 399–400
  goals and, 7–10
  hierarchical structure of, 93–95
  intrinsic, 215
  personalizing, 216
  personal striving and, 95–96
  possible selves and, 214–17, 227–35

potential, 170–73, 185–96, 199–203
  subjective effects and, 203–6
  relating to goal-means-outcome relation, 400–401
  self-efficacy beliefs and, 29–36
  self-knowledge and, 398–401
  for self-relevant behavior, 268–70
  task-centered, 399–400
  unconscious, achievement, 20–22, 58–59
  to understand social situation, 400
  work
    need-based theories of, 292–94
    organizational behavior modification and, 297
    value-based theories of, 294–97
Motivation: The Organization of Action (Mook), 216
Motivational theories, history of, 1–12
Motivational transformations, 344, 345, 351
Motivation and Cognition (Sorrentino & Higgins), 216
Motive disposition concept, 88–89, 112
Multiple selves, 431
Muscle, priming of, 234–35

N

Need(s), 118–19, 195, 200, 202–7, 211, 269–70, 435, 461
Need-based theories of work motivation, 292
Need integrate, 461
Negative feedback control system, 36–39
Neo-Hullian theories, 202
Network analysis, 391
Nomothetic-idiographic properties, 88–91, 95, 98, 100, 460, 463
Nomothetic properties of interpersonalism, 463
Normative framework of life tasks, 147–49, 154–55
Norms, social, 436–37

O

Optimism, 139
Organizational accomplishments, 50–57
Organizational behavior modification, 297

Other(s)
    meta-cognitive abilities of, 440–41
    perceiving and understanding, 435–50
        culturally shared knowledge and, 436–41
        explaining the unexpected and, 446–50
        idiographic knowledge and, 441–44
        interaction models and, 444–45
        meaning of actions and, 435–36
    reference, 251
    self-identification and, 251
    understanding of, 393–94
Other-directedness, 141–44
Other schemas, 440
Other variable approach, 404
Outcome expectations, 19
    performance and, 218, 277–79
    self-identification and, 277–79
Overt interpersonal goal conflict, 346–47

PQ

Parsimony principle, 445
Participative decision making (PDM), 308–10, 315
"Passive" self-identification, 271–81
Peer pressure, 306–7, 318
Penetration, social, 342
Perceived self-efficacy. *See* Self-efficacy beliefs
Perception, 457
Performance, 9–10, 20–21. *See also* Job performance
    achievement motivation and, 58–59
    affect and, 230–31
    audience and assessment of, 252
    consistency with claims and, 262–65
    effort and, 24–25
    feedback, 27–28
    goal challenge and, 43–44
    goal discrepancies and, 33
    goal proximity and, 48
    in groups, 52–53
    outcome expectations and, 218, 277–79
    possible selves and, 218, 220–24
    private attributions and, 267
    self-efficacy beliefs and, 31–32
    strategy development for, 310–11

Persistence, accepted goals and, 310
Person, coherence and integration of, 432–33
Personal causation, 215
Personal dispositions, 95. *See also* Personal strivings
Personal frameworks of life tasks, 149–50
Personality, inter-personalism and, 465–66
Personality and Assessment (Mischel), 88
Personality theory(ies), 460–62. *See also* Inter-personalism; Personal strivings
    around concept of will, 215
    implicit, 374, 377
Personality variables, 313–14
Personal project concept, 88, 89–90, 120–21, 130, 217
Personal resources, 419–21
Personal Striving Assessment Packet (PSAP), 96–99, 102, 110, 118
Personal strivings, 87–126, 130, 217, 432
    action identification theory and, 114–16
    assessing, 96–101
        coding of striving, 100
        generation of striving lists, 96–97
        instrumentality matrix, 99
        scales, 98–99
        striving specification task, 97–98
        unconscious motivation and self-deception, 100–101
    clinical implications, 117–18
    current conceptions of motivation, 88–91
    definition of, 92–95, 112
    historical background, 91
    origin of, 118–20
    relation to motives and values, 95–96
    self-complexity and affective reactivity, 109–11
    self-concept and, 116–17
    traits and, 111–14
    as units of analysis, 92–95
    well-being and
        conflict among, 103–6
        conflict over expression and, 106–8
        subjective, 102–3
Personified images. *See* Imago

SUBJECT INDEX

Person impression, 388
Person knowledge, 373–89, 392, 396, 447
  within actor schemata, 376–77
  general, 377–84
  individualized, 377, 384–89
  leit-motives of, 378
  polymorphic structure of, 385
Person structure(s), 427–33, 442, 461–62, 465
  idiographic configurations, 427
  integration and coherence of persons and, 432–33
  interpersonal themes, 432
  life tasks, 432
  life themes, 432
  personal strivings, 432
  possible selves, 431
  radial structures, 431
  relational structures, 433
  roles themes, 432
  traits, 428–30
Pessimism, defensive, 132, 139, 140–41, 145, 152, 153–54, 157–58, 161, 231
Physical resources, 421
Physiologic reactivity, 180–84, 187–89, 190–91, 194, 199, 231–35
Plans and the Structures of Behavior (Milla, Galanter & Pribram), 6, 330
Plans/planning, 7, 247, 252, 415, 416–17, 418, 426, 437–38, 449–60, 462
  goal proximity vs., 47
Position, social, 420
Possessions, 420
Possible selves, 4, 9, 211–43, 402, 431, 433, 451
  affective consequences of, 230–31
  balance factor in, 224–27
  cognitive consequences of, 228–30
  controlling behavior and, 223–24
  delinquency and, 224–27
  empirical studies, 219–27
  goal-directed behavior and, 219
  goal effectiveness and, 218–19
  goal framing in terms of, 217–19
  goals representation within, 212–14
  motivation and, 214–17, 227–35
  performance and, 218
  somatic consequences of, 231–35
  task performance and, 220–24
  working self-concept and, 213–14

Potential motivation, 170–73, 185–96, 199–203
  subjective effects and, 203–6
Preservation goal, 424
Pressure, peer and group, 306–7, 318
Priming in impression formation, 380–84
Problem schema, 397
Problem solving, complex pragmatics of, 157–58. *See also* Life tasks
Proximity, goal, 44–48
PSAP, 96–99, 102, 110, 118
Psychological resources, 421
Psychosomatic illness inhibition model, 105–6, 108
Punishment
  dehumanization and, 73–74
  diffusion of responsibility and, 70, 71
Purposive behavior, 3–4, 5, 7, 9
Q-sort procedures, 139, 143

R

Radial structures, 431
Rational-emotive therapy, 117
Reality, social, 365. *See also* Knowledge
Reference others, 251
Relational resources, 421–22
Relational structures, 433
Relationships. *See also* Inter-personalism
  alienation in, 352
  congenial, 352
  contentious, 352
  feedback loops in, 352
  growth in, 352
  methodology for study of, 336–37
  stable in, 352
  stages of, 342–46
  structural improvement of, 351
  unstable, 352
Representation of knowledge, action-oriented, 364–66. *See also* Goal categories
Repression, 202
Resolution, conflict, 339, 349, 350–51, 352, 358
Resources, 415, 418–25, 433, 454–55
Responsibility
  diffusion of, 70, 71
  displacement of, 68–70
Rewards, 307, 314
Role actor schema, 378–79

Roles, 434
  sociological concepts of, 398
Rules, 436–37

S

Satisfaction, social, 144
Schemata, 228, 366. *See also* Knowledge
  action-oriented, 366–68
    self-knowledge in, 395–98
  actor, 388, 393, 396, 397, 399
    person knowledge within, 376–77
  of event, 370, 371–73, 377
  other, 440
  problem, 397
  self, 440
  unit, 389–90, 393, 396, 405
    moral knowledge within, 390–93
    understanding others and, 393–94
Schematics, 213
Scientific management, 299
Scripts, 228, 247, 271, 342, 364, 437–38, 447, 455
  identity images as, 253
Self/selves
  creative, 399
  doer's, 399
  inter-personalism and, 465
  multiple, 431
  possible, 4
Self-completion theory, 399
Self-complexity, 109–11
Self-concept(s), 249–50, 431, 453, 465.
  See also Possible selves
  challenges to, 160
  discrepancy in, 116–17, 139–40, 159–60
  personal striving and, 116–17
  self-identifications as expressions of, 247
  working, 213–14, 219–20, 221, 223, 224
Self-consciousness, 432, 465
Self-deception, 243
  disengagement of, 76–78
  unconscious motivation and, 100–101
  self-deception and, 100–101
Self-demoralization, 47
Self-disclosure, 243
Self-efficacy beliefs, 24, 25–26, 153, 217
  affective and achievement benefits of optimistic, 40–41

depression and, 59–64
effort attributions and, 21–22
environmental factors in, 55–57
goal adjustment and, 38–39
goal challenge and, 43–44
goal discrepancy and, 40–42
goal setting and, 307
organizational accomplishments and, 52, 53
participative decision making and, 309
performance and, 31–32
personal control of motivation and, 29 36
variability of, 159
Self-esteem, 225, 266, 314, 432
  motivational bias to boost, 255–57
Self-exoneration, 75
Self-identification, 243–90
  accounting in, 276–77
  "active" and "passive," 271–81
  claim-performance consistency and, 262–65
  communicability of, 259
  confident and persuasive assertion of, 260–61
  consensual validation of, 259–60
  in context, 246–47
  control of environment and, 244
  definition of, 245
  desired, 253–71
    believability of, 257–61
    beneficiality of, 255–57
    cognition and affect, 270–71
    in context, 261–65
    motive for, 268–70
    positivity vs., 265–66
    response bias vs., private belief in, 266–68
  determinants of, 247–53
    audience, 251–52
    packaging, 252–53
    person, 249–50
    situation, 250–51
  empirical consistency of, 258
  expressiveness vs. self-presentation, 279–81
  fit with prevailing assumptions and values, 259
  identity images, 246, 253
  intensified information processing, 274–75

internal consistency of, 258–59
nature of, 244–53
outcome expectations, 245, 277–79
self-regulation and, 244
shifts in, 262
simplicity of, 259
strategic activities in, 277
Self-identity, 399
Self-images, 249–50
Self-involvement, conditions of, 373
Self-knowledge, 394–403, 404
  in action-oriented schemata, 395–98
  motivation and, 398–401
  polymorphic structure of, 398
  processes of, 401–3
Self-management, goal setting and, 317–18
Self-motivation, 400
  goal properties and, 42–48
Self-narratives, 402
Self-presentation, 243, 260, 263–64, 266, 428–30
  expressiveness vs., 279–81
Self-reactive influences, 26–36
Self-reflection, 243, 266
Self-regulation, 19–86, 94, 457
  absence of, 117
  attribution theory, 20–22
  expectancy-value theory, 22–26
  forms of cognitive motivation and, 19–20
  goal theory, 26–64
    affective consequences of goal discrepancies, 59–64
    aspirational standards, achievement motives and external incentives, 58–59
    generic goal orientation, 49–50
    hierarchical structure of goal systems, 44, 48–49
    negative feedback control system, 36–39
    organizational accomplishments and, 50–57
    self-efficacy and goal discrepancy, 40–42
    self-motivation and, 42–48
    self-reactive influences, 26–36
  misregulation, 117
  self-evaluation and, 251
  self-identification and, 244

through moral standards, 64–78
  advantageous comparison, 68
  attribution of blame, 75–76
  dehumanization, 72–75
  diffusion of responsibility, 70
  disengagement of self-sanctions and self-deception, 76–78
  displacement of responsibility, 68–70
  disregard or distortion of consequences, 70–72
  euphemistic labeling, 67–68
  moral justification, 67
  selective activation and disengagement of internal standards, 66–67
Self-sanctions, disengagement of, 76–78
Self-schemas, 212–13, 224, 399, 440. *See also* Self-images
Self-system, production and control of action and, 236. *See also* Possible selves
Self-understanding processes, 401–3
Semantic links between psychological traits, 388–89
"Similarity" hypothesis of mate selection, 343–44
Situational knowledge, 447, 454
Situational resources, 420–21
Situational structures, 434–35, 443, 462, 464
Situations, self-identifications and, 250–51
Sociability, 428–30, 464
Social cognition, 381
  goals and, 10–12
Social constraints, 132, 139, 141–45, 158, 162
Social intelligence, 419–20, 453
Social intelligence framework of life tasks, 145–62
  autobiographical frameworks, 151, 153, 158
  complex pragmatics of problem solving, 157–58
  context sensitivity of, 153–57
  evaluation of, 158–62
  independence and lost identities, 150–51
  normative framework, 147–49, 154–55
  personal frameworks, 149–50

Social interaction, 328, 338–42, 365, 426, 434–35, 458, 465. *See also* Interpersonal goal conflict; Interpersonalism
Social knowledge, 436–41, 451. *See also* Knowledge
Social norms, 436–37
Social organization knowledge, 389–94
Social penetration theory, 342
Social reality, 365. *See also* Knowledge
Social satisfaction, 144
Social skills, 419–20
Social stereotypes, 438–40
Social validation, 340–41
Somatic consequences of possible selves, 231–35
Specialized talents and abilities, 419
Specificity, 299–304, 318
Stability
  in inter-personalism, 463–64
  in relationships, 352
Standards
  aspirational, 58–59
  internal, selective activation and disengagement of, 66–67
Status, social, 420
Stereotypes, social, 438–40
Strategies, 415, 416–17
  in goal-based structures, 416–17
  in inter-personalism, 415, 416–17
  job performance and, 314–15
  life task, 129–32, 139, 140–45
  for performance, 310–11
  in self-identification, 277
Stress, global measures of, 158–60
Striving Assessment Scales (SAS), 98–99
Striving Instrumentality Matrix (SIM), 99
Structural change model, 348–49
Structural improvement of relationships, 351
Structure(s), cognitive
  goal-based, 415–27
    behavior and, 422–27
    beliefs, 417–18
    goals, 416
    plans and strategies, 416–17
    resources, 418–22
  person, 427–33, 442, 461–62, 465
    idiographic configurations, 427
    integration and coherence of persons and, 432–33

interpersonal themes, 432
life tasks, 432
life themes, 432
personal strivings, 432
possible selves, 431
radial structures, 431
relational structures, 433
roles themes, 432
traits, 428–30
relational, 433
situational, 434–35, 443, 462, 464
Students
  goal discrepancies and, 61–62
  life tasks of, 133–38
  selves of, 139–40
Subgoal-realization episode forms, 372
Subgoals, 44, 45–48
Support resources, 421

T

Tacit knowledge, 402–3
Talents, specialized, 419
Task(s)
  complexity of, 307, 314, 320
  energization and difficulty of, 173–85, 207
  financial, 317
  strategy development for performing, 310–11
Teleonomic trend concept, 91
Themes, life, 437–38
Time, as resource, 420
Trait inferences, 438–40
Traits, 5–6, 415, 428–30, 434, 445, 451, 460, 464
  attribution theory and, 10
  definition of, 112
  goal relations and, 430
  personal striving and, 111–14
  self-ratings and perceived importance of, 266–67
  semantic links between, 388–89
  social stereotypes and, 438–40
  theoretical inadequacy of, 91
Transactional memories, 421
Transformation(s)
  cognitive, 340–41
  dispositional, 345, 351
  motivational, 344, 345, 351
Transgressive conduct, 64
Type A personality, 313–14

U

Understanding others, unit schemata and, 393–94
Unexpected, explaining the, 446–50
Unit schema, 389–90, 393, 396, 405
  moral knowledge within, 390–93
  understanding others and, 393–94

V

Validation, social, 340–41
Value-based theories of work motivation, 294–97
Values, 4
  personal striving and, 95–96
Variable, personality, 313–14
Volition, 2–3, 214–15, 314

WY

Well being
  conflict among personal striving and, 103–6
  conflict over expressing emotion and, 106–8
  global measures of, 158–60
  subjective, 102–3
Will, 2–3, 214–15, 314
Working self-concept, 213–14, 219–20, 221, 223, 224
Work motivation. *See also* Job performance; Goal setting
  need-based theories of, 292–94
  organizational behavior modification and, 297
  value-based theories of, 294–97
Yerkes-Dodson principle, 184–85